The Last Dance

SIXTH EDITION

Encountering Death and Dying

LYNNE ANN DeSPELDER
Cabrillo College

ALBERT LEE STRICKLAND

Boston   Burr Ridge, IL   Dubuque, IA   Madison, WI   New York
San Francisco   St. Louis   Bangkok   Bogotá   Caracas   Kuala Lumpur
Lisbon   London   Madrid   Mexico City   Milan   Montreal   New Delhi
Santiago   Seoul   Singapore   Sydney   Taipei   Toronto

McGraw-Hill Higher Education

A Division of The **McGraw-Hill** *Companies*

3 4 5 6 7 8 9 0 DOC/DOC 0 9 8 7 6 5 4 3 2

Library of Congress Cataloging-in-Publication Data

DeSpelder, Lynne Ann
    The last dance : encountering death and dying / Lynne Ann DeSpelder, Albert Lee Strickland—6th ed.
      p. cm.
    Includes bibliographical references and indexes.
    ISBN 0-7674-2162-0
      1. Death—Psychological aspects.   2. Death—Social aspects.   I. Strickland, Albert Lee.   II. Title.

BF789.D4 D53 2001
155.9'37—dc21   2001030424

Sponsoring editor, Franklin C. Graham; *production editor,* April Wells-Hayes; *manuscript editor,* Carol Dondrea; *design manager,* Susan Breitbard; *cover designer,* Lisa Buckley; *art and photo researchers,* Lynne Ann DeSpelder and Albert Lee Strickland; *computer illustrator,* Joan Carol; *manufacturing manager,* Randy Hurst. The text was set in 10/12 Baskerville by Thompson Type and printed on 45# Scholarly Matte by R.R. Donnelley and Sons.

Text credits appear on a continuation of the copyright page, pages 631–633.

www.mhhe.com

To our parents

Bruce Erwin DeSpelder
and
Dorothy Roediger DeSpelder

Luther Leander Strickland (1896–1966)
and
Bertha Wittenburg Strickland (1905–1985)

who gave us our first "Golden Books" and shared with us the
joys of reading

Contents

CHAPTER I

CHAPTER 9

The Law and Death

CHAPTER 10

Death in the Lives of Children and Adolescents

CHAPTER 11

Death in the Lives of Adults   *383*

CHAPTER 15

Preface

*T*he study of death is concerned with questions that are rooted at the center of human experience. Thus, the person who sets out to increase his or her knowledge of death and dying is embarking on an exploration that is partly a journey of personal discovery. In writing *The Last Dance: Encountering Death and Dying,* our aim is to offer a comprehensive and readable introduction to the study of death and dying, one that highlights the main issues and questions. We are sensitive to the need for a text that balances intensity with relief and detailed investigations of specific issues with general discussions of broader topics. This book embodies an approach to the study of death and dying that combines the intellectual and the emotional, the social and the individual, the experiential and the scholarly.

The Last Dance: Encountering Death and Dying provides a solid grounding in theory and research as well as in methods for applying what is learned to readers' own situations, personal and professional. It encourages readers to engage in a constructive process of self-discovery. The text is not an indoctrination to any one point of view, but an introduction to diverse points of view. It emphasizes the positive values of compassion, listening, and tolerance of the views of others. Readers may well form their own opinions, but, when they do, it is hoped that they do so only after considering other possibilities in a spirit of open-mindedness. Unbiased investigation leads to choices that might otherwise be neglected because of ignorance or prejudice.

While retaining all of the popular features of earlier editions, the sixth edition of *The Last Dance: Encountering Death and Dying* reflects the ongoing evolution of death studies. Every chapter has been carefully revised to enhance clarity of presentation and integrate the latest research, practices, and ideas. New to this edition is a *Student Study Guide to Accompany The Last Dance: Encountering Death and Dying,* which offers a wealth of learning activities and additional resources—including chapter summaries—to promote mastery of the material covered in the text itself.

The study of death is unavoidably multidisciplinary. Accordingly, contributions from medicine, the humanities, and the social sciences are all found here in their relevant contexts. Throughout the book, principles and concepts are made meaningful by extensive use of examples and anecdotes. Boxed material, photographs, and other illustrative materials expand upon and provide counterpoint to the textual presentation. We urge readers to make use of these materials. Specialized terms, when needed, are clearly defined. For those who wish to pursue further study of particular topics, a list of recommended readings is provided at the end of each chapter, and citations given in the chapter notes offer a guide to additional sources and references, including pertinent selections in the companion volume to this text, *The Path Ahead: Readings in Death and Dying* (Mayfield, 1995). Thus, while being introduced to a broad range of topics in death studies, readers are also encouraged to investigate more deeply those topics that evoke special interest.

The influence of historical and sociocultural forces on our understanding of death forms a central theme of the book's first three chapters. These chapters provide a solid foundation for appreciating how specific issues in death, dying, and bereavement are dealt with in distinctive ways by different individuals, families, and social groups. Indeed, throughout the text, attention is given to the importance of ethnic traditions in shaping our relationship with death in culturally diverse societies.

The changing nature of health care, especially care of the dying, is given detailed coverage in Chapters 4 and 5. Ongoing developments in hospice, palliative medicine, and home care are discussed, along with the impact of managed care. Special attention is given to new insights about the various ways individuals and families cope with life-threatening illness, from the time of initial diagnosis to the final stages of the dying trajectory. The discussion of options for treating life-threatening illnesses includes up-to-date coverage of complementary therapies and pain management. Learning about issues related to care of the seriously ill and dying leads naturally to a concern with ethical questions that occur in the context of modern medicine. Chapter 6 explores such concerns, including informed consent, truth-telling, assisted suicide, euthanasia, organ donation and transplantation, and the impact of medical technologies on the definition of death. Considered as a unit, Chapters 4 to 6 focus on critical issues in end-of-life care.

Bereavement, grief, and mourning are pervasive concerns in death studies. Chapter 7 provides an in-depth discussion of grief, ways of coping with it, and how a variety of psychosocial factors influence its expression. Particular emphasis is given to recent advances in our understanding of bereavement, grief, and mourning; conventional models are swiftly being replaced or augmented by models that offer a more encompassing and accurate understanding of how human beings experience and cope with grief. Chapter 8 examines the ceremonies and rites enacted by individuals and social groups in the wake of a close death, with a focus on how such death customs create opportunities for expressing grief and integrating loss. Chapter 9 examines how the legal system influences our understanding and practices relative to dying and death. Major topics in this chapter include advance directives, laws and court decisions concerning physician-assisted suicide, death certification, and practices surrounding wills and probate.

Making use of a lifespan perspective, Chapters 10 and 11 deal with a variety of death-related issues that are associated with different stages of life, from childhood through old age. The discussion in these chapters is based on an understanding of human development that draws on both theoretical work and clinical findings. Chapter 10 includes examples of typical childhood encounters with death as well as guidelines for helping children cope with loss. Chapter 11 includes detailed discussions about parental bereavement, the deaths of parents, and spousal bereavement, as well as about grief in response to the death of a friend and the losses associated with aging.

Building on an understanding of normative patterns throughout the life cycle, Chapter 12 takes up the subject of suicide as a mode of death that occurs in the context of various risk factors, many of which have special relevance at different stages of life. Topics discussed in this chapter include using psychological autopsies as a means of investigating the antecedents of suicidal behavior, as well as alleviating suicidal tendencies through timely prevention and intervention.

Broadening the scope of death-related risks, Chapter 13 addresses a number of important topics that are crucial to a comprehensive understanding of death and dying. These topics include accidents, disasters, violence, homicide, capital punishment, war, and emerging diseases. This last category includes AIDS, which continues to threaten the health of many people around the world even as some people with AIDS are experiencing an unexpected extension of life due to innovative medicines and improved treatments.

Questions about the meaning of human mortality are at the forefront in the final two chapters of the book. Chapter 14 draws on a variety of religious and secular traditions, as well as accounts of near-death experiences, to present a wide-ranging survey of concepts and beliefs that humans hold regarding immortality and the afterlife. Whether death is viewed as a wall or as a door can have important consequences for how we live our lives. Chapter 15 emphasizes the personal and social values that can be enhanced through death education. Bringing together a host of topics covered in the text, the chapter stimulates readers to consider how a "good death" might be defined.

The Last Dance has been reviewed by professors in a broad range of academic disciplines. Their suggestions have helped to make this text an outstanding teaching tool. Formal reviews have been provided by Lisa Angermeier, Indiana University at Bloomington; Thomas Attig, Bowling Green State University; Ronald K. Barrett, Loyola Marymount University, Los Angeles; Michael Beechem, University of West Florida, Pensacola; Laura Billings, Belleville Area Community College, Illinois; John B. Bond, The University of Manitoba; Sandor B. Brent, Wayne State University; Tom Bruce, Sacramento City College; Richard Cording, Sam Houston State University; Charles A. Corr, Southern Illinois University; Gerry R. Cox, Fort Hays State University; Steven A. Dennis, Utah State University; Kenneth J. Doka, College of New Rochelle; Stephen J. Fleming, York University, Toronto; Audrey K. Gordon, Oakton Community College; Debra Bence Grow, Pennsylvania State University; John Harvey, Western Illinois University; Russell G. Henke, Towson State University; David D. Karnos, Eastern Montana College; Linda C. Kinrade, California State University, Hayward; Anthony Lenzer, University of Hawaii at Manoa; J. Davis Mannino, Santa Rosa Junior College; Wendy Martyna, University of California, Santa Cruz; Marsha McGee, Northeast Louisiana University; Walter L. Moore, Florida State University, Tallahassee; Vincent M. Rolletta, Erie Community College; Lee Ross, Frostburg State University, Maryland; Rita S. Santanello,

Belleville Area Community College, Illinois; Thomas W. Satre, Sam Houston State University; Edwin S. Shneidman, University of California, Los Angeles; Judith M. Stillion, Western Carolina University; Jeffrey S. Turner, Mitchell College; Hannelore Wass, University of Florida, Gainesville; Jack Borden Watson, Stephen F. Austin State University, Nacodoches, Texas; John B. Williamson, Boston College; C. Ray Wingrove, University of Richmond; Robert Wrenn, University of Arizona, Tucson; Joseph M. Yonder, Villa Maria College of Buffalo; and Andrew Scott Ziner, University of North Dakota. In addition, many other colleagues and students have informally shared ideas for enhancing the text. We extend our appreciation to all who have offered helpful suggestions about the book through its successive incarnations.

Our collaborators on various editions of the *Instructor's Guide* for this text deserve special thanks, and we express our gratitude to Barbara Jade Sironen, Patrick Vernon Dean, Robert James Baugher, and Carol Fern Berns. We also thank Matt Strickland for his expertise in producing the test bank that accompanies the *Instructor's Guide*. In addition, we are grateful to staff members at many museums, libraries, and governmental institutions, who have assisted us in our research and in gathering both text and art resources over the years.

In our association with Mayfield Publishing Company over the course of six editions of *The Last Dance*, we have had the pleasure of collaborating with many talented people who exemplify excellence in publishing. Very special thanks are due Franklin C. Graham, our sponsoring editor, whose breadth of vision and warm friendship inspire and sustain us; and Linda Toy, head of Mayfield's production department, who unfailingly cheers us with uncommon calm despite pressing deadlines. In preparing this new edition, we also thank Lynn Rabin Bauer and April Wells-Hayes, who managed the production of this book with consummate professionalism; Carol Dondrea, whose expert copyediting consistently improved the original manuscript; Robin Mouat, who skillfully sheperded the book's illustration program through production; Jeanne Schreiber and Susan Breitbard for their expert design management; Kate Schubert, whose rapid-response editorial assistance provided timely answers to a variety of questions; and Jay Bauer, whose promotional efforts on behalf of the book are always appreciated. To all whose help was instrumental in bringing this edition of *The Last Dance* to readers, our heartfelt thanks.

L. A. D.
A. L. S.

P R O L O G U E

I don't know how much time I have left. I've spent my life dispensing salves and purgatives, potions and incantations—miracles of nature (though I admit that some were pure medicine-show snake oil). Actually, half the time all I offered was just plain common sense. Over the years, every kind of suffering person has made his or her way here. Some had broken limbs or broken bodies . . . or hearts. Often their sorrow was an ailing son or daughter. It was always so hard when they'd lose a child. I never did get used to that. And then there were the young lovers. Obtaining their heart's desire was so important to them. I had to smile. I always made them sweat and beg for their handful of bark, and for those willful tortures I'll probably go to hell . . . if there is one. My God, how long has it been since I had those feelings myself? The fever, the lump in the throat, the yearning. I can't remember. A long time . . . maybe never. Well, there have been other passions for me. There's my dusty legion of jars. Each one holds its little secret. Barks, roots, soils, leaves, flowers, mushrooms, bugs—magic dust, every bit of it. There's my book—my "rudder," a ship's pilot would call it. That's a good name for it. Every salve, every purgative . . . they're all in there. (Everything, that is, except my stained beard, scraggly hair, and flowing robes—they'll have to figure those out on their own.) And then there's my walking stick (always faithful) . . . and the ballerina. And ten thousand mornings, ten thousand afternoons, ten thousand nights. And the stars. Oh, I have had my loves.

It hurts to move. My shelf and jars seem so far away, though I know that if I tried I could reach them. But no. It's enough and it's time . . . almost. I hope he makes it back in time. He burst through my door only two days ago. A young man, well spoken. Tears were streaming down his face. He looked so bent and beaten that I could not refuse him. He told me that his wife had died over a month ago and that he had been inconsolable since.

"Please help me," he pleaded, "or kill me." He covered his face with his hands. "Perhaps they're the same thing. I don't know anymore."

I let him cry a while so I could watch him, gauge him. When at last he looked up, with my good hand I motioned him to take a seat. Then, between coughing fits, I went to work. "Do you see that toy there?" I said. "The little ballerina . . . yes, that's it. Pick it up."

"Pick it up?"

"It won't bite. Pick it up." (He probably thought it was a trick—that's what they expect.) He grasped it carefully, with one hand, then wiped his eyes with the other. "That's better," I continued. "that's just a toy to you. You don't know what meaning to put to it, yet. So I want you to look at that ballerina."

He was hesitant, but I waited, stubbornly, until he looked down and fixed his attention on the little toy dancer. I went on: "I knew a young man once who was very handsome—always had been. He not only turned every head, he was strong and smart, and his family was wealthy. His main concern each day was which girl he should court that evening. He had planned that after several seasons of playing at love he would marry a beautiful girl, have beautiful children, and settle down to spend the money his father had promised him. And he had plans for that money. He had already purchased the land he wanted to live on and was having built there the biggest house in the area. He was going to raise and race horses, I think. One morning he got on his favorite horse and went for a ride. He whipped that horse into a gallop; it stepped in a hole and threw him. The young man broke his neck, and died." I stared at my guest and waited.

"That's a tragedy," he finally croaked.

"For whom? For those he left behind, perhaps. But was it for him? When he opened his eyes that morning, he didn't know he would die that day. He had no intention of dying for another sixty years—if then. None of us does." The young man looked confused. "His mistake was that he forgot that he could die that day."

"That's a morbid thought," he replied, and he looked as though he had just smelled something putrid.

"Is it? A moment ago you asked me to end your grieving by ending your own life. Suppose I oblige?" I stared at him for a few moments with my most practiced penetrating glare. "Suppose I did agree to kill you. How would you spend your last few minutes?"

He was still a little wary of me, but relieved that I seemed to be suggesting a hypothetical situation, rather than a serious course of action. He considered the possibilities for a while, then straightened in his chair: "Well, I guess I would step outside and take a last, best look at the sky, the clouds, the trees."

"Suppose you lived that way all the time?" He stared at me, then looked down at his hands, searching them. "That young man I told you about . . . perhaps the tragedy for him was not that he died, but that he failed to use the eventual certainty of his death to make him live! Did he woo each of those ladies as though it might be his last romance? Did he build that house as though it might be his last creation? Did he ride that horse as though it would be his last ride? I don't know; I hope so." My young guest nodded, but he was still sad. I pointed to the toy ballerina he was holding. "That was given to me by a young lady who understood these things."

He looked at the figure closely. "Is she a dancer?"

"Yes, she is, and she is dead." The young man looked up, once again off balance. "She has been dead for, oh, a very long time." After all these years, a tear fell onto my cheek. I let it go. "She was many things. A child, a woman, a cook and a gardener, a friend, lover, daughter. . . . But what she really was—who she was—was a dancer. When she was dying, she gave that doll to me, smiled, and whispered, 'At the moment of my death, I will take all of my dancing and put it in here, so my dancing can live on.'"

Tears welled in my guest's eyes.

"I can help you," I said, "but first there is something that you must do." He became very attentive. "Go to town and knock on the door of the first house you come to. Ask the people inside if their family has ever been touched by death. If so, go to the next house. When you find a family that has not been touched by death, bring them to me. Do you understand?" He nodded, and I sighed: "I'm tired now."

He got up, set the ballerina back on the table, and started for the door. I stopped him. "Young man!" He faced me from the doorway. "Come back as soon as you can."

David Gordon

*In a Spanish village, neighbors and relatives peer through the doorway
upon the deathbed scene of a villager.*

Attitudes Toward Death: A Climate of Change

Of all human experiences, none is more overwhelming in its implications than death. Yet, for most of us, death remains a shadowy figure whose presence is only vaguely acknowledged. We tend to relegate death to the periphery of our lives, as if it can be kept out of sight, out of mind.[1] Some believe that we seem to deny death even while we are obsessed with its mastery, seeking to control it through belief in the almost limitless possibilities of medical technology.[2]

According to sociologist Talcott Parsons, the attitude toward death in modern societies involves death denial less than it does "bringing to bear every possible resource to prolong active and healthful life" and accepting death only when "it is felt to be inevitable."[3] It has been argued that individuals and societies must, in fact, both accept and deny death.[4] We must accept death if we wish to maintain a grasp on reality. Yet, it must be denied if we are to go about our daily lives with a sense of commitment to a future that is inevitably limited by our mortality. The attempt to deny death or make it invisible is changing as more people explore their options with respect to dying, death, and bereavement.

Consider how our experiences with dying and death have changed over the last hundred years.[5] During the nineteenth century, most Americans lived in rural areas. People usually died at home, often surrounded by an extended family that spanned several generations. As death drew near, relatives and friends gathered to maintain a vigil at the

5

bedside. Afterward, they washed and prepared the body for burial. A home-built coffin was placed in the parlor of the house so friends and relatives could participate in a wake and share in mourning the deceased. In close-knit communities, a death bell might toll the age of the deceased, giving notification of the death so that others in the community could join in the rituals marking the deceased's passing (see Figure 1-1). Children were included in activities surrounding the dead, keeping vigil alongside adults and sometimes sleeping in the same room as the corpse. Later, in a family plot at the homeplace or a nearby churchyard cemetery, the coffin was lowered into the grave and those closest to the deceased filled in the grave. Throughout this process, from caring for the dying person through the burial, death was within the realm of the family.

If you were a person of the nineteenth century suddenly transported to the present, you would find modern funeral practices a rich source of information about current attitudes toward death. You would likely experience culture shock as you walked into the "slumber room" of a typical mortuary. There, in place of a simple, wooden coffin, you view a more elaborate casket. The corpse shows the mortician's skill in cosmetic restoration. At the funeral, you watch as relatives and friends eulogize the deceased. Ah, that's familiar, you say—but where is the dear departed? Off to the side a bit, the casket remains closed, death tastefully concealed. At the graveside committal, as the service concludes, you are amazed to see mourners leaving while the casket lies yet unburied; the cemetery crew will complete the actual burial. As a nineteenth-century observer at a modern funeral, you may be most impressed by the fact that the deceased's family and friends are spectators rather than participants. The tasks of preparing the dead for burial and managing the rites of passage are carried out by hired professionals.

Not so long ago, the skills appropriate to caring for the dying and the dead were an ordinary part of domestic life. Now, comparatively few people know how to provide such care. By learning about how people believed, behaved, and felt about death in earlier times, we can appreciate how our personal attitudes are influenced by social forces that shape our relationships with dying and death.

You can feel the silence pass over the community as all activity is stopped and the number of rings is counted. One, two, three—it must be the Myer's baby that has the fever. No, it's still tolling—four, five, six. There is another pause at twenty—could that be Molly Shields? Her baby is due at any time now—no, it's still tolling. Will it never stop? Thirty-eight, thirty-nine, another pause—who? It couldn't be Ben; he was here just yesterday; said he was feeling fit as a fiddle—no, it's starting again. Seventy, seventy-one, seventy-two. Silence. You listen, but there is no sound—only silence. Isaac Tipton. He has been ailing for two weeks now. It must be Isaac.

Figure 1-1 *Tolling the Bell*

Gordon Parks, FSA Collection, Library of Congress

Five generations of the Machado family form an extended family network rarely seen today. Firsthand experiences of death in such a family come through the closeness of multigenerational living.

Factors Affecting Familiarity With Death

During the past hundred years, there has been a dramatic change in the size, shape, and distribution of the American population—that is, its *demographics.* These changes—the most notable of which involve increased life expectancy and lower mortality rates—affect our expectations about death. In addition, the typical household of the nineteenth century included parents, uncles,

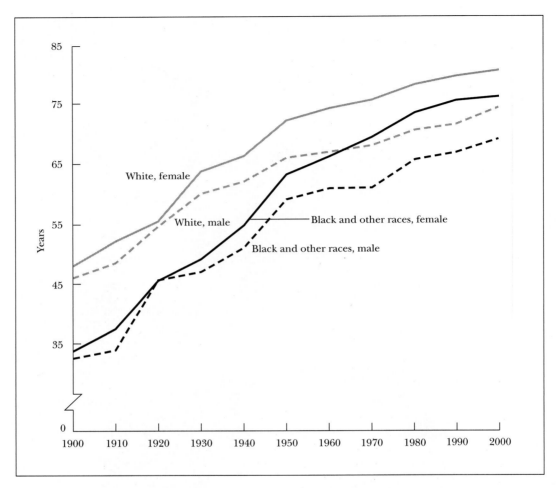

Figure 1-2 *Life Expectancy at Birth, by Race and Sex, 1900–2000*
Source: U.S. Census Bureau, *Statistical Abstract of the United States: 1999,* pp. 93, 874.

aunts, and aged grandparents, as well as children of varying ages. Such extended families, with several generations living together under the same roof,
are rare today. Most of us live in smaller families and have fewer opportunities
to experience our relatives' deaths firsthand. Greater geographical mobility
also makes it less likely that we will be present when relatives die. Medical
technologies, of course, strongly influence both how a person dies and the
setting where death takes place. In our encounters with death, we call upon
professionals—from the cardiologist to the coroner to the cremator—to act
as our go-betweens. The net result is that, for most of us, death is unfamiliar.

Life Expectancy and Mortality Rates

Since 1900, average life expectancy in the United States has increased
from forty-seven to seventy-six years (see Figure 1-2).[6] Today, we tend to as-

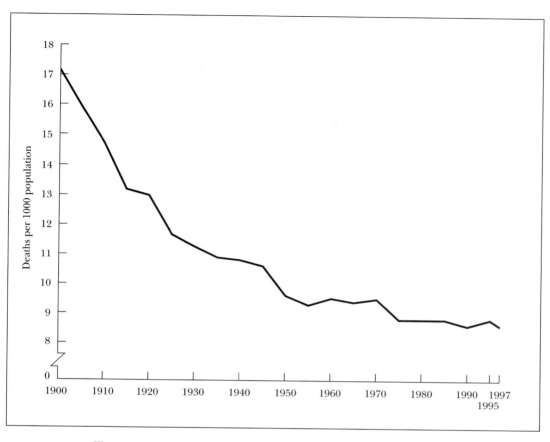

Figure *1-3 Death Rates, 1900–1997*
Sources: U.S. Census Bureau, *Historical Statistics of the United States, Colonial Times to 1970*
(Washington, D.C.: Government Printing Office, 1975), p. 59; and *Statistical Abstract
of the United States: 1999,* p. 95.

sume that a newborn child will live into his or her seventh or eighth decade,
perhaps longer.[7] This was not the case in 1900. Over half of the deaths in 1900
occurred among children age fourteen and younger; now, less than 2 percent
of deaths occur among this age group.[8] This fact influences how we think (or
don't think) about death.

Another way to appreciate the changing impact of death is to examine
death rates, which are typically stated as the number of individuals dying per
1000 population in a given year. In 1900, the death rate in America was about
17 per 1000; today, it is about 8.6 per 1000 (see Figure 1-3).[9] Imagine yourself
in an environment where death at an early age is common. Think about how
different the experience of death and dying was for our ancestors. The high
percentage of infant deaths was generally considered a matter of "fate," which
could not be averted.[10] Both young and old were familiar with death as a
natural part of the human condition. Mothers died in childbirth; babies were

stillborn; one or both parents might die before their children had grown to adolescence. Surviving siblings often had a postmortem photograph of a dead brother or sister displayed on the bedroom wall, a memorial to the deceased and testament to the integrity of the family.[11] Living with such awareness of mortality, our ancestors could hardly deny the fact of death.

Causes of Death

Changes in life expectancy and mortality rates are largely due to shifting patterns in the causes of death. In the early years of the twentieth century, death was typically caused by an acute infectious disease such as tuberculosis, typhoid fever, diphtheria, streptococcal septicemia, syphilis, or pneumonia. Most of these diseases came on suddenly, and death soon followed. Today, death usually occurs as the result of a chronic illness such as heart disease or cancer, and it typically follows a slow, progressive course that may last weeks, months, or even years (see Table 1-1).

This historical shift in disease patterns is termed an *epidemiologic transition* and is characterized mainly by a redistribution of deaths from the young to the old.[12] (Epidemiology is the study of the patterns of health and disease.) With a reduced risk of dying at a young age from infectious diseases, people survive into older ages, where they tend to die from degenerative diseases. This shift results in a growing proportion of aged people in the population. In 1900, people sixty-five or older made up 4 percent of the population in the United States; today, they comprise 13 percent. In 1900, people sixty-five or older accounted for about 17 percent of deaths; today, 74 percent of the 2.3 million deaths each year in the United States occurs among people in this age group.[13] Because of changes over the last century in the most common causes of death, we tend to think that death is something that happens in old age.

TABLE *1-1   Leading Causes of Death, 1998*

Cause of Death	Death Rate Per 100,000	% of Total
All Causes	864.7	100.0
Diseases of heart	268.2	31.0
Cancer	200.3	23.1
Stroke	58.6	6.7
Lung disease	41.7	4.8
Accidents	36.2	4.1
Pneumonia and influenza	34.0	3.9
Diabetes	24.0	2.7
Suicide	11.3	1.3
Kidney disease	9.7	1.1
Liver disease	9.3	1.0

Source: Sherry L. Murphy, "Deaths: Final Data for 1998," *National Vital Statistics Reports* 48, no. 11 (2000), p. 5.

I often wonder what it would be like to be born and raised and live one's whole life in the same zip code. I wonder what it would be like to be able to dial all of one's family and friends without an area code. What it would be like not to always be missing one person or the other, one place or the other. What it would be like to return to a family home in which one grew up and still had things stored in the attic.

My family is in area code 405 and my best friend's in 415 and I'm living in 212. The in-laws are in 203. And there are other friends in 213 and 202, in 412 and 214.

Beverly Stephen, "A Mobile Generation in Search of Roots"

Geographical Mobility

Each year, more than one-sixth of the American population is on the move.[14] People pull up stakes and say goodbye to friends, neighbors, and relatives. Relationships historically have been closely tied to place and kinship; now they depend more on present function than on a lifetime of shared experiences. Children, once grown, rarely live in the same house with their parents or, even more rarely, with their brothers and sisters in an extended family. Very few college friendships continue through marriage and the child-rearing years into retirement. There is a corresponding loss in the sharing of death rituals.

Because of such mobility, people are unlikely to be present at the deaths of relatives or friends. Even when the cost of travel is not an issue, most people cannot take off long periods of time from work or other responsibilities to care for dying relatives or friends or to attend funerals. Indeed, with more people living at a distance from their loved ones, the issue of bereavement leave is becoming an increasingly hot topic in the workplace.[15]

Many families do try to maintain close relations, even when they don't share the same dwelling or live in the same town. It is also true that the mobile pattern of living varies among individuals and groups. The members of some ethnic and cultural groups, for example, place a high value on maintaining strong family ties despite general trends in society. Even so, geographical mobility tends to make death less familiar for most Americans.

Displacement of Death from the Home

In the not too distant past, most people died in their own beds, at home, surrounded by loved ones. In 1900, about 80 percent of deaths in the United States occurred at home. Now, we find the reverse, with about 80 percent of all deaths occurring in institutional settings, mainly hospitals and nursing homes. Death was moved from the home for a variety of reasons—the expansion of medical technology and demographic changes foremost among them—thereby adding yet another explanation for our comparative unfamiliarity with death and dying.

For a variety of reasons, there is less intermingling of the generations, a normal part of daily life in earlier times. Consider the experience of two small children on a Halloween trek, going door to door. After knocking on several well-lighted doors in a seniors-only mobile-home park and receiving no response, their cries of "Trick or treat!" were answered by a woman who said, "You'll not get any Halloween treats in this place. Only old people live here, and they leave their lights on for security and safety, not to welcome children on Halloween!"

Most people say they would prefer to live out their last days amid the familiar surroundings of home, but the nature of a final illness or lack of social support can make this choice difficult or impossible to implement. This situation is changing as advocates for improving end-of-life care help make home care a realistic option once again. Still, for many people, a long-distance phone call announcing the passing of grandma substitutes for the intimate experience of a loved one's death.

Life-Extending Technologies

In institutional settings, a dying person may be surrounded by an astonishing array of machinery designed to monitor life until the last impulse fades. Sophisticated machines monitor biological functions such as brain wave activity, heart rate, body temperature, respiration, blood pressure, pulse, and blood chemistry. Signaling changes in body function by light, sound, and computer printout, such devices can make a crucial difference in situations of life or death.

But the advanced medical technology that seems to one person a godsend, extending life, may seem to another a curse that only prolongs dying. Dignity may be devalued amid technology focused exclusively on the biological organism. What are the trade-offs in applying medical technologies to the end stage of life? The conventional definition of death as "the cessation of life, the total and permanent cessation of all vital functions" is now accompanied by a medicolegal definition that acknowledges the fact that life can be sustained artificially. Our modern definition of death is not always as simple as the child's statement, "When you're dead, you're dead."

Medical technology has become yet another factor in our lessened familiarity with dying and death. The attitude that "what can be done, should be done" increases the likelihood that technological fixes will be tried even when success or cure is unlikely. Family and friends may be distanced from the patient who is dying. When death does come, it may seem unexpected. There is a tendency to view death as an event that can be deferred indefinitely rather than as part of life.

The latest stage of the North American story regarding death might be termed "managed death." Even when a person's dying has been accepted and further treatments intended to cure have been put aside, there can be a strong desire to manage the situation so that it comes out "right." One expression of this desire involves ending treatment just at the proper moment and allowing the person to die a quiet death. Another involves the attempt to control death even more completely through physician-assisted suicide or euthanasia. Whether something is missing in such efforts to manage death is a question that should be considered. In responding to what some believe are excesses in applying medical technologies, others may be turning death into "just one

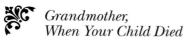

Grandmother, When Your Child Died

Grandmother, when your child died
hot beside you
in your narrow bed,
his labored breathing kept
you restless
and woke you when
it sighed,
and stopped.

You held him through the bitter dawn
and in the morning
dressed him, combed his hair,
your tears welled, but you didn't weep
until at last he lay
among the wild iris in the sod,
his soul gone inexplicably to God. Amen.

But grandmother, when my child died
sweet Jesus, he died hard.
A motor beside
his sterile cot
groaned, and hissed, and whirred
while he sang his pain—
low notes and high notes
in slow measures
slipping through the drug-cloud.
My tears, redundant,
dropped slow
like glucose or blood
from a bottle.
And when he died
my eyes were dry
and gods wearing white coats
turned away.

Joan Neet George

more choice-and-efficiency issue, to be domesticated along with traffic jams and other excesses of modern life."[16]

Expressions of Attitudes Toward Death

By assessing our past experiences and projecting our imaginations into the future, we arrive at attitudes that help us respond to the varied situations we encounter in life. Attitudes toward death become evident when we look at how they reveal themselves in social interactions through the language people use when talking about death and the humor employed in response to it, as well as how death is portrayed by the media and in music, literature, and the visual arts. Direct, firsthand experience with death is rare for most people in modern societies, yet death still has a significant, even if unacknowledged, place in our cultural environment.

Language

When people talk about dying or death, the language used is often indirect. The words *dead* or *dying* tend to be avoided; instead, loved ones "pass away" and the deceased is "laid to rest." Burial becomes "interment," and the undertaker is transformed into a "funeral director." Such terms suggest a well-choreographed production in caring for the dead. Listening carefully, you will probably notice that euphemisms, metaphors, and slang comprise a large part of "death talk" (see Table 1-2). Euphemisms—substitutions of indirect or vague words and phrases for ones considered harsh or blunt—may be used to keep death at arm's length by masking its reality.

Using euphemisms and metaphors does not always imply an impulse to deny death or avoid talking about it, however. Sometimes these terms reveal

TABLE 1-2   *Death Talk: Metaphors, Euphemisms, and Slang*

Passed on	Made the change
Croaked	Taking the dirt nap
Kicked the bucket	On the other side
Gone to heaven	God took him/her
Gone home	Asleep in Christ
Expired	Departed
Breathed the last	Transcended
Succumbed	Bought the farm
Left us	With the angels
Went to his/her eternal reward	Feeling no pain
Lost	Offed himself/herself
Met his/her Maker	His/her time was up
Wasted	Cashed in
Checked out	Crossed over Jordan
Eternal rest	Perished
Laid to rest	Ate it
Pushing up daisies	Was done in
Called home	Translated into glory
Was a goner	Returned to dust
Came to an end	Withered away
Bit the dust	In the arms of the Father
Annihilated	Gave it up
Liquidated	It was curtains
Terminated	A long sleep
Gave up the ghost	On the heavenly shores
Left this world	Out of his/her misery
Rubbed out	Ended it all
Snuffed	Angels carried him/her away
Six feet under	Resting in peace
Passing	Changed form
Found everlasting peace	Dropped the body
Went to a new life	Returned to the source
In the great beyond	That was all she wrote
No longer with us	Passed away

subtler and deeper meanings. Among members of some religious and ethnic traditions, for example, terms like "passing" convey an understanding of death as a spiritual transition. At other times, however, euphemisms are used to devalue and depersonalize death. This occurs when soldiers killed in battle are described as "being wasted" or civilian deaths are termed "collateral damage." Plain talk about death can be subverted by a lexicon of substitutions that cite "body counts" or "KIAs" (killed in action). When used in this way, euphemisms replace accurate descriptions of the horror of death in war.

Another arena of social interaction in which death is typically mentioned indirectly involves the use of sympathy and condolence cards. Generally, such cards allow us to express our condolences to the bereaved without directly mentioning death.[17] Death may be referred to metaphorically, as in sentiments like "What is death but a long sleep?" or apparently denied in verses like "He is not dead, he is just away." Images of sunsets and flowers convey an impression of peace, quiet, and perhaps a return to nature. The deceased may be mentioned within the context of the bereaved person's memories or the healing process of time. Sympathy cards are designed to let us acknowledge the reality of loss by doing so in a sensitive and gentle fashion intended to comfort the bereaved.

Among the Yorubas of southwestern Nigeria, "greeting formulas"—which are in some ways similar to the expressions of condolence offered with sympathy cards—allow friends and relatives of the bereaved to distinguish between different circumstances surrounding a loss.[18] For example, the death of a child, spouse, parent, or sister calls for a particular type of bereavement greeting. The age of the person who died, cause of death, and circumstances surrounding the death are all considered in choosing the right greeting. Expressing the appropriate bereavement greeting is an important part of Yoruba mourning rituals, which help the bereaved feel supported and comforted. Perhaps a similar intention is evident in the recent release of a Hallmark card focusing specifically on comforting persons who are bereaved as a result of a loved one's suicide.[19]

The intensity and immediacy of a person's encounter with death can also be revealed through the language used. In "danger of death" narratives—stories about close calls with death—a tense shift typically occurs when the narrator comes to the crucial point in his or her story, the point when death seems imminent and unavoidable. In one instance, a man who had experienced a frightening incident some years earlier while driving in a snowstorm began his story in the past tense as he described the circumstances. But as he came to the point in the story when his car went out of control on an icy curve and slid into the opposing lane of traffic, he switched to the present tense. It was as if he were *reliving* the experience of watching the oncoming car heading straight for him and believing in that moment that he was about to die.[20]

Word choices can also reveal subtle changes in the way death is experienced at different times. For example, after the bombing of the federal building in Oklahoma City, when the focus of rescue efforts changed, so did the language used to describe the work of emergency personnel and search-and-rescue teams. As hours stretched into days, *rescue* work became *recovery* work.

Similarly, people who experience the same death-related event from different perspectives may choose different ways of talking about it. When Kurt Cobain of the rock group Nirvana committed suicide, the language used by fans and by the media showed interesting contrasts. Whereas Cobain's fans expressed their shock by saying, "Can you believe it? He offed himself; he actually blew himself away," reporters used formal language to describe Cobain's death by "suicide" from "gunshot."

Look again at the words and phrases used in death talk (see Table 1-2). Notice how language offers clues about the manner of death and a speaker's attitude toward the death. Subtle distinctions can reflect very different attitudes. Sometimes these distinctions involve spiritual or cultural frameworks. Consider, for instance, the subtle differences between "passed away" and "passed on." Paying attention to the metaphors, euphemisms, slang, and other linguistic devices people use to talk about death increases our understanding about the variety and range of attitudes toward death.

Humor

Serious and somber matters can be easier to deal with when there is comedic relief. Laughter defuses some of the anxiety about death. Humor puts fearful possibilities into manageable perspective. Death-related humor comes in many different forms, from funny epitaphs to so-called black or gallows humor. On a highway not long ago, passing motorists were taken aback by a gleaming white hearse with the cryptic license plates, "Not Yett."

Mary Hall observes that "what is humorous to each of us depends on our particular cultural set, our own experience, and our personal inclination."[21] Humor functions in several ways relative to death: First, it raises our consciousness about a taboo subject and gives us a way to talk about it. Second, it presents an opportunity to rise above sadness, providing a release from pain and promoting a sense of control over a traumatic situation, even if we cannot change it. Third, humor is a great leveler; it treats everyone alike and sends the message that there are no exemptions from the human predicament. Thus, it binds us together and encourages the intimacy we need to face what is unknown or distressing. After death has occurred, humor can comfort survivors as they recall the funny as well as painful events of a loved one's life. A sense of humor can moderate the intensity of negative life events.[22]

For people with serious illness, humor is a way to cope with the effects of a shattering diagnosis. It can provide another perspective on a painful situation, as in the jest, "Halitosis is better than no breath at all." When things are bad, humor doesn't necessarily make the situation better, but it can serve a protective psychological function and help people keep their equilibrium.[23]

Individuals who care for the dying or encounter death on their jobs, as, for example, emergency services personnel, use humor to distance themselves from

---

 The Undertakers

Old Pops had been stone cold dead for two days. He was rigid, gruesome and had turned slightly green and now he lay on a slab at the undertakers, about to be embalmed by two lovable old morticians.

"At least he lived to a ripe age," said one.

"Yep," said the other. "Well, let's get to 'er."

Suddenly, Old Pops bolted upright and without opening his eyes, began to utter this story:

"In 1743, Captain Rice set sail from England with an unreliable and mutinous crew. After three days at sea, the mast of the mainsail splintered, and then broke completely in half. The ship tossed about at sea for two days; the men mutinied, and the ship tossed about for another two days. At the end of the third day, a ship appeared on the horizon and rescued them and good Captain Rice failed to mention to the admiral the incident of mutiny, and his crew became faithful and hardworking and devoted themselves to their captain."

Old Pops laid back down on the marble.

"Well," said one mortician, "there goes the old saying, 'dead men tell no tales'!"

Steve Martin, *Cruel Shoes*

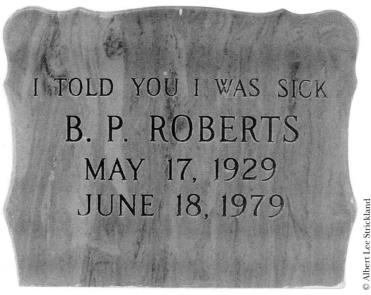

I TOLD YOU I WAS SICK

B. P. ROBERTS

MAY 17, 1929
JUNE 18, 1979

© Albert Lee Strickland

In place of the conventional sentiment usually engraved on tombstones, a touch of whimsy adorns this memorial to B. P. Roberts at a cemetery in Key West, Florida.

horror as well as to rebond after traumatic incidents. A firm that provides instructional materials for emergency medical technicians includes in its catalog a musical recording entitled "You Respond to Everyone But Me." In another example, a group of doctors at a medical center avoided using the word "death" when a patient died because of concern that other patients might become alarmed. One day, as a medical team was examining a patient, an intern came to the door with information about the death of a patient. Knowing that the word "death" was taboo and finding no ready substitute, she announced, "Guess who's not going to shop at Wal-Mart any more?" This phrase quickly became the standard way for staff members to convey the news of a patient's death.

The things we find funny about death can reveal a good deal about our attitudes. A joke that is shared gleefully by some people may be shocking to others. In short, as is easily seen when jokes are told, there are constraints on the kinds of humor that a particular person or group finds acceptable. Nevertheless, humor can be a useful tool that helps us cope with painful situations. It can be an aid in confronting our fears and gaining a sense of mastery over the unknown. Finding humorous aspects to death, casting it in an unconventional light, can remove some of the anxiety that accompanies awareness of our mortality.

Mass Media

Modern communication technology has the potential to make us all instantaneous survivors, as news of disaster, terrorism, war, and political assassination is flashed around the world. Stunned viewers watch in disbelief as the

Drawing by Frank Cotham, © 1999 The New Yorker Collection

"Before we continue, is there anyone else present who has never seen a dead person?"

terrible event unfolds. Crises produce huge audiences for the mass media, and people look to the media as sources of information when situations involve some perceived threat.[24] Because our attitudes are influenced significantly by the vicarious experiences offered by the mass media, we need to ask ourselves: What do these secondhand sources tell us about death and dying?

In the News

As you read the daily newspaper, what kinds of encounters with death vie for your attention? Scanning the day's news, you find an assortment of accidents, murders, suicides, and disasters involving violent deaths. A jetliner crashes, and the news is announced with banner headlines. Here you see a story describing how a family perished when trapped inside their burning home; in another, a family's vacation comes to an untimely end due to a fatal collision on the interstate.

Then there are the deaths of the famous. The death of the average Joe or Jill tends to be made known through *death notices*—brief, standardized statements, usually printed in small type and listed alphabetically in a column of vital statistics "as uniform as a row of tiny grave plots."[25] The deaths of the famous, however, are announced by lengthier *obituaries*.[26] Prefaced by individual headlines and set in the larger type used for feature stories, obituaries indicate the degree of newsworthiness that editors attribute to the deaths of famous people. Indeed, most news organizations maintain files of pending obituaries for individuals whose deaths will be newsworthy, and these obituaries are updated periodically so they are ready for publication or broadcast when the occasion demands.

The death of a neighbor or colleague at work is not likely to be reported with such emphasis. On the contrary, when "ordinary" people try to obtain an obituary rather than a death notice for a loved one, their efforts may meet with resistance. When one young woman died of Hodgkin's disease, her family delivered a brief account of her life and her photo to their local newspaper, asking that these items be used in announcing her death. Despite their efforts, and the efforts of others in the community who knew of the young woman's accomplishments, a newspaper spokesperson held to the position that it was against policy to run obituaries instead of death notices in such cases. Ordinary deaths—the kind most of us will experience—are ignored or mentioned only in routine fashion. When it comes to reports of death in the media, the spectacular obscures the ordinary.

Whether routine or extraordinary, our encounters with death in the news media influence the way we think about and respond to death. News reports may have less to do with the *event* than with how that event is *perceived*. Jack Lule illustrates this point by citing the manner in which Huey Newton's death was reported in newspapers across the country.[27] As cofounder of the Black Panther Party, Newton's public career spanned two decades and he occupied various roles; yet, in the main, his death was reported in ways that disavowed and debased his accomplishments as well as his standing as a political figure. Most reports focused on the violent nature of Newton's demise while ignoring other aspects of his life and, indeed, the tragic nature of his death. The implicit message seemed to be: "He who lives by the sword dies by the sword."

A very different perception was conveyed by the media in reporting the explosion of the space shuttle *Challenger,* which caused the deaths of seven crew members (including Christa McAuliffe, a schoolteacher). This event was portrayed as a tragedy for the whole country, evoking a sense of shared grief, and television was likened to a national hearth around which Americans symbolically gathered to collectively work through their shock and grief.

Whether television is best characterized as a national hearth or as simply another household appliance, people look to the media not only for information about events but also for clues about their meaning. This can present problems when trying to determine what is appropriate coverage of stories involving death. During the memorial service for the *Challenger* crew, for example, the grieving families were repeatedly shown in close-up views. Is such coverage an intrusion on the private sorrow of bereaved families, or is it legitimate news? The distinction between *public* event and *private* loss sometimes blurs.

When a Canadian newspaper published a photograph of a distraught mother as she learned of her daughter's fatal injuries in an accident, many readers expressed outrage, characterizing the photograph as "a blatant example of morbid ludicrousness" and "the highest order of poor taste and insensitivity."[28] The mother, interestingly enough, did not share these feelings. Seeing the photo, she said, helped her comprehend what had happened. Actually, this mother's reaction was not unusual. People who are bereaved by sudden, unexpected death often want to obtain details to help them reconstruct the events surrounding the death, as an aid in coping with the reality of their loss. So, was the newspaper correct in publishing the photo? Or were outraged readers correctly defending the rights of a grief-stricken mother, who appeared to have been victimized by an intrusive press? Or, yet again, did such volatile emotion result from the readers' own uncomfortable feelings about death? It seems that, because most people are not familiar with death and the emotions it elicits, they sometimes ascribe emotions to the grief-stricken that are not really present.

Even so, there are clearly times when media coverage does cause a "revictimization" or "second trauma" after the initial trauma of the horrible event itself. Because of television's visual power and immediacy, questions about privacy and propriety are especially relevant to this medium. Reporters may seek to capture the experience of a tragedy at the expense of victims. The journalistic stance, "if it bleeds, it leads," sets the priorities for much news reporting. (To be fair, this stance is a response to the human tendency toward voyeurism—our desire to have a close-up view of what's going on in other people's lives, a trait apparently shared with our primate cousins.[29] The media's eagerness to characterize events like the Oklahoma City bombing and the death of Princess Diana as "defining moments" plays to our yearning to escape rather humdrum lives and feel that we are living in extraordinary times.[30])

We might also question whether the media seek to help us explore the meaning of death, or merely want to grab our attention with a sensationalistic news flash. Robert Fulton and Greg Owen point out that the media often "submerge the human meaning of death while depersonalizing the event further by sandwiching actual reports of loss of life between commercials or other mundane items."[31] News of a bus crash or mine disaster is interposed between reports about the stock market or factory layoffs. The ensuing grief and disruption of survivors' lives is generally given scant attention. Recall your own experiences relative to deaths reported in the media and how reporters presented such information. Although there are exceptions, it seems that most media reports of death and dying bear little resemblance to the losses we experience in our own lives.

Entertaining Death

With an average of 2.4 television sets in American households, television's pervasive influence on our lives is solidly established.[32] Television is a significant agent of socialization, influencing our beliefs, attitudes, and practices. In a typical week's listings in *TV Guide,* about one-third describe programs in which death or dying features in some way. Far from being ignored, death is a central theme of much television programming. Besides its depiction in mov-

Relative News Values

ies of the week and on crime and adventure series, death is a staple of newscasts (typically, several stories involving death are featured in each broadcast), nature programs (death in the animal kingdom), children's cartoons (caricatures of death), soap operas (which seem always to have some character dying), sports (with descriptions such as "the ball is dead" and "the other team is killing them"), and religious programs (with theological and anecdotal mention of death). Yet these diverse images of death seldom add to our knowledge of its reality. Few programs deal with such real-life topics as how people cope with a loved one's death or confront their own dying.

Recall the Saturday morning cartoon depiction of death. Daffy Duck is pressed to a thin sheet by a steamroller, only to pop up again a moment later. Elmer Fudd aims his shotgun at Bugs Bunny, pulls the trigger, bang! Bugs, unmarked by the rifle blast, clutches his throat, spins around several times, and mutters, "It's all getting dark now, Elmer . . . I'm going . . ." Bugs falls to the ground, both feet still in the air. As his eyes close, his feet finally hit the dirt. But wait! Now Bugs pops up, good as new. Reversible death!

Or consider the western or detective story, which glazes over the reality of death by describing the bad guy as "kicking the bucket"—relegated, no doubt, to Boot Hill at the edge of town, where the deceased "pushes up daisies." Perhaps the camera pans from the dying person's face and torso to a close-up of hands twitching—then all movement ceases as the person's breathing fades away in perfect harmony with the musical score. Or, more likely, the death is violent: the cowboy gunfight at the OK Corral, high noon. The gent with the slower draw is hit, reels, falls, his body convulsing into cold silence.

People who have been present as a person dies describe a very different picture. Many recall the gurgling, gasping sounds as the last breath rattles through the throat; the changes in body color as flesh tones tinge blue; the feeling of a once warm and flexible body growing cold and flaccid. They often say, "Death is not at all what I thought it would be like; it doesn't look or sound or feel like anything I see on television or in movies!"

When told of his grandfather's death, one modern seven-year-old asked, "Who did it to him?" The image of death in the media is that it comes from outside, often violently. Such notions of death reinforce the belief that dying is something that *happens* to us, rather than something we *do*. Such portrayals affect our attitudes. Death is seen as an accidental rather than a natural process.

Unrealistic portrayals of violence can make viewers less sensitive to both real violence and its victims, increase unwarranted fears of becoming a victim, and contribute to aggressive behavior.[33] Media analyst George Gerbner observes that most television portrayals of death are embedded in a structure of violence that conveys "a heightened sense of danger, insecurity, and mistrust."[34] Such portrayals reflect a "mean world" syndrome, in which the symbolic use of death contributes to an "irrational dread of dying and thus to diminished vitality and self-direction in life." Depictions of violence often fail to show the real harm to victims, their pain, or appropriate punishment for perpetrators.

The portrayal of a "mean world" is found not only in fictional stories but also in news reports and other fact-based programming. True-crime television shows, for example, reinforce the viewer's perception of a dangerous world.[35] Crime reports on television news are presented as a kind of modern play in which the "devil" is symbolically cast out from society by its "guardians"—the police and the judiciary. Because so-called blue-collar crimes, such as murder and robbery, are more exciting to depict than white-collar crimes, such as embezzlement or bribery, the overall picture of both the nature of crime and of the criminal population is likely to be misleading. Yet, regular viewers come to believe that the real world is much like the television world.[36] The notion that we live in a dangerous world is also communicated by reports of environmental or health hazards that are alarmist rather than reassuring, reports that rarely use statistical measures to express degree of risk.[37] As our firsthand *experiences* of death and violence have diminished, *representations* of death and violence in the media have increased in sensationalism.[38]

Turning to the cinema, we find that death is a major theme in movies, although fantasy generally replaces reality to enhance the story line. Films often exhibit what critic Roger Ebert calls "Ali McGraw Disease" (alluding to the actress's character in *Love Story*), in which people with terminal illness are depicted as becoming more and more beautiful until ultimately "they're so great that they die."[39]

Thrillers featuring extreme violence have become a profitable genre for moviemakers. The road to more "blood and gore" in popular films was paved in part by the success of "slasher" films like *Friday the 13th* and *Nightmare on Elm Street*. Critics note that, in traditional horror films, the audience usually views the action through the eyes of the victim and thus identifies with his or her fate. In recent films, however, viewers are asked to identify with the attacker.[40] A similar phenomenon of identification is seen in video game violence, which has progressively become more vivid.[41] Games like "Postal," "Grand Theft Auto," "Duke Nukem," "Doom," "Quake," "Death Rally," and "Redneck Rampage" have prompted debate about potentially adverse effects on young players.

In February 2000, a cable television channel in Eugene, Oregon, aired a video showing people how to commit suicide and how to help others commit suicide using lethal drugs.[42] Written and narrated by Derek Humphry, founder of the Hemlock Society, "Final Exit" added to the ongoing debate about ethical issues involved in physician-assisted suicide and end-of-life care. The program raised concerns that uncontrolled public access to this kind of information could influence children or other individuals who were at risk to take steps toward suicide. Later that year, end-of-life care was examined from a different perspective in a four-part television series, "On Our Own Terms," hosted by Bill Moyers.[43] Featuring a number of experts in palliative medicine and hospice care, the series provided a window into the experience of patients and their caregivers. Two hundred hours of film were shot to create the six-hour series, which emphasized the importance of talking about issues related to dying and death. After doing the program, Moyers said, "I realized that each day of filming was one day closer to my own death," and "looking at dying taught me about living."

"On Our Own Terms" was acclaimed for bringing public attention to an important issue for individuals, families, and society as a whole. In the larger picture of media presentations involving dying or death, such positive contributions tend to be buried under an avalanche of messages about death that bear scant resemblance to its reality. As is readily seen, there is no shortage of death symbolism in the entertainment media. But relatively few stories include themes that deal with rebirth, continuation, or other positive aspects of death and dying.[44]

Music

Within the human mind, the power and significance of music has essential meaning. Even in the dark days of the Nazi Holocaust, music in the camps and ghettos provided hope and comfort. It helped sustain a sense of community and elicited at least a momentary sense of well-being.[45] Our liking for particular kinds of music relates to our basic sociocultural values.[46] In fact, music can be a kind of "badge" that serves to communicate our values, attitudes, and opinions to others.[47] In all musical styles, however, themes of death and loss can be heard and, indeed, are likely to be quite common.

Murder, mayhem, and misery have long been staples of American music. In traditional American folk music, for example, there are ballads describing premonitions of death, deathbed scenes, last wishes of the dying, the sorrow and grief of mourners, admonitions about caring for a person's gravesite, and expectations about the afterlife.[48] Themes of suicide and murder are also expressed in song, especially when they conjoin love and death. Consider the themes in such songs as "Where Have All the Flowers Gone?" (war), "Long Black Veil" (mourning), "Casey Jones" (accidental death), "The TB Is Whipping Me" (life-threatening illness), and "John Henry" (occupational hazards).

In rock and other forms of popular music, death themes are also standard fare (see Table 1-3). Some commentators even argue that the death imagery in rock music played a role in breaking the taboo against public mention of death. Support for this thesis can be found in a survey of the "Top 40" songs from the mid-50s to the 90s.[49] In so-called heavy metal, the lyrics often convey striking images of homicide and suicide.[50] Songs like "Skeleton on Your Shoulder" by a group called Coroner celebrate death. In the genres of rap and hip-hop music, there is also an obvious focus on themes involving dying and death. Coolio describes a "Gangsta's Paradise," while Puff Daddy grieves over a close friend's death in "I'll be Missing You."

In American blues music, the predominant themes involve loss and longing, trials and tribulations, separations and death. In "See That My Grave Is Kept Clean," Blind Lemon Jefferson expresses a universal human desire to be remembered after death. Son House expresses regret in the wake of a loved one's unexpected death in his "Death Letter." The legendary Robert Johnson's "Crossroad Blues" conveys a sense of the singer's pervasive spiritual and existential unease. In "I Feel Like Going Home," Muddy Waters tells us that death sometimes ushers in relief from overwhelming pain. For the student of death themes in music, the treasure trove of blues music offers numerous examples, including Bessie Smith's "Nobody Knows You When You're Down and Out" (economic reversal), T-Bone Walker's "Call It Stormy Monday" (lost love), John Mayall's "The Death of J. B. Lenoir" (death of a friend in a car accident), and Otis Spann's "The Blues Never Die" (consolation in loss). Even though the lyrics in blues often express regret and sadness, the music itself generally conveys a sense of ultimate well-being, testifying to our inherent capacity to cope with even the most painful tragedies of human life.

Sometimes characterized as the flip side of the blues, traditional gospel music expresses many images of loss and grief. Here are just a few examples: "Will the Circle Be Unbroken" (death of family members), "Oh, Mary Don't You Weep" (mourning), "This May Be the Last Time" (impermanence of life), "Known Only to Him" (facing death), "When the Saints Go Marching In" (afterlife), "If I Could Hear My Mother Pray Again" (parent's death), and "Precious Memories" (adjustment to loss and sustaining bonds with the deceased).

Turning to classical music, death themes are heard in both religious and secular compositions. Leonard Bernstein's *Symphony No. 3* (Kaddish) is based on the Jewish prayer for the dead. The Requiem Mass (Mass for the Dead) has

TABLE 1-3   *Death Themes in Contemporary Popular Music*

Performer	Song	Theme
Tori Amos	Little Earthquakes	Multiple losses
Beatles	Eleanor Rigby	Aging and loss
Boyz II Men	Say Goodbye to Yesterday	Loss and grief
Garth Brooks	One Night a Day	Coping with grief
Jackson Browne	For a Dancer	Eulogy
Eric Clapton	Tears in Heaven	Death of young son
Elvis Costello	Waiting for the End of the World	Threat of death
Rodney Crowell	Things I Wish I'd Said	Cherishing memories
Joe Diffie	Almost Home	Anticipating father's death
Dion	Abraham, Martin, and John	Political assassination
Doors	The End	Murder
Bob Dylan	Knockin' on Heaven's Door	Last words / Death scene
Grateful Dead	Black Peter	Social support in dying
Jimi Hendrix	Mother Earth	Inevitability of death
Indigo Girls	Pushing the Needle Too Far	Drug-related death
Elton John	Candle in the Wind	Death of Marilyn Monroe
The Judds	Guardian Angels	Ancestors
Kenny Loggins	My Father's House	A father's death
Patty Loveless	How Can I Help You to Say Goodbye?	A mother's dying
Madonna	Promise to Try	Mother's death
Metallica	Fight Fire with Fire	Nuclear catastrophe
Mike and the Mechanics	The Living Years	Father's death
Morrissey	Angel, Angel, Down We Go	Suicide intervention
Holly Near	The Letter	Friend dying of AIDS
Sinead O'Connor	I Am Stretched on Your Grave	Mourning behavior
Oingo Boingo	No One Lives Forever	Facing death stoically
Pink Floyd	Dogs of War	War-related deaths
The Police	Murder by Numbers	Political killings
Elvis Presley	In the Ghetto	Violent death and grief
Queen	Another One Bites the Dust	Violent death
Lou Reed	Sword of Damocles	Coping with terminal illness
Henry Rollins	Drive-by Shooting	Satire on death by random violence
Carly Simon	Life Is Eternal	Desire for immortality
Snoop Doggy Dogg	Murder Was the Case	Urban homicide and justice system
Bruce Springsteen	Streets of Philadelphia	Dying of AIDS
James Taylor	Fire and Rain	Suicide
Stevie Wonder	My Love Is with You	Violent death of a child

racted composers like Mozart, Berlioz, and Verdi, among others. One section of the Requiem Mass, the *Dies irae* ("Day of Wrath"), is a musical symbol for death in works by many composers. In Berlioz's *Symphonie Fantastique* (1830), this theme is heard, first following an ominous tolling of bells and then, as the music reaches its climax, in counterpoint to the frenzied dancing of witches at a *sabbat*. Berlioz's *Symphonie* tells the story of a young musician who, spurned by his beloved, attempts suicide with an overdose of opium. In a narcotic coma, he experiences fantastic dreams that include a nightmarish march to the gallows. The *Dies irae* is also heard in Saint-Saëns' *Danse Macabre* (1874) and Liszt's *Totentanz* (1849), two of the best-known musical renditions of the Dance of Death. Opera, which combines drama with music, commonly includes themes of murder and suicide.[51] A recent symphony by John Corigliano is composed as a musical response to the AIDS epidemic. Epic in scope and formal in structure, the symphony has no real finale; rather, it just stops, a musical statement of the fact that, as yet, there is no real resolution to this devastating disease. A companion piece, a choral work entitled "Of Rage and Remembrance," was inspired partly by the Names Project AIDS Memorial Quilt.[52]

The *dirge* is a musical form associated with funeral processions and burials. Beethoven, Schubert, Schumann, Strauss, Brahms, Mahler, and Stravinsky all wrote dirges. The jazz funeral of New Orleans is a well-known example of a popular interpretation of the dirge. Related to this musical form are *elegies* and *laments*—musical settings for poems commemorating a person's death. The lament is a musical expression of ritual leave-taking that is found in many cultural settings, one example being Scottish clan funerals, where bagpipes are played. Vocally, the characteristic lament is an expression of mourning called "keening," an emotionally moving expression of loss and longing. Besides being a way to mourn the dead, laments may display a future orientation, in which the bereaved identify their altered social status and seek sympathetic understanding from the community.[53]

In traditional Hawaiian culture, chants known as *mele kanikau* were the traditional lament for commemorating a person's death.[54] Some *kanikau* were carefully composed; others were chanted spontaneously during the funeral procession. Imagery of the natural world is called upon to portray the writer's experience of loss.[55] Memories of shared experiences amid natural surroundings are mentioned: "My companion in the chill of Manoa" or "My companion in the forest of Makiki." Such chants fondly recall the things that bind together the deceased and his or her survivors. The message of the Hawaiian lament was not "I am bereft without you" but rather "These are the things I cherish about you."

As you listen to your favorite styles of music, notice the references to dying and death. What messages are being conveyed? What attitudes are being expressed? Whatever your musical taste, you will find a wealth of information about individual and cultural attitudes toward death.

Literature

From the epic poetry of Homer's *Iliad* and the classic drama of Sophocles' *Oedipus the King* and Shakespeare's *King Lear,* through modern stories like Leo Tolstoy's "The Death of Ivan Ilych," James Agee's *Death in the Family,* and Ernest J. Gaines's *A Lesson Before Dying,* writers treat death as a significant event

One Tree Hill

We turn away to face the cold, enduring chill
As the day begs the night for mercy
Your sun so bright it leaves no shadows, only scars
Carved into stone on the face of earth
The moon is up and over One Tree Hill
We see the sun go down in your eyes
You ran like a river to the sea
Like a river to the sea
And in our world a heart of darkness, a firezone
Where poets speak their hearts, then bleed for it
Jara sang, his song a weapon, in the hands of love
You know his blood still cries from the ground
It runs like a river to the sea
Like a river to the sea
I don't believe in painted roses or bleeding hearts
While bullets rape the night of the merciful
I'll see you again when the stars fall from the sky
And the moon has turned red over One Tree Hill
We run like a river to the sea
Like a river to the sea

Bono, U2. For the funeral of Greg Carroll
(1960–1986), Wanganui, New Zealand,
July 10, 1986.

in human experience. The meaning of death is often explored as it relates to society as well as the individual. Recall for a moment a favorite novel or short story. Was death an element of the plot? How did the author portray dying or death in the story?

Writers have also depicted the trauma of combat and the various ways individuals struggle to find meaning in shattering experiences of loss. More than just war stories, many of these accounts illustrate a basic human need to make sense of traumatic loss, to confront and cope with the overwhelming grief that war brings to both individuals and societies. Holocaust literature is of special interest in this regard. Devastating experiences of horror and mass death are dealt with in victims' diaries, as well as in novels and psychological studies.[56] Examples include Chaim Kaplan's *Warsaw Diary*, Charlotte Delbo's *None of Us Will Return*, Elie Wiesel's *Night*, and Anne Frank's *Diary of a Young Girl*. Writings like these lead readers to contemplate essential aspects of human nature and spirit.

Modern literature often attempts to explore the meaning of death in situations that are seemingly incomprehensible. The existential works of Jean-Paul Sartre (*Nausea, No Exit*) and Albert Camus (*The Plague, The Stranger*) are examples. In the genre of "vigilante" stories, which characterize modern detective novels, the hero sets out to avenge evil but is often corrupted by a self-

Buffalo Bill's
defunct
              who used to
              ride a watersmooth-silver
                                    stallion
and break onetwothreefourfive pigeonsjustlikethat
                                              Jesus
he was a handsome man
                              and what i want to know is
how do you like your blueeyed boy
Mister Death

              e.e. cummings

justifying morality that only perpetuates violence.[57] Modern literature, it seems, often focuses on a "landscape of violence."[58] The fictional hero tries to come to terms with sudden and violent death in situations that allow no time for survivors to express their grief or mourn their dead.[59] Finding meaning in death is problematic, as violence reduces persons to the status of *things*.

Uncertainty about death is also found in the *elegy*. Jahan Ramazani says, "The poetry of mourning for the dead assumes in the modern period an extraordinary diversity and range, incorporating more anger and skepticism, more conflict and anxiety than ever before."[60] Modern elegies include Wilfred Owen's poems of moral objection to the pain wrought by industrialized warfare; Langston Hughes's "blues poems," expressing the soul-weariness of African Americans in their encounters with racial injustice; Allen Ginsberg's *Kaddish* after the death of his mother; Seamus Heaney's memorials to the suffering caused by political violence in Ireland; and the "parental elegies" in the poetry of Sylvia Plath, Anne Sexton, and Adrienne Rich. Ramazani observes that poetry is an important "cultural space for mourning the dead," as writers search for "credible responses to loss in the modern world."

Literature dealing with dying and death is increasingly finding a place in training programs for physicians, nurses, and other health professionals. Technical information about dying and death is balanced by the humanistic insights found in literary works. By exploring the impact of frightening diseases and unsettling circumstances through stories and poems, abstract clinical descriptions are humanized and made more personal.[61]

Visual Arts

In the visual arts, death themes are revealed through symbols, signs, and images.[62] In Western European art, these themes are usually expressed in ways that are based on classical mythology and the Judeo-Christian tradition. Comparable sources inspire artists of other cultures. The scenes inscribed in relief on ancient Egyptian sarcophagi attest to that culture's beliefs about the afterlife. Graphically portrayed on these limestone coffins is the expectation that, after death, a person will be judged according to his or her deeds during earthly life. Artistic themes that draw upon natural processes of life, growth, decay, and death transcend cultural boundaries and are universally found in art.

During the Middle Ages, there arose in Western Europe one of the most arresting expressions of dying and death ever to emerge in the graphic arts: the *Dance of Death.* Growing out of widespread fears about the spread of bubonic plague, the Black Death, the images associated with the Dance of Death testify to a preoccupation with mortality and fear of sudden, unexpected death. This theme captures the attention of artists in our own time, as seen in Fritz Eichenberg's woodcuts depicting the fears of our era: annihilation caused by total war, environmental catastrophe, and epidemic diseases such as AIDS.[63]

Franco José de Goya's *Self-Portrait with Dr. Arieta* exemplifies an artistic genre that depicts deathbed scenes and persons *in extremis.* Completed for the doctor who aided Goya's recovery from a life-threatening illness, this painting shows the doctor holding medicine to Goya's lips while the figure of Death is depicted next to people who are thought to be Goya's priest and his housekeeper. Suicide is another theme dealt with by artists of virtually all eras and cultures. In *The Death of Lucretia,* for example, Rembrandt van Rijn portrays Lucretia with a tear in her eye, moments after she has stabbed herself with a dagger. Painted shortly after the deaths of Rembrandt's wife and one of his sons, the work reflects the artist's saddened mental state.

Art can give us a window into the customs and beliefs of other ages and places. The customs and beliefs of the American colonial period, for instance, are illustrated in Charles Wilson Peale's *Rachel Weeping* (1772 and 1776). In this deathbed scene, a mother is shown mourning her dead child. The child's jaw is wrapped with a fabric strap to keep it closed. Her arms are bound with cord to keep them at her sides. Medicines, all of which have proved ineffective, sit on a bedside table. As the mother gazes heavenward, she holds a handkerchief to wipe away the tears streaming down her face, her expression of grief a marked contrast to the dead child's peaceful face.

Art can be a vehicle for expressing the powerful impact of personal loss, as in the lithographs, etchings, and woodcuts of Käthe Kollwitz, which depict parental grief evoked by the death of a child. Other artists have taken on the mission of using art to communicate the horror of the Nazi Holocaust, with the aim of ensuring that the slaughter of millions of innocent people will not be forgotten.[64] Edvard Munch's *The Dance of Life,* which appears on the cover of this text, represents the artist's summing up of human fate: "Love and death, beginnings and endings, are fused in a roundel that joins private lives and lusts to the larger, inexorable cycle of ongoing generations."[65] In some art, we find a whimsical attitude toward death, as in the engravings of Mexican artist Antonio Guadalupe Posada, which contain skeletal figures from all walks of life engaged in daily routines, or in American sculptor Richard Shaw's *Walking Skeleton,* with the skeleton composed of twigs, bottles, playing cards, and similar found objects.

Käthe Kollwitz, Library of Congress

Of the modern artists who have expressed death themes in art, few have done so more frequently or more powerfully than German artist Käthe Kollwitz—as in this 1925 woodcut, Proletariat—Child's Coffin.

Within the context of nineteenth-century mourning customs, ordinary Americans incorporated both classical and Christian symbols of death to memorialize public figures as well as family members.[66] Embroidered memorials to the dead were hung in the parlor, the most important room of the house, and elaborate quilts were sewn into designs that celebrated the life of the deceased. Such mourning art provided not only a way to perpetuate memories of a loved one, but also a focus for physically working through grief, an opportunity to actively grieve by doing something.

Similar motives were behind the making of a massive quilt to commemorate individuals who have died from AIDS: The Names Project AIDS Memorial Quilt.[67] Within the context of American folk art, quilts represent family and community. As the largest ongoing community arts project in America, the AIDS Quilt has become a symbol of collective, national unity. It has also motivated people to seek information and make positive behavioral changes to counteract a devastating disease.[68] As an artistic response to AIDS, the Names Quilt reaffirms the value of creative expression as a means of coping with loss. Maxine Junge points out:

> Creativity in the face of death offers a spectrum of life-enhancing possibilities. These possibilities can ward off a meaningless conclusion to a life, give meaning and hope to a life lived and to a future in which the dead, through memory, still exist.[69]

In responding to AIDS, the artistic community has expressed its anger and grief through activist art with a political edge, as well as through mourning art that tries to convey the magnitude of loss.[70]

The Vietnam Veterans Memorial Wall in Washington, D.C., designed by architect Maya Lin, is another outstanding example of contemporary mourning art. It, like the AIDS Quilt, counters the anonymity of lives lost. The impetus for creating the memorial came from bereaved individuals who felt the need to honor loved ones who died while serving their country in a largely unpopular war. On the wall, the names of the dead are listed chronologically by the date of their death, not alphabetically, presenting a chronicle of the war that vividly depicts the scale of losses. As *sites of memory,* both the AIDS Quilt and the Vietnam Veterans Memorial are focal points for mourning. They exemplify how the social taboo against open mourning can be resisted when people defy the suppression of grief and create new modes for its expression.

The Present Milieu: Death Attitudes and Awareness

Historian David Stannard tells us that in societies in which each individual is unique, important, and irreplaceable, death is not ignored but is marked by a "community-wide outpouring of grief for what is a genuine social loss."[71] Conversely, in societies where people feel that "little damage is done to the social fabric by the loss of an individual," outside of that individual's immediate circle, death receives little or no acknowledgment.

A first step toward gaining new choices about death is to recognize that avoiding or denying it estranges us from an integral aspect of human life. The

Smithsonian Institution

© Albert Lee Strickland

The making of a memorial quilt was among the elaborate personal and social mechanisms for dealing with grief widely practiced during the nineteenth century, as in this example memorializing a granddaughter who died in infancy. This traditional mourning custom was revived recently to commemorate and remember persons who died from AIDS; in the example shown here, words and symbols express beloved qualities of Joe's life. For survivors, the creation of such memorials provides not only a focus for physically working through grief, but also a means of perpetuating the memory of the loved one.

term *thanatology* is usually defined as the "study of death"; but, as Robert Kastenbaum suggests, it is perhaps better defined as "the study of life, with death left in."[72] As eloquently stated by the Mexican poet and social philosopher Octavio Paz: "A civilization that denies death ends by denying life."[73]

Pioneers in Death Studies

Herman Feifel's book, *The Meaning of Death,* published in 1959, provides a convenient watershed from which to date the modern study of death and dying. Based on a symposium held in 1956, Feifel's book brought together authorities from different disciplines whose essays encompassed theoretical approaches, cultural studies, and clinical insights. Death was shown to be an important topic for public and scholarly consideration. This was no easy feat, considering the prevailing resistance to discussing death. Feifel says:

> The realization soon began to sink in that what I was up against were not idiosyncratic personal quirks, the usual administrative vicissitudes, pique, or nonacceptance of an inadequate research design. Rather, it was personal position, bolstered by cultural structuring, that death is a dark symbol not to be stirred—not even touched—an obscenity to be avoided.[74]

Feifel recalls that he was emphatically told that "the one thing you never do is to discuss death with a patient."

The same message was communicated to Elisabeth Kübler-Ross, whose book, *On Death and Dying* (1969), became the first bestseller about death and helped create demand for a new approach to caring for dying patients. Cicely Saunders addressed similar issues ten years earlier in her pioneering work, *Care of the Dying* (1959), which sparked interest in hospice care. In the same era, literary works such as C. S. Lewis's *A Grief Observed* (1961) brought greater prominence to bereavement issues.

During this pioneering era in death studies, Geoffrey Gorer's essay, "The Pornography of Death" (1955), focused attention on social issues and questioned how society was dealing with death at midcentury. In "Death in American Society" (1963), sociologist Talcott Parsons looked at the impact of social forces, especially technological advances in public health and medicine, on dying in America. At the same time, Jacques Choron wrote about death and dying from a philosophical vantage point in his *Death and Western Thought* (1963) and *Death and Modern Man* (1964). Soon, Robert Fulton brought together a group of scholars and practitioners to address both theoretical and practical issues in his compilation, *Death and Identity* (1965), and John Hinton's *Dying* (1967) offered a review of contemporary attitudes toward death.

Also during the 1960s, Barney G. Glaser and Anselm L. Strauss applied the tools of sociology to study how the awareness of dying affected patients, hospital staff, and family members. Their studies revealed that caregivers were reluctant to discuss death and avoided telling patients that they were dying. Glaser and Strauss's *Awareness of Dying* (1965) and *Time for Dying* (1968) are classics in the early literature of thanatology, as is Jeanne Quint Benoliel's pioneering work, *The Nurse and the Dying Patient* (1967), in which she called for systematic death education for nurses. In *On Dying and Denying: A Psychiatric Study of Terminality* (1972), Avery D. Weisman shed light on the dying process by astutely combining research skills and clinical experience with dying patients. Ernest Becker's *The Denial of Death* (1973) drew upon psychological and theological insights to analyze the "terror" of death in human life and suggest a more "heroic" response.

At about the same time, contemporary funerals were being critiqued in Jessica Mitford's *The American Way of Death* and Ruth Harmer's *The High Cost of Dying*, both published in 1963. Some time earlier, in *The Loved One* (1948), novelist Evelyn Waugh had employed satire to shed light on hypocritical and death-avoiding attitudes relative to funeral practices. Such publications sparked efforts by consumer advocates to institute governmental regulation of funeral businesses.

These pioneering works provide a foundation for death studies that remains valuable today. In the decades since their publication, scholarly and academic studies of dying and death have been joined by hundreds of books and articles on the subject aimed at the general public. Each new publishing season brings additional offerings of advice for the bereaved, the dying, and their caregivers. Nor has the scholarly and academic literature lagged behind. Several journals are published with a specific concern for thanatological studies, including *Omega: Journal of Death and Dying, Death Studies, Journal of Personal and Interpersonal Loss, Mortality,* and *Illness, Crisis, and Loss.* Scholarly books and monographs appear with such regularity that it is difficult to review them all. In addition, technology has made a considerable amount of information about death and dying available to both professionals and the general public on the Internet.[75] In short, from the seeds planted just a few decades ago by pioneering contributors to the field, interest in death and dying appears to be blossoming.

The Rise of Death Education

Take a death and dying course or read a book like this and someone will probably ask, "Why would you want to take a class about death?" or "Why are you reading about death?" Despite increasing interest in death-related issues, many people still display attitudes of avoidance or denial when it comes to death. In our cultural relationship with death, we seem to be in a period of transition.

Ambivalent attitudes toward death are evident when one educator applauds the study of death as the "last of the old taboos to fall," while another contends that death is "not a fit subject for the curriculum." As Patrick Dean observes, if death education is viewed by some as a "bastard child of the curriculum, hidden in the closet," then those who value death education should be grateful to the critics who create opportunities for highlighting the importance of death education as preparation for living.[76] Dean says that death education could appropriately be renamed "life and loss education," because "only through awareness of our lifelong losses and appreciation of our mortality are we free to be in the present, to live fully."

Considered broadly, death education encompasses formal instruction as well as informal discussion of dying, grief, and related topics. Informal death education occurs in the context of "teachable moments" that arise out of events in daily life. The precipitating event may be the death of a gerbil in an elementary school classroom, or it may be an event experienced more widely, such as the *Challenger* accident or death of Princess Diana. Diana's funeral was broadcast live around the world and reportedly was watched by more than 2 billion viewers, the largest audience in television history. Much the same kind of media attention was given to the July 1999 deaths of John F. Kennedy, Jr., his wife Carolyn Bessette Kennedy, and sister-in-law Lauren Bessette in a plane crash offshore from Martha's Vineyard. The story of their deaths unfolded during a five-day period of search and recovery by the Navy and Coast Guard, which culminated in the scattering of their cremated remains at sea from the deck of the USS *Briscoe*.[77]

The first formal course in death education at an American university was initiated by Robert Fulton at the University of Minnesota in the spring of 1963.[78] The first conference on death education was held at Hamline University in Minnesota in 1970. From the beginning, the study of death has embraced a wide range of issues and topics, from the nuts-and-bolts issues of selecting mortuary services or probating an estate, to more philosophical matters such as speculation about what happens after death.

Because death education addresses both objective facts and subjective concerns, it receives broad academic support, with courses offered in a variety of disciplines.[79] In most courses, mastery of facts is enhanced by personal narratives that describe the myriad ways human beings encounter and cope with death.[80] The arts and humanities are drawn upon to balance scientific and technical perspectives. The arts and humanities constitute the "language of the soul," and their images, symbols, and sounds express themes of life, death, and transcendence that allow for other ways of knowing and learning.[81]

Death education benefits from the collegiality offered by organizations that promote interaction and communication around issues of mutual interest. One such organization, which includes special programs for college and university students, is the Association for Death Education and Counseling (ADEC).[82] Another organization, the International Work Group on Death, Dying, and Bereavement (IWG), provides a forum for creating and disseminating policy statements concerning issues of widespread interest in the field.[83]

The larger picture of death education includes training for physicians, nurses, allied health personnel, funeral directors, and other professionals whose duties involve contact with dying and bereaved individuals.[84] This includes police officers, fire fighters, and emergency medical technicians (EMTs). As witnesses to human tragedy in the line of duty, they are called upon to comfort victims and survivors. The stoic image of the police officer, EMT, or fire fighter who "keeps it all in," never showing emotion, is challenged by the recognition that such a strategy is physically and psychologically harmful.

Death education has achieved many milestones over the past decades, yet it remains a work in progress that is welcoming to the ideas and visions of new

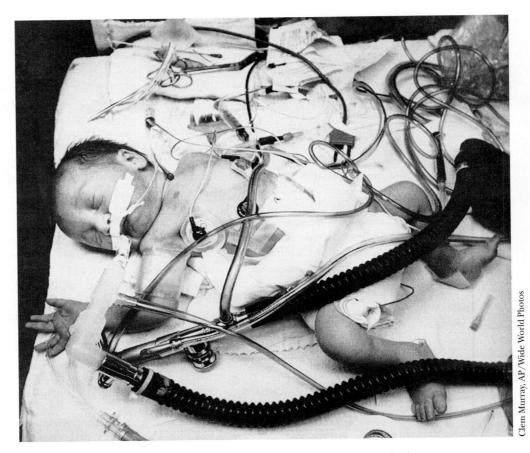

Clem Murray, AP/Wide World Photos

Lifelines—tubes and wires monitoring heartbeat, breathing, and blood pressure—increase this premature baby's chances of survival in the intensive care unit of Philadelphia's Children's Hospital. The special-care nursery often becomes an arena for many of the most difficult ethical decisions in medicine.

contributors. Hannelore Wass observes that the study of death and dying has the potential to help individuals and societies "leap from a parochial to a global view," transcending self-interest in favor of concern for others.[85] The ultimate rationale for death studies, Wass says, "is about love, care, and compassion; it is about helping and healing."

Is Death Out of the Closet?

Where death is concerned, the adage, "What you don't know won't hurt you," is false. Death is unavoidably part of our lives. People living in modern times have been described as *hibakusha,* a Japanese word meaning "explosion-affected." Used originally to describe survivors of the atomic bombing of Hiroshima, the term connotes pervasive anxiety about the threat of annihilation.

In this regard, the horrors of war, violence, and terrorism have been joined more recently by the specter of emerging diseases like AIDS.

Not thinking or talking about death doesn't remove us from its power. Such ostrichlike behavior only limits our choices for coping effectively. When we bring death out of the closet, we give ourselves an opportunity to clear away the accumulated rubbish and keep what is valuable. As pioneering death educator Robert Kavanaugh said, "The unexamined death is not worth dying."[86] In assessing death avoidance, we should consider the role of *institutional denial.* One student said: "Sometimes I feel there's too little space in our society for a person to scream, to cry, to shout, to sing, to touch, to be human." Death evokes all these aspects of human behavior.

Medical technologies have had a major impact on how we die. Urbanization and other social changes have affected how we care for our dead. These effects have been so thorough and rapid that our personal and social responses have not always kept pace with innovation. *Cultural lag* is a term used by social scientists to describe the phenomenon of societies falling behind in dealing with the new social problems that result from technological advances. It is possible that we are in a period of cultural lag with respect to how we deal with dying and death.

According to some scholars, we now live in a *postmodern* era, "surrounded by images and artifacts from all periods and of all geographical and cultural locations."[87] In part, this means that we have the opportunity to become "aware of the entire experience of the human race in ways that were not available to previous generations." This awareness is reflected in the eclecticism readily seen in contemporary art, philosophy, ethics, social and political matters, and life styles. Capitalizing on the postmodern perspective may lead to the possibility of selecting pertinent ideas and practices from all historical periods and cultures, thereby enabling us to create a synthesis that is personally and socially appropriate for the times in which we live and die.

Examining Assumptions

As we journey into the early years of the twenty-first century, many people are examining their assumptions about death and dying. The quest for a personally meaningful response to these central human questions leads different individuals to different outcomes. For example, questions about the conventional funeral cause some people to favor swift and inexpensive disposition of the body in place of traditional practices. Others maintain that conventional funerals provide a crucial framework for meeting the social and psychological needs of survivors (see Figure 1-4). At some level, or at some time, we all need to ask: What is important about participating in a ceremony commemorating the death of a loved one, and is something of value lost when survivors have no opportunity to engage in such ritual?

Among the Amish community, which maintains traditional beliefs and practices, death is part of the natural rhythm of life. A person's death initiates an outpouring of social support, for the bereaved family and for the wider

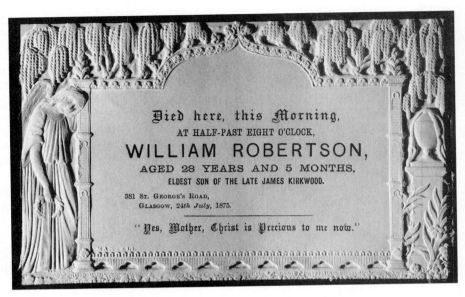

Figure *1-4* *Embossed Linen Death Notification, 1875*
This card exemplifies the formality of nineteenth-century mourning customs. The etiquette books of the period often devoted considerable space
to the procedural details associated with the wearing of mourning clothes,
the issuance of funeral invitations, and other behaviors appropriate to the
survivors of a death.

society. The social patterns that the Amish find helpful in coping with death
include open communication about the process of dying; maintaining, to the
extent possible, a normal life style during the course of the final illness; commitment to the independence of the dying person; and community support
of the bereaved.[88]

These qualities of care and community are being adapted to very different
cultural settings through such initiatives as hospice and palliative care, which
aim to provide total care for the dying person and his or her family. Recent
programs sponsored by George Soros's "Project on Death in America" and
the Robert Wood Johnson Foundation's "Last Acts Program" seek to advance
these initiatives to improve care of the dying.[89] Meanwhile, a new service industry appears to be forming, one composed of "personal death consultants"
who, for a fee, will help people create custom-made deathbed rituals or
conduct do-it-yourself funerals, all designed to "achieve a good death" and
"healthy grief."[90]

As individuals and societies begin to face dying and death more openly,
we can expect to see a variety of ideas and practices put forward. In taking
what may be halting steps toward finding a place for death in our lives, we will
find that some proposals and plans are more valuable than others. Our journey is likely to include restoring or rediscovering appropriate elements of

attitudes and customs that prevailed in the past. In examining our assumptions about death and dying, and in creating a synthesis of old and new that fits who we are and our place in society, we do well to consider both our individual preferences and cultural perspectives. Andrew Ziner says:

> Like nearly every other aspect of our lives, our understandings and feelings about dying and death are derived from our involvement in the myriad of groups, organizations, and institutions that represent our communities and, ultimately, constitute our society. As these religious, economic, legal, and familial structures change over time, we also change. This is because, as social beings, all of the meanings we attach to personal and cultural concerns—including dying and death—are inexorably tied to our social worlds. For example, how do you feel when you hear the word *death*? If you were born a century earlier, would you feel the same way? Is the difference due to individual or social factors?[91]

Death is intrinsic to human experience. Yet we may wish to cram it into a dark closet and shut the door. There it stays until, bursting the hinges, the door flies open and death is forced upon our awareness. Death is like a mysterious stranger at a costume ball, whose mask conceals the face beneath. Perhaps the disguise is more terrifying than the reality, yet how can we know unless we risk uncovering the face hidden behind the mask? Learning about death and dying helps us identify attitudes and behaviors that keep us from lifting the mask and confronting death in a way that is meaningful for our own lives.

Further Readings

Patricia Anderson. *All of Us: Americans Talk About the Meaning of Death.* New York: Delacorte, 1996.

Martha Cooper and Joseph Sciorra. *R.I.P.: Memorial Wall Art.* New York: Henry Holt, 1994.

James K. Crissman. *Death and Dying in Central Appalachia: Changing Attitudes and Practices.* Urbana: University of Illinois Press, 1994.

Lynne Ann DeSpelder and Albert Lee Strickland, eds. *The Path Ahead: Readings in Death and Dying.* Mountain View, Calif.: Mayfield, 1995.

Anthony Elliott. *The Mourning of John Lennon.* Berkeley: University of California Press, 1999.

Donald Heinz. *The Last Passage: Recovering a Death of Our Own.* New York: Oxford University Press, 1999.

Lawrence L. Langer, ed. *Art from the Ashes: A Holocaust Anthology.* New York: Oxford University Press, 1995.

Dan Nimmo and James E. Combs. *Nightly Horrors: Crisis Coverage by Television Network News.* Knoxville: University of Tennessee Press, 1985.

Howard M. Spiro, Mary G. McCrea Curnen, and Lee Palmer Wandel, eds. *Facing Death: Where Culture, Religion, and Medicine Meet.* New Haven, Conn.: Yale University Press, 1996.

Tony Walter. *The Revival of Death.* New York: Routledge, 1994.

Robert F. Weir, ed. *Death in Literature.* New York: Columbia University Press, 1980.

In January 1879, frontier photographer L. A. Huffman recorded this scene showing the burial platform of a Sioux warrior who had died and been placed on the scaffold only a few days before. Surrounding the gravesite is a vast plain, crisscrossed with the trails of wild herds of buffalo.

C H A P T E R 2

Perspectives on Death:
Cross-Cultural and Historical

*D*eath is a universal human experience; yet our response to it is shaped by the attitudes of a particular culture. Attitudes reflect the characteristic orientation or "posture" of a given individual or society; they include components of belief, emotion, and behavior. The shared consciousness among its members makes a culture distinct; it gives a particular cast to experiences and the meanings ascribed to them. The term *culture* is a kind of shorthand for talking about the way of life of a given group of people. Understanding how other people relate to death can shed light on our own beliefs and behaviors. Various cultures can be ranged on a continuum from "death-welcoming" to "death-denying." In thinking about the cultures discussed in this chapter, consider where each might be placed on the welcoming–denying continuum. Consider, too, where your own "cultures"—the national, ethnic, and family groups of which you are a member—might fit on such a continuum.

Dying and death are more than biological events; they have social and spiritual dimensions. Questions about the meaning of death and what happens when we die are central concerns to people in every culture and have been since time immemorial. An essential concern for living well—and dying well—is present in all human cultures.

Death in Early and Traditional Cultures

Human concern for the dead predates written history. In Bronze Age burials, archeologists have found evidence of floral tributes.[1] The even older burials of Neanderthals, who began to inhabit Europe about 150,000 years ago, contain ornamental shells, stone implements, and food buried with the dead, implying a belief that such items would be useful in the passage from the land of the living to the land of the dead. In many such burials, the corpse is stained with red ochre and placed in a fetal posture, suggesting ideas about revitalization of the body and rebirth (see Figure 2-1).[2]

In traditional cultures, death is typically viewed not as an end but as a change of status, a transition from the land of the living to the world of the dead. The living are careful to help the dead in their journey to the other world. Sometimes precautions are taken to offset fears about the potential malevolence of the dead, who may harm the living if not shown respect. The foundations for human attitudes, values, and behaviors in traditional cultures are generally found in myths—that is, stories that explain beliefs or ideas.[3] A given culture's understanding of death and its meaning in people's lives are therefore revealed through its rituals and stories.

Figure 2-1 *Neanderthal Burial*

When the first man, the father of the human race, was being buried, a god passed by the grave and inquired what it meant, for he had never seen a grave before. Upon receiving the information from those about the place of interment that they had just buried their father, he said: "Do not bury him, dig up the body again." "No," they replied, "we cannot do that. He has been dead for four days and smells." "Not so," entreated the god, "dig him up and I promise you that he will live again." But they refused to carry out the divine injunction. Then the god declared, "By disobeying me, you have sealed your own fate. Had you dug up your ancestor, you would have found him alive, and you yourselves when you passed from this world should have been buried as bananas are for four days, after which you shall have been dug up, not rotten, but ripe. But now, as a punishment for your disobedience, you shall die and rot." And whenever they hear this sad tale the Fijians say: "Oh, that those children had dug up that body!"

Figure 2-2 *Fijian Story (Traditional): The Origin of Death*

Origin of Death

Why is there death? How did it become part of human experience? Looking at the big picture, we see that death promotes variety through the evolution of species. The human lifespan is long enough to allow us to reproduce ourselves and ensure that the lineage of our species continues. Yet it is brief enough to allow for new genetic combinations that provide a means of adaptation to changing conditions in the environment. From the perspective of species survival, death makes sense. But this explanation offers little comfort when death touches our own lives.

For people living in early and traditional societies, the origin of death is explained through stories or myths.[4] In some stories, death becomes part of human experience because ancestral parents or an archetypal figure transgressed divine or natural law, either through poor judgment or disobedience (see Figure 2-2). The stories sometimes involve a test of some person or group. When the test is failed, death becomes a reality. A story told by the Luba of Africa describes how god created a paradise for the first human beings and endowed it with everything needed for their sustenance; however, they were forbidden to eat of the bananas in the middle of the field. When the humans ate the bananas, it was decreed that humankind would die after a lifetime of toil. This motif is akin to the biblical story of Adam and Eve's transgression in the Garden of Eden, an account of death's origin that persists in the religious traditions of Judaism, Christianity, and Islam.

In some myths, a crucial act that would have ensured immortality was not properly carried out; an *omission* rather than an *action* introduces death to humankind. Some stories tell of a messenger who was supposed to deliver the message of eternal life but the message was garbled due to malice or forgetfulness, or it did not arrive on time. Among the Winnebago of North America, the trickster figure, Hare, is an example of this motif (see Figure 2-3).

When Hare heard of Death, he started for his lodge & arrived there crying, shriek-ing, *My uncles & my aunts must not die!* And then the thought assailed him: *To all things death will come!* He cast his thoughts upon the precipices & they began to fall & crumble. Upon the rocks he cast his thoughts & they became shattered. Under the earth he cast his thoughts & all the things living there stopped moving & their limbs stiffened in death. Up above, toward the skies, he cast his thoughts & the birds flying there suddenly fell to the earth & were dead.

After he entered his lodge he took his blanket and, wrapping it around him, lay down crying. *Not the whole earth will suffice for all those who will die. Oh, there will not be enough earth for them in many places!* There he lay in his corner wrapped up in his blanket, silent.

Figure 2-3 *Winnebago Myth: When Hare Heard of Death*

Momentarily forgetting his purpose, Hare failed to deliver the life-saving message. In a variant of this motif, two messengers were sent—one bringing immortality, the other bringing death—and the messenger bringing death arrived first.

In the "death in a bundle" motif, death is introduced into human expe-rience when a bundle containing the mortal fate of all humankind is opened, either inadvertently or because of poor choice. A story from Greek mythology told by Aesop is a variant of this theme (see Figure 2-4). Another motif de-scribes how a message of immortality was addressed to human beings, but people were not awake to receive it.

Although most myths portray death as unwelcome, some describe how it is actively pursued because of weariness with life or disgust with its misery. In these stories, people barter for or buy death from the gods so life does not go on interminably, or death is obtained as a remedy for overpopulation.

All of these myths echo a theme that is surprisingly familiar: Death comes from outside; it cuts short an existence that would otherwise be immortal. This notion still influences our attitudes to some degree. We can understand the biological processes of disease and aging, yet still feel that, if only this defect could be repaired, we could remain alive. We find ourselves believing that death is foreign, not really part of us. It seems an anomaly.

Ultimately, of course, we cannot avoid the recognition of our own mortal-ity. The epic of Gilgamesh tells the story of a king who sets off on a journey to find the secret of immortality, a journey undertaken because of the death of his friend, Enkidu. After overcoming great perils while searching for the power to renew one's youth, Gilgamesh returns from his quest empty-handed. Finally, grieving the death of his beloved friend, Gilgamesh realizes that he too will die. As was true of Gilgamesh, our mortality may be acknowledged most profoundly in grieving the death of a loved one.

Causes of Death

Even when we find a meaningful explanation about how death came into the world, there remains the question: What causes *individual* human

It was a hot, sultry summer afternoon, and Eros, tired with play and faint from the heat, took shelter in a cool, dark cave. It happened to be the cave of Death himself.

Eros, wanting only to rest, threw himself down carelessly—so carelessly that all his arrows fell out of his quiver.

When he woke he found they had mingled with the arrows of Death, which lay scattered about the floor of the cave. They were so alike Eros could not tell the difference. He knew, however, how many had been in his quiver, and eventually he gathered up the right number.

Of course, Eros took some that belonged to Death and left some of his own behind.

And so it is today that we often see the hearts of the old and the dying struck by bolts of Love; and sometimes we see the hearts of the young captured by Death.

Figure 2-4 *Aesop: Eros and Death*

beings to die? In most traditional cultures, an unexpected death is viewed as unnatural. The immediate cause of a death from accidental injuries or wounds sustained in battle is clear, but its ultimate cause is open to question: Why did this fatal event happen to this person at this particular time? Might it be due to some evil influence, possibly shaped by magic? Supernatural causes may provide an explanation for untimely death. Such explanations do not lend themselves to proof or disproof, of course, but they can comfort the bereaved by helping make sense of what otherwise seems inexplicable.

Among the Senufo people of Africa's Ivory Coast, for example, the death of a child is considered to be unnatural. It is disturbing to the whole community. Survivors must discover the cause of such misfortune. Actions must be taken to go beyond the obvious cause and uncover what lies behind it. Any instance of sudden death—whether due to violence or accident—threatens the welfare of the whole community. To restore a sense of security and proper order, sacrifices are offered to purify and protect the community from further calamity.[5]

In seeking the causes of death, traditional societies typically embrace an ecological orientation.[6] They look to the supernatural and investigate the possible role of such phenomena as the wind or moon, heredity, and behavioral excesses, such as not getting enough sleep. A variety of socioeconomic and psychosocial factors are explored. The cause of death may be related to the person's social interactions. Was anger, anxiety, fright, or envy involved? Did the person offend the ancestors or neglect to carry out the prescribed rites for the dead? The search for answers takes place within an environment that encompasses both the living and the dead. Illness and death signal the fact that something is "out of balance." Because of this, illness and death are public, not private, events. The health of the whole community depends on maintaining a proper relationship with the environment, including its unseen aspects.

Power of the Dead

In cultures that maintain strong bonds between the living and the dead, "the land echoes with the voices of the ancestors."[7] Together, the living and the dead comprise the clan, the tribe, the people. The bond between living and dead is a sign that the community endures beyond the limits of death. In Balinese society, the village territory belongs to the ancestors, and the living members of the community maintain contact with them to ensure their livelihood and well-being.[8] The community is a partnership of the living and the dead. This understanding is implicit when people refer to the "founding fathers" of a nation or college, who are spoken of metaphorically as "being with us in spirit" as living members of the group meet to celebrate their common purpose with those who preceded them.

In traditional societies, grief may be expressed with loud wails or with silent tears, but almost always there is deep respect for the still-powerful soul of the deceased. If the soul or spirit of the deceased is not treated properly, harm may result. Conducting the prescribed funeral rites ensures the successful journey of the soul into the realm of the dead, a journey that benefits the living. Of special concern are evil-intentioned spirits that wander about aimlessly, seeking to disrupt the well-being of the living. Such spirits are often associated with catastrophic deaths, such as deaths in childbirth.

In traditional cultures, people generally do not shun their dead. In the rhythm and flow of communal life, the deceased—in death as in life—is part of the whole. As unseen members of an ongoing social order, the dead are often allies who can perform services for the living—as interpreters, intermediaries, and ambassadors in the realm beyond the reach of our physical senses. Such communication with the dead is often facilitated by a *shaman,* a visionary in the community who projects his or her consciousness to the other realm and acts as an intermediary between the worlds of living and dead.[9] Because the dead are not bound by human time, *necromancy* (from the Greek, meaning "corpse-prophecy") offers access to past and future events.[10] By entering into a trance, a shaman contacts the dead and reports back the prophetic message that will benefit the living.

Among traditional Hawaiians, the intimate relationships of the *'ohana,* or family clan, involved close bonds between living family members and their ancestors.[11] Ancestors could serve as role models and uphold standards of conduct. In doing so, they formed a crucial spiritual link between human beings and powerful—but distant and impersonal—gods. Keeping alive the memory of one's ancestors and calling upon them to intercede with the gods allows individuals to sustain family loyalties beyond death.

Names of the Dead

If calling a person's name is a way of summoning the person, then refraining from using a name will presumably leave its bearer undisturbed. Hence, a common practice related to the dead is name avoidance: The deceased is never again mentioned or is referred to only obliquely, never by name. For example, the deceased might be referred to as "that one" or allusions may be made to particular traits or special qualities a person was known for during his or her lifetime. Thus, "Uncle Joe," who gained renown as an expert fisherman, might be referred to after his death as "that relative who caught many fish." A woman who had displayed extraordinary bravery might be referred to as "that one who showed courage." In some cultures, the deceased is referred to by his or her relationship to the speaker.

Name avoidance can be so thorough that living people with the same name as the deceased must adopt new names. Among the Penan Geng of central Borneo, naming practices involving death are incorporated into all forms of social discourse.[12] When a person dies, "death names" are given to closest kin. Thus, as a person goes through life, he or she may take on a series of names and titles that refer to different categories of relationship to the deceased.

Some cultures give special emphasis to the deceased's name, rather than avoiding it. For example, the deceased's name may be conferred on a newborn child. Such naming may reflect a desire to honor the memory of a loved one or to ensure that the soul of the dead person is reincarnated. In some cultures, when a woman nears the time to give birth, a deceased ancestor appears in a dream and tells her which of her ancestors is to be reborn; the dream determines the name her new baby receives.[13] Among Hawaiians, children may be named for ancestors or even named by the gods. The names bestowed by gods, which are communicated through dreams, are especially important. The name of a child who died earlier is sometimes given to a child born later. Naming a child for a relative who has died allows the name to live again.[14]

Respect for the dead or anxiety about provoking spirits may prompt name avoidance in traditional cultures. In modern societies, however, people avoid mentioning the deceased's name at times to prevent conjuring up painful reminders of the loss. In both situations, name avoidance may be a way of managing grief. Similarly, when a child is named after a beloved grandparent or respected friend, aren't the parents hoping that some of the qualities valued in the namesake will be "reborn" in the child? Although cultural forms differ, we find common threads that run through all human experience.

Death and Dying in Western Culture

Beginning in the early Middle Ages, about the year 400, and continuing for a thousand years, people living in Western European culture shared a view of the universe as bound together by natural and divine law. The teachings of the Church influenced the manner in which people died and offered hope for the afterlife. An acceptance of death associated with this outlook generally prevailed until the European cultural Renaissance, or rebirth, in the 1400s and 1500s. This period has been characterized by historian Philippe Ariès as one of "tamed death."[15]

In the earlier centuries of this period, people viewed death with the understanding that "we shall all die." This understanding reflected a sense of death as the collective destiny of humankind. The end of life was not thought to be synonymous with physical death; rather, the dead were "asleep" in the Church's keeping with assurance of resurrection at the apocalyptic return of Christ. With this faith, people tended not to fear what awaited them after death.

Death Knells

During many centuries one item of expense for survivors was the fee that must be paid for the ringing of the soul bell. Every cathedral and church of medieval Christendom had such a bell, almost always the largest one in the bell tower.

By the time John Donne wrote the immortal line "for whom the bell tolls," ringing of the soul bell—in a distinctive pattern, or knell—was popularly taken to be merely a public notice that a death had occurred. This use of the soul bell came into importance relatively late, however.

Not simply in Christian Europe but also among primitive tribes and highly developed non-Christian cultures of the Orient, bells have been linked with death. Notes from bells (rung in special fashion) served to help convince a spirit that there was no need to remain close to a useless dead body. At the same time, noise made by bells was considered to be especially effective in driving away the evil spirits who prowled about hoping to seize a newly released soul or to put obstacles in its path.

Ringing of the soul (or passing) bell was long considered so vital that bell ringers demanded, and got, big fees for using it. Still in general use by the British as late as the era of King Charles II in the seventeenth century, bell ringers then regulated the number of strokes of the passing bell so that the general public could determine the age, sex, and social status of the deceased.

Webb Garrison,
Strange Facts About Death

This sense of a common, collective destiny began to change during the period of the High Middle Ages, about 1000–1450, being transformed into an emphasis on the destiny of the individual. The collective idea that "everyone dies" was replaced by the individual acknowledgment, "I will die my own death." This transformation occurred over the course of several centuries and coincided with a general enrichment of life and culture. The achievements of this period include the building of the great cathedrals of Notre Dame and Chartres in France, Canterbury in England, and Cologne in Germany, as well as the creation of literary works such as Dante's *Divine Comedy* and Chaucer's *Canterbury Tales.*

Whereas, during the earlier period, residing in the bosom of the Church had been enough to provide assurance of resurrection on the Last Day and entry into Heaven, people now became personally anxious about Judgment Day, the cosmic event that would separate the just from the damned. An individual's good or bad deeds, not the community's faith, would determine his or her ultimate and eternal fate. The *liber vitae,* or Book of Life, which previously had been pictured as a sort of vast cosmic census, was now imagined to contain the biographies of individual lives, a kind of balance sheet by which each person's soul would be weighed. Even with this change, however, the dominant cultural attitude toward death throughout the Middle Ages fits into Ariès's category of "tamed death."

The period of Renaissance and religious reformation, beginning about 1450, has aptly been called an "age of transition." Gutenberg's *Bible* went to press in 1456 and, in 1517, Luther nailed his Ninety-Five Theses to the door of the church at Wittenberg Castle, inaugurating the Protestant reformation. During this period, the dominant trends of thought became increasingly humanistic, secular, and individualistic. Geographic boundaries fell away, with explorations such as Columbus's voyage to America in 1492, and a scientific revolution ensued with publication in 1543 of Copernicus's *On the Revolution of the Heavenly Spheres,* which posited the radical notion that the earth revolves around the sun. This was a time of experimentation and pluralism, as many of the certainties of the earlier era were reexamined.

Transformations in cultural and intellectual life were accompanied by changes in how people related to death. The conventional wisdom was challenged by competing ideas in the religious marketplace and by the revolutionary discoveries of scientists and explorers. Traditional answers about the shape of the cosmos and the place of human beings within it were still backed by the authority of the Church. But the reassuring notions of earlier centuries were questioned as people began to feel more ambivalent about death and the afterlife. The scientific revolution of the 1500s and 1600s challenged traditional notions of authority and ushered in an age of "enlightenment" in the 1700s, with an emphasis on reason and intellect. Individuals living at this time were present at the creation of a modern worldview. Death was no longer something to be contemplated or dealt with only in the realm of the sacred. It became an event that could be manipulated and shaped by human beings.

These modernizing trends accelerated with an industrial revolution, from about 1750 to 1900. This 150-year period was a time of rapid technological innovation, mechanization, and urbanization, accompanied by progress in public health and medicine. Ariès describes the predominant attitude toward death during this period as emphasizing the death of the other, "thy death." Thus, in the outline devised by Ariès, "we shall all die" had gradually evolved to an emphasis on "my own death," and now the focus became "thy death."

This new emphasis was, at least partly, a reaction to the scientific rationalism that had arisen with the age of enlightenment in the 1700s. It occurred in connection with the Romantic movement in literature and the arts, a movement characterized by fascination with acts of chivalry, as well as with mystery and the supernatural.[16] Secular notions about death and the afterlife began to replace (or coexist with) religious concepts. Nature symbolism was increasingly used in death-related art and memorials, and there was widespread interest in spirits and spiritualism. The Romantic period is characterized by a search for spiritual reality, a search that no longer seemed adequately resolved by the answers found in Christianity.

Within the context of this emphasis on "thy death," death meant separation from the beloved, giving rise to impassioned expressions of grief and desires to memorialize the dead. Hence was born the ideal of the "beautiful death," in which the sad beauty of a loved one's death elicits feelings of melancholy, tinged with optimism for eventual reunion with the beloved in a Heavenly home. With the death of her prince consort, Albert, in 1861, Queen Victoria of Great Britain set the trend for elaborate funeral etiquette and mourning customs, as well as for a cult of widowhood.[17] She wore a black mourning bonnet for the rest of her life and often communed with Prince Albert at his grave in the Royal Mausoleum, where she herself would be laid to rest after her death in 1901, the couple side by side, their heads slightly inclined toward one another.

Through more than a thousand years in Western culture, attitudes toward death reflected a more or less gradual progression from an emphasis on collective destiny in which "we all shall die," to the more personal awareness of "one's own death," and then finally to a preoccupation with the deaths of loved ones, "thy death." Despite these changes of emphasis, Ariès characterizes virtually the whole of this period as one of "tamed death." In other words, death was an ordinary human experience, not something to be hidden away from view or excluded from social life.

According to Ariès, the era of "tamed death" came to an end in the twentieth century. World War I (1914–1918) was a major turning point in modern history. It marked the advent of "total war," affecting civilians as well as soldiers. It also exemplified the increasing importance of technology in virtually every aspect of life. In the area of health care, technology brought about the "medicalization" of dying and death. Death had been a public and communal event; now it became private.[18] Events that had been part of people's ordinary lives were placed under the control of professionals. The deathbed was moved from home to hospital. Funerals became more discrete; the customary signs of mourning all but disappeared. The prevailing attitude toward death began to be described as "forbidden death," "invisible death," and "death denied."

With this historical summary in mind, we can now take a closer look at the impact of changing attitudes toward death on specific customs and practices. Specially, we focus on how these changes affected the manner of dying and the deathbed scene, burial customs and memorialization of the deceased, and the cultural expression of the Dance of Death.

Dying and the Deathbed Scene

"I see and know that my death is near": Thus did the dying person during the Middle Ages acknowledge impending death. On pious deathbeds, the dying offered their suffering to God, expecting only to die in the customary manner. Sudden death was rare; even wounds received in battle seldom brought instantaneous death. (The possibility of sudden, unexpected death was fearful because it caught victims unaware and unable to properly close earthly accounts and turn toward the divine.) Those who stood around the deathbed could say with confidence that the dying person "feels her time has come" or "knows he will soon be dead." Anticipated by natural signs or by inner certainty, death was understood as manageable.

A person's dying occurred within the context of familiar practices, marked by simple and solemn ceremony. Ariès describes the main features of a typical Christian death during the early Middle Ages: Lying down, with the head facing east toward Jerusalem and arms crossed over the chest, the dying person

This deathbed vigil in a Spanish village is characteristic of the way in which human beings have responded to death for thousands of years. Only recently have such scenes been superseded in modern societies by the specter of dying alone, perhaps unconscious, amid the impersonal technological gadgetry of an unfamiliar institutional environment.

expressed sadness at his or her impending end and began "a discreet recollection of beloved beings and things." Family and friends gathered around the deathbed to receive the dying person's pardon for any wrongs they might have done, and all were commended to God. Next, the dying person turned his or her attention away from the earthly realm and toward the divine. Prayer requesting divine grace followed confession of sins to a priest, and then the priest granted absolution. With the customary rites complete, nothing more need be said: The dying person was prepared for death. If death came more slowly than expected, the dying person simply waited in silence. Elizabeth Hallam writes: "The deathbed was a space which developed a rich visual and aural texture where each word and gesture became meaningful in physical, social, and spiritual terms."[19]

The recumbent figure in the deathbed, surrounded by parents, friends, family, children, and even mere passersby, remained the customary deathbed scene until modern times. Dying was more or less a public ceremony, with the dying person in charge. Nevertheless, with the growing emphasis on the destiny of the individual around the twelfth century, the scene around the deathbed began to change subtly. In addition to the entourage of public participants, there now hovered an invisible army of celestial figures, angels and demons, battling for possession of the dying person's soul. *How* a person died became profoundly important. Death became the *speculum mortis,* the mirror in which the dying person could discover his or her destiny by tallying the moral balance sheet of his or her life. Thus, the time of dying was seen as a unique opportunity to review one's actions and make a final decision for good or ill. The moment of death became the supreme challenge and ultimate test of an entire lifetime. This emphasis on individual responsibility for the destiny of one's soul was communicated in the *memento mori* of the time, "Remember, you must die!"

In later centuries, as a scientific orientation became prominent in society, rationalism came to share the stage with religion. There was little change in the outward aspects of the deathbed scene; family and friends still gathered as participants in the public ritual of a person's dying. But religion was less prominent in the thoughts of the dying person or the grief of survivors. A secular hope for immortality and eventual reunion with loved ones became more important than the images of Heaven and Hell portrayed in the iconography of the Church. Whereas people in earlier centuries meditated on the torments of a fiery Hell as prods to good behavior, people now compared the act of dying to the emergence of a butterfly from its cocoon. Over time, the focus changed from the dying person to his or her survivors.

By the mid-twentieth century, the rituals of dying that guided our ancestors had been overtaken by a technological process in which death occurs by "a series of little steps." Ariès says, "All these little silent deaths have replaced and erased the great dramatic act of death." Writing in the 1970s, he added, "No one any longer has the strength or patience to wait over a period of weeks for a moment which has lost a part of its meaning." This assessment is now being challenged by the philosophy of hospice and palliative care, which seeks to provide opportunities for persons who are dying and their families to discover essential meaning in the last acts of a human life.

Burial Customs

As with the deathbed scene, changes in burial customs reveal transformations in attitudes toward death over time. In the Roman era, graveyards were situated on the outskirts of the settlements they served, and burial within the town's precincts was permitted only as a special honor.[20] These practices were followed by the early Christians, who were at first buried in what were then mostly pagan cemeteries. In the early Middle Ages, however, these practices were altered as believers began to adopt the notion that the saintliness of Christian martyrs was powerful, even in death.[21] The idea developed that these saints of the Church could help others avoid the pitfalls of sin and the horrors of hell. For this reason, it became advantageous to be buried near the grave of a martyr to gain merit by proximity. (A modern analogy might be that of a movie fan being buried near a film star at Forest Lawn or a veteran requesting burial near a Medal of Honor winner, although medieval folk were generally more concerned with the welfare of their soul than with earthly prestige.)

As Christian pilgrims began journeying to venerate and honor the martyrs, altars, chapels, and eventually churches were built on or near the martyrs' graves. Initially, only notables and saints of the Church were eligible for such burial, but eventually even ordinary folk came to be buried in common graves located in the churchyards and surrounds of churches and cathedrals. In later centuries, the great urban cathedrals allowed burials within their precincts. In this way, the state of the dead was intimately linked with the Church.

Charnel Houses

Burial within churchyards led to the development of *charnel houses,* arcades and galleries where the bones of the dead were entrusted to the Church. Limbs and skulls were arranged along various parts of the churchyard, as well as within and near the church. (In Paris, tourists visit catacombs where, as one visitor exclaimed, "piles of femurs and skulls" are "stacked eight feet high and ten yards deep, as neatly as lumber in an Oregon mill yard."[22]) The bones in these charnels came from the common graves, which were periodically opened so that the bones could be safely kept by the Church until the Resurrection.

The public nature of these charnel houses reflects the general familiarity with death and with the dead. As the Romans before them had congregated in the Forum, so their counterparts in the Middle Ages met in charnel houses, which functioned as public squares. There, they would find shops and merchants, conduct business, dance, gamble, or simply enjoy being together.

"As yet unborn," Ariès says, "was the modern idea that the dead person should be installed in a sort of house unto himself, a house of which he was the perpetual owner or at least the long-term tenant, a house in which he would be at home and from which he could not be evicted."

Memorializing the Dead

About the twelfth century, as individualism started to take hold, there arose a desire to preserve the identity of the person buried in a particular place. Before this time, except for burials of the upper classes or notables of the Church, graves had no markers identifying who was buried there. Now, simple grave markers of the "Here lies John Doe" variety began to appear, as did elaborate effigies of the dead at the burials of notables. The thirteenth-century sepulchral effigy of Jean d'Alluye depicts a recumbent knight in chain mail, sword girded and shield at his side, feet resting on the image of a lion, a vivid expression of the intellectual and social milieu of the age of chivalry, with its tension between faith and heroism. Although effigies were created only for people at the highest social rank, they give us clues about how people of the time viewed death.

Effigies reflect the emerging belief that the bereaved could maintain bonds with the deceased by perpetuating their *memory.* Over time, such memorialization became increasingly important. By the time of the Renaissance,

Library of Congress

This ossuary located at a European monastery is a survival of the medieval charnel house, a gallery of skeletons and skulls and bones.

as secular ideas competed with religious beliefs, burials began to take place in cemeteries that were not associated with churches. The opening of the Cemetery of Père Lachaise outside Paris in 1804 signaled the culmination of a radical change in Western attitudes toward life and death.[23]

The rural cemetery movement, which began in the United States in the 1830s, had the effect of replacing the simple, untended graveyards of the Puritans with lush, well-kept cemeteries like Mount Auburn in Cambridge,

Massachusetts, and Woodlawn in New York City. In parklike settings, the bereaved visited private graves and communed in memory with the deceased.[24] Ornate monuments were erected to honor the dead, and elaborate funeral rituals included an extensive assortment of mourning paraphernalia. The deceased were imagined to be in a heaven where survivors hoped to eventually be reunited with their loved ones. These nineteenth-century mourning customs are marked by a sense of sentimentality that made the finality of death seem less severe.

In the twentieth century, such "excessive" mourning customs gave way to an apparent desire to mute the reality of death. Except for occasional memorials to the war dead, most cemeteries today do not encourage monuments that interrupt the flat expanses of embedded "grave markers." Architectural historian James Curl says,

> The neglected cemeteries, poorly designed crematoria, and abysmal tombstone designs of the present insult life itself, for death is an inevitable consequence of birth. By treating the disposal of the dead as though the problem were one of refuse-collection, society devalues life.[25]

The Dance of Death

With origins in the ecstatic dances of pre-Christian times, artistic themes involving the *danse macabre,* or Dance of Death, came to fullest expression in the late thirteenth and early fourteenth centuries. Partly a reaction to the horrors of war, famine, and poverty, it was influenced primarily by the mass deaths caused by the plague, or Black Death, which came to Europe via a Black Sea port in 1347. When the first wave of pestilence ended in 1351, a quarter of the population in Europe had died. The Dance of Death reflects a conjoining of ideas relating to the *inevitability* and *impartiality* of death.

The *danse macabre* was expressed through drama, poetry, music, and the visual arts. It was sometimes performed as a masque, a short entertainment in which actors costumed as skeletons danced gaily with figures representing people at all levels of society. Paintings of the Dance of Death depict individuals being escorted to graveyards by skeletons and corpses, a grim reminder of the universality and imminence of death. The Dance of Death conveys the notion that, regardless of rank or status, death comes to *all* people and to *each* person. In the oldest versions of the Dance of Death, the figure of death seems scarcely to touch the living as it singles them out. Death has a personal meaning but is part of the natural order. In later versions, people are depicted as being forcibly taken by death.

By about the fifteenth century, death is portrayed as causing a radical, violent, and complete break between the living and the dead. This is reflected in macabre themes that involve cadavers and the deterioration of the corpse. Along with the display of skeletons, naked corpses, and figures of the grim reaper, the Dance of Death eventually includes erotic connotations. The radical disruption of death is likened to the "small deaths" that occur during sexual intercourse, when there is a momentary break with ordinary consciousness.[26] It's as if the grim reaper has become a deadly lover.

This is also the era of public anatomy dissections, which were attended by ordinary townspeople as well as surgeons and medical students. At the University of Leiden, an "Anatomical Theater" was held in the apse of a church, where human remains were artistically displayed and posed in dramatic gestures. Frank Gonzalez-Crussi cites the example of a child's arm "clad in an infant's lace sleeve," and, held in the child's hand, "between thumb and index finger—as gracefully as an artist's model might hold a flower by the stem—a human eye by the optical nerve."[27]

By the eighteenth and nineteenth centuries, the blatant eroticism in the Dance of Death had become sublimated into an obsession with the "beautiful death." The relationship between love and death, which had been confined mostly to religious martyrdom, was extended to include romantic love. Antecedents of this notion are found in the code of chivalry and in the ideals of courtly love. Romances like those of Tristan and Isolde or Romeo and Juliet promoted the idea that, where there is love, death can be beautiful, even desirable.

Originally a reaction to people's fears of sudden death caused by an epidemic, the *danse macabre* emphasized the uncertainties of human mortality,

Hans Holbein the Younger, authors' collection

MIGUEL Y LA CRIADA.

Antonio Guadalupe Posada, Swann Collection, Library of Congress

The somber mood of Hans Holbein's depiction of Die Totentanz, *or Dance of Death, contrasts with the treatment of the same theme by Mexican artist Antonio Guadalupe Posada. In Holbein's medieval woodblock print,* The Child, *we see the anxiety of family members as the skeletal figure of Death ominously takes a child; in Posada's print, there is a sense of gaiety and festivity. Although expressed differently, the two works convey a common message: Death comes to people in all walks of life; no one is exempt.*

that death can come when least expected and disrupt the most loving relationships. These themes of death's universality and inevitability are still portrayed in the Mexican celebration of *el Día de los Muertos,* the Day of the Dead, and artists have drawn upon themes based on the Dance of Death to convey the epidemic nature of AIDS as well as the threatening qualities of other potential catastrophes faced by human beings. More subtly, images associated with the *danse macabre* persist in the form of skeletons and other scary regalia found on children's Halloween costumes.

Invisible Death?

In tracing the manner in which attitudes and behaviors change relative to dying and death, a common theme emerges: Human beings seek to manage death in ways appropriate for their cultural and historical circumstances. Comparing present practices with those of earlier centuries in Western culture, dying and death are in many respects less visible, less part of our common experience. Care of the dying and the dead is now largely the domain of hired professionals. Deathbed scenes are often dominated by efforts to delay death. The role of family and friends as witnesses to a loved one's dying has diminished. The elaborate mourning customs of the past now appear excessive. Thus, funerals and memorial services are shorter, more discreet, and private. Grief, a natural response to loss, is becoming medicalized; the bereaved now require expert help to guide them through "therapeutic" mourning. These trends, which perhaps reached an apex in the last part of the twentieth century, represent yet another way that human beings have attempted to manage death and dying.

The evolution of death-related attitudes and practices continues, however. At the beginning of the new millennium, there are signs that the tendency to compartmentalize dying and death is no longer effective or satisfactory. There is, as yet, no consensus about many of the issues related to dying and death. But, increasingly, people are engaging in discussions about these issues. Many wish to reverse the patterns of alienation associated with the medicalization of dying. Various movements promote death with dignity. "Death denied" may be outmoded as a way to describe the present era, even as the term "invisible death" still applies in many respects. During an extended period in the history of Western culture, a mostly uniform set of beliefs and customs satisfactorily served the needs of most people. Today, however, our beliefs and customs for dealing with dying and death are likely to involve considerable variation and diversity. It behooves us, then, to consider how human beings have found meaningful ways of encountering death, not only historically but also cross-culturally.

Four Cultural Case Studies

Cross-cultural comparisons give us perspectives that allow both appreciation and criticism of our own beliefs and customs.[28] Although some death customs are shared widely among different cultures, they occur in distinct ways in each society. For example, ancestors are important to all of the cultures discussed in this section; yet, each one has distinctive attitudes and behaviors toward them. At first glance, the four cultures examined here may seem exotic, their customs quite different from those typical of North American society. Nevertheless, it is possible to identify significant correspondences between the "foreign" and the "familiar"—correspondences that can evoke insights about behaviors and attitudes that, because they are familiar to us, we may not have closely considered. Exploring dying and death in other cultures creates possibilities for enlivening customs that have become a matter of rote rather than choice in our own encounters with death.

Native American Traditions

Within Native American societies, death tends to be seen as a natural event. The emphasis is on "living one day at a time, with purpose, grateful for life's blessings, in the knowledge that it could all end abruptly."[29] This way of relating to death is typified in the Lakota battle cry: "It's a good day to die!" This phrase encapsulates the notion that death may come at any time; it is wise to be prepared. This outlook on life is evident in the emphasis the Cree people place on making sure to say farewells before going away on a lengthy or difficult journey; unforeseen death may intervene.[30]

There are numerous stories of Native Americans whose preparation for death enabled them to face it stoically, even indifferently. Many composed "death songs" as they confronted their own death. In some cases, a death song was "composed spontaneously at the very moment of death" and "chanted with the last breath of the dying person."[31] These death songs express a resolve to meet death fully, to accept it with one's whole being, not in defeat and desperation, but with equanimity and composure. Death songs summarize a person's life and acknowledge death as the completion of being, the final act in the drama of earthly existence.

Among most Native Americans, time is not considered to be linear, but rather a recurring cycle. Åke Hultkrantz says that Native Americans are "mainly interested in how this cycle affects people in this life and have only a vague notion of another existence after death."[32] Rigid beliefs about the state of the dead or the afterlife tend to be of little or no importance. Instead, says Hultkrantz, "One individual might hold several ideas about the dead at the same time [because] different situations call for different interpretations of the fate of humans after death." The Wind River Shoshoni, for example, have

---

 Two Death Songs

In the great night my heart will go out
Toward me the darkness comes rattling
In the great night my heart will go out

Papago song by Juana Manwell
(Owl Woman)

The odor of death,
I smell the odor of death
In front of my body.

A song of the Dakota tribe

© Lawrence Migdale

Among members of the Northwest Coast culture, which extends more than 2000 miles from the northern limits of California to the panhandle of Alaska, the potlatch, or "giveaway" ceremony, reinforces tribal identity and helps determine an individual's rank and prestige in the community. This potlatch was given by David Baxley, a totem-pole carver of the Tsimshian on the island of Metlakatla in southeastern Alaska, to honor his grandfather, who would have been 100 years old. The old man had died two years earlier. Marked by the host's lavish distribution of gifts, which may take months or years to accumulate, the potlatch is a celebration of life, a way of honoring the deceased as well as others in the community, and saying "thank you."

a variety of beliefs about death: The dead may travel to another world or may remain on earth as ghosts; they may be born again as people or may transmigrate into "insects, birds, or even inanimate objects like wood and rocks." Hultkrantz says that "most Shoshoni express only a slight interest in the next life and often declare that they know nothing about it."

Cherokee elders describe a multiple-soul concept that involves four souls and four stages of death.[33] The "soul of conscious life" leaves the body at death and stays nearby for a time as a harmless ghost before traveling the "trail of Kanati" to the land of the dead. When this soul departs the body at the moment of death, the other three souls begin to die. The second soul, located in the liver, takes about a week to die; the third soul, located in the heart and concerned with bodily circulation, takes about a month to die; the fourth soul, located in the bones, takes a year to die. In light of this understanding, the Cherokee elders say that graves should be tended for a year after death but can be neglected afterward "because there is nothing of any significance left in the grave." Formal mourning ends after a year because the process that separates the dead from the living is complete.

The indigenous peoples of North America exhibit great diversity in their beliefs and customs.[34] Furthermore, most traditional practices were altered dramatically by the upheavals that occurred with the "westward expansionism" of white society.[35] Even within a particular tribal group or culture area, traditional beliefs and practices have undergone change. Generally, however, Native Americans honor their dead, believing them to be guardian spirits or special envoys to the spirit world. Places of burial are usually considered sacred. This reverence toward the dead is stated eloquently in the words of Chief Seattle: "To us the ashes of our ancestors are sacred and their resting place is hallowed ground. . . . Be just and deal kindly with my people, for the dead are not powerless. Dead, did I say? There is no death, only a change of worlds."[36]

Among some tribal groups, the soul or spirit of the deceased is thought to linger for several days near the site of death before passing on to the other world. Great care is required during this period, both to ensure the progress of the deceased toward the supernatural realm and to safeguard the living. The Ohlone of the California coast adorned the corpse with feathers, flowers, and beads, and then wrapped it in blankets and skins. Dance regalia, weapons, medicine bundle, and other items owned by the deceased were gathered together and, with the corpse, placed on a funeral pyre. Destroying the deceased's possessions helped to facilitate the soul's journey to the "Island of the Dead." It also removed reminders of the deceased that might cause the ghost to remain near the living. This belief is echoed in a Yokut funeral chant that says: "You are going where you are going; don't look back for your family." During the dangerous period, which lasted from six months to a year, the Ohlone considered it disrespectful to utter the deceased's name. In *The Ohlone Way*, Malcolm Margolin writes: "While the mere thought of a dead person brought sorrow, the mention of a dead person's name brought absolute dread."[37] By destroying the deceased's belongings and avoiding his or her name, the survivors confirmed the separation of the dead from the living.

In the Great Plains, it was customary among Native Americans to expose the corpse on a platform aboveground or to place it in the limbs of a tree. This form of burial not only hastened the decomposition of the body, it aided the soul's journey to the spirit world. Later the sun-bleached skeleton would be retrieved for burial in sacred grounds. As Old Chief Joseph of the Nez Percé lay dying, he told his son, "Never forget my dying words. This country holds your father's body. Never sell the bones of your father and mother." These words were remembered by Younger Chief Joseph as he led warriors into battle to preserve the sanctity of the lands that held the bones of the ancestral dead. In recent years, disputes have centered on the disposition of artifacts and bones retrieved from such sacred burial places by archaeologists and other scholars.[38] In the 1990s, the U.S. Congress passed the Native American Graves Protection and Repatriation Act with the purpose of reuniting Native American skeletal remains, funerary items, and ceremonial objects with living members of the cultures that produced them.[39]

Warrior Song

I shall vanish and be no more
But the land over which I now roam
Shall remain
And change not.

Hethúshka Society, Omaha tribe

Tribes that are sedentary, such as the Pueblo and Navajo, seem to fear the dead more than tribes that are hunters and gatherers, such as the Sioux and Apache.[40] A study by David Mandelbaum of the Cocopa and Hopi presents informative contrasts.[41] When a Cocopa dies, surviving family members wail in an "ecstasy of violent grief behavior" that lasts twenty-four hours or more and continues until the body is cremated. Clothes, food, and other articles are burned with the body. The deceased will need these items in the afterlife, but the Cocopa also hope their actions help persuade the spirit of the dead person to pass on from the earth. Later, a ceremony is held to mourn and commemorate the deceased. Although the deceased's name cannot be spoken at other times, at this special mourning ceremony, relatives who have passed into the spirit world are publicly summoned, and their presence may be impersonated by living members of the tribe. A house constructed especially for the spirits may be burned as a gift. The mourning ceremony is conducted to both honor the dead and persuade lurking spirits to come out in the open and leave the earthly realm. Whereas the initial cremation ritual is focused on the grief of the bereaved family, the subsequent mourning ceremony is focused on affirming the integrity of the family and the community.

Unlike the Cocopa, the Hopi keep death at a distance. Death threatens the Hopi "middle way" of order, control, and measured deliberation. This attitude is reflected in Hopi funeral rituals, which are attended by few people and held privately. Mourners are reticent about expressing grief. The Hopi want the whole matter to be "quickly over and best forgotten." The Hopi do not wish to invite ancestors to a communal gathering. Once a person's spirit leaves the body, it is a different class of being, no longer Hopi. Thus, it is important to make sure that the "dichotomy of quick and dead is sharp and clear."

As these descriptions of the Cocopa and the Hopi show, even within similar cultural settings, different social groups create distinctive responses to death. Both the Hopi and the Cocopa fear the dead, but they cope with this fear differently: The Hopi wish to avoid the dead completely, whereas the Cocopa invite the spirits of the dead to join them in ritual celebration, even if only temporarily and under controlled circumstances.

Although the rites of passage surrounding death share common elements—themes of separation, transition, and reincorporation—the way in which these elements are realized through ceremony and other mourning

Burial Oration

You are dead.
You will go above there to the trail.
That is the spirit trail.
Go there to the beautiful trail.
May it please you not to walk about where I am.
You are dead.
Go there to the beautiful trail above.
That is your way.
Look at the place where you used to wander.
The north trail, the mountains where you used to wander, you
     are leaving.
Listen to me: go there!

Wintu tribe

behaviors reflects a society's unique path toward resolution when death comes to a member of the community. Reflecting on the different emphases within the Hopi and Cocopa societies can help us evaluate our own attitudes and values relative to death. What do you find valuable about each of these ways of coming to terms with death?

African Traditions

The term *ancestor worship* is sometimes used to label customs that are more accurately described as reverence for the deceased members of a community. In African societies, this communion with the "living dead" can be compared to our own relationships to deceased loved ones. When some event or stimulus evokes the memory of a person who was dear to us, we may pause a moment and think about the qualities that made that person beloved. Such momentary reverie often evokes a sense of communion with the deceased, and it may bring insights that are helpful in our lives.

Reverence for the dead in African culture involves the deceased members of a community who are still remembered by name. As generations come and go, and memory fades, the long-dead ancestral members of the community are replaced by the more recently deceased.[42] Thus, the ongoing community of the "living dead" consists of ancestors who are recalled in the minds of the living. This is illustrated by the system of age grouping. As practiced by the Nandi in Kenya, once past childhood, a male member of the tribe moves through the junior and senior warrior levels and eventually enters the age group of senior elders; he next becomes an old man and ultimately, at death, an ancestor, one of the living dead, whose personality is remembered by survivors. When he is no longer remembered, he merges with the anonymous dead. The Nandi believe that, by this time, the dead person's "soul stuff" may have reappeared in a newborn child of the tribe, thus continuing the recurrent pattern of a person's passage through the levels of the age-group system.[43]

Kofi Asare Opoku says that the traditional African attitude toward death is essentially positive because "it is comprehensively integrated into the totality of life."[44] In the African tradition, "the opposite of death is birth, and birth is the one event that links every human being, on the one hand, with all those who have gone before and, on the other, with all those who will come after." This basically optimistic attitude can be found in the festive sounds of trumpets and drums played at African funerals. "Music," says Francis Bebey, "is a challenge to human destiny; a refusal to accept the transience of this life; and an attempt to transform the finality of death into another kind of living."[45]

African funeral rituals prepare the dead to enter the abode of the ancestors. Mourners may give messages to the deceased to take to the other side, just as one might give a message to a person going on a trip to convey to those he meets at his destination. The traditional African concept of the afterlife reflects a "this-world orientation." Kwasi Wiredu says, "The land of the dead is geographically similar to our own [and] its population is rather like us."[46] It has been said that, for Africans, life is afterlife.[47]

Reverence toward the dead is still important. When the body of a Nigerian villager of the Ibo people was shipped by air from the United States to her home village, the coffin arrived in a damaged condition. Somewhere in transit her body had been wrapped in burlap and turned upside down—violating strict tribal taboos concerning abuse of a corpse. Despite the family's offerings of yams, money, and wine to appease the insult, members of the tribe reported seeing the woman's spirit roaming about, and relatives began to experience various reversals of fortune, which they characterized as a "curse" due to mistreatment of their dead relative. The woman's son said, "My mother was treated as if she were nothing." Thus, her spirit was angry and not at peace. In bringing suit against the airline to which the body had been entrusted, the son said, "If this had been done to us by an individual, my whole tribe would have gone to war. If I win the case, it would be like bringing back someone's head. It would prove I'm a warrior . . . it will show the gods I have done something against someone who shamed my mother."[48]

Examining funeral customs among the LoDagaa of Northern Ghana provides insight into the richness of African mourning customs.[49] Among the LoDagaa, funeral ceremonies span at least a six-month period and sometimes continue over several years. They occur in four distinct, successive phases, each focusing on specific aspects of death and bereavement.

The first stage begins at a person's death and lasts six or seven days. During the first several days, the body is prepared for burial, the deceased is mourned by the community, rites are performed to acknowledge the separation of the deceased from the living, kinship ties are affirmed, and some of the social and family roles occupied by the deceased are redistributed. The public ceremonies, which last about three days, conclude with the burial of the corpse. The remaining three or four days of this first stage are devoted to private ceremonies in which preparations are made for redistributing the dead person's property.

About three weeks later, in a second ceremony, the cause of death is established. Rather than considering a snakebite, for example, to be the cause of a

Delmar Lipp, Eliot Elisofon Archives, National Museum of African Art

A woman and child in mourning are depicted in this Yombe memorial figure from Zaire. Installed in a shed constructed on the grave, such adornments are thought to provide the deceased with companionship or protection in the afterlife.

person's death, the LoDagaa view the bite as an intermediate agent but not the final cause of death. The real cause of death lies in the network of spiritual and human relationships. Inquiries are made to uncover any tension that may have existed between the deceased and others.

At the beginning of the rainy season, a third stage of the funeral is held. These rites mark a transitional period in the deceased's passing from the role of the living to that of an ancestor. At this stage, a provisional ancestral shrine is placed on the grave.

The fourth and final stage of LoDagaa ceremonies occurs after the harvest. A final ancestral shrine is constructed and placed on the grave, and the

> If we knew the home of Death, we would set it on fire.
>
> Acholi funeral song

close relatives of the deceased are formally released from mourning. The care of offspring is formally transferred to the deceased's tribal "brothers," and final rites conclude redistribution of the deceased's property.

These extended mourning ceremonies serve two purposes: First, they *separate* the dead person from the bereaved family and from the wider community of the living; social roles formerly held by the deceased are assigned to living persons. Second, they gather together, or *aggregate;* that is, the dead person joins with the ancestors and the bereaved are reincorporated into the community in a way that reflects their new status. This rhythm of separation and gathering together is common to all funeral rites. Those of the LoDagaa are noteworthy because of the formality with which these essential functions are accomplished. They provide a model of explicitness in mourning that can be compared and contrasted with our own.

The explicitness of LoDagaa mourning is evident in the use of "mourning restraints" made of leather, fabric, and string. These restraints, which are generally tied around a person's wrist, indicate the degree of relationship of the bereaved to the deceased. At a man's funeral, for example, his father, mother, and widow wear restraints made of hide; his brothers and sisters wear fiber restraints; and his children wear restraints made of string, tied around the ankle. Notice that the strongest restraints are provided to mourners who had the closest relationship with the deceased, usually through kinship and marriage but sometimes through friendship bonds. Persons with less intimate relationships to the deceased wear weaker mourning restraints. In all cases, one end of the mourning restraint is attached to the bereaved while the other end is held by a "mourning companion," who assumes responsibility for the bereaved's behavior during the period of intense grief.

The LoDagaa mourning restraints serve two related purposes. First, as objects that can be seen and felt, they validate that the bereaved person's expression of grief is commensurate with the intensity of his or her relationship with the deceased. Second, they discourage expressions of grief that exceed the norms of the LoDagaa community.

Traditional African funeral ceremonies are threatened by the encroachment of modernity, which exerts intense pressure to give up the old ways. Conversely, traditional death customs can help people maintain their culture in the face of change. The Sakalava of Madagascar, for example, continue to organize their lives around royal ancestors who once governed them, participating only minimally in the current political and economic life of the country.[50] In doing so, they resist destruction of their indigenous institutions by "hiding" their values in the now-illicit realm of the dead. Colonization and subsequent political independence has brought major social changes to the

Sakalava, but ancestral tradition is still considered the ideal guide to action. In the traditional African worldview, concern about one's ancestors remains an important sanction that constrains the actions of the living.[51]

Traditional customs can be carried forward in various ways. Among the Yoruba of southwestern Nigeria, obituary publication provides a modern forum for an ancient custom. In newspaper obituaries paid for by family and friends, the deceased's status and prestige are denoted by, among other things, the size of the obituary, which can occupy a full page. Olatunde Bayo Lawuyi says it is common to "mark the return of the dead [through obituary publications] every ten years," although this practice lessens over time.[52] For the Yoruba, Lawuyi says, the publication of obituaries "demonstrates the possibility of continuity in ancestral beliefs" and "is a symbolic manifestation of a tradition that has taken a new cultural form."

Traditions such as those discussed here are part of the heritage of African Americans. The black church testifies to an ongoing emphasis on community values and high levels of religious involvement among African Americans.[53] It has provided social, political, economic, and other opportunities for participation in American society, even when racial segregation and prejudice restricted such functions.[54] Although there is not just one "black church," but many different denominations, death tends to be a recurrent theme among African-American congregations. Pastors, sermons, and songs frequently refer to themes involving death and dying and "homegoing." As Mary Abrums points out, the terminology of dying—that is, the common use of the terms *passed* or *crossed over*—evokes "an image of passing across a fragile invisible line, almost a sleight of hand, where the loved one walked gently into an invisible space."[55] Members of the black church often express belief in the possibility of an ongoing relationship with someone who has passed and of one day being reunited with their loved ones. Visitations from family and friends who have crossed over are related to such beliefs.

In recent years, the black church—itself a hybrid of Protestantism and West African traditionalism—is being joined by newer religious communities with roots in African traditions. These include the Afro-Caribbean religions of *Santería, Espiritismo,* and *Orisha-Voodoo,* as well as traditional Yoruba religion (*Anago*). As these traditions become part of today's world, the Internet is playing an important role in facilitating development of new African-American religious communities.[56] This example suggests the possibility of combining traditional worldviews and present circumstances to create a response to dying and death that is personally and culturally meaningful.

Mexican Traditions

From early times, Mexican culture has embodied themes of death, sacrifice, and destiny. For the Aztecs, the very creation of the world was made possible by sacrificial rites enacted by the gods, and human beings were obliged to return the favor. Sacrificial victims in Aztec rites were termed *teomic-queh,* the "divine dead." Within the divine–human covenant, they were participants in a destiny determined at the origin of the world. Through such

An ironic attitude toward death characterizes the Day of the Dead fiesta in Mexico. Death is satirized while memories of deceased loved ones are cherished by the living. Family members often place the names of deceased relatives on ornaments such as this candy skull and these candy coffins. This practice assures the spirits of the dead that they have not been forgotten by the living and provides solace to the living in the form of tangible symbols of the presence of deceased loved ones.

sacrifice, human beings could take part in sustaining life on earth as well as in the heavens and the underworld.[57] When the Spanish came to Mexico, they brought a cult of immortality that in some ways resembled indigenous beliefs. A sense of destiny, along with a willingness to die for ideals, is exemplified in Spanish history by the mass suicide at Sagunto in 219 B.C., when the city's leading citizens demonstrated by their sacrifice that death was preferable to capture by the Carthaginians.

Mexican culture abounds with symbols of death. The suffering Savior is portrayed with bloody vividness; glass-topped coffins display the remains of martyrs, saints, and notables of the Church. A striking awareness of death is displayed in graffiti and ornaments that decorate cars and buses. Newspapers revel in accounts of violent deaths, and obituaries framed with conspicuous black borders call attention to death. Mexican poetry is filled with similes comparing life's fragility to a dream, a flower, a river, or a passing breeze.[58] Death is described as awakening from a dreamlike existence.[59]

In Mexican culture, death is often confronted with humorous sarcasm. Death is cast as an equalizer that not even the wealthiest can escape. The emotional response to death is characterized by impatience, disdain, or irony. The popular engravings of Mexican artist Antonio Guadalupe Posada superficially resemble the woodcuts of the medieval *danse macabre,* in which people from all walks of life danced fearfully with their own skeletons, although Posada's skeletons seem to have no anxious premonition about death.[60]

Commenting on how these themes manifest themselves in modern-day Mexico, Octavio Paz says, "Death defines life. . . . Each of us dies the death he has made for himself. . . . Death, like life, is not transferable."[61] Folk sayings confirm this connection between death and identity: "Tell me how you die and I will tell you who you are." In the Mexican consciousness, death mirrors a person's life. Surrounded by references to death, the Mexican, says Paz, "jokes about it, caresses it, sleeps with it, celebrates it [and makes it] one of his favorite toys and his steadfast love."

Every year, Mexicans celebrate death in a national fiesta known as *el Día de los Muertos,* the Day of the Dead. Occurring in November, it coincides with All Souls' Day, the Christian feast of commemoration for the dead. Blending indigenous ritual and Church dogma, the fiesta is a unique occasion for communion between the living and the dead. Bread in the shape of human bones is eaten; sugar-candy skulls and tissue-paper skeletons poke fun at death and flaunt it. Celebrated throughout Mexico, the most traditional observances of the fiesta are found on the Island of Janitzio in Michoacán and in the Zapotec villages in the Valley of Oaxaca.[62] The following account of *el Día de los Muertos* in the village of Mixquic is representative of observances throughout the country.[63]

The fiesta begins at midday on October 31, as bells toll to mark the return of dead children. In each house, the family "sets a table adorned with white flowers, glasses of water, plates with salt (for good luck), and a candle for each dead child." The next day families gather at San Andres Church. Bells are rung at noon to signify the departure of the "small defunct ones" and the return of the "big defunct ones." Then, before nightfall, several thousand graves near the church are swept clean and decorated with ribbons, foil, and marigold-like cempasuchil flowers. Maria Nuñez, a caretaker of the village, says:

> The celebration kicks into high gear on the evening of November 1 and into the next morning, when thousands file into the small candle-illuminated graveyard carrying tamales, pumpkin marmalade, chicken with "mole"—a spicy sauce of some 50 ingredients including chili peppers, peanuts, and chocolate—and "pan de muerto," or bread of the dead—sweet rolls decorated with "bones" made of sugar. People sit on the graves and eat the food along with the dead ones. They bring guitars and violins and sing songs. There are stands for selling food for the visitors. It goes on all night. It's a happy occasion—a fiesta, not a time of mourning.[64]

Octavio Paz observes that *el Día de los Muertos* is a time for revolting against ordinary modes of thought and action; the celebration reunites "contradictory elements and principles in order to bring about a renascence of life."[65] Celebrants challenge the boundaries that ordinarily separate the dead from the living. It is important that families pay their respects to the dead, but mourners are cautioned against shedding too many tears; excessive grief may make the pathway traveled by the dead slippery, burdening them with a tortuous journey as they return to the world of the living at this special time of celebration. Although a heightened awareness of death is part of everyday life in Mexican culture, it is given particular emphasis during *el Día de los Muertos* as people gather to commemorate enduring ties between the living and the dead.

Asian Traditions

In European and American societies, ancestors are usually thought of as part of a person's biological and social past, but they tend to be of little importance in one's daily life. In Asian societies, ancestors maintain a central place as members of the household who are dead and who are cared for by the living.[66] In rituals for the dead, the Chinese concept of *yin-yang* duality is conceptualized as forming a whole that includes the world of the dead and the world of the living. The *yin-yang* symbolizes the eternal reciprocity between dead ancestors and their heirs.[67]

One becomes an ancestor not through his or her own achievements or virtue, but through the rites performed by family members and priests. Funeral and memorial rituals transform the ancestors into sources of blessing for their descendants. As Dennis Klass points out in discussing Japanese customs, "The dead still care for the living, not by granting favors like Western saints,

Chuang Tzu's wife died. When Hui Tzu went to convey his condolences, he found Chuang Tzu sitting with his legs sprawled out, pounding on a tub and singing.

"You lived with her, she brought up your children, and grew old," said Hui Tzu. "It should be enough simply not to weep at her death. But pounding on a tub and singing—this is going too far, isn't it?"

Chuang Tzu said, "You're wrong. When she first died, do you think I didn't grieve like anyone else? But I looked back to her beginning and the time before she was born. Not only the time before she was born, but the time before she had a body. Not only the time before she had a body, but the time before she had a spirit. In the midst of the jumble of wonder and mystery, a change took place and she had a spirit. Another change and she had a body. Another change and she was born. Now there's been another change and she's dead. It's just like the progression of the four seasons, spring, summer, fall, winter.

"Now she's going to lie down peacefully in a vast room. If I were to follow after her bawling and sobbing, it would show that I don't understand anything about fate. So I stopped."

Chuang Tzu

but in the sense that the dead share the joys of any positive achievement of a family member, and indeed may be given credit for their success."[68]

A key concept in Asian philosophy is *harmony,* which is manifested in proper conduct, especially in interpersonal relationships. This importance placed on harmony stems from the ancestral cult, with descendants of a common ancestor sharing a lineage that often dates back centuries. In traditional Chinese funeral rites, specific mourning garments highlight the degree of kinship between the bereaved and the deceased (much as the mourning restraints used by the LoDagaa in Africa indicate a mourner's relationship to the deceased).

The motive for such practices is found in the Chinese ideal of *hsiao,* which translates as filiality or filial piety. The living and the dead are dependent on each other; the living perform the necessary ancestral rites while the dead dispense blessings to their descendants. In traditional Chinese society, the family is, in effect, a religious institution. The Chinese philosopher Mencius said that the most unfilial act was to leave no heirs because there would be no one to perform the necessary ancestral rites.

Following Taoist traditions, Chinese death rituals apply the ancient principles of *fěng-shui* (literally, "wind-water"), an art of divination concerned with the proper positioning of elements in harmonious relation to one another. It is crucial to determine the most auspicious siting of human dwellings, both for the living and the dead; failure to do so can cause sorrow. Chinese cemeteries are usually situated on elevated, sloping ground—preferably with mountains in back and the sea in front—with a view of fertile fields the ancestors are leaving to their descendants. During funeral ceremonies, the foot of the casket is usually positioned facing the door so that the spirit or soul of the deceased will have an unobstructed pathway into the next world. Attention to such details assures the bereaved family that everything has been done in the proper way to facilitate the ancestor's journey to the afterlife.

The Chinese celebrate the return of deceased ancestors in a festival known as *ch'ing ming,* which has been called a kind of Chinese Memorial Day. Families visit graves and burn paper replicas of money, clothes, jewelry, and even modern necessities like video cameras and cell phones as a way of showing regard and care for their ancestors.

The Japanese festival of *bon* or *o-bon* is similar in many respects to the Chinese *ch'ing ming.* Usually observed each year in August, *o-bon* marks the return of ancestral spirits to their families. Known in English as the Festival of the Dead, the Feast of Lanterns (because lamps are lit to guide the spirits on their journeys home), the Feast of All Souls, or simply as the midsummer festival, *o-bon* is a modern expression of ancient customs relating to the souls of the dead and the reverence due them by the living.

O-bon is a fusion of indigenous Japanese beliefs and Buddhist concepts. Based on a sutra, or discourse of the Buddha, known as the *urabon-kyo,* the festival weaves together traditions from Indian Buddhism, Chinese Taoism and Confucianism, and Shinto, Japan's indigenous religion. The strands of these various traditions are woven almost seamlessly into "the Japanese way."

Empty-handed I entered the world
Barefoot I leave it.
My coming, my going—
Two simple happenings
That got entangled

Kozan Ichikyo

In Japan, practicing one religious tradition does not mean rejecting all others. A person might feel close to a number of different traditions insofar as they become an integral part of his or her way of life.

Japanese funeral and memorial practices, like those of other Asian societies, are notable for both their duration and the strong association between the ancestor's spirit and the well-being of the family. Following a death, the family invites Buddhist priests to the home for prayers that help emancipate the deceased's spirit. After the body is cremated, the ashes and some pieces of bone are placed in an urn, which will be interred at the family's grave. Prior to interment, a funeral service is held, during which incense is offered and priests read Buddhist scriptures. At this time, the deceased is given a special posthumous or "Buddhist name," which indicates that the material aspect of the person is extinguished. This name (*kaimyo*) is eventually inscribed on an *ihai,* or memorial tablet, that is placed in the family's *butsudan,* or household altar.

The Funeral (1987), a Japanese film directed by Juzo Itami, offers a glimpse into Japanese death rites, along with elements of comic relief, through its portrayal of a modern family's experiences in rural Japan. American viewers have noted particularly how young children are incorporated into rituals and taught the proper way to behave. For example, after the coffin is closed but before it is taken from the family home, each member of the family uses a stone to strike a blow on the lid of the coffin, symbolically sealing it. A child of perhaps three or four, apparently fond of the sound the stone makes as it hits the wood, starts banging the stone on the coffin lid repeatedly, whereupon he is admonished kindly by an older relative, and the stone is passed along to the next family member.

In the traditional view, the spirit of the dead is thought to linger at the family home for the first forty-nine days after death. During this period, rites are held to remove the pollution of death and prepare the soul for enshrinement in the *butsudan,* where the family's ancestors are honored. Although these rites may be abbreviated today, they traditionally include seven weekly ceremonies, culminating, on the forty-ninth day after death, in the deceased person's transformation into a benevolent ancestor.

Memorial services continue to be held for the deceased at periodic intervals—typically, on the hundredth day after death, on the first anniversary, the third anniversary, and at fixed intervals thereafter (the seventh, thirteenth,

This butsudan, *prominently situated in the home of a Japanese-American family in California, is representative of altars found in Japanese homes, where deceased relatives and ancestors are honored through prayers, gifts of food, and other ways of showing respect. As a focal point for ongoing relationships between the living and dead members of a household, the* butsudan *is a place where such relationships are demonstrated through concrete actions.*

and twenty-third), until the thirty-third, or sometimes the fiftieth, anniversary. The memorial tablets (*ihai*) placed in the Buddhist altar in the home are regularly honored by the family with simple offerings and scripture read-

Death-Song

If they ask for me
  Say: He had some
  Business
In another world.

      Sokan

ings. In addition, the priest of the family's parish temple may, upon request, perform memorial masses in the home, especially on anniversaries of the person's death.

Besides the family *butsudan* in the home, the other main focus of Japanese ancestral rites is the *haka,* the family grave, where ashes of family members are interred. The grave must be maintained properly, which includes cleaning it and making offerings to the dead. As with the *butsudan,* the *haka* is a place of ritual. Incense and flowers are offered to the ancestors, and water is poured over the gravestone, a gesture of purification that dates back to Japanese antiquity and that some people now perform without fully recognizing its ancient meaning and symbolism. For the Japanese, it is quite an ordinary thing to talk to their ancestors, either at the gravesite or at the family altar in the home, often in very conversational ways, telling the deceased about things that are going on in life or asking for advice. The connection between the dead and the living is maintained through such activities.

The Chinese follow similar practices in honoring their ancestors. Traditionally, each ancestor's soul was embodied in a spirit tablet—a rectangular piece of wood, upon which was engraved the deceased's name, title, and birth and death dates—which was kept on the family's home altar. Even today, Chinese families often maintain memorial walls in their homes, sometimes substituting photographs for the former spirit tablets, as a way to maintain the presence of the dead within the family.

Of particular importance in Chinese traditions is the ultimate destination of the deceased's bones. Many Chinese immigrants to America believed that their souls would not rest unless they had living descendants to care for their spirit tablets and graves. To allay such concerns, the passage contracts for Chinese workers often contained a clause specifying that, if they died while in the United States, their remains would be returned to ancestral plots in China.[69] Among overseas Chinese, it was customary to exhume the bones of ancestors after ten or twenty years and send them back to their ancestral villages in China. However, it sometimes happened that lack of funds or health department rules caused the bones to remain in America. For this reason, Chinese cemeteries in the United States often have a "Bone House," where the bones of deceased Chinese patiently await return to the homeland.

The annual observances of festivals like *ch'ing ming* and *o-bon* attest to the central role of ancestors in Asian cultures. Although the roots of such

© Albert Lee Strickland

For individuals whose deaths occurred away from their ancestral villages, traditional Chinese custom involved disinterring the bones after perhaps ten years of burial and eventually returning them to the village where the person wsa born. In the interim, the bones were kept in a structure like this one at the Ket-On Society cemetery in Hawaii.

observances are found in ancient religious beliefs, people today sometimes see them simply as social and cultural events that center on family obligations and traditions. The importance of such traditions, and the centrality of the ancestors in Asian cultures generally, can serve as a reminder that the social forms of mourning always have their foundation in broader cultural meanings. The Asian attitude of respect toward the dead supports the idea that survivors tend not to actually sever their bonds with deceased loved ones; rather, in a variety of ways, the dead continue to play an active role in the ongoing life of the bereaved.

Rediscovering the Commemoration of Death

Shared experiences and a sense of community shape the customs and beliefs of a particular society. Traditionally, ancestors have been viewed as fulfilling important roles in the lives of the living. Ceremonies and rituals of various kinds provide opportunities for communities to define and celebrate this relationship between the living and the dead. In modern societies, however, there are few such opportunities to commemorate the dead or honor our ancestors.

The profound thoughts and feelings associated with the dead have typically been expressed with the aid of religious faith. But, in secular and pluralistic societies, religion has a problematic role in communal life, although it can be significant to individuals. Can we devise rituals that serve present needs while making use of traditional insights? One should not imagine that the customs of traditional peoples can be lifted from one society and placed unthinkingly into another, quite different society. We must be careful about any temptation to take "recipes" for coping with death from other cultures or a nostalgic past.[70] Nevertheless, it is possible to gain an appreciation of how other cultures deal with death and to adapt into one's own life appropriate aspects that are felt to be worthwhile. As implied in the root meaning of *tradition,* "to hand down," the ways we cope with death are not created out of thin air. Each generation receives culture from the one preceding, alters it a bit, and passes it on.

When it comes to present-day funeral rites, probably the most frequently heard question is: "Should the children be allowed to attend?" In answering this question, it is important to acknowledge the fact that children are not just members of a community, they are also its future. Through the processes of socialization, children learn the concepts and conventions that have currency in a particular society. What do we want to teach our children about dying and death? In the next chapter, we look at the way sociocultural forces influence a person's attitudes, beliefs, and values toward death.

Further Readings

Philippe Ariès. *Images of Man and Death.* Cambridge, Mass.: Harvard University Press, 1985.

Carol Beckwith and Angela Fisher. *African Ceremonies.* New York: Abrams, 1999.

Paul Binsky. *Medieval Death: Ritual and Representation.* London: British Museum Press, 1996.

Patrick J. Geary. *Living with the Dead in the Middle Ages.* Ithaca, N.Y.: Cornell University Press, 1994.

John Greenleigh and Rosalind Rosoff Beimler. *The Days of the Dead: Mexico's Festival of Communion with the Departed.* San Francisco: HarperCollins, 1991.

Yoel Hoffman. *Japanese Death Poems.* Rutland, Vt.: Charles E. Tuttle, 1986.

Åke Hultkrantz. *Shamanic Healing and Ritual Drama: Health and Medicine in Native North American Religious Tradition.* New York: Crossroad, 1992.

Patricia Jalland. *Death in the Victorian Family.* New York: Oxford University Press, 1996.

Frederick S. Paxton. *Christianizing Death: The Creation of a Ritual Process in Early Medieval Europe.* New York: Cornell University Press, 1990.

Colin Platt. *King Death: The Black Death and Its Aftermath in Late-Medieval England.* London: University College of London Press, 1996.

James L. Watson and Evelyn S. Rawski, eds. *Death Ritual in Late Imperial and Modern China.* Berkeley: University of California Press, 1988.

A father and son make an offering at the grave of their Chinese ancestors during village cremation ceremonies held in 1994 in Peliatan, Bali. In this way, religious and cultural traditions are passed along to successive generations through socializing processes that are important to the ongoing life of the community.

C H A P T E R 3

Learning About Death: The Influence of Sociocultural Forces

*I*magine yourself as a child. Someone says, "Everybody's going to ziss one of these days. It happens to all of us. You, too, will ziss." Or, one day as you're playing, you are told, "Don't touch that, it's zissed!" Being an observant child, you notice that, when a person zisses, other people cry and appear to be sad. Over time, as you put together all your experiences of "zissing," you begin to develop some personal feelings and thoughts about what it means to ziss.

The understanding of death evolves in much this way. As a child grows older, incorporating varied experiences of death, his or her concepts and emotional responses to death begin to resemble those of the adults in the culture. Just as a child's understanding of "money" changes over time—at first it is a matter of little or no concern; later it seems to come into the child's experience almost magically; and finally, it engages the child's attention and participation in many different ways—so, too, does the child develop new understandings about the meaning of death. Like other aspects of human development, the understanding of death evolves as experiences stimulate reevaluation of previously held knowledge, beliefs, and attitudes.

A Mature Concept of Death

A child's understanding of death evolves greatly from about ages 5 to 9. During this period, most children come to understand that death is final, universal, and inevitable. A child who consciously recognizes these facts is said to possess a mature understanding of death. This understanding is further refined during the years of adolescence and young adulthood, as individuals consider the impact of death on close relationships and contemplate the value of religious or philosophical answers to the enigma of death.

In observing and interacting with children at different ages, psychologists have developed a description of how children evolve toward a mature concept of death. In reviewing more than 100 such studies, Mark Speece and Sandor Brent conclude that "[i]t is now generally accepted that the concept of death is not a single, unidimensional concept but is, rather, made up of several relatively distinct subconcepts."[1] A formal statement of the empirical, or observable, facts about death includes four components:

1. *Universality.* All living things eventually die. Death is all-inclusive, inevitable, and unavoidable (although unpredictable with respect to its exact timing).
2. *Irreversibility.* Organisms that die cannot be made alive again.
3. *Nonfunctionality.* Death involves the cessation of all physiological functioning, or signs of life.
4. *Causality.* There are biological reasons for the occurrence of death.

It is important to add, however, that individuals who possess a mature understanding of death typically hold nonempirical ideas about it as well.[2] Such nonempirical ideas—that is, ideas not subject to scientific proof—deal mainly with the notion that human beings survive in some form beyond the death of the physical body. What happens to an individual's "personality" after he or she dies? Does the self or soul continue to exist after the death of the physical body? If so, what is the nature of this "afterlife"? Developing personally satisfying answers to such questions, which involve what Speece and Brent term "noncorporeal continuity," is part of the process of acquiring a mature understanding of death.

What a person "knows" about death may change from time to time. We may hold conflicting or contradictory notions about death, especially our own. When facing a distressing situation, an understanding of the facts may give way to a more childlike attitude, such as the notion that we can bargain where death is concerned. A patient told that he or she has only six months to live may imagine that by some "magical" act, some bargain with God or the universe, the death sentence can be postponed. Thus, although the main evolution toward a mature understanding of death occurs during childhood, how a person understands death fluctuates among different ways of knowing throughout life.

Children who experience the death of someone close may look to adults for models of appropriate behavior. Amidst the regalia of high military and political office that characterized the funeral of President John F. Kennedy, young John F. Kennedy, Jr., salutes the flag-draped coffin containing his father's body as it is transported from St. Matthew's Cathedral to Arlington National Cemetery. The day also marked John-John's third birthday.

Sociocultural Influences on Our Understanding of Death

Acquiring a mature understanding of death is part of the developmental process known as *socialization*. This process involves learning and internalizing the norms, rules, and values of the society in which we live. Through socialization, younger members of a society acquire knowledge, behavior, and ideals from older generations. Socialization does not stop with childhood's end, but continues throughout life. As the "wheel of life" turns, people develop new social roles and values.[3] Nor is it a one-way process whereby individuals simply learn to fit into society. Society's norms and values are modified as its members redefine their social roles and obligations.

Society can be defined as "a group of people who share a common culture, a common territory, and a common identity; and who feel themselves to constitute a unified and distinct entity which involves interacting in socially structured relationships."[4] The social systems and institutions of a society give it a distinctive flavor and set it apart from other societies. This sense of distinctiveness is captured in the term *culture,* which refers to all the ways of thinking, feeling, and acting that people have as members of a given society. We often refer to societies in ways that highlight this distinctiveness—for example, Japanese culture, Western European culture, and the like.

Culture can be defined as "all that in human society which is socially rather than biologically transmitted."[5] This definition encompasses both material and nonmaterial components. Material culture consists of "things"— that is, manufactured objects (for example, buildings and consumer goods) or physical manifestations of the life of a people. Nonmaterial aspects of culture lie in the realm of ideas, beliefs, values, and customs (see Table 3-1). These elements of culture are dynamic; that is, they are subject to change as the members of a society reevaluate inherited beliefs, values, customs, and so on in light of circumstances and experiences. Recall the discussion in Chapter 2 describing how the death customs of Western European culture changed from the early Middle Ages to the present. Researchers point out that culture operates as a framing device in the sense that it channels, not determines, attitudes and behaviors.[6]

T A B L E *3-1* | *Nonmaterial Aspects of Culture*

Knowledge: Conclusions based on empirical evidence.
Beliefs: Conclusions for which there is not sufficient empirical evidence for them to be seen as necessarily true.
Values: Abstract ideas about what is good and desirable.
Norms: Social rules and guidelines that prescribe appropriate behavior in particular situations.
Signs and symbols: Representations that stand for something else; this category includes language and gestures.

Source: Adapted from Norman Goodman, *Introduction to Sociology* (New York: HarperCollins, 1992), pp. 31–34.

Agents of Socialization

Cultural influences are expressed within particular social settings. Individuals come of age in a particular community, school, and family. Socialization involves a variety of influences, beginning with the family and extending to the mass media. Children today are exposed to a broader range of influences on their socialization than at any other time in history. As Hannelore Wass says, "Children adopt many values and beliefs from significant adults in their world [including] parents, teachers, public figures, sports heroes, and famous entertainers."[7]

Although the main phases of socialization occur during the years of childhood, the process continues lifelong. *Resocialization,* a term that refers to the "uprooting and restructuring of basic attitudes, values, or identities," occurs when adults take on new roles that require replacing their existing values and modes of behavior.[8] This occurs with religious conversion, starting a new job, getting married, having children, or surviving the death of a mate. Widowhood involves dramatic changes in many areas of life, as new roles and activities are taken on.[9] Rapid social change leads to resocialization, as, for example, in the case of women's roles in the recent past. Resocialization also takes place as the norms and values we learn in childhood are modified later in life.

People tend to acquire their learning about dying and death on an ad hoc basis—that is, in a disorganized and impromptu fashion. Formal education about death is offered through courses, seminars, and the like, but these avenues of socialization are not part of most people's experience. The term *tactical socialization* refers to strategies that hospice caregivers, for example, use to informally teach people about death and dying.[10] It involves a deliberate and active effort to change other people's perceptions and behaviors about some aspect of their social world.

It is not always possible to pinpoint the genesis of ideas that an individual acquires about death. Consider the following incident, involving two siblings, ages eight and ten. When asked to draw a picture of a funeral (see Figure 3-1), they got out their colored pencils and immersed themselves in the task. After a while, Heather (ten) said to Matt (eight), "Hey, you've got smiles on those faces! This is supposed to be a funeral. What are they doing with smiles on their faces?" In her model of appropriate death-related behavior, people don't smile at funerals; to her younger brother, smiles were perfectly acceptable. One can only guess the influences that provoke such strong statements about what kind of behavior is appropriate at funerals. It is in interactions like this that attitudes about death are incorporated into a child's understanding of death.

Family

The family is the foundational social institution in all societies although the definition of "family" varies from place to place and time to time.[11] In the routines and events of daily life, the beliefs and values of parents are transmitted to their children.[12] Think back to your own childhood. What messages did

Figure *3-1*   *Children's Drawings of a Funeral*

Instructed to draw a picture of a funeral, a sister (age ten) and brother (eight) did so. The ten-year-old, whose drawing is A, emphasizes the emotional responses of the survivors. We see the picture as if we are looking in (and down) upon their grief. The figures in the first two pews have tears streaming down their faces and one woman shouts "No!" At ten, this child reflects on the sorrowful and unwelcome nature of death. When questioned about the empty pews, she said they were for anyone who came late.

     The eight-year-old's drawing (B) is viewed from a similar perspective (looking in and down at the scene). Here we see the survivors grouped around a flag-draped and flower-bedecked coffin. The figures are portrayed with smiles on their faces. The focus in this drawing is on the symbols of death (for example, the casket) and the ceremony rather than emotions. During the drawing session, the older sister commented that her brother's picture was "too happy" for a funeral scene.

you receive about death that remain to this day in the back of your mind? Possibly some messages were conveyed directly: "This is what death is" or "This is how we behave in relation to death." Perhaps some messages were indirect: "Let's not talk about it. . . ." How would the rest of that sentence go? Let's not talk about it . . . because it's not something that people talk about? When, as a child, one woman encountered a dead animal on the highway, she was told, "You shouldn't look at it." Her mother admonished, "Put your head down; children shouldn't see that." That is a parental message about what constitutes appropriate behavior toward death.

Other parental messages about death may be communicated unconsciously. Consider the notion of replaceability. A child's pet dies, and the parent says, "It's okay, dear, we'll get another one." Children differ in their emotional response to the death of a family pet; some grieve intensely when a

 ## The Dead Mouse

We had been out of town and the neighbors had been caring for our various pets. When we returned, we found that our cat had, as cats will, caught and killed a mouse and had laid it out ceremoniously in front of his bowl in the garage. I discovered that that had happened when I heard loud screams from the garage. "Pudley's killed a mouse. There's a dead mouse in the garage!" Loud screams, for the whole neighborhood to hear. I went downstairs. It was the first time that I had a chance to observe how my children dealt with death. I said, "Oh, there is?" "Right here," they said. "Look!" They began to tell me how they had determined it was dead. It was not moving. They had poked at it several times and it didn't move. Matthew, who was five years old, added that it didn't look like it was ever going to move again. That was his judgment that the mouse was dead.

I said to him, "Well, what are we going to do?" I could feel myself being slightly repulsed; my fingers went to my nose. It was obvious to me that the mouse was dead—it had started to decay. Matt said very matter-of-factly, "Well, we'll have to bury it." Heather, seven, climbed on a chair and announced, "Not me. I'm not going to touch it. Don't bring it around here. Aughhh, dead mouse!" At that time, she was intent on being what she thought was feminine, and part of the stereotype involved not getting herself dirty.

So Matt volunteered for the job. "I'm going to need a shovel," he said. I stood back and watched, interested to see what would happen. I noticed that he didn't touch the mouse. From somewhere he already had gotten the idea that it wasn't appropriate to touch dead things. He carefully lifted it with the shovel and took it into the backyard to dig a hole. Heather peered around and watched at a safe distance.

After the mouse was buried, Matt came back and said, "I'm going to need some wood, a hammer, and a nail." I thought, "Oh great! He's going to perform some kind of little ceremony and place a symbol of some kind on the grave." Matt went to the woodpile and carefully selected a piece of wood maybe two inches long and another piece a bit wider, perhaps three inches wide and about four or five inches long. I thought, "Tombstone?" He got the nail and put the pieces of wood together in the shape of a cross.

beloved pet dies. Quickly replacing a deceased pet may not allow sufficient time for acknowledging the loss. What lesson about death is taught when a parent acts hastily to replace a pet that has died? Imagine a situation in which a mother's grief over her mate's death is interrupted by her child's remark, "Don't worry, Mommy, we'll get you another one."

The lessons about death that are learned in the family are conveyed by actions as well as words. A woman now in her thirties tells the following story: "I remember a time when my mother ran over a cat. I wasn't with her in the car, but I recall my mother coming home and just totally falling apart. She ran into the bedroom and cried for hours. Since that time, I've been extremely conscientious about not killing anything. If there's an insect on me or in my house, I'll pick it up and carry it outside." Parental attitudes, and the attitudes of other family members, shape the values and behaviors not only of the child

---

I thought, "Oh. A cross, religious symbol, burial, funeral—all the things I knew about what happens with a dead body." Matt picked up a marking pen and wrote on the front of the cross: "DEAD MOUSE, KEEP OUT!" And he pounded it into the ground in front of where the mouse was buried. I thought, "What's going on in this kid's mind?"

I asked him, "Does that mean that when I die there should be a sign saying, "Dead Mommie. Keep out"? He put his hand on his hip and looked at me with that disgust that five-year-olds can muster for somebody who is *so* dumb, and said, "Of course not. You're going to be buried in one of those places where they have bodies. This is a backyard. Kids could ride their bikes over it. Who would know that there is a mouse buried back here?" I was flabbergasted.

A few weeks later there was a long discussion about what the mouse would look like at that time. My first thoughts were, "Don't do that! You can't dig it up. It's not nice. It's not good. The mouse has to rest his spirit." Then I realized that all those things were coming from that place in me that didn't want to see what a month-old dead mouse looked like.

So I kept quiet. They dug and dug, and I could feel the sweat dripping off me. They dug a huge hole, but could find no remnants of the mouse. I was a bit relieved. But that brought up all kinds of questions about what happened to the mouse. I made this elaborate picture of a compost pile, really a lengthy explanation. Finally I realized that they didn't understand at all and that what I was saying was of no interest to them.

I said, "Well, it's like if you buried an orange." Something safe, I thought, something I can deal with that can be dug up day by day by day to see how it goes back into the earth.

They buried an orange and dug it up and dug it up and dug it up. And it wasn't an orange anymore.

I came away from that experience thinking, "Where did they learn all that? Matt's behavior, particularly. . . . Where did he get that from?"

© Carol A. Foote

Childhood activities such as "playing dead" can be a means of experimenting with various concepts, trying them on for size, and thus arriving at a more comprehensive and manageable sense of reality.

but also of the adult that the child will become, and they influence how that adult conveys attitudes toward death to his or her own children.

School and Peers

Schools teach more than "reading, 'riting, and 'rithmetic." The social world of a child is dramatically broadened during the school years, partly because of greater opportunity for interactions with peers. Even before the school years, children enter the social world of their peer group as they play with other children of the same age and general social status. Sports and hobbies also involve children in a social world, connecting them to a community and a set of social norms.[13] Socialization about death occurs in such groups when, for example, a member or leader dies. With the broadening of an individual's social network, there is a corresponding increase in possible encounters with death.

In a study of junior high students, males and females expressed different attitudes toward death, and these differences generally reflected traditional sex roles.[14] Girls tended to place higher value on funerals and express more concern about what happens to bodies after death. On the issue of capital punishment, boys were about equally divided, pro and con; girls tended to express uncertainty or opposition. Asked to describe their beliefs about life after death, boys were "more decisive" and girls "more variable" in their beliefs. Such gender-related differences result from a child's social encounters in a variety of contexts and are significantly influenced by the attitudes found among their peers.

Although the way we learn about death tends to be less a result of systematic instruction than of happenstance, cultural attitudes are sometimes communicated through programs designed especially to provide opportunities for discussing the topics of dying and death. This was the case, for instance, when the Boston Children's Museum presented a show entitled "Endings: An Exhibit About Death and Loss." In this participatory exhibit, parents and children shared their thoughts and feelings about death through songs, stories, games, videotapes, and other resources.

Mass Media

Television, movies, radio, newspapers, magazines, books, videos, records, cassettes, and compact discs—these media have a powerful socializing influence on both children and adults. Media messages communicate cultural attitudes toward death to children, even when the message is not purposely directed to them, as in the case of news reports of disasters. This influence is usually an unintentional by-product of the primary message or story. How children relate to such messages depends on their cognitive development as well as their individual life experiences. When President John F. Kennedy was assassinated, from the details presented by the media, children tended to select certain aspects that were consistent with their own developmental concerns.[15] For instance, young children were worried about the appearance of the president's body and the effects of the death on his family; older children expressed concerns about the impact of Kennedy's death on the political system.

Developmentally related concerns also surfaced in children's reactions to the deaths of the *Challenger* astronauts. When first graders were asked to draw pictures of the shuttle accident, many showed the astronauts returning safely to earth, where rescue teams could revive them.[16] One child depicted the astronauts coming down in parachutes. Another showed all seven astronauts in the water, apparently waiting to be rescued. Some drawings depicted the astronauts' bodies in pieces, but the child-artists said rescue crews or hospital workers could make them whole again. One boy drew a picture of an astronaut in the grass and told his teacher that rescue crews would find the astronaut and take him to a hospital where he would be made well again. This interest in the condition of the astronauts' bodies and in rescue is normal for children of this age group. (Developmental issues during childhood and adolescence are discussed in Chapter 10.)

Children's literature is another source of messages about death. Many classic children's stories depict death, near deaths, or the threat of death. Elizabeth Lamers notes that, because of its ubiquity and drama, death has often had a place in children's stories, and this is especially true of the earliest versions of familiar stories that parents and other adults share with children. Lamers says, "American children taught to read with textbooks such as

Recently my seven-year-old son hopped in my lap and we watched the evening news together. The concluding line of a report on environmental pollution was a quote from U.N. scientists predicting that in twenty years the world would be uninhabitable. As the TV switched to a Madison Avenue jingle designed to encourage us to purchase a non-greasy hair tonic, my son turned to me with a terribly small voice and asked: "Dad, how old will I be when we all die?"

Robert D. Barr, *The Social Studies Professional*

McGuffey's Eclectic Readers found that death was presented as tragic, but inevitable, and many of the death-related stories conveyed a moral lesson."[17] In the nineteenth century, the violence in children's stories was usually graphic and gory so that it would make the desired moral impression.[18] As with *McGuffey's*, the manner in which death is presented communicates cultural values. Consider, for example, the contrasts between the European and Chinese versions of the tale of Little Red Riding-Hood.

In the Western version, Little Red Riding-Hood goes by herself to visit her grandmother, encounters the wolf, and is tricked into believing the wolf is her grandmother. In the traditional version of the story, the wolf eats Little Red Riding-Hood, but she is saved by a woodsman who kills the wolf and slits its stomach, allowing Little Red Riding-Hood to emerge unharmed. In more recent versions, Little Red Riding-Hood's screams alert the woodsman, who chases the wolf and then returns to announce that she will be bothered no more (the killing of the wolf occurs off-stage and is not mentioned).[19]

The Chinese tale of *Lon Po Po* (Granny Wolf) comes from an oral tradition thought to be over a thousand years old. In this version of the story, three young children are left by themselves while their mother goes away to visit their grandmother. The wolf, disguised as Po Po (Grandmother), persuades the children to open the locked door of their house. When they do, he quickly blows out the light. By making perceptive inquiries, however, the oldest child cleverly discovers the wolf's true identity and, with her younger siblings, escapes to the top of a gingko tree. Through trickery, the children convince the wolf to step into a basket so they can haul him up to enjoy the gingko nuts. Joining together, the children start hauling up the basket. But, just as it nearly reaches the top of the tree, they let the basket drop to the ground. The story says, "Not only did the wolf bump his head, but he broke his heart to pieces."[20] Climbing down to the branches just above the wolf, the children discover that he is "truly dead." Unlike the European version, which has a solitary child facing the threat of the wolf by herself and ultimately being saved by someone else, the Chinese folk tale emphasizes the value of being part of a group effort to do away with the wolf.

Some children's stories are written with the aim of answering their questions about dying and death. In many such books, especially those for young children, death is presented as part of the natural cycle. These stories often express the idea that, like the transition from one season to the next, each

Little Red Riding-Hood

. . . "Dear me, Grandmamma, what great arms you have!"
    The wolf replied:
    "They are so much better to hug you with, my child."
    "Why, Grandmamma, what great legs you have got!"
    "That is to run the better, my child!"
    "But, Grandmamma, what great ears you've got!"
    "That is to hear the better, my child."
    "But, Grandmamma, what great eyes you've got!"
    "They are so much better to see you with, my child."
    Then the little girl, who was now very much frightened, said:
    "Oh, Grandmamma, what great teeth you have got!"
    "THEY ARE THE BETTER TO EAT YOU UP!"
    With these words the wicked wolf fell upon Little Red Riding-Hood and ate her
up in a moment.

Journeys Through Bookland, Volume One

ending in life is followed by renewal. (A selected list of children's books about death is included in Chapter 10.)

Lullabies also contain themes of death and violence.[21] Adults have always sung to children—in every human culture and in every historical period. Some songs for infants communicate emotional information.[22] And a surprising number of these contain messages about death. Consider the message in the following well-known lullaby:

Rockabye baby, in the treetops.
When the wind blows, the cradle will rock.
When the bough breaks, the cradle will fall.
Down will come baby, cradle and all.

Some lullabies are "mourning songs," which describe the death or funeral of a child; others are "threat" songs that warn of violence if a child does not go to sleep or perform some other action in the expected manner. In studying infant songs and lullabies, scholars note that changes occur with respect to the subject matter and manner of presentation as higher standards of living and a more secure sense of the future evolve in societies and among social groups.

Nursery rhymes also contain death imagery. Of two hundred nursery rhymes examined in one study, about half described the wonder and beauty of life, whereas the other half dealt with the ways in which humans and animals die or are mistreated.[23] Death-related themes in these rhymes include accounts of murder, choking to death, torment and cruelty, maiming, misery and sorrow, stories of lost or abandoned children, and themes depicting poverty and want.

Religion

As psychologist Robert Emmons points out, "Spirituality and religion are an integral part of human culture, and as such, have the potential to shape

T A B L E   3-2   *Four Functions of Religion in Societies*

1. Religion provides a shared set of beliefs, values, and norms around which people can form a common identity. Thus, religion is a unifier, "the social glue that binds a group together by giving it a common set of values."
2. Religion provides answers to the "big questions" about human existence and purpose. It addresses issues of life and death, outlines the kind of life people are expected to lead, and explains what happens to them after they die.
3. Religion often provides a foundation for the norms and laws of a society. Laws acquire a moral as well as legal force when they are embedded in religious values.
4. Religion is a source of emotional and psychological support to people, especially at times of crisis.

Source: Adapted from Norman Goodman, *Introduction to Sociology* (New York: HarperCollins, 1992), pp. 205–206.

individual lives and personalities."[24] Determining one's place in the universe is a crucial aspect of human development. Religion results from the efforts of individuals and societies to make sense of the world and human existence.[25] Religion is a basis for morality and human relationships; it enables humankind to live in harmony with the gods, and gives meaning to life.[26]

For children as well as adults, spirituality and religion can be important avenues for understanding and coping with dying and death.[27] Religion can offer solace, suggest some meaning in dying, and provide mourning rituals that ease the pangs of grief. Vernon Reynolds and Ralph Tanner note that religion is concerned with "ministering to the dying person, preparing him or her for the world to come, generally being involved with his physical needs and psychological feelings at this time, and likewise helping those who are especially close."[28]

Even in modern secular societies, religion plays a major role in shaping our attitudes and behaviors toward death (see Table 3-2). More than 90 percent of Americans are affiliated with a religious tradition.[29] A national survey indicates that 95 percent of American teenagers believe in God and about one-quarter consider religious faith more important to them than it is to their parents.[30]

In considering the impact of religion in the lives of individuals, it is useful to distinguish between two related concepts: *religious affiliation* and *religiosity*. Two members of the same religious group share the same religious affiliation, but their religiosity—that is, the relative importance of religion in their lives—may differ. When death intrudes, the person who attends religious services as an opportunity for social interaction may experience the consolations of religion differently than the person who participates in religious activities because of deep personal meaning in creeds and beliefs. The concept of religiosity embraces several dimensions, including:[31]

1. Experiential religiosity (emotional ties to a religion)
2. Ritualistic religiosity (participation in the religion)
3. Ideological religiosity (religious commitment)

4. Consequential religiosity (degree to which religion is integrated into the person's daily life)
5. Intellectual religiosity (range and depth of the person's knowledge about the religion's traditions, beliefs, and practices)

Any or all of these dimensions can have an impact on a person's way of facing death and coping with loss. For example, a young Filipino-American man whose father died talked about the comfort he felt in connection with a funeral mass held in the church where his family worshiped. Commenting on the language and other symbols present in the service, he said, "You know, I've never thought much about what those prayers are about, but the soothing rhythms of the chants and the pungent smell of the incense caused me to feel that my dad is somehow still being cared for, that he's really okay." In this young man's experience, we detect elements of experiential, ritualistic, and consequential religiosity.

Dying and death are more than biological events; they have social and spiritual dimensions. Our beliefs—religious or philosophical—can be a key to how we relate to the prospect of our own death as well as the deaths of others.

Teachable Moments

Throughout the course of life, opportunities abound for children to learn about dying and death.[32] Consider, for example, a mother who discovers her eleven-year-old son sitting at her new computer writing his will. Taken aback,

 I recall with utter clarity the first great shock of my life. A scream came from the cottage next door. I rushed into the room, as familiar as my own home. The Larkin kids, Conor, Liam and Brigid, all hovered about the alcove in which a mattress of bog fir bedded old Kilty. They stood in gape-mouthed awe.

I stole up next to Conor. "Grandfar is dead," he said.

Their ma, Finola, who was eight months pregnant, knelt with her head pressed against the old man's heart. It was my very first sight of a dead person. He was a waxy, bony specimen lying there with his open mouth showing no teeth at all and his glazed eyes staring up at me and me staring back until I felt my own ready to pop out of their sockets.

Oh, it was a terrible moment of revelation for me. All of us kids thought old Kilty had the magic of the fairies and would live forever, a tale fortified by the fact that he was the oldest survivor of the great famine, to say nothing of being a hero of the Fenian Rising of '67 who had been jailed and fearfully tortured for his efforts.

I was eleven years old at that moment. Kilty had been daft as long as I could recall, always huddled near the fire mumbling incoherently. He was an ancient old dear, ancient beyond age, but nobody ever gave serious consideration to the fact he might die.

Leon Uris, *Trinity*

she pauses for a moment as thoughts race through her head: Why is he writing a will? How did an eleven-year-old become interested in giving away his favorite treasures? Does he believe he is going to die soon? What should I do? What can I say? Gathering her courage, she cautiously adjusts her tone to suggest a neutral inquisitiveness and asks, "What has made you think about writing a will?"

Turning to her, the joy of accomplishment lighting up his face, the boy says, "I was looking at the menu on your computer and found *Willmaker 5*. The program came up and all I have to do is fill in the blanks. It's easy, see? Then I can print out my very own will."

Thus we encounter the concept of a "teachable moment," a phrase used by educators to describe opportunities for learning that arise out of ordinary experiences. Because of their immediacy, such naturally occurring events are ideal vehicles for learning. The learner's questions, enthusiasm, and motivation guide the educational process. If we assume that learning always flows in a single direction, from adult to child, we miss the quintessential quality of education as an interactive process. In the example of the young boy filling in the blanks of a computerized will-making program, the mother appears to occupy most clearly the role of the learner. She learns something about her son's exploration of the new computer and, more important, she learns the crucial lesson of gathering information before reacting.

Suppose this mother, acting out of initial shock at her son's apparent interest in death, had hastily responded, "Stop that! Children shouldn't be thinking about wills or about dying!" A lesson about death would surely be taught, but it wouldn't promote a healthy understanding of death. So, in applying the principle of teachable moments as a way of guiding children in their understanding of death, it is useful to ask: *What* is being taught? Does the "teaching" result from a conscious design? Or is it unintentionally conveying unhealthy messages about death?

Let's return to our story of the mother and son. Having elicited information without acting on her initial anxiety, the mother can use this conversation as an opportunity to discuss death with her son in a nonthreatening and unemotional context. She might call attention to the entry for "Designated Guardian for Minor Children," informing her son about the steps she has taken to ensure his well-being ("Did I tell you that Aunt Martha and Uncle John are listed in my will as your guardians?") as well as to respond to his concerns ("No, I do not intend to die for a long time."). They might spend a few minutes talking about other aspects of death and how people prepare for it. Much learning can take place in a brief conversation. An atmosphere of openness is promoted as information is exchanged between adult and child.

Teachable moments are often defined in the context of unplanned or unexpected occurrences, but it is useful to recognize that parents, educators, and other adults can create situations that encourage such opportunities for learning about death.[33] There is no rule that we must wait until such events happen spontaneously. Indeed, in the example given earlier, the mother used her son's experience with the computer program as a way of introducing their subsequent discussion about death. Similarly, in films produced for children, death is frequently part of the plot, and this can lead to a natural discussion about how grief, for example, is portrayed among the various characters.[34] The key to making the most of such opportunities is adequate preparation by trusted adults in the child's environment.

Opportunities for "teachable moments" take place not only between adults and children, but also between adults. While on an airplane trip, an executive for a large corporation engaged one of this book's authors in conversation. Upon learning the subject of this textbook, his tone changed a bit as he said, "Could I ask your opinion on a personal matter?" The question involved a family dispute about whether the man's five-year-old son should attend his grandfather's burial ceremony at Arlington National Cemetery. He was concerned that the military ceremony—with uniforms, soldiers, and a twenty-one gun salute—would frighten his son unnecessarily. After he shared additional information about his family and child, suggestions were offered about some ways that parental support could be provided to the child during the funeral rites. Hearing these suggestions made it possible for the man to reconsider his earlier decision to exclude the child. With specific recommendations in hand, he decided that the child should be present at his grandfather's funeral. You do not have to be the author of a textbook to offer information that is helpful to people who are coping with death-related issues. In reading this book, you will gain information that can be appropriately offered.

Early Experiences With Death

Because personal experiences are crucial in shaping an individual's attitudes and behaviors, it is important to recognize each person's unique experiences with dying and death. When children are included in activities surrounding the death of a close family member or friend, they usually acquire an understanding of death that is associated with children at a later stage of development. One six-year-old who witnessed the accidental death of her sibling expressed a clear understanding that death is final, that people die, and that she herself could die. She was concerned about how she could protect herself and her friends from the dangerous circumstances that led to her brother's death. Her attitude was displayed in admonitions to schoolmates that they should try to prevent accidents. Her attitude toward death resulted from the particulars of her experience.

Self-concept affects a child's ability to cope with death. Children (and adults) who are comfortable with themselves, who see themselves as active, vital, and interesting, and who have caring relationships with others tend to be less fearful about dying and death.[35] Consider the responses to death that you have observed. Whereas one person is curious to know all the details about a death, someone else prefers to know as little as possible. A ten-year-old's phrase, "It's sickening, don't talk about it!" can survive into adulthood.

Encounters with violent death can powerfully alter a child's understanding of death. Drawings made by Cambodian children in refugee camps depict

Cpl. Edward Belfer, U.S. Army Photo

Children experience the impact of war on their lives in a variety of ways. For the German child seen here, war brought a stark encounter with death. This child was one of many German citizens who, at the end of World War II, were ordered by the provisional military government of the U.S. Third Army to view the exhumed bodies of Russians, Poles, and Czechs killed while imprisoned in the concentration camp at Flossenberg. For Amanda Wille (facing page), the impact of war was felt in terms of the anticipated loss of her father, a Navy computer technician, as he prepared to board the USS John F. Kennedy for service during the Persian Gulf War. Understanding only that her father was going away, the three-year-old seemed anxious and bewildered until she found a piece of string on the Norfolk, Virginia, dock. After her father broke the string and tied one piece around his wrist and the other around hers, Amanda cried and hugged him goodbye.

death as the predominant theme.[36] Having seen the deaths of parents and others from starvation, children responded to that traumatic experience in their drawings. One such picture shows a woman in the midst of six smaller bodies with the caption, "Mother's Dead Children." James Garbarino says, "Few issues challenge our moral, intellectual, and political resources as does the topic of children and community violence—war, violent crime on the streets, and other forms of armed conflict."[37]

A diary written by a young girl in war-torn Sarajevo highlights the effects of violence on children. Zlata Filipovic's diary displays an evolution from the ordinary concerns of teenage life to a shattering preoccupation with destruction and death as warfare disrupts normal life. In one entry, Zlata writes: "War has crossed out the day and replaced it with horror, and now horrors are unfolding instead of days."[38] Many children and teenagers growing up in America's cities experience warlike disruptions due to the prevalence of drug-related violence and gang warfare, a situation that writer and musician Ice T characterizes as "the killing fields" of America.[39]

Catastrophic experiences of death influence children's understandings of death. In addition to acquiring a more mature conceptual orientation toward death, children who experience firsthand the reality of death through war or pervasive violence, or in connection with other forms of catastrophic death, often exhibit a fatalistic attitude toward death that contrasts with children whose experiences of death occur in more benign circumstances. When questioned about the "ways people die," children in violent or death-saturated environments tend to answer quite differently from children whose lives are comparatively sheltered from such experiences (see Figures 3-2 and 3-3).

When children in a lower-middle-class urban school in Germany were asked about the ways people die, the responses corresponded to their environment. Violent deaths were described as being caused by "weapons" and "sharp knives." Conspicuously absent was any use of the word *gun*.[40] In Germany, handguns, being illegal, are not available to the general populace. Environmental factors play an important role in determining how people think about and respond to death.

Take a moment to consider your own circumstances. Do you live in a rural, urban, or small town environment? What region of the country do you live in? The North, East, South, or West? Was your school environment ethnically and religiously diverse? Your response to death is likely to be influenced by such factors. Life experiences—particularly those that involve an encounter with significant loss or death—are powerful in shaping a person's attitudes and beliefs about death. In some cases, especially when such experiences occur in early childhood, it is only as an adult that a person becomes fully aware of the impact.

Theoretical Perspectives

Sociology provides useful tools for understanding how social and cultural factors affect people's attitudes and behaviors relative to death. The three theoretical perspectives that follow provide different vantage points about how

cut your head off

Figure 3-2 *Ways People Die: Children's Images*
Above: A seven-year-old African-American boy in a large Midwestern city draws a picture of murder by decapitation. (In separate incidents, two young girls in his city had been recently killed in this manner.)
Below: In contrast, the drawing created by a seven-year-old Caucasian boy attending Catholic school in a small California town portrays the child's concept that people die when "God calls you home." Notice the child's depiction of the voice of God and heavenly "pearly gates."

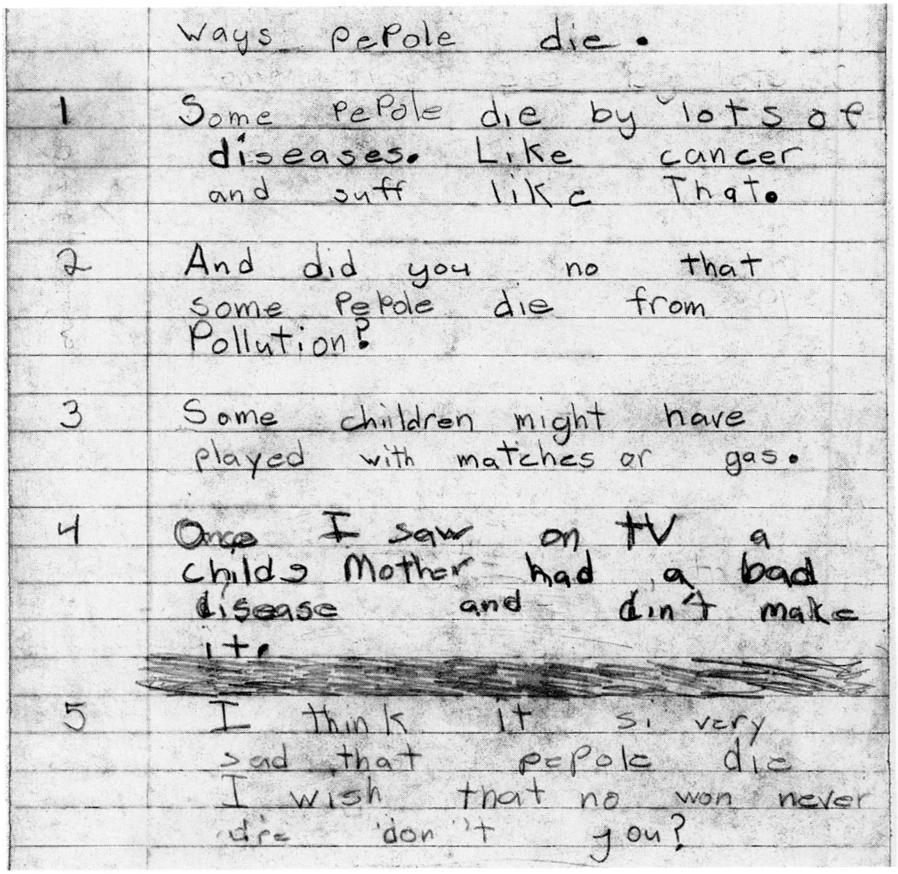
Ways pepole die.
1 Some pepole die by lots of diseases. Like cancer and suff like That.
2 And did you no that some pepole die from Pollution?
3 Some children might have played with matches or gas.
4 Once I saw on TV a childs Mother had a bad disease and din't make it.
5 I think it si very sad that pepole die I wish that no won never die don't you?

Figure 3-3 *Ways People Die: Children's Explanations*
Environment, including both time and place, influences a child's understanding of death. The impact of environment on children's views of death can be evoked by asking them to make a list or draw a picture in response to the question: "What are the ways people die?" The list shown above was written in 1978 by a seven-year-old Caucasian girl living in a small coastal California town. It stands in sharp contrast to the 13-item response (*facing page*) written in 1995 by a seven-year-old African-American boy living in a major Midwestern city. Although both lists were created by children of the same age, the second list reflects both the passage of time (17 years) and the circumstances of life in an inner-city metropolitan environment. Whereas the first child's list focuses on diseases and accidents, the second child's explanation shows familiarity with a broad range of causes of death, few of which relate to "natural" events. His illustration of item number 11, "cut your head off," is shown in Figure 3-2.

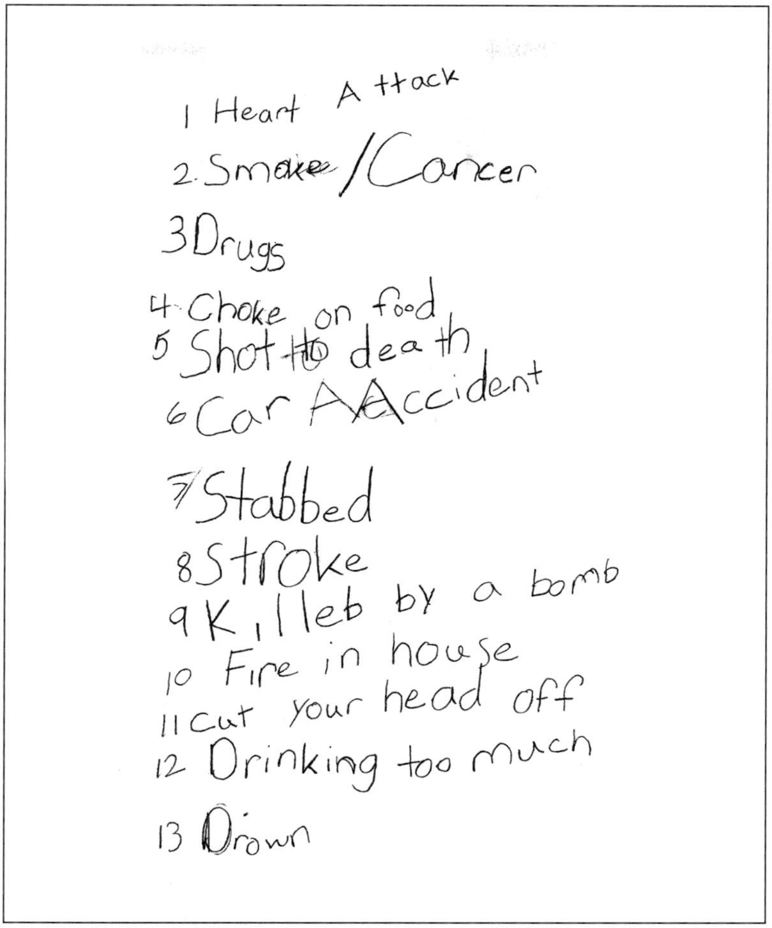

1 Heart A ttack
2. Smoke / Cancer
3 Drugs
4. Choke on food
5 Shot to death
6 Car A Accident

7 Stabbed
8 Stroke
9 Killed by a bomb
10 Fire in house
11 Cut your head off
12 Drinking too much

13 Drown

societies work. The first takes a broad view of social structures and institutions. It emphasizes the interrelationships among major elements of society, including the family, the economy, and the political system. The second focuses on social relations and interactions among members of a society. This theory calls attention to the way people shape and are shaped by the social world in which they live, as well as the ways in which social meaning is created and shared. The third explanation provides a model of how people become members of a society through the interplay of personality, behavior, and environment.

The Structural-Functionalist Approach

Much as in studying the human body, where we look at the structure and function of various organs and their interrelationships, we can view society as an organic whole, with constituent parts working together to maintain each other and the whole society. The patterns of interaction among the members of a society are part of that society's *social structure*. Essentially, social structures are aspects of social life that influence other aspects of social life, making it orderly and predictable.

Sociologists usually delineate five major social institutions: (1) the economy, (2) the educational system, (3) the family, (4) the political system, and (5) religion. These institutions are related in such a way that a change in one leads to changes in others (see Figure 3-4). For example, in northeastern Brazil, a region where many people live in extreme poverty, political authorities do not bother to keep accurate statistics about infant mortality among the poor.[41] In this example, the economy has an impact on the political system, with consequences that, in turn, affect the social reality of poor Brazilian families.

The view of society provided by a structural-functionalist approach helps us appreciate the institutionalized bases of attitudes and behaviors toward death. In North America, cultural expectations about death reflect a social reality consistent with a technology-oriented and bureaucratic society. An appropriate death is one that occurs naturally and is correctly timed—that is, occurs in old age.[42] The bureaucratic aspect of death in modern societies is designed to prevent disruptions and preserve the equilibrium of social life.[43] In this structural framework, death tends to be moved to the periphery of social life.[44]

Robert Kastenbaum introduced the concept of the "death system" to describe the elements of society that have an impact on how people deal with dying and death. According to Kastenbaum, the components of a death system include *people* (for example, funeral directors, life insurance agents, weapons designers, people who operate slaughterhouses, as well as medical personnel who care for the dying), *places* (for example, cemeteries, funeral homes, battlefields, war memorials, disaster sites), *times* (for example, memorial days and religious commemorations such as Good Friday, anniversaries of important battles), *objects* (for example, obituaries, tombstones, hearses, the electric chair), and *symbols* (for example, black armbands, funeral music, skull and crossbones symbols, language used to talk about death).[45]

All death systems serve important functions in society although how these functions are accomplished varies "from one society to another and from one time to another in the same society." These functions include (1) warnings and predictions about life-threatening events (such as disasters); (2) preventing death (for example, emergency and acute medical care, public health initiatives); (3) care of the dying; (4) disposing of the dead; (5) social consolidation after death (for example, dealing with grief, maintaining the community); (6) making sense of death (for example, through religion, scientific explanations); and (7) killing (for example, hunting, raising and marketing of animals, capital punishment).

This listing of what constitutes a death system appears to touch on virtually every aspect of social life. Kastenbaum says, "Everything that makes a

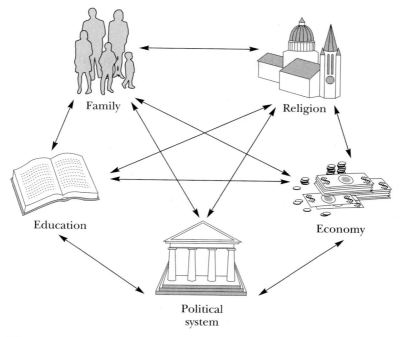

Figure *3-4* *Structural-Functionalist Approach*

collection of individuals into a society and keeps that society going has implications for our relationship with death."[46]

> In practice there are many interconnections and mutual influences among these
> functions. For example, at a particular phase in his/her illness, a person may be
> perceived as a candidate for prevention or for palliative care. . . . Similarly, the
> case for physician-assisted death would be seen in a more favorable light if inter-
> preted as part of "caring for the dying," and in a less favorable light if interpreted
> as "killing."[47]

Symbolic Interactionism

The theoretical approach known as *symbolic interactionism* "seeks to explain
human action and behavior as the result of the meanings which human beings
attach to action and things."[48] Symbolic interactionism emphasizes "the freedom of individuals to construct their own reality as well as to potentially reconstruct that which has been inherited."[49] People are seen not as passive
elements in society but as beings actively responsive to the social structures
and processes in their lives. This theory highlights the fact that socialization is
a two-way process; it is not simply "putting in" information at one end and
"getting out" a finished product at the other.

Commenting on the findings from her study of terminally ill children in
a leukemia ward, Myra Bluebond-Langner says that we limit our perspective

when we define children in terms of "what they will become" while viewing adults as the active "agents" of their socialization.[50] Bluebond-Langner's remarks apply not only to the socialization of children, but also to interactions between adults. This is illustrated in a study of dying and grieving among Native Canadian patients and their families in urban hospital settings.[51] Euro-Canadian caregivers and Native Canadian patients bring to their encounters differing interpretations of appropriate care for patients and families. By engaging one another in interactions to resolve the conflict between these different views, there is a change in attitudes and behaviors on both sides. New "meanings" emerge; as a result, the hospital "culture" is changed.

This process is referred to by social scientists as the *social construction of reality*.

> Each society constructs its own version of the world, its "truths." In some societies the guiding forces of the world are seen as supernatural; in others they are the impersonal forces of nature. Some individuals structure their lives around their belief in a personal deity. . . . For others no such supreme being exists. Different versions of reality are not limited to weighty issues like religion. They also come into play in everyday events in people's lives.[52]

As Robert Fulton and Robert Bendiksen point out, "the 'meaning' that death has for anyone is a result of the socially inherited ideas and assumptions that have been formed over the lifetime of the society in which one lives."[53]

Grief is expressed in ways that reflect the influence of cultural norms that prescribe certain emotions as appropriate for a given social situation.[54] Studies indicate that the human response to loss is culturally learned. In short, people do not "naturally" grieve any more than they "naturally" laugh or cry.[55] Wolfgang and Margaret Stroebe point out:

> Grief is channeled in all cultures along specified lines [and] there are substantial differences in the rules laid down by cultures as to how long the deceased should be grieved over and how long mourning should last. . . . What is sanctioned or prohibited in one culture may differ dramatically from what is or is not permitted in another.[56]

Although death is a biological fact, socially shaped ideas and assumptions create its meaning. This is borne out in the experiences of the Hmong who immigrated to North America from Southeast Asia. Their traditional funeral customs practiced in the mountains of northern Laos, which included firing of mortars to alert the village that a death had occurred and slaughtering oxen and buffalo for the funeral ceremony, have been significantly altered in the very different social setting of their new homeland.[57] The traditional elements of Hmong funeral ritual cannot readily be accomplished in urban settings in North America.

In much the same fashion, migrant Muslims in Germany are being pressured to adapt their funeral ceremonies to European cultural norms and practices. Islamic religious leaders must "carry out a balancing act in order to adapt to the new situation without violating the ritual which holds their community together," a cultural dilemma that has been characterized as "the knife's edge."[58]

Hindus living in England encounter similar cultural imperatives related to death rituals.[59] In India, there are very few undertakers or funeral directors. Because funeral arrangements in India are made by the deceased's family, funeral directors would be redundant. Cremation is a public event in India, and a principal mourner lights the sacred flame of the funeral pyre; in Britain, the body is placed inside a coffin and further concealed from view inside the cremator, with the cremator operated by employees of the crematorium. "For the mourners there is neither the smoke to sting their eyes, nor the fire to singe their hair, nor the smell of burning flesh to bring the poignant immediacy and reality of the experience to their consciousness." Living in a very different cultural environment, some Hindus feel that they are giving up a communal and spiritual ceremony and, in its stead, being left with an anonymous, individualistic, materialist, and bureaucratic procedure. The examples of the Hmong in North America, Muslims in Germany, and Hindus in Britain illustrate the increasingly multicultural nature of modern societies. Whether, or how, such societies find ways to accommodate such diversity of belief and practice is an important question.

The Social Learning Approach

According to social learning theory, we learn through conditioning how to behave as members of a society. Behavior is shaped "by the stimuli that

Two great fears of the traditional Aboriginals are to be hospitalized away from their homelands and to die in the hospital and/or meet the "mamu" spirits of people who have died in the hospital. Aboriginals believe that good health results from harmonious relationships among physical, human, and supernatural environments; sickness results from disruption in these relationships and is directly attributable to the intervention of supernatural forces. These forces are known by various names, one of the most common is "mamu."

Generally, there are two types of forces, and both are potentially dangerous. The first is a kind of "devil," an indeterminate being capable of moving around the same space as ordinary people. . . . The second mamu is more fearful, from the adult Aboriginal's point of view. It is the spirit of the dead, particularly the recent dead. Although not hostile to people, these spirits are dangerous because they seek to rejoin the living. . . . This belief impels people to avoid using the dead person's name and to move camp as soon as a relative dies in camp, as the spirit will look for relatives in the last place they were seen in life.

Death at the time of hospitalization, in a hospital miles from home . . . means that the spirit of the Aboriginal child who dies cannot find its way to the tribal territory to await rebirth. It also means that the life force of adults who die, particularly those who have been repositories of tribal law and knowledge, are separated from their country; the strength of dreaming is weakened, to the eternal loss of all survivors. And a hospital in which many have died becomes a terrifying threat to Aboriginal patients because of the concentration of the mamu spirits of those who died and were unable to find their way back to their individual homelands.

Ruth Walker and Brenda Gameau, "Australia: Its Land, Its People, Its Health Care System, and Unique Health Issues"

follow or are consequences of the behavior, and by imitation or modeling of others' behavior."[60] When we conform to social norms, our behavior is rewarded; when we fail to conform, our behavior is punished or goes unrewarded. This conditioning mechanism is obvious as parents discipline their children for certain behaviors and reward them for others, according to the norms and standards that the parents want the children to learn and emulate.

Much of our learning about social norms occurs through reinforcement, imitation, interaction, rationalization, and other such behavioral and cognitive processes. We may not even be aware that we are conforming to some social norms because they are embedded in our way of life. We accept them as natural, "the way things work." For instance, in modern societies, people are unlikely to consider disposing of a relative's corpse by placing it on a scaffold outdoors where it will gradually decompose; yet, to the Native Americans living on the Great Plains in the nineteenth century, platform burial was a normal and natural part of that society's norms. A person with a different cultural orientation may perceive as deviant the norms we accept uncritically. Ronald Akers says:

Every society and group has a set of social norms, some applying to everyone in the system, some to almost everyone, and others only to persons in particular age, sex, class, ethnic, or religious categories. Some norms apply to a wide range of situations; others govern specific situations. In a heterogeneous society, different systems of normative standards exist side by side, and one may automatically violate the expectations of one group simply by conforming to those of another.[61]

In a culturally diverse society like the United States, we have ample opportunities to apply the insights of social learning theory to expand our understanding of customs and behaviors associated with dying, death, and bereavement. A young Hispanic-American woman who had recently attended her first "Anglo" funeral said that she was "genuinely puzzled" at the absence of storytelling and gentle humor about the deceased's life. "Everyone was respectful of the family," she said, "but I was surprised that it was all so serious. I'm used to people talking and laughing at funerals." By recognizing that social norms function much like the rules of a game or the script of a drama, we can observe their influence in the ways people grieve and the ceremonies they enact to commemorate death.

Death in Contemporary Multicultural Societies

Most modern societies are composed of a number of social groups with distinctive customs and life styles. The United States, for example, is characterized as a "nation of immigrants," a term that reflects cultural diversity. Groups that share a distinctive identity and life style within a larger society are called *subcultures*. In some cases, a subculture shares a specific ethnic heritage; in other instances, a subculture is unique because of its history, place of origin, or economic circumstances. Subcultures often share a distinctive language or, if they have the same language as the wider culture, a distinctive jargon or slang. Scholars note that, in modern societies, "[g]roups as diverse as Punks, Freemasons, and Rastafarians could be classed as subcultures."[62] Although differences among subcultures sometimes result in tension and discord within societies, the presence of a "cultural mosaic" created by different ethnic and cultural groups can be enriching to a society.[63] In some cases, subcultures influence mainstream culture through such avenues as music, fashion, advertising, and the media.

Distinctive Traditions: Ethnicity and Pluralism

Death is the ultimate challenge to human pretensions. "In the last analysis," says sociologist David Clark, "human societies are merely men and women banded together in the face of death."[64] How individuals cope with this challenge is revealed in their cultural life. Despite various signs that death is pushed aside and avoided in modern societies, closer examination reveals that the social practices for dealing with death are not uniform. A set of attitudes and behaviors may be characterized as "The American Way of Death," but this phrase conceals the fact that there are many different "ways of death," reflecting the beliefs and customs of diverse groups within American society. In describing American families, David Olson and John DeFrain remind us that "tremendous diversity exists among people who are commonly grouped together."[65]

The extent to which different groups maintain distinctive cultural patterns varies widely, both among the different ethnic groups and among individuals who share a particular ethnic heritage. Nevertheless, ethnic and other subcultural differences are often influential with respect to such matters as methods of coping with life-threatening illness, the perception of pain, social support for the dying, behavioral manifestations of grief, mourning styles, and funeral customs. A comparison of bereavement practices among ethnic and cultural groups in the United States shows that, "while adapting partly to Western patterns, these groups also adhere to the bereavement procedures of their own cultures."[66]

African-American funerals and mourning illustrate how traditional customs can persist despite time and changed circumstance. Ronald Barrett points out that elements of traditional West African practices retain their importance for many African Americans.[67] This is exemplified in customs such as gathering at the gravesite to bid godspeed to the deceased and relating to funerals as a "home-going" ceremony honoring the spirit of the deceased. David Roediger says these views on death "grew from deep African roots, gained a paradoxical strength and resilience from the horrors of mid-passage, and flowered in the slave funeral—a value laden and unifying social event which the slave community in the United States was able to preserve from both physical and ideological onslaughts of the master class."[68]

Similarly, the Spanish-speaking people of northern New Mexico continue to practice traditional forms of *recuerdo,* or remembrance, which memorialize the dead and comfort the bereaved. Often presented as a written narrative, the *recuerdo* tells the story of a person's life in an epic, lyrical, and heroic manner. It is a kind of farewell, a leave-taking or *la despedida,* on behalf of a deceased person. Such memorials frequently contain reminders of the transitory nature of life and express the notion that life is on loan from God for only a short time, that we are only shadows. The poignant beauty of the *recuerdo,* which is given to the bereaved family and often published in local newspapers, suggests that life has meaning because there is death. Alvin Korte says, "[T]he wisdom of the culture has provided many termini [points on the journey] where family, friends, and community may take their leave and depart from a deceased person."[69] He adds that "It is critical that persons become involved in the process so that the final letting go or *despedida* can be accomplished with ease and lack of guilt."

Encouraging diversity in death attitudes and customs can benefit society as a whole by making available a wealth of cultural resources for coping with death. Yet, diversity also presents challenges in pluralistic societies. When everyone in a society shares essentially the same beliefs and customs, there are known and socially accepted ways of dealing with death and grief. This comforting situation is jeopardized by diversity because there may be less agreement about which practices are socially sanctioned for managing death and minimizing "existential dread."[70] This kind of uncertainty about the social

The Shroud

A mother once had a little seven-year-old boy with such a sweet, beautiful face that no one could look at him without loving him, and she loved him more than anything in the world. Suddenly, the child fell sick, and God took him. The mother was inconsolable and wept day and night. Soon after he was buried, the child began to appear in places where he had sat playing in his lifetime. When his mother wept, he too wept, and when morning came he vanished. Then when the mother could not stop crying, he appeared one night wrapped in the little white shroud he had been buried in and wearing a wreath of flowers on his head. He sat down at her feet and said: "Oh, mother, if you don't stop crying I won't be able to sleep in my coffin, for my shroud is wet with all the tears that fall on it." When she heard that, the mother was horrified, and from then on she shed no tears. The next night the child came again. He held a candle in his hand and said: "You see, my shroud is almost dry. Now I can rest in my grave." After that, the mother gave her grief into God's keeping and bore it silently and patiently. The child never came again, but slept in his little bed under the ground.

Grimm's Tales for Young and Old

norms for dealing with death is evident when people at modern funerals feel anxious about how they should act or what they should say to the bereaved. This was the situation faced by the man who was unsure about whether or not to permit his young son to attend his grandfather's military burial service. People living in modern societies find themselves in a situation where socially sanctioned rites for dealing with death are in flux.

Mixed Plate: Cultural Diversity in Hawaii

Eleanor Nordyke points out that Hawaii "is the only region where all racial groups are minorities and where the majority of the population has its roots in the Pacific Islands or Asia instead of Europe or Africa."[71] Hawaii was settled by Polynesians who sailed their canoes to the Hawaiian archipelago.[72] Their first contact with Europeans came in 1778 with exploration of the Pacific by Captain James Cook. Later, successive waves of immigrants came—including Chinese, Japanese, Portuguese, Okinawans, Koreans, and Filipinos—many arriving as temporary laborers in sugar cane fields and then remaining to make Hawaii their home.[73] Today's residents include Caucasians from both North America and Europe, Samoans, Vietnamese, Laotians, and Cambodians, as well as African Americans, Latin Americans, Pakistanis, Tongans, Fijians, Micronesians, people from other parts of Oceania, and others.

The population of Hawaii represents a rich ethnic and cultural blend. Each group has its own story, unique history, and corresponding traditions. Most groups also have their own cultural networks, with their own ways of keeping story, history, and tradition alive, as well as providing mutual support in times of need. With the Japanese, it's kin groups; the Portuguese have the church; the Chinese, clubs; and Filipinos have provincial clubs.[74] With its diversity and intermingling of different cultural traditions, Hawaii is a model for societies that wish to preserve the cultural richness of distinctive traditions by accommodating and, indeed, welcoming their expression.

Characteristics of Hawaii's Peoples

Among native Hawaiians, the extended family group, or *'ohana,* is at the center of traditional values.[75] Children are given an important place in all family gatherings, including funeral rituals. Ancestral remains are considered sacred, especially those of the *ali'i,* members of the royal family. Indeed, the Hawaiians' love of family is the basis of their love of the land. George Kanahele says,

> In a religious society in which ancestors were deified as *'aumakua* [gods] and genealogy elevated to prominent status, a place, a home, was much more valued because of its ties with the ancestors. A Hawaiian's birthplace was celebrated not simply because he happened to be born there, but because it was also the place where so many generations of his ancestors were born before him. It was a constant reminder of the vitality of the bloodline and of the preciousness of life past, present, and future.[76]

Hawaiians have a profound capacity for experiencing the sacred and expressing—through myth, symbolism, and ritual—the transcendent realities of life. In the spring of 1994, the Hawaiian community was shocked into mourning when two *ka'ai,* or woven caskets, containing bones believed to be those of deified Hawaiian chiefs were taken from the Bishop Museum in Honolulu.[77] A grief-filled ceremony was held at the Royal Mausoleum to inform the ancestors of the missing bones and express the desire for the bones' safe return. Chants and wailing laments asking the ancestors' forgiveness formed part of a ceremony that was said to have been last held a hundred years ago.

The Chinese were among the earliest immigrants to Hawaii.[78] Like native Hawaiians, the Chinese embody cultural values stressing the importance of family and relationships. They also retain core elements of traditional funerals and mourning.[79] For example, in accordance with the belief that the needs of the dead resemble those of the living, Chinese funerals in Hawaii typically include offerings of food, money, and other items that will be needed by the deceased in the afterlife. Papier-mâché "servant dolls," placed in front of the casket, are given chanted instructions by a Taoist priest about how to take care of the deceased in Heaven. The boy servant might be told, "Take care of your master; fetch him water and firewood." To the girl servant, the priest might say, "Keep the house clean and, when you go shopping, don't waste your master's money." In the Taoist funeral, which lasts nearly all day, the priest chants and musicians play instruments while family members perform rituals at the priest's direction. Symbolic money (sometimes called "Hell Notes"), which the dead person will spend in the other world, is contributed by mourners and burned in a container during the service. The more money burned, the more the deceased has in the next life. As these ritual activities are per-

© Albert Lee Strickland

Located in a setting of great natural beauty on the Hawaiian island of Oahu, this Chinese cemetery is situated on a hillside that gently slopes down toward the city of Honolulu and the ocean beyond. Following Chinese custom, care is taken to ensure proper siting of the grave so that the deceased's spirit can easily depart this world. As in the case of this cemetery, located above a bustling, metropolitan city, certain aspects of traditional practices retain their importance even in modern social settings.

formed, relatives and friends visit and express condolences. Following Taoist traditions, the ancient divinatory art of *fĕng-shui* is called upon for auspicious placement of the casket during the service. Similarly, Chinese cemeteries in Hawaii are situated amid great natural beauty and on sloping ground, in accord with the principles of *fĕng-shui*. A burial that meets these requirements facilitates the journey of the deceased's spirit to the afterlife.

As with the Hawaiians and the Chinese, Japanese place high value on the family and its extended household.[80] Unlike the Chinese, who typically choose ground burial, the Japanese generally prefer cremation and then interment of the remains in a *haka,* or family memorial, which often has space for a dozen or more urns. At funerals, the primary mourner is often given *koden*— contributions of money to help defray the expenses—with the donation increasing as kinship ties become closer. An elder son, for example, makes a larger contribution than, say, a cousin. Most Japanese homes in Hawaii have a *butsudan* as a focal point for honoring the family's ancestors. In Hawaii, the midsummer *o-bon* festival (discussed in Chapter 2) is celebrated widely, not just by Japanese families. In Hawaii, celebrations like *o-bon,* as well as the Chinese festival *ch'ing ming,* are community affairs, with people of varied backgrounds and traditions participating.

Most cultural groups living in Hawaii share a valuing of family ties and respect for ancestors. John F. McDermott says,

> In all groups, except perhaps the Caucasian, the extended family plays a central role. There is an emphasis on the family as a key social unit, and on family cohesion, family interdependence, and loyalty to the family as central guiding values. The individual is seen as part of a larger network, and duties and obligations, as well as much of the sense of personal security, derive from that context. . . . Caucasians, too, value the family, but they face the world as individuals.[81]

Euro-American culture plays a major role in modern Hawaii although it is appropriate to think of Caucasians not as the dominant force but as one of many groups that constitute the "ethnic mosaic" of the islands. Newcomers often find that this social reality requires some adjustment. Caucasians who move to Hawaii from the mainland United States generally do not think of themselves as migrants; rather, they view themselves as representing mainstream culture and expect others to adapt, not themselves.[82]

Assimilation and Accommodation in Death Rites

The various groups in Hawaii tend to maintain their own distinctive identity and culture while sharing elements of their identity and culture with the overall community. As different ethnic groups became part of the cultural mix in Hawaii, a common language, called "pidgin," developed and became a symbol of local identity. Pidgin borrows words and grammar from the native tongues of its speakers. It is not only an expressive means of communication among people of disparate backgrounds, but a way for people to identify with their adopted homeland. Today, speaking pidgin allows people to transcend cultural boundaries and establish rapport with each other on the basis of "local" identity.

A Caucasian nurse in Hawaii describes how she used pidgin in talking with a Filipino man who was dying. As the man's body wasted away from disease, he was frightened of dying. Offering comfort, the nurse told him, "Spirit good, body *pau* [finished]." In using a pidgin word, which had been borrowed from the Hawaiian language, she was able to affirm, in a culturally appropriate and comforting way, the strength of the patient's spirit while acknowledging that the life in his body was being consumed by disease.

Local identity is fostered by familiarity with customs practiced by other ethnic groups and flexibility in adopting elements of those customs in one's own life. For instance, the native Hawaiian tradition of feasting at important ceremonial events, such as those commemorating birth and death, is widespread among Hawaii's residents. At funerals, mourners often gather after the ritual to share food and conversation. In fact, mortuaries in Hawaii accommodate this custom by having kitchen and dining facilities where food can be prepared, brought by mourners (pot luck), or catered and served to gathered family and friends.

Similarly, funeral announcements in Hawaii usually include the notice, "Aloha attire requested," to which mourners respond by wearing colorful shirts or *mu'u mu'u* (long "missionary" dresses), along with beautiful and fragrant flower leis. The lei is very special in Hawaiian culture, and different flowers and leis carry symbolic meanings. For example, a *hala* lei is associated with the breath (*ha*) and connotes passing away or dying. The ginger, or *'awapuhi,* lei is a symbol of things that pass too soon, as indicated in the Hawaiian folk saying, "*'Awapuhi lau pala wale,*" or "Ginger leaves yellow too quickly."[83] In the customs of "feasting" after a funeral and wearing flower leis with symbolic meanings, traditions associated with the indigenous Hawaiians have been adopted as expressions of local identity and community feeling.

Given the varied religions practiced in Hawaii—Christianity, Buddhism, and Taoism, among others—mortuaries are generally set up to offer appropriate accoutrements and symbols for all these traditions. The central portion of the altar at one mortuary is designed as a revolving display so that the images and symbols of the appropriate religious tradition can be easily provided—whether it is Catholic, Protestant, Buddhist, or whatever.

The creation of Hawaii's ethnic mosaic and sense of local identity involves both assimilation and accommodation. In this context, *assimilation* "refers to the incorporation of the values of a new group by the dominant existing group so that it fits into the existing social network, while *accommodation* suggests movement in the other direction, that is, a new individual or group adapting to the existing or dominant group values by changing in order to continue to live with them."[84] The boundaries between different groups have become loosened through social interaction among the groups, so that they are "soft instead of hard, often overlapping rather than sharply defined," resulting in a unique situation wherein "no group has totally surrendered the core of its traditional cultural identity."[85]

The fastest growing ethnic group in Hawaii is "mixed race," or *hapa.*[86] When people marry outside their heritage group, thereby joining in kinship with families from different cultural traditions, their customs, beliefs, and practices blend together in a new family. As spouses from different traditions adopt elements of each other's culture, their children become acquainted with both cultures. Hawaii's diverse inhabitants have not minimized differences between different ethnic groups so much as learned how to appreciate and make room for their expression.

The Mature Concept of Death Revisited

The process of socialization is both complex and ongoing. Our understanding of death evolves throughout the life course. As we experience loss in our lives, we modify previously held beliefs, exchanging them for new ones that provide

© Patrick Dean

In this celebration of el Día de los Muertos, *or Day of the Dead, held in a Califor-nia community, a child enters into the festivities by drawing a skull, an activity that reinforces her identity as a participant in age-old traditions that mark her culture's particular attitudes and behaviors relative to death. In pluralistic societies, such cele-brations both perpetuate cultural traditions and allow them to be shared with people from the wider community, who may choose to adopt elements of those traditions in their own lives, thereby creating a distinctive sense of local identity with respect to death-related customs and practices.*

a better fit with our current understanding of death and its meaning in our lives. A "mature" concept of death, acquired in childhood, becomes the foundation for further development on into adulthood.[87] Sandor Brent and Mark Speece note that this basic understanding of death is "the stable nucleus, or core, of a connotational sphere that the child continues to enrich and elaborate throughout the remainder of life by the addition of all kinds of exceptions, conditions, questions, doubts, and so forth." Instead of the "neat, clean, sharply delineated concepts of formal scientific theories of reality," the end result of this process may be a kind of "fuzzy" concept that acknowledges the reality of death while leaving room for a variety of elaborations about its meaning. The binary "either/or" logic that young children use to grasp the core components of a mature concept of death is a precursor to the greater sophistication in understanding death that develops later in life.[88]

As this process unfolds, the agencies of socialization discussed in this chapter exert a powerful influence on beliefs and behaviors. Broadening our perspective on dying and death to include cultures other than our own increases the range of choices available in our encounters with death. David Plath says,

> We are born alone and we die alone, each an organism genetically unique. But we mature or decline together: In the company of others we mutually domesticate the wild genetic pulse as we go about shaping ourselves into persons after the vision of our group's heritage. Perhaps the growth and aging of an organism can be described well enough in terms of stages and transitions within the individual as a monad entity. But in a social animal the life courses have to be described in terms of a collective fabricating of selves, a mutual building of biographies.[89]

Enlarging our perspective and engaging the ideas and customs of other cultures are the antidote to ethnocentrism—that is, the fallacy of making judgments about others solely in terms of one's own cultural assumptions and biases. People tend to view the world from a single perspective—their own. By understanding ourselves as ethnic/cultural beings, we can more accurately understand others as ethnic/cultural beings.[90] We should be careful of the tendency to use our own cultural criteria as benchmarks for judging the worth of other communities. There may be more differences within cultural groups than between cultural groups.

In becoming more culturally sensitive, we need to be careful about stereotyping others. Stereotypes are often used as a learning strategy to organize and interpret information.[91] But it is important to keep in mind, first, that culture is a continuum; and, second, that culture is not defined simply by ethnicity. The fact is, especially within culturally diverse societies, we can expect to find great variation within each ethnic group.[92] Identity is situational and adaptive, and it can serve multiple purposes.[93] The meanings people attach to a particular cultural identity vary within cultural groups.[94] Furthermore, discrepancies may exist between *expressed* norms and *observed* behaviors within groups.[95] Even though we may be identified with a particular group, we are also individuals who sometimes do things our own way. Seeing others as they see themselves, sharing in some way their perceptions

© Patrick Dean

In contemporary societies, where a variety of cultural traditions are practiced by different ethnic and subcultural groups, people may find themselves "trying on" customs and practices that differ from those of their own heritage group. The opportunity to participate in the rites and ceremonies of other cultures, to assume a "local identity," even if only temporarily, can broaden our understanding and expand our range of choices for revitalizing even those customs with which we are most familiar.

and customs, enriches individual as well as social life, and, indeed, may be the essence of education.

Further Readings

Nigel Barley. *Grave Matters: A Lively History of Death Around the World.* New York: Henry Holt, 1997.

David Clark, ed. *The Sociology of Death: Theory, Culture, Practice.* Cambridge, Mass.: Blackwell, 1993.

David R. Counts and Dorothy A. Counts, eds. *Coping with the Final Tragedy: Cultural Variation in Dying and Grieving.* Amityville, N.Y.: Baywood, 1991.

Geri-Ann Galanti. *Caring for Patients from Different Cultures: Case Studies from American Hospitals,* 2d ed. Philadelphia: University of Pennsylvania Press, 1997.

Artin Göncü, ed. *Children's Engagement in the World: Sociocultural Perspectives.* New York: Cambridge University Press, 1999.

Donald P. Irish, Kathleen F. Lundquist, and Vivian Jenkins Nelsen, eds. *Ethnic Variation in Dying, Death, and Grief.* Washington, D.C.: Taylor and Francis, 1993.

Colin Murray Parkes, Pittu Laungani, and Bill Young, eds. *Death and Bereavement Across Cultures.* New York: Routledge, 1997.

Clive F. Seale. *Constructing Death: The Sociology of Dying and Bereavement.* Cambridge: Cambridge University Press, 1998.

Robert S. Siegler. *Emerging Minds: The Process of Change in Children's Thinking.* New York: Oxford University Press, 1996.

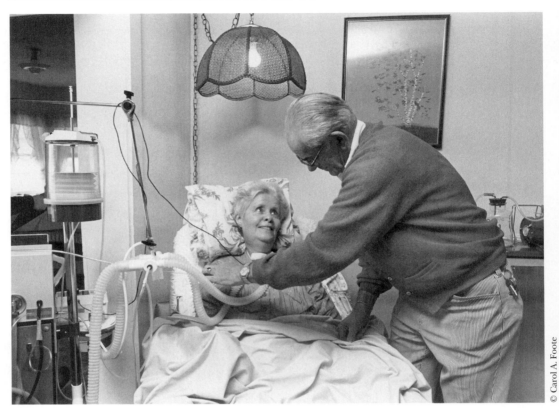

*Home care may not come immediately to mind when one thinks of health
care systems, yet this centuries-old tradition of care for the ill and the dying
is once again emerging as an option for many. Innovations in sophisticated
medical life-support equipment often make it possible for the seriously ill to
be cared for at a high level of medical technology within the home.*

Health Care Systems: Patients, Staff, and Institutions

*M*edical institutions are designed to soothe and heal; yet their salve is not always comforting for the dying. Oriented toward the goal of sustaining life, the medical system sometimes falls short in meeting the needs of dying patients and their families. In the modern hospital, death may be treated as an anomaly. Think about the end of your own life. What are your fears about dying? Many people say that they fear dying in pain, hooked up to machines in an impersonal institutional setting. All too often, there is an "interventional cascade" that surrounds people with more technology as they die. A century ago, physicians did as much to console as to cure patients. Indeed, consolation and comfort were often all that medical practitioners could offer. Today, because of our higher expectations of medicine, if a cure does not result, we may feel cheated. Indeed, doctors may become scapegoats if treatment does not lead to the desired outcome.

Each of the three major categories of institutional medical care—hospitals, nursing homes, and hospices—is designed to optimally serve a specific purpose within the overall health care delivery system. Patients with life-threatening illness usually receive a combination of acute and supportive care. As conditions change, institutional care may alternate with home care.

Hospitals are devoted mainly to acute intensive care of a limited duration. Aggressive techniques are employed to diagnose symptoms, provide treatment, and sustain life. The typical patient expects to regain well-being after a short period of treatment and then return to normal life. Patients with chronic or terminal disease may alternate occasional acute care stays in the hospital with care received in nursing homes, hospices, or at home.

Hospitals face challenges related to changing patterns of disease and health care economics. The acute care focus of hospitals appears to be giving way to a more integrated system in which outpatient and extended care, as well as home and hospice care, play important roles.[1] In effect, hospitals are changing from "monolithic" centers focusing on acute care to institutions that offer a "portfolio" of health care services.[2]

Nursing homes (a category that includes convalescent and extended-care facilities) are designed to provide long-term residential care for the chronically ill. In 1997, about 1.6 million residents were receiving care in 17,000 nursing homes.[3] The level of care provided in such facilities is less sophisticated than that in hospitals. About three-quarters of nursing home patients eventually return to the community; the remaining one-quarter includes both patients who require ongoing nursing care and those who die while in a nursing home. Nursing homes designated as skilled nursing facilities have a registered nurse on duty around the clock and a paramedical staff. There is a trend toward lower utilization of nursing homes as some of the same health care services are being provided by home health care agencies.

Hospice care is distinguished by its orientation toward the needs of dying patients and their families. The central mission of hospice care is to comfort the patient, rather than cure a disease. Unlike hospitals and nursing homes, hospice is not necessarily a place, but a program of caring. Hospice care may be provided in a community hospice program, in a palliative medicine department within a hospital, in a nursing care or residential care facility, or at home. We look at these options in greater detail later in this chapter.

Modern Health Care

A person is admitted to a health care facility to receive medical and nursing care appropriate to a particular malady. The kind and quality of care provided depends on the relationships among the patient, the staff, and the institution. Each side of this health care triangle—patient, staff, and institution—contributes to the overall shape of health care. Because providing health care for large numbers of people requires efficient use of staff and facilities, procedures are standardized and routine. Thus, the institution's capacity for meeting the needs of each patient is inherently limited. When the elderly aunt was dying at home, she could be spoon-fed her favorite homemade soup by a member of her family. In a hospital or nursing home, she is likely to be fed a standardized diet, perhaps served impersonally by a harried and overworked aide. The trade-off for sophisticated health care may be less personal comfort. In an institutional setting, the patient's experience is influenced by rules, regulations, and conventions—written and unwritten.

Unwritten rules, no less faithfully executed than written ones, can contribute to a sense of alienation in institutional settings. The family of a dying

"I think in the next 10–20 years we'll have 'warehouses' with patients on life support systems, if the American public and physicians don't come to grips with and resolve the inherent conflicts involved in the present 'common' method for handling the terminally ill patient." *General practitioner*

"I do not think anybody should have the right to be God and decide death. In view of age and circumstances life may be prolonged to the benefit of patient and family." *Orthopedic surgeon*

"I am a doctor and I feel I should do all in my power to diagnose disease and sustain life." *Internist*

"We should not prolong misery when it's not indicated for other reasons. Everyone has a time to die and should be allowed to die with some dignity." *Urologist*

"The Physician Speaks,"
The Newsletter of Physician Attitudes

patient may be relegated to maintaining a deathwatch in the corridor or the waiting room down the hall, with one family member at a time squeezing into the patient's room to keep a bedside vigil. There may be no private space where relatives can gather to discuss their concerns with staff members. Meetings with doctors or nurses in hospital corridors symbolize this sense of impersonality. In such public settings, grieving relatives may feel obliged to contain or repress their emotions. These examples reflect a medical model in which patient and staff are central while the family is much less important. As a patient nears death, however, this focus may need to change: "The goal must not be simply to provide expert medical care to an individual patient, but to help give voice and connection and meaning to a family."[4]

Depersonalization and abstraction are part of the scientific method, which is responsible for many of the medical advances we applaud. Yet these mechanisms can make medicine less humane. Depersonalization is most common when a disease is not well understood; physicians may exhibit greater interest in the disease than in the patient. Some studies have found that nurses take longer to answer the bedside calls of terminally ill patients than to answer the calls of patients less severely ill.[5] This is not always the case, of course, but such avoidance is lamentable whenever it occurs. Charles Rosenberg observes that "we expect a great deal of our hospitals: alleviation of pain, extension of life, [and] management of death and the awkward and painful circumstances surrounding its approach."[6]

Health Care Financing

Individual and social choices about financing health care influence the options available for care of the seriously ill and dying. After 25 years of double-digit annual growth in national health expenditures, the rate of growth slowed during the 1990s although the United States continues to spend more on health than any other industrialized country. In 1997, the most recent year for which statistics are available, national health expenditures totaled almost $1.1 trillion, nearly 14 percent of the gross domestic product.[7] Health economists observe that there seems to be no limit to spending for health care, "the richer a country becomes, the more it will tend to spend."[8]

The rapid rise in health care expenditures has occurred during a period when medical coverage is being extended to more people while at the same time attempts are being made to control health care costs—goals that may be incompatible. In 1965, the federal government created the Medicare and Medicaid programs to provide health care coverage to underserved populations, especially the elderly and poor. These programs are now an integral part of the health care system in the United States. During the 1980s, steps were taken to contain costs associated with these programs and with health care generally, the most important step being the institution of diagnosis-related groups (DRGs) and prospective payment. The idea behind DRGs is that costs can be controlled by using a predetermined schedule of fees for reimbursements to health care providers. Basing such fees on a patient's disease, procedure, and medical history, DRGs and prospective payment combine to create a system whereby hospitals are compensated a set amount that depends on the complexity of services used by a patient.

Recent developments in managed health care have troubling side effects. Medical care is increasingly viewed in terms of standardized "products." Physicians are now "providers" and patients are "consumers."[9] Patients may be forgotten if "dollars saved" becomes the primary measure of outcome. All managed care plans (by definition) involve efforts to control where, when, and from whom medical services can be obtained. The health care system in the United States is currently undergoing massive restructuring. As this restructuring proceeds, it must be kept in mind that the "medical encounter" is more complex than the models of consumerism found in other commercial transactions.[10]

A "technological imperative" is driving up the cost of medical care. Scientific research promises an unprecedented range of tools for combating disease.[11] On the horizon are designer antibodies to fight cancer. The cloning of a Scottish mountain sheep named Dolly portends the creation of custom-designed animals that can produce medically useful proteins and perhaps generate tissues for organ replacement. Gene therapy promises to radically change medicine as the genetic mechanisms of diseases are discovered. Surgeons are adopting noninvasive techniques that speed healing. Access to current information via the Internet and satellite communications is helping physicians and other health care personnel stay abreast of the rapid changes in medicine, an advance that is especially appreciated by those who care for patients in remote or rural areas. Patients themselves are accessing medical information on-line through databases maintained by the National Library of Medicine, the National Institutes of Health (NIH), and other electronic services, thereby assuming a more central role in determining their own care. Given the rapid pace of change in medicine, however, "[l]ast year's advance may be this year's error."[12]

Innovations in medical care can be a mixed blessing. Earlier detection of disease, for example, may lead to a cure that would not have been possible otherwise, or it may just mean that the patient knows about his or her disease for a longer period of time.[13] As health technologies allow earlier diagnosis of life-threatening conditions and more success in mitigating the effects of these conditions, the process of dying is likely to be longer now than in past decades; indeed, a terminal illness can last as long as 15 years.[14]

High-quality patient care requires ongoing capital investment.[15] Do larger investments in medical technology result in a better quality of care? The answer seems to be yes.[16] As the costs of medical care rise, however, more people are questioning whether society is obligated to provide every intervention that a patient believes might be beneficial. To alleviate pressures on the health care system, some experts suggest that resources must be rationed.

Rationing Scarce Resources

Rationing refers to the allocation of scarce resources among competing individuals. In health care, it is defined as any system that limits the amount of health care a person can receive. Rationing occurs when not all care expected to be beneficial is provided to all patients and, in particular, when a medical benefit valued by a patient must be withheld because of cost.[17] Doctors have always been "gatekeepers," providing access to treatments and procedures that serve the patient's welfare. In an era of managed care, however, physicians are increasingly being asked to engage in "restrictive" gatekeeping and "bedside" rationing, roles that many physicians believe are morally illegitimate and unacceptable in the practice of medicine.[18]

The scarcity of health care resources is driven by an aging society as well as a growing population of "potentially salvageable" patients. Daniel Callahan suggests that a "principle of symmetry" could help people acknowledge the inherent limits of medical progress.[19] In Callahan's view, "A technology should be judged by its likelihood of enhancing a good balance between the extension and saving of life and the quality of life." Conversely, "a health care system that develops and institutionalizes a life-saving technology which has the common result of leaving people chronically ill or with poor quality of life ignores the principle of symmetry."

A yardstick of some kind is needed to measure the outcomes of health care choices in relation to available resources.[20] One such measure involves the use of "quality-adjusted life years" (or QALYs) to find a balance between length of life and quality of life.[21] The idea behind QALYs is that people may be willing to accept a trade-off. For example, a person might equate the prospect of living *fewer* years in *perfect* health with the prospect of living *more* years in *less than perfect* health. Depending on the outcome of such decisions, an individual or society as a whole might choose to pay for some health expenditures but not others.

Decisions about allocating scarce medical resources are not just a matter for experts and legislators to consider. The choices we make in pursuit of our own well-being affect the health care system and ultimately shape its character. For example, rather than undergoing expensive and futile treatments at the end of life, some people choose to complete advance directives that make known their wishes about the use of life-sustaining medical technologies. "Medicine overreaches itself," Daniel Callahan says, "when it sets as its implicit goal that of curing all diseases and infinitely forestalling death."

The Caregiver–Patient Relationship

Physicians occupy a place of honor in society. Aesculapius, the first physician according to Greek legend, was elevated to the pantheon of gods and, along with Hygeia and Panacea, ruled over health and illness in Greek mythology. Given its association with the elemental experiences of birth, life, and death, medicine carries high symbolic importance. But the "Aesculapian authority" of physicians is changing due to the impact of managed care and a greater emphasis on patients' rights. Managed care is a reminder that the physician–patient relationship is influenced by its institutional and economic context.[22] Excessive *paternalism,* the assumption of parentlike authority by medical practitioners, infringes on a patient's autonomy or freedom to make medical decisions.

The social contract between physicians and patients includes qualities of a *covenantal* relationship, which implies a mutuality of interests between health care providers and patients, and between medical professionals and society.[23] Stanley Joel Reiser suggests that patients' experiences in coping with illness can help shape the missions of health care.[24] Ideally, the physician–patient relationship is an alliance wherein the physician is an educator, counselor, and expert, but not the sole decision maker. Shared decision making is the goal of good medical care.[25] Patient participation in decision making is crucial in palliative care programs and end-of-life care generally. It is facilitated when caregivers get to know the patient, empower the patient to share in decision making, and work within the constraints of the situation to respect and accommodate patient choices.[26]

With the advent of managed care, patients are being required to take a more active role in decision making, sometimes becoming their own advocates for desired treatment options. Preferences or questions about end-of-life care should be part of any discussion when choosing a doctor.[27] Does the doctor have experience caring for people at the end of life? Is he or she willing and able to provide care in all settings—hospital, nursing home, hospice, or at home? Is the doctor familiar with home health and other resources available in the community? Financial issues should be discussed, as should any preferences about limiting treatment at the end of life. The bottom line is: (1) Will the patient and his or her family be supported medically, emotionally, and financially within the system? and (2) Will the system accommodate their specific preferences and plans? These issues are too important to leave to chance.

Disclosing a Life-Threatening Diagnosis

If you were diagnosed as having a life-threatening illness, would you want to know about it? Some people say, "Of course, I want to know about

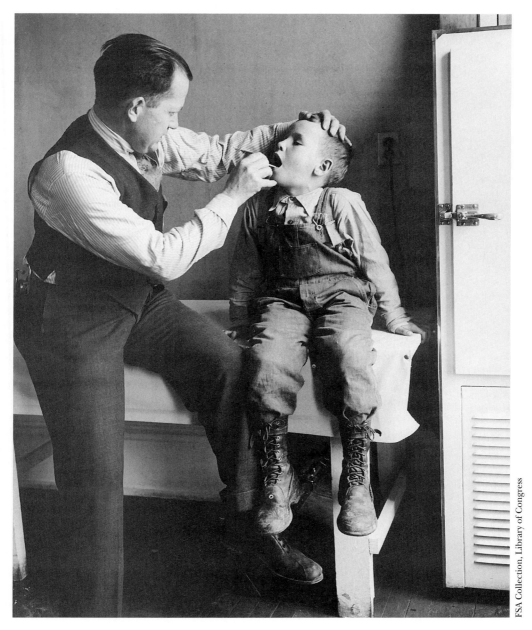

In 1935, medical care in Reedsville, West Virginia, seems less formal than that received in the urban clinics and hospitals of today. Although the practice of medicine has been enhanced by new methods of diagnosis and treatment, most people still believe that the relationship between physician and patient is central to the outcome of an illness.

I clearly made Dr. Mueh nervous. He was clearly up to his ears in patients and spread very thin.

He took 90 minutes to talk to me and my wife about my disease. He started out with terminal care and told me I'd get all the narcotics I would need to eliminate pain and that tubes could be used to provide nourishment.

I was amazed that he talked that way, as if I were dying.

Pierre Bowman, Honolulu *Star-Bulletin*

everything that's going on with me!" Others answer, "If I could be spared the truth, I'd rather not know that I'm about to die; ignorance is bliss." Consider your own attitudes and preferences. The person who has spent a lifetime as a fighter against the odds is likely to have a very different response from the person whose typical pattern of coping with difficulties involves efforts to shun stress.

Surveys indicate that most people do want to be told if diagnosed with a life-threatening illness, but the questions of *when* and *how* such information should be communicated are more difficult to answer. Physicians need to present the news of a life-threatening diagnosis in a manner that will serve the best interests of the patient. In deciding how this should be done, the patient's personality, emotional constitution, and capacity for continued function under stress must all be carefully considered.

Doctors may worry that knowing all the details about a life-threatening illness could adversely affect a patient's ability to cope. Is minimizing the threat of an illness sometimes in a patient's best interest? Physicians generally subscribe to the belief that reassurance and support must be sustained. Hopefulness must be encouraged. Thus, although the general facts of a life-threatening illness are likely to be disclosed by physicians, some details may be withheld until the patient takes the initiative by asking specific questions. Cultural factors are also a consideration. Members of some ethnic groups have a preference for "concealment," rather than complete disclosure, when diagnosed with serious illness.[28] In China, for example, protecting patients from possible psychological harm after learning about a critical condition is considered more important than information disclosure. Furthermore, a patient may not be the one making decisions about his or her medical care; family members may have the largest say.[29]

In cases of serious illness, communicating the diagnosis is a critical event in patient care. How this is done can influence a patient's attitude toward the illness, response to treatment, and ability to cope. What is said depends on a number of factors, including the doctor's preferences for breaking bad news, the patient's receptivity to the facts, and the expected prognosis. In conversations that involve breaking the bad news of a terminal diagnosis, both physicians and patients tend to be cautious in how they discuss dying and death.[30] Because uncertainty is inherent in medical practice, physicians who openly

There are some people who really can't deal with being told the truth about their illness. If you tell them at the wrong time or in the wrong way, it's too devastating for them.

First of all, get to know the patient. Sit down and talk with him, not about his illness particularly, but general topics. Very soon you get a feeling as to whether or not the patient wants to know. There are two groups: those who want to know and don't mind knowing, and those who very plainly don't want to know. There are some patients who have been told they have cancer, hear doctors discussing it, see their charts, and will still turn around and deny that they have cancer. And, of course, that's a gray area. You're not sure if they want to know. If they want to know, tell them. Don't hide the fact.

Quoted from *Death and Dying: The Physician's Perspective,* a videotape by Elizabeth Bradbury

discuss these issues with patients may actually promote trust and realistic expectations.[31]

Generally, doctors should provide a truthful report of the diagnosis and advice about the proposed course of treatment, providing as much detail as the patient desires. Time should be made available to explore the patient's questions and concerns.[32] When initially informed of a diagnosis of serious illness, patients may be too shocked to ask questions that will occur to them later; detailed information may need to be given in segments.[33] It is also important to recognize that family members typically form an integral part of a patient's care from the moment of the diagnosis, and friends may be closely involved as well.

Achieving Clear Communication

Achieving clear communication in the physician–patient relationship does not happen automatically. There is an asymmetry in physician–patient communications that challenges both parties to the dialogue.[34] Candace West, a sociologist who conducted a five-year study of how doctors and patients relate to each other, found what she calls a "communications chasm" that hinders the healing process.[35] In particular, she observed a lack of "social cement"—the introductions, greetings, laughter, and use of patients' names—that are part of ordinary social interactions. West also found that physicians tend to "advance questions which restrict patients' options for answers," whereas patients tend to be hesitant about questioning their doctors.

Physicians should "listen" with their eyes as well as their ears, paying attention to the nonverbal communication of gestures and body language that reveal a patient's unease or anxiety about what is being discussed. Highly technical diagnostic and therapeutic interventions can themselves be obstacles to effective communication.[36] The knowledge base required to master modern medicine can itself become an instrument of bewilderment. Speaking

" WHY, YOUR FEVER'S WAY DOWN. "

as a doctor, Richard Sandor says, "We detect subtle disturbances of heart rhythm, manipulate faltering blood pressure to within a few millimeters of mercury, and regulate minute changes in blood chemistry, but what about the *person* who is dying?"[37] In practicing the art of medicine, "Accurate communication is the single most valuable asset of the skilled doctor."[38]

Communication is an interactive and transactional process: One cannot *not* communicate. Consider the role that nonverbal communication plays in the health care setting. Such communication includes not only facial expressions, gestures, and body postures, but also *iconics*—that is, objects that convey meaningful information. Labels such as M.D. and R.N., as well as titles such as doctor, nurse, and patient, are examples of symbolic identifiers that can influence the process of communication.[39] For instance, in most medical communications, patients are addressed by their first names whereas doctors are addressed by their titles.[40]

Trained to save lives, medical and nursing personnel may feel helpless when they are unable to offer a cure. When dying patients express a desire to talk about death, various strategies may be used, with the effect of either curtailing or encouraging such conversations, including (1) reassurance ("You're doing so well"); (2) denial ("Oh, you'll live to be a hundred"); (3) changing the subject ("Let's talk about something more cheerful"); (4) fatalism ("Well, we all have to die sometime"); (5) discussion ("What happened to make you feel that way?"). Jeanne Quint Benoliel points out that, in their relationships with dying patients, caregivers need to be aware that "open communication does not necessarily mean open talk about death, but it does mean openness to the patient's verbalized concerns."[41]

Responding to the emotional and spiritual needs of patients and their families can be as important as caring for physical needs. A nurse who steps into the room, sits down by the patient's bed, and displays a willingness to listen is likely to be more effective in providing comfort than one who breezes in, remains standing, and quips, "How're we today? Did we sleep well?" Skillful communication is crucial in attaining the goals of health care for the whole person.

Depending on how it is conducted, medical communication can promote either a positive attitude, with faith in the ultimate outcome, or a negative attitude, with corresponding feelings of despondency and despair. Writing about his own experiences with serious illness, Norman Cousins points out that a life-threatening diagnosis can be communicated as a "challenge rather than a verdict."[42] Clear communication can play an important role in motivating the patient's own "healing system," thereby creating the potential for a positive outcome regardless of the ultimate prognosis.

Providing Total Care

Caring for seriously ill and dying patients is not just a matter of attending to a patient's physical needs; the patient's personality—a unique combination of mental, emotional, and spiritual needs—must also be considered in the context of total patient care (see Figure 4-1).[43] Such care requires continuity of contact between at least one caregiver and the patient, opportunity for the patient to remain informed of his or her condition and outlook, patient participation in decisions that affect him or her, and behavior by staff members that elicits the patient's trust and confidence.[44] When these guidelines are followed, caregivers are in a position to provide care that is both *personal* and *comprehensive.*

Accommodations sometimes must be made to help patients cope with inconvenient aspects of an illness. For example, it may be possible to adjust treatment schedules so that patients can continue to work, go to school, or care for their families. The entire family unit is affected when one of its members is seriously ill. As death becomes more imminent, the patient's family is likely to experience a transition that involves the patient's "fading away."[45] A period of chaos, confusion, fear, and uncertainty may ensue: "Nothing feels solid anymore." This transition involves a task of redefinition that requires family members to cope with the burden of letting go of the old before picking up the new. Families often find themselves coping with the paradox of caring for a dying loved one while simultaneously trying to carry on with the normal business of life. Thus, a model of total care also includes attending to the needs of the patient's family.

Caregiver Stress

Physicians, nurses, and other health care professionals work in environments where death is more commonplace than it is in most walks of life. This

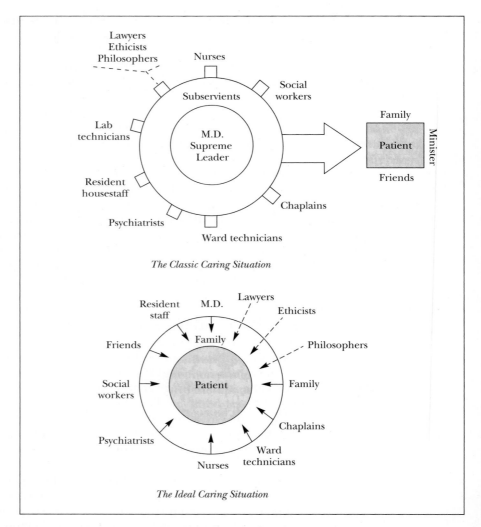

Figure 4-1 *Classic and Ideal Caring Situations*
Source: David Barton, ed., *Dying and Death: A Clinical Guide for Caregivers* (Baltimore: Williams & Wilkins, 1977), p. 181.

observation also applies to "first-responders," such as emergency medical technicians (EMTs), paramedics, and search-and-rescue personnel, as well as firefighters and police officers who are on the scene at accidents or disasters. The impact of working in a death-saturated environment was evident on the faces of rescue personnel in the aftermath of the Oklahoma City bombing in 1995. Although caring for seriously ill and dying may make death more familiar, it is nonetheless stressful.

Caregivers may perceive the inability to produce a cure as an inability to provide adequate care. In fact, however, both "cure" and "care" are focused on maintaining an optimal level of care for patients.[46] The most stressful situations tend to be those where caregivers feel helpless, unable to do anything that would significantly improve the situation. Working with patients who suffer intractable pain or who are obviously afraid to die can increase the stress on caregivers.[47] The main sources of caregiver stress include feelings of inadequacy, nonreciprocal giving, and too many demands. Caregivers may also experience the "what-ifs" when losses occur. Was there something else that could have been done? The impact of AIDS has burdened caregivers with yet more stress. The danger of exposure to AIDS from needle sticks is just one example.

In hospitals, nurses are likely to have more contact with patients than their physicians do. Yet, as nurses are forced to take on more administrative duties, they end up spending more time at desks and less time at patients' bedsides. One doctor says, "We've devalued nurses by turning them into record keepers, and we've devalued patients, who need and deserve the attention of professional nurses."[48] The changing face of modern medical care can be an additional source of stress for caregivers.

How much should a doctor, nurse, or other professional caregiver personally care about a dying patient? What is the proper degree of personal involvement with a patient? When caring is defined as curing, caregivers are vulnerable to feelings of failure when a patient dies.[49] A study of nurses in an intensive care unit found that the death of a patient usually evoked grief.[50] Working with seriously ill and dying patients, burdened by fatigue and grief, caregivers are sometimes tempted to take refuge in hospital routine and standardized policies as a way of coping. If constructive ways to deal with stress are not pursued, the result can be emotional exhaustion and depersonalization, a state known as "burnout," which is defined as a reaction to stress in which a caregiver moves beyond exhaustion and depression to being "past caring." Caregivers must find ways to replenish themselves in order to maintain empathy.

To cope with the stresses of providing care to seriously ill and dying patients, it is crucial that a supportive environment be established in which death can be discussed openly. For example, policies can be set up that encourage caregivers to come together on a regular basis to discuss their feelings and issues related to caregiving. Social support is an antidote to harmful stress. In one nursing home, schedules are rotated so that, when a patient's death is imminent, someone on the staff is with the patient almost all the time. The patient's family is notified and, if the patient or family wishes, a member of the clergy is called. If no relatives live nearby, the staff offers assistance in making arrangements for the funeral and disposition of the body. Staff members who had developed a close relationship with the patient are given time off for funeral services if they wish to attend. Other patients who knew the deceased and express an interest are informed of the death. Shortly after a patient's death, everyone who provided care for the patient in any way— nurses, housekeeping staff, dietitians, recreational and special service personnel—gather to talk about their responses to the patient's illness and death. Although it is impossible to completely eliminate stress from their working environment, as long as caregivers have empathy for the patients

Members of the Newburgh, New York, Volunteer Ambulance Corps are overcome with tears at the end of a memorial held for seven children killed at a local elementary school by a tornado. Emergency personnel who work in closely knit communities often have personal relationships with those they serve, and thus may experience the tragedies that befall their neighbors with special intensity.

under their care, it is possible to find and institute constructive methods for coping with it.

Care of the Dying

When Elisabeth Kübler-Ross set out years ago to educate interns in an urban hospital about the needs of the dying, she wanted to let terminally ill patients make their own case. When she told staff members of her plan, however, she was informed that no one was dying on their wards; there were only some patients who were "very critically ill."[51] Kübler-Ross's efforts in bringing attention to the needs of terminally ill patients became a springboard for a growing movement toward compassionate care of the dying.

Caregivers must put aside their own beliefs to discover what's appropriate for a particular person in a particular situation. There must be an ongoing search for answers to the question of how best to provide care—physical, emotional, and spiritual—for the whole person. Dying, like birthing, is a natural event, perhaps better witnessed than managed. Care of the dying, as Balfour Mount observes, involves both heart and mind: "The dying need the friendship of the heart with its caring, acceptance, vulnerability and reciprocity. They also need the skills of the mind embodied in competent medical care. Neither alone is sufficient."[52]

Would you prefer to spend your last days or weeks at home, cared for by relatives and friends? Or would you rather have access to the sophisticated medical technologies available in the hospital? Would hospice care, with its emphasis on alleviating pain and on family involvement, be your choice for care at the end of life? The unpredictable course of a disease may not allow a person to choose the place where he or she will die, or the exact nature of the medical care received. Even so, we can and should consider the alternatives. When death is expected, perhaps coming as the final chapter of a long illness, there is usually some degree of choice about where death will occur. End-of-life care may involve a combination of home care, hospital stays, and hospice or palliative care. Learning about our options empowers us to make informed, meaningful choices (see Table 4-1).

Hospice and Palliative Care

According to the National Hospice and Palliative Care Organization (NHPCO), about 3000 hospice programs in the United States provided care to some 700,000 patients in 1999, roughly 30 percent of all Americans who died in that year.[53] NHPCO reports that hospices now care for over half of all

TABLE 4-1 *Principles of a Good Death*

- To know that death is coming and to understand what can be expected.
- To be able to retain reasonable control of what happens.
- To be afforded dignity and privacy.
- To have adequate control over pain relief and other symptoms.
- To have choice about where death occurs (home or elsewhere).
- To have access to information and expertise of whatever kind is needed.
- To have access to desired spiritual and emotional support.
- To have access to hospice or palliative care in any location (home, hospital, or elsewhere).
- To have a say about who is present and who shares the end.
- To be able to issue advance directives that ensure wishes are respected.
- To have time to say goodbye.
- To be able to leave when it is time to go and not have life prolonged pointlessly.

Source: Adapted from Richard Smith, "A Good Death," *British Medical Journal* 320 (January 15, 2000): 129–130.

Americans who die from cancer. The goals and methods of hospice are reflected in the term *palliative care,* which comes from the Latin *palliatus,* meaning to cloak or conceal and, by extension, to moderate or reduce the severity of an event or situation. This term encompasses end-of-life care provided to patients in hospitals, nursing homes, and their own homes by conventional hospice programs, as well as by specialists in palliative medicine. As defined by the World Health Organization, *palliative care* refers to "the active total care of patients whose disease is not responsive to curative treatment."[54] The increasing demand for such care—and the principles it promotes—reflects changing social expectations about health care at the end of life, "from cure to care, extension of life to quality of life."[55]

The Principles of Hospice and Palliative Care

Unlike acute care, which involves taking measures to sustain life, palliative care focuses on controlling pain and relieving suffering by caring for the physical, psychological, spiritual, and existential needs of the patient.[56] The main aim of palliative care is to control pain and other physical symptoms commonly experienced by people who are dying.[57] As the concept of "total care" suggests, however, its overall mission is broader. Palliative care embodies the idea that the ultimate goal of medicine is *healing* rather than *curing* disease. "Healing involves restoring, or preserving, a sense of equanimity and personal integrity in the face of the many and varied disturbances in living that are necessarily caused by illness."[58] At the end of life, the patient's personal story tends to be more important than what's written on the medical chart. Thus, palliative care aims to relieve not just physical pain or clinical distress, but suffering in all the ways it may be experienced. Palliative care is not "passive"; measures are actively taken to relieve pain and suffering so that the dying person can go on *living* until his or her death. An important feature of palliative care is its response to the conventional message heard by dying patients and their families that "nothing more can be done."[59] Much can be done even when recovery or cure is not a realistic possibility.

Hospice care and palliative medicine involve a team approach that typically includes physicians, nurses, social workers, pharmacists, physical and occupational therapists, chaplains, home health aides, and trained volunteers, as well family members and friends. This team-oriented approach is intended to provide state-of-the-art care to prevent or relieve pain and other distressing symptoms, as well as to provide emotional and spiritual support tailored to the needs of the patient and his or her family.

The primary aim of hospice and palliative care is to help people live as fully as possible until the end of their lives.[60] In addition to its goal of helping patients achieve a "good" or "peaceful" death, an important gift of such care is the potential to help patients and families discover how much can be shared at the end of life through personal and spiritual connections that might not have been possible otherwise. As hospice and palliative care physician Ira Byock says, "Even when it is not possible to add many days to life, the opportunity exists to add life to one's days."[61]

The Origins of Hospice and Palliative Care

The roots of hospice and palliative care are found in age-old customs of hospitality and in "places of welcome" maintained by early Christians to care for pilgrims and travelers.[62] (The words *hotel, hospice,* and *hospital* derive from the Latin *hospitium,* meaning a place that receives guests.) Whereas Roman hospitals were built on a "military model of efficiency" to provide quick repair of gladiators and slaves, Christian hospices aided injured travelers, the hopelessly ill, and victims of disasters. The dying received special honor, for they were seen as spiritual pilgrims who were close to God. Among the earliest hospices were those founded in the fourth century by a disciple of Saint Jerome named Fabiola, a wealthy Roman widow who became both patron and nurse in caring for the sick and dying. Within the Judeo-Christian tradition, the basis for hospice care is found in the concepts of *diakonia* (serving and caring for others), *metanoia* (turning within to a deeper self or divine power), and *kairos* (a unique moment of fulfillment).[63]

The most influential model of modern hospice care is St. Christopher's Hospice in Sydenham, England, founded in 1967 by Dr. Cicely Saunders.[64] During the 1940s, while training as a medical social worker, Saunders met David Tasma, a Jewish refugee from Poland who was dying of inoperable cancer. Together, they formulated the vision of a haven where people could find relief from pain and die with dignity. When Tasma died in 1948, he left a small bequest to Saunders, saying "I'll be a window in your home." Nineteen years later, with the opening of St. Christopher's Hospice, the vision became a reality as a window was dedicated to Tasma's memory.[65]

Named for the patron saint of travelers, St. Christopher's draws most of its patients from within a six-mile radius of the hospice, an area with about 1.5 million inhabitants. The wards and rooms at St. Christopher's are filled with flowers, photographs, and personal items. Patients are encouraged to pursue their familiar interests and pleasures. Extensive visiting hours allow for interaction between patients and their families, including children and even family pets. St. Christopher's promotes an aura of tranquillity and an acceptance of dying. With the largest portion of operating costs allocated to staff salaries, St. Christopher's reflects what Dr. Saunders calls a "high person, low technology and hardware" system of health care.[66] When a patient is dying, family, friends, and staff members gather around the bed for farewells. Relatives spend time with the deceased's body if they wish. Then the body is bathed and taken to a small chapel. Death is treated familiarly at St. Christopher's.

Home care is an important adjunct to residential care at St. Christopher's; it allows the benefits of hospice care to be extended to nonresidential patients and families. Home care serves people who have never been residential patients, as well as former residential patients who have been discharged to their homes. The hospice staff plans medication schedules, and hospice nurses regularly visit patients to monitor their conditions. A nurse is on call around the clock to answer questions from patients and family members. Over the years, St. Christopher's has exemplified many of the features associated with hospice

Dr. Elisabeth Kübler-Ross, seen here with a patient who has been diagnosed with a life-threatening illness, is widely recognized for her pioneering efforts toward increased awareness on the part of the patient, family, and medical staff relative to the issues that arise in caring for the dying.

care, such as providing adequate pain control, treating the patient and his or her family as the unit of care, and achieving the best possible quality of life for dying patients.

In 1963, a visit by Cicely Saunders to the school of nursing at Yale University stimulated interest in hospice care in the United States. When Saunders again visited Yale in 1966, Florence Wald, as dean of Yale's graduate school of nursing, organized a meeting attended by Saunders, Elisabeth Kübler-Ross,

Colin Murray Parkes, and others interested in improving care of the dying. Wald, who had worked with terminally ill patients and their families for more than a decade, was instrumental in establishing the first American hospice, which opened in New Haven, Connecticut, in 1974. Its first medical director was Dr. Sylvia Lack, who had previously served at St. Christopher's.

Besides the opening of St. Christopher's Hospice in England in 1967, other key events in the advent of hospice and palliative care include establishment of a hospital-based palliative care team at St. Luke's Hospital in New York City in 1974 and publication of assumptions and principles for terminal care by the International Work Group on Death, Dying, and Bereavement in 1979.[67] Also, in the early 1970s, at Hospice of Marin in California, Dr. William Lamers developed innovative approaches to home care for terminally ill patients. Hospice programs, Lamers says, were created out of a desire to improve the quality of life for patients with incurable illness, patients who were being "slighted in a health care system that stressed aggressive therapies aimed at cure or rehabilitation, but that seemed to offer disincentives for care aimed at relief of illness."[68]

Hospice Programs

As a comprehensive program of care offering a set of services designed to support terminally ill patients and their families, hospice is a well-known form of palliative care. Although the terms *hospice care* and *palliative care* are often used interchangeably, they can be differentiated by defining hospice care as a type of palliative care that focuses specifically on patients who are terminally ill.[69] Although the term *hospice* may refer to a residential facility to which terminally ill patients are admitted, most hospice care takes place in patients' homes with family members as primary caregivers. "Entering hospice care" usually means affiliating with a *hospice program*—that is, arranging to receive the services of a local hospice. Hospice programs are usually community-based organizations designed to coordinate a wide range of palliative care services that are provided in nursing homes, residential-care facilities, senior housing, and hospitals, as well as in patients' homes. As is true of palliative care generally, hospice programs emphasize doing everything possible to keep patients free of pain and suffering at the end of life. Whereas other categories of palliative care may be provided to patients who are not terminally ill, hospice is designed specifically for those who are in the final stages of a terminal illness and who agree to refrain from medical interventions intended to extend life. Hospice, then, is a special form of palliative care for terminally ill patients. Although hospice programs have sometimes been accused of fostering an idealized "happy death," hospice care is not about prescribing a particular "way of dying."[70] It is about creating an environment in which the "seemingly disordered process of dying" can be lived out in a manner that fits the needs and beliefs of the person who is dying.[71]

In San Francisco, an innovative approach to care of people with AIDS provides palliative care to residents of an inner-city, single-occupancy hotel. Many residents are HIV-positive, and most are active users of speed, heroin,

"As you can see, we've transferred your husband from intensive to casual care."

crack, or alcohol. The "Hotel Project," as the program is called, is meeting the needs of individuals who are at the margins of society.[72]

Palliative Care in Hospitals

Although hospitals are primarily organized around the goals of short-term intensive treatment for acute injury and illness, they are increasingly adopting the principles of palliative care for patients who require comprehensive care at the end of life. In some cases, palliative therapies are combined with cure-oriented treatment approaches, allowing patients to battle their disease while receiving palliative care to improve their quality of life. In all cases, however, the goal of palliative care is to achieve the best possible *quality of life* for patients and their families.

The conventional mission of hospitals as medical institutions devoted to acute care is expanding to encompass various kinds of outpatient and extended care, as well as home and hospice care.[73] In hospitals where nurses have time to get to know dying patients, where caregivers are assigned responsibility for individual patients rather than tasks, where supportive relationships exist among staff members, and where there is a policy of open disclosure of diagnosis and prognosis, care of the dying reflects the ideals of hospice.[74]

T A B L E   4-2   *Questions for Contemporary Hospices*

1. *The question of access.* Is hospice care available to everyone who desires it? How can access to hospice care be improved for underserved populations such as minorities and people with AIDS?
2. *The question of spiritual care.* Is care related to the spiritual dimensions of life—that which "connects an individual to a sphere beyond himself or herself"—being adequately addressed by hospice?
3. *The question of finances.* What is the effect of the increasing imposition of bureaucratic regulation and budgetary controls on hospice care?
4. *The question of innovation.* How should present hospice services be expanded and new services created?
5. *The question of choice.* What is the role of hospice care in the growing debate about quality of life, euthanasia, and physican-assisted suicide?

Source: Adapted from Inge Baer Corless, "A New Decade for Hospice," in *A Challenge for Living: Dying, Death, and Bereavement,* ed. Inge B. Corless, Barbara B. Germino, and Mary A. Pittman (Boston: Jones and Bartlett, 1995), pp. 77–94.

Challenges to Hospice and Palliative Care

Demand for hospice and palliative care is growing, but there are challenges that must be faced if this kind of compassionate, comprehensive care at life's end is to become more widely available (see Table 4-2). Because most hospice care is provided in patients' homes, a virtual requirement is the presence of a primary caregiver who is available 24 hours a day. This may be the patient's spouse, partner, or parent, although other relatives—as well as someone paid by the family or funded by public agencies—can fulfill this role. For men, the primary caregiver is usually a spouse; for women, it is usually another relative, often a child or child-in-law. Home care is provided mostly by unpaid family members and friends, only secondarily by paid workers.[75] In caring for patients at home, family members or significant others are called on to perform health tasks of a complex nature, including monitoring vital signs, assessing pain, and administering proper dosages of medications.[76]

Another challenge involves funding for hospice care. Although hospice services are covered by Medicare/Medicaid programs, as well as by most private health plans, there are restraints on who qualifies. Under the Medicare Hospice Benefit, enacted by the U.S. Congress in 1982, one requirement in qualifying for hospice care is a doctor's certification that a patient's life expectancy is six months or less if the illness runs its normal course. Patients and their physicians must also agree to stop treatment aimed at prolonging life.[77] Because it is difficult to certify a less-than-six-months' prognosis, especially in noncancer diseases, the "six-month" rule tends to exclude patients with conditions that are difficult to predict. It also results in patients entering hospice care at a later stage of illness than is preferable; in fact, the primary reason for nonadmission to a hospice program is death: The patient died before he or she could be certified as meeting the life-expectancy requirement.[78]

The six-month rule causes hospice officials to be wary of government auditors questioning whether patients are sick enough to qualify for hospice

The Patient's Story

In learning to think like a medical scientist, I was forgetting the whole patient. To help the patient in times of suffering, the physician must know the patient: not only as a case but as a person. Each patient has a history, a unique story to tell, which goes beyond the information in the medical history. Different patients have different senses of what makes life important to them, what they want out of life, and how far they are willing to go to preserve it. The patient's full story, like any person's story, includes his or her cultural background, childhood circumstances, career, family, religious life, and so on. It includes the patient's self-understanding, appearance, manner of expression, temperament, and character. In short, it includes those attributes that make the patient a person—and not only a person, but this particular person.

Richard B. Gunderman,
"Medicine and the Question of Suffering"

care and cracking down when patients don't die on schedule.[79] Some doctors and hospices discharge patients from hospice care when they live longer than six months. In response to these concerns, the head of the federal Health Care Financing Administration, which administers the hospice benefit, recently stated that it is a misperception that patients who outlive their six-month prognosis automatically lose their coverage. "In no way," she said, "are hospice beneficiaries restricted to six months of coverage," pointing out that the pertinent part of the law states "six months or less *if the illness runs its normal course.*" Nevertheless, hospice officials say that, up to this time, the government has mainly emphasized the six-month part of the law.[80] In addition to uncertainties about the six-month rule, program of prospective payment for hospice services, by which a fixed reimbursement is set in advance, can create funding problems when hospice patients need extra services or have unexpected complications.

Yet another challenge to hospice and palliative care is broadening its access to underserved patient populations. Since its inception, hospice has expanded to serve diverse patient populations, including children.[81] But ethnic groups and minorities continue to be underrepresented in hospice care. In 1999, the most recent year for which statistics are available, 83 percent of hospice patients were white, 8 percent were African American, 3 percent were Hispanic, and 6 percent were identified as "other."[82] Many ethnic groups have strong traditions of family and community support in the face of illness and death, whereas hospice has generally reflected white, middle-class values.[83] Psychologist Ronald Barrett points out that, in addition to a traditional preference for dying at home cared for by relatives, people of color, for historical reasons, tend not to trust social institutions.[84] Inequalities in health care provided to ethnic groups and minorities have been well documented.[85] For example, African-American and Hispanic patients with severe pain are less likely than white patients to receive commonly prescribed pain medicines.

Injustices in health care over time have caused some members of ethnic groups to be suspicious about choices that others welcome in the area of end-of-life care. Richard Payne, chief of the pain and palliative care service at New York's Memorial Sloan-Kettering Cancer Center points out:

> African Americans are significantly less likely to prepare a living will, to talk to their doctors about end-of-life care, or to participate in a hospice program. When death is inevitable and imminent, blacks are twice as likely as whites to request life-sustaining treatments that can make dying a miserable experience for both patients and their families. . . . In my experience, many patients, especially African Americans and members of other medically underserved minority groups, tend to think of "palliative care" as "giving up hope." I suspect this is so because many African Americans fear their cultural and personal values will not be respected when they are dying.[86]

The challenge of accommodating the cultural and personal values of underserved people must become a priority for hospices and palliative medicine.

As hospice has become a more regulated industry, it faces the challenge of excessive bureaucracy that can lead to routinization of care. Some see parallels between the evolution of hospice and the development of community-based AIDS services.[87] In their early years, both had informal structures as pioneer-activists provided services not available through mainstream social service agencies or in conventional medical settings. As these organizations grew, however, they became more formalized, a progression viewed as necessary for offering reliable services. Inge Corless asks: In our zeal to provide hospice care, are we becoming as paternalistic as the medical practices we oft criticize? Do patients need to comply with hospice ideology to receive services? Must all hospice clients engage in a dialogue about death? What gives us the hubris to think we know best?[88] Some observers believe that there has been a subtle shift from the broad concept of striving for a "good" death to a more prescriptive "peaceful" death.[89] Early hospices were in a position to experiment with different approaches to delivering their services; now, as Corless observes, the "politicization of reimbursement for hospice care" is bringing in regulations that require all programs wishing to obtain certification "to comply with a set of standards based on one model of care."[90] If hospice becomes simply another item in a menu of medical options for terminal care, can its commitment to a unique philosophy of care for the dying be sustained despite bureaucratic red tape?

A final challenge for hospice and palliative medicine involves education about end-of-life care for both the public and professional caregivers. Despite several decades of expanding interest in learning how to provide quality care for persons who are terminally ill, there are still deficiencies in nursing textbooks with respect to topics relating to end-of-life care and death and dying.[91] If the goal of providing excellent care to dying patients and their families is to be achieved, health care professionals must not only acquire the necessary technical skills, but also learn to recognize and effectively deal with their own feelings about dying and death.[92] Recent initiatives, such as the Robert

Wood Johnson Foundation's "Last Acts Program," are providing much needed education. In Michigan, for example, this program is funding an end-of-life commission that will coordinate the construction of two walk-in consumer education centers on death and dying issues, the creation of model pain-management guidelines for nursing homes, and the design of curricula on end-of-life care for medical, nursing, pharmacy, and other health care schools.[93]

In looking to the future of hospice, pioneering hospice physician Bill Lamers suggests that new types of hospice care may be needed to meet some of the challenges discussed here.[94] He outlines three "levels" of hospice care that could be provided:

1. *Traditional* hospice care for persons with fairly definable short-term prognoses (for example, persons with advanced, incurable cancers).
2. *Long-term* hospice care for persons with an indeterminate diagnosis who do not require expensive therapies to improve quality of life during a prolonged period of dying (for example, persons with chronic, incurable neurologic disorders, such as Alzheimer's and ALS).
3. *High-tech* hospice care for persons who require expensive therapies to maintain reasonable relief of symptoms in the face of a limited, although uncertain, prognosis (for example, persons with advanced AIDS).

The reciprocal influences of hospice and mainstream medicine in the development of palliative medicine may be bringing about a variety of compassionate options for care at the end of life, thereby adding to our choices. Noting that there is something paradoxical about creating a specialty for something that happens to us all, Richard Smith, editor of the *British Medical Journal,* says that "the trend now is for the lessons learnt by palliative care physicians to be reclaimed by everybody."[95] These lessons include appreciating the importance of effectively managing pain and suffering not just in hospices, but in all areas of medical practice. The emphasis on "total care" in hospice and palliative care can be extended beyond the arena of terminal care to health care generally.

Home Care

Many people express a preference to be cared for at home during the end-stage of a terminal illness. An obvious advantage of home care is the fact that the dying person is in a familiar setting, ideally in the company of family and friends. Instead of following a schedule of visiting hours and other rules determined by institutional routine, the patient and his or her family have greater flexibility in setting their own timetable. For home care to be an option, however, support generally must be provided not only by family and friends, but also by skilled, professional caregivers. In the United States, more than 80 percent of the time, hospice care is provided by visiting nurses and other staff in patients' own homes.[96] In fact, home care is one of the fastest-growing segments of the U.S. health care industry.[97] Although many home-care nurses provide an array of hospicelike services, experts believe there

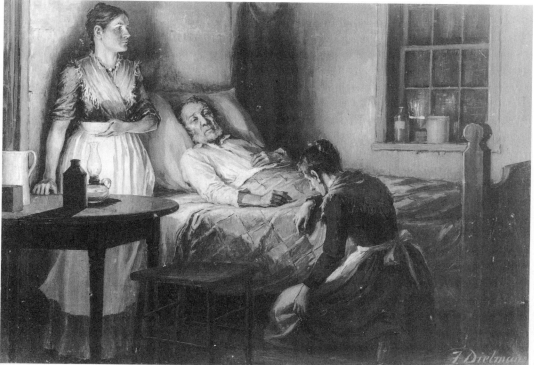

This 1895 illustration captures, in posture and expression, the weariness that accompanies round-the-clock care for the seriously ill and dying. Today's caregivers may feel this burden as much as ever while expecting themselves to put such feelings aside to conform to an image of professionalism.

needs to be better integration between home-care services and hospice programs.[98]

Successful home care depends on adequate preparation and commitment. It isn't always possible to provide the necessary level of care in the home. When a patient requires sophisticated medical procedures, does not have access to qualified caregivers, or intends to be an organ donor, other types of care may be more appropriate. In short, meeting the requirements for home care is not always possible. When it is appropriate, however, home care can be the best option for care as a person's life comes to a close.

Simply defined, home care is medically supervised care that is provided in a person's home. In the United States, palliative care at home is referred to as "hospice home care." Such care is directed by physicians, coordinated by nurses, and usually supported by an interdisciplinary team that may include volunteers, family members, and friends.[99] Despite its low-key connotations, home care is increasingly "high-tech," as central and peripheral intravenous lines are used to administer fluids, drugs, and nutrition, and as caregivers manage side effects and complications.[100] There can be disruptions to usual household routines as special equipment is set up and maintained, furniture moved or stored, and rooms rearranged so that the patient's needs are met. Although the term "home care" may sound domestic and low key, it is bearing massive burdens in the health care system.[101]

Home care offers a number of possible advantages as a setting for terminal care, including the obvious fact that the patient is *at home,* which, for most people, is a "center of meaningful activity and connectedness to family, friends, and community."[102] Home care offers a sense of normalcy, with more opportunities for the patient to maintain relationships and exercise self-determination. Home care lessens the need to "live to a timetable," as is the case in hospitals with scheduled routines. Home care also allows for reciprocity, a mutuality of care and concern, which families often find gratifying in caring for an ailing family member.

However, to realize these attractive features, home care requires adequate support. Home care is a 24-hour-a-day job. Whether family member, friend, paid home health aide, or outside volunteer, someone must attend to the various tasks that constitute appropriate care of the patient. AIDS has had a significant impact on expanding such "informal caregiving."[103] The work load of patient care can be alleviated by outside support services provided by visiting nurses and other caregivers. Periods of home care may alternate with stays in the hospital or other health care facility. There may be times when respite care—temporary care that gives family members or other caregivers a break— is needed, and it may be provided in a hospital, nursing home, hospice facility, or even in the home. Although home care is not an option for everyone, many people who have cared for a seriously ill or dying relative at home report that the experience was a positive one.

Social Support for the Dying

Social support is a key component in caring for the dying patient. Organizations dedicated to helping people with a specific disease, such as cancer or heart disease, can be found on the national level as well as through hospitals and other community agencies. These organizations help patients gain better understanding of the disease affecting them and provide a forum for sharing ways to cope with fears and enhance their sense of physical and emotional well-being.[104] Patient and family education programs are offered through lectures, reading materials, and audiovisual media, as well as through the direct sharing of concerns by participants. Support programs aim to decrease feelings of helplessness while increasing self-esteem and confidence.

Support groups supplement services provided by other programs of terminal care. This is illustrated by the Zen Hospice Project, a program established in 1987 under the auspices of the San Francisco Zen Center.[105] At Zen Hospice Project, volunteers receive extensive training in the fundamentals of hospice work, which equips them to provide practical, emotional, and spiritual

I Know (I'm Losing You)

Have you ever touched your father's back? No, my fingers tell me, as they try to pull up a similar memory.

There are none. This is a place we have never traveled to, as I try to lift his weary body onto the bedpan.

I recall a photo of him standing in front of our house. He is large, healthy, a stocky body in a dark blue suit.

And now his bowels panic, feed his mind phony information, and as I try to position him, my hands shift and the news shocks me more than the sight of his balls.

O, bag of bones, this is all I'll know of his body, the sharp ridge of spine, the bedsores, the ribs rising up in place like new islands.

I feel him strain as he pushes, for nothing, feel his fingers grip my shoulders. *He is slipping to dust,* my hands inform me, *you'd better remember this.*

Cornelius Eady

support to individuals who are in the final weeks of their lives. About 30 percent of the people served have been diagnosed with cancer; the other 70 percent have AIDS. Volunteers care for patients at the Project's Guest House (a homelike residence providing 24-hour care that serves about 30 individuals annually) and at Laguna Honda Hospital (a large public facility with a 28-bed hospice and AIDS unit). Although the predominant spiritual practice of volunteers is Buddhist, other religions are represented. Services are provided without regard for religious or sexual preference, gender, ethnicity, age, national origin, or ability to pay. Inspired by a 2500-year-old tradition, Zen Hospice Project aims to foster awareness and compassion in the lives of caregivers and to provide sensitive care for people approaching death. To this end, each caregiver cultivates the "listening mind" through regular meditation or spiritual practice. Frank Ostaseski, Director of Zen Hospice Project, says: "As hospice workers, one of our central tasks is to be available when stories are ready to be told."[106]

Trauma and Emergency Care

Over half of the deaths resulting from trauma occur instantly after injury.[107] For those who survive, time is the enemy. Immediate surgery is usually required, often to stop internal bleeding. Experts in trauma and emergency care refer to a critical "golden hour" following injury, of which the first fifteen minutes are particularly crucial. Among people who receive appropriate care during this period, the survival rate is about 90 percent.[108] Timely treatment is critical.

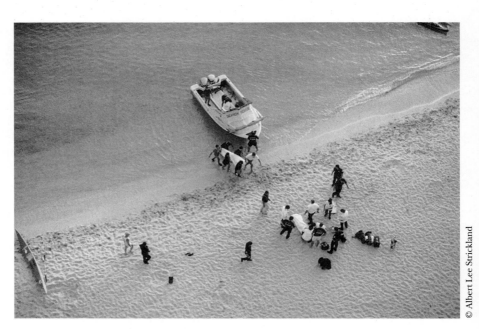

© Albert Lee Strickland

Emergency personnel, including search-and-rescue workers and police officers, engage in the grim task of recovering and identifying the bodies of two people who died in the crash of a helicopter about a thousand yards offshore. Such work is stressful and involves an extensive network of helping professionals who typically receive little or no formal training in methods of coping with the impact of multiple encounters with death, which occurs in the performance of their duties.

The roots of modern trauma care can be traced back to the Civil War, when Army Major John Letterman developed the "triage" system for evacuating casualties. Aimed at reducing the time between injury and care, triage involves assigning priorities to patients based on the seriousness of their injuries. Highest priority is given to patients whose injuries are serious but survivable. Lower priorities are assigned to patients with only a remote chance of survival and to those with comparatively minor injuries. Many of the procedures that are commonplace in trauma care were adapted from techniques used by the military in combat situations. These include the use of helicopter air ambulances, advances in team surgery and orthopedics, and treatment for burns and shock.

Modern hospital-based trauma care was initiated in 1966 by Robert Freeark at Cook County Hospital in Chicago and William Blaisdell at San Francisco General Hospital. In 1969, R. Adams Cowley formed a comprehensive system of trauma and emergency care by bringing together the Maryland State Police and the Maryland Institute for Emergency Medical Services to create the first civilian helicopter medevac program. The first hospital-based helicopter program was established in 1972 at St. Anthony's Hospital in Denver.

Currently, over 92,000 Americans die from injuries sustained in accidents each year.[109] Nearly half of these deaths involve motor vehicles, with falls, drownings, fires, and poisonings accounting for most of the rest. Traumatic injury has been called "the principal public health problem in America today," yet trauma care receives scant funding in comparison with other public health programs. Donald Trunkey, a trauma surgeon, says that "the current status of trauma care in the United States is less than optimal."[110] Results would be better if trauma care were more widely available; however, financing of trauma care remains a significant barrier to expanding services across the United States. "The lack of a system," some experts believe, "is killing people."[111]

Think about the compelling images associated with the drama of immediate responses to life-or-death situations in the emergency room. The pressure to perform is intense. As an ER staffer at one hospital put it, "You can be sitting there almost lulled to sleep during a quiet period, then suddenly everything is happening at once because there's just been a five-car crackup." Interventions must be rapidly and efficiently mobilized if life is to be sustained. For some caregivers, the pressure is overwhelming; the rhythm of patient care in other wards is less stressful. Others gain professional satisfaction from participating in situations in which their skills must be quickly brought to bear to save lives.

Trauma patients are frequently comatose or incoherent due to shock. Often, the ER staff must take action that can make the difference between life and death while receiving little or no feedback from the patient. The patient who survives and is transferred to intensive care may not be seen again by those who labored so conscientiously to save his or her life.

Frequent exposure to death in the ER is stressful. The notion that every patient can be saved may be a worthy goal, but it is not realistic in the context of trauma care. When the circumstances of a death provoke the caregiver's own anxieties about death, or when a death is exceptionally tragic—the death of a child, for example, or the death of a family in an automobile accident on Christmas Eve—caregivers are likely to be affected profoundly.

When a patient dies, ER staff members face the task of delivering bad news to relatives. The manner in which such news is communicated will remain with the survivors and, if handled badly, may leave emotional scars.[112] A doctor usually provides news of a patient's death, perhaps with other staff members on hand. The communication of information about a patient's death must be presented in a way that is tailored to fit the situation.

Being With Someone Who Is Dying

People often feel uncomfortable in the presence of a person who has been diagnosed with a life-threatening illness. What can we say? How ought we to act? It may seem that anything we might think of to express our feelings is

Generally, the doctor's announcement of the death was made within the first or first two sentences, usually in the course of one long sentence. An interesting feature of his presentation, more common in the DOA situation than in announcements of the deaths of hospital patients, was that in announcing the death he provided, in some way, that the death be presented as having followed a course of "dying." In nearly every scene I witnessed, the doctor's opening remarks contained an historical reference. . . . This was true in accident as well as "natural" deaths, and true whether or not the physician had any basis for assuming a likely cause of death. . . . Physicians seem to feel in such situations that historicizing their delivery of news, no matter how much their limited knowledge of the case may restrict the range of possibilities, helps not only reduce some of the shock value of "sudden deaths" but aids in the very grasp of the news. The correctness of the physician's supposed cause of death is of secondary significance relative to the sheer fact that he provides some sequential formulation of its generation, some means whereby the occurrence can be placed in a sequence of natural or accidental events. This is felt particularly to be necessary in the DOA circumstance, where many deaths occur with no apparent "reason," particularly the so-called "sudden unexpected death," not uncommon among young adults.

David Sudnow,
Passing On: The Social Organization of Dying

nothing more than a stale platitude. We may shy away from real communication. Discomfort and uncertainty may be exhibited through either excessive sympathy or obsessive avoidance. As an antidote to such responses, it is helpful to keep in mind that the essence of caregiving is to leave your own agenda at the door and be present to whatever the person needs. Charles Garfield says that one of the subtlest skills is knowing when to encourage someone to fight for life and when to accompany him or her to death's door.[113]

Life review, a counseling tool used widely with older people, often opens up possibilities for discussing issues that are of concern to someone facing death. Reviewing the course of a person's life can empower that person to make the choices he or she values in completing the last chapter of life.[114] Reviewing past relationships and events, the person has an opportunity to complete unfinished business. Often, the only task that matters in being with someone who is dying is to sit still and listen to the stories. In a talk to volunteers at San Francisco's Zen Hospice Project, Tenshin Reb Anderson expressed that task this way: "Stay close and do nothing."[115]

Being with someone who is seriously ill or dying, we also confront our own mortality. We appreciate how precious life is and how uncertain. Few opportunities in life present us with the chance to be as vulnerable to those aspects of ourselves that are usually kept hidden. In describing her mother's illness and death, Janmarie Silvera describes how the blossoming of a "huge, luminous full moon" through a hospital window becomes an occasion of "wonderment," a moment of intimacy that acknowledges both life and death.[116]

A person's in the room with me and they're very close to dying and afraid. I can feel the fear of death in myself. I'm working through my fear. I give them an opportunity, silent though it may be, to work through theirs. If I come into a room saying, "Oh, there's nothing to be afraid of. We go through death and then into another rebirth," that's not very useful. That's a way of not dealing with the power of the moment—the suffering in that room in the fellow on the bed, and the suffering in the mind of the fellow next to the bed.

Stephen Levine, *A Gradual Awakening*

Further Readings

Ira Byock. *Dying Well: The Prospect for Growth at the End of Life.* New York: Riverhead Books, 1997.

Daniel Callahan. *What Kind of Life: The Limits of Medical Progress.* New York: Simon & Schuster, 1990.

Stephen R. Connor. *Hospice: Practice, Pitfalls, Promise.* Washington, D.C.: Taylor & Francis, 1998.

Mickey Eisenberg. *Life in the Balance: Emergency Medicine and the Quest to Reverse Sudden Death.* New York: Oxford University Press, 1997.

Marilyn J. Field and Christine K. Cassel, eds. *Approaching Death: Improving Care at the End of Life.* Washington, D.C.: National Academy Press, 1997.

John D. Lantos. *Do We Still Need Doctors?* New York: Routledge, 1997.

Dale G. Larson. *The Helper's Journey: Working with People Facing Grief, Loss, and Life-Threatening Illness.* Champaign, Ill.: Research Press, 1993.

Marcia Lattanzi-Licht, John J. Mahoney, and Galen W. Miller. *The Hospice Choice: In Pursuit of a Peaceful Death.* New York: Fireside, 1998.

Rodger McFarlane and Philip Bashe. *The Complete Bedside Companion: No-Nonsense Advice on Caring for the Seriously Ill.* New York: Simon & Schuster, 1998.

Fiona Randall and R. S. Downie. *Palliative Care Ethics: A Good Companion.* New York: Oxford University Press, 1996.

Cecily Saunders and Robert Kastenbaum. *Hospice Care on the International Scene.* New York: Springer, 1997.

Virginia F. Sendor and Patrice M. O'Connor. *Hospice & Palliative Care: Questions and Answers.* Lanham, Md.: Scarecrow Press, 1997.

Howard Spiro, Mary G. McCrea Curnen, Enid Peschel, and Deborah St. James, eds. *Empathy and the Practice of Medicine: Beyond Pills and the Scalpel.* New Haven, Conn.: Yale University Press, 1993.

Carolyn L. Wiener and Anselm L. Strauss, eds. *Where Medicine Fails,* 5th ed. New Brunswick, N.J.: Transaction, 1997.

Total care for the patient with a life-threatening illness includes warm, intimate contact with caring persons who are able to listen and share the patient's concerns.

C H A P T E R 5

Facing Death:
Living With
Life-Threatening Illness

One day you wake up and notice symptoms in your body that you associate with a serious illness. What goes through your mind? Perhaps you just barely admit to yourself the possibility that you're "really sick," then quickly push away such thoughts and go on with your day's activities. "After all," you say, "there's no reason to suspect it's anything serious; it's probably just something minor." You don't want to tempt fate by looking too closely.

You forget about it for a while. But, more and more persistently, the symptoms demand your attention. "This better not be anything serious," you tell yourself, "I've got too much to do." Yet, in some part of your mind, you recognize that it could be serious. You begin to admit to your concern, feeling a bit anxious about what the symptoms might mean, how they might affect your life.

So you make an appointment with your doctor, describe your symptoms, submit to an examination, and wait for the results. Perhaps right away, or maybe only after additional tests are ordered, you learn the diagnosis. Your doctor informs you that you have a tumor, a malignancy. Cancer.

Now your thoughts and emotions really become agitated. "What can be done? How are the doctors going to treat this illness? What kind of changes will I have to make in my life? Should I postpone the trip I've been planning? What course of treatment should be followed? Are there side effects? Can this kind of cancer be cured? What about the pain? Will

I die?" As the drama unfolds, you find ways to cope with the crisis. Earlier fears about symptoms are transformed into concerns about diagnosis, treatment, and outcome.

As time passes, you experience a remission: The tumor appears to have stopped growing. The doctors are optimistic. Still, you wonder whether the cancer is really gone for good or just temporarily. You are in limbo. You're happy that things seem to be going well, but optimism is mixed with uncertainty and fear. Perhaps after a while you begin to relax and feel less anxious about the cancer returning. Relieved, it seems "your" cancer was curable.

However, you may sooner or later again notice the onset of symptoms, signaling the cancer's return. You may fear metastasis, the spreading of the cancer to other areas of your body, as you wrestle with the questions, "Is it going to be painful? What parts of my body will be affected? Am I going to die? How long do I have to live?"

Some cancers can be cured by relatively simple treatment. Others persist for a time and, with treatment, diminish or become stabilized. With yet others, there is little hope of survival. To the extent that cancer threatens one's well-being, the foregoing scenario resembles the patient's experience and, by extension, the experience of anyone diagnosed with life-threatening illness.

Once a disease is determined to be incurable, a person's fears may be focused on the uncertainty surrounding dying and death. These fears probably have been present from the first, underlying the changing concerns about symptoms, diagnosis, and treatment. Yet, when life-threatening disease was just a possibility represented by a particular set of symptoms, attention was focused on what the symptoms might mean. After the disease has been diagnosed and as treatment proceeds, thoughts of death may become more predominant, although fear is balanced by hope. Attention is focused on carrying out all the various activities that accompany the role of being a patient with a life-threatening illness.

 I'm forty. So, obviously things happened to me before I came in here. . . . I was married—I had a wife, and I had a son. But my wife divorced me. I was served with the papers the day I went to the hospital for the operation. My son will be twelve this October, I guess. I've never seen him since.

In the beginning, I was bewildered-like. I didn't know what the hell was happening to me. I didn't know what was wrong. And I kept going from doctor to doctor—and getting worse all the time. Slipping and slipping. I was like up in a cloud—and I was cross then. And bitter. I couldn't see why God had made such a big decision on me. I saw my brothers and sisters walking around so healthy-like—and I couldn't understand why it had happened to me and not to them. Things like that. . . . But, after a while, I decided you've got to take what the Lord decides, and make the best of it. . . .

Quoted in Renee Fox, *Experiment Perilous*

When nothing more can be done to stop the progression of the disease, the prospect of death is difficult to avoid. Still, feelings of hopefulness may remain—the hope for a last-minute remission, some change for the better that the doctors haven't foreseen. We may fight to the end with the attitude, "I've always outwitted the percentages. Why not now?" Or we may take a very different approach, coping with the end of life by making the most of the time we have left, being surrounded by those closest to us, and accepting our fate. The way we cope with dying will likely reflect the ways we've coped with living, the ways we've coped with other losses and changes in our lives.

Personal and Social Meanings of Life-Threatening Illness

A patient with acute leukemia compared her experience to that of someone with the plague, which was caused by the Black Death during the fourteenth century in Europe. The origin of the disease is mysterious, the result of causes not easily discernible or completely understood. Nature seems somehow to have gotten out of control. Not fully comprehending the chain of events that led to such a bleak fortune, the patient feels responsible for putting things right. Cancer symbolizes the worst fears of our age: pain, wasting away, suffering, and death.

People coping with life-threatening illness may feel an additional burden of social stigma. Because such diseases do not fit our idealized view of how things should be, they are sometimes treated as taboo (from the Polynesian word, *tapu,* meaning "marked off"), as if fraught with mystical danger.[1] This can lead to avoidance of people, places, and objects associated with the forbidden condition. Kay Toombs says,

> Diagnoses are permeated with personal and cultural meanings. The dread diseases—cancer, heart disease, AIDS—carry with them a particularly powerful symbolic significance. In living an illness, one is forced not only to deal with the physical symptoms of disease but also to confront the meanings associated with the diagnosis—particularly with respect to the response of others.[2]

Life-threatening diseases represent a confrontation with our own mortality, exposing our anxiety about being separated from all that we love, our fear of pain, and the imagined horror of dying. They challenge our image of ourselves and threaten our plans for the future.

A pattern of taboo and avoidance can cause friends and relatives, as well as caregivers, to abandon the patient, creating a kind of "social death," with the patient feeling "walled off" from the rest of society. People with serious illnesses may be socially defined as "non-persons" or as somehow "in-valid."[3] Negativity about the disease can lead to avoiding the patient altogether.[4]

The "meaning" of a life-threatening illness is determined to a significant extent by the individual's social environment.[5] In societies that place high value on health, the pursuit of wellness becomes a kind of moral virtue, a way to set oneself among the "righteous."[6] A person who fails to achieve or retain good health may feel guilty: "Am I somehow responsible for bringing this

I remember her as she lay in her hospital bed in July. Unable finally to deny the pain. And for the first time in our relationship of 21 years forced to allow someone else to take care of her. My father could not stand the sight and so he stayed outside, pacing up and down in the hallways. I could not help staring at her. Disbelief that this person with tubes running in and out like entrances and exits on a freeway was the same woman who just six months before had laughed gaily and danced at my wedding.

Ruth Kramer Ziony, "Scream of Consciousness"

illness on myself?" In this regard, simplistic concepts about how the mind influences the body can be detrimental.

Magical thinking—assuming oneself responsible though it's unclear just how—can place an additional burden on the patient with life-threatening illness: "What did I do to bring this condition upon myself? If I had done this, or not done that, maybe I wouldn't be in this predicament." The person may feel a pervasive sense of helplessness, trying to combat natural forces that have gone awry, forces that seem bent on destroying one's body. Anxiety about treatment may compound fears about the disease itself.

Life-threatening diseases such as heart disease and cancer are expensive, with costs related to hospitalization, outpatient therapy, office visits, and medications. Besides medical care, there are incidental costs associated with transportation, support services, child care, and temporary housing for patients who must travel long distances to receive specialized care. Time lost from work often results in lost earnings. The patient's family shares these burdens. Looking at the family as a "system," as the illness affects family life, there is a reciprocal impact on the patient.[7]

Therapeutic tools—including education, counseling, support groups, and communication skills—can help people cope with the experience of life-threatening illness. Acquiring information about the disease and its treatment, sharing experiences with others in an atmosphere of mutual support, using counseling services to clarify personal and emotional issues, and finding ways of communicating more effectively with caregivers as well as family members and friends—all these are examples of positive approaches to dealing with life-threatening illness.[8] They can contribute to a way of understanding that places the crisis in a more affirmative context, making the experience less confusing, perhaps less melodramatic, and restoring a sense of personal control over one's life.

Coping With Life-Threatening Illness

There is no one right way to live with or die from a life-threatening illness. Every disease has its own set of problems and challenges, and each person copes with these problems and challenges in his or her own way. The ways

When I first realized that I might have cancer, I felt immediately that I had entered a special place, a place I came to call "The Land of Sick People." The most disconcerting thing, however, was not that I found that place terrifying and unfamiliar, but that I found it so ordinary, so banal. I didn't feel different, didn't feel that my life had radically changed at the moment the word *cancer* became attached to it. The same rules still held. What had changed, however, was other people's perceptions of me. Unconsciously, even with a certain amount of kindness, everyone—with the single rather extraordinary exception of my husband—regarded me as someone who had been altered irrevocably. I don't want to exaggerate my feeling of alienation or to give the impression that it was in any way dramatic. I have no horror stories of the kind I read a few years ago in the *New York Times*; people didn't move their desks away from me at the office or refuse to let their children play with my children at school because they thought that cancer was catching. My friends are all too sophisticated and too sensitive for that kind of behavior. Their distance from me was marked most of all by their inability to understand the ordinariness, the banality of what was happening to me. They marveled at how well I was "coping with cancer." I had become special, no longer like them.

> Alice Stewart Trillin,
> "Of Dragons and Garden Peas:
> A Cancer Patient Talks to Doctors"

patients respond to experiences of illness result from such factors as personality, psychological makeup, family and social patterns, and environment. It is said that doctors treat disease; people suffer from illness.[9] Much of the suffering experienced by people with life-threatening illness comes from overwhelming feelings of loss on all levels. Carl May says, "At the moment a diagnosis is confirmed and a lethal disorder identified, the patient becomes the focus of a potentially dramatic set of events."[10] The response to such a diagnosis often includes fears related to the possibility of physical discomfort and pain, the unknown risks associated with dying, the threat to personal integrity, and uncertainty about life after death. It takes courage to master such fears. Facing the prospect of dying and affirming this reality is not easy. As Joseph Campbell says,

> We always affirm with conditions. I affirm the world on condition that it gets to be the way Santa Claus told me it ought to be. But affirming it the way it is—that's the hard thing.[11]

Yet, as Arthur Frank points out, "Critical illness teaches us that to be alive is to be constantly at risk, but the risk greater than dying is living less than well."[12]

For many people, religious faith is an important ally in coping with life-threatening illness.[13] Patients and their families may be comforted by a faith that helps them face the abyss of inevitable death and somehow make sense of existence, even when it includes one's own death and the death of loved ones.[14] Religious belief can promote a sense of self-confidence, peacefulness,

---

 Your Caring Presence: Ways of Effectively Providing Support to Others

1. Be honest about your own thoughts, concerns, and feelings.
2. When in doubt, ask questions:
   How is that for you?
   How do you feel right now?
   Can you tell me more about that?
   Am I intruding?
   What do you need?
   What are the ways you can take care of yourself?
3. When you are responding to a person facing a crisis situation, be sure to use statements such as:
   I feel _____
   I believe _____
   I would want _____
   Rather than:
   You should
   That's wrong
   Everything will be ok.
   which are statements that may not give the person the opportunity to express his/her own unique needs and feelings.
4. Stay in the present as much as possible: How do you feel RIGHT NOW? What do you need RIGHT NOW?
5. Listening is profoundly healing. You don't have to make it better. You don't have to have the answers. You don't have to take away the pain. It's his pain. He needs to experience it in his own time and in his own way.
6. People in crisis need to know they have decision-making power. It may be appropriate to point out alternatives.
7. Offer any practical assistance that you feel comfortable giving.
8. If the situation warrants it, feel free to refer individual to appropriate agency.

The Centre for Living with Dying

---

and purpose.[15] Indeed, "surrender to God" may be an additional coping style.[16] Through religious faith or other avenues of psychosocial support, many people with serious or life-threatening illness find constructive ways of adapting and, over time, come to see themselves as better adjusted than they were before their illness.[17]

Awareness of Dying

Observing family interactions in response to life-threatening illness, sociologists Barney Glaser and Anselm Strauss noted four distinctive ways in which a context of awareness about dying shapes communication styles.[18] In the *closed awareness* context, the dying person is not aware of his or her impending death, although others may know. This context is characterized by a lack of communication about the person's illness or the prospect of his or her death.

In the *suspected awareness* context, a person suspects that his or her prognosis involves death, but this suspicion is not verified by those who know. The dying person may try to confirm or deny his or her suspicions by testing family members, friends, and medical staff in an effort to elicit information known by others but not openly shared. Despite this secrecy, the patient observes the disruptions in family communication patterns caused by the illness and senses others' anxiety about the illness, thus tending to confirm suspicions.

The *mutual pretense* context is like a dance in which participants sidestep direct communication about the patient's condition. This can lead to complicated, though usually unspoken, rules of behavior intended to sustain the illusion that the patient is getting well. Everyone, the patient included, recognizes the fact that death will be the outcome, but all act as if the patient will recover. Mutual pretense may be carried on right to the end, even when the unspoken rules are occasionally violated in ways that might have revealed the patient's condition.

Underlying mutual pretense is the notion that everyone should avoid "dangerous" or "threatening" topics, such as facts about the disease, its prognosis, medical procedures, the deaths of other patients with the same disease, and future plans and events that will likely occur after the patient dies. This eliminates from discussion a considerable portion of the patient's experience. Participants exchange subtle signals that the style of communication used to cope with the crisis is to pretend that things are normal.

When something happens that threatens to break the fiction and disclose the reality of the situation, the parties to mutual pretense act as if the threatening event did not occur. Distancing strategies preserve the illusion that the person is not seriously ill. People may respond to the risk of disclosure by becoming angry or withdrawn, or they may avoid further communication by saying they need to go out for a walk or make a phone call. In the short term, mutual pretense can be a useful strategy for coping with a difficult and painful situation.

Glaser and Strauss's fourth designation, the context of *open awareness,* is one in which death is acknowledged and discussed. Open awareness does not necessarily make death easier to accept, but it does allow for the possibility of sharing support in ways that are not readily available with the other awareness contexts. As new information about the course of the disease is presented to the patient or family members, the context of awareness may change. For example, mutual pretense may dominate through a succession of medical procedures; then, with receipt of new test results, the participants may begin to openly acknowledge the illness as life threatening. As circumstances change, awareness context may shift.

Agreement between beliefs and actions is an important determinant of how a crisis is experienced. If, in your belief system, mutual pretense is a useful way of coping with threatening or discomforting situations, and if this style of communication is customary in your family's interactions, then pretense may be an effective and helpful way to cope. Suppose, conversely, that you place a high value on openness and honesty, and your family has always been

"Bloom County," drawing by Berke Breathed, © 1985 by Washington Post Writers Group

scrupulously honest with one another. If someone in your family is dying, yet everyone is pretending that this is really not happening—that the person is getting well—anxiety about the crisis will probably be made even more unbearable because of the conflict between beliefs and actions.

Adapting to "Living-Dying"

Living with an illness that is life-threatening and incurable can be described as a "living-dying" experience, during which patients and their families fluctuate between denial and acceptance as circumstances—and their responses to circumstances—change.[19] Psychiatrist Avery Weisman described this process of coping as involving *middle knowledge,* with patients and their families seeking a balance between sustaining hope and acknowledging the reality.[20]

On the basis of her work with dying patients, Elisabeth Kübler-Ross developed the best-known description of the emotional and psychological responses to life-threatening illness.[21] Because this description has been discussed so widely, many people have some acquaintance with the "five stages" associated with Kübler-Ross's model: denial, anger, bargaining, depression, and acceptance. The notion that these stages occur in a linear progression has become a kind of modern myth of how people *ought* to cope with dying. Unfortunately, this can lead to the idea that it is a person's "task" to move sequentially through these stages, one after another; and, if this is not accomplished, the person has somehow failed. In fact, however, Kübler-Ross said that individuals go back and forth among the stages during the course of an illness and different stages can occur simultaneously.

In the initial confrontation with death, a person may respond with avoidance or denial, suppressing the truth or excluding it from consciousness. Even after the truth is acknowledged, feelings of anger, vulnerability, and dependency may be present. Anger is sometimes manifested as displaced hostility: "Maybe I could've done something to keep this from happening to me, but, damn it, if it isn't safe, why doesn't the government put a stop to it!" The object of such displaced hostility is often the person's caregiver. Anger may be exhibited in complaints about food or other aspects of care: "Why can't you fix me a good cup of tea? You know I can't do it for myself!" Difficult and possibly painful for patient and caregiver alike, such expressions of anger can mask anxiety about the underlying problem: the confrontation with serious illness and what it means for one's continued existence.

Bargaining, attempting to strike a deal with fate or with God, is yet another response that may occur as the patient tries to find some way to postpone or avoid the inevitable. Perhaps "good behavior" can be exchanged for an extension of life. As illness progresses and the body weakens, efforts to be stoic in the face of reality may be replaced by depression, a profound sense of loss. Kübler-Ross distinguished two kinds of depression: a *reactive* depression to the disruptions caused by the disease and a *preparatory* depression related to the awareness that one must prepare for death.

Ultimately, as the person copes with the predicament of loss, there may be some resolution that leads to acceptance. This does not mean giving up or losing all hope; rather, it implies that the person faces his or her mortality in a manner that is essentially positive. Consider the words of Harold Brodkey as he faces the prospect of dying from AIDS:

> I have liked my life. I like my life at present, being ill. I like the people I deal with. I don't feel I am being whisked off the stage or murdered and stuffed in a laundry hamper while my life is incomplete. It's my turn to die—I can see that that is interesting to some people but not that it is tragic. Yes, I was left out of some things and was cheated over a lifetime in a bad way but who isn't and so what? I had a lot of privileges as well. Sometimes I'm sad about its being over but I'm that way about books and sunsets and conversations.[22]

In coping with death, each person's pathway is determined by such factors as the specific nature of the illness, his or her personality, and the helping resources available in his or her environment (see Figure 5-1).

66—Real Estate Wanted

FORMER President — Major Manufacturing Company. age 56, with possible terminal disease interested in lease purchase of old home. Reasonably large. Farm house with property, condos, land with run down cabin or home in total disrepair. Probably in foothills between Santa Cruz and Castroville. Option period 18 months or final diagnosis — whichever is first. Any remodeling by permission of owner in his name. Will arrive from Seattle on Tuesday evening. Please leave number at Box 9, c/o this newspaper.

Figure *5-1 Life Change with Life-Threatening Illness: Real Estate Want Ad*
The confrontation with a life-threatening illness may activate desires to accomplish in the present plans that previously had been visualized as occurring in the future.
Source: *Register-Pajaronian* (Watsonville, Calif.), March 11, 1981.

The stage-based model of coping with dying devised by Kübler-Ross more than three decades ago has been a stimulus toward a better understanding of how people cope with dying. But this, or any, model of how people cope with loss should not be applied indiscriminately. For example, in the stage-based model proposed by Kübler-Ross, many people interpret denial as a "bad thing," something that the dying person should move beyond. But this interpretation ignores the fact that denial can be an effective coping mechanism. Life may be intolerable without illusion. Denial involves refusing to admit the truth or reality of a troubling situation.[23] But whether denial is adaptive or maladaptive depends on the timing and duration of its use and on the nature of the perceived threat. Appropriate use of avoidance and repression can help maintain a healthy mental balance. Facing reality about impending death is not always the best approach; there are times when "game-playing," or acting "as if" the situation were otherwise, is appropriate.[24]

Many different emotions and thoughts may be experienced as a person copes with the changing circumstances of life-threatening illness. But there is no set *sequence* in which these emotions and thoughts are experienced and expressed. Herman Feifel emphasizes that "[c]oping with a life-threatening illness or death threat varies in significant fashion not only among differing groups but among situations."[25] From the moment one notices unusual symptoms and questions what they mean, through the ups and downs of treatment, and on to the final moments of life, hope and honesty are often delicately balanced—honesty to face reality as it is, hope that the outcome is positive. The object of hope changes over time. The hope that the symptoms really mean nothing gives way to hope that there will be a cure. When the illness is labeled incurable, one hopes for more time. When time runs out, one hopes for a pain-free and appropriate death (see Figure 5-2). When hope no longer includes the expectation of a cure, it is important for people not to give up, but to retain other kinds of hope by focusing on meaningful aspects of life.[26]

Although Kübler-Ross's "stage theory" was an early effort toward understanding how people cope with life-threatening illness, more recent approaches offer insights, or different angles of vision, that contribute to a more well-rounded and complete picture. For example, Charles Corr's model provides a holistic view that distinguishes four primary dimensions in coping with dying: physical, psychological, social, and spiritual (see Table 5-1).[27] In this model, the spiritual dimension is not to be interpreted as exclusively religious; rather, it embraces a person's basic values and centers of meaning about life and death. Incorporating an inclusive and broad view of the dying process, Corr's model helps us shift our perspective from a linear or sequential view of the dying process to one that is less prescriptive.

Avery Weisman observed that effectively coping with life-threatening illness involves three interrelated tasks: (1) confronting the problem and revising one's plans as necessary, (2) keeping communication open and wisely using the help offered by others, and (3) maintaining a sense of optimism and hope.[28] In addition, Weisman suggested that the process of coping with a terminal illness could be divided into three phases: (1) from the time symptoms

Dear Friends,

In company with our dear Mother Earth, I have arrived at the time of autumn in my worldly life, that time of transition between life and death. Before long, just as the leaves drop from the trees to continue Life's cycle of generation and regeneration, so will my body be shed and become part of the muttering earth. Like the tree gathering in energy to prepare itself for winter, I feel a need to gather energy for the process of dying. Also, I want to share a last celebration with you dear friends. To do this, I have planned a ritual of transition to take place on Sunday, November 3, at 2:30 p.m. here at my home.

I would love it if you can participate with your presence; and if you cannot, I would appreciate your joining us in spirit with loving energy via the ethers that afternoon.

If you can come, please bring a pillow to sit on and a symbolic gift of your energy and blessing for me in this process I am going through—something from nature (rock, shell, feather, etc.); a poem, picture or song; something written or drawn; or whatever you are inspired to bring. Please also bring a casserole, salad or dessert or beverage to contribute to our potluck supper following the ritual.

There is a new joy that is beginning to be realized in me as I acknowledge the prospect of having a spirit float free of my tired body. I look forward to sharing this with you too.

Love and blessings,

Joan Conn

Figure 5-2 *Invitation to a Going-Away Party*
Ritual and companionship can assist in dealing with impending death. This celebration was attended by close friends and family, who said the occasion was an extremely moving experience. Knowing that she would soon die from cancer, Joan created a ritual that involved drawing a line on the floor and, in her weakened condition, she was helped across it by her ex-husband and her children while members of the gathering played music and sang. Although such an event would not be appropriate for everyone, Joan's farewell party aptly reflected her life style and values. She died seven months later.

TABLE *5-1*   *Four Primary Dimensions in Coping with Dying*

1. *Physical.* Involves satisfying bodily needs and minimizing physical distress in ways consistent with other values.
2. *Psychological.* Involves maximizing psychological security, autonomy, and richness in living.
3. *Social.* Involves sustaining and enhancing significant interpersonal relationships; and addressing the social implications of dying.
4. *Spiritual.* Involves identifying, developing, or reaffirming sources of spiritual energy or meaning and, in so doing, fostering hope.

Source: Adapted from Charles A. Corr, "A Task-Based Approach to Coping with Dying," *Omega: Journal of Death and Dying* 24, no. 2 (1991–1992): 81–94.

are noticed until the diagnosis is confirmed, (2) the time between diagnosis and the final decline, and (3) from decline to death.[29] Some of the "landmarks" through these three phases include the following:

1. *Existential plight.* A crisis of self-identity begins with the initial shock of diagnosis as the person attempts to come to terms with the life-altering news.
2. *Mitigation and accommodation.* As treatment begins, the reality of the illness becomes part of the person's life as adjustments and accommodations are made.
3. *Preterminality and terminality.* When no cure or extension of life is in the offing, the individual confronts progressive decline and deterioration as the limits of life become increasingly clear. As the end draws near, palliative care replaces curative therapy as the dying person prepares for death.

In addition to the models discussed thus far, Therese Rando identifies three major psychological and behavioral *patterns* that individuals use in coping with the threat of death: (1) retreat and conservation of energy, (2) exclusion from the threat of death, and (3) attempting to master or control the threat of death.[30]

With any model, we need to keep in mind the highly individual nature of coping styles and also the fact that an individual may have various ways of effectively coping with life-threatening illness. Kenneth Doka describes how the tasks involved in coping change at the different phases of an illness (see Table 5-2). These include an *acute* phase, initiated by the diagnosis; a *chronic* phase of living with the disease; and a *terminal* phase that involves coping with impending death.[31] In some situations, there may be two other phases: first, a *prediagnostic* phase, during which a person suspects the illness and may seek medical attention; and, second, a *recovery* phase following a cure or remission of a previously life-threatening disease. Even as the threat of death recedes into the background, however, there can be a need to cope with the fact that one has had a potentially terminal illness. In commenting on this model, Doka says:

> Life-threatening illness is only part of life. Throughout the time of the illness, at whatever phase, individuals continue to meet many needs and to cope with all the

issues and problems that they had prior to the diagnosis. . . . [Of course,] the experience of illness may affect the perception of these needs and issues. . . . All the previous challenges of life—dealing with family and friends, coping with work and finances, even keeping up with the demands of a home or apartment—remain an ongoing part of the larger struggle of life and living.[32]

In reviewing the various models of dying that have been proposed over the past few decades, Robert Kastenbaum and Sharon Thuell note that, despite these contributions to our understanding, important issues remain.[33] For example, none of the approaches takes full account of the dying person's physical condition; there is a tendency to "construct a generic dying person," with cancer as the model for the dying process. In fact, different types of cancer, not to mention other life-threatening diseases, may evoke different coping mechanisms. Furthermore, little attention is directed to changes that occur in the person's socioenvironmental context during the dying process. Kastenbaum and Thuell suggest that "[a] useful contextual theory of dying might well take the form of an evolving narrative . . . an active model of all the key people in the situation as they continue to respond to their challenges and consult their deepest personal values."[34]

To avoid mistaking the map for the territory, it is crucial to remember that a person's death is as unique as his or her life.[35] Thus, we cannot rely solely on

TABLE   5-2   *Tasks in Coping with Life-Threatening Illness*

Acute Phase	Chronic Phase	Terminal Phase
Understand the disease.	Manage symptoms and side effects.	Manage discomfort, pain, incapacitation, other symptoms.
Maximize health and life style.	Carry out health regimens.	Cope with health procedures and institutional stress.
Optimize coping strengths.	Manage stress and examine coping behaviors.	Manage stress and examine coping behaviors.
Develop strategies to deal with issues created by disease.	Normalize life to extent possible in face of disease.	Prepare for death and saying goodbye.
Explore effect of diagnosis on self and others.	Maximize social support and preserve self-concept.	Sustain self-concept and appropriate relationships with others.
Express feelings and fears.	Express feelings and fears.	Express feelings and fears.
Integrate present reality into sense of past and future.	Find meaning in uncertainty and suffering.	Find meaning in life and death.

Adapted from Kenneth J. Doka, "Coping with Life-Threatening Illness: A Task Model," *Omega: Journal of Death and Dying* 32, no. 2 (1995–1996): 111–122.

some "standard model" of the dying process. All models must be balanced by paying attention to the dying person's own *life story.*

Patterns of Coping

When confronted by a stressful situation, our first response is to appraise the situation. Whether or not we are fully aware of this process, we evaluate the significance of the threatening situation and assess our resources for coping with it. Our appraisal influences the way we subsequently cope.[36] The concept of coping describes not only psychological (cognitive and emotional) processes, but also behavioral efforts.[37]

The threat of a potentially fatal illness evokes a variety of responses to make the threat somehow manageable. These responses can be divided into two main categories: defense mechanisms and coping strategies.[38] *Defense mechanisms* occur unintentionally and without conscious effort or awareness; they function to change a person's internal psychological states, not the external reality. *Coping strategies* involve conscious, purposeful effort; they are employed with the intention of solving a problem situation. Although coping strategies are generally viewed more positively than defense mechanisms, both involve psychological processes that can help ease a distressful situation. Denial, for example, is a defense mechanism that is sometimes adaptive and sometimes not, depending on the person and the situation. In the short term, denial can give a person "breathing room" in living with a distressing situation; over the longer term, however, such defenses may hinder a positive outcome if they prevent a person from mobilizing needed resources and taking appropriate action. Consider, for example, a person who uses denial to delay seeking medical attention because of his or her fear about illness.[39]

The main aim of the mental processes and behaviors involved in coping is to establish control over a stressful situation.[40] Achieving this typically requires different coping strategies working in concert. As with an orchestra, wherein particular instruments come to the fore at a given time while other instruments await their turn, the various coping strategies may be employed at different times to achieve different purposes. One way of distinguishing different strategies is to examine their purpose and focus. *Emotion-focused coping,* for example, helps regulate the level of distress. It allows a person to escape the impact of the stressful situation by reframing it or distancing oneself from it. Reframing a situation to put it in a positive light can reduce the sense of threat. Another strategy, *problem-focused coping,* deals with managing the problem that is causing distress. A cancer patient who seeks out information about her disease and takes an active role in determining her options is engaging in problem-focused coping. A hallmark of this style of coping is the person's pursuit of personally meaningful goals. Recalling that the main aim of coping is to establish a sense of control, it is worth mentioning that a greater sense of control is associated with problem-focused coping, whereas less control is associated with emotion-focused coping. Even so, each of these strategies has a role in coping. A third strategy, *meaning-based coping,* is employed to maintain a person's sense of positive well-being. Examples include giving up goals that

Playboy: It's been five years since you found out you are HIV-positive, right?

Kramer: I found out more than that I was positive. In 1988 I found out that I have liver disease from hepatitis B. They gave me two years to live. I learned this in the hospital, and it was very scary. For whatever reason, I am still here and I feel terrific. But it made me forcefully comprehend the fragility of life and the importance of making use of every remaining minute of it.

Playboy: By 1988 you had helped put most AIDS issues on the table. What was it like to hear the bad news yourself?

Kramer: I remember standing on a street corner near the building where I was given the news and just being overwhelmed with a sort of awe that it finally had happened. It felt like an affirmation of something I knew was probably going to happen. So I accepted it, I think, with a surprising ease. I was prepared for it. I didn't break down or go into depression. There was a moment of overwhelming readjustment. It forced upon me the necessity of making calculated, determined decisions. I had to assume I had only so many years and so much energy left, so what would I do with that?

Playboy: And what did you decide to do?

Kramer: I became obsessed with my work. Nothing has made me so productive as learning I am HIV-positive. Since 1988, when I had my face right straight up to death, I've worked hard all the time. Time is precious to me. I don't waste time like I used to, letting days go by without working, finding excuses to do something else. I work every day, seven days a week.

> Excerpt from *Playboy* interview with
> Larry Kramer by David Nimmons

are no longer achievable and formulating new ones, making some sense of what is happening, and, where possible, finding benefit in the distressing situation. In this search for meaning, people often turn to spiritual beliefs for insight in making the best of a bad situation. Finding some redeeming value in loss can make the burden easier to bear.

What people do in response to stress is largely determined by who they are—by their enduring dispositions and personalities.[41] People vary their styles of coping depending on the opportunities for problem solving in a situation, the intensity of their emotional responses and their ability to regulate them, and the changes in their environment as the distressing situation unfolds. Thus, the various coping strategies are dynamic rather than static, with the overall pattern of coping resembling a more or less continual flow or rhythm among the various styles. It is a mistake to pit one style against another because they are interdependent and work together, each supplementing the others.[42] Also, we should be careful about judging the coping process of another person as good or bad.[43]

People who apparently cope best with life-threatening illness often exhibit a "fighting spirit" that views the illness not only as a threat, but also as a challenge.[44] These people strive to inform themselves about their illness and

But You Look So Good

It's with me each day.
I wake, thinking
Today it will go away.
But the pain seems to stay . . .
Persistent, resistant, consistent.
People say,
But you look so good.
If only I could
Feel like I look.
Or, should
I look bad?
So they'll know
How I feel
is real.
Do they doubt?
I wish the pain
Was on the outside—
something you see.
Not only the pain
Do I need to survive,
But also my
Paranoid imaginings
Of others' disbelief.

Judy Ellsworth

take an active part in treatment decisions. They are optimistic and have a capacity to discover positive meaning in ordinary events. Holding to a positive outlook despite distressing circumstances involves creating a sense of meaning that is bigger than the threat. In the context of life-threatening illness, this encompasses a person's ability to comprehend the implications an illness has for the future, as well as for his or her ability to accomplish goals, maintain relationships, and sustain a sense of personal vitality, competence, and power. Although life-threatening illness disrupts virtually all aspects of a person's life, there is a vital link between finding meaning and achieving a sense of mastery.[45]

Maintaining Coping Potency

The capacity to maintain a sense of self-worth, to set goals and strive to meet them, to exercise choice out of an awareness of one's power to meet challenges, to engage in active interactions with one's environment—all of these reflect a "coping potency" that sustains the will to live in the face of death. Reportedly, both John Adams and Thomas Jefferson, although gravely ill, managed to live until July 4, 1826, the fiftieth anniversary of the signing of the Declaration of Independence. According to his physician, Jefferson's last words were, "Is it the Fourth?" This story illustrates how human beings appear to have a capacity for sustaining life against the odds to mark an anniversary or other important event before dying.[46]

It has long been a truism in medicine that hope plays a key role in a patient's ability to cope with illness. Doctors often attempt to instill hope in patients by the manner in which they discuss a disease and its treatment. In difficult cases, doctors may talk about taking things "one step at a time," first controlling the pain or other symptoms and then working on various treatment options. Or they may liken the process of coping with a serious illness to climbing a mountain, which can be arduous but potentially successful if one keeps advancing to the top. This metaphor suggests that the doctor can help "pull the patient to safer, higher ground." As one oncologist explains, "You have to give people something to wake up for in the morning, otherwise they might as well take some cyanide."[47] In putting the best face on bad news, doctors see themselves in the role of "the patient's cheerleader." Yet, it is also the case that "sometimes the only real hope you can offer a dying person is that you will accompany them to their death and respect their wishes to the best of your ability."[48]

Essential to maintaining a positive attitude despite the stress of life-threatening illness is the patient's self-image. The late Orville Kelly, founder of Make Today Count, described his own response and the reactions of others after he was diagnosed with cancer.[49] Given a terminal prognosis, Kelly contemplated suicide, fearing that he might become a burden to his family. Relatives and friends were uncomfortable in his presence. One woman asked his wife, "How is he?"—although Kelly was just a few feet away. Though still alive, he was experiencing a kind of social death. Despite the frightening prognosis, Kelly soon realized that in fact he was still alive. He could still love and be loved. No matter how short a time he might have to live, he could make the most of each day. Recognizing that the mortality rate of every generation is 100 percent, Kelly began to talk about his feelings and express his concerns as a person with terminal illness. An article he wrote for his local newspaper elicited such a positive and sizable response that it led to Kelly's founding of Make Today Count, a nationwide support group for the terminally ill. Kelly's message is a crucial one: Everyone, whether diagnosed with terminal illness or not, is challenged to make each day count.

Treatment Options and Issues

The options for treating life-threatening illness vary with the nature of the disease and the patient's particular situation. As new medical technologies become available, treatment options may change drastically. Yet, the range of life-saving choices for treating disease also depends in part on decisions made by society at large. Sudden cardiac death is a case in point.[50] Heart attack—which typically occurs when a blockage in a coronary artery cuts off the blood supply to a region of the heart—is a medical emergency. Half of the deaths

© Burton Steele, *Times-Picayune*

With her seriously ill daughter, this mother waits for the test results that will help determine the next step in care and treatment.

from heart attack occur in the first three to four hours after the onset of symptoms. The sooner treatment begins, the better the chances of survival.[51] Heart attack victims who reach a hospital and receive early treatment can look forward to a survival rate of about 90 percent.[52] Many heart attacks occur suddenly and without warning. The key to life-saving help is a rapid, coordinated emergency response. Some communities, recognizing that sudden cardiac death is a pressing public health problem, have funded sophisticated mobile cardiac care units; other communities consider these units too costly. Such decisions affect a patient's options for treatment and may determine whether the outcome is life or death.

In the discussion that follows, we focus particularly on cancer and its treatment. As a general term, *cancer* encompasses many types of malignant, or potentially lethal, growths that occur in the body. Briefly defined, a cancerous cell is one that has lost its normal control mechanisms and thus has unregulated growth. Such cells can develop in any tissue within any organ. Cancerous cells reproduce in a manner unregulated by the body's normal controls on cell growth. First affecting tissues in one part of the body, cancer may spread either by invading adjacent tissues or by *metastasis*, a process whereby diseased cells travel in the blood or lymph system or through body tracts, to more distant parts of the body. Successful treatment of cancer requires the destruction or removal of all cancerous tissue; otherwise, the disease recurs.

There are many categories and types of cancer. Because of this variety, some experts propose that cancer should be interpreted as a process, with *time* as a critical dimension.[53] Cancerous growths can be fast or slow; their development may take weeks or years. The speed at which cancer progresses affects how the patient copes with the illness.[54]

Treatment of cancer is focused on the primary tumor and its metastases. Some cancers respond best to a combination of therapies, including surgery, radiation, and chemotherapy. No single therapy is effective for all types of cancer. A therapy that results in a high success rate with one type of cancer may be ineffective with another. Cancer therapies often require *adjunctive therapies* to counteract the side effects of the primary treatment. (Key terms used in cancer care are defined in Table 5-3.) If a cure is not possible, palliation of symptoms using some or all of these therapies may improve the quality and duration of life.[55] In making decisions about a proposed treatment, patients should have enough information to clearly understand the risks and benefits of proceeding with the treatment, as well as the consequences of pursuing a different course of action.[56]

Surgery

Surgery is the oldest effective form of cancer therapy, and some cancers are curable in early stages with surgery alone.[57] The diagnosis of cancer is usually established by a biopsy, a tissue sample surgically removed and examined for the presence of cancerous cells. Surgery is not only the most common treatment for cancer, it is sometimes the only treatment, as with some tumors in the gastrointestinal tract and advanced cancers of the head and neck.[58]

Although most people recognize that surgery is a routine medical practice, some fear it as a "violation of the body." Even when surgery is successful in curing a life-threatening disease, its side effects may include disfigurement, disability, or loss of bodily function. To stop the growth of cancer and prevent it from spreading, surgery may involve the removal of not only the malignant organ or tissue, but also adjacent healthy tissue.

Radiation Therapy

Soon after the discovery of radium in 1898, it was recognized that radiation could be used to treat cancer. Radiation therapy uses ionizing radiation to preferentially destroy cells that divide rapidly.[59] Although radiation affects both normal and cancerous tissues, cancer cells usually grow more rapidly than normal cells and are more seriously damaged.

Radiation plays a key role in the treatment of Hodgkin's disease, early non-Hodgkin's lymphoma, squamous cell cancer of the head and neck, seminoma (a testicular cancer), localized prostate and bladder cancers, and early-stage breast cancer, among others. It is used as an adjunct to chemotherapy in some cancers, such as acute lymphoblastic leukemia.

Even when radiation does not offer a cure, it may relieve symptoms and improve quality of life. Radiation is used as palliative therapy to reduce symptoms in prostate cancer and breast cancer when bone metastases are present

T A B L E   *5-3*   *Medical Treatment Word List*

Alkylating agents: A family of chemotherapeutic drugs that combine with DNA (genetic substance) to prevent normal cell division.

Analgesic: A drug used for reducing pain.

Antimetabolites: A family of chemotherapeutic drugs that interfere with the processes of DNA production, and thus prevent normal cell division.

Benign: Not malignant.

Biopsy: The surgical removal of a small portion of tissue for diagnosis.

Blood count: A laboratory study to evaluate the number of white cells, red cells, and platelets.

Bone marrow: A soft substance found within bone cavities, ordinarily composed of fat and developing red cells, white cells, and platelets.

Cancer: A condition in which there is the proliferation of malignant cells that are capable of invading normal tissues.

Chemotherapy: The treatment of disease by chemicals (drugs) introduced into the bloodstream by injection or taken by mouth as tablets.

Cobalt treatment: Radiotherapy using gamma rays generated from the breakdown of radioactive cobalt-60.

Colostomy: Surgical formation of an artificial anus in the abdominal wall, so the colon can drain feces into a bag.

Coma: A condition of decreased mental function in which the individual is incapable of responding to any stimulus, including painful stimuli.

Cyanotic: A blue appearance of the skin, lips, or fingernails as the result of low oxygen content of the circulating blood.

Diagnosis: The process by which a disease is identified.

DNA: Abbreviation for deoxyribonucleic acid, the building block of the genes, responsible for the passing of hereditary characteristics from cell to cell.

Hodgkin's disease: A form of tumor that arises in a single lymph node and may spread to local and then distant lymph nodes and finally to other tissues, commonly including the spleen, liver, and bone marrow.

Immunotherapy: A method of cancer therapy that stimulates the body defenses (the immune system) to attack cancer cells or modify a specific disease state.

Intravenous (IV): Describing the administration of a drug or of fluid directly into a vein.

Leukemia: A malignant proliferation of white blood cells in the bone marrow; cancer of the blood cells.

Lymph nodes: Organized clusters of lymphocytes through which the tissue fluids drain upon returning to the blood circulation; they act as the first line of defense, filtering out and destroying infective organisms or cancer cells and initiating the generalized immune response.

Malignant: Having the potentiality of being lethal if not successfully treated. All cancers are malignant by definition.

and in brain metastases, as well as in cases of multiple myeloma, advanced lung and esophagopharyngeal cancer, gastric cancer, and sarcomas.

Most patients who receive radiation are scheduled for frequent treatments over a period of several months. The side effects of radiation therapy depend on the region being radiated and on how particular tissues tolerate the effects of radiation. Side effects can include nausea, vomiting, tiredness, and general weakness. The radiation dose is prescribed on the basis of the stage of the disease and the patient's ability to withstand the side effects. As with all cancer

TABLE 5-3 *(continued)*

Melanoma: A cancer of the pigment cells of the skin, usually arising in a preexisting pigmented area (mole).

Metastasis: The establishment of a secondary site or multiple sites of cancer separate from the primary or original site.

Multimodality therapy: The use of more than one modality for cure or palliation (abatement) of cancer.

Myelogram: The introduction of radiopaque dye into the sac surrounding the spinal cord, a process that makes it possible to see tumor involvement of the spinal cord or nerve roots on X-ray.

Oncologist: An internist (specialist in internal medicine dealing with nonsurgical treatment of disease) who has subspecialized in cancer therapy and has expertise in both chemotherapy and the handling of problems arising during the course of the disease.

Parkinson's disease: Degenerative disease of the brain resulting in tremor and rigid muscles.

Prognosis: An estimate of the outcome of a disease based on the status of the patient and accumulated information about the disease and its treatment.

Prosthesis: An artificial structure designed to replace or approximate a normal one.

Regression: The diminution of cancerous involvement, usually as the result of therapy; it is manifested by decreased size of the tumor (or tumors) or its clinical evidence in fewer locations.

Relapse: The reappearance of cancer following a period of remission.

Remission: The temporary disappearance of evident active cancer, occurring either spontaneously or as the result of therapy.

Sarcoma: A cancer of connective tissue, bone, cartilage, fat, muscle, nerve sheath, blood vessels, or lymphoid system.

Subcutaneous cyst: A cyst located beneath the skin; usually benign.

Symptom: A manifestation or complaint of disease as described by the patient, as opposed to one found by the doctor's examination; the latter is referred to as a sign.

Terminal: Describing a condition of decline toward death, from which not even a brief reversal can be expected.

Therapeutic procedure: A procedure intended to offer palliation (abatement) or cure of a condition or disease.

Toxicity: The property of producing unpleasant or dangerous side effects.

Tumor: A mass or swelling. A tumor can be either benign or malignant.

Source: Excerpted and adapted from Ernest H. Rosenbaum, M.D., *Living with Cancer: A Guide for the Patient, the Family and Friends* (St. Louis: C. V. Mosby, 1982).

therapies, new techniques are constantly being developed to make radiation therapy more effective in fighting cancer and less stressful for patients.[60]

Chemotherapy

Chemotherapy is the use of toxic drugs to kill cancer cells. It originated from the observation that the toxic effects of mustard gases during World War I included damage to bone marrow. Clinical trials with chemotherapy began after World War II. Today, many different chemotherapeutic agents are employed in various combinations for treating cancer. Chemotherapy has been called the leading weapon for increasing the number of patients who can be

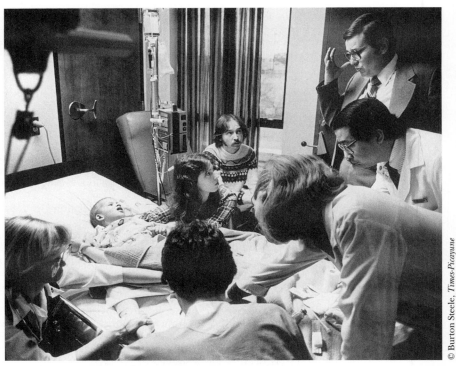

Family members and consulting physicians gathered around the bedside of a seriously ill child discuss the impending brain surgery that everyone hopes will bring a favorable prognosis.

cured of cancer. The dose must be strong enough to kill the cancer or slow its growth but not so potent that it seriously harms the patient. The ideal chemotherapeutic agent would attack cancerous cells in the body without affecting healthy tissue.

Some cancers respond to chemotherapy; others improve but aren't cured; and yet others are resistant.[61] In some cases, there is a good initial response to chemotherapy, but after repeated treatment the cancer develops resistance to the drugs. Chemotherapy is an important treatment in germ-cell tumors and some leukemias and lymphomas, as well as in ovarian cancer (after surgery), among others; it also has a role in treating some breast cancers, advanced myeloma, sarcomas, and some childhood cancers, such as Wilms' tumor of the kidney. In some forms of cancer, chemotherapy has palliative effects that help patients lead relatively normal, even prolonged, lives.

All chemotherapeutic agents basically work by blocking the metabolic processes involved in cellular division. Because cancer cells divide more rapidly than do most normal cells, the agents used in chemotherapy are designed to preferentially affect the cancerous cells. Whether the particular drug used in chemotherapy prevents cells from making genetic material (DNA), blocks nucleic acid synthesis, or stops cell division and induces other cellular changes, chemotherapeutic agents owe their effectiveness to the fact that they are poison. As a result, they damage normal as well as diseased tissue. Because chemotherapeutic agents generally destroy only the portion of the cell population that is undergoing division, several drugs that act on cells in different ways are usually administered in combination.

Chemotherapy may cause discomforting side effects, including hair loss, nausea, sleeplessness, problems with eating and digestion, mouth sores, ulceration and bleeding in the gastrointestinal tract, and other toxic effects. Other drugs may be given to counteract side effects of the chemotherapeutic agents.

Alternative Therapies

Many people find mainstream medicine lacking in its ability to address the patient as a whole person, not just the recipient of a "doctor-centered" treatment regimen. As a result, there is growing interest in so-called *alternative therapies*. Some of these therapies are associated with traditional medical practices that date back hundreds or thousands of years; others are newcomers on the scene. Alternative health care encompasses a broad range of therapeutic approaches (see Table 5-4).[62]

Cross-cultural issues are becoming more important in medicine as immigrants to industrialized countries bring a variety of indigenous and folk beliefs to their encounters with mainstream medical practitioners.[63] Rather than viewing such beliefs as foreign, irrational, or wrong, physicians are increasingly recognizing that optimal care is often achieved by judiciously combining conventional biomedicine and various folk beliefs, or *ethnomedicine*. Physician Lori Arviso Alvord, for example, combines tribal beliefs with medical training to offer a holistic approach to her Navajo patients.[64] Modern biomedicine itself can be viewed as a highly refined form of folk medicine. Individuals from ethnic or cultural groups who have practiced "ethnomedicine" all their lives may feel intimidated or ignored by Western biomedicine. Others, raised in societies where biomedicine dominates, may be interested in expanding their choices by investigating alternatives. The importance of such issues to contemporary health care is seen in the recent establishment of the Office of Alternative Medicine within the National Institutes of Health and in medical texts that support tolerance of alternatives to conventional approaches. After all, "If the goal is the maintenance of or a return to health, all available mechanisms should be used."[65]

Among Hmong immigrants in Kansas City, traditional healing methods, including massage and herbalism, are combined with modern Western medicine.[66] Similarly, among recent Mexican immigrants and some Mexican Americans, the traditional folk practice of *curanderismo* (from the Spanish verb *curar*, "to heal") is an important part of total health care.[67] As Kaja Finkler reports in a study comparing sacred folk healing and biomedicine as practiced in Mexico, "In the search for the alleviation of pain, pragmatism prevails; people judge the treatments they are given by their effects."[68] Indeed, in the United

TABLE 5-4   *Alternative and Complementary Therapies*

Mind–Body Interventions	Systems-Oriented Approaches	Manual Healing Methods
Psychotherapy and support groups	Traditional Chinese medicine	Osteopathic medicine
Meditation	Acupuncture and acupressure	Chiropractic treatment
Imagery	Herbal medicine and diet/ nutritional approaches	Massage therapy
Hypnosis and biofeedback	Community-based practices (for example, Native American "sweat lodges" and Latin American *curanderismo*)	Biofield therapeutics (that is, laying on of hands)
Yoga, dance therapy, other movement therapies	Ayurveda (India)	Reflexology
Music therapy and art therapy	Homeopathic medicine	"Body work" (for example, Rolfing, Trager, Feldenkrais method, Alexander technique, Shiatsu)
Prayer and mental healing	Naturopathic medicine	Bioenergetics

States, one of every three individuals uses some kind of alternative therapy to treat illnesses.[69] People who seek alternative health care are not necessarily dissatisfied with conventional biomedicine; they may simply appreciate the personal attention they are given by practitioners of alternative medicine.[70]

Nevertheless, the popularity of alternative approaches to health care raises questions about people getting ripped off by quacks and charlatans. Quacks exploit people's misery while jeopardizing their health, and charlatans promise miracle cures for those with sufficient money. Even in the best of circumstances, alternative approaches typically make use of unproved therapies— that is, therapies that have not undergone rigorous scientific testing. Physicians warn that "Patients with terminal cancer, often grasping at straws, need to be informed and wary of those who falsely promise cure."[71] The practice of standard biomedicine is based on randomized clinical trials and on "evidence-based medicine," whereby scientific method establishes the efficacy, or value, of therapies. Lawrence Schneiderman says, "Respect for multiculturalism should not be used as a sentimental excuse to abandon one's professional obligation to serve the patient's best interest."[72]

In the following sections, we look first at some therapies that may be used in conjunction with conventional biomedical therapies and then at some ap-

"Next, an example of the very same procedure when done correctly."

Drawing by Tom Cheney, © 1998 The New Yorker Collection

proaches that are characterized as "unorthodox" because of their unproved nature.

Complementary Therapies

Many of the alternative medical practices listed in Table 5-4 are used alongside conventional approaches to treating illness. In pain management, for example, these adjunctive or auxiliary methods may include psychotherapy and other mind–body interventions (meditation, imagery, biofeedback, and so on), as well as physical therapy and other forms of manual healing. In using *visualization* as an adjunct to chemotherapy, for example, the patient visualizes the therapeutic agent inside the body as it diminishes the cancer and helps to restore well-being. Thus, the patient mobilizes his or her inner

Figure 5-3 *Good Cells and Bad Cells: A Child's Drawing*
In this drawing by a child with cancer, the health-giving good cells are
depicted as being victorious over the diseased bad cells. Such imaginative
techniques can be ways of enlisting the patient's internal resources as an
adjunct to conventional therapies.
Source: Center for Attitudinal Healing, *There Is a Rainbow Behind Every Dark Cloud* (Millbrae,
Calif.: Celestial Arts, 1978), p. 71.

healing resources by imagining the diseased parts of the body becoming well
again (see Figure 5-3).

At Shibata Hospital in Japan, conventional treatment for cancer is accompanied by a psychotherapeutic technique called *ikigai ryoho,* or meaningful-
life therapy.[73] The theory behind meaningful-life therapy is that, despite fears
or quirks of personality, even when we are terminally ill, we can "take responsibility for what to do in the time remaining to us." Thus, cancer patients at
Shibata Hospital begin by acknowledging their own suffering and gradually
proceed, first, to the recognition that others also suffer, then to an acceptance
of the reality of the illness and the fight that must be carried on, and, finally,
to "an ability to live fully and deeply within the realistic limits posed by the
illness."

Anson Shupe and Jeffrey Hadden have proposed the term *symbolic healing*
to identify the varied therapies known under such names as "faith healing,"
"supernatural healing," and "folk healing."[74] What we take to be meaningful—

what we believe—potentially affects the functioning of our bodies. As human beings, we function within a series of overlapping environments: biological, social, and cultural. Looked at cross-culturally, most healing systems describe illness as "an imbalance among different realms of a patient's life." When alternative therapies help restore this balance, they serve an important function as an adjunct to conventional medical treatment.

Adjunctive therapies of the kind mentioned are often characterized as "complementary therapies." Whereas some kinds of alternative therapy may be harmful, complementary therapies of various kinds are used in conjunction with conventional medicine. As one physician points out, complementary therapies only become "alternative," in a negative sense, when they are promoted as "cure-oriented alternatives to conventional treatment."[75]

Unorthodox Treatment

What comes to mind when you hear the word *unorthodox?* Outside the establishment? Ineffective? Unorthodox therapies are methods of treatment that the medical establishment considers unproved or potentially harmful. The advocates of such remedies may be branded as quacks or charlatans, and their methods characterized as updated editions of Dr. Feelgood's Medicine Show, a form of snake oil medicine that, even if intrinsically harmless, diverts individuals from conventional medicine, which could help them.

That a cure for cancer could be found in the pits of apricots or shark cartilage stretches credibility; and, indeed, such "cures" may be not only controversial, but dangerous. Yet, many of our most common medications derive from seemingly unlikely sources. Digitalis, in continuous use for more than two hundred years and prescribed for heart ailments, derives from the plant foxglove. Penicillin is naturally produced from molds. The active ingredient of common aspirin is close kin to a substance found in the bark and leaves of the white willow. It seems that the source of a proposed medicinal substance ought to concern us less than the question: Does it work? In China, about 1700 plants are commonly used as medicines and, in India, that number is about 2500. The study of medicinal plants is increasingly important to pharmacology, as scientists wonder how many "undiscovered" drugs are used effectively by healers around the world.[76] The debate over the medical use of marijuana has involved conflicts between law and medicine because the substance in question is not only an unproved therapy but an illegal one.[77]

Some patients are willing to try anything to "beat" a terminal prognosis, taking on an attitude of "heroic self-healing" that defies the odds.[78] Shortly before his death, Norman Cousins said, "The great tragedy of life is not death but what dies inside us while we live."[79] The shock of a terminal diagnosis and the reality of living with serious illness can wreak damage on the human spirit. Conventional medical therapies alone may not repair this damage. It may be a mistake to confront patients with an "either/or" situation, forcing them to choose between orthodox or alternative treatments. Indeed, there may be times when rigidly defending standard practices can do more harm than good.

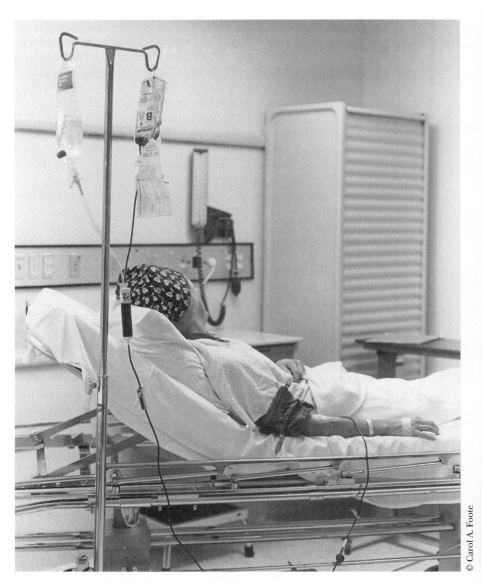

© Carol A. Foote

As part of her medical treatment, this chemotherapy patient is receiving a blood transfusion. Some treatments of life-threatening illness create the need for adjunctive therapies to counteract the side effects of the primary mode of treatment.

Pain Management

Pain is the most common symptom in terminally ill patients.[80] The advocates of hospice and palliative care highlight the need for adequate pain management, not only for patients with terminal illness, but for all patients

> The family of an elderly terminal cancer patient sued a nursing home that unilaterally reduced his pain medication without seeking approval from his doctor, a decision that caused the 75-year-old patient increased suffering. Deciding that the patient was "addicted to morphine," the nursing home staff substituted a "mild tranquilizer," which failed to control his pain. In response to the lawsuit, the nursing director at the facility said: "I have never heard of giving such high doses, at such frequent intervals. . . . The staff and I did not think he needed that much morphine."
>
> Maureen Cushing, "Pain Management on Trial"

with untreated or undertreated pain and suffering. Increasingly, pain is viewed as a "fifth vital sign," one that should be added to the four vital signs—temperature, pulse, respiration, and blood pressure—now recorded and assessed as a standard part of patient care.[81] Unfortunately, there is tremendous variation among health care providers with respect to assessing and managing pain adequately. Inadequate pain management has been called "the shame of American medicine."[82]

Pain is a complex, multidimensional phenomenon; the type and severity of pain can be an important diagnostic tool.[83] Two main types of pain can be distinguished: *Acute pain* is "an essential biological signal of the potential for or the extent of injury."[84] Acute pain is a protective mechanism insofar as it causes the sufferer to remove or withdraw from the source.[85] *Chronic pain* is usually defined as pain that persists longer than three to six months. When pain lasts this long, it loses its adaptive biologic role. Chronic pain may be accompanied by sleep disturbances, loss of appetite, weight loss, diminished sexual interest, and depression. It may result from physical mechanisms (somatogenic pain), psychological mechanisms (psychogenic pain), the activation of pain-sensitive nerve fibers (nociceptive pain), or nerve-tissue damage (neuropathic pain).

The treatment of pain requires attention to its severity, location, quality, duration, and course, among other factors, including the "meaning" of the pain to the patient. Furthermore, it is important to distinguish between pain and suffering, especially in the case of cancer patients, "whose suffering may be due as much to loss of function and fear of impending death as to pain."[86]

Pain is generally managed in a "stepwise approach," beginning with basic non-opioid pain medications and, if necessary, moving on to powerful opioids like codeine and morphine.[87] Morphine is the drug most commonly used to treat severe cancer pain. It affects both the perception of pain and the emotional response to it. The good news is that (1) it is not especially difficult to assess and treat cancer pain, and (2) more attention is being paid to pain.[88] The not-so-good news is that there are doctors, nurses, and pharmacists whose misunderstandings about opioid analgesics, such as morphine, prevent patients from receiving adequate pain control. This is partly because many caregivers underestimate the pain experienced by patients and partly because of unfounded concerns about patients becoming addicted to such opioids. Strangely, there are even some hospice nurses who worry about the possibility of addiction in their dying patients.[89]

Pain experts point to a fundamental distinction between addiction (in which drug-seeking behavior occurs in an effort to reproduce the "high") and physical dependence (which simply results in an "abstinence syndrome" after the patient stops taking the drug). In fact, patients who experience severe pain rarely obtain pleasant, euphoric sensations from drugs. Morphine works effectively in managing pain because it taps into the body's own pain relief system, the neurotransmitters, one class of which is chemically similar to morphine. Heroin, which has an ill-deserved reputation as the "hardest drug" known to humankind, is another useful remedy in pain control. It is considered by many experts to be indispensable for managing pain, and many argue that it should be available to physicians in the United States, as it is in Great Britain.[90] Pain specialists say that medicine has the means to alleviate the pain and suffering of almost all dying patients, but the will to treat pain effectively is lacking (see Table 5-5). Thus, the "politics of pain management" may determine whether pain is treated adequately.

The technology of pain management is advancing as the pathways of pain and its mechanisms are understood more completely.[91] Epidural and intraspinal drug delivery—placing a slow, steady stream of morphine directly into the spinal column—provides effective control of pain and is often used with late-stage cancer patients.[92] "Drug cocktails"—small amounts of several different drug compounds—are used to block different pain channels in the body. Patient-controlled analgesia, a mechanism that allows patients to determine for themselves the best timing of pain relief, is often more effective than relying on others for an injection or a tablet after pain has worsened. Pain is also treated with a variety of other medical techniques, including nerve blocks,

TABLE 5-5   *Factors That Inhibit Adequate Pain Control*

- Medical personnel have concerns that patients may become addicted, so they either don't prescribe appropriate drugs or prescribe only low, insufficient doses of medications that would be helpful in adequate dosages.
- Physicians are afraid to prescribe powerful narcotics due to concern about prosecution by overzealous law enforcers.
- Patients feel they should silently live with pain as a sign of moral strength or stoicism.
- Patients worry that, if they use strong painkillers now, nothing will be available later when pain may become worse; in fact, however, for most people there is no upper limit to the ability of narcotics like morphine to control pain.
- Many doctors really don't know much about how to control pain. There is a severe lack of training and information about the principles of pain management and palliative medicine.

Adapted from Shannon Brownlee and Joannie M. Schrof, "The Quality of Mercy" (Special Feature), *U.S. News & World Report,* 17 March 1997, 54–67.

electrical stimulation of nerves, acupuncture, and neurosurgery. In addition to controlling pain per se, antidepressants and other drugs can be prescribed to relieve anxiety, confusion, and depression that may be experienced by terminally ill patients.[93] Finally, drugs can be given to minimize the discomforting effects of constipation, nausea, respiratory depression, and other physical symptoms commonly experienced by dying patients.

People often speak of pain as if it were a well-defined entity, but, in fact, as Linda Garro points out, pain is "subjective in nature and ultimately unshareable."[94] Garro says, "Pain cannot be directly measured or observed; it is a perceptual experience that can only be communicated through verbal means and/or by behavior interpreted as indicating pain." Culturally related belief systems have a dramatic impact on how patients "represent" their illness, as well as on their coping responses.[95]

Languages differ in their "lexicon" for talking about pain. When describing pain, English speakers use such terms as *pain, hurt, sore,* and *ache.* Qualifiers are added to make the description match the actual experience. We talk about having a "burning" or "stabbing" pain, or about "unbearable ache" or "soreness in the shoulder." Notice the tendency to treat pain as an object: "I have a pain." For Thai speakers, however, the basic terms for describing pain are verbs. They refer to the active perception of sensations and often convey the location of the pain as well; for example, "suffering focused abdominal pain" or "feeling irritated by an abrasion." Thus, pain is described not as an object but as a perceptual process. Language reveals how our response to pain is, at least in part, culturally shaped.

Hospice and palliative care practitioners have taken a leading role in bringing greater attention to adequate pain management. Especially important has been hospice's insistence on the need to respond to the dying person's "total pain," which includes physical, psychological, social, and spiritual components. Managing pain effectively requires specialized attention by skilled professionals. Controlling pain in patients who are nearing the end of life can be a formidable challenge. Techniques for adequate pain control are known and accessible. Ignorance of these options on the part of both medical practitioners and society at large, and a shared failure to institute adequate delivery systems that would make them widely available, perpetuates situations in which people die in needless pain.

The Dying Trajectory

Our expectations about dying may be quite different from what most people actually experience. Young adults tend to imagine themselves living into old age and then quickly dying at home, alert and lucid until the end.[96] The pain and other discomforts of dying tend to be absent from these imagined deathbed scenes. Our pictures of dying may be influenced more by images in the media than by what is likely to actually occur.

The concept of a *trajectory of dying* is useful for understanding patients' experiences as they near death. Although sudden death from an unexpected

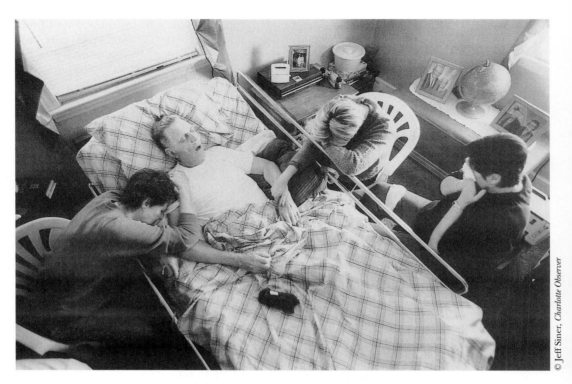

After being diagnosed with a recurrence of cancer, Vernon Nantz chose to be cared for at home by family and friends, with the support of hospice. In his last days, Vernon's family united in tears and prayers, sharing a vigil around his bedside, as he drifted away to the peaceful end he sought.

cause—a massive heart attack or an accident, for example—is one type of dying trajectory, our focus here is on deaths that occur when there is forewarning. Among these, some trajectories involve a steady and fairly predictable decline. This is the case with many cancers, which tend to follow the course of a progressive disease with a terminal phase. Other kinds of advanced, chronic illness involve a long period of slow decline marked by episodes of crisis, the last of which proves to be "suddenly" fatal.

We can also distinguish between different stages in a dying trajectory—namely, a period when a person is known to be terminally ill but is living with a life expectancy of perhaps weeks or months, possibly years; and a later period when dying is imminent and the person is described as "actively dying." The way in which such trajectories are estimated—their duration and expected course—can affect both patients and caregivers and influence their actions. Deaths that occur "out of time" (too quickly or too slowly) may pose special difficulties.

Two patterns of "dying trajectories" are particularly important: (1) the *lingering* trajectory, when a patient's life fades away slowly and inevitably, and

TABLE *5-6   Signs of "Active Dying"*

Common Symptoms During Last Days or Hours . . .
- Body systems slow down
- Breathing pattern changes and becomes irregular (for example, shallow breaths followed by deep breath; periods of panting)
- Difficulty breathing (dyspnea)
- Congestion (noisy and moist breathing; gurgling sounds)
- Decrease in appetite and thirst
- Nausea and vomiting
- Incontinence
- Sweating
- Restlessness and agitation (for example, jerking, twitching, pulling at bed linen or clothing)
- Disorientation and confusion (for example, about time, place, identity of people)
- Decreased socialization; progressive detachment
- Changes in skin color as circulation decreases (limbs may become cool and perhaps bluish or mottled)
- Increasing sleeping
- Decrease in consciousness

At Time of Death . . .
- Relaxing of the throat muscles or secretions in the throat may cause noisy breathing ("the death rattle")
- Breathing ceases
- Muscle contractions may occur and the chest may heave as if to breathe
- Heart may beat a few minutes after breathing stops, and a brief seizure may occur
- Heartbeat ceases
- Person cannot be aroused
- Eyelids may be partly open with the eyes in a fixed stare
- Mouth may fall open as the jaw relaxes
- Bowel and bladder contents may be released

Adapted from "Preparing for the Death of a Loved One," *American Journal of Hospice and Palliative Care* 9, no. 4 (1992): 14–16; Robert Berkow, ed., *The Merck Manual of Medical Information: Home Edition* (Whitehouse Station, N.J.: Merck Research Laboratories, 1997), p. 21; and Robert E. Enck, "The Last Few Days," *American Journal of Hospice and Palliative Care* 9, no. 4 (1992): 11–13.

(2) the *expected quick* trajectory, when an individual makes a sudden exit, as in emergency situations where life or death hang in the balance.[97] The expectations that medical professionals, family members, and others have about a patient's course toward death are likely to be important in determining the nature and kind of care received by the dying person. Although proposals appear from time to time concerning an *ars moriendi,* or right way to die, the notion that there is an "art of dying" that applies to everyone is probably not valid within modern pluralistic societies that place a high value on individualism.[98]

When a person is at the end stage of a terminal illness, death is expected to occur within hours or, at most, a few days.[99] The end of life is characterized by what is termed "active dying" (see Table 5-6). During the last phase of a fatal illness, a dying person may exhibit irregular breathing or shortness of breath, decreased appetite and thirst, nausea and vomiting, incontinence, restlessness and agitation, disorientation and confusion, and diminished consciousness. These symptoms usually can be managed by skilled palliative care. Pain, if it is present, should be treated aggressively as part of a comprehensive approach to comfort care. Even when pain can be controlled by drugs and other therapies, some patients, even as they near death, still have concerns about addiction or want to delay pain medication "until it is really needed," or they want to maintain control by "using the pain as a reminder that they are still living."[100] The dying patient may also experience depression, anxiety, confusion, delirium, and unconsciousness.[101] Because most dying patients are more comfortable without eating or drinking at the end of life, forcing food or liquids is usually not beneficial. The stopping of eating and drinking has always been part of the last phase of a terminal condition. Near the time of death, relaxation of the throat muscles or secretions in the throat may cause the person's breathing to become noisy, resulting in a sound called the "death rattle." Most dying patients are not aware of this noisy breathing. If it unnerves family or caregivers, medication or repositioning the person can help. Just before death, the person may take a breath and sigh or shudder. After death, unless the person had a rare infectious disease, family and friends may stay with the body for a time as they make their farewells.

The Social Role of the Dying Patient

When death is made to seem less a natural event than a medical failure, biological death, the cessation of physical functions, may be preceded by *social death*. Eric Cassell writes: "There are two distinct things happening to the terminally ill: the death of the body and the passing of the person."[102] The death of the body is a physical phenomenon, whereas the passing of the person is a nonphysical (social, emotional, psychological, spiritual) one; yet, these aspects sometimes become confused.

As a person begins to recognize his or her impending death, this acknowledgment may stimulate a period of life review, an assessment of one's accomplishments in life: What have I achieved or failed to achieve? How have I contributed to others' well-being or to the betterment of humankind? Have I met my expectations for a life well lived? How will my reputation fare after I'm gone? Has life been "fair"? Has my "good luck" outweighed the bad? In short, what is the "balance sheet" of my life?[103] The answers to such questions influence the person's attitude. As a person realizes that he or she is nearing the end of life, the most important thing may be "to believe that life has, if not a purpose, at least a singularity that makes it memorable."[104] The story, or "narrative," of a person's life is extremely important.

In coping with life-threatening illness, individuals often find ways of redefining their situation so that they still feel "healthy." A woman with metastatic cancer said: "I am really very healthy. I just have this problem, but I am still me." Her statement shows a sense of self-integrity that demonstrates an ability to go on with life despite the disease.[105] Cultural models of health and illness affect the way we relate to the meaning of an illness and cope with its reality.[106] "Being healthy" is a vital characteristic of our social world.[107] The obligation of the sick person is to engage in a supervised attempt to get well.

Sociologist Talcott Parsons argues that a particular social role accompanies illness.[108] Like all social roles—parent, child, student, employee, spouse—the role of the "person who is sick" includes rights and responsibilities. When we are ill, we are exempt from our usual tasks. We may stay home from work, and someone else may take on our share of domestic or social commitments. We are granted the right to be sick. Other people make allowances for our behavior. Whereas taking off from work just to enjoy a day in the sun is frowned upon, absence due to illness elicits sympathy rather than reprimands. The sick person not only enjoys exemptions from usual social obligations, he or she is given special consideration and care. Such care is part of the social role of being sick, of being a patient. But these rights are balanced by responsibilities. The sick person must cooperate with caregivers. You've got to take your medicine.

The social role of a person who is dying does not fit neatly the usual parameters of the "sick role" described by Parsons. A terminal illness is not a temporary condition followed by a return to wellness. However, a social role for the dying person is not well defined in our society. Even when circumstances are clearly contrary, the dying person may be urged to hope for recovery, to deny the reality of his or her experience. The lack of a consensus about the role of a dying patient sometimes results in actions that are incongruous. Consider, for example, the situation of an end-stage terminally ill person being rushed to the ICU (intensive care unit) and subjected to heroic medical attempts to sustain life.

What would an appropriate social role for the dying look like? First, the dying person would not be expected to maintain an appearance of expecting to live forever, of getting well again, of sustaining false hope. He or she would be encouraged to mobilize the necessary resources for attending to the prospect of death. Relatives and friends, accepting this changed perspective as natural, would allow the patient to set his or her own agenda about activities and relationships as the end of life draws near.[109] In a study of "farewells by the dying," most wanted to express their farewells through giving gifts, writing letters, and informal conversations with those closest to them.[110] Valued relationships are important for most people right to the end of life.

The social role of the dying encompasses spiritual as well as physical and emotional needs. These include:[111]

1. *The need for meaning and purpose.* This involves reviewing one's life (including relationships, work, other achievements, and religious concerns) and attempting to make sense of it, to place it within a larger perspective that has meaning.
2. *The need for hope and creativity.* Whereas the first item on this list involves looking back over one's life to discover meaning and purpose, this need

There Are Days Now

There are days now
when I can see
the souls of elephants
being towed to heaven;
and the whales, the whales,
those hulls full of sadness!
Soon the trees will be loosed from their moorings
and sail off
like a chorus of Greek Women
rigid with grief.

I am resigned to this,
and yet
with each of their passings
there is a crumbling
along the banks of my bloodstream.
So if I touched you now,
my friend,
how could it be with my whole hand,
the fat resting firm beneath the palm,
and not with a clutch of fingers,
as though I had grabbed you in passing
and were holding on?

Morton Marcus

is oriented toward the future. It may involve the aspiration for improved well-being, to be free of pain; the desire to accomplish a personal goal or to achieve reconciliation with others; or it may involve the hope of an afterlife. This need may also center on the hope, as Roderick Cosh puts it, "that that which has been of meaning and purpose to the individual may be affirmed by those who are important to him or her."[112]

3. *The need to give and receive love.* As Cosh says, "We all need to be reassured that we are loved and that others need our love." Reconciliation is a key element in satisfying this human spiritual need.

In an essay, "The Eyes of a Dying Man," Japanese writer Yasunari Kawabata suggests that the human longing for beauty is realized in a special way by persons who are dying, and this theme is echoed in his stories: In "The Moon in the Water," a dying man finds an enhanced appreciation of the beauty of nature; in *The Sound of the Mountain,* an aged man, approaching death, enjoys an intensified awareness of the beauty of the heroine Kikuko; in *The House of the Sleeping Beauties,* the "beauties" are all the more beautiful because they are seen through the eyes of old Eguchi, who knows his days are numbered.[113]

Further Readings

Mitch Albom. *Tuesdays with Morrie: An Old Man, A Young Man, and Life's Greatest Lesson.* New York: Doubleday, 1997.

Maggie Callanan and Patricia Kelley. *Final Gifts: Understanding the Special Awareness, Needs, and Communications of the Dying.* New York: Bantam, 1997.

Roger S. Cicala. *The Heart Disease Sourcebook.* Los Angeles: Lowell House, 1997.

Geoffrey M. Cooper. *The Cancer Book: A Guide to Understanding the Causes, Prevention, and Treatment of Cancer.* Boston: Jones and Bartlett, 1993.

Charles A. Corr, Kenneth J. Doka, and Robert Kastenbaum. "Dying and Its Interpreters: A Review of Selected Literature and Some Comments on the State of the Field." *Omega: Journal of Death and Dying* 39, no. 4 (1999): 239–259.

Kenneth J. Doka. *Living with Life-Threatening Illness: A Guide for Patients, Their Families, and Caregivers.* New York: Lexington, 1993.

Kenneth J. Doka and Joyce Davidson, eds. *Living with Grief When Illness Is Prolonged.* Washington, D.C.: Hospice Foundation of America, 1997.

Jerome Groopman. *The Measure of Our Days: New Beginnings at Life's End.* New York: Viking, 1997.

Marie de Hennezel. *Intimate Death: How the Dying Teach Us to Live.* New York: Alfred A. Knopf, 1997.

Bert Keizer. *Dancing with Mister D: Notes on Life and Death.* New York: Doubleday, 1997.

Joanne Lynn and Joan Harrold, eds. *Handbook for Mortals: Guidance for People Facing Serious Illness.* New York: Oxford University Press, 1999.

David B. Morris. *The Culture of Pain.* Berkeley: University of California Press, 1991.

Sherwin B. Nuland. *How We Die: Reflections on Life's Final Chapter.* New York: Alfred A. Knopf, 1994.

Arthur Selzer. *Understanding Heart Disease.* Berkeley: University of California Press, 1992.

"What You Need to Know About Cancer" (Special Issue). *Scientific American* 275, no. 3 (September 1996).

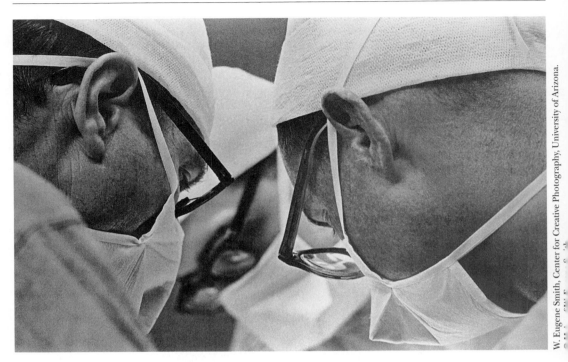

At the Hospital for Special Surgery, physicians use medical techniques that call for teamwork and expertise. Life-sustaining interventions made possible by advances in medical technologies require physicians and society as a whole to consider difficult issues of medical ethics.

Medical Ethics: Dying in a Technological Age

Great-grandpa was born before Henry Ford put his first automobile on the road, and he died shortly after Neil Armstrong set foot on the moon. From Michigan to outer space, he experienced an unprecedented advance in the technological capacities of our society. At the time of his death, he was surrounded by technological innovations. The canvas-topped, hand-cranked, two-seater car he hand-built in 1922 had been replaced by a factory-built, vinyl-topped, four-door automatic, with power steering and power brakes. A retired autoworker, he had begun to question the consequences of the automobile on the quality of his life. If he had been conscious as he lay dying, he might have talked about the consequences the machines sustaining his life were having on the quality of his death.

Advances in biomedical technology present us with new and sometimes confusing choices. Medical advances take place because physicians take seriously the Hippocratic obligation to keep people alive. Named for the ancient Greek physician Hippocrates, the Hippocratic oath has been an enduring guide for the conduct of physicians since the fourth century B.C. But practicing this worthy maxim can lead to difficult choices. Techniques for cardiopulmonary resuscitation (CPR) and artificial respiration allow physicians to intervene in the "normal" dying process. (The portrayal of CPR on television medical shows, however, presents a misleading picture of the frequency with which such resuscitation results in "miracles."[1]) Patients who are saved by such techniques may have their cardiac and respiratory

The Oath of Hippocrates

I swear by Apollo the physician, and by Aesculapius [god of medicine], Hygeia [goddess of health], and Panacea [goddess of healing], and all the gods and goddesses, that, to the best of my ability and judgment, I will keep this oath and agreement: to regard my teacher in this art as equal to my own parents; to share my living with him and provide for him in need; to treat his children as my own and teach them this art if they wish to learn it, without payment or obligation; to give guidance, explanations, and every other kind of instruction to my own children and those of my teacher, and to students who subscribe to the Physician's Oath, but to nobody else.

I will prescribe treatment to the best of my ability and judgment for the benefit of my patients and will abstain from whatever is harmful or pernicious. I will give no poisonous or deadly medicine, even if asked to, nor make any such suggestion; neither will I give any woman a pessary to produce an abortion. I will both live and work in purity and holiness. I will not operate, not even on patients suffering from the stone, but will leave this to specialists who are skilled in this work. Into whatever houses I enter, I will make the patient's good my principal aim and will avoid all deliberate harm or corruption, especially from sexual relations with women or men, bond or free. Whatever I see or hear about people, whether in the course of my practice or outside it, if it should not be made public, I will keep it to myself and treat it as an inviolable secret.

While I abide by this oath and never violate it, may all people hold me in esteem for all time on account of my life and work; but if I break this oath, let the reverse be my fate.

functions restored but suffer irreversible damage to the brain. The human organism can be kept functioning despite the cessation of normal heart, brain, respiratory, or kidney function. Does the Hippocratic obligation to keep people alive apply when a person is saved only to be maintained in a hopeless condition? When medical technologies spare patients' lives and enable them to resume more or less normal functioning, the results are gratifying. But the same technologies that prolong life can also prolong our dying.

In a climate of managed medical care, traditional "virtue-centered" ethics are challenged by the "businessification" of medicine.[2] Medical decisions ideally are made by individuals, families, and caregivers, who, acting together, form a community of interest, with firsthand knowledge about a particular case and the will to make moral decisions.[3] Physician John Lantos says, "The goal of medical ethics, it seems, should not be to develop rules that will minimize the need for individual virtues but to develop virtues that will minimize the need for rules."[4]

Fundamental Ethical Principles

To provide a framework for discussing informed consent, withdrawing or withholding medical treatment, euthanasia (defined as bringing about a gentle or peaceful death), and other issues in medical ethics, we must examine what it means to behave ethically or morally. To begin, *ethics* is concerned with the investigation of what is good and bad, especially as these concepts relate to moral duties and obligations. Such an investigation results in a set of moral principles or values that guide proper behavior. When we think of *morals,* or moral principles, we are dealing essentially with notions of right and wrong. Although the two terms—*morals* and *ethics*—are closely related, we can distinguish them, in one way, by noting that morals involve conforming to established codes or accepted notions of right and wrong, whereas ethics involve more subtle or challenging questions. The pursuit of ethics is characterized by efforts to answer the question, "What is the good?" and its corollary, "What is to be done?"

In applying ethical principles to the realm of medicine, several concepts have major importance. The first of these, *autonomy,* refers to an individual's right to be self-governing—that is, to exercise self-direction, freedom, and moral independence. Our personal autonomy is limited by the rights of others to exercise their autonomy, and it also may be limited by society, which exercises rights in the name of the community at large. A common example is the requirement that a traveler must obtain inoculations before being granted a visa to enter certain countries; the traveler's autonomy is restricted by concerns about public health imposed by the larger community. Personal autonomy is complex and often ambiguous.

A person may limit the extent to which his or her autonomy will be exercised. For example, the principle of autonomy should not be used to impose a burden of self-determination on individuals who prefer to have physicians or family members assume a major role in making medical decisions. Religious and cultural beliefs can affect the degree to which individuals exercise personal autonomy.[5] For some individuals and cultural groups, family members have a primary, or at least equal, voice in decisions about a patient's care. Individual autonomy is balanced by respect for the values of others, especially those with whom one has a significant relationship. If decisions are made without considering their effect on the "family commons," some people believe those choices may be overridden.[6] Thus, within certain limits, the principle of autonomy promotes "respect for persons" as people negotiate the medical system.

Another fundamental principle in medical care is *beneficence,* which involves doing good or conferring benefits that enhance personal or social well-being. This principle is sometimes expressed by its counterpart, *nonmaleficence,* or the injunction to "do no harm." In the context of physician–patient relationships, this principle requires that physicians not abandon a patient even when a patient makes decisions or takes actions that the physician believes are ill advised.[7]

Finally, medical ethics is fundamentally concerned with the principle of *justice.* Like "the good," justice is not an easy concept to define, although it includes qualities of impartiality and fairness, as well as right and proper action. Justice implies going beyond one's own feelings, prejudices, and desires to find an appropriate balance among conflicting interests. As you consider the ethical issues discussed in this chapter, keep in mind these fundamental principles of medical ethics: autonomy, beneficence, and justice.

Informed Consent to Treatment

The relationship between patient and physician implies a contract whereby each party agrees to perform certain acts designed to achieve the desired results. Informed consent is generally considered essential to this contract. Patients have a right to be fully informed about a proposed plan of treatment so they can decide whether to go forward with it. In practice, most people tend to rely on the physician's judgment, accepting the diagnosis and going along with the proposed course of treatment. We see our doctor to obtain medication to cure the flu or mend a broken arm, and we give little thought to other possible treatments. By following the doctor's advice, we expect to achieve a more or less speedy recovery. The etiology, or cause, of the disease or injury generally concerns us less than obtaining relief from its symptoms. However, when an illness is serious or life threatening, a patient's consent to treatment becomes more significant. Several treatment plans may be presented, each with its own set of potential risks and benefits. There may be uncertainty about which course of treatment promises the best results or concerns about potential side effects.

Informed consent is based on three legal principles: First, the patient must be *competent* to give consent. Second, consent must be given *freely*. Third, consent must be based on an *adequate understanding* of the proposed treatment, including potential risks. Although the phrase "informed consent" did not achieve legal definition until 1957, the antecedents of informed consent go back hundreds of years to English common law. The President's Commission for the Study of Ethical Problems in Medicine noted that "the legal doctrine of informed consent imposes on physicians two general duties: to disclose information about treatment to patients and to obtain their consent before proceeding with treatment."[8]

Informed consent ideally occurs within a process of shared decision making based on mutual respect and participation. Because people differ in their attitudes toward personal autonomy relative to medical care, the process of obtaining informed consent must be flexible. Physicians can find themselves in the difficult position of balancing disclosure of the facts and sensitivity to a patient's wishes. Some studies indicate that patients are more interested in being *informed* than in being fully involved in *decision making*; this seems to occur most often when decisions involve a serious health risk.[9]

Most physicians believe they have a duty to truthfully inform patients about a life-threatening condition, but this has not always been the case. A study in 1961 found that most doctors had a strong and general tendency to *withhold* information.[10] None of the doctors surveyed at that time reported a policy of telling every patient about a life-threatening diagnosis. Only about 12 percent said they would usually inform patients about a diagnosis of incurable cancer. Even when patients were informed, the disease was often de-

Informed consent is a fundamental ethical principle in medicine. Even fairly routine procedures, such as mending a small fracture, may become complicated when the patient is leukemic, as is this child: Alternatives must be weighed more carefully before a course of treatment is chosen.

scribed euphemistically. Doctors might tell the patient that he or she had a "lesion" or a "mass." Some doctors were more precise, using a description such as "growth," "tumor," or "hyperplastic tissue." In many instances, the description was phrased to suggest that the cancer was benign, and adjectives were used to temper the impact of the diagnosis. Thus, a tumor was said to be "suspicious" or "degenerated." Such descriptions allowed physicians to give a general explanation about the medical situation while eliciting the patient's cooperation in the proposed course of treatment.

By the late 1970s, the climate of truth telling had changed significantly. A study done in 1977 found an almost complete reversal of attitudes, with about 97 percent of the doctors surveyed reporting that they would usually tell patients the truth about a diagnosis.[11] In a follow-up study, however, doctors reported that they were willing to engage in some deception when situations involved complicated or very sensitive ethical issues.[12] Researchers said that physicians "appear to justify their decisions in terms of the consequences and to place a higher value on their patients' welfare and keeping patients' confidences than truth telling for its own sake." Offering information about *prognosis*—that is, the expected course of the disease—can be especially problematic. Predicting how long a particular person can expect to live is difficult. Statistics about the usual course of a disease can provide a rough idea of the odds of survival, and a doctor's clinical experience may be a guide. Still, when there is uncertainty, "Some doctors prefer to offer hope by describing remarkable recoveries without also mentioning the high likelihood that most people who have such a condition will die."[13]

Although some patients may not completely understand all of the medical information presented to them, most grasp the significant aspects of their condition and treatment when doctors allow sufficient time and make the effort to provide a clear explanation. Obtaining informed consent can be especially important when medical care is provided by a team of specialists whose responsibilities are defined less by the needs of the patient than by particular diseases or organ systems. In some cases, it may seem as if no doctor has responsibility for the overall care of the patient. Thus, there is no familiar person the patient can turn to for information and advice. Situations like this can pose a threat to the patient's well-being.

To the extent that a course of treatment is elective, the outcome uncertain, and the procedure experimental, informed consent becomes correspondingly more important. For example, drawing a blood sample is a common procedure that entails little risk to the patient. Consequently, we do not expect to receive a detailed explanation of risks when we roll up our sleeve for the insertion of the needle. However, a complicated surgical procedure, one that involves a nearly equal proportion of risks and benefits, makes a patient's informed consent crucial.

A gray area involving informed consent is the use of *placebos* in medical practice. A placebo is defined as "an inert substance given as a medicine for its suggestive effect."[14] Placebos are commonly used in testing new drugs to provide an evaluation by comparison, and such use is not normally questioned. In contrast, when doctors prescribe placebos in routine medical care, it raises questions about deceiving patients, even if the aim is worthy. Typically, placebos are prescribed when no organic cause for an ailment is found, and it is believed that the placebo will have a beneficial psychological effect. Some authorities estimate that perhaps one-third of all prescriptions are essentially

The doctor who fears being subjected to a malpractice suit if he doesn't tell the worst, and who tells the worst, may actually help to bring on the worst. . . . A serious diagnosis can be communicated as a challenge rather than as a verdict. The physician who volunteers a terminal date, for example, or allows himself to be pressured into offering a terminal date may actually be putting a hex on the patient.

Norman Cousins, "Tapping Human Potential"

placebos. David Towle says that "those physicians who use placebos argue that the end, curing the patient, takes precedence over the means: in this case, the deception of the patient."[15]

What constitutes sufficient information on which the patient can base a decision? Some patients take an active role in their treatment, even proposing methods of treatment to their physician. Others prefer to follow the treatment plan suggested by their doctor; they really don't want to know about potential risks or the percentage of failures. Full disclosure is a help to some patients, a hindrance to others. Such variation among patient attitudes presents a dilemma for the medical practitioner.

Sometimes members of a patient's family have an agenda of their own that complicates issues of informed consent and medical decision making. Margot White and John Fletcher describe a case in which the spouse of a dying patient told doctors: "You can't tell my husband he's dying; it will kill him."[16] She insisted that the truth of her husband's illness be withheld from him, refusing the doctors' requests to speak with him about his condition and preferences for treatment. From the wife's point of view, she knew her husband better than anyone—certainly better than the doctors—and she knew what was best for him. For the staff, however, her "interference" created concerns about whether the patient's autonomy was being compromised. It is sometimes difficult to find solutions that satisfy all concerned parties.

Informed consent is closely tied to the quality of communication between caregivers and patients. A recent study to assess end-of-life care found shortcomings in communication between physicians and seriously ill patients. (The study, known by its acronym, SUPPORT, was conducted as a multicenter "Study to Understand Prognoses and Preferences for Outcomes and Risks of Treatment.") Fewer than half of the physicians were aware of their patients' preferences for or against CPR (cardiopulmonary resuscitation).[17] In the second phase of the SUPPORT study, researchers gave specific information to physicians and patients about the survival prospects of each patient. Yet, even with the added guidance of this intervention, designed to enhance physician–patient communication, there was no improvement in physicians' knowledge about patients' CPR preferences. Other studies appear to confirm these findings in the clinical setting.[18]

Patients at the end-stage of life may express their desire to avoid disruptive medical interventions and be allowed to die as peacefully as possible. This preference can be recognized in the medical setting by designating the patient as "DNR" (Do Not Resuscitate), "No Code," or "CMO" (Comfort Measures Only)—all of which are intended to inform medical and nursing staff that the patient does not want any attempts made to revive him or her in the event of cardiac or respiratory failure.[19] Unless a physician has written a DNR order, however, hospital policies generally require that CPR be initiated immediately if the patient experiences cardiac arrest or respiratory failure.

Even when a physician has entered a DNR order on the patient's chart, it may not contain specific guidance about which treatments should be initiated and which withheld. Does the order not to initiate CPR mean that *other* life-saving medical interventions should be done? Or should *all* such interventions be withheld? If medical heroics are to be avoided, who decides whether a particular intervention is "heroic" or "ordinary" in a given set of circumstances? When a patient's attending physician is not on the scene to determine the appropriate level of treatment, it can put other medical and nursing staff in a quandary about what to do.[20] It is not always possible to simply "follow doctor's orders."

The SUPPORT study shows that physicians are rarely aware of their patients' preferences regarding resuscitation and that lack of communication may cause DNR orders to be ignored even when they exist. Many physicians have not been trained to move from aggressive to palliative care, nor are they familiar with the principles of care associated with palliative medicine.[21] The momentum in medicine naturally moves toward providing life-sustaining treatment. Thus, a patient's wish to refuse CPR and other life-sustaining interventions at the end of life may be an issue that is simply not on a doctor's "radar screen."

Although forced, coercive treatment is rare, caregivers can—unwittingly or not—exert undue influence on patients by means of subtle or overt manip-

---

Nurse: Did they mention anything about a tube through your nose?

Patient: Yes, I'm gonna have a tube in my nose.

Nurse: You're going to have the tube down for a couple of days or longer. It depends. So you're going to be NPO, nothing by mouth, and also you're going to have IV fluid.

Patient: I know. For three or four days, they told me that already. I don't like it, though.

Nurse: You don't have any choice.

Patient: Yes, I don't have any choice, I know.

Nurse: Like it or not, you don't have any choice. (laughter) After you come back, we'll ask you to do a lot of coughing and deep breathing to exercise your lungs.

Patient: Oh, we'll see how I feel.

Nurse: (emphasis) No matter how you feel, you have to do that!

> President's Commission for the Study of Ethical Problems in Medicine and Biomedical and Behavioral Research, *Making Health Care Decisions: A Report on the Ethical and Legal Implications of the Patient–Practitioner Relationship*

ulation. Once the patient is admitted to a health care institution, cooperation with caregivers is expected. The tacit communication may be that the patient has no choice. There is a tendency to assume that conventional medical practices are to be faithfully followed as a matter of routine, without considering whether these conventions match the patient's preferences. In the SUPPORT study, for example, it seems that physicians tended to be oblivious to the fact that some patients, nearing the end of their lives, would not want CPR administered. Truly informed consent requires cooperation between patient and physician in seeking the common goal of optimal, and appropriate, health care. In achieving this goal, the communication process is likely to be the crucial factor.

Choosing Death

The conventional understanding of the Hippocratic oath acknowledges that in some circumstances medical treatment is futile; that is, it has no reasonable possibility to "cure, ameliorate, improve, or restore a quality of life that would be satisfactory to the patient."[22] With the advent of modern medical technologies, however, the slogan often seems to be: "Keep the patient alive at all costs." What is the proper balance between preserving life and preventing suffering when further treatment is likely to be futile? Medical technologies offer seemingly miraculous possibilities for sustaining life, but what is the effect of life-sustaining technologies on the *quality* of patients' lives? There is a growing recognition that, for some patients, "[t]he available choices are between dying sooner but remaining comfortable and living slightly longer by receiving aggressive therapy, which may prolong the dying process, increase discomfort and dependence, and decrease the quality of life."[23]

If you were given a prognosis of only a very short time to live and told that any further treatment toward a cure was useless, would you want aggressive treatment to keep you alive, even if it meant that your vital bodily functions were maintained on life-support systems? The decision to limit treatment, to stop "doing everything that can be done," is often difficult for patients and their families. Although many people owe their lives to advanced medical technologies, a stance that strives to keep people alive by all means and at any cost is increasingly questioned. Reviewing the range of modern medical technologies, the President's Commission for the Study of Ethical Problems in Medicine concluded: "For almost any life-threatening condition, some intervention is capable of delaying the moment of death. . . . Matters that were once the province of fate have now become a matter of human choice."[24]

When suffering outweighs the benefits of continued existence, some argue that individuals have a "right to die."[25] Surrounded by an array of machinery and tubes, the patient may seem less a human person than an objectified extension of medical technology. Patients themselves may "swallow Kleenex to suffocate themselves, or jerk tubes out of their noses or veins, in a cat-and-mouse game of life and death which is neither merciful nor meaningful."[26]

Should futile treatments be withheld or withdrawn, even when such actions are virtually certain to result in the patient's death? Should treatment be continued even when the patient is in a persistent vegetative state—that is, profoundly unconscious, lacking any sign of normal reflexes controlled by the brain stem or spinal cord, unresponsive to all external stimuli, and with no reasonable hope of any improvement? Are there circumstances in which a physician should actively hasten or assist in bringing about a patient's death?[27]

Ethical questions about the "right to die" have become prominent since the landmark case of Karen Ann Quinlan in 1975. On April 15 of that year, at age twenty-one, Karen was admitted to the intensive care unit of a New Jersey hospital. She was in a comatose state, and soon her breathing was being artificially sustained by a mechanical MA-1 respirator. When she remained unresponsive in a persistent vegetative state, her parents asked that the respirator be disconnected so that nature could take its course. But the medical staff responsible for Karen's care denied their request. The request to withdraw treatment eventually reached the New Jersey Supreme Court, which ruled that artificial respiration could be discontinued.[28] It was discontinued and Karen was transferred to a nursing care facility. She died in June 1985 at age thirty-one, having become a focal point for issues pertaining to "death with dignity."

Since the Quinlan case, both state and federal courts have issued rulings concerned with removing other types of life-sustaining treatment, including artificial feeding mechanisms that supply nutrition and hydration to patients. Most notable was the case of Nancy Beth Cruzan, heard before the United States Supreme Court in 1990.[29] As a result of injuries sustained in an automobile accident in 1983, when she was twenty-five, Nancy was in a persistent vegetative state. Paramedics restored her breathing, but her brain had been deprived of oxygen for so long that she never regained consciousness. To provide nourishment, Nancy's physicians implanted a feeding tube in her stomach, the only form of life support she was receiving, a treatment that physicians said could prolong her life for as long as thirty years.

Nancy's parents, as her guardians, requested that the feeding tube be taken out, asserting her right to be free from "unwarranted bodily intrusions." The Missouri Supreme Court denied this petition, holding that, without Nancy's express consent, her parents could not exercise her right to refuse treatment. Therefore, the state's "unqualified" interest in preserving life should prevail. The state's decision was appealed to the United States Supreme Court.

In the Cruzan case, the U. S. Supreme Court ruled that the right to refuse unwanted treatment, even if it is life sustaining, is constitutionally protected. However, the court said that states are justified in requiring that only the patient herself or himself can make a decision to refuse treatment. Because Nancy apparently had not provided a clear expression of her wishes prior to her injury and her ensuing comatose state, Missouri was not bound to honor her parents' request.

A few months later, however, in light of new testimony from several of Nancy's friends that she had expressed her wish "not to live like a vegetable," a Missouri state court ruled that the legal standard of "clear and convincing" evidence of Nancy's wishes had been met, and permission was granted for

A number of years ago, before all the discussion about defining brain death and maintaining life on a respirator and so on, a patient of mine, a young pregnant woman at term, suddenly developed extremely high blood pressure. Then she had a stroke and the baby's heartbeat stopped, so we supported her by artifically maintaining blood pressure and other vital functions, including breathing. But she had had a complete brain death immediately. And she had lost the baby. We got an EEG [electroencephalogram], and it was completely flat. We repeated it twenty-four hours later, and again it was completely flat.

It was the worst tragedy I've ever seen, because in just a few minutes she was gone and the baby was gone—just within moments. I talked with her husband, her mother, and her father. (Now, this was long before the issues surrounding definition of death had become so contentious that the lawyers got involved.) I told them that the thing to do was turn off the machine. Just as I had not read about all this, they as a family had not read about it. It seemed quite logical to me.

So we picked a time when we were going to do it, and they all came and waited outside the door. I told them again what I was going to do, and they said to go ahead and do it. I went in and turned off the machine. The nurse and I watched her, and in five minutes her pulse rate had stopped. I think this is the proper way to handle this sort of situation when brain death is involved. I think it has a negative effect to continue life support systems for weeks and months. It was a tragedy, and given the tragedy, what options do you have? Continue the life support system or don't continue it. To me, there's no argument whatsoever to continue the life support system.

Quoted from *Death and Dying: The Physician's Perspective,* a videotape by Elizabeth Bradbury

removal of the feeding tube. Thirteen days later, Nancy Cruzan died. In a statement to the press, her family said: "She showed no sign of discomfort or distress in any way. . . . Knowing Nancy as only a family can, there remains no question that we made the choice she would want." The Cruzan case emphasizes how important it can be to express one's preferences about life-sustaining treatment—preferably in writing—before the need arises. (Advance directives are discussed in Chapter 9.)

Withholding or Withdrawing Treatment

The right of a competent patient to refuse unwanted treatment is now generally established in both law and medical practice. This can mean withholding (not starting) a treatment or withdrawing (stopping) a treatment once it has been started. The consensus is that there is no medical or ethical distinction between withholding or withdrawing treatment. The choice to forgo life-sustaining treatment involves refusing treatments that would be expected to extend life. Such treatments include cardiopulmonary resuscitation (CPR), advanced cardiac life support, renal dialysis, nutritional support and hydration, mechanical ventilation, organ transplantation and other surgery, pacemakers, chemotherapy, and antibiotics.[30] The right to refuse treatment

remains constitutionally protected even when a patient is unable to communicate. Although specific requirements vary, all of the states authorize some
type of written advance directive to honor decisions of individuals unable to
speak for themselves, but who have previously recorded their wishes in an
appropriate legal document.

The distinction between "allowing to die" (withholding or withdrawing
treatment) and "helping to die" (actively taking steps to cause a patient's
death) is important in discussions about whether patients have a right to die,
with many ethicists and physicians willing to permit the former but not the
latter. When a treatment that could potentially sustain life is withheld or withdrawn, this practice is sometimes termed *passive euthanasia,* although many
people consider this term a misnomer because it tends to confuse the widely
accepted practice of withholding or withdrawing treatment with the generally
unacceptable and unlawful practice of taking active steps to cause death. It
can be argued that "passive euthanasia" is not euthanasia at all but rather
letting nature take its course. This distinction is sometimes phrased as the
difference between "killing" and "allowing to die" (see Figure 6-1). As you
look at this figure, consider your own attitudes about the various treatment
options that may hasten death.

Assisted Suicide and Active Euthanasia

In contrast to withdrawing or withholding treatment, assisted suicide and
active euthanasia refer to practices that intentionally hasten the death of a
person. Although some ethicists argue that the constitutional basis for the
right to refuse treatment provides the same basis for a right to active euthanasia, this argument has not been accepted by the U.S. Supreme Court nor by
most health care practitioners.[31] Arthur Berger says, "Choosing to die naturally is one thing [but] asking the assistance of others to terminate a life is
quite another."[32] Nevertheless, there appears to be growing public acceptance
of the belief that it is permissible for physicians to assist their patients in
choosing death.[33]

Assisted suicide refers to providing someone with the means to commit
suicide, knowing that the recipient intends to use them to end his or her life.
In *physician-assisted suicide (PAS),* a physician intentionally helps a patient hasten his or her death by providing lethal drugs or other interventions—at the
patient's explicit request—with the understanding that the patient plans to
use them to end his or her life.[34] The patient, not the doctor, administers
the fatal dose. (Legal issues in physician-assisted death are discussed in Chapter 9.)

Unlike physician-assisted suicide, *active euthanasia* involves a deliberate act
to end another person's life. Generally, it is understood as the intentional act
of killing someone who would otherwise suffer from an incurable and painful
disease. An example of active euthanasia is the case of "Debbie," a twenty-year-
old woman with terminal ovarian cancer whose death was hastened by her
physician because he "wanted to help put her out of her misery."[35] It is important to recognize that active euthanasia can be involuntary, nonvoluntary, or
voluntary. Involuntary euthanasia (or involuntary active euthanasia) refers to

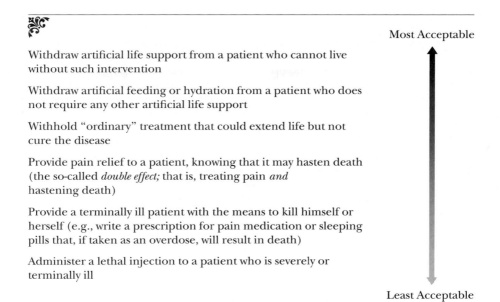

Figure *6-1* *Public Acceptance of Hastening Death*
Note: Involuntary euthanasia occurs when someone acts arbitrarily, without the patient's consent, to end the patient's life.

the death of a patient by a medical practitioner *without* the patient's consent. The most notorious example of this is the medicalized killing programs of the Nazi regime. Nonvoluntary euthanasia occurs when a surrogate decision maker (not the patient himself or herself) asks a physician for assistance to end another person's life.

Voluntary euthanasia (also known as voluntary active euthanasia, or VAE) is the intentional termination of life at the patient's request by someone other than the patient. In practice, this generally means that a competent patient requests direct assistance to die, and he or she receives assistance from a qualified medical practitioner.

At present, active euthanasia has found greatest acceptance in the Netherlands, where physicians are legally permitted to give lethal injections to patients who request death.[36] The guidelines for VAE in the Netherlands include the presence of a terminal diagnosis, the patient's unwavering desire to die, the presence of suffering that the patient finds unbearable, and a second medical opinion. Voluntary active euthanasia is currently unlawful in the United States. Taking active steps to end someone's life is a crime—even if the motive for doing so results from good intentions as an act of mercy.

Palliative Care and the Right to Die

Many people believe that the movement toward public acceptance of physician-assisted suicide and active euthanasia is due to lack of attention to the

When I was a junior physician in a hospital, we were once called urgently to the bedside of a lady of ninety. The nurse had used the term "cardiac arrest"—the old lady's heart had stopped (as hearts are apt to do, around ninety!). But because the cardiac arrest alarm was raised, I and the other houseman launched into a full-scale resuscitation. With violent drugs injected directly into the heart, blasts of electric current through her chest, noise and chaos, she had anything but a peaceful death. On reflection we realized that all this had been inappropriate, but nothing in our medical student training gave us any guide. Indeed once the emergency is in the air, there is not time to weigh up the pros and cons. The decision is rarely a doctor's anyway, because usually the only person on the scene when an emergency occurs is a nurse—probably a relatively junior one if it is night time—and she decides whether or not to resuscitate. Needless to say, it is a very courageous nurse who decides not to. Once things have started, it is very difficult for the doctor when he arrives to stop everything, particularly if the patient is showing signs of reviving.

Richard Lamerton, *Care of the Dying*

needs of the dying, particularly with respect to relieving pain and suffering at the end of life. Decisions about prolonging life or hastening death are regularly arrived at on the basis of the pain and suffering experienced by the patient or perceived by caregivers and family members. In thinking about our options, we need to recognize that a "one size fits all" approach to medical treatment and decision making is likely to fit relatively few. Our preferences about these matters are influenced by both our individual beliefs and the cultural or ethnic traditions that help define who we are as human beings.[37]

David Roy, director of the Center for Bioethics in Montreal and editor of the *Journal of Palliative Care,* argues that the distinction between allowing to die and active euthanasia should be maintained: "This distinction is a recognition of the limits of modern medicine's power, and of the limits of the medical profession's mandate; a recognition also that horrible and intolerable abuse is as much a possibility for us today as it has already proved to be a reality in the past."[38] The challenge, Roy says, is not to legalize euthanasia, but to transform care of the dying. Dame Cicely Saunders, founder of St. Christopher's Hospice, says

> We certainly cannot be complacent as we look at the pressures in hospital wards and nursing care facilities, the lack of community support for many in their own homes, and the frequently indifferent or negative attitudes toward the increasing number of elderly people. But surely this is the very climate in which euthanasia would not remain voluntary for long! Is there a society that will not exert pressure, however subtle, on the dependent to believe they are merely burdens with the responsibility to opt out or for exhausted care providers to beg or to act for their joint release?[39]

Proponents of euthanasia argue that it is morally permissible when it prevents an even greater cruelty—namely, preventing a person who is in unremitting pain or suffering from obtaining the release offered by death. Critics respond that, if euthanasia did become a routine policy, it is likely to create significant ethical problems. How will physicians and others make sure that a patient has given his or her clear consent to a hastened death? What about the risk of an erroneous diagnosis? Objections to euthanasia also take the form of the "wedge" or "slippery slope" argument: One should not permit acts that, even if moral in themselves, would pave the way for subsequent acts that would be immoral. If euthanasia is permitted for people with incurable illness, it could be expanded to the aged, the mentally incompetent, the severely handicapped, or other "burdens on society," with the result that such acts become motivated by caprice or whim, or darker motives.

Charles Dougherty argues that questions about taking steps to intentionally hasten death should be placed within the context of society's "common good."[40] Excessive emphasis on individual choice can cause us to lose sight of the fact that no aspect of human experience is wholly personal and private. In fact, says Dougherty, "The way we die—when, under what circumstances, and from what cause or reason—is shaped in profound ways by relationships with others and by large social and institutional forces." If dying in the medical setting is accurately characterized as involving pain and suffering, and costs too much, the common good of society could be served best by taking measures that "add simplicity and dignity to the process of dying and contain unnecessary spending." Dougherty suggests that practical steps toward realizing this common good include:

1. Increasing the use of home hospice care
2. Developing strategies for more aggressive pain management
3. Refining protocols for timely diagnosis of terminal illness
4. Making the right to refuse extraordinary care universally available to patients
5. Expanding the use of DNR orders to avoid prolonged, expensive, and unnecessary care at the end of life
6. Providing universal access to an appropriate combination of care options (home, hospice, and so on)
7. Instituting a health insurance system that ensures adequate and appropriate care for everyone

Nutrition and Hydration

The right of a competent patient to refuse unwanted treatment is generally established in both law and medicine. But should an exception be made for artificial nutrition and hydration? Answering this question requires examining the distinction between ordinary and extraordinary care. *Ordinary care* is generally defined as the use of conventional, proven therapies. In contrast, *extraordinary measures* usually involve some kind of life-sustaining intervention. Such measures are usually done as a temporary measure until the patient's own restorative powers allow the resumption of normal biological functioning.

Of course, therapies that are usually considered "ordinary" may be "extraordinary," or even intrusive, depending on the circumstances. Using antibiotics to treat pneumonia, a practice that generally fits into the category of ordinary care, may be viewed as extraordinary when such drugs are administered to a person who is actively dying. The distinction between ordinary and extraordinary therapies also becomes blurred in situations where a series of medical interventions, each one in itself "ordinary," combine in such a way that the net result is an "extraordinary" effort to sustain life. Although some argue that a clear dividing line is needed between ordinary and extraordinary treatment, Thomas Attig makes the point that, in reality, it is likely that "a definitive rule dividing ordinary and extraordinary treatment will forever elude us."[41]

Removing artificial nutrition and hydration tends to evoke deep-rooted human feelings about the provision of food and drink, as well as the image of "starving" a person to death. This causes some people to believe that removal of artificial nutrition and hydration is really intentional killing. The symbolic significance of nourishment seems to justify the continuation of artificial nourishment even when all other medical treatments have been stopped.

Those who disagree with this view argue that our normal, everyday sentiments about the symbolic meaning of food and water "cannot be transferred without distortion to the hospital world," and that, indeed, "authentic sentiment may demand discontinuance of artificial feeding."[42] Because we think of nourishment as ordinary care, withholding such nourishment brings up im-

© Carol A. Foote

Assistance in providing nutrition to chronically ill and dying patients ranges from help with eating, as seen here in the case of these nursing home residents, to total reliance on artificial feeding. The issue of artificially providing nutrition to comatose, hopelessly ill patients is one of the newest ethical issues in medicine.

ages of causing the patient's death by starvation.[43] But these images may be inaccurate for several reasons. First, the invasive nature of delivering such nourishment, and the skills required to administer it, argue against the perception that artificial nourishment is merely providing simple care. Second, artificial nourishment causes discomfort to many patients, especially those who are close to dying. Feeding tubes and intravenous lines may actually add to a patient's suffering at the end of life. Acknowledging that issues around providing nourishment are highly charged emotionally, Dena Davis says, "We need to be very careful to sort out the physiological aspects of providing nutrition from the social phenomenon of 'feeding.'"[44] When a person is actively dying, the removal of artificial nutrition and hydration can actually be good palliative care.

Seriously Ill Newborns

Ethical issues that focus on the dilemma of whether to sustain life or to allow death are perhaps most sensitively realized in the case of seriously ill newborns. In hospitals with specialized neonatal intensive care units (NICUs), the lives of newborns who are born prematurely or with other serious medical problems are saved routinely. Unfortunately, some babies whose lives are spared will never be capable of living what most people consider a normal human life. These infants suffer from cardiopulmonary ailments, brain damage, or other serious congenital dysfunction. In the past, such conditions would have quickly resulted in death. Now, because of highly specialized neonatal care, babies born with life-threatening conditions often survive.

These medical miracles raise questions, however. In saving seriously ill newborns, should the infant's probable quality of life be considered? Is medical intervention the best or right course of action in every case? For example, should a newborn with an intestinal blockage be spared by surgical intervention? Is the answer always "Yes, life should be saved," or does the answer change according to circumstances? Is the answer the same if the infant with intestinal blockage is also severely brain-damaged?

Consider the following case: An infant was born with his entire left side malformed, with no left eye and very little of a left ear; his left hand was deformed, and some of his vertebrae were not fused. Also afflicted with a tracheo-esophageal fistula (an abnormality of the windpipe and the canal that leads to the stomach), he could not be fed by mouth. Air leaked into his stomach instead of going to the lungs, and fluid from the stomach pushed up into the lungs. One doctor commented, "It takes little imagination to think there were further internal difficulties as well." In the ensuing days, the infant's condition steadily worsened. Pneumonia set in; his reflexes became impaired; and, because of poor circulation, severe brain damage was suspected. But despite the seriousness of all these factors taken together, the immediate threat to his survival, the tracheo-esophageal fistula, could be corrected by a fairly easy surgical procedure. The debate began when the parents refused to give their consent to surgery. Some of the doctors treating the child believed that surgery was warranted and took the case to court. The judge ordered the surgery, ruling that "at the moment of live birth, there exists a human being entitled to the fullest protection of the law."[45]

In another case, which provides some contrasts to the one just cited, the mother of a premature baby overheard the doctor describing her infant as having Down's syndrome, with the added complication that the intestines were blocked. This kind of blockage can be corrected by ordinary surgery; without correction, the child could not be fed and would die. The mother felt that "it would be unfair" to her other children if a retarded child were brought into the home. Her husband supported this decision, and they refused their consent for surgery.

One of the physicians argued that the degree of mental retardation in children with Down's syndrome cannot be predicted; and, in the physician's words: "They're almost always trainable. They can hold simple jobs, and they're famous for being happy children. They're perennially happy and usually a great joy. When further complications do not appear, a long life can be anticipated." However, in this case, the hospital staff did not seek a court order to override the parents' decision against surgical intervention. As a result, the child was placed in a side room and, over the following eleven days, starved to death.

Think about the differences between these two cases. In the first case, the severely malformed infant seemed to have less chance of survival or of living a normal life than the afflicted infant in the second example. Yet, the hospital staff in the first case chose to seek a court order granting treatment, whereas the staff at the second hospital chose to abide by the parents' wishes, even though the child could probably have been saved. In the second case, did the physicians and the parents adequately explore the child's right to life? From the doctors' point of view, once the decision was made not to proceed with the operation, the child became terminal, and further means of sustaining life were therefore unwarranted. It could be argued, however, that the withholding of ordinary means of treatment (that is, surgery) was in fact an *extraordinary* nonintervention.

Whatever our feelings about the decisions described, a distinction between ethical issues involving infants and those involving adults should be noted. Generally, in the latter case, all procedures that might prolong life have been tried, or at least presented to the patient as options. In cases involving newborns, the question of whether to treat or withhold treatment cannot be discussed with the patient; thus, the decision is made by others, who will, it is hoped, act in the child's best interest. The tough part, of course, is defining "the child's best interest."[46]

The hard choices inherent in making decisions about the treatment of seriously ill newborns were highlighted in the study by the President's Commission for the Study of Ethical Problems in Medicine. While affirming that parents should have the power of decision making in most cases, the Commission also stated that medical institutions should pursue the best interests of an infant "when those interests are clear."[47] Using the example of an otherwise healthy Down's syndrome child whose life is threatened by a surgically correctable condition, the Commission said that such an infant should receive surgery because he or she would benefit. While stating that therapies expected to be futile need not be provided, the Commission added that, even in cases when no beneficial therapy is available, actions should be taken to ensure the infant's comfort.

Organ Transplantation and Organ Donation

One of the most dramatic medical techniques for saving patients who were once considered hopelessly ill is organ transplantation, which is defined as "the transfer of living tissues or cells from a donor to a recipient, with the intention of maintaining the functional integrity of the transplanted tissue in the recipient."[48] In the years since the first kidney transplant, from one identical twin to another, in 1954 at Peter Bent Brigham Hospital in Boston, organ transplantation has become part of standard medical practice. Public interest in organ transplantation grew more widespread in 1967, when Christiaan Barnard accomplished the first successful adult heart transplant. Other noteworthy events in the history of transplantation include agreement on the definition of brain death in 1968 and discovery of the immunosuppressive drug cyclosporine in 1976.[49] The acceptance of transplantation is indicated by an increasing number of patients on waiting lists for transplants involving the heart, kidney, liver, pancreas, and lung. Much of the current success of organ transplantation is due to newer immunosuppressants, better patient selection, and earlier intervention, as well as better understanding of the issues related to histocompatibility, the ability of tissues to accept a transplant from a different individual without rejecting it. Rejection is still the greatest obstacle to transplantation, although this barrier is falling as medical science learns more about the body's immune response.[50]

The ideal candidate for a transplant is a patient whose condition is deteriorating despite the best conventional medical treatment available and for whom a transplant offers a reasonable likelihood of recovery—in other words, someone who is likely to die without an organ transplant. Once a prospective recipient is certified as physically suitable for a transplant, other factors are considered. Emotional stability, age, and ability to deal with stress influence the chances of achieving a successful outcome. Because not enough organs are donated to meet the demand, physicians are "gatekeepers" in choosing among prospective recipients.

For some organ transplants, the donor is a living person; sometimes donor and recipient are members of the same family. When a living donor is unavailable, or when the needed organ—a heart, for example—cannot be taken from a living human being, organs are harvested from the body of a person who has been declared dead. Donated organs may come from a person who agreed before his or her death to allow organs to be taken for transplantation, or the deceased's next of kin may give permission. Organs are kept viable for transplantation by sustaining physiological functions in the body of a person who has been declared dead.

A scarcity of human organs for transplantation has led to research into *xenotransplantation,* the use of animals—including baboons, chimpanzees, and pigs—as sources for needed organs. The main technical difficulty in such

At the Stanford University Medical Center, Dr. Norman Shumway and his colleagues perform open-heart surgery. Advances in transplantation procedures and related medical therapies make such operations more feasible, yet they also raise questions that are difficult, at times quite painful, to resolve.

T A B L E 6-1 *Major Provisions of the Uniform Anatomical Gift Act*

1. Any person over eighteen may donate all or part of his or her body for education, research, therapeutic, or transplantation purposes.
2. If the person has not made a donation before death, the next of kin can make it unless there was a known objection by the deceased.
3. If the person has made such a gift, it cannot be revoked by his or her relatives.
4. If there is more than one person of the same degree of kinship, the gift from relatives shall not be accepted if there is a known objection by one of them.
5. The gift can be authorized by a card carried by the individual or by written or recorded verbal communication from a relative.
6. The gift can be amended or revoked at any time before the death of the donor.
7. The time of death must be determined by a physician who is not involved in any transplantation.

cross-species transplants, as with transplantation generally, is rejection of donor tissue by the recipient's immune system. Genetically engineered "transgenic animals" may circumvent this problem. The goal of substituting xenotransplants for human organs may not be achieved for years, if at all, but scientists believe a more limited objective of transplanting isolated cells and tissues is on the near horizon of medical practice.[51]

The Uniform Anatomical Gift Act, approved in 1968 by the National Conference of Commissions on Uniform State Laws and enacted in some form in all fifty states, provides for the donation of the body or specific body parts upon the death of the donor.[52] The main provisions of the Gift Act are presented in Table 6-1. Due to a chronic shortage of donated organs, the Gift Act was revised in 1987 to simplify organ donation by removing requirements that the next of kin give consent and that the document be witnessed. This revision also included a "required request" provision that requires hospitals to have procedures that encourage organ donations. Near the time of death, hospital personnel must ask if the patient agreed to be an organ donor; and, if not, the family must be informed about the option to donate organs and tissues.

Organ donations can be made by completing a form such as the uniform donor card (see Figure 6-2). A donor may specify that *any* needed organs or body parts may be taken or that only certain body parts or organs are to be harvested. Besides specifying how one's body may be used after death, the donor may also specify the final disposition of his or her remains once the donation has been effected. Although not legally required, most hospitals obtain consent from the donor's next of kin. Hospitals are unlikely to insist on organ donation if relatives disagree with the deceased's wishes. Thus, plans for organ donation should be discussed with family members.[53]

In 1984, the U.S. Congress enacted the National Organ Transplant Act, which instituted a central office to help match donated organs with potential recipients. The United Network for Organ Sharing (UNOS), under a contract with the federal government, maintains lists of people waiting for transplants and tracks the status of all donated organs to ensure both the fairness of

DONOR

STATE OF CALIFORNIA
DMV
DEPARTMENT OF MOTOR VEHICLES

Pursuant to the Uniform Anatomical Gift Act.
I hereby give, effective upon my death:
A ____ Any needed organ or parts
B ____ Parts or organs listed ____________

____

____
Signature of Donor

____
DL-290 (REV 10/86) DATE

DETACH HERE

To pledge a donation, fill out this card. Remove "DONOR" dot and affix it on the front of your license or I.D. card as shown in the diagram. Affix the card on the reverse of your license or I.D. card. If you change your mind, peel off the card and the dot. Whole Body donations require separate arrangements.
If you are unable to sign, instruct two witnesses to sign this card in your presence.

DMV CALIFORNIA
Driver License
DONOR DOT

NOTICE

If you are at least 18, you may designate on your driver license or I.D. card a donation of any needed organs or tissues for medical transplantation. Under the Uniform Anatomical Gift Act (Sec. 7150, Health & Safety Code) donation takes effect upon your death.
NEXT OF KIN (OPTIONAL)

NAME ____________________

ADDRESS ____________________

TELEPHONE NO. ____________________

DETACH HERE

Additional information regarding the Donor program may be obtained by writing or calling The Gift of Life:

National Kidney Foundation of Southern California
6820 La Tijera Blvd., Suite 111
Los Angeles, CA 90045
(213) 641-5245

3430 Fifth Ave., Suite C
San Diego, CA 92103
(619) 297-2470

National Kidney Foundation of Northern California
856 Stanton Road
Burlingame, CA 94010
(415) 697-0110

Figure 6-2 *Donor Card*
Source: California Department of Motor Vehicles.

distribution and the competence of medical centers where organ transplants are performed.

Each day about 60 people receive an organ transplant while another 16 people on the waiting list die because not enough organs are available.[54] Because many patients are waiting for donated organs, and some die while waiting, questions have been raised about the voluntary approach embedded in the Uniform Anatomical Gift Act. One suggested answer involves changing the law so that it would *require* organ donation except when an individual specifically "opts out" by signing an objection on his or her driver's license or other designated document. This suggestion is based on the idea that donating one's organs after death is a moral duty.

Another suggestion would make commerce in human organs legal. A human body is a valuable resource. Under provisions of the National Organ Transplant Act, it is illegal to buy or sell human organs and tissues (except blood). If this suggestion were adopted, however, a person's heirs might earn money through selling the deceased's vital organs. It is possible to imagine a "futures market" in human organs, as prices fluctuate according to supply and demand. As a result of market forces, proponents of this plan argue, shortages or surpluses would be eliminated. In some countries, there is already an active

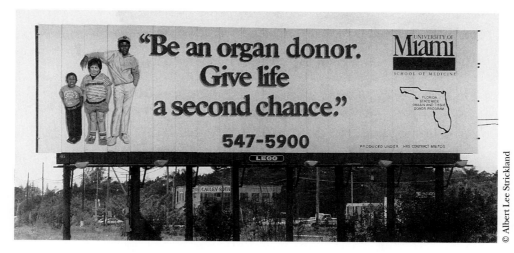

Designed to increase public awareness of organ donation, this billboard on a Florida highway calls particular attention to donations that can save the lives of children.

"black market" in transplantable organs (notably kidneys). Generally, however, the present consensus is that commercialization is not "ethically preferable to the gift model of organ donation."[55]

Many transplanted organs are taken from donors who are declared legally dead but whose heartbeat and respiration are maintained artificially until organs to be donated and transplanted are removed. Two issues are critical in such cases: (1) determining when death occurs, and (2) deciding when it is permissible to remove the deceased's organs for transplantation. The advent of organ transplantation has been an impetus for developing a new definition of death. Once a person is placed on a device that artificially sustains his or her vital functions, a number of complex medical, legal, and ethical questions impinge on how death is defined.

Defining Death

On the face of it, the definition of death might seem obvious: A person dies, is dead, and the corpse is disposed of. But as soon as someone asks, "What do you mean by 'a person dies'?" this definition begins to unravel. What at first seems simple turns out to be quite complex. Indeed, there are historical accounts of people being thought dead who, in fact, were in a state that only mimicked biological death. A state of unconsciousness or an extreme slowing of body functions may cause the appearance of death. As a safeguard against the threat of being buried alive, people in earlier times sometimes arranged for their bodies to be placed in coffins with bells or some other attention-getting device that the "corpse" could activate after burial should consciousness return after a mistaken determination of death (see Figure 6-3).

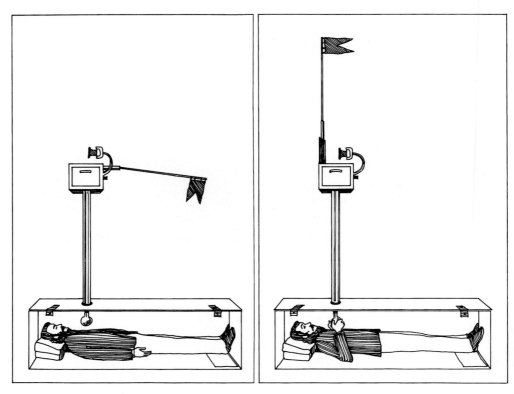

Figure 6-3 *Coffin Bell-Pull Device*
To prevent premature burial in cases of doubtful death, devices such as this French "life-preserving" coffin were invented and patented. If activated, the box above the ground opened to let in air and light, the flag raised, a bell rang, and a light came on to signal that the buried person was still alive. The person who had been mistaken for dead could also call out, and his or her voice would be amplified by the device. The fear of being buried alive stemmed from the period of great plagues and epidemics when, in the hasty disposition of the dead, a mistaken determination of death might result from a state of illness that only mimicked death.

Think for a moment. When would you consider yourself to be dead? How would you know that death had occurred in someone else? The answers to these questions range from the definite ("when decay and putrefaction have set in") to the subtler ("when I can no longer take care of myself"). A person using the first method for making a determination of death would hardly be pleased to be judged dead by the standards of the second.

The present concern with defining death is, of course, more sophisticated, taking into account scientific data. Although we still determine when death has occurred by observing certain signs that life has ceased, these signs can be interpreted differently depending on how death is defined. In other words, our definition of death establishes the criteria to be used in determining that a person has died. We can distinguish five steps in the process of making decisions about the death of a human being:[56]

1. Establish a conceptual understanding of what constitutes death—that is, a *definition of death.*
2. Decide upon the *criteria and procedures that will be used in making a determination* that death has occurred.
3. Apply these criteria and procedures *in a particular case* to determine if a person's condition meets the criteria.
4. If the criteria are met, the person is *pronounced dead.*
5. Attest the person's death on *a certificate of record*

Conventional Signs of Death and New Technology

Historically, the death of the human organism has been determined by the absence of heartbeat and breathing. With the cessation of these vital signs, and as the cells and tissues of the body die, advanced signs of death become evident: the lack of certain reflexes in the eyes, the fall of body temperature (algor mortis), the purple-red discoloration of parts of the body as blood settles (livor mortis), and the rigidity of muscles (rigor mortis). Most deaths are determined by the absence of vital signs.

However, when respirators and other life-support systems are used to artificially sustain vital physiological processes, the conventional means of determining death are inadequate. Using the traditional criteria, a patient in an irreversible coma with no brain wave activity could be termed alive on the basis of *artificially* maintained breathing and heartbeat. Thus has developed the concept of "brain death" to determine whether a person is alive or dead when the conventional vital signs are ambiguous because of supportive medical technology.

Medical practitioners have adopted a definition of death that equates it with irreversible coma, as determined by a flat electroencephalogram (EEG) reading. Confirmatory signs of irreversible or terminal coma include lack of response to all external stimuli and lack of any sign of normal reflexes controlled by the brain stem or spinal cord. (When a comatose state persists longer than a month or so, it is described as a "persistent vegetative state" [PVS] and is usually considered irreversible.[57]) Rather than replacing the conventional clinical criteria for determining death—pulse, heartbeat, and respiration—the criteria for "brain death" supplement them.

In contrast to *clinical death,* which is determined by either the cessation of heartbeat and breathing or the criteria for establishing brain death, *cellular death* refers to a gradual process that results when heartbeat, respiration, and brain activity cease. When a person's breathing and heartbeat ceases temporarily, as during certain surgical procedures, it is possible to say that he or she was "clinically dead." When a cessation of vital functions is reversible, however, it is really imprecise or unwarranted to term such a cessation "clinical death."

Cellular death encompasses the breakdown of metabolic processes and results in complete nonfunctionality at the cellular level. Living cells require a continuous input of energy; without it, they degrade into a nonliving collection of molecules. Without oxygen, cells vary in their survival potential. The cells of skin and connective tissues may survive for several hours; the neurons of the brain last only five to eight minutes. When there is a loss of neurons in the midbrain and medulla, the brain center that controls breathing is destroyed; the death of neurons in the cerebral cortex destroys intellectual capacity. Cellular death is an irreversible process of deterioration in the body's systems and organs. The breakdown of these processes, the sum of which is life, causes a loss of organic functions—that is, death. As cellular death progresses, such phenomena as algor mortis, livor mortis, and rigor mortis can be observed in the body. In a biological sense, therefore, death can be defined as the cessation of life due to irreversible changes in cell metabolism.

Modern medicine now makes it possible to manipulate the dying process in such a way that some parts of the body stop functioning while other parts can be artificially maintained. Thus, cell death may affect some organs of the body, causing irreversible breakdown, while other organs of the body are still functioning. The capacity of modern medicine to alter the natural sequence and process of cellular death has created a need to rethink how death is defined and institute new procedures for determining when death has occurred.

Conceptual and Empirical Criteria

What is death? How can it be determined that a person has died? These questions, though closely related, involve separate issues that must be distinguished. Robert Veatch outlines four levels that must be addressed in our inquiry concerning the definition and determination of death.[58] The first level involves formally defining *death*. Essentially, this is a conceptual or philosophical endeavor. According to Veatch, "Death means a complete change in the status of a living entity characterized by the irreversible loss of those characteristics that are essentially significant to it." Although this definition may sound rather abstract on first reading, it is really quite precise. It encompasses the deaths not only of human beings, but also of nonhuman animals, plants, cells, and indeed can even be understood metaphorically as applying to a social phenomenon such as the organization of a society or culture.

To flesh out this definition, we must turn to Veatch's second level of inquiry, again a conceptual or philosophical question: What is so essentially significant about life that its loss is termed *death*? Some possible answers include the flow of vital bodily fluids (breath and blood, for example), the soul, and, in more recent definitions, consciousness. Each of these possible answers will be examined more closely in a moment.

The third level that Veatch distinguishes has to do with the *locus* of death: Where in the organism should one look to determine whether death has occurred? This question moves us from the conceptual realm to an empirical inquiry—that is, one based on observation or experience. Notice, however, that the answer to this question depends on the conceptual understanding used to define death.

Veatch's fourth level deals with the following question: What technical tests must be applied at the locus of death to determine if an individual is living or dead?

So, to recap these levels of inquiry: Step one involves formally defining death. Step two adds further content to the definition by pinpointing the significant difference between life and death. Step three locates where one should look for signs of this significant change. And step four gives us some tests, or a set of criteria, that can be used to finally determine whether an organism is alive or dead. With this process firmly in mind, we now have the tools to examine four different approaches to the definition and determination of death.

Four Approaches to the Definition and Determination of Death

All four of the following approaches to defining and determining death begin with the formal definition of death given by Veatch: "Death means a complete change in the status of a living entity characterized by the irreversible loss of those characteristics that are essentially significant to it." From that shared beginning, however, each approach wends its own way through subsequent levels of inquiry. As you'll see, each of these approaches relates death to a loss: the first, of the flow of vital fluids; the second, of the soul by the body; the third, of the capacity for bodily integration; the fourth, of the capacity for social interaction. In considering the merits of the various approaches, notice how death is determined according to the way it is defined.

Irreversible Loss of Flow of Vital Fluids

The first approach pertains to the cessation of the flow of vital bodily fluids. With this conceptual understanding of death, one looks to the heart, blood vessels, lungs, and respiratory tract as the locus of death. To determine whether an individual is alive or dead, one would observe the breathing, feel the pulse, and listen to the heartbeat. The more sophisticated modern methods of electrocardiogram and direct measurement of oxygen and carbon dioxide levels in the blood can be added to these traditional tests because they focus on the same loci and criteria for determining death.

This approach to defining death is adequate for making a determination of death in most cases, even today. When vital functions are artificially sustained by machines, however, no clear determination of death can be made by this definition. For instance, a patient is connected to a heart–lung machine that keeps the vital fluids of blood and breath flowing through the body. According to this definition, the patient is alive. If the patient is disconnected from the machine, these vital functions cease and, by this definition, the patient is dead. Yet during open-heart surgery, these circulatory systems are interrupted, making it possible to consider the patient clinically dead under this definition. But we know the patient is not dead because such temporary cessation is simply part of the surgical procedure.

The ambiguity of this first approach to defining death results from defining death on the basis of physiological criteria that, although intimately related to life processes, do not seem to constitute the most significant criteria for identifying human life.

Irreversible Loss of the Soul from the Body

In the second approach to defining death—one used in many cultures worldwide and from time immemorial—the criterion is the presence or absence of the soul in the body. Within this framework, as long as the soul is present, the person is alive; when the soul leaves, the body dies. Indeed, some traditions define death in precisely this way. The *Tibetan Book of the Dead,* for example, presents the view that life is terminated in a series of gradual steps, from a state of life to the state we call death. Christian theologians and other religious ethicists also grapple with this question.

This second conceptual definition of death, then, involves the irreversible loss of the soul from the body. The locus of the soul has not been scientifically established (nor has its existence), although some believe the soul is related to the breath or the heart, or perhaps, as seventeenth-century philosopher René Descartes believed, to the pineal body, a small protrusion from the center of the brain. For those who hold this concept, the criteria for determining death would presumably involve some means of ascertaining death at the particular locus where the soul is thought to reside. For example, if the soul is thought to be coincident with the breath, then absence of breath would indicate the loss of the soul and, hence, death. In a study conducted in 1907, dying people were placed on a very sensitive scale to determine whether any weight loss occurs at the moment of death. Researchers noted a loss, averaging from 1 to 2 ounces, leading to speculations about whether the loss indicated the departure of the soul from the body at death.[59]

To most people living in modern, urban-technological societies, in which secular beliefs are prominent, this approach to defining death is simply not relevant. Our first difficulty would be to adequately define the soul. And even if this difficulty could be surmounted, we would need some way to ascertain whether the soul was present or absent at a given time. Moreover, this definition of death forces an examination of whether death occurs because the soul departs from the body, or, conversely, whether the soul departs from the body because death has occurred. In other words, does the soul "animate" the body, giving it life, or do the physiological processes of vitality in the body provide a vessel wherein the soul resides? Such questions may elicit fascinating speculations, but they bear little relevance to the dilemmas posed by modern medical practice in a scientific age.

Irreversible Loss of the Capacity for Bodily Integration

In the third approach, death can be defined as the irreversible loss of the capacity for bodily integration. This approach is more sophisticated than the first because it refers not simply to the traditional physiological signs of vitality in the body (the flow of breath and blood), but to the more generalized capability of the body to regulate its own functioning. The approach recognizes the fact that a human being is an integrated organism with capacities for internal regulation through complex homeostatic feedback mechanisms.

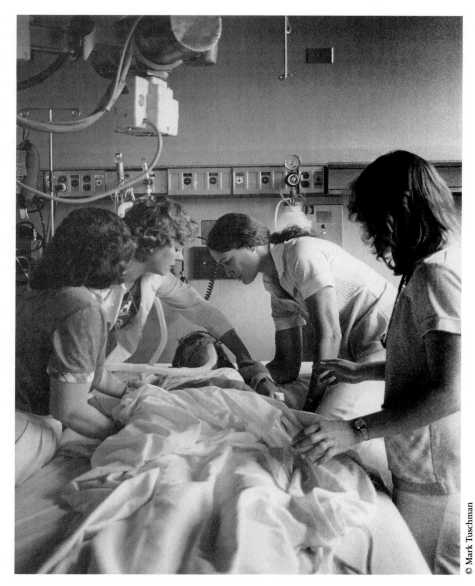

© Mark Tuschman

In the intensive care unit, both human and technical considerations combine to make necessary the evaluation of ethical questions regarding the meaning of life and death.

This definition at least partly resolves the ambiguity of the first definition, for a determination of death would not be made merely because a person's physiological functioning was being maintained by a machine. Rather, a determination of death could be made when the organism itself was no longer capable of bodily integration. In other words, artificial life support would not constitute the determining factor; rather, only with the irreversible loss of the capacity for bodily integration could there be a determination of death. The locus for such a determination is currently considered by clinicians to be the central nervous system—more specifically, the brain. The determination of death that results from this definition is often characterized as "brain death" (although this term is possibly misleading because it focuses attention on the death of a part of the organism, not the whole organism).

According to the standards published in 1968 by the Harvard Medical School Ad Hoc Committee to Examine the Definition of Brain Death, "brain death" involves four essential criteria for brain death: (1) lack of receptivity and response to external stimuli; (2) absence of spontaneous muscular movement and spontaneous breathing; (3) absence of observable reflexes, including brain and spinal reflexes; and (4) absence of brain activity, as signified by a flat electroencephalogram (EEG). The Harvard criteria require a second set of tests to be performed after twenty-four hours have elapsed, and they exclude cases of hypothermia (body temperature below 90 degrees Fahrenheit) as well as situations involving central nervous system depressants such as barbiturates. Notice that these criteria incorporate the traditional means of determining death—absence of heartbeat and blood flow. Procedures for applying these criteria, also known as the "whole-brain" definition of death, have been widely adopted for cases in which the traditional means of determining death are inconclusive.

Recently, evidence has been accumulating that the current tests for "brain death" do not truly meet all of the criteria; specifically, varying amounts and kinds of brain function have been found in those diagnosed as brain dead by the standard tests, suggesting that "permanent cessation of functioning of the entire brain" is not met by those standard tests. Some medical practitioners and ethicists are advocating a return to the older cardiorespiratory death as the definition of death.[60] This suggestion is problematic, however, because organ donation would then become a form of legally sanctioned killing.

Irreversible Loss of the Capacity for Consciousness or Social Interaction

Although the Harvard criteria have gained wide acceptance in clinical settings, some argue that they fail to specify what is *significant* about human life. Veatch, for example, says that it is the higher functions of the brain—not merely reflex networks that regulate such physiological processes as blood pressure and respiration—that define the essential characteristics of a human being. Thus, the fourth approach to defining death emphasizes the capacity for consciousness and social interaction. The implicit premise of this approach is that for a person to be fully human, not only must certain biological processes operate, but the social dimension of life—consciousness or personhood—must be present. Being alive implies the capacity for conscious interaction with one's environment and with other human beings. According to this definition, when the capacity for social interaction is irreversibly lost, a determination of death would follow.

Using this approach, where should one look to determine whether an individual is alive or dead? Current scientific evidence points to the neocortex, the outer surface of the brain, where processes essential to consciousness and social interaction are located. If this supposition is correct, the EEG alone would provide an adequate measure for determining death.

In the theoretical debate regarding how death should be defined, this fourth approach is known as a "higher-brain" theory, in contrast with the "whole-brain" theory advocated by those who define death as the irreversible loss of function of the organism as a whole. As Karen Gervais points out, "By emphasizing the brain's integrating role in the human organism, the whole-brain theory of death reduces to a lower-brain theory of death."[61] In Gervais's view, "it is loss of consciousness and not loss of biological functioning that should determine when human life is over." According to the so-called higher-brain theory, the death of a *person* is synonymous with the death of a human being. In commenting on the search for a more precise definition of human death, Gervais concludes that we are left with a basic choice about the definition of human life—namely, whether we consider a human being as an *organism* or as a *person*.

Robert Veatch points out that the current whole-brain definition establishes a view of what is *essential* to being alive that is not shared by all ethnic or religious groups.[62] In a pluralistic society, therefore, individuals with conflicting beliefs should perhaps have the right to "opt out" of having a whole-brain definition of death apply to them. Clearly, then, although the Harvard criteria for establishing brain death have been practiced in clinical settings for more than thirty years, questions about how death should be defined are far from completely settled.

Medical Ethics: A Cross-Cultural Example

In Japan, ethical, moral, and legal questions involving brain death and organ transplantation have been matters of public controversy for three decades.[63] Debate began in 1968, when Japanese surgeon Dr. Jurō Wada performed the world's second heart transplant using an organ from a brain-dead donor. Initially hailed for his scientific achievement, Wada was soon subjected to intense questioning about mismanagement of the procedure and alleged disregard for the rights of both donor and recipient. He was accused of illegal human experimentation and of poor judgment in the manner in which he made a determination of the donor's death. At the time, the criteria for establishing brain death were quite new, and no public consensus existed in Japan concerning this new definition of death. The Wada case left a legacy of mistrust about brain death and transplantation in Japan.

Among technologically advanced countries, Japan is unique in its reliance on living donors. Recent statistics indicate that, in Japan, about 70 percent of transplanted kidneys and liver segments are taken from live donors, an almost mirror image of the situation in the United States, where most such organs are harvested from brain-dead donors. Although most scientific and technological advances have been eagerly adopted in Japan, persistent questions about brain death have resulted in a reluctance to actively pursue organ transplantation. Only in 1997 did Japan pass an Organ Transplant Law that legalizes organ procurement from brain-dead donors. Even with passage of this law, however, sixteen months elapsed before the first *legal* heart and liver transplantation was performed using organs from a brain-dead donor.

Japan's debate regarding brain death and organ transplantation illustrates how culture influences attitudes and practices related to dying and death. Although the circumstances surrounding the Wada case have had a lingering effect, a sense of mistrust between physicians and patients has long been prevalent in Japan. Until quite recently, most physicians practiced a kind of "closed door" medicine in which patients were neither given information about their health nor permitted to criticize their physicians. In the Japanese medical system, the consensus has been that patients should leave their decision making to others. To many people in Japan, this kind of paternalism is especially worrisome in the context of transplantation procedures. It is feared that, in determining brain death, doctors might give no information to family members and perhaps even lie to them. People also worry that the criteria for brain death may be applied too readily. There is widespread feeling that the definition of brain death is such a critical issue that it should not be decided solely by physicians. In addition, long-term mistrust raises concerns that a market for organs could provoke abuses by physicians.

Traditional beliefs about death may have an even more important influence on Japanese attitudes about brain death and transplantation. In Japan, death has been traditionally viewed as a social process, not a medically determined phenomenon. The respect shown to ancestors through various practices attests to an extended process of social death. Physicians may alter the conventional definition of death, but the persistence of traditional views reveals diverse opinions about the meaning of death.

Many Japanese are concerned about keeping the body intact, not only during life but also after death. The body is viewed as a gift from one's parents, one's ancestors. Removal of organs from brain-dead bodies violates the integrity of the body. An aversion to tampering with the corpse of a loved one is related to beliefs that body and soul must be intact as the person goes to the next world. The body must be perfect, or the soul may become unhappy. Organ transplantation is viewed as involving mutilation of the body. Whereas Americans tend to think of body organs as replaceable parts, the Japanese tend to find in every part of a deceased person's body a fragment of his or her mind and spirit. Related to this issue is Japan's historical concern about impurity. From this viewpoint, procedures involved in organ donation and transplantation defile the body. A person considering organ donation may be dissuaded by the notion that, if organs are taken, "My body is no longer mine."

Another important issue has to do with differing cultural ideas about the "seat of the soul" or "center of the self." In Western biomedicine, the brain—the locus of rational thought—tends to occupy the most important place among the various body parts. As the "seat of the mind," it represents the essence of humanness. In other traditions, the heart, not the brain, is considered the seat of life. Equating life with the functioning of the brain is alien to

Knowing What a Human Being Is

Rolling Thunder often repeated, "We do so many unnatural things, we don't know what's natural anymore." One day he and I were sitting on the ground out in the desert. He was describing a young Indian apprentice from another tribe and making designs in the sand with a stick. Suddenly he said, "You people don't even know what a human being is!" I did not see the connection between the subject at hand and that sudden exclamation, but I had learned to understand what he meant by "you people." It was not a judgmental finger-pointing to be taken personally, but a sort of generalized identification to be applied wherever it fit. "You can look right at someone's empty body and think that you're lookin' at the person when they're not even there. Time and time again, you people speed to the scene of an accident, pick up an empty body and take it down the highway at eighty miles an hour, leaving the person miles behind, not knowing what the heck is going on!"

As an example, he then described to me an episode in which he went into the hospital to assist a young lady—a friend of friends—who had been in a head-on collision and was a long time in a coma.

"But the moment I took a good look at the body, I could see she wasn't even there. I had to find her—go get her—and she was way out in the field where the car'd flipped over the cliff, and she was sittin' on a rock. Her friend who was driving was killed. And this one sittin' on the rock, she didn't even know where she was. But, boy, she was determined to stay there. She was totally disoriented. I had to pull her, nearly force her back. Only time we can do that is when we know their own will isn't working—otherwise we always leave it up to their own choice.

"Well, in the early days, most everyone could tell when a person wasn't in their body. That was just natural to see that. That's been lost now, mostly. Only thing I can say is, until you learn to understand these things, you should never, never move an unconscious body. Unconscious means the person is not in there. So treat the body on the scene and never, never move it. Not until you learn how. People can't find their own way back to the body—not when they've been pulled loose that way by some accident or something. Time and time again, traumatized people get abandoned that way. Time and time again, people die in a coma because of that."

Quoted in Doug Boyd, *Mystics, Magicians,*
and Medicine People: Tales of a Wanderer

many Japanese, who place equal if not greater symbolic importance on the heart. A person's true center of spirit and consciousness, the "heart-mind," is traditionally located in the *hara*, or belly.

As this example illustrates, the notion of brain death is culturally constructed. The criteria for brain death focus on cessation of brain function while other vital functions continue. However, the notion of death as absence of brain function, separate from other bodily functions, is inconsistent with the Japanese perspective on death of the whole person. Making a determination of brain death creates confusion because there remains a beating heart and a warm body. For many Japanese, the procedures involved in organ donation and transplantation result in a "death that cannot be seen," an invisible death. Furthermore, many people in Japan refuse to recognize brain death as biological death because they are skeptical about whether brain death can be determined with certainty and whether those who make such a determination can be fully trusted.

In addition to the cultural factors already mentioned, Japanese concerns about organ donation and transplantation also relate to traditional practices involving the exchange of gifts. In Japan, there are fine-tuned rules governing the flow of gifts and gift exchange. Receiving a gift incurs an obligation to return the favor. With organ donation, giving is viewed as one-way. The recipient of an organ donation cannot offer a countergift. There is no way of repaying such a valuable gift, even to the family of the brain-dead person. Moreover, the absence of a social relationship between donor and receiver clouds organ donation with a sense of commercialization.

Interestingly, surveys indicate that about half of the Japanese people are willing to equate brain death with human death, a figure similar to that reported in Western countries, where there has been no parallel outcry about the appropriateness of organ donation. In interpreting these findings, it is noteworthy that many Japanese view brain death and organ transplantation as reflecting Western influences. According to this view, transplantation in countries like the United States is aimed at recycling all possible organs from brain-dead donors, regarding them as exchangeable body parts, as "cogwheels inside a clock." Many Japanese believe this kind of system could lead to a more inhumane society in which every person is regarded as an "exchangeable cogwheel" of the total social system.

The maintenance of cultural identity is important to most Japanese. Unquestioningly adopting Western practices of organ donation and transplantation would involve abandoning history and thereby diminishing cultural distinctiveness. From this perspective, bioethics in Japan should be culturally relevant, not merely a reflection of Euro-American values. Developing a culturally appropriate bioethics would therefore incorporate the influences of Shinto, Buddhist, and Confucian thought, as well as modern Western traditions. In reflecting on the Japanese example presented here, we see that cultural differences with respect to ethical issues need not be viewed as barriers that must somehow be overcome, but as opportunities for learning about different ways that people deal with the complex issues surrounding dying and death.

Considering Ethical Issues in Medicine

In reviewing the rapidity with which issues of medical ethics have come to the forefront of discussion during the past three decades, Leon Kass observes that "today the ethics business is booming," with medical schools offering courses in medical ethics, hospitals establishing ethics committees, courts adjudicating ethical conflicts, and blue-ribbon commissions analyzing and pronouncing on ethical issues.[64] Yet, Kass argues, much of this "action" is really just talk—

philosophical theorizing and rational analysis—with comparatively little time devoted to "what genuinely moves people to act—their motives and passions." This is not to say that analysis and theorizing are irrelevant, but the "morality of ordinary practice" is where the rubber meets the road. Kass points out that every human encounter is an ethical encounter, an occasion for the practice and cultivation of virtue and respect.

Our choices result not only from a unique blend of our personal values, but also from values present within our own particular ethnic or cultural group. Different value systems produce distinctive and diverse attitudes toward the role of biomedical interventions.[65] The discussion in this chapter can form a basis for intelligent consideration of ethical issues in medicine, especially as they affect the dying and their families. Many of us will grapple with such issues at a personal level. The issues surrounding euthanasia and physician-assisted suicide have been characterized as "the abortion debate of the next century."[66] Concerns about such issues affect not just the realm of public policy, but also bear directly, often poignantly, on the lives of individuals and families.

Further Readings

Renee Anspach. *Deciding Who Lives: Fateful Choices in the Intensive Care Nursery.* Berkeley: University of California Press, 1993.

Michael C. Brannigan and Judith A. Boss. *Healthcare Ethics in a Diverse Society.* Mountain View, Calif.: Mayfield, 2001.

Peter G. Filene. *In the Arms of Others: A Cultural History of the Right-to-Die in America.* Chicago: Ivan R. Dee, 1998.

Herbert Hendin. *Seduced by Death: Doctors, Patients, and the Dutch Cure.* New York: Norton, 1996.

Albert R. Jonsen. *The Birth of Bioethics.* New York: Oxford University Press, 1998.

Patricia A. King and Leslie E. Wolf. "Lessons for Physician-Assisted Suicide from the African-American Experience." In *Physician-Assisted Suicide: Expanding the Debate,* edited by Margaret P. Battin, Rosamond Rhodes, and Anita Silvers, pp. 91–112. New York: Routledge, 1998.

Edmund D. Pellegrino and David C. Thomasma. *The Virtues in Medical Practice.* New York: Oxford University Press, 1993.

Robert M. Veatch. *Cross Cultural Perspectives in Medical Ethics.* Boston: Jones and Bartlett, 1989.

Robert M. Veatch, ed. *Medical Ethics.* 2d ed. Boston: Jones and Bartlett, 1997.

Robert F. Weir, ed. *Physician-Assisted Suicide.* Bloomington: Indiana University Press, 1997.

Stuart J. Youngner, Robert M. Arnold, and Renie Schapiro, eds. *The Definition of Death: Contemporary Controversies.* Baltimore: Johns Hopkins University Press, 1999.

Stuart J. Youngner, Renée C. Fox, and Laurence J. O'Connell, eds. *Organ Transplantation: Meanings and Realities.* Madison: University of Wisconsin Press, 1996.

Robert Zussman. *Intensive Care: Medical Ethics and the Medical Profession.* Chicago: University of Chicago Press, 1992.

Funeral traditions provide an opportunity for mourners to publicly acknowledge their loss. Here, bereaved family members walk behind the horse-drawn carriage bearing the casket of Diana, Princess of Wales, as it slowly winds through the streets of London on the way to her funeral at Westminster Abbey. In the somber expressions of Prince Philip, Prince William, Earl Spencer, Prince Harry, and Prince Charles, we see a blending of private grief and public mourning.

CHAPTER 7

Survivors: Understanding the Experience of Loss

*W*e are all survivors. Even if we have not experienced the death of someone close, we are survivors of losses that occur in our lives because of changes and endings. The loss of a job, the ending of a relationship, transitions from one school or neighborhood to another—these are examples of the kinds of losses that occur in all our lives. Such losses are sometimes called "little deaths," and, in varying degrees, they all involve grief. As you recall some of the "little deaths" in your own life, think about how you responded. Shock, disbelief, anger, sadness, and relief are all natural reactions. Generally, the more emotionally charged an experience or relationship, the greater a person's reaction to its loss.

A study of the "sport career deaths" of college athletes found that grief was experienced by athletes who abruptly made an involuntary and unanticipated exit from college sports due to being cut from the team or suffering a career-ending injury, or because their sport program or team was terminated. In transitioning to the status of a "normal student," these athletes mourned the loss of camaraderie with teammates, loss of self-image and social reputation as athletes, and the loss of "what might have been."[1]

Similarly, when the Chicago White Sox played their last game at Old Comiskey Park, many fans were acutely aware of their grief as a response to losses associated with their memories of attending games at "the world's greatest baseball palace."[2] One fan recalled attending a game at the Park with six of his friends before leaving for Vietnam. He said,

"Three of those guys eventually were killed over there and I guess I'm sayin' goodbye to them. This Park was my bond with them and now I'm gonna lose that tie." Another fan said that his fondest memories of his father were associated with the ball games they attended together at the Park. He said, "As a son, I went back to recapture the warmth and contentment I always had felt sitting in those 'special' seats—I went back to visit my father. . . . When Old Comiskey closed that autumn day . . . I lost something. I lost a very real connection to the feelings a six-year-old boy has for his father."

Bereavement, Grief, and Mourning

Knowing the definitions of bereavement, grief, and mourning broadens our understanding of what it means to be a survivor. Although these terms are often used somewhat interchangeably, each refers to a distinct aspect of the encounter with loss.

Bereavement is defined simply as the objective event of loss. It comes from a root word meaning "shorn off or torn up"—as if something precious had been suddenly yanked away by a disruptive force. Thus, at root, bereavement conveys a sense of being deprived, of having some part of ourselves stripped away against our will, of being robbed. Although bereavement can be defined as an event that disrupts our lives, it is also appropriate to define it as an event that is normal in human experience. To understand bereavement, these two definitions need to be kept in balance.

Grief is the reaction to loss. It encompasses thoughts and feelings, as well as physical, behavioral, and spiritual responses. Mental distress may involve disbelief, confusion, anxiety, disorganization, and depression. The emotions in grief can include not only sorrow and sadness, but also relief, anger, and self-pity, among others. By recognizing that grief can involve many feelings, even conflicting ones, we become better able to cope with it. Behaviors associated with grief include crying and "searching" for the deceased. Many bereaved people talk incessantly about the deceased and the circumstances of the death. They may be restless, as if not knowing what to do with themselves. Physically, grief typically involves frequent sighing, insomnia, and loss of appetite. Grief may also evoke a reexamination of religious or spiritual beliefs in the attempt to make meaning of the loss. Limiting our definition of grief reduces our chances of accepting all of the responses that can be present.

Mourning is closely related to grief and is often used as a synonym for it. However, mourning refers not so much to the *reaction* to loss, but to the *process* by which a bereaved person integrates the loss into his or her ongoing life. How this process is managed is determined, at least partly, by social and cultural norms for expressing grief.[3] Considered jointly, grief and mourning are the means to healing the pain of loss.

Mourning behavior includes wearing black armbands or clothes of subdued colors and, if the deceased was a public figure, flying the national flag at half-mast. Following the death of George Washington, Congress led the nation in a thirty-day period of mourning, during which citizens wore black bands on which were stamped in white letters the inscription that appeared on the President's coffin plate: "General George Washington—Departed this life on the 14th of December, 1799."[4] In some cultures, widows wear black for years following the death of a spouse, thereby acknowledging their loss, their changed status, and their grief. The *mater dolorosa,* a veiled woman dressed in black clothing, was a socially prescribed way of mourning in the late nineteenth century. The practice of altering one's appearance in some way as a sign of mourning occurs in many societies. Among some Native American cultures, a person's hair is shorn as a way of signifying that he or she is mourning. Long hair is a sign of status and wealth. Thus, as Terry Tafoya says, "To cut the hair short is a symbolic and actual sacrifice in memory and respect of the one lost. It is also an immediate sign to visitors that such a loss has taken place. It is a strong visual symbol of grief."[5]

There is a common theme to mourning behaviors cross-culturally—namely, that the bereaved are "different" and that this difference usually diminishes with time.[6] This is seen in customs that involve seclusion of the bereaved for a designated period of time. Seclusion enforces on survivors a period of abstinence from social relationships. Perhaps you have heard someone say, "That family experienced a death in the family and is in mourning; they aren't going out socially." Philippe Ariès concludes that, historically, seclusion serves two purposes during the mourning period: First, it allows survivors to shelter their grief from the world, and, second, it prevents survivors from forgetting the deceased too quickly.[7]

Contemporary mourning customs are generally not as formal or as socially regulated as the customs found in traditional cultures. Lacking rigorous social rules, people who are recently bereaved may experience conflict about what constitutes appropriate mourning behavior, as illustrated by the following anecdote: A young girl wrote to an advice columnist about a "sweet sixteen" party that her dying father asked the family to celebrate for her, even if the party should occur on the day of his funeral. The girl said that she had not felt like having a party, but the family decided to honor the promise to her father. So the party was held two days after her father's death, and it turned out to be a good experience for all who attended. The problem arose when several relatives became horrified because, in their view, enjoying a party was inappropriate during a time of mourning. What advice would you have given to this girl?

"Appropriate" mourning behavior is difficult to define in modern societies, especially those where diverse cultural groups and influences are present. It is useful, therefore, to suspend judgments about what is "correct," recognizing that many different kinds of mourning behaviors can be appropriate for different people and circumstances.

The Experience of Grief and Mourning

Newly bereaved persons may be alarmed by the flood of physical, mental, emotional, and behavioral reactions they experience. Stephen Fleming and Paul Robinson point out, "Grief, at times, may be experienced as frightening,

Grief may indeed range the gamut. It may be shrill and maniacal; it may be subdued and reflective; it may be philosophical. The recording of grief and of the response to it, of the sadness that is virtually physiological and is certainly deeply mysterious in its fullest psychological character, serves, as Aristotle and the later students of tragic cartharsis have suggested, as a kind of purgation, as a means of releasing the terrible suppressed tensions, fears, anxieties, deeply fearsome in their potential for still greater unknown effect. Identifying the full range and depth of the symptoms must always come first, must be the basis on which understanding, management, and assimilation of grief into the totality of living rests.

Morris Freedman, "Notes on Grief in Literature"

overwhelming, even 'crazy-making.' "[8] People often ask, What is normal grief? How long should a person mourn? What is the normal course of grief? If the bereaved is not "over" the loss by a certain time, does that mean he or she is experiencing pathological grief or mourning inappropriately? Questions like these reflect natural human concerns. Any attempt to understand grief and mourning must take into account the circumstances of a death, as well as other variables that influence a particular person's experience. In addition, it is necessary to have a basic understanding of the typical course of grief and how it is likely to be expressed.

Manifestations of Grief

William Lamers says, "On experiencing loss, people begin passing through an irregular continuum that encompasses thoughts, feelings, physiological responses, and observable behavioral changes."[9] The somatic, or physical, disturbances that typically occur include tightness of the throat, choking, shortness of breath, frequent sighing, a feeling of emptiness in the abdomen, muscle weakness, chills, tremors, nervous system hyperactivity, insomnia or other sleep disruptions, and changes in appetite.

Mental or cognitive distress may manifest as confusion, disbelief, anxiety, tension or pain, and a pervasive sense of disorganization. Survivors may seem depressed, especially in the early period following loss (grief-related depression is distinguished from clinically defined depression).[10] Events may seem unreal, sensory responses undependable and erratic. The bereaved may experience periods of euphoria, with heightened perceptual and emotional sensitivity to people and events. Survivors may be preoccupied with images of the deceased, experienced in dreams, hallucinations, or a vague sense of the deceased's presence. Paranormal or psychic experiences in which the dead appear to the living or seem to communicate with the living are not unusual in grief.[11]

A very wide range of emotions can be experienced in grief, especially during the early period. Sadness, longing, loneliness, sorrow, and anguish are commonly experienced, as well as guilt or anger. The bereaved may express outrage at the apparent injustice of the loss. Survivors often feel a great sense of frustration and impotence at their inability to control events. If the world could be arranged more to the bereaved's liking, it would not have included this loss.

Behaviors commonly associated with grief include crying and searching for the deceased. At times, survivors may be highly irritable or even hostile. They may talk incessantly about the deceased. Or they may talk about everything but the loss, the circumstances of the death, and the deceased. There is often a kind of frenetic overactivity and general restlessness, as if survivors don't know what to do with themselves.

This brief survey does not exhaust the list of possible manifestations of grief, but it is evident that a broad range of responses—physical, mental, emotional, and behavioral—may be associated with bereavement. However, no particular survivor will necessarily experience all of them, nor must all be present. If a person has mental images of the deceased and says, "Oh no, I shouldn't be thinking like this," denial of the experience may create conflicts that impede healthy resolution. In contrast, if a survivor is aware that many kinds of feelings, thoughts, and behaviors are a normal part of grief, the experience is likely to be more easily accepted.

The signs of grief may appear immediately after the bereaved learns of the death, or they may be delayed; they may even be absent. Grief is highly variable. It is a complex, evolving process with multiple dimensions. As Dennis Klass observes, "Bereavement is complex, for it reaches to the heart of what it means to be human and what it means to have a relationship."[12]

The Course of Grief

Attempts to categorize the course of grief by imposing a set of discrete "phases" on the process of mourning are somewhat arbitrary, reflecting different observers' viewpoints. Nevertheless, most studies indicate that the course of grief, or mourning, follows a generally consistent overall pattern.[13] To describe the course of mourning as a set of stages or phases seems to suggest a linear progression from the first stage, through the second, and so on, until the process has been completed. This approach might be comforting to those who would like to have a ready-made schema for evaluating a survivor's journey after loss, but we need to be cautious in applying any such schema to the experience of a particular survivor. Grieving, like dying, is highly individualistic.

In the first hours or days following a death, grief usually manifests in shock and numbness, feelings of being stunned, as well as of disbelief. There may be an expression of denial—"No! This can't be true!"—especially if the death was unexpected. Even when a death is anticipated, however, grief is not necessarily diminished when the loss becomes real. During the initial period of mourning, there is often a sense of confusion and disorganization that can be overwhelming, as if the bereaved person, motionless and helpless, is stranded in the middle of a fast-flowing stream while water and debris rush about him or her. Bewildered by the shock of the loss, the bereaved may feel vulnerable and seek protection by withdrawing. The confusion of this early phase of grief is set against the need for survivors to attend to decisions and actions concerning the disposition of the deceased's body. This is normally a time when the bereaved are occupied with arranging for funeral services, as well as starting

Tears stream down the face of accordion player Graham Jackson as the body of President Franklin Delano Roosevelt is carried to the train at Warm Springs, Georgia, the day after his death—a poignant example of how bereaved persons express their loss in public as well as private.

to sort out the deceased's personal and family affairs. The funeral service can be a focal point that helps reintegrate the distraught and disoriented family members after the disruption caused by death.[14] As family and friends gather to offer mutual support, the funeral rituals take place. Engaging in such activities promotes acceptance of the reality of the death and allows the survivors to begin to move beyond the acute period of grief.

In its middle phase, mourning is characterized by anxiety, apathy, and pining for the deceased. Despair is likely to be felt, as "the feelings of disbelief give way to the realization that there will be no reprieve and that the reality is neither a horrible hoax nor a bad dream."[15] The pangs of grief are felt as the bereaved deeply experiences the pain of separation and yearns intensely for the person who died. Bereaved individuals may repeatedly go over the events surrounding the loss, wishing to undo the calamity and make everything as it was before. Rage and resentment may be felt toward persons or institutions that might have somehow prevented the death, "if only things had been different," and even toward the deceased whose "abandonment" causes such pain. Hostile or negative feelings directed toward the deceased may, in turn, give rise to guilt. In beginning to accept the unwelcome fact that the loss is real and cannot be changed, the bereaved is likely to review and sort through all the "bits" of interaction that created his or her relationship with the deceased. This can involve an intense reexperiencing of the history of the relationship and the bonds of attachment.

During this phase, which can last quite some time, survivors often experience volatile emotions, which suggests the image of a volcano, at times giving off steam, at other times appearing relatively dormant. Anger is commonly experienced, with the object of the anger being the deceased loved one ("How could you abandon me?"), God ("How could you let this happen?"), or the situation itself ("How could this happen to me?"). Family or friends may be the target of displaced anger. However, the predominant feeling is likely to be sadness. Feelings of longing and loneliness are common, as needs and dependencies that had been satisfied by the deceased become painfully apparent. Much of this time is filled with "if-onlys" and "what-ifs," as the bereaved comes to terms with the reality that is: The person is dead. Over a period of weeks or months, the mourning process goes on, as the bonds of the relationship that *was* are gradually undone and a new relationship with the deceased is created as part of the survivor's ongoing life.

This can be a difficult time in grieving. Yet the bereaved often find themselves without the social support of relatives and friends who were present during the earlier period. Once the funeral is over, the bereaved may be left alone with his or her grief. In supporting a grieving person, we should remember that a lack of social support at this crucial time can limit the bereaved's opportunities for talking about the loss and expressing grief.

There is no predetermined timetable for completing the mourning process. In moving toward the restoration of one's well-being, however, the last phase of "active" grief is marked by a sense of resolution, recovery, reintegration, and transformation as the bereaved person moves forward with a life that is irrevocably changed but worth living. The turmoil of grief subsides; actively mourning no longer dominates every waking hour. Physical and mental balance is reestablished. Sadness doesn't go away completely, but it gradually recedes into the background. Grief is no longer so "heavy"; a weight has been lifted. Although reminders of the loss stimulate active grieving from time to time, the main focus is the present, not the past. Anniversaries or new losses can reactivate grief for a loss previously mourned. Adjusting to loss may at times feel like a betrayal of the deceased loved one, but it is healthy for the bereaved person to engage again in his or her ongoing life and become oriented toward the future.

Coming to terms with loss doesn't mean forgetting our loved one or minimizing the significance of the lost relationship. It is not a matter of "getting over the grief" in some absolute or final sense, but a process whereby the present concerns of life become the foreground. Making the journey of grief allows us to incorporate the loss into our ongoing lives. We maintain connections with deceased loved ones through memories and other means that sustain relationships beyond the grave. There is no absolute endpoint so long as the deceased is kept alive in our memory.

When you remember a loss in your life, you may recall some of the emotions, thoughts, physical reactions, and behaviors associated with the various phases of grief. But perhaps it felt as if all these reactions were happening at once. Part of you may have been in shock while another part was calm. Distinguishing specific aspects in the mourning process is an aid in comprehending "how grief works" and its effects on survivors. Although descriptions of grief help to delineate elements of grief that are normally experienced by survivors, the actual experience resembles a series of dance steps more than it does a cross-country walk. As Sandra Bertman says, the phases of grief "may overlap, may be of varying and unpredictable duration, occur in any order, may be present simultaneously, and may disappear or reappear at random."[16]

Complicated Mourning

The journey through grief may be affected by various influences that hamper its satisfactory resolution and the adjustment of the bereaved to life without the deceased. Because the duration of grief varies so widely, the idea that a person might be experiencing "prolonged grief" has become problematic, and the term itself is difficult to define. In some studies, normal grief was reported as lasting only a short time, perhaps six months to a year. As the knowledge base concerning bereavement has expanded, however, the notion of a "standard duration" of grief has largely been put aside. Generally speaking, concerns about "prolonged grief" have been dropped in favor of an emphasis on the factors that "complicate" grief or that may result in "pathological" grief. As the understanding of grief has become less categorical, there is a more cautious attitude with respect to labeling particular manifestations of grief as pathological or abnormal.[17]

Regarding "prolonged" or "delayed" grief, for example, the onset of intense pain years after a loss may be mistaken as abnormal when it is in fact a normal response to a "new" death or loss and, thus, a time-appropriate, rather than delayed, response.[18] To illustrate, a young woman whose husband had died nearly four years earlier reported a bout of intense grief. Bewildered by the experience, she said, "I don't understand myself; it feels almost like the day he died." In conversation with her counselor, she discovered the event triggering her pain: Within a few days, the couple's seven-year-old daughter would be celebrating her first communion. Although happily remarried, successfully back to work, and obviously healing from her loss, this devoutly religious woman grieved the absence of her child's father from a celebration that had been discussed and anticipated since the child's birth.

Survivors may experience a recurrence of grief for a significant loss at various times throughout their lives. Some event brings freshly to mind the recognition that what once was is no more. For example, a person who was bereaved as a child by a parent's death may grieve that death anew many years later when his or her own child is born. A study of bereaved spouses found that the effects of loss can be sustained over an extended period of time that is more appropriately termed a "life transition" than a "life crisis," with survivors grieving in some fashion for the rest of their lives.[19] Commonly, the experience of loss has an ongoing developmental quality; it corresponds to the situation in which a person finds himself or herself at different stages of life.

Perhaps in your own life you recognize a recurrence of grief for earlier losses. At various times, people may grieve the loss of childhood and its experiences. A woman mentioned visiting her parents after some years of living on her own, and, one day, while poking around in the attic, her mother opened a trunk and pulled out a collection of dolls that had belonged to the daughter when she was a child. Seeing the dolls evoked grief for the childhood that had ended years earlier. She said, "I looked at those dolls and their tiny clothes, and I got in touch with the loss of that time in my life when my mother had taken care of me and had made clothes for my dolls. There I was, sitting in the attic, just bawling." Most of us have experienced similar situations in our own lives. Some event, picture, place, melody, or other stimulus has provoked grief related to something or someone no longer present in our lives.

Recurrences of grief such as those described are normal and present no cause for alarm. When signs of acute grief persist for an abnormally long time, however, they may indicate the presence of some form of pathological grief. For example, severe and sustained depression—especially when accompanied by serious emotional problems, substance abuse, or suicidal imagery—can be a correlate of complicated or pathological grief. Nevertheless, to avoid misdiagnosis and inappropriate treatment, care should be taken to distinguish between normal grief and clinical depression.[20] *Persistent* problems with sleeplessness or loss of appetite may be symptomatic of problems, as may medical complaints, such as, in some cases, ulcerative colitis, rheumatoid arthritis, or asthma. Although one should not rush to judgment and become unnecessarily anxious, it is a good idea to seek expert counsel or intervention when there is an underlying reason for difficulty in coming to terms with a loss.

Complicated mourning can occur when high-risk factors are present in the bereaved's experience of loss. Therese Rando says, "In all forms of complicated mourning, there are attempts to do two things: (1) to deny, repress, or avoid aspects of the loss, its pain, and the full realization of its implications for the mourner; and (2) to hold onto, and avoid relinquishing, the lost loved one."[21] Rando provides the following list of factors that may especially complicate grief:

1. Sudden and unanticipated death, especially when it is traumatic, violent, mutilating, or random
2. Death from an overly lengthy illness
3. Loss of a child
4. The bereaved's perception that the death was somehow preventable
5. A relationship between the bereaved and the deceased that was markedly angry or ambivalent, or markedly dependent
6. The bereaved's prior or concurrent mental health problems or unaccommodated losses and stresses
7. The bereaved's perceived lack of social support

Bereaved persons in most cultures may dream that a beloved person has come back. In the early stages of bereavement, this, as well as hallucinating the dead, is a normal manifestation of grieving. However, Hawaiians usually see the dead in dreams more often, for more reasons, and for longer periods after a death than do, for example, Western Caucasians. In modern Western culture, when dreams (or hallucinations) of the dead continue too long, they are usually symptoms of pathological grief: the process or "work" of grieving has not progressed through the normal stages.

For the Hawaiian who is emotionally close to his ethnic roots, such prolonged dreaming or envisioning of the dead may or may not be a sign of blocked grief work. In the Hawaiian tradition, the dead do return: in dreams and visions, in sensations of skin, in hearing the voice or smelling the perfume or body odor of the one who has died.

The difference between what is culturally normal and what may be pathological is only partly spelled out by the dream content. We must also know what is going on in the life and family life of the dreamer; we must know how much and what kind of emotion the dream aroused. Especially, we must know what were the relationships in life between the one who died and the survivor who dreams.

Mary Kawena Pukui, E. W. Haertig, and
Catherine A. Lee, *Nana I Ke Kumu (Look to the Source)*

You may notice from this brief overview that assessing whether a person is indeed experiencing complicated mourning is not as simple as just going down a checklist and marking off the appropriate items. For example, how should the bereaved "relinquish the lost loved one" while yet maintaining, in some way, bonds with the deceased? Or, to take another example, does the death of a child always result in complicated mourning? As Rando says, "What may be an appropriate response in one circumstance for an individual mourner may be a highly pathological response for a different mourner in other circumstances." We do not have the convenience of using X-rays or similar diagnostic tools to determine the presence or absence of pathology in grief.

Nevertheless, when the natural expression of grief is suppressed and emotional engagement with the loss is lacking, or when grief is so boundless that it becomes totally overwhelming, it sets the stage for a poor outcome.[22] In reviewing the factors, or situations, that Rando identifies as potentially complicating mourning, notice that they do not necessarily justify labeling the mourner's grief as "dysfunctional" or "pathological." For example, the parent who experiences the death of a child as a result of random violence certainly faces a bereavement that is inherently complicated, but this complexity does not necessarily result in dysfunctional grieving. In Rando's view, the prevalence of complicated mourning is increasing due to a variety of social processes associated with modern societies, including urbanization, secularization, and deritualization, as well as violence, the availability of guns, social alienation, substance abuse, and a sense of hopelessness, among others.

A recent initiative directed by Holly Prigerson at Yale University School of Medicine is developing criteria for making a psychiatric diagnosis of *traumatic grief*.[23] These criteria include symptoms of both "separation distress" and "traumatic distress." Although the criteria have yet to be finalized, many of the *symptoms* planned for inclusion in the definition of traumatic grief appear to be virtually indistinguishable from the *signs* of normal grief. These include such common grief reactions as yearning, longing, or searching for the deceased; a sense of shock, numbness, or disbelief; feeling that part of oneself has died; and irritability or anger related to the death. According to the criteria being considered, if such reactions persist longer than two months—and if the bereaved has a "clinically significant impairment in social, occupational, or other areas of functioning"—a diagnosis of traumatic grief could be made. In developing these criteria, Prigerson and her colleagues aim to identify individuals who are "at risk" because of abnormal grieving. Others question whether this proposal is a step toward "medicalizing" grief, especially if the label of dysfunctionality is eventually applied to what has conventionally been considered normal grief and mourning. Additional field studies are currently being done to gather data that is needed before final criteria can be proposed. One of the main questions about the criteria as they now stand is the issue of whether a bereaved person should be expected to not display the "symptoms" mentioned above within as short a time as two months after a significant loss. Another important question involves the definition of "clinically significant impairment" in the context of a person experiencing acute grief in the early period of bereavement. Because the criteria for traumatic grief were developed on the basis of a consensus reached by a panel of experts, this initiative bears watching as it could have an impact on the way we—as well as physicians and psychologists—think about grief and mourning.

The Mortality of Bereavement

The biology of grief may have life-threatening consequences. In an early study of a small community in Wales, W. D. Rees and S. G. Lutkins found that the death rate among bereaved individuals during the first year of bereavement was nearly seven times that of the general population.[24] Other research has shown a higher incidence of some chronic diseases in the recently bereaved.[25] A study by Marvin Stein at Mount Sinai School of Medicine found that there was a diminished immune response among widowers during the first few months following bereavement.[26] Other studies have shown significant depression of lymphocyte (T-cell) function following bereavement.[27] Although no direct cause-and-effect link has been established between bereavement and the onset of disease, there is evidence suggesting that the reaction to loss can contribute to morbidity and even mortality, illness and death.

In some cases, the stress of bereavement appears to aggravate a physical condition that may have been latent, causing symptoms to manifest or develop more rapidly. Hans Selye's studies point to the existence of an acute alarm reaction, or mobilization of the body's resources, in situations of high emotional stress.[28] According to Selye, the alarm reaction is a "generalized call to arms" of the body's defenses, and it manifests in various physiological changes that prepare the organism to cope with the agent or situation eliciting the reaction. If this reaction is not followed by either adaptation or resistance to the agent eliciting it, dysfunction or death may ensue.

George Engel investigated the possible relationship between stress and sudden death.[29] After compiling a number of case reports, Engel classified the various stressful situations into eight categories, four of which can be considered as either a direct or an indirect component of grief and mourning: (1) the impact of the death of a close person, (2) the stress of acute grief, (3) the stress that occurs with mourning, and (4) the loss of status or self-esteem following bereavement.

At first, loss of self-esteem may not seem especially relevant to bereavement. Guilt, however, tends to lower self-esteem, and guilt is a common component of grief. Consider the bereaved person who says, "If only I had tried harder or done something differently, my loved one might not have died." The changed circumstances of daily life may also tend to lower a survivor's self-esteem. A widower who used to attend social functions with his spouse may now be left off the guest list; a widow may decline social events that she believes are for "couples only." Handling financial problems after a death can be stressful. If self-worth depends on a certain income level, then less money and tighter finances may lower self-esteem. Loss of status that had been enjoyed due to a deceased mate's professional or community standing may have a similar effect.

Can a bereaved person die of a "broken heart"? During the fifteenth century, grief was a legal cause of death that could be listed on death certificates. Although the notion that severe grief can damage the heart has been around a long time, Colin Murray Parkes notes that "the fact that bereavement may be followed by death from heart disease does not prove that grief itself is a cause of death."[30]

Stephen Oppenheimer, a neurologist, says, "It's an old wives' tale that a person can die of a broken heart. . . . But, many old wives' tales are true."[31] Oppenheimer believes that unresolved mental stress can throw the heart into an irregular and fatal heartbeat. To confirm or deny this belief, he is studying the brain's insular cortex, an area of the nervous system that controls breathing and heartbeat and that links up with the limbic system, which deals with anger, fear, sadness, and other emotions. Damage to the insular cortex may possibly render a person susceptible to a chaotic heartbeat called ventricular fibrillation, leading to cardiac arrest, and, thus, a "broken heart."

The death of a loved one involves many concurrent changes, or "secondary losses," that can increase a survivor's vulnerability. What determines the outcome is not so much stress itself as the person's ability to cope with it. How a person copes with devastating losses—the death of a mate, close friend, or family member—tends to be consistent in many ways with how that person copes with the everyday stresses and small losses of daily living. In many instances, social support is the key to helping bereaved individuals mitigate potentially harmful effects of grief.[32]

Funeral Blues

Stop all the clocks, cut off the telephone,
Prevent the dog from barking with a juicy bone,
Silence the pianos and with muffled drum
Bring out the coffin, let the mourners come.

Let aeroplanes circle moaning overhead
Scribbling on the sky the message He Is Dead,
Put crêpe bows round the white necks of the public doves,
Let the traffic policemen wear black cotton gloves.

He was my North, my South, my East and West,
My working week and my Sunday rest,
My noon, my midnight, my talk, my song;
I thought that love would last for ever: I was wrong.

The stars are not wanted now; put out every one;
Pack up the moon and dismantle the sun;
Pour away the ocean and sweep up the wood;
For nothing now can ever come to any good.

  W. H. Auden

In reviewing the "broken heart" phenomenon, Margaret Stroebe concludes that "both the direct consequences of loss of a loved one, or a broken heart, and secondary effects, or the stress of bereavement, are responsible for the bereavement-mortality relationship."[33] She adds, "When extreme grief coincides with severe life stresses during bereavement, the risk to life is likely to be greatest of all."

Intellectual Versus Emotional Responses

When there is a substantial difference between a survivor's emotional and intellectual responses to death, and the survivor believes that only one response can be right, the result is conflict. To expect the head and the heart to react the same to loss is unrealistic; disparity between feelings and thoughts is likely. In mourning a loss, many different emotions will be felt, and many different thoughts will arise. By allowing them all and withholding judgment as to the rightness and wrongness of particular emotions or thoughts, the survivor is more likely to experience grief as healing.

Survivors often have rigid rules about what kind of emotions can be expressed in grief, and when—such as where and when it is acceptable to be angry, or to open to the pain and release an intense outburst of sadness.

Permission to have and express feelings is of immense importance in dealing with the issues of survivorship. Intellectually, we may think, "How can I be mad at someone for dying?" Yet anger may indeed be a component of grief; consider the example of someone who died because of driving while intoxicated, or by committing suicide. Of course, anger may be present even if death was seemingly unavoidable and beyond the victim's control. One young mother told of walking past a photograph of her recently deceased child and noticing, amid the grief and pain, a small voice within her blurting out, "Brat! How could you die and leave me as you did!" In a purely intellectual sense, we might be tempted to think this mother's behavior out of place. How could she be angry at her child for dying? Yet a sense of rage or frustrated anger is common in the experience of survivors. Survivors should allow themselves to experience those feelings, to feel anger at the person for having died and anger at themselves for not having been able to prevent the death—indeed, they must give themselves permission to experience all the feelings that arise. Thus, they need not judge themselves as uncaring or bad.

Models of Grief

The belief that there is a consistent pattern to grief and mourning may bring solace to bereaved people.[34] It seems that human beings have an affinity for patterns and models that appear to help make sense of complex phenomena. Many people are aware of the "five stages" of coping with loss—denial, anger, bargaining, depression, and acceptance—described by Elisabeth Kübler-Ross. This model has been portrayed in cartoons and on the television program, *The Simpsons*. The acronym DABDA is even used by medical students while preparing for their examinations. But are grief and mourning really this stereotypical?

Models can provide a "snapshot" of a dynamic process, but they can also oversimplify and distort reality. This is surely the case with a complex phenomenon like grief. Over the past few decades, various models have been proposed and refined, as theorists attempt to describe how people grieve. It is exciting to see these pictures develop, even as we recognize that they are not yet complete.

Working Through Grief

The concept of "working through grief" has been an important theoretical perspective at least since Sigmund Freud's 1917 paper, "Mourning and Melancholia."[35] The central message of the "grief work" perspective, as it is

Working through our endings allows us to redefine
our relationships, to surrender what is dead
and to accept what is alive,
and to be in the world more fully to face the
new situation.

Stanley Keleman,
Living Your Dying

usually understood, is that the bereaved must "let go" of his or her bonds of attachment to the deceased by gradually "working through" these attachments and relinquishing them. Therese Rando points out that, according to this model,

> Mourning is initiated by the need to detach from the lost object, and the reason mourning is such a struggle is that the human being never willingly abandons an emotional attachment, and only does so when he or she learns that it is better to relinquish the object than to try to hold on to it now that it is lost.[36]

The nature of our attachments and the process by which those attachments are relinquished were central concerns in the work of John Bowlby.[37] According to *attachment theory,* when a person recognizes that an object (someone loved) to which he or she is attached no longer exists, grief arises, along with a defensive psychological demand to withdraw libido (energy) from the object. This demand to withdraw energy that had previously been invested in the object is likely to meet with resistance, causing the survivor to temporarily turn away from reality in an attempt to cling to the lost object. By continuing to do "grief work," the energy previously invested eventually becomes detached from the love object, and the ego (personality) is freed of its attachment so that new relationships can be formed.[38]

In "The Symptomatology and Management of Acute Grief," a landmark article published in 1944 and based on the author's involvement as a psychiatrist in treating the survivors of a nightclub fire in which 492 people died, Erich Lindemann observed:

> The duration of a grief reaction seems to depend upon the success with which a person does the *grief work,* namely, emancipation from the bondage to the deceased, readjustment to the environment in which the deceased is missing, and the formation of new relationships.[39]

Lindemann added that the main obstacle to successful grief work was the fact that many people "try to avoid the intense distress connected with the grief experience and to avoid the expression of emotion necessary for it."

The grief-work model incorporates several important points about mourning a loss: First, it describes grief as an *adaptive response* to loss. Second, it states that the reality of the loss must be *confronted and accepted.* Third, it acknowledges that grieving is an *active process that occurs over time.*

The grief-work model has been widely accepted as the "standard" formulation for understanding and helping people accommodate to loss. However, its apparent emphasis on the need for bereaved individuals to break their relational bonds with the deceased has been questioned. Colin Murray Parkes points out: "Each love relationship is unique, and theoretical models which assume that libido can be withdrawn from one object in order to become invested in another similar object, fail to recognize this uniqueness."[40]

As the contributions of earlier grief theorists are examined more closely in the light of recent contributions to our understanding of grief, it appears that their views about "breaking bonds" may not have been expressed quite as

> Comparing the extent and form of emotional responses to announcements of death in various circumstances, I found a considerable amount of variability. On some occasions there was no crying whatever; the doctor's mention of the death was responded to with downward looking silence. On other occasions, his utterance "passed away" or "died" spontaneously produced hysterical crying, screaming, moaning, trembling, etc. . . . In numerous instances I have seen men and women tear at themselves, pulling their hair, tugging at their garments, biting their lips.
>
> David Sudnow,
> *Passing On: The Social Organization of Dying*

dogmatically as some later interpreters have thought. With recent studies offering evidence that accommodation to loss is more complex than simply severing affectional bonds with the deceased and getting on with one's life, a review of the literature finds similar ideas, albeit expressed less prominently, in the writings of many early theorists. Nevertheless, as the grief-work model is reexamined in the light of newer perspectives, our conventional views of bereavement, grief, and mourning are being revised.

In a comprehensive review of the literature on grief, Margaret Stroebe points to a number of significant questions about the grief-work model: Is it really necessary to work through grief in order to adapt to a loss? Could suppression not lead to recovery? Are there occasions when, or persons for whom, grief work is not adaptive? And where does one draw the line between healthy grief work and unhealthy rumination?

The conventional formulation of the grief-work model seems to imply that "one size fits all," that everyone needs to work through grief in a similar fashion to recover from a loss. Cross-cultural studies, however, attest to diversity in grief and mourning.[41] Although certain patterns of grief are commonly found within a particular social or cultural group, there may be no universal or standard process of coping with grief. The idea that there is some standard method of grieving is being replaced by the recognition that grief is both highly individualistic and influenced by a variety of situational factors, such as the type of death, circumstances of the loss, and so on. Stroebe says, "Within the range of normal grief reactions, it is possible that suppression or avoidance of confrontation with memories related to the deceased can be as effective a strategy as 'working through' grief. For some people, and in some circumstances, it may even be more effective."[42] In short, there is more than one way to cope effectively with loss.

It may be helpful to think of bereavement, as Colin Murray Parkes suggests, as one category of "psychosocial transition." We need not discard the grief-work model. To do so would be to lose the insights it offers. Rather than assuming it is the *only* model of grief, however, it is more appropriate to view it as one among many, each of which adds to our knowledge and ability to respond to our own losses and console others in their losses. As one bereaved father said, "Living without my son has meant adding another room onto the house in my mind; not so I can shut the door on his death, but so I can move in and out of the experience of my loss."[43]

Tasks of Mourning

In psychologist William Worden's description of the "tasks of mourning," the first task involves *accepting the reality* of the loss.[44] Even when death is anticipated, the reality may be difficult to accept fully. "Denying the facts of the loss," says Worden, "can vary in degree from a slight distortion to a full-blown delusion." One signpost at this point in the journey is the survivor's choice of words when talking about the deceased person. Most significant is the transition from present to past tense, from *is* to *was,* as, for example, from "Randy is a wonderful carpenter" to "Randy was a wonderful carpenter."

The second task involves *working through the pain* of grief. This includes physical as well as emotional and behavioral pain. As Worden says, "Not everyone experiences the same intensity of pain or feels it in the same way, but it is impossible to lose someone you have been deeply attached to without experiencing some level of pain." In accomplishing this task, humor can lighten the weight of grief, providing respite as survivors cope with loss.

The third task involves *adjusting to a changed environment* in which the deceased is missing. It takes time to make this adjustment, especially when a relationship was of long duration and exceptional closeness. The many roles fulfilled by the deceased in the bereaved's life may not be fully recognized until after the loss. The "changed environment" encompasses physical, emotional, mental, behavioral, and spiritual dimensions of life. Changes in one's environment are symbolized by actions such as rearranging the furniture or changing the place settings at the dining table.

The fourth task has to do with *emotionally relocating the deceased and moving on with life.* Accomplishing this task involves the recognition that, although one does not forget or necessarily stop loving the deceased person, there are other people one can love.

Psychologist Therese Rando offers another perspective on the tasks of mourning essential for healthy accommodation of loss.[45] Briefly stated, these include:

1. Recognize the loss (acknowledge and understand the death).
2. React to the separation (experience the pain; feel, identify, accept, and express the reaction to loss; and identify and mourn secondary losses).
3. Recollect and reexperience the deceased and the relationship (review and remember realistically; revive and reexperience the feelings).
4. Relinquish the old attachments to the deceased and the old assumptive world.
5. Readjust to move adaptively into the new world without forgetting the old (develop a new relationship with the deceased, adopt new ways of being in the world, form a new identity).
6. Reinvest.

In the tasks of mourning outlined by both Worden and Rando, notice that accomplishing these tasks involves "relocating" the deceased in one's ongoing life and "developing a new relationship" with the deceased.

Maintaining Bonds With the Deceased

The view that coping with grief means relinquishing affectional ties with the deceased is giving way to a paradigm that is both more encompassing and more accurate in describing the range of behaviors and emotions elicited by loss. Recognizing the variability in grief, we need to be cautious about generalizing. Phyllis Silverman observes that our way of talking about grief influences both how we understand it and how we cope with it.[46] What expectations do we communicate to the bereaved when we speak about grief as a "time of healing" and talk about "getting over it" or "working through it"? By focusing exclusively on "resolving" grief, Silverman says, we may unwittingly perpetuate "a major deception of the bereaved as they try to conform to the expectations of their social network." When it turns out that grief is not so readily "resolved," the bereaved may feel somehow deficient, as if "something must be wrong with them."

Margaret Stroebe and her colleagues suggest that we must "search for an appreciative understanding of grief in all its varieties."[47] In counseling the bereaved, "this would mean curtailing the search for ideal therapeutic practices and focusing instead on tailor-made treatments." There is a growing recognition that, rather than severing ties with the deceased, grief usually involves a process whereby the bereaved person incorporates the loss of a loved one into his or her ongoing life. In some cultural settings, this occurs in the context of rituals that locate the deceased in the realm of beloved ancestors. In others, it means keeping a special place for the deceased in one's heart and mind.[48]

Maintaining a bond with the deceased is not an example of dysfunctional mourning that must be corrected; rather, it is testimony to the enduring strength of love. Based on an extensive survey of "communications" between the living and the dead as expressed in art, literature, and song, Sandra Bertman observes that "[t]he dead do not disappear from the lives of the living. They stay connected; and lively communications continue between the two worlds."[49] Determining whether maintaining continuing bonds with the deceased reflects a "healthy" adjustment to loss may depend on two criteria: First, does the mourner truly recognize that the person is dead and understand the implications of the death? Second, is the mourner moving forward adaptively into his or her new life?[50]

Dennis Klass says that bereaved parents often find solace by maintaining continuing bonds with their children who died untimely deaths.[51] "Memory," Klass says, "binds family and communities together." Through religious beliefs and objects that link the parents' with their memories of the child, a kind of immortality is granted to the child in the lives of surviving family members. Klass points out that the death of a child challenges parents' worldviews—that is, their basic assumptions about how the universe functions and their place in the world. Making sense of such a loss is facilitated by maintaining an "inner

The nineteenth-century Romantic view of death is reflected in the Lawson memorial, which characterizes both the devotion of the bereaved to the deceased and the belief that loving relationships continue beyond the mortal framework of the human lifespan.

Contemporary memorial stones often reflect a similar emphasis on the unending love felt by survivors for the deceased and on the faith that bonds forged during a person's lifetime can remain strong despite death.

representation" of the dead child that allows for continuing interactions so that the significance of the child's life is not forgotten or diminished.[52]

Work done by Phyllis Silverman, Steven Nickman, and William Worden in the Child Bereavement Study supports the notion that children likewise maintain connections with deceased parents through memories and linking objects.[53] Furthermore, David Balk and Nancy Hogan point out that "[a] remarkable bit of evidence for ongoing attachment is the millions and millions who visit the Vietnam War Memorial each year to remember and leave literally tons of connections for their deceased loved ones."[54] Therese Rando says, "The development of a healthy new relationship with the deceased is a crucial part of the mourning process when the person lost has been integral to the mourner's life."[55]

Although the value of maintaining bonds with the deceased has only recently been addressed prominently in the literature on grief, it would not be particularly surprising to people living in cultures where ties between the living and the dead are sustained as a matter of tradition. Recall, for example, the Japanese custom of maintaining a household shrine to the ancestors or African traditions that celebrate relationships with the "living-dead." In commenting on the social bond between human beings and the relationship of that bond to loss, Lyn Lofland suggests that the following are just some of the "threads of connectedness" or "ties that bind" us to one another:

> We are linked to others by the *roles* we play, by the *help* we receive, by the wider *network* of others made available to us, by the *selves* others create and sustain, by the comforting *myths* they allow us, by the *reality* they validate for us, and by the *futures* they make possible.[56]

Telling the "Story": Narrative Approaches

When someone we love dies, we face the prospect of revising and re-forming our life story. John Kelly suggests that, by viewing our lives as "stories," we can cast a more expansive light on grief and mourning.[57] By contemplating mourning in terms of a narrative, or story, we find a way to cope with loss by re-forming our story so that we integrate the deceased into our lives in a new way and adjust our relationships in ways that restore wholeness.

Carolyn Ellis describes how telling the story of her brother's death resulting from an Air Florida crash into the Potomac River after takeoff from Washington National Airport not only gives meaning to the loss, but also helps in "reconstructing" her life.

> Each writing and reading of my text has permitted me to relive my brother's death from an aesthetic distance, a place that allows me to experience the experience but with an awareness that I am not actually again *in* this situation, and thus I muster the courage to continue grieving.[58]

In telling the story of loss, Ellis says, "We can make true a plot in which we play the part of, and become in the playing, actual 'survivors.'"

The story of grief can be told by bereaved persons without the constraint of having to conform to a particular model of how it should be or what it should feel like or what should be thought. In a sense, it is the "real" story. In telling and retelling it, the story gradually reveals the varied dimensions of grief in a way that allows survivors to carry on despite loss. Mary Anne Sedney and her colleagues note that "[e]very death creates a story, or a set of stories, to tell."[59] Sharing the story of a loss provides emotional relief, promotes the search for meaning, and brings people together in mutual support of one another.

Part of coping with grief is talking about the dead. Through conversations with others, we not only gain a fuller appreciation of the deceased's life, but also come to a revised assessment of our own life. Describing how this process occurred with the death of a former girlfriend, Tony Walter says, "This was not social support for an intrinsically personal grief process, but an intrinsically social process in which we negotiated and re-negotiated who Corina was, how she had died, and what she had meant to us."[60] In proposing a model of grief that makes use of biography and storytelling, Walter says that one way we "keep" those we have lost to death is to talk honestly about them with family, friends, and neighbors who knew them.

In emphasizing the *personal meaning* of a loss, Stephen Fleming and Paul Robinson observe,

> It is our opinion that survivors seldom, if ever, are able to make sense of a loss or find meaning in a death. . . . You do not find meaning in *death,* you find meaning

in the *life* that was lived. Central to the struggle to find meaning in the life that was lived is the notion of the deceased's legacy. The legacy is the appreciation of how knowing and loving the deceased has irrevocably changed the survivor, thus realizing the transition from losing what one has to having what one has lost.[61]

"Giving grief voice" by telling our stories about the dead and listening to the stories that others tell helps us move on with our lives without leaving our loved ones behind.

Toward an Integrated Model of Grief

Until recently, most of the notions circulating about grief were based on a Western model; and this model was then usually interpreted, rightly or wrongly, as prescribing or delineating acceptable and unacceptable ways of coping with loss. There has been a tendency to medicalize grief, to make grief something to be "cured" so that the bereaved could get back to "normal" as quickly as possible. This understanding of grief can result in theories and interventions that do not match the way grief is actually experienced, even by many people who are themselves situated within the Western cultural tradition.

In reformulating our understanding of the conventional models of grief, greater attention is being given to the important role of the family system in coping with loss. Nancy Moos says, "Families and family grief processes are inextricably linked to individual grief and recovery."[62] In thinking about the tasks of mourning, it can be worthwhile to reframe them in such a way that the bereaved's family is clearly embraced as part of the process. David Kissane and Sidney Bloch emphasize how the family and its patterns of interaction are often crucial determinants of whether grief is dealt with in a healthy or a dysfunctional manner.[63]

In this connection, it is important to understand that, although gender influences patterns of grief and mourning, it does not determine them. People sometimes believe that "men don't cry, women do," thus associating with only one gender a behavior that applies to human beings generally. Because of gender stereotypes, women are often portrayed as readier to express emotion than men, a notion that is sometimes interpreted as a sign that women are better able to cope with grief. Terry Martin and Kenneth Doka point out, however, that there are many effective ways of expressing and adapting to loss, and that women as well as men make use of various coping patterns.[64] In particular, they identify two patterns of grieving: *intuitive* and *instrumental*. In the first, individuals experience and express grief in an affective way; in the second, grief is experienced physically, such as in restlessness or mental activity. Although the first pattern tends to be associated with women and the second with men, Martin and Doka reject the notion that one pattern is inherently better than the other, along with the bias that correlates these patterns with gender. In fact, both patterns can be effective ways of coping, and both men and women make use of them.

In developing a comprehensive understanding of how people cope with bereavement, one of the most interesting contributions is the dual process model proposed by Margaret Stroebe and Henk Schut.[65] According to this model, the bereaved person expresses, in varying proportions (depending on individual as well as cultural variations) both *loss-oriented* and *restoration-oriented* coping behaviors. In acknowledging both of these aspects of coping, this model avoids getting stuck in an "either/or" framework whereby the bereaved must either "let go" of the deceased or "hold on" to memories. Instead, there is "oscillation" between the two forms of coping.

Examples of loss-oriented coping include the grief work of conventional theories: yearning for the deceased, looking at old photographs, crying about the death, and so on. Restoration-oriented coping includes mastering tasks that had been taken care of by the deceased (such as cooking or handling the finances), dealing with arrangements for reorganizing one's life (such as selling the house or moving to another area), developing a new identity (such as changing status from spouse to widower or from parent to parent of deceased child), and so on.

Thus, on the one hand, loss-oriented coping involves "concentrating on, dealing with, [or] processing some aspect of the loss experience." Restoration-oriented coping, on the other hand, involves making the changes that are required to cope with the "secondary consequences" of loss—all those aspects of the bereaved's life that require rearrangement in the wake of the loss.

Central to this model is the understanding that grief is a dynamic process. It involves movement—"oscillation" or alternation—between loss-oriented and restoration-oriented coping. In coping with loss, the bereaved at times will be actively confronting the loss; at other times, he or she will avoid troubling memories, be distracted, or seek relief by turning attention to other things. Over time, oscillation between these ways of coping leads to optimal adjustment.

As a theoretical construct, the dual process model of coping has a broad range of applications. Particularly important is its ability to help explain patterns of grief in diverse cultural settings as well as at different times within the same person. It is perhaps the most value-free model of grief presented to date, and it promises to be an important tool for furthering our understanding of the many ways people respond to loss.

Grief always occurs within a particular social or cultural context, and individual grievers differ in their particular styles of grieving. This leads to the recognition that there is no standard way of coping with loss. Colin Murray Parkes points to three main influences on a person's course of grieving:[66]

1. The urge to look back, cry, and search for what is lost
2. The urge to look forward, explore the world that emerges out of the loss, and discover what can be carried forward from the past into the future
3. The social and cultural pressures that influence how the first two urges are inhibited or expressed

As these influences interact in various ways, at times the bereaved tries to avoid the pain of grief and at other times confronts it. The goal is to achieve a balance between avoidance and confrontation that facilitates coming to terms with the loss and accommodating it in our lives.

The upper middles would probably drink themselves silly at the funeral. Although a few years ago this would have been frowned on. When my husband in the sixties announced that he intended to leave £200 in his will for a booze-up for his friends, his lawyer talked him out of it, saying it was in bad taste and would upset people. The same year his grandmother died, and after the funeral, recovering from the innate vulgarity of the cremation service when the gramophone record stuck on 'Abi-abi-abi-abi-de with me', the whole family trooped home and discovered some crates of Australian burgundy under the stairs. A rip-roaring party ensued and soon a lower middle busybody who lived next door came bustling over to see if anything was wrong. Whereupon my father-in-law, holding a glass and seeing her coming up the path, uttered the immortal line: 'Who is this intruding on our grief?'

Jilly Cooper, *Class*

Variables Influencing Grief

Just as no two persons are alike, no two experiences of grief are alike. The circumstances of death, the personality and social roles of the bereaved, the relationship with the deceased—these are among the factors that influence grief and mourning. These factors offer clues about why some deaths are especially devastating to survivors. In thinking about some of the variables that can influence a survivor's grief, the following are some basic questions: Who died? How did the death occur? What was the quality of the survivor's relationship to the deceased? Is there still "unfinished business" from the relationship? What prior losses has the survivor experienced? Were there any complicating factors about the death? Was this loss socially sanctioned? What financial and legal matters remain to be dealt with in the wake of the death? Each of these questions opens up an area for further consideration.

Survivor's Model of the World

A survivor's response to loss is conditioned to a significant extent by his or her model of the world—that is, by his or her perception of reality and judgment about how the world works. In considering how a person's model of the world applies to bereavement, four factors identified by Edgar Jackson are singled out as especially important: personality, social roles, perception of the deceased's importance, and values.[67]

Personality

Our personality influences how we relate to life experiences generally: Some people seem to ride easily over large bumps but receive quite a jolt from a small shock; for others, the situation is reversed. In this respect, self-concept is an important determinant of how a person responds to death. The person with an immature or dependent personality is especially vulnerable to the loss of someone in whom much emotional capital has been invested, perhaps in an attempt to compensate for feelings of inadequacy by projecting part of his or her identity onto the other person. With the death of that person, more of the survivor's projected self is involved in the loss. In contrast, the person with greater self-esteem and stronger self-concept is not as prone to such overcompensation; thus, grief is likely to be less devastating. People who report a high degree of purpose in life tend to cope more effectively with bereavement than do people who report a low purpose in life.[68]

Cultural Context and Social Roles

Grief is shaped by the social context in which it occurs.[69] In examining the dimensions of bereavement and loss in two Muslim communities—one in Egypt, the other in Bali—Unni Wikan concludes that culture is a potent shaper and organizer of how people in a given society respond to loss.[70] Although both societies share a common religious heritage, one encourages mourners to express their sorrow in wails and lamentations, whereas the other encourages mourners to contain their sorrow and maintain a quiet and essentially cheerful countenance. Culture provides a framework wherein we cope with grief. What does society say about a survivor's response to death in general or to a particular type of death? In combat, a soldier is expected to perform his duties despite personally grieving when comrades die. In some societies, a widow knows well in advance what kind of behavior is expected when her husband dies, and the members of her society gather to ensure that her grief is expressed in specific and appropriate ways. People who live in modern societies generally have greater flexibility in determining for themselves what behavior is appropriate in different social contexts. Even so, the cultural environment is an important factor in shaping a person's grief and mourning.

Perceived Relationship With Deceased

The survivor's perception of the relative importance of the deceased also conditions and shapes the experience of grief. Was the deceased an important person in the bereaved's life? Is the bereaved's life likely to be significantly changed by the death? Think for a moment about the various relationships in your life—parents, children, neighbors, coworkers, teachers, friends, lovers, and so on. Generally speaking, the death of a family member or other close relative is perceived as more important than the death of a coworker or neighbor. But the outward form of the relationship is not the only determinant of the deceased's importance to a survivor. The death of a close friend may parallel the mourning patterns associated with surviving a death within the family.[71]

Whatever the outward form—kin, friend, neighbor, or mate—relationships vary according to degree of intimacy, perception of each other's roles, expectations of the other person, and the quality of the relationship itself. In Bali, family members and other kin are rarely referred to by their *personal* names, but rather by the *degree of relationship,* thus emphasizing how their social roles are perceived.

In some instances, a person's relationship with his or her parents may reflect socially defined roles of "parent" and "child" more than feelings of friendship or personal intimacy. For others, a parent may occupy the addi-

David Des Granges, Tate Gallery, London

This portrait of the Saltonstall family, painted in 1611 by David Des Granges, provides a record of living family members and their relational links with the deceased, whose influence is still felt. The husband and father, Sir Richard, is portrayed as if standing at the bedside of his dead wife, whose arm reaches toward their two children. Seated in the chair and holding her baby, the newest member of the family, is Sir Richard's second wife, whom he married three years after the death of his first wife.

tional roles of business associate, neighbor, and close friend. These differing roles and expectations result in different perceptions about the importance of the parent in one's life and, in turn, are likely to shape the experience of grief when the parent dies.

The deaths of family members and close friends usually cause the deepest grief, but the deaths of those who have been significant in other ways can also evoke powerful grief reactions. Consider the outpouring of grief over the deaths of President John F. Kennedy, Robert Kennedy, and Martin Luther King, Jr., or, more recently, Princess Diana and John F. Kennedy, Jr.—even though the vast majority of mourners had never met any of them personally.

As we see, then, a number of factors determine whether a relationship is central or peripheral to a person's life. In his 1977 paper, "Human Grief: A Model for Prediction and Intervention," Larry Bugen observed that a death involving someone central to the survivor's life generally will be more affecting than the death of someone who is perceived to be on the periphery.[72] Bugen added that grief can also be predicted to some extent by a survivor's belief about the circumstances of the death—that is, whether the death was preventable or unpreventable. For instance, given a *central* relationship between the survivor and the deceased and the belief that the death was *preventable,* mourning would be expected to be both intense and prolonged. However, if a survivor had a *peripheral* relationship with the deceased and also believed that the death was *not preventable,* mourning would be expected to be less intense as well as of shorter duration.

The deceased's importance may also be considered in terms of a survivor's *perceived similarity* to the deceased. This hypothesis suggests that the more similar to the deceased a survivor believes he or she is, the greater is likely to be the grief reaction.[73] (Perceived similarity is also a factor in the formation of support groups that are composed of people who have experienced similar losses.)

In discussing the influence of a survivor's perception of the deceased's importance on subsequent grief at the death of that person, it is important to also mention the role of *ambivalence* on the course of grief. Ambivalence about a relationship reflects a push-pull struggle between love and hate, and it may be subtle or dramatic. Perhaps no relationship is entirely free of ambivalence, but when such feelings are intense and continue over a long period of time, confusing emotions can complicate grieving.

Relationship issues and the circumstances of a death appear to influence whether a particular death is likely to involve *high grief* or *low grief.*[74] A high-grief death is characterized by intense reactions; a low-grief death is perceived as less devastating, and thus grief is likely to be less intense. The death of a child is often cited as the classic example of a high-grief death.

Values and Beliefs

A person's value structure—that is, the relative worth he or she assigns to different experiences and outcomes based on his or her model of the world—is another influence on the course of grief. We sometimes hear people say things like, "Of course, his wife misses him terribly, but she is also relieved that he is no longer enduring such pain and suffering." In other words, knowing the husband's suffering is over mitigates the wife's grief at his death. Edgar Jackson cites the example of a husband who, knowing that he will soon die from a terminal illness, prepares his wife for the time when he will not be present to manage their financial affairs. The value this couple placed on being prepared was therefore a conditioning factor in their grief as they faced the husband's dying and, subsequently, in the wife's grief after his death.

More generally, value structures that include a place for death in a person's philosophy of life can be an important determinant of how that person experiences loss and grief. Religious and spiritual beliefs, for example, influence how individuals relate to the meaning of death and, thus, play a role in shaping the experience of loss and grief. Even when there is hope of an eventual reunion with the deceased loved one, however, the immediate reality must be recognized. Richard Leliaert says: "To suggest that faith itself can drive out the pain of bereavement is to counsel badly."[75] Although religious faith can be

Many people believe the death of a young child to be the most heartrending of all bereavement experiences—what researchers term a high-grief death because it tends to elicit a tremendous sense of loss.

consoling and comforting, the path of grief still must be trod. Leliaert says, "Good spiritual caregiving for bereaved persons needs a fine balance between the human need to grieve adequately and the spiritual grounds for hope provided by formal religions or spiritual belief systems."

Mode of Death

How a person dies affects a survivor's grief. Consider the ways in which people die: the aged grandmother, dying quietly in her sleep; the young child pronounced DOA after a bicycle crash; the innocent bystander caught in the crossfire of violence; the despondent executive who dies by suicide; the chronically ill person who dies a "lingering death." The mode of death—natural, accidental, homicide, or suicide—has an impact on the nature of grief, as does the survivor's previous experience with that type of death.[76]

Anticipated Death

The phenomenon of *anticipatory mourning* can be understood as a reaction to being aware of an impending loss. Therese Rando defines anticipatory mourning as encompassing both the awareness of an impending loss and the recognition of associated losses.[77] Some people believe a death that is anticipated, as in the case of chronic or long-term illness, is easier to cope with than a death that occurs suddenly, without warning.[78] Others argue that grief experienced before a death occurs does not significantly diminish the grief experienced when the anticipated loss becomes an objective fact. Nevertheless, it is generally agreed that the elements of shock and disbelief are more intense and overwhelming when a death is unexpected.

A phenomenon associated with anticipatory mourning is *secondary morbidity*, which refers to "difficulties in the physical, cognitive, emotional, or social spheres of functioning that may be experienced by those closely involved with the terminally ill person."[79] The strain of caring for a dying relative may cause the caregiver to be inattentive to his or her own health care needs, with the result that the caregiver becomes sick or "run down." Secondary morbidity can affect professional or volunteer caregivers as well as family members and friends of the dying person.

Sudden Death

In an address before a group of death educators and counselors, Yvonne Ameche described her experience on the night two policemen came to her door with news of her son's unexpected death. Despite having experienced the deaths of her grandparents during her childhood and, later, the deaths of both her parents, Ameche said, "I don't know if anything prepared me for the knock on the door the night Paul died. . . . I remember reeling back [and feeling] like I had been physically assaulted."[80] The sense of overwhelming shock caused by the unexpected nature of her son's death was accompanied by feelings that her own familiar sense of self had been "lost" as well. The journey of survivorship from head to heart, as Ameche describes it, "where I started to internalize what I had so carefully intellectualized," took a long time and, she adds, "it was a long time before I felt like myself."

Sudden deaths that occur in the context of specific kinds of events—war, for example—result in a particular set of circumstances surrounding death, and this constellation of circumstances affects how survivors deal with the loss.[81] Survivors who are bereft because of a sudden death usually want information as quickly as possible—and often in considerable detail—about what caused the death, to help them begin to make sense of the loss. Hospital staff, emergency personnel, and others who deal with traumatic deaths need to offer this information in a sensitive, compassionate manner and provide a supportive environment for the grief that ensues following a notification of sudden death.[82] The abrupt breaking of ties between the deceased and his or her survivors makes sudden deaths a category of bereavement that many people consider especially difficult.

A Letter from the Canadian Prairie

Heather Brae, Alberta
January 12, 1906

Miss Jennie Magee
Dear Sister:

You will be surprised to hear from me after so many years. Well I have bad news for you. My Dear little wife is Dead and I am the lonelyist Man in all the world. She gave Birth to little Daughter on the 27th of December three Days after she went out of her mind and on the 7th of January she took Pnumonia and Died about half past three in the afternoon. We buried her tuesday afternoon in a little cemetary on the Prarry about 15 miles from here. I am writing to you to see if you will come and keep house for me and raise my little Baby. I would not like to influence you in any way as I am afraid you would be lonely when I have to go from home as I will now and again. You are used to so much stir in the city. I have 400 acres of Land and I have 9 or ten cows and some hens. If you come you can make all you can out of the Butter and eggs and I might be able to Pay you a small wage . . . Write and let me know as soon as Possible what you think about the Proposition. I am writing to the rest tonight to let them know the bad news. I think this is all at Present from your affectionate Brother.

William Magee

Linda Rasmussen, Lorna Rasumssen,
Candace Savage, and Anne Wheeler,
A Harvest Yet to Reap: A History of Prairie Women

Suicide

People who survive a loved one's death by suicide are often left feeling bewildered, "Oh, my God, he did it to himself!" The impact of suicide can intensify survivors' feelings of blame and guilt.[83] If someone close to us was in such pain that he or she chose suicide, we may be burdened with guilty questions: "Why didn't I see the predicament and do more to help? What could have been done to respond to the cry for help?" In a series of interviews with survivors of suicide, Carol Van Dongen concluded:

> A consistent theme throughout survivors' experiences was an intense need to understand why the suicide had occurred and what were the implications of the death for themselves and their family. Survivors agonized over possible reasons for the suicide, as well as how the death was affecting them now and what it might mean in the future.[84]

Besides guilt and self-questioning, the survivor may direct strong feelings of anger and blame toward the person who died by suicide. Suicide is seen as the ultimate affront, the final insult—one that, because it cannot be answered, compounds the survivor's frustration and anger. When the suicide is actually witnessed by family or friends, they are likely to be especially traumatized by the loss.[85]

The other day I heard the father of a boy who had committed suicide say, "Everyone has a skeleton in their closet. But the person who kills themselves leaves their skeleton in another's closet." The grief and guilt that arise in the wake of suicide often leave a legacy of guilt and confusion. Each loved one wracks the mind and tears the heart questioning, "What could I have done to prevent this?"

Stephen Levine, *Who Dies? An Investigation of Conscious Living and Conscious Dying*

Moreover, feelings of guilt and blame may be made more difficult to cope with because of societal attitudes. Survivors are more likely to be "held responsible" for a death by suicide than for a death by illness. Negative reactions to suicide survivors may be especially directed toward the parents of a child who died by suicide.[86] Gordon Thornton and his colleagues point out that such attitudes can result in a comparative lack of social support for individuals who are bereaved by suicide.[87] As with other categories of sudden death, because suicide is usually unexpected, the shock magnifies the bereaved's sense that the death occurred "out of time" or was inappropriate.

Homicide

When a loved one dies as a victim of homicide, the survivor may experience the world as dangerous and cruel, unsafe and unfair. The suddenness and apparent injustice of a violent death have an impact on the experience of grief. Furthermore, as Lula Redmond points out, "the raw wound of the grieving homicide survivor is overtly and covertly affected by the performance of law enforcement officials, criminal justice practitioners, media personnel, and others after a murder."[88] Dealing with the criminal justice system extends the normal mourning period as the case drags on, with no assurance that the result will give the survivor a sense of justice being done. Among the "trigger events" that Redmond cites as restimulating grief in such cases are:

1. Identification of the assailant
2. Sensing (hearing, smelling, and so on) something that elicits recollection of an experience acutely associated with the traumatic event
3. Anniversaries of the event
4. Holidays and other significant events in the life of the family (such as birthdays)
5. Hearings, trials, appeals, and other criminal justice proceedings
6. Media reports about the event or about similar events

Redmond points out that survivors of someone who was murdered face a number of obstacles in adjusting to the loss. The survivor may have to cope with giving depositions to attorneys and possibly giving testimony in court. He or she may be surprised to learn that the charge of murder is a crime against the *state,* not against the *loved one* for whom the survivor grieves. Prosecutors may decide to plea bargain or reduce the charge to a lesser offense, and they may do so without consulting bereaved family members. As the case proceeds through the judicial system, survivors can find themselves facing the defendant in the courtroom or in the corridor or waiting room. They may hear the defendant described as a good and honorable person by character witnesses. Finally, they may have to contend with the defendant receiving a light sentence or even being released. In other instances, the crime may never be solved, or it may not be prosecuted because there is insufficient evidence to bring the case to trial.

In considering the effects of homicide on survivors, we should also think about those who deal with such deaths in an official capacity. Although dealing with violent death becomes a way of life for those who investigate homicides, the constant exposure to death is not only stressful but can evoke intense feelings of grief. One homicide detective says, "Every cop maintains that detachment is the key, but the truth is that he gives up a section of his soul to every corpse and he dies a little death at the beginning of every case."[89]

Disaster

People who survive a disaster in which others died become survivors twice over—survivors of a catastrophic event that could have ended their own lives and survivors of the deaths of others, often friends or relatives.[90] Because such survivors may feel that they did not deserve to live when others did not survive, a sense of profound guilt can accompany the anguish and sorrow of grief. Relief at having survived catastrophic and threatening circumstances—a natural human response—may be accompanied by intense questioning: Why did I survive while others very much like me perished? Survivors of the Nazi Holocaust, for example, often express a deep sense of guilt about having survived the camps and torture while others were not as fortunate.[91] Combat veterans whose comrades were killed in war often feel much the same way. Although such feelings are intensified by catastrophic events that involve the untimely or unwarranted deaths of others, *survivor guilt* at being alive while others died can be felt, in varying degrees, in other situations.

For example, parents who survive the death of a child often feel that they have become survivors of an untimely and unwarranted death. A child's death upsets the usual expectation that, in the natural cycles of life and death, the old die first and are replaced by the young. Also, if the basic function of parenting is to protect one's child and nurture his or her well-being, this responsibility is thwarted by the child's death, potentially resulting in feelings of guilt.

When children are involved in a disaster that attracts the attention of the news media, coverage of the crisis may have both potential benefits and negative consequences.[92] Some children seem to enjoy the "instant celebrity status." Others feel "ripped off" or portrayed in an unflattering light that causes additional anguish beyond the traumatic event itself. The media's tendency to emphasize the child's "helplessness" in the context of the disaster is of particular concern, as it may impede healthy mourning at a difficult time.

All that day I walked alone. In the afternoon I looked for a church, went into a cafe, and finally left on the bus, carrying with me more grief and sorrow than I had ever borne before, my body in tatters and my whole life a moan.

Oscar Lewis, *A Death in the Sanchez Family*

Multiple Losses and Bereavement Burnout

The experience of multiple losses can intensify grief and mourning. Catastrophe, whether natural or human-caused, can result in multiple losses that complicate mourning. Overwhelmed by loss, survivors can be so devastated that they become emotionally numb and disoriented, preventing the expression of normal grief.

Genocide, the systematic destruction of a racial or cultural group, is often an accompaniment to war, as in the Nazi Holocaust and, more recently, in the mass killing of Cambodians at the hands of the Khmer Rouge. Terry Tafoya points out that Native Americans "hold in common a heritage of death following initial contact with Europeans."[93] Within two generations of white contact, it is estimated that 80 percent of the Native people of the Pacific Northwest had died in the encounter from newly introduced diseases to which they had no immunity. Native peoples throughout the Americas experienced a similar pattern.

In the wake of the multiple losses experienced by many people because of AIDS, some survivors feel that they have "run out of tears," that they are bereft of emotional resources to express further feelings of grief.[94] Experiencing multiple losses can result in what has been termed *bereavement burnout*. It's as if the normal expression of grief is short-circuited by the ongoing experience of loss.

Social Support and Disenfranchised Grief

The experience of grief and mourning also varies according to the kind of social support available to the bereaved. In some communities and religious traditions, such social support is provided within an organized framework that ensures caring concern for the bereaved. Among Jewish religious families, for example, there are specific customs associated with *Aninut,* the period between death and interment; *Kreiah,* the rending of the garment by the bereaved, which allows expression of deep anger in response to grief in a controlled, religiously sanctioned manner; the *Hesped,* or eulogy, in which the virtues of the deceased are recounted in a way that elicits the natural expression of grief; *Seudat Havraah,* the meal of condolence, which recognizes that the first meal after the interment should be provided by the mourner's friends or neighbors as a way of offering consolation; the *Kaddish* prayer, which subliminally transfers the focus from the deceased to the living; and *Shiva,* the seven days of mourning that give structure to the early period of grief.[95] Social support of this kind can be immensely helpful to mourners.

Conversely, when social support is lacking, mourners may experience an added burden in dealing with a loss. For example, after the death of an unborn child, whether through miscarriage or induced abortion, bereaved persons may receive little or no social support of the kind that comforts survivors of other types of bereavement. In most cases, there is no funeral or other formal observance of the death; the loss may not be acknowledged at all by the larger community. Occurrences of this kind may involve what has been termed *disenfranchised grief*—that is, grief experienced in connection with a loss that is not socially supported or acknowledged through the usual rituals.[96]

When grief is disenfranchised, either because the significance of the loss is not recognized or because the relationship between the deceased and the bereaved is not socially sanctioned, the bereaved person has little or no opportunity to mourn publicly. Bereaved same-sex mates of persons who die may face this situation. Survivors may receive comparatively little support from the broader community as they cope with their loss. How many community resources, such as spousal support groups, are welcoming of persons with a different sexual orientation? Obviously, the answer to this question varies depending on the community and the mind-set of a particular support group. For example, in one community, a support group for parents who experienced neonatal loss integrated a lesbian couple whose baby died, thus providing a measure of community support. When a death is treated by society as if it were not a significant loss, the process of adjustment is unnecessarily made difficult for survivors.

Grief may also be disenfranchised not because of the circumstances of the loss, but because of certain qualities that others may wittingly or unwittingly associate with the bereaved himself or herself. Darlene Kloeppel and Sheila Hollins point out that complications may occur when a death in the family is combined with a family member having a mental handicap.[97] These complications may affect both the family's functioning and the handicapped person's mourning. Kloeppel and Hollins add that "death and mental retardation are both taboo subjects in our society," and that "taboos elicit fear and avoidance."

Family support can be a key factor in determining whether the bereaved feels encouraged to cope not only with grief per se, but also with practical issues that follow bereavement. The situation faced by widows in Western Nigeria is an example. The rule is that a widow has no rights of inheritance to her deceased husband's estate; all of their possessions revert to the husband's family. Kemi Adamolekun points out that the social support provided by in-laws, or the lack of it, is an important factor in how these widows mourn their loss.[98] Indeed, a common saying is that widowhood should not be wished even for an enemy. Complicated grieving was especially noted when in-laws held the widow somehow responsible for her husband's death and when in-laws acted to dispossess the widow and her children of property. One observer at an African funeral said, "When a widow cries uncontrollably at her husband's burial, she is not crying only for the loss, but for herself, because of the ordeal ahead of her."

An Elegy on the Death of John Keats

Ah, woe is me! Winter is come and gone,
But grief returns with the revolving year;
The airs and streams renew their joyous tone:
The ants, the bees, the swallows reappear;
Fresh leaves and flowers deck the dead Seasons' bier;
The amorous birds now pair in every brake,
And build their mossy homes in field and brere;
And the green lizard, and the golden snake,
Like unimprisoned flames, out of their trance awake.

Alas! that all we loved of him should be
But for our grief, as if it had not been,
And grief itself be mortal! Woe is me!
Whence are we, and why are we? of what scene
The actors or spectators? Great and mean
Meet massed in death, who lends what life must borrow.
As long as skies are blue, and fields are green,
Evening must usher night, night urge the morrow,
Month follow month with woe, and year wake year to sorrow.

Percy Bysshe Shelley, "Adonais"
(excerpt)

Unfinished Business

Unfinished business can be aptly termed "business that goes on after death." Something is incomplete. The content of unfinished business, how it is handled, and how the survivor is affected by it all have an impact on mourning. Unfinished business can be thought of in one or both of two ways relative to its effect on survivors: first is the fact of death itself; second is the relationship between deceased and survivor. As to the first, perhaps an earlier death of a parent, child, sibling, or someone else close continues to be a vivid reminder of the survivor's uncertainty and fears about death. Regardless of an individual's particular beliefs or values, the more "finished" the business of death is—that is, the more a survivor feels resolved within himself or herself toward it—the easier it will be to accept death and to cope with it. If a person rails against death, refusing to make a place for it, grief is likely to be more difficult to accept. Accepting death, giving it a place in our lives, allows us to be finished with otherwise unresolved issues about death itself.

Second, and perhaps more crucial, is the unfinished business between the deceased and the survivor. Something in the relationship was left incomplete—perhaps some long-standing conflict was never resolved while the deceased was alive, and now it's too late. Unfinished business can include things that were and were not said, things done or not done. Bereaved people often say that the things left unsaid or undone seem to come back to haunt them and make mourning more painful. The sense of never being able to resolve conflicts left by unfinished business amplifies the suffering. Consider the image of a son standing over his father's grave saying, "If only we had been closer, Dad. We ought to have taken more time to visit each other." It may be possible to resolve unfinished business by dealing with unresolved issues with the help of creative or therapeutic interventions, but it is generally better to try to resolve unfinished business daily, in all our relationships and especially our intimate ones.

Another category of unfinished business relates to the plans and dreams that the bereaved person had shared with the deceased. Perhaps there were places they talked about going together at some time in the future; now, these travel plans will never be fulfilled. Perhaps the survivor and the deceased shared dreams related to family matters—plans about their children or "retirement years," for example. Perhaps they shared plans relating to starting or building a business together. Such plans and dreams can touch on a number of areas in a survivor's life. Death brings an end to all the plans and dreams that had involved the deceased being present.

Deathbed promises constitute a particular kind of unfinished business. Picture the classic scene in which the person who is dying elicits some promise from the survivor to perform a particular action after the person dies. Most survivors agree to enact the promise, whether or not they really want to comply with the deathbed request. Thus, a deathbed promise can later create conflict for the survivor, who may be torn between fulfilling the promise and taking another course of action. Whereas some people carry through a deathbed promise and find it to be a gratifying choice, others find that deathbed promises need to be reevaluated in the light of their own wishes and circumstances.

Support for the Bereaved

When a person experiences a significant loss, he or she may initially feel and behave much like a frightened child. A hug may be more comforting than words. Having someone who can "simply listen" can be helpful. The key to being a good listener is to refrain from making judgments about whether the feelings expressed by a bereaved person are "right" or "wrong," "good" or "bad." The emotions, thoughts, and behaviors evoked by loss may not be the ones we would expect, but they can be valid and appropriate within a survivor's experience.

Bereaved persons should not be urged to hold back their feelings or be "strong" and "brave." Talking and crying, even yelling in rage, are ways of coping with intense emotions. Expressing grief is healing. However, there is no reason for the bereaved to pretend or exaggerate emotions just to satisfy others' expectations. The role of the wake in traditional Hawaiian culture illustrates how the support of others can provide an opportunity for the bereaved to engage in a "controlled expression of anger and hostility, and also for a lessening of guilt and anxiety."[99] Everyone in the *ohana*, or extended family, attended the wake, including children. With each new arrival, a relative would say—as if telling the dead person—"Here comes Keone, your old fishing companion," or "Tutu is coming in now; remember how she used to massage you when you were sick." The assembled mourners addressed the dead, recalling their memories and sometimes describing their feelings of abandonment or even scolding the deceased. A fishing companion might exclaim, "Why you mean, go off when we gon' go fishing! Now who I go fish with?" Or a wife might say, "You had no business to go. You should be ashamed. We need you."[100] Scolding the corpse allowed survivors to vent hostility toward the dead who had abandoned them. What a contrast to the idea that one should "not speak ill of the dead," which encourages suppressing feelings of anger at the deceased.

As a culturally condoned vehicle for expressing grief, funerals and other death-related community gatherings facilitate mourning by providing a social framework for coping with the fact of death. Funerals and other rituals can help survivors gain a sense of closure and begin to integrate a loss into their lives. For some, funerals are occasions of weeping and wailing; for others, stoic and subdued emotions are the rule. Different styles of mourning behavior can be equally valid and appropriate. Whereas dense social networks—small or medium-sized Israeli kibbutzim, for example—have social structures that allow mourning to take place within an intimate circle of family, friends, neighbors, and coworkers, looser social networks may need funerals and other rituals to provide a structure wherein support can be offered to the bereaved.[101]

Social support is every bit as critical during the later course of grief as it is during the first days. Bereaved people should be able to rely on receiving support from those they trust. They may need to be reassured that grief is normal and that it is appropriate to express grief. They may also need permission to occasionally give themselves a break from grieving. As they move forward in life, the bereaved person may need encouragement from others to face the world confidently. The need for this kind of support can extend through the first year or two of mourning. The first anniversary following a significant loss is generally a time of renewed grieving, when the support of others is important and appreciated. Knowing that others remember and acknowledge the loss, and that they take time to "touch base," is usually perceived as very supportive.

Besides receiving social support from individuals who form their network of friends and relations, bereaved people may want to share their stories and concerns through organized support groups. Most such groups are based on perceived similarity. Having experienced similar losses, members of support groups come together to talk with each other as they integrate those losses into their lives. Widow-to-widow groups, for example, provide opportunities for women to share experiences of being a woman alone and encourage one another in the task of coping with the death of a spouse. Military families receive bereavement support through the Tragedy Assistance Program for Survivors (T.A.P.S.), which offers peer-to-peer support, counseling referrals, survivor seminars, and other types of help.[102] Other organizations, such as The

Family members leave the church after attending the funeral of a son and brother.
As a focus of familial and community support for the bereaved, the funeral ceremony
performs a unique function among the social rituals devised to mark significant
events in the lives of members of a community.

Compassionate Friends and Bereaved Families of Ontario (BFO), assist families who are coping with the death of a child. BFO also provides assistance
to children, adolescents, and young adults who lose a parent or sibling. In
describing the aims of BFO, Stephen Fleming and Leslie Balmer note that
it is "designed to facilitate the grieving process, emancipate the bereaved
from crippling attachments to the deceased, assuage fears that one is 'going

crazy,' educate the survivors about the nature and dynamics of grief to normalize their experience, and promote the usual curative qualities found in groups (the installation of hope, altruism, group cohesiveness, catharsis, and insight)."[103]

The meetings of some support groups resemble encounter sessions, the rule being to accept and express feelings. Others function more as social groups, providing a place for the survivor to come and be with others who have had similar experiences. Some groups are composed entirely of peers; others are facilitated by a trained professional or lay counselor. Many hospice and palliative care programs, for example, have specially trained volunteers to help families cope with grief.[104]

Bereaved people may also find solace through leave-taking rituals that differ from, or become an adjunct to, conventional funerals and memorial services. These forms of "directive mourning therapy" allow the grieving survivor to take symbolic leave of the deceased.[105] Therapeutic ritual can also help individuals move from a maladaptive to an adaptive style of grieving.[106] These rituals typically use *linking objects* that symbolize in some way the relationship between the bereaved and the deceased.[107] An example is writing a farewell letter to the deceased and subsequently burying or burning it. An activity like this can be followed by a "reunion" ritual, perhaps in the form of a ceremonial dinner with family and friends. In this way, the rhythms of separation and joining found in traditional rituals can be adapted to the circumstances of a particular survivor.

People who are recently bereaved must deal with the impact of change, which may affect virtually every detail of life: The family unit is different; social realities have changed; legal and financial matters require attention. Newly

 Advice for the Bereaved

Realize and recognize the loss.
Take time for nature's slow, sure, stuttering process of healing.
Give yourself massive doses of restful relaxation and routine busy-ness.
Know that powerful, overwhelming feelings will lessen with time.
Be vulnerable, share your pain, and be humble enough to accept support.
Surround yourself with life: plants, animals, and friends.
Use mementos to help your mourning, not to live in the dead past.
Avoid rebound relationships, big decisions, and anything addictive.
Keep a diary and record successes, memories, and struggles.
Prepare for change, new interests, new friends, solitude, creativity, growth.
Recognize that forgiveness (of ourselves and others) is a vital part of the healing process.
Know that holidays and anniversaries can bring up the painful feelings you thought you had successfully worked through.
Realize that any new death-related crisis will bring up feelings about past losses.

The Centre for Living with Dying

bereaved people face the question, "How can I make the necessary adjustment in each of these areas?" Survivors are sometimes urged to take a hand in the practical management of their everyday affairs soon after bereavement, but it can be useful to limit, insofar as possible, the number of changes made, especially in the first few months after loss. It is usually appropriate to strike a balance between the *linking* activities that maintain the survivor's familiar ties to the past and the *bridging* activities that lead the survivor to a future without the deceased.

Bereavement As an Opportunity for Growth

Viewing bereavement as an opportunity for growth can be difficult at first, but this perspective can promote gradual movement toward accommodating the loss. As the bereaved person begins to reformulate the loss, it frees up energy that had been bound to the past. As John Schneider says, "There is a change in perceptual set from focusing on limits to focusing on potential; from coping to growth; and from problems to challenges."[108] The tragic event of a loved one's death is reformulated in a way that doesn't shut out new possibilities. This reframing can carry over into other areas of the person's life, so that beliefs and assumptions that were once limiting are reassessed with greater self-confidence and self-awareness, making possible significant and rewarding life changes.

The loss is transformed in a way that places it within a context of growth. Grief becomes a unifying rather than alienating human experience. The lost relationship is changed but not ended. Becoming a survivor can allow for changes in beliefs and values—understanding about death and about life— that might not have been possible otherwise. Recalling their grief and mourning, bereaved individuals often describe themselves as stronger, more competent, more mature, more independent, better able to face other crises; and, for many, bereavement leads to more positive experiences in the context of family and friends.[109] George Bataille writes:

> It is a naive opinion that links death closely to sorrow. The tears of the living, which respond to its coming, are themselves far from having a meaning opposite to joy. Far from being sorrowful, the tears are the expression of a keen awareness of shared life grasped in its intimacy.[110]

Turning to inner sources of creativity gives form to the experience of grief. Creatively responding to loss can bring forth remarkable results. Those who work with the bereaved can spark a grieving person's creative response, as in the case of a young woman who had experienced the sudden, unexpected death of her son at birth. Overwhelmed by feelings of sadness, depression, and an inability to do anything other than grieve, she was despairing of words to communicate her feelings. In a counseling session six months after her son's death, she remarked, "I haven't touched a lump of clay since Justin died." The obvious question was: What had she done with clay before his death? She said that her sculptures of whales and seals had sold at a local

Figure 7-1(a) *Anguish of loss*

Figure 7-1(b) *Sharing the grief*

Figure 7-1(c) *Collapsing*

"The anguish of loss is overpowering and vast," begins the prose accompanying the sculpture by Julie Fritsch pictured here, part of the series created following the death of her son. "Sharing the grief" states the theme of the second sculpture, acknowledging that "together we must comfort and be comforted." The third sculpture portrays the bereaved artist "collapsing from the weight of emotions I cannot control." The prose accompanying this sculpture continues: "Drained of any ability to cope or carry on, I must collapse now. And feel myself overcome by absolute grief."

seaside crafts shop. The counselor pointed out that the reason for her inability to return to her art might lie in the source of her creative energies. Although whales and seals might one day reemerge from the lumps of clay, her creativity at present might take a different form. The client agreed to find a quiet moment when she would put her hands to the lump of clay as an experiment to see what might emerge.

Both the bereaved mother and the counselor were amazed at the results (see Figures 7-1a,b,c). Over the course of twelve months, a series of some twenty-two figures emerged. The earliest were naked, later works were draped with blankets, and, with the final pieces, the fabric of the blankets had been turned into clothing. The mother's creativity not only gave form to her loss, but also manifested an unconscious understanding of the process of recovery and the integration of her loss. Subsequently, the sculptures were photographed and published, along with her prose, giving comfort to other survivors.[111]

Death is a community event. People maintain connections with deceased loved ones through memories, as well as through personal and social rituals that provide a "space" in their ongoing lives for acknowledging affection and love for the deceased. Bereavement, grief, and mourning are complementary threads in the fabric of life, part of the warp and weft of human experience.

Further Readings

John Archer. *The Nature of Grief: The Evolution and Psychology of Reactions to Loss.* New York: Routledge, 1999.

Thomas Attig. *The Heart of Grief: Death and the Search for Lasting Love.* New York: Oxford University Press, 2000.

Sandra L. Bertman, ed. *Grief and the Healing Arts: Creativity As Therapy.* Amityville, N.Y.: Baywood, 1999.

Kenneth J. Doka and Joyce D. Davidson, eds. *Living with Grief: Who We Are, How We Grieve.* Washington, D.C.: Hospice Foundation of America, 1998.

John H. Harvey. *Give Sorrow Words: Perspectives on Loss and Trauma.* Philadephia: Brunner/ Mazel, 2000.

Dennis Klass, Phyllis R. Silverman, and Steven Nickman, eds. *Continuing Bonds: New Understandings of Grief.* Washington, D.C.: Taylor & Francis, 1996.

Terry L. Martin and Kenneth J. Doka. *Men Don't Cry . . . Women Do: Transcending Gender Stereotypes of Grief.* Philadelphia: Brunner/Mazel, 2000.

Janice Winchester Nadeau. *Families Making Sense of Death.* Thousand Oaks, Calif.: Sage, 1997.

Robert A. Neimeyer, ed. *Meaning Reconstruction and the Experience of Loss.* Washington, D.C.: American Psychologial Association, 2001.

Colin Murray Parkes. *Bereavement: Studies of Grief in Adult Life.* 3d ed. New York: Routledge, 1996.

Therese Rando. *Grieving: How to Go On Living When Someone You Love Dies.* Lexington, Mass.: Lexington Books, 1988.

Margaret S. Stroebe, Robert O. Hansson, Wolfgang Stroebe, and Henk Schut, eds. *Handbook of Bereavement Research: Consequences, Coping, and Care.* Washington, D.C.: American Psychological Association, 2001.

Tony Walter. *On Bereavement: The Culture of Grief.* Philadelphia: Open University Press, 1999.

Familiarity with the choices available in funeral services can help us appreciate our many options, perhaps alleviating some of the stress of making such choices in the midst of crisis. The roles of the funeral director and others who can provide assistance in coping with the practical matters of death may also be better understood.

CHAPTER *8*

Last Rites: Funerals and Body Disposition

*O*ur choices regarding last rites tell something about our attitudes and beliefs about death. The ceremonies that a community enacts to mark the passing of one of its members express, through symbol and metaphor, how death is perceived within a particular social group. A young musician describes the ceremony he would choose to mark his death: "My body would be cremated and the ashes put into an Egyptian urn. My friends would place the urn on stage at a concert and, as the band plays on, everyone will dance and celebrate the changes that we all must pass through eventually."

Some people find the musician's choice lacking in solemnity. "That's not a funeral," they say. "It's a party." The friends of the musician, however, might respond that his death style is consistent with his life style. His funeral celebrates the joys of life. His preference for cremation reflects a belief that existence is transitory. It's as if he were saying, "Life is a passing show. When the movie's over for me, why should my body be preserved?" The urn in which the ashes are placed symbolizes the view that he is part of a historical continuity that transcends death. Each part of the musician's death ceremony tells us something about his concept of death.

As you begin to think about the significance of funeral ceremonies, consider these questions: Who does the funeral serve—the living or the dead? What is the purpose—socially and psychologically—of last rites? What are the essential elements of ceremonies that

The presence of mortuary goods helped ensure a pleasant afterlife for the ancient Egyptians. Dating from the Eleventh Dynasty, about two thousand years before the present era, this funerary model of a paddling yacht comes from the tomb of Meket-Re.

mark the passing of a member of the community? What do the funeral customs of other cultures tell us about their attitudes toward death?

Examining the death customs of the ancient Egyptians, we see a culture preoccupied with acquiring mortuary goods and preparing for the afterlife.[1] A dominant theme in Egyptian religion was belief in life after death. The body was mortal. Yet within it were immortal elements: the *Ba,* a soul or psychic force, and the *Ka,* a spiritual double representing the creative and sustaining power of life. At death, the *Ka* flew to the afterlife while the *Ba* lived on in the body.

As the permanent dwelling place of the *Ba,* the body was preserved by mummification and protected by wooden coffins, sometimes placed within stone sarcophagi. The tomb was built to resemble an earthly home. By providing a home for the *Ba* (often depicted in the form of a bird hovering above the mummy of the deceased), continued enjoyment of the afterlife was ensured. However, if the *Ba* were destroyed, one would suffer "the second death, the death that really did come as the end." Thus, preserving the physical form, as mummy or statue, was necessary for survival.

In contrast to cultures in which the funeral is seen as a vehicle for preparing the dead to successfully migrate to the afterworld, the American funeral is largely focused on the welfare of the survivors. Socially, funerals provide a setting wherein the bereaved family makes a public statement that one of its members has died. The wider community uses the occasion to respond with sympathy and support for the bereaved. According to Vanderlyn Pine, the funeral has historically addressed four major social functions:[2]

1. It serves to acknowledge and commemorate a person's death.
2. It provides a setting for the disposition of the dead body.
3. It assists in reorienting the bereaved to their lives, which have been ruptured by the death.
4. It demonstrates reciprocal economic and social obligations between the bereaved and their social world.

Traditionally, funeral rites begin with the gathering of family and friends for a "deathwatch" to say farewells and accompany the dying person in his or her last hours of life, and they formally end with the disposition of the corpse (see Table 8-1). The various elements of funeral ritual have both social and psychological significance in helping the bereaved deal with a loved one's death. Modern funerals do not always include all of the traditional elements, or some of them may be abbreviated, depending on individual and cultural preferences. Review the descriptions given in Table 8-1 and consider which of the elements you believe would have value in planning a funeral for a loved one or which you would want to have included as part of your own last rites.

Psychosocial Aspects of Last Rites

Just as people gather to commemorate other major transitions in a person's life, such as birth and marriage, funerals and memorial services are rites of passage that commemorate a person's life in a community and acknowledge his or her passing from that community. Funerals and memorial services provide a framework that allows survivors to support one another as they cope with the fact of their loss and express their grief. The presence of death rites in every human culture suggests that they serve innate human needs. Thomas Lynch, author of *The Undertaking: Life Studies from the Dismal Trade,* makes the observation that "[f]unerals are the way we close the gap between the death that happens and the death that matters."[3]

Death Notification

When a person dies, the first to learn about it, besides the attending medical team, are usually members of the person's immediate family. Then, in a widening circle of relatives, friends, and acquaintances, others affected by the death are notified. In his classic study, *Passing On: The Social Organization of Dying,* David Sudnow observed that death notification generally occurs in a consistent pattern from the immediate family to the wider community (see Figure 8-1).[4] Those with closest relationships to the deceased are notified first, followed by those with less intimate relationships. Sudnow also found that death notification generally takes place between people in a peer relationship. For example, a bereaved mother might first call the child who had been closest

T A B L E 8-1   *Elements of Funeral Ritual*

1. *Deathwatch* (also known as the "death vigil" or "sitting up"). As death nears, relatives and friends gather to say farewells and show respect for the dying person, as well as give support and care to his or her family. Historically, a deathwatch might continue for hours, days, or even weeks or months.
2. *Preparation of the deceased.* Involves various tasks associated with preparing the corpse for ultimate disposition, usually burial or cremation.
3. *Wake* (also known as "visitation" or "calling hours"). Traditionally held on the night after death occurs, this practice involves laying out the corpse and keeping a watch or "wake" over it. Historically, wakes were observed as a safeguard against premature burial, as an opportunity for paying respects to the deceased, and, in some cultures, as an occasion for lively festivities focused on allaying fears by "rousing the ghost."

   With changes in the social patterns of mourning, the traditional wake has been transformed into the practice of setting aside time for viewing of the body prior to the funeral service. As with traditional wakes, the modern "visitation" offers opportunities for social interactions that can be healing in the aftermath of loss.
4. *Funeral.* As the "centerpiece" of the ritual surrounding death, the funeral is a rite of passage for both the deceased and his or her survivors. Services are usually held in a mortuary chapel or church, although they may be held in the home or at the gravesite. The body may or may not be present; if it is present, the casket may be open or closed. Funeral services typically include music, prayers, readings from scripture or other poetry or prose, a eulogy honoring the life of the deceased, and, less frequently, a funeral sermon focusing on the role of death in human life generally. In modern times, funerals are usually held within a few days after death, and they are increasingly scheduled in the evening or on weekends so mourners who work during the week can attend the service.
5. *Procession.* Traditionally, funerals include a procession conveying the corpse from the site of the funeral to the place of burial. It is considered an honor to be among the friends and relatives chosen to carry the deceased's body to its final resting place. Funerals for national leaders and other notables may include a lengthy procession, or cortege, with the corpse attended by honorary pallbearers.
6. *Committal.* A ceremony held at the grave or crematorium, the committal service is held after, or sometimes in lieu of, the funeral service. When it follows a funeral service, it usually consists of a brief ceremony focusing on disposition of the deceased's remains.
7. *Disposal of the corpse.* In modern societies, disposition usually means burial or cremation.

to the deceased, and that person then calls the other brothers and sisters. They, in turn, notify more distant kin. A similar pattern of notification occurs among people not directly related to the deceased. For instance, a coworker or neighbor informed about the death notifies others who had a similar relationship with the deceased. Ideally, this process of notification—taking in a gradually widening circle of relatives, friends, and acquaintances—continues until everyone affected by the death is notified.

   Notification also takes place by means of death notices and obituaries that appear in newspapers (see Figure 8-2). Human beings have an inherent need

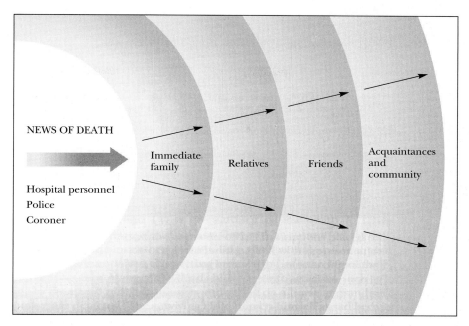

Figure *8-1 Widening Circles of Death Notification*

to respond to the death of someone significant to them. Thus, it is important for the notification process to occur in a timely fashion, so that those affected by the death are able to come together in a spirit of mutual support to grieve their loss. When an announcement of death does not appear in a timely fashion, it can be upsetting. The following complaint is typical: "The obituary did not appear in the newspaper until the morning of the funeral. . . . We had a number of calls and letters from people who didn't know about the funeral until it was too late to attend."

The person who learns about a death only after the final disposition of the body may be saddened at not having been able to participate in the funeral ceremonies. Because the mutual support of the community of bereaved persons is not likely to be as available after the initial period of mourning has passed, the belatedly notified person may feel that he or she is alone in dealing with grief. The value placed on timely notification within the African-American community is emphasized by Ronald Barrett. He says: "The immediacy of notification is equated with importance and respect. To not be informed of the death in a timely manner is considered insensitive, lacking respect, and an insult."[5]

When the deceased is well known, news of the death is broadcast more widely because it affects more people. Thus, notification about the deaths of public figures is carried out on a grand scale. The death of President John F.

Obituaries

Spirit Bird Benton

HAYWARD – Spirit Bird Benton, 17, Rt. 5, Hayward, died Friday, April 19, 1991, in Albuquerque, N.M. in an automobile accident.

Spirit Bird was born August 22, 1973 in St. Paul, Minn., the son of Edward J. and Delma (Arrow) Benton. He was a student at Lac Courte Oreilles High School.

He is survived by his father, Edward, Hayward; his mother, Delma, Tama, Iowa; three brothers, John Wedward and Ramon, both of Hayward and Eddie, Green Bay; four sisters, Marilyn, Nancy and Sherrole, all of Hayward and Natalie, Oneida; and a grandmother, Elizabeth Arrow, White River, S.D.

Tribal rites were held on Tuesday, April 23 at the Eagle Lodge, Hayward. Burial was in the Hayward Indian Cemetery in Historyland.

Anderson-Nathan Funeral Home of Hayward was in charge of arrangements.

Figure 8-2 *Newspaper Obituary*
Source: The County Journal (Bayfield County, Cable, Wis.), April 25, 1991.

Kennedy, for example, was known by about 90 percent of the American people within an hour of its official pronouncement at Parkland Hospital in Dallas.[6] A similar social response occurred with the deaths of Diana, Princess of Wales, and John F. Kennedy, Jr.

The process of death notification also helps to set apart the bereaved during the period of mourning. In some societies, the black armband, mourning colors and garb, as well as various other signs and symbols, distinguish the bereaved person from those not in mourning. Such traditional signs of mourning have all but vanished in North America. Yet most people still feel that the bereaved deserve special consideration during their distress.

A woman who became involved in a minor automobile accident several days after the death of her child said later that she wished she could have had a banner proclaiming her status as a "mother whose child has just died." With no outward symbol of her bereavement, she was subjected, as any of us would be, to the strain of waiting around and filling in seemingly endless accident report forms. Had she lived in a small town, the process of notification itself might have set her apart in such a way that the task of completing the paperwork would have been made easier.

The process of death notification is important. It can elicit support that is helpful to survivors in dealing with their loss, and it provides an impetus for coming to terms with the fact that a significant loss has taken place.

Mutual Support

When people learn about the death of a person who is significant to them, they tend to gather together, closing ranks to provide support and comfort in their mutual bereavement. This emotional and social support is directed primarily toward the bereaved family. When a small child asked her mother why they were going to visit a bereaved family, the mother replied, "It's important for people to know that you care." What we think we can or cannot do for the bereaved family matters little; what counts is that we show our care and concern. J. Z. Young says, "Probably the very act of coming together symbolizes communication."[7] Assembling as a community reassures us that we are part of a larger whole, thereby strengthening our individual lives.

Funeral rituals embody the rhythms of separation and integration. Death is a change of status both for the person who dies and for his or her survivors. This change of status is reflected in language when we refer to someone as a "widow" or "widower." This use of a special designation for a bereaved spouse affirms the social and psychological impact associated with the death of a mate. Based on a cross-cultural investigation of funeral rites, Vernon Reynolds and Ralph Tanner conclude:

> The importance of the rituals of death is that they are socioreligious requirements which have to be carried out by the bereaved within the social context of friends, relatives, and neighbors who are less bereaved. The bereaved are not left alone to generate and multiply the psychosomatic symptoms of their grief, but are required to be active, and in many cultures there is a special role for bereaved persons over quite a long period . . . at the end of which their recovery from bereavement is well advanced.[8]

Gathering at the home of the bereaved is a unique social occasion. Some people stay only a short while, express their condolences, and leave. Others, usually relatives or close friends, stay for a longer time, perhaps assisting with

---

 Visiting with a family in a funeral home one night, we witnessed a woman enter the visiting room. She approached the casket and burst into convulsive tears. Two men stood up and supported her on either side as she sobbed loudly. The mother of the deceased man leaned over to me and said, "Brother Wayne, do you know that woman?" I had never seen her before. Everyone in the room was whispering and looking. "Who is that?" they were asking.

After this loud display, the men escorted the woman to a folding chair, where she gradually calmed herself. Finally, one of the men asked her how she was acquainted with his brother, Bill.

She raised her head and asked, "Bill?"

"Yes, that's my brother Bill."

The mystery lady stood, looked in the casket, and said, "Oh, I'm sorry . . . I'm in the wrong room," and quickly exited.

As we all doubled over with laughter, Bill's widow said, "I was fixin' to get up there and find out WHO she was and WHY she was so upset that Bill was dead!"

Wayne Delk, *U.S. Gospel News*

the preparation of food, caring for children, helping with funeral arrangements, greeting visitors, and doing whatever else needs doing. This process of gathering together to support and comfort the bereaved continues throughout the events of the funeral. Such social interaction is psychologically important for the bereaved. It corroborates the fact that a loved one has died. The coming together of the friends and relatives to support one another confirms the significance of that loss.

Impetus for Coping With Loss

The death of a loved one is confronted not only within the social setting in which it occurs, but also within the psyche of the bereaved person. Death notification, visitation, and other after-death rituals are forms of social interaction that provide a potent psychological impetus for coming to terms with a loss.

When death occurs, one of the immediate concerns of survivors is the disposition of the corpse. This involves both a mental process (deciding what is to be done) and a physical activity (carrying out the action decided upon). The final disposition of a dead body is surrounded by a web of social, cultural, religious, psychological, and personal considerations that determine how this task is accomplished. Making arrangements for the final disposition of the body engages survivors in a process that helps reinforce the recognition that the deceased person is really dead. This acknowledgment of the loss occurs whether the survivor simply talks with someone about funeral arrangements or actively constructs the coffin and digs the grave.

The funeral itself offers a range of opportunities for the bereaved to engage in activities that promote expression of grief. For example, survivors often place items that are somehow significant to the deceased in the casket. The practice of burying "grave goods," or funerary artifacts, with the dead is found in many cultures.[9] Jewelry, photographs, rosaries, Bibles, favorite hats, military medals, stuffed animals, and organizational emblems are among the items commonly placed in the casket or buried with the deceased. Tobacco, alcohol, and articles related to a favorite activity such as golf or fishing are other examples of grave goods. The placing of such grave goods is a mourning practice that can be very meaningful to survivors. Funeral rituals give significance to the activities connected with the final disposition of the deceased's body and, in so doing, provide a structure for experiencing and expressing grief.

The American Funeral

Few people personally care for their own dead in modern societies. Most of us hire professionals, known as funeral directors or morticians, to provide services and merchandise for conducting a funeral service and handling various tasks involved in caring for the dead. As a result, the funeral business is generally viewed as a "mystery business," about which the average person knows little. Critics of the modern American funeral claim that, because of this widespread lack of familiarity, funeral directors are in a position to take advantage of their customers. This claim is made despite the fact that most people give funeral directors high marks for the services they provide at a distressing time.

To counteract the potential for abuses, however, the U.S. Federal Trade Commission (FTC) implemented the "Trade Regulation Rule on Funeral Industry Practices" in 1984.[10] The Funeral Rule, as it is called, stipulates that funeral service providers must give detailed information about prices and legal requirements to people who are arranging funerals. It requires the disclosure of itemized prices, both over the telephone and in writing. Misrepresentations about the disposition of human remains are prohibited, as are certain practices such as embalming for a fee without prior permission, requiring customers to purchase caskets for a direct cremation, or making the purchase of any funeral good or service conditional on the purchase of any other funeral good or service. The FTC Funeral Rule can be viewed as the natural outcome of a historical process that removed death from the purview of family and friends and placed it in the hands of professionals.

The Rise of Professional Funeral Services

When families themselves took care of the disposition of their dead, any criticism would have been irrelevant. And, of course, there was no profit motive. Disposition of the dead was simply a human task to be carried out by the

 If you have an uncomfortable feeling about funerals, which are the accepted social pattern for confronting death in our culture, if you try to avoid or eliminate them, that might be a sign that you're dealing with major residual death anxiety. That's one of the things that shows up in our culture: the way people delude themselves and retreat from the major therapeutic resources that are provided culturally. There's a notion that if we have a mini-funeral, we'll have mini-grief. But we know that the exact opposite is true.

The more you reduce your emotional acting out at the time of the event, the more you prolong the pain of grief and postpone the therapeutic work of mourning.

That's why in a culture such as ours, where you have an unwise management of grief, you have a very large proportion of illness responses after the death experience. People act it out physically, rather than doing it psychologically or socially. That's a very heavy weight.

But in primitive cultures, such as the aboriginals in Australia, where you have almost a two-week funeral process, where there are all kinds of acting out of deep feelings, you come to the end of that two weeks and a major portion of the grief work has been done, and the survivor is ready to move into the period of resolution through the mourning process, which takes quite a bit longer usually.

Edgar N. Jackson, from an interview with the authors

Thousands of American citizens joined in the funeral observance honoring the Unknown Serviceman of the Vietnam Era. Here the procession is crossing Memorial Bridge between a Marine honor cordon, on its way to Arlington National Cemetery. Replete with full military honors, the funeral was an occasion for expressing national gratitude and grief in response to the ultimate sacrifice of those who died in the wartime service of their country.

family and community in a spirit of respect. At a time when the family's ceremonial occasions involving death were held within the home, the "undertaker" mainly functioned as a merchant who supplied materials and funeral
paraphernalia—such items as the casket and carriage, door badges and
scarves, special clothing, memorial cards and announcements, chairs, robes,
pillows, gauze, candles, ornaments, and so on—that were used for mourning
rituals (see Figure 8-3). From such humble beginnings, the funeral service
"industry" began to become more commercialized.

By the later decades of the nineteenth century, undertakers were assuming a larger role in caring for the dead. No longer merely a tradesman who
furnished goods to bereaved families, the undertaker had become a provider
of services. He began to actually take part in the disposition of the dead: laying
out the body for the wake, transporting it to the church for the funeral, and,
finally, taking it to the cemetery for burial. With the coming of smaller houses
and increased urbanization, the viewing of the body moved from the parlor of
the family home to a room reserved for such use by the tradesman-undertaker.
The funeral "parlor" in town became a substitute for the ceremonial room
that people no longer had in their own homes. This one-room funeral parlor
was the forerunner of the present-day funeral home or mortuary.

Also around this time, undertakers were becoming "morticians" and were
starting to view themselves as "funeral *directors.*" The Funeral Directors' National Association, established in the 1880s—now the National Funeral Directors Association (NFDA)—was among the first of the new trade organizations
designed to promote funeral service businesses as well as establish standards.
Early trade publications, such as *The Casket* and *Sunnyside,* helped to facilitate
communication among funeral directors.

Professionalism in funeral service continued with the founding, in 1917,
of the National Selected Morticians, a limited-membership group dedicated
to the ideal of excellent service. In 1945, the National Foundation of Funeral
Service was formed to conduct research, establish a library of funeral service
information, and sponsor an institute providing professional education for
funeral directors.

More recently, many funeral directors have expanded their services to
include "aftercare" programs, which can range from simply telephoning a
bereaved spouse to see how he or she is doing to offering counseling or support groups for bereaved individuals. Staff members may attend training programs to prepare themselves for offering aftercare and, in some cases, the
funeral establishment hires a certified psychologist or grief counselor to manage such services. In some communities, a local hospice and funeral home
join forces in providing support groups for the community. Many funeral
directors view this offering of aftercare service—this extension of their professional services—as a contemporary expression of "old-fashioned neighborly
concern."[11]

Traditionally, the clergy has played a large role in assisting bereaved families in making funeral arrangements. Whereas funerals were once commonly
held in churches, they are now more likely to be held in funeral homes.

The move from church to mortuary chapel (along with the more dominant role of mortuary personnel) has sometimes put a strain on relationships between clergy and funeral directors. Some members of the clergy are now bringing funeral services back into church and generally assuming a greater presence in the whole matter of funeral arrangements. In fact, some churches have started operating their own "funeral businesses" or have contracted with corporations that agree to provide funerals for parishioners at a discounted cost.

Conglomeration in the funeral industry has become a major trend, and much-debated topic, over the past decade or so. Large multinational corporations that own hundreds of funeral homes are purchasing neighborhood "mom-and-pop" funeral homes, many of which have been family owned and operated for generations. Many observers wonder whether the "personal touch" identified with locally owned funeral homes will be lost with corporate ownership. In some communities, long-time customers of funeral homes that were once family owned but are now owned by corporations are "voting with their feet" as they switch to mortuary establishments that remain devoted to local ownership and personal service.

The commercialization of funeral services over the past century or so has attracted a number of criticisms. Even though we are now accustomed to turning over care of our dead to professionals, the idea of profiting from such services may seem somehow macabre. Discomfort about the "funeral industry" may also relate to a sense of anxiety that is likely to be more prevalent among people who have little personal contact with death. When a corpse belongs to someone we loved, the common aversion to touching a dead body may be mixed with guilt. Unconscious resentment may be felt toward the funeral director or mortician who prepares the body of our loved one for final disposition. Pulled in opposing directions, we may experience a confusing range of emotions regarding our dead: aversion, guilt, resentment, anxiety, and affection. In some cases, our relative lack of familiarity with the dead can make funeral directors and funeral establishments a lightning rod for criticisms.

Figure 8-3 *City Directory Listing for a Cabinet Maker and Supplier of Funeral Furnishings, circa 1850*

"Now, Mr. Barlow, what had you in mind? Embalmment of course, and after that incineration or not, according to taste. Our crematory is on scientific principles, the heat is so intense that all inessentials are volatilized. Some people did not like the thought that ashes of the casket and clothing were mixed with the Loved One's. Normal disposal is by inhumement, entombment, inurnment or immurement, but many people just lately prefer insarcophagusment. That is *very* individual. The casket is placed inside a sealed sarcophagus, marble or bronze, and rests permanently above ground in a niche in the mausoleum, with or without a personal stained-glass window above. That, of course, is for those with whom price is not a primary consideration."

Evelyn Waugh, *The Loved One*

Criticisms of Funeral Practices

Funerals have attracted criticism of various kinds since ancient times. The Greek philosopher Herodotus, in the fourth century B.C., spoke critically about what he called lavish displays for the dead. American funeral practices have attracted their share of criticism as well, especially since the early decades of the twentieth century, as funeral ceremonies and care of the dead became professionalized, no longer a standard part of domestic life. In the wake of these changes, one of the earliest criticisms was directed not just at American funeral practices, but at the funeral itself. Published in 1926, Bertram Puckle's *Funeral Customs: Their Origin and Development* argued that the modern funeral was merely the vestige of a "pagan" superstitious fear of the dead. Like Herodotus, Puckle was especially critical of elaborate ceremonies for the dead.

In 1959, the commercialism and conspicuous display connected with funerals were documented by LeRoy Bowman in *The American Funeral: A Study in Guilt, Extravagance, and Sublimity*.[12] Bowman was especially interested in the social and psychological value of funerals, and he was concerned that modern funerals were overlaid with such ostentation that the essential meaning and dignity of funeral rites had all but disappeared. The American funeral, Bowman said, "appears to be an anachronism, an elaboration of early customs rather than the adaptation to modern needs that it should be." In Bowman's view, the funeral director was a tradesman, often selling wares that were unnecessary and unwanted. Bowman believed that consumers could avoid the potential for exploitation associated with the materialistic features of contemporary practices by becoming aware of the essential social, psychological, and spiritual functions of funeral rituals. The function of the funeral director, said Bowman, should be to help the family fulfill its own wishes. He also argued for greater flexibility in funeral service: "The uniformity of present usage," he said, "should give way to individually adapted procedures, whatever they may be."

In 1963, two books appeared that brought considerable public attention to the American funeral: Jessica Mitford's *The American Way of Death* and Ruth

"Eddie was a simple man and, in the end, an eminently practical one."

Drawing by Jack Ziegler, © 1997 The New Yorker Collection

M. Harmer's *The High Cost of Dying.* Both of these books criticized the materialism of modern funerals and appealed for reforms. To Mitford, conventional funeral practices were bizarre and morbid; efforts to disguise and prettify death only made it more grotesque. She took issue with the euphemisms employed to soften the reality of death: the metamorphosis of coffins into "caskets," hearses into "coaches," flowers into "floral tributes," and cremated ashes into "cremains." The language of funeral service businesses came under especially heavy assault by Mitford's penetrating wit. The corpse lies in state in the "slumber room." The undertaker, now a "funeral director," displays a solid-copper "Colonial Classic Beauty" casket, replete with "Perfect-Posture" adjustable mattress, in a choice of "60 color-matched shades." The deceased wears "handmade original fashions" from a "gravewear couturiere" and "Nature-Glo, the ultimate in cosmetic grooming."[13]

Despite the criticisms of American funeral practices by Mitford and others, most people appear to be satisfied with the quality of service provided by their local mortuaries. Funeral directors often receive expressions of gratitude from the people they serve. Their immediate help in sorting out the events of the days following the death of a loved one provides stability and reassurance. The typical funeral director is committed to meeting the needs and wishes of bereaved families, even when they vary from "standard" practices, as the following story illustrates.

When a Dutch couple died unexpectedly while traveling in South America, their relatives felt that the couple's intimacy and sharing in life should be carried through to their death rites. They wanted the couple buried together in one coffin, and in one grave. Although this request had never been made before, the funeral establishment checked applicable laws and found that they did not prohibit the family's wishes being carried out. There were practical problems, however. No company made a double casket. Acting quickly, the funeral home found a craftsman who was able to make a special casket by working overtime and, with a few adjustments, all went smoothly. The funeral director said, "We are proud that we have been able to arrange this committal for the couple in which, for the children, the love between their parents was confirmed."[14] A willingness to "go the extra mile" is typical of most funeral directors.

Selecting Funeral Services

In commemorating a person's life and death, the choice of last rites may involve a traditional funeral ceremony or a simple memorial service. Whereas the casketed body is typically present at a funeral, it is not at a memorial service. In some cases, both a funeral and a memorial service are held, the former occurring within a few days after death and the latter being held sometime later (perhaps in a different town, where the deceased had a large social network). Although it is becoming more common for individuals and families to express a preference for no services, bereaved relatives and friends can experience important benefits from having an opportunity to honor the deceased and express their grief through ceremony.

Decisions about one's own last rites are ideally made with a view to the needs and wishes of one's survivors. It can be worthwhile to consider such decisions early in life, while it's possible to gather information about options, and to discuss plans with family members. In making plans or arrangements, you may want to review the various elements that are traditionally part of after-death rituals (see Table 8-1, presented earlier in this chapter). Religious and cultural or ethnic traditions play a major role in shaping the way people honor their dead. The diversity of life and death in the United States calls for a diversity of rites. A meaningful funeral or memorial service can be designed in many different ways.

The purchase of funeral services is a transaction unique in commerce. Most people give it little or no thought until they find themselves in the midst of an emotional crisis. As with other purchases, however, the customer who winds up with the fewest regrets is likely to be the one who takes time beforehand to investigate his or her options. When arrangements for funeral services are made during a time of crisis and confusion, the customer must make an on-the-spot decision about a purchase that cannot be returned. Caskets do not bear a notice saying, "Return in thirty days if not completely satisfied." Once made, the decision is final. Lack of information, coupled with lack of forethought about funerals or body disposition, may lead to choices that are regretted later.

Selecting funeral services differs from the way we make most other purchases. When purchasing a new car, for example, you can shop around and test-drive various makes and models. If you encounter a salesperson who uses high-pressure tactics, you can either submit or walk away: You have a clear choice. Yet, the emotional circumstances surrounding the purchase of funeral services rarely allow for such objectivity or coolheadedness. The bereaved is usually not in a position to simply walk away and compare prices elsewhere. In some towns, there is just one funeral business to serve the entire community. Once a death has occurred, it may be too late to fully investigate the options.

It is unfortunate when an expensive casket or lavish display becomes the focal point of a funeral merely because survivors are attempting to assuage guilt or compensate for unresolved conflict with the deceased. Spending a huge sum of money on a funeral may, in some circumstances, thwart the real purpose of last rites—namely, to effect closure on the deceased's life and comfort the bereaved. As Thomas Lynch, a funeral director and poet-essayist, says, "In even the best of caskets, it never all fits—all that we'd like to bury in them: the hurt and forgiveness, the anger and pain, the praise and thanksgiving, the emptiness and exaltations, the untidy feelings when someone dies."[15]

The funeral is a setting for private sorrow and public loss in which the burden of grief is reduced by sharing with others. It effects the disposition of the corpse while acknowledging that indeed a life has been lived. The funeral is a statement from the family to the community: "We have lost someone, and we are grieving." Ideally, it is a personal statement based on felt needs and values. It is worth remembering that the purpose of the funeral can be realized whether it is garnished with diamonds and rubies, or with poetry and a song.

Funeral Service Charges

The National Funeral Directors Association distinguishes four categories of costs related to the conventional American funeral. The first category includes services provided by the funeral director and mortuary staff, the use of mortuary facilities and equipment, and the casket and any other funeral merchandise selected by the customer.

The second category pertains to the disposition of the body. This can include the purchase of a gravesite and costs for opening and closing the grave; or, if aboveground entombment is chosen, the cost of a mausoleum crypt; or, if the body is cremated, the cost of cremation and subsequent interment, entombment, or scattering of the cremated remains, as well as the cost of an urn to hold the ashes, if desired.

The third category involves costs related to memorialization. For burials, this can include a monument or marker for the grave; for cremated remains, it can include an inscription or plaque for the niche (recessed compartment)

What sounds downright oxymoronic to most of the subspecies—a *good* funeral—is, among undertakers, a typical idiom. And though I'll grant some are pulled into the undertaking by big cars and black suits and rumors of riches, the attrition rate is high among those who do not like what they are doing. Unless the novice mortician finds satisfaction in helping others at a time of need, or "serving the living by caring for the dead" as one of our slogans goes, he or she will never stick it. Unless, of course, they make a pile of money early on. But most of us who can afford to send our kids to the orthodonist but not to boarding schools, who are tied to our brick and mortar and cash-flow worries, who live with the business phone next to our beds, whose dinners and intimacies are always being interrupted by the needs of others, would not do so unless there were satisfactions beyond the fee schedule. Most of the known world could not be paid enough to embalm a neighbor on Christmas or stand with an old widower at his wife's open casket or talk with a leukemic mother about her fears for her children to be motherless. The ones who last in this work are the ones who believe what they do is not only good for business and the bottom line, but good, after everything, for the species.

Thomas Lynch,
The Undertaking: Life Studies from the Dismal Trade

in a *columbarium,* an aboveground structure with a series of niches for urns.

The fourth category involves miscellaneous expenses either paid directly by the family or reimbursed to the undertaker. These may include a clergy member's honorarium, the use of limousines and additional vehicles (if not included in the funeral services category), flowers, death notices in newspapers, and transportation of the body outside the local area, if necessary.

Until the early 1980s, the funeral director's portion of these expenses might be quoted to customers in various ways. The most widespread form of pricing, and the simplest, was the single-unit method: A single price was quoted for a standard funeral; the specifics of the service and the total price depended on the type of casket selected. A more expensive casket thus became the centerpiece of a correspondingly more ornate and elaborate ceremony.

With the advent of the Federal Trade Commission's Funeral Rule in 1984, it has become a requirement for all funeral businesses to provide itemized price information on a general price list so that customers can compare prices or choose only those elements of a funeral they want. It is important to note that FTC requirements do not prohibit funeral directors from also offering "package" funerals for a single price.

Funeral costs vary among regions of the country, as well as between rural and metropolitan areas. The average cost of an adult funeral, including casket but excluding cemetery costs, is now about $5500.[16] With about 2.3 million Americans dying each year, expenditures for funeral services total about $11 billion.[17] Although many funeral service firms are small businesses, considered in the aggregate, disposition of the dead is clearly big business.

TABLE 8-2   *Funeral Service Prices*

Services

Professional service charges	$965–$1290
Embalming	$320–$465
Other preparations (cosmetology, hair, etc.)	$110–$180
Visitation/Viewing	$175–$375
Funeral at mortuary	$275–$380
Memorial service	$310–$400
Graveside service	$240–$435
Transfer of remains to mortuary	$115–$175
Hearse	$135–$185
Limousine	$70–$170
Service car/van	$65–$135
Direct cremation	$1145–$1545
Immediate burial	$1175–$1980
Forwarding remains to another funeral home	$1075–$1340
Receiving remains from another funeral home	$915–$1135

Merchandise

Acknowledgment cards	$15–$95
Casket (selected woods)	$1590–$3280
Casket (selected metals)	$880–$6230
Burial vault	$505–$2180

Comparing the Costs

Even when itemized, costs quoted by different funeral homes may be difficult to compare. Funeral providers do not always offer exactly the same goods and services, and they may have different ways of presenting prices. Nevertheless, it is useful to distinguish the usual charges that may be assessed. (In reading the following discussion of funeral goods and services, you can refer to Table 8-2, which shows the national ranges for funeral services and merchandise.)

Professional Services

Funeral costs include a basic charge for the services provided by mortuary staff, such as arranging the funeral, consulting with family members and clergy, directing the visitation and funeral ceremony, and preparing and filing necessary notices and authorizations related to body disposition. The latter may include filing the death certificate and certain claims for death benefits.

The fee for professional services also must cover a share of the overhead and business expenses required to maintain facilities and staff. Mortuary facilities usually require a large capital investment because of their specialized design. The typical funeral business is located in a large, possibly colonial style, building. The floor plan may be designed especially to function as a funeral home. Funerals have been compared to theatrical presentations, with certain activities taking place "off stage." The backstage area, hidden away from the public's gaze, is where the body is prepared by embalming and application of cosmetics for its eventual role in the funeral drama. There is generally no hint of these backstage regions to those who enter by the front door. The funeral chapel itself has been described as "a model of theatrical perfection" that might well "make a Broadway star envious."[18] Usually arranged in such a way that there are several entrances and exits, it "may be served by back doors, halls, tunnels, and passageways that lead from the preparation room without ever trespassing frontstage areas."

Besides the fee for professional services, mortuaries usually charge an "intake fee" for transferring remains from the place of death to the mortuary, and there may be a surcharge for after-hours (night or weekend) pickup. In addition, cemetery or crematory services, flowers, placement of newspaper notices, and other incidental costs are usually billed separately.

As an alternative pricing method, the FTC rule allows funeral providers to include the professional service fee as part of the cost of caskets. When this is done, however, a description of such services must appear on the casket price list.

The FTC Funeral Rule also specifies that, with direct cremation or immediate burial, the fee for professional services must be included in the price quoted for those methods of disposition. Similarly, the fee for professional services must be included in prices quoted for forwarding remains to another funeral home or receiving remains from another funeral home.

Embalming

A body destined for burial or cremation may or may not be embalmed. If the body is to be viewed during a wake or present at the funeral, however, embalming is generally done (although facilities with "cold rooms" may substitute for embalming). Embalming methods have differed among cultures, with correspondingly varied results with respect to preservation of the corpse. In *Death to Dust,* Kenneth Iserson says, "Originally, embalming meant placing balm, essentially natural sap and aromatic substances, on a corpse."[19] In modern usage, embalming involves removing the blood and other fluids in the body and replacing them with chemicals to disinfect and temporarily retard deterioration of the corpse.

In the United States, embalming was adopted around the time of the Civil War, as funeral homes like Brown & Alexander in Washington, D.C., began to make embalming available to their clientele. Brown was a medical doctor whose interest in embalming grew out of his training in anatomy and his marriage to the daughter of the founder of the oldest present-day continuously operating funeral home in the United States, Kirk & Nice in Philadelphia. After witnessing embalming demonstrations by a French doctor in New York City, Brown decided to offer this service at no charge to "soldiers who may be so unfortunate as to die or be killed while at the seat of war and away from their families and friends."[20] The funeral procession for President Abraham Lincoln, which traveled by train from Washington, D.C., to Springfield,

Illinois, was a public event that greatly increased awareness of the practice of embalming.[21] During this period, however, other means of temporarily retarding decomposition of the corpse remained in use (see Figure 8-4).

Embalming is such an accepted practice in America that few people question it, and it is usually considered a practical necessity by most mortuary establishments when a body will be viewed. With few exceptions, however, the FTC rule requires that mortuaries obtain express permission to embalm from the family in order to charge a fee for the procedure.[22] Furthermore, the mortuary's price list must include the following disclosure next to the price for embalming:

> Except in certain special cases, embalming is not required by law. Embalming may be necessary, however, if you select certain funeral arrangements, such as a funeral with viewing. If you do not want embalming, you usually have the right to choose an arrangement which does not require you to pay for it, such as direct cremation or immediate burial.

Some mortuaries have a combined fee for both embalming and body preparation; others itemize the procedures separately. In addition to basic antiseptic

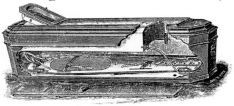

J. C. TAYLOR & SON'S
PATENT IMPROVED ICE CASKETS,
FOR PRESERVING THE DEAD BY COLD AIR.

The Pioneer Corpse Preserver, Over 3,500 in Use.

⁓ PRICES AND SIZES: ⁓

6 Feet 4 Inches Long, 20 Inches Wide, $60 00.   4 Feet 10 Inches Long, 17 Inches Wide, $48 00.
5 " 10 "   "   20 "   "   58 00.   3 " 10 "   "   15 "   "   42 00.

Send for Illustrated and Descriptive Price-List, Containing full Particulars.

FOR SALE AT MANUFACTURERS' PRICES, BY

Paxson, Comfort & Co., 523 Market St., Philadelphia.

Figure 8-4 *Refrigerated Casket Advertisement, 1881*
Undertakers of the 1880s could keep a body for viewing over a longer period of time by using an ice casket, such as the one shown in this advertisement. When embalming became widespread, these cold-air preservation devices became obsolete.

hygiene procedures, body preparation services may include cosmetology, hair styling, and manicuring, as well as dressing the body, placing it in the casket, and composing it for viewing.

If refrigeration or a "cold room" is available, a mortuary may offer the alternative of storing a body for a short time without embalming. A refrigerated, unembalmed body will remain relatively preserved for about three days, although some mortuaries stipulate that they will not hold an unembalmed body for longer than forty-eight hours. Refrigeration usually costs somewhat less than embalming.

Caskets

Most people feel that the casket is the centerpiece of a funeral because of its symbolic and emotional value in honoring the deceased. The average amount spent on a casket is about $2200. However, when it comes to buying a casket, customers have a wide range of choices, and prices are highly variable. Choices range from inexpensive cardboard containers all the way to solid mahogany, copper, or bronze caskets that cost thousands of dollars. Depending on the socioeconomic status of their clientele, most funeral homes display caskets in a range of prices. Because funeral businesses determine their own methods of pricing caskets, customers may find that a casket selling for $1500 in one funeral home costs twice that amount in another. This price difference may be due to a higher markup by the second funeral home; or, as mentioned earlier, the fee for professional services may be included in the casket price rather than charged separately.

Caskets at the lower end of the price range are typically made of cloth-covered plywood or pressboard and contain a mattress that is likely to be made of straw covered with an acetate sheet. At the next pricing level, from about $1500 to several thousand dollars, certain refinements appear. The casket may be covered with copper or bronze sheathing, and the mattress is probably constructed with springs and topped by a layer of foam rubber with a covering of acetate material. In this mid-range, gasketed steel caskets are available with devices intended to ensure an airtight environment within the casket. (Although this provides solace for some people, any added protection is debatable.) The gasketed steel casket is most popular with Americans.[23]

The price for a "top-of-the-line" casket ranges from about $5000 upward to $25,000 or more. For this sum, there are caskets constructed of mahogany, copper, or bronze and fitted out with all the embellishments of the casket manufacturer's art. Deluxe models feature an adjustable boxspring mattress that can be tilted to enhance the display of the corpse.

The FTC rule requires funeral providers to supply customers with a list of the prices and descriptions of available caskets. This may be done either on the general price list or on a separate casket price list. In addition, the FTC rule stipulates that customers have the right to buy a casket from a different supplier than the funeral home contracted to handle all the other aspects of the funeral service and burial. In 1993, the FTC reaffirmed this rule when a customer of Al Tacker's Family Heritage Casket Gallery in Memphis,

Library of Congress

The funeral has traditionally been a time when family and friends come together to pay respects and to say farewells. It is a time of mutual support for the bereaved and of tribute to the deceased. The display of flowers surrounding this coffin bespeaks the affection felt for the deceased while she was alive and the sense of loss at her absence from the community.

Tennessee, filed a complaint with the FTC claiming that a funeral home refused to accept a casket bought from Tacker's shop (a discount casket retailer).[24] In addition, funeral homes may not charge handling fees on caskets purchased elsewhere.

This 1993 ruling has led to an increase in the number of casket discounters, some of which are operated as small chains. Although many are storefront businesses or are even located in shopping malls, some discounters are set up so that customers can order caskets via an 800 number or on the Internet. Some mortuaries are following this trend by opening their own "funeral shops," where caskets and funeral accessories are sold at discounted prices.[25] Customers now have the opportunity to avoid part of the markup on caskets charged by funeral homes, but it is not clear that most people will feel comfortable purchasing funeral merchandise from discounters. Funeral homes provide "one-stop shopping" for merchandise and services. Furthermore, people may be uncomfortable with the idea of "skimping" on a loved one's funeral. Nevertheless, for some, casket retailers appear to be an idea whose time has come. The Regale Funeral Store in London, England, a "funeral supermarket," offers flowers, memorials, caskets, urns, and other funeral paraphernalia in a supermarket-style shopping hall, with the prices of all products and services clearly itemized and priced.[26]

People are usually surprised to learn that there is no law requiring that a body destined for cremation must be placed in a casket. Most crematoria require only that the body be delivered in a rigid container. Mortuaries can provide a body-sized cardboard box that suffices for this purpose. The FTC rule prohibits funeral providers from telling consumers that state or local law requires them to purchase a casket when they want to arrange a direct cremation (that is, a cremation that occurs without formal viewing of the remains or any visitation or ceremony with the body present). The FTC rule stipulates that firms offering direct cremation provide the following disclosure:

> If you want to arrange a direct cremation, you can use an unfinished wood box or an alternative container. Alternative containers can be made of materials like heavy cardboard or composition materials (with or without an outside covering), or pouches of canvas.

Outer Burial Containers

If outer burial containers (vaults or grave liners) are offered for sale by a funeral home, prices must be listed, either separately or on the general price list, and the following disclosure must be made:

> In most areas of the country, no state or local law makes you buy a container to surround the casket in the grave. However, many cemeteries require that you have such a container so that the grave will not sink in. Either a burial vault or a grave liner will satisfy these requirements.

Because many funeral businesses do not sell burial vaults or grave liners, this item may not appear on the price lists of mortuaries in your area.

Facilities and Vehicles

The use of a "visitation" or "viewing" room is a common component of most American funerals. In the itemized listing of prices, the funeral establishment may use whatever method of pricing it prefers or follow common practice in its area. For example, various settings in the funeral home might be listed, along with the charges for each by day, half day, or hour. Similarly, if funeral ceremonies can be held in a chapel at the funeral home, a charge for its use will be specified. When other facilities are made available to customers (for example, tent and chairs for graveside services), the charges must be stated on the price list.

According to the FTC rule, charges for the use of a hearse, limousine, or other automotive equipment provided by the mortuary must be itemized separately on the general price list. Family members, pallbearers, or other participants such as clergy often use vehicles provided by a funeral home. A "flower car" (or van) may be engaged to transport floral arrangements from the place where the funeral is held to the cemetery or crematorium. A fee will also be assessed when a motorcycle escort is hired to be part of the procession.

Miscellaneous Charges

In the miscellaneous category are charges for goods or services provided directly by the funeral home, as well as charges incurred on behalf of the customer from outside sources. The latter include "cash-advance" items, such as floral arrangements and newspaper notices. Customer may be billed for the actual amounts of the items, or the funeral provider may add a surcharge for arranging these cash-advance items. If an additional charge is made, a notice to that effect must be shown on the general price list.

The FTC rule specifically mentions that acknowledgment cards must be itemized if the funeral provider sells those items or performs the service of filling out and sending them for customers.

The "miscellaneous charges" category may also include the cost of burial garments purchased from the mortuary, any fees or honoraria for pallbearers, or an honorarium for the clergyperson who conducts the funeral service.

Direct Cremations and Immediate Burials

Not all funeral homes offer direct cremations and immediate burials to customers, but most now do offer these options. These methods of body disposition generally do not involve any formal viewing of the remains or any visitation or ceremony with the body present. (Some mortuaries respond to requests for viewing or informal ceremonies by placing the body on a cloth-covered gurney.)

If direct cremation or immediate burial is offered by a funeral home, the cost—which includes the fee for professional services—is shown on the general price list. When direct cremation is selected, the customer must be given the option of providing the container or of purchasing an unfinished pine box or alternative container (such as a box made of cardboard, plywood, or composition material). Similarly, for immediate burials, the customer can provide a container or purchase a simple casket, such as one made of wood and covered with cloth. (If a funeral home offers immediate burials but does not offer direct cremations, the FTC rule does not require the firm to make available an alternative container or unfinished wood box, although a funeral director might choose to do so.)

Funeral and Memorial Societies

Funeral and memorial societies are non-profit, cooperative organizations that offer body disposition to members at a reduced cost by arranging with a mortuary or crematorium to provide services based on volume purchasing. There are currently about 200 societies in the United States and Canada. Most advocate simplicity and economy in after-death arrangements. They generally follow a minimalist plan with respect to disposition of the corpse—either immediate cremation or immediate burial—although some offer other op-

Assume that we are confronted with the dead body of a man. What disposition shall we make of it? Shall we lay it in a boat that is set adrift? Shall we take the heart from it and bury it in one place and the rest of the body in another? Shall we expose it to wild animals? Burn it on a pyre? Push it into a pit to rot with other bodies? Boil it until the flesh falls off the bones, and throw the flesh away and treasure the bones? Such questions provoke others which may not be consciously articulated, such as: "What do men generally think this body is?" And, "What do they think is a proper way of dealing with it?"

Robert W. Habenstein and William M. Lamers,
The History of American Funeral Directing

tions at a higher cost. Funeral and memorial societies represent a response to consumers' wishes for low-cost and simple methods of body disposition.

Body Disposition

Think for a moment about the manner you would choose for the disposition of your body after you die. Corpses must be disposed of for sanitary reasons, though it is unlikely that a person's choice of *how* to accomplish disposition is influenced by that fact. The method chosen is more likely to involve social, cultural, religious, psychological, and personal considerations. Reynolds and Tanner point out that "Dead bodies have to be disposed of and religions often provide the rules and personnel for this, even when the dead and their survivors are not specifically religious."[27] When Americans are asked their preferences, responses usually fall into one of the following categories: earth burial, entombment in a mausoleum crypt, cremation, or donation to science.

Religious beliefs often influence the method of body disposition. For example, Judaism, Christianity, and Islam typically practice ground burial, whereas Hindus and Buddhists prefer cremation. Each method of disposing of the corpse has symbolic meanings that are important to followers of the respective religions. For example, among Hindus, cremation is seen as a gesture of purification and symbol of the transitory nature of human life. Orthodox Judaism, in contrast, views cremation as a form of idolatry; burial returns the body to the "dust" from whence it was created by God. Other branches of Judaism have a less strict view of the ban on cremation. The Christian prohibition against cremation is no longer universal, having been replaced by a diversity of viewpoints; some churches support or at least tolerate cremation whereas others require, or strongly prefer, ground burial.

In *Death to Dust,* Kenneth Iserson reports that "[a]n unembalmed body buried six-feet deep in ordinary soil without a coffin normally takes ten to twelve years to decompose down to the bony skeleton; a child's body takes about half that time."[28] Environmental conditions can delay or hasten decomposition; for example, corpses buried in coffins or caskets take longer to decompose than those buried without such containers, and bodies exposed to the environment will generally be reduced to skeletons rather quickly.

The decomposition of the body is hastened in some societies by washing the flesh from the bones when the corpse is partially decomposed; parts of the body are then retained as a memorial. In other societies, open-air disposal is practiced, with the body left to the elements, where it generally decomposes quite rapidly (except in very dry, desert climates, where heat removes the moisture from the body, acting thereby to preserve it). Some Indian tribes of the American plains constructed platforms on which the corpse was exposed to the effects of the sun, wind, and rain. In some societies, vultures or other animals consume the remains of the dead. In India, for example, one can see scaffolds known as high *dakhmas* (towers of silence) on Bombay's fashionable Marabar Hill, where the Parsi community disposes of its dead by leaving corpses to be devoured by birds of prey. As followers of Zoroaster, they regard earth, fire, and water as sacred; and, therefore, not to be defiled by the dead.

A method of body disposal practiced by mariners since ancient times is water burial, or burial at sea. Depending on circumstances and cultural practices, this form of body disposition might involve either ceremonially sliding the corpse off the side of a ship or placing the corpse inside a boat that is set aflame and then set adrift. The Norwegian ship burials of the Viking Age present an interesting twist on this method of body disposal by combining the "burial at sea" theme with ground burial.[29] The dead were laid in a wooden grave chamber and placed in a ship along with grave goods, and the whole was covered by an earthen mound.

Donation to medical science is another method of body disposition. The person who chooses this method may gain satisfaction from the notion that he or she is making a contribution to the advancement of knowledge: "My body will serve a useful function even after I'm gone." This is a somewhat limited option, however, because most medical schools and other such institutions require few cadavers. Thus, the option of donating one's body to medical science may be difficult to implement. When a body has been donated to science, the final disposition of the remains may be left to the discretion of the institution that has the body. The next of kin is usually given a say in determining the final disposition once the medical or scientific purposes of the donation have been achieved. When the next of kin does not request return of the remains for private disposition, most medical schools and other such institutions have policies to ensure that cadavers are treated ethically and that human remains are disposed of properly. In some cases, a memorial service is held to acknowledge the gift that is represented by the donation of the body to science.[30]

Cryogenic suspension is not a method of body disposal in the sense used so far, but it has nevertheless attracted attention as a unique way to deal with a body after death. Cryogenic suspension involves preserving a corpse by freezing it to the temperature of solid carbon dioxide and keeping the body frozen until some future time when medical science is sophisticated enough to allow for resuscitation of the body and continued life.

U.S. Navy Photo

Burial at sea is a naval tradition the world over, particularly during times of war. Here the body of a seaman is committed to the deep during burial services aboard the USS Ranger *in 1963.*

From the burials of prehistory to space-age cryonics, human beings have chosen from a variety of alternatives for disposing of the dead. Although few people give much thought to the subject of body disposition, it is nonetheless fraught with emotional and psychological importance, as the following story illustrates: When Major Edward Strombeck was killed in a plane crash while on duty in Vietnam, the military cremated his body and forwarded the ashes, by mail, to his home in Hawaii.[31] Shocked at the lack of proper ceremony, his mother and other family members expressed their dismay and gained the attention of U.S. Senator Daniel Inouye. The result was a change in policy, which ordered that the ashes of military personnel must be escorted home with dignity and honor. Proper disposition of human remains is a matter of considerable significance not only to the immediate survivors, but also to the larger community. What do your own preferences regarding body disposition tell you about your attitudes and beliefs toward death?

Burial

In the Western European tradition, and in most societies associated with that tradition, including the United States, the preferred method for disposing

© Albert Lee Strickland

Burial vaults, such as those seen here in Oaxaca, Mexico, represent an alternative to underground burial that is found in many parts of the world. When space is at a premium, bodies may be removed from the vaults after a certain period of time and given underground burial.

of the corpse has been burial, at least until recently. Now, with a growing number of cremations, traditional cemetery burial is becoming more of a life-style choice.[32] *Burial* usually involves a grave dug into the soil or entombment in a mausoleum, although the term itself encompasses a wide range of practices. It may involve digging a single grave in the soil, or it may refer to entombment in a mausoleum (of which the Taj Mahal and the pyramids are examples). The whole body can be buried, or just the bones or even cremated remains. In some parts of the world, cemetery plots are purchased outright; elsewhere, a burial plot is merely rented for a number of years.[33] In some cemeteries, we are all equal in death; in others, the social distinctions that held sway in life are perpetuated by dividing burial space into classes with better placement of graves for those who occupy the first-class ranks.[34]

In addition to the cost of a cemetery plot, which can range from less than $100 to more than $5000, cemeteries usually require a grave liner or vault to support the earth around and above the casket. This adds about $500–$800 to the cost of ground burial, although certain vaults that are designed (but not guaranteed) to seal out moisture cost substantially more.

The cost of entombment in a mausoleum or outdoor crypt averages about $2000 although, again, prices vary. Historically, the term *crypt* denotes a subterranean burial vault or chamber, often situated beneath the floor of a church. In modern usage, the term also refers to space in a *mausoleum,* an aboveground structure of concrete, marble, or other stone in which one or more bodies are entombed. The most expensive crypt spaces are usually those at eye level, with less expensive spaces at the top and bottom. (The Queen of Heaven mausoleum complex in Chicago, the world's largest Catholic mausoleum, has space for 33,000 bodies.[35]) The opening and closing of a grave or crypt normally involves additional charges, which range from about $75 to $350, depending on the particular facility.

Simple bronze or stone grave markers generally cost about $300, with nameplates for mausoleum crypts costing a bit less. More elaborate memorials, if they are permitted by a cemetery (some permit only flat-on-the-ground markers), cost from several hundred to many thousands of dollars.

Finally, some cemeteries assess an endowment or "perpetual care cost" that subsidizes upkeep of the cemetery. These costs range upward of $100, although this fee is sometimes included in the basic cost for burial or entombment.

Cremation

Cremation involves subjecting a body to intense heat, thereby reducing its organic components to a mineralized skeleton. In the United States, the practice of cremation as a method of body disposal dates from the nineteenth century (although it had been customary for some Native American cultural groups for centuries, of course). In Europe, the practice is considerably older, going back at least to the Bronze Age. Cremation is the most common method of body disposal in many countries, including India and Japan, and it has found growing acceptance in the United States in recent decades. Currently, cremation is the method of body disposition chosen in about one-quarter of the deaths in the United States.[36]

Cremation involves a process of dehydration and oxidation of the organic components of the body by subjecting a corpse to extreme heat, approximately 2000 to 2500 degrees Fahrenheit. Cremation has been accomplished by means ranging from a simple wood fire to sophisticated electric or gas retorts. In the United States, natural gas is the most commonly used fuel. An average-size body takes about one and one-half hours to be reduced to a mineralized skeleton, which is put through a "cremulator" that reduces the bone fragments to a granular state, often referred to as "ashes." (The term *ashes* leads some people to believe that the cremated remains will look and feel like wood or paper ashes. Actually, they include pieces of bone, which look and feel like coarse coral sands whose shell-like components are worn by the wind and waves.)

Cremated remains can be buried, placed in a columbarium niche, put into an urn kept by the family or interred in an urn garden, or scattered at sea or on land. State and local laws may restrict how some of these options are carried out. Although scattering cremated remains is a popular method of final disposition, and usually the least costly, some people who have decided

Elmer Ruiz: Gravedigger

Not anybody can be a gravedigger. You can dig a hole any way they come. A grave-digger, you have to make a neat job. I had a fella once, he wanted to see a grave. He was a fella that digged sewers. He was impressed when he seen me diggin' this grave—how square and how perfect it was. A human body is goin' into this grave. That's why you need skill when you're gonna dig a grave.

The gravedigger today, they have to be somebody to operate a machine. You just use a shovel to push the dirt loose. Otherwise you don't use 'em. We're tryin' a new machine, a ground hog. This machine is supposed to go through heavy frost. It do very good job so far. When the weather is mild, like fifteen degrees above zero, you can do it very easy.

But when the weather is below zero, believe me, you just really workin' hard. I have to use a mask. Your skin hurts so much when it's cold—like you put a hot flame near your face. I'm talkin' about two, three hours standin' outside. You have to wear a mask, otherwise you can't stand it at all. . . .

The most graves I dig is about six, seven a day. This is in the summer. In the winter it's a little difficult. In the winter you have four funerals, that's a pretty busy day. . . .

The grave will be covered in less than two minutes, complete. We just open the hoppers with the right amount of earth. We just press it and then we lay out a layer of black earth. Then we put the sod that belongs there. After a couple of weeks you wouldn't know it's a grave there. It's complete flat. Very rarely you see a grave that is sunk. . . .

I usually tell 'em I'm a caretaker. I don't think the name sound as bad. I have to look at the park, so after the day's over that everything's closed, that nobody do damage to the park. Some occasions some people just come and steal and loot and do bad things in the park, destroy some things. I believe it would be some young fellas. A man with responsibility, he wouldn't do things like that. Finally we had to put up some gates and close 'em at sundown. Before, we didn't, no. We have a fence of roses. Always in cars you can come after sundown. . . .

A gravedigger is a very important person. You must have hear about the strike we had in New York about two years ago. There were twenty thousand bodies layin'

to scatter "ashes" later regret it because, as one woman said about her husband, "I have no place to take him a flower." When remains are scattered at sea, over a forest, or in some similar locale, people may find that they miss the emotional power of a *specific place* where one can visit the deceased loved one. In Japanese cemeteries, *haka*—small, private family mausolea that fit on a standard cemetery plot—hold a dozen crematory urns. This setting has been called "the Asian equivalent of a European family plot with a hedge growing around it."[37] As land for burials becomes more expensive, mainstream cemeteries may respond to the increasing popularity of cremation by offering land-scaped "garden" plots that have space for several urns, thereby allowing several generations to be buried and memorialized in a family plot.

Survivors may choose to memorialize the deceased in conjunction with cremation, just as with traditional burials. Urns to hold cremated remains can and nobody could bury'em. The cost of funerals they raised and they didn't want to raise the price of the workers. The way they're livin', everything wanna go up, and I don't know what's gonna happen.

Can you imagine if I wouldn't show up tomorrow morning and this other fella—he usually comes late—and sometimes he don't show. We have a funeral for eleven o'clock. Imagine what happens? The funeral arrive and where you gonna bury it? . . .

There are some funerals, they really affect you. Some young kid. We buried lots of young. You have emotions, you turn in, believe me, you turn. I had a burial about two years ago of teen-agers, a young boy and a young girl. This was a real sad funeral because there was nobody but young teen-agers. I'm so used to going to funerals every day—of course, it bothers me—but I don't feel as bad as when I bury a young child. You really turn. . . .

This grief that I see every day, I'm really used to somebody's crying every day. But there is some that are real bad, when you just have to take it. Some people just don't want to give up. You have to understand that when somebody pass away, there's nothing you can do and you have to take it. If you don't want to take it, you're just gonna make your life worse, become sick. People seems to take it more easier these days. They miss the person, but not as much.

There's some funerals that people, they show they're not sad. This is different kinds of people. I believe they are happy to see this person—not in a way of singing—because this person is out of his sufferin' in this world. This person is gone and at rest for the rest of his life. I have this question lots of times: "How can I take it?" They ask if I'm calm when I bury people. If you stop and think, a funeral is one of the natural things in the world. . .

I believe I'm gonna have to stay here probably until I die. It's not gonna be too bad for me because I been livin' twelve years already in the cemetery. I'm still gonna be livin' in the cemetery. (Laughs.) So that's gonna be all right with me whenever I go. I think I may be buried here, it look like.

Quoted in Studs Terkel, *Working*

be purchased at prices from about $50 to $400, though more expensive urns are available. If ashes are to be entombed, columbarium niches (a small vault in which the urn is placed) are available, with the cost depending on the size and location of the niche. Among some families and ethnic groups, a family tomb is the resting place for the ashes of several generations of the dead.

Memorialization

Grave markers and monuments are examples of ways in which people have traditionally chosen to honor and remember their dead. For cremated remains, such memorialization may include an inscription or plaque on a columbarium niche or a special urn to hold the ashes. With the growing popularity of cremation, entrepreneurs have developed, or rediscovered, innovative ways of memorializing a deceased loved one. For example, several firms offer "cremation jewelry," locket-style pendants that hold a small bit of cremated remains. These pendants can be worn around the neck or displayed in special holders.

Recently, in some inner-city areas, T-shirts are being worn as a way of memorializing victims of violence, as well as persons who died in accidents or from illnesses. The custom apparently began in New Orleans and has since been adopted elsewhere. As "wearable tombstones," these shirts are characterized as "a uniquely modern twist on the ancient ritual of honoring the dead." One young woman in her early twenties has memorial T-shirts for eight family members and friends murdered in and around her neighborhood. A man in his early thirties says, "Now I got more T-shirts than friends." The shirts are worn to wakes and funerals, on the anniversaries of the deaths, the victim's birthday, when visiting the gravesite, or just when someone is missed.[38]

High-tech innovations are resulting in new styles of "electronic" gravesite memorials. One such offering allows survivors to compile a "visual eulogy" of the deceased loved one, whereby photographs, his or her life story and family history, and other such gleanings of a life well lived are electronically stored and can be displayed on a small video monitor that is installed into a traditional grave marker. Containing up to 250 pages of information, this personalized memorial "allows a person's life story to be remembered for generations to come."[39]

Laws Regulating Body Disposition

As a general rule, the deceased's next of kin is responsible for arranging for the final disposition of the body. State laws and local ordinances, however, may govern the manner in which disposition can be effected. For example, some communities have ordinances prohibiting burial within city limits.

When the deceased has left no money to cover the cost of body disposition, and his or her relatives are unwilling or unable to pay, the state may be forced to step in and handle the details. Counties generally have an "indigent burial fund" for such cases. Depending on the circumstances, the public administrator's office may make a determination that distinguishes between "inconvenient to pay" and "unable to pay." When funds are not available from private sources, the county picks up the cost. The county may have a contract with a local mortuary that provides direct cremation and burial of the cremated remains. If the next of kin opposes cremation, the corpse may be placed in a casket and buried in a plot donated by a cemetery for indigent burials (or, again, paid for out of community funds).

Making Meaningful Choices

The funeral has been defined as "an organized, purposeful, time-limited, flexible, group-centered response to death."[40] In light of the varied and diverse styles of funeral service now available, does this definition apply to our current approaches to caring for the dead? What values guide our actions in memori-

A papier-mâché bull symbolizing the deceased's caste is a focal point of this cremation ceremony in a Balinese village. According to local custom, corpses are buried until families accumulate the necessary funds to pay for the cremation ritual; at that time, the body is disinterred, wrapped in cloth, and placed, along with various offerings, in ritual objects such as the bull shown here at the cremation site.

alizing the dead and meeting the emotional needs of survivors? The choices we make concerning funerals and body disposition increasingly reflect personal rather than community judgments. Yet, if the monolithic, and perhaps stereotypical, "American funeral" is disappearing from the scene, it is being replaced by a much broader range of options. Reflecting the cultural diversity in modern societies, most funeral directors now have at least some familiarity

Epitaph

The Body of
B. Franklin, Printer,
(Like the cover of an Old Book
Its contents torn out
And stript of its Lettering and Gilding)
Lies here, Food for Worms.
But the work shall not be lost;
For it will, (as he believ'd) appear
once more
In a new and more elegant Edition
Revised and Corrected
By the Author.

not only with the varied rituals practiced in dozens of Christian denominations, but also with essential aspects of Buddhist, Hindu, and Muslim services, as well as nonreligious humanistic and fraternal rites.[41] Thus, rather than being locked into a "conventional funeral" that fails to meet their needs, people can choose from a wide range of resources that allow them to create or adapt funeral customs from both religious and secular traditions.[42]

In pluralistic societies, there are many ways to deal meaningfully and appropriately with death. Some people prefer a minimal role in caring for their dead; others seek to participate actively. Becoming aware of the alternatives enables us to make meaningful choices. The experience of a family following the death of a young son is illustrative. There were no plans for a formal funeral ceremony. The body would be cremated and the ashes scattered. On the day before the body was to be cremated, the family found themselves experiencing the acute grief that comes with a sudden and intimate loss.

As they tried to come to terms with their emotions and the loss of their son, someone in their circle of friends suggested that they put their energy into building a coffin. Soon, friends and members of the family, including the five-year-old brother of the child who was killed, were busily engaged in the task of constructing a coffin. Later they said they were relieved to have had the opportunity to "do something" (see Figure 8-5). Building the coffin became a meaningful way to honor the dead child as well as a means of working through their feelings.

If funeral rituals provide closure on the deceased's life for survivors and allow the community to affirm the timeless rhythms of separation and integration, then what should our feelings be when the traditional social elements of a funeral are absent, as with some "take-out-and-cremate" practices? Can the emotional and psychological issues of bereavement be resolved satisfactorily? Many of those who counsel grieving people would answer in the negative. Psychiatrist William Lamers, for example, points out that substituting a "memorial service" for a traditional funeral is lacking in several respects: First, it usually does not take place when feelings about a loss are most intense. Second, members of the family are not as exposed to the fact that death has occurred, nor do they participate as fully as they would in making funeral arrangements and going through the funeralization process. Third, the body is not present at a memorial service, thus removing the therapeutic benefit that comes with fixing the fact of death in the minds of mourners.[43] Alan Wolfelt, Director of the Center for Loss and Life Transition, says, "Opponents of viewing [the body] often describe it as unseemly, expensive, undignified, and unnecessary. Yet, seeing and spending time with the body allows for last good-byes and visual confirmation that someone loved is indeed dead."[44]

At Pütz-Roth, an innovative funeral establishment in Bergisch Gladbach, Germany, mourners are encouraged to give themselves sufficient time to grieve after a loved one's death. In a homelike environment, the bereaved family and friends are offered the opportunity to spend time with the deceased's body over a period of several days prior to final disposition of the remains (see Figure 8-6). At Pütz-Roth, the bodies of the dead are not embalmed but are instead kept in a "cool room" between visits by the bereaved. When family and friends wish to come, the body is moved to a sitting room, where the bereaved have access to a kitchen facility for keeping beverages or making snacks. In addition to comfortable seating and soothing artworks, each sitting room has windows that look out on natural surroundings and that also let in the sounds of running water and birdsong. Amid this natural setting, as the body begins to show signs of deterioration, the mourners are subtly encouraged to recognize that all things have a beginning and an ending, and that grief involves letting go of the physical aspects of the deceased loved one while finding a "place in the heart for grief."[45]

The fast pace of modern life directly influences the way we choose to honor our dead. Attendance at funerals is down; fewer people seem to "have the time" to take off from work or other pressing activities for a mourning ceremony that seems somehow optional. Yet the desire to participate in such ceremonies persists, as is evident in the advent of new technologies that allow distant mourners to feel they are included even when they can't be physically present at the funeral itself. Videotapes may be provided for friends and relatives who are unable to attend the funeral. Cameras in the funeral chapel can transmit live video of the funeral to "cybermourners" via the Internet.[46] Memorial pages on the Internet allow mourners to post their condolences and share their grief on-line. Web sites known as "virtual cemeteries" provide space for photographs and biographical information about the dead, and visitors have opportunities to sign the guest book and leave "digital flowers." One web site offers a choice of virtual cemeteries to accommodate people from "all walks of life, including those with religious, ethnic, military, national, and alternative lifestyle affiliations."[47] Thus, a person who was both Catholic and a Navy veteran might have a memorial placed on both the "Catholic" and "U.S. Navy Veterans" virtual cemeteries.

Figure *8-5 Three Views of a Child's Coffin*
Top View: When the wooden coffin constructed by the family and friends
had been completed, the surviving child ran his hand over the surface and
voiced his approval but said that it "needs something more." He gathered
his marking pens and began to ornament the coffin with drawings. The
inscriptions on the outer surface of the lid show the child's interest in identifying by name and by picture the fact that this coffin was built for his
brother. His own participation in the making of the coffin is also connoted
by the inclusion of his name and by the demonstration of his newly developed skills with the use of numerals and letters.
Detail of Lid Interior: In this closeup of a portion of the interior lid, viewed
from left to right, one can see a chrysalis—indicating a transition from caterpillar to butterfly—along with some of the younger brother's favorite television characters: Big Bird, Oscar the Grouch, and the Cookie Monster.

Interior of Lid: In contrast to the matter-of-fact inscriptions placed on the outer surface, the inside of the coffin lid is filled with representations of experiences, events, and objects that brought joy into the life of the child's younger brother. Many of the dead child's favorite activities, such as listening to the stereo with headphones and sitting on a horse at grandma's house, are depicted. The surviving child depicts himself as sad because of his brother's death, yet also as happy because of the shared experiences he enjoyed with his brother. It is interesting to notice the degree of detail and the variety of images placed on the interior of the coffin lid.

Internet memorial pages and other high-tech options appear to meet a basic human need for participation in rituals surrounding death. Whether these options are adequate substitutes for the intimate, face-to-face social support provided by conventional funeral services is an open question. What does it say about how we manage our lives when we are too busy to join together with other mourners to acknowledge the passing of a person who was loved and respected as part of our community of friends and family? These new options attest to the strength of the bonds between the living and the dead and the human desire to make connections with others in our bereavement.

The social support that accompanies meaningful ritual need not be limited to the period immediately following a death. In traditional Hawaiian culture, for example, the bereaved community holds a memorial feast on the first-year anniversary of the day of death for any person—man, woman, child, even a newborn baby.[48] For the extended family, this is considered "one of the three greatest occasions, the others being the feasts of rejoicing for the first-born and the marriage festival." Although this memorial occasion is called the *'aha'aina waimaka* or "feast of tears," because it embraces everyone who had shed tears out of respect and love for the deceased, it is in fact "a happy occasion, a joyful reunion of all who had previously shed tears together." In the words of one participant: "There was drinking, eating, singing and dancing. We had a *lu'au* when all the grief was done."

Figure *8-6* Mourners at Pütz-Roth in Bergisch Gladbach, Germany, are given opportunities to sit with their deceased loved ones in a serene, home-like environment that aids their coming to terms with the death. This innovative funeral establishment is a model for helping the bereaved find a place in the heart for grief.

Further Readings

Vernel Bagneris. *Rejoice When You Die: The New Orleans Jazz Funerals.* Baton Rouge: Louisiana State University, 1998.

Xavier A. Cronin. *Grave Exodus: Tending to Our Dead in the 21st Century.* New York: Barricade Books, 1996.

Robert W. Habenstein and William M. Lamers. *Funeral Customs the World Over.* Rev. ed. Milwaukee: Bulfin Printers, 1974.

Robert W. Habenstein and William M. Lamers. *The History of American Funeral Directing.* Milwaukee: Bulfin Printers, 1962.

Glennys Howarth. *Last Rites: The Work of the Modern Funeral Director.* Amityville, N.Y.: Baywood, 1996.

Kenneth T. Jackson and Camilo José Vegara. *Silent Cities: The Evolution of the American Cemetery.* New York: Princeton Architectural Press, 1996.

Douglas Keister. *Going Out in Style: The Architecture of Eternity.* New York: Facts on File, 1997.

Thomas Lynch. *The Undertaking: Life Studies from the Dismal Trade.* New York: Norton, 1997.

Elaine Nichols, ed. *The Last Miles of the Way: African-American Homegoing Traditions, 1890–Present.* Columbia: South Carolina State Museum, 1989.

Stephen Prothero. *Purified by Fire: A History of Cremation in America.* Berkeley: University of California Press, 2001.

Seen here testifying in a Michigan courtroom, Dr. Jack Kevorkian has become a symbol of the debate over the ethical and legal issues that pertain to physician-assisted death. The legal system touches on many aspects of dying and death, from advance directives and death certification to the making of wills and settling of estates.

C H A P T E R 9

The Law and Death

*F*rom the relative simplicity of filing a death certificate to the settling of a complicated estate, the law impinges upon our experiences of death and dying. In some cases, laws serve to increase our options; in other cases, they restrict them. In the case of advance directives, for example, our options for dealing with death are expanded. In other areas, such as physician-assisted suicide, the law constrains our behavior and choices. In this chapter, we examine a variety of legal issues related to dying and death.

We begin with a discussion of several issues that have become prominent in the public arena, including legislation defining death, the use of advance directives in health care, and physician-assisted suicide. The next section of the chapter deals with the question: How are societal interests in the circumstances of death reflected in governmental and institutional policies and procedures? This section provides an overview of the legal and administrative aspects of death certification, the role of the coroner and the medical examiner, and autopsies. Finally, we examine the procedures involved in making a will, probating an estate, and claiming death benefits. Most of the topics covered in this chapter pertain to matters that should be considered before death occurs.

Acknowledging the inevitability of death allows us to plan for it. Adequate planning can help ensure that a sudden, unexpected death is not made even more difficult for survivors. Even when sudden death is not the issue, persons who have serious or debilitating illness may become unable to make decisions that could have been made before the onset of crisis. Although some decisions cannot be made until one is actually in a particular situation, many decisions relating to dying and death can be anticipated, considered, and discussed with close relatives and friends. Advance planning can potentially ease what otherwise would be difficult and painful decisions for both our survivors and ourselves.

Basic tasks in planning for death include making a will to specify how property will be distributed after we die, anticipating medical care needs and expressing preferences for end-of-life care, and helping our survivors plan tasks that will be carried out after we die. It is reasonable to begin such planning and decision making during the college years and to periodically review and revise one's choices throughout life.[1]

Legal Issues in the Public Arena

Public concerns about legal issues involving dying and death are currently focused mainly in three areas: defining death in a way that responds to the impact of modern life-support technology on care of the dying; creating a way for individuals to express their wishes about medical treatment at the end of life through advance directives; and shaping policies about physician-assisted suicide, or aid-in-dying, when a person is seriously ill and wants to exercise control over when and how death occurs. Whereas legalities involving wills, probate, autopsies, and the role of the coroner have a long history in Western societies, these three issues are of recent vintage and have become a matter of public debate mainly because of the modern encounter with sophisticated medical technologies.

Legislation Defining Death

The definition of death touches upon many aspects of our lives. Criminal prosecution, inheritance, taxation, treatment of the corpse, and mourning are all affected by the way society "draws the dividing line between life and death."[2] The conventional definition of death—that is, as the cessation of breathing and heartbeat—is sometimes not adequate for defining when death has occurred when current medical technology is used to artificially sustain life.

The clock wound by Elizabeth still ticked, storing in its spring the pressure of her hand.

Life cannot be cut off quickly. One cannot be dead until the things he changed are dead. His effect is the only evidence of his life. While there remains even a plaintive memory a person cannot be cut off, dead. A man's life dies as a commotion in a still pool dies, in little waves, spreading and growing back towards stillness.

John Steinbeck, *To a God Unknown*

Following publication of the criteria for establishing brain death proposed by a Harvard Medical School Ad Hoc Committee in 1968, public discussion began to take place concerning the need to revise the legal definition of death so as to reflect medical realities. In 1970, Kansas became the first state to adopt a statute that included brain-based criteria for determining death, and a number of other states subsequently adopted similar laws. These early statutes were criticized as potentially confusing, however, because they contained dual definitions for determining death: one based on cessation of vital functions and the other on brain functions. In 1972, Alexander Capron and Leon Kass offered a proposal that related the two standards.[3] Capron and Kass said that the statute should:

1. Concern the death of a human being, not the death of cells, tissues, or organs; and not the death or cessation of a person's role as a fully functioning member of his or her family or community.
2. Move incrementally, supplementing rather than replacing older cardio-pulmonary (heartbeat and breathing) standards.
3. Avoid serving as a special definition for a special function such as organ transplantation.
4. Apply uniformly to all persons.
5. Be flexible, leaving specific criteria to the judgment of physicians.

This proposal was adopted, with various modifications, by several states. But it was criticized for not addressing the issues raised by organ transplantation. Specifically, it did not require at least two physicians to participate jointly in determining death, nor did it stipulate that the physician who pronounces death could not be a member of the medical team seeking organs for transplantation. Capron and Kass replied that transplant considerations should be dealt with in separate legislation, such as the Uniform Anatomical Gift Act (dicussed in Chapter 6).

In 1975, the American Bar Association proposed its own model statute. It offered a definition of death "for all legal purposes." This proposal virtually ignored conventional cardiopulmonary criteria and focused instead on "irreversible cessation of total brain function." The ABA proposal, either verbatim or with modification, was, like its predecessors, adopted by a number of states. In 1978, yet another proposal was contained in a model statute that was part of the Uniform Brain Death Act. That model was followed the next year by a statute proposed by the American Medical Association. The number of model statutes proposed during the 1970s suggests the struggle to come to terms with new medical technologies and their impact on determining when a person could (or should) be declared dead.

Finally, in the early 1980s, the President's Commission for the Study of Ethical Problems in Medicine proposed a model statute that found broad acceptance: the Uniform Determination of Death Act (see Figure 9-1). This model was endorsed by the American Bar Association and the American Medical Association, both of which substituted it for their own earlier efforts. The Uniform Determination of Death Act eased the enactment of uniform law throughout the United States.

Uniform Determination of Death Act

1. [*Determination of Death.*] An individual who has sustained either (1) irreversible cessation of circulatory and respiratory functions, or (2) irreversible cessation of all functions of the entire brain, including the brain stem, is dead. A determination of death must be made in accordance with accepted medical standards.
2. [*Uniformity of Construction and Application.*] This act shall be applied and construed to effectuate its general purpose to make uniform the law with respect to the subject of this Act among states enacting it.

Figure 9-1   *Uniform Determination of Death Act*
Source: President's Commission for the Study of Ethical Problems in Medicine and Biomedical and Behavioral Research, *Defining Death: A Report on the Medical, Legal and Ethical Issues in the Determination of Death* (Washington: Government Printing Office, 1981), p. 73.

In its report, the President's Commission remarked that the Uniform Determination of Death Act "addresses the matter of 'defining' death at the level of general physiological standards rather than at the level of more abstract concepts or the level of more precise criteria and tests," because these change over time as knowledge and techniques are refined.[4] Because irreversible circulatory and respiratory cessation provide the obvious and sufficient basis for diagnosing death in most cases, the Uniform Determination of Death Act acknowledges that fact. In such cases, death is determined on the basis that breathing and blood flow have ceased and cannot be restored. If a patient is not supported on a respirator, there is no need to evaluate brain function before making a determination of death.

The Commission said that a statutory definition of death should be separate and distinct from any provisions concerning organ donation. In contrast to earlier proposals, which stated that a person would be "considered dead" when their stated criteria were met, the language of the Uniform Determination of Death Act is clearer and more direct. It states that a person who meets the standards set forth in the law "is dead."

Confusion about the definition of death had arisen, the Commission said, "because the same technology not only keeps heart and lungs functioning in some who have irretrievably lost all brain functions but also sustains other, less severely injured patients." The result is a "blurring of the important distinction between patients who are *dead* and those who are or may be *dying*." The Commission concluded that "proof of an irreversible absence of functions in the entire brain, including the brain stem, provides a highly reliable means of declaring death for respirator-maintained bodies."

The Commission noted that the 1968 Harvard Ad Hoc Committee's definition of irreversible coma as brain death had been reliable and added that "no case has yet been found that met these criteria and regained any brain functions despite continuation of respirator support." Nevertheless, the Commission felt that the phrase "irreversible coma" is misleading because *coma* refers to a condition of a living person, whereas "a body without any brain functions is dead and thus *beyond* any coma." This observation reflects the Commission's emphasis on a "whole-brain" definition of death rather than a "higher-brain" definition, whereby the loss of cognitive function or "person-hood" is equated with death.

(Irreversible loss of functions of the whole brain is usually due to (1) direct trauma to the head, such as from a motor vehicle accident or gunshot wound, (2) massive hemorrhage into the brain from a ruptured aneurysm or from complications of high blood pressure, or (3) anoxic damage from cardiac or respiratory arrest or severely reduced blood pressure.)

Death is an absolute and single phenomenon, the Commission said, arguing that it would radically change the meaning of death to expand the definition of death to include persons who have lost all *cognitive* functions but still are able to breath spontaneously. When brain stem functions remain—for example, when respiration occurs naturally but there is no cognitive awareness—the patient's condition can be described as a "persistent vegetative or noncognitive state." Although one may observe involuntary movements and unassisted breathing in a person's body, the lack of higher brain functions indicates no awareness of self or the environment. Sustained by medical and nursing care, including artificial feeding and antibiotics to fight recurrent infections, such patients may survive for years without a respirator. (The longest such survival, according to the Commission's report, was over thirty-seven years.)

The Commission cited the nearly universal acceptance of the "whole-brain" concept by both the medical community and the general public. A higher brain formulation, which would require agreement about the meaning of personhood, does not enjoy such consensus. At the present level of understanding and technique, the Commission said, "the 'higher brain' may well exist only as a metaphorical concept, not in reality."

As Albert Jonsen, a medical ethicist and historian, points out, the work of the President's Commission for the Study of Ethical Problems in Medicine "brought conceptual clarity to a confused issue and helped to make good law."[5] Jonsen adds that the Commission made a crucial contribution to the field of medical ethics in demonstrating the value of combining the logic of philosophical discourse and the needs of practical public policy.

Advance Directives

To make our preferences known to health care providers and others who should be aware of them, it is important to document them through a written *advance directive*. In a general sense, an advance directive is any statement made by a competent person about choices for medical treatment should he or she become unable to make such decisions or communicate them at some time in the future. Anticipating potential crises and planning for them can reduce the sense of "emergency" that can occur without such planning. Advance directives have become increasingly important in medical decision making, but they were actually quite controversial just a few years ago (see the letters in Figure 9-2). Opponents argued that advance directives represented a step

Editor: If the governor signs the bill currently before him, this will become the first state to legalize suicide.

I believe this measure is immoral, bizarre, and tainted with Mephisthophelian connotations.

Legislators, at all levels, should legislate laws pertaining only to life, as we know it. Death, in any manner, is nature's absolute domain, and no one should attempt to trespass on that domain.

I trust the governor is wise enough and sane enough to veto the bill presently lying heavily and cadaverously on his desk.

Editor: We have explored this bill and its implications in death and fully support the right of an individual, who wishes to do so, to be allowed to make a legally recognized written directive requesting withdrawal of life-support systems when these procedures would serve no purpose except to artificially delay the moment of death.

We reiterate our belief in the basic human right of an individual to control his destiny. We have communicated our support of this bill to the legislature and to the governor.

Editor: This bill, and all other natural-death or death-with-dignity bills, is based on a faulty premise. For when we react to tubes, oxygen and other paraphernalia, our concern is with daintiness, not dignity.

Dignity is the quality of mind having to do with worth, nobility, and forbearance. The dying, with the help of the living, can have dignity—no matter what functions of control are lost.

Instead of unplugging and abandoning our dying patients, we should work to achieve truly compassionate care for them in hospices like those in London, England, and New Haven, Connecticut.

Editor: No physician is required by law to use extraordinary means of preserving life, and none has ever been convicted for failing to do so.

So the real purpose of death-with-dignity or natural-death bills must be to set the stage for letting doctors take positive action: giving lethal injections or denying ordinary means of care to patients who may be handicapped or burdensome to society.

We must be suspicious of any trend which offers death as a solution to problems, no matter how heart-rending those problems may be.

Editor: The bill allowing an adult of sound mind to refuse extraordinary life-preservation measures reaffirms for me the value of life. Life is active choosing toward greater fulfillment and reduced suffering, not the beating of a heart in a pain-wracked and hopeless body. This bill is a public and legal recognition of that principle.

Figure 9-2 *Letters in Response to Living Will Legislation*

toward active euthanasia, whereas proponents argued that advance directives could safeguard patients' rights to determine the manner of their care at the end of life.

Two forms of advance directives are legally important. First is the *living will,* which enables individuals to provide instructions about the kind of medical care they wish to receive if they become incapacitated or otherwise unable to participate in treatment decisions. Many people believe that living wills are appropriate only for stating a desire to forgo life-sustaining procedures or to avoid medical heroics when death is imminent; and, indeed, most "standard" forms for completing a living will reflect this purpose. In fact, however, a living will can be drafted to express very different ideas about the kinds of treatment a person would or would not want, and they can be written to cover various contingencies. Living wills were originally proposed in 1967 by Louis Kutner as a way for patients with terminal illness to document their wishes regarding medical care in the event of their incapacitation.[6] Although living wills originally had no force in law, provisions for advance directives now exist in every state.[7]

The second important form of advance directive is the *health care proxy*, which is also known as a durable power of attorney for health care. This document makes it possible to appoint another person to make decisions about medical treatment if you become unable to do so. This decision maker is also known as a *surrogate*. He or she may be a family member, close friend, or attorney with whom you have discussed your treatment preferences. The proxy is expected to act in accordance with your wishes as stated in an advance directive or as otherwise made known. A court may take away the surrogate's power to make decisions if he or she: (1) authorizes any illegal act; (2) acts contrary to the patient's known desires; or (3) where those desires are not known, does anything clearly contrary to the patient's best interests. Completing a health care proxy can be an additional safeguard that preferences about life-sustaining treatment will be followed.

California was the first state to adopt a Natural Death Act, which permitted an individual to sign a declaration expressing his or her wishes for treatment and to appoint a health care proxy. The laws governing living wills and health care proxies vary somewhat for the different states, making it important to be sure you complete the proper forms that apply where you live (current forms can be obtained on-line at www.partnershipforcaring.org). An example of the forms used in New York is shown in Figure 9-3.

Using Advance Directives

For advance directives to be of value, we must do more than merely complete the paperwork. Completing a living will and health care proxy is one step toward improving the chances that our treatment preferences will be honored if we become incapacitated. But physicians and other medical staff cannot follow advance directives if they don't know about them, or if the instructions are too vague to give the necessary direction about what should be done. Also, because state laws may differ, if you have completed an advance directive in one state and subsequently move to another state, you should find out whether the requirements in your new residence require additional action on your part. Indeed, after one has completed an advance directive, it is always a good idea to revisit the issue occasionally to be sure the preferences expressed in the directive continue to match your wishes.

Whether a patient's wishes, as expressed in a living will or health care proxy, are followed can depend on the policies of a given health care institution and the circumstances that bring the advance directive into play. Uncertainty about the course of a disease may cause doctors to be wary of deciding that a patient is in a terminal condition. In some cases, a living will may be less a directive than a request. Individuals should discuss issues of end-of-life care with their primary doctor and other physicians from whom they receive treatment, as well as with family members, *before* a situation comes up in which the

NEW YORK
HEALTH CARE PROXY

INSTRUCTIONS

PRINT YOUR NAME

(1) I, _____, hereby appoint:

(name)

PRINT NAME, HOME ADDRESS AND TELEPHONE NUMBER OF YOUR AGENT

_____

(name, home address and telephone number of agent)

_____

as my health care agent to make any and all health care decisions for me, except to the extent that I state otherwise.

This Health Care Proxy shall take effect in the event I become unable to make my own health care decisions.

ADD PERSONAL INSTRUCTIONS (IF ANY)

(2) Optional instructions: I direct my agent to make health care decisions in accord with my wishes and limitations as stated below, or as he or she otherwise knows.

(Unless your agent knows your wishes about artificial nutrition and hydration [feeding tubes], your agent will not be allowed to make decisions about artificial nutrition and hydration.)

© 2000
PARTNERSHIP FOR CARING, INC.

Figure 9-3 *Advance Directives for Use in New York State*

PRINT NAME, HOME ADDRESS AND TELEPHONE NUMBER OF YOUR ALTERNATE AGENT

(3) Name of substitute or fill-in agent if the person I appoint above is unable, unwilling or unavailable to act as my health care agent.

_____

(name, home address and telephone number of alternate agent)

_____

ENTER A DURATION OR A CONDITION (IF ANY)

(4) Unless I revoke it, this proxy shall remain in effect indefinitely, or until the date or condition I have stated below. This proxy shall expire (specific date or conditions, if desired): _____

_____

SIGN AND DATE THE DOCUMENT AND PRINT YOUR ADDRESS

(5) Signature _____ Date _____

Address _____

WITNESSING PROCEDURE

Statement by Witnesses (must be 18 or older)

I declare that the person who signed this document appeared to execute the proxy willingly and free from duress. He or she signed (or asked another to sign for him or her) this document in my presence. I am not the person appointed as proxy by this document.

YOUR WITNESSES MUST SIGN AND PRINT THEIR ADDRESSES

Witness 1 _____

Address _____

Witness 2 _____

Address _____

NEW YORK LIVING WILL

This Living Will has been prepared to conform to the law in the State of New York, as set forth in the case <u>In re Westchester County Medical Center</u>, 72 N.Y.2d 517 (1988). In that case the Court established the need for "clear and convincing" evidence of a patient's wishes and stated that the "ideal situation is one in which the patient's wishes were expressed in some form of writing, perhaps a 'living will.'"

I, _____, being of sound mind, make this statement as a directive to be followed if I become permanently unable to participate in decisions regarding my medical care. These instructions reflect my firm and settled commitment to decline medical treatment under the circumstances indicated below:

I direct my attending physician to withhold or withdraw treatment that merely prolongs my dying, if I should be in an **incurable or irreversible mental or physical condition with no reasonable expectation of recovery,** including but not limited to: (a) **a terminal condition;** (b) **a permanently unconscious condition;** or (c) **a minimally conscious condition in which I am permanently unable to make decisions or express my wishes.**

I direct that my treatment be limited to measures to keep me comfortable and to relieve pain, including any pain that might occur by withholding or withdrawing treatment.

While I understand that I am not legally required to be specific about future treatments **if I am in the condition(s) described above I feel especially strongly about the following forms of treatment:**

I do not want cardiac resuscitation.
I do not want mechanical respiration.
I do not want artificial nutrition and hydration.
I do not want antibiotics.

However, I **do want** maximum pain relief, even if it may hasten my death.

Figure 9-3 *(continued)*

NEW YORK LIVING WILL — PAGE 2 OF 2

ADD PERSONAL INSTRUCTIONS (IF ANY)

Other directions:

These directions express my legal right to refuse treatment, under the law of New York. I intend my instructions to be carried out, unless I have rescinded them in a new writing or by clearly indicating that I have changed my mind.

SIGN AND DATE THE DOCUMENT AND PRINT YOUR ADDRESS

Signed _____ Date _____

Address _____

WITNESSING PROCEDURE

I declare that the person who signed this document appeared to execute the living will willingly and free from duress. He or she signed (or asked another to sign for him or her) this document in my presence.

YOUR WITNESSES MUST SIGN AND PRINT THEIR ADDRESSES

Witness 1 _____

Address _____

Witness 2 _____

Address _____

Courtesy of **Partnership for Caring, Inc.**   6/96
1035 30th Street, NW Washington, DC 20007 800-989-9455

provisions of an advance directive become effective.[8] It is possible to construct advance directives initially as a general statement of one's goals and philosophy and then make them more specific as a disease progressively becomes more debilitating or likely to result in death. Although advance directives are a valuable tool, clear communication between the patient and his or her physician, a letter written by a patient, or documentation of the patient's directives in a medical chart may be all that is really needed.[9]

Because advance directives are designed to become effective when a patient is unable to communicate his or her wishes, and when some medical intervention is needed to sustain life, there is also the possibility that advance directives might be implemented in a situation that the patient had not foreseen.[10] For example, a woman in her seventies entered a hospital for hip replacement surgery and, along with other admission forms, was given a living will to sign. While recovering from surgery, she had an unexpected cardiac arrest. Rather than attempting to save her, however, the medical staff assumed that—because she had signed a living will—she wanted no efforts at resuscitation, and the woman died. Although this woman was not terminally ill when she signed the living will, by providing evidence that she did not want to be kept alive if in a grave medical condition, the power to interpret her wishes was effectively put into the hands of the medical staff. Was the outcome in this case truly what this woman intended when she signed the living will?

In 1990, the United States Congress enacted the Patient Self-Determination Act (PSDA).[11] It requires providers of services under the Medicare and Medicaid programs to inform patients of their rights to appoint a health care proxy and draw up written instructions concerning limits to medical care to be activated if they become incapacitated.[12] Health care providers are required to document in the patient's medical record whether the patient has executed an advance directive and ensure compliance with requirements of state law with respect to advance directives. The PSDA has been described as a "medical Miranda warning" (referring to the requirement that police officers advise arrested suspects of their rights) due to its requirement that patients be advised of their rights regarding advance directives and life-sustaining treatment.

Although the intent of the Patient Self-Determination Act is to help individuals determine their own medical care, some people are concerned that it contributes to devaluing the goal of sustaining life. Another concern is that patients may become unduly alarmed about the state of their health after being questioned about whether they have completed an advance directive. The elderly widow, for example, who enters a nursing home following the death of her husband may be frightened by what she perceives as a warning that she, too, is about to die, thus adding to the anxiety and depression caused by disruptions in her life. Thus, the PSDA—and matters pertaining to advance directives more generally—should be handled with sensitivity to the circumstances affecting a particular patient.

One should not be complacent in thinking that all will necessarily go smoothly so long as an advance directive has been completed and signed. Zelda Foster, a social worker and educator, has written poignantly about her struggles to ensure that her 93-year-old father's wishes were respected by medical personnel after he was brought to an emergency room and attached to life-support machines.[13] Despite having her father's health care proxy in hand, the staff seemed to be unfamiliar with its purpose and hospital administrators insisted that Foster's family obtain a court order to enforce the proxy's provisions. Ms. Foster noted that "the hospital has created one obstacle after another to challenge our rightful request that our father be allowed to die with dignity." As the Supreme Court decision made clear in the case of Nancy Beth Cruzan (discussed in Chapter 6), advance directives offer a means for providing "clear and convincing evidence" about one's wishes for life-sustaining treatment in critical situations; however, they are not a panacea that solves all the difficulties that may accompany end-of-life care.

Advance Directives and Emergency Care

It is important to recognize the distinction between advance directives and do-not-resuscitate (DNR) orders. Failure to do so can result in unwanted treatment being administered to a terminally ill patient when emergency personnel arrive in response to a 911 call. Emergency care provided by EMTs and other such personnel is considered a boon when it helps save lives, but it can be less welcome when it results in interventions that save the lives of those who would rather die naturally. Once 911 is dialed, however, it sets in motion a response intended to save life. Emergency personnel are generally not in a position to make decisions about who wants to be saved and who doesn't. In fact, EMTs are legally *required* to initiate CPR (cardiopulmonary resuscitation) unless there is clear evidence that a patient has a DNR order provided by his or her physician. A DNR order is written only when a patient is in the end-stage of a terminal illness.

Imagine a dying person, at home surrounded by family and close friends, prepared to let nature take it course. When the person begins to experience difficulty breathing, however, some of those watching this course unfold toward death may have an impulse to *do* something to relieve the apparent suffering. Unless preparations have been made ahead of time to avoid such a possibility, a spontaneous call to 911 can result in the dying person being resuscitated by paramedics only to be placed on life-support equipment, where the last hours or days of life are played out as a crisis.

To prevent this scenario, people who do not want CPR or other life-saving interventions must ensure that they have a valid DNR order that it is readily available to emergency personnel who may be called to the scene. Wallet cards or Medic-Alert bracelets may be useful in signaling the fact that a person should not receive CPR. Because situations vary, patients who want to avoid such life-sustaining interventions should prepare ahead of time and make sure that all the necessary documents have been completed and are in place.

Physician-Assisted Suicide

Publicity surrounding the cases of physician-assisted suicide (PAS) conducted by Michigan pathologist Jack Kevorkian brought issues concerning intentionally hastened deaths of patients to widespread media and public attention. At the time of his sentencing in April 1999 for the second-degree murder of Thomas Youk, Dr. Kevorkian had provided aid-in-dying to more than 100 individuals since he began his active crusade to legalize physician-assisted suicide in 1990.

In 1997, the U.S. Supreme Court reviewed two cases relating to physician-assisted suicide.[14] The decisions in these cases (Washington *v.* Glucksberg and Vacco *v.* Quill) are important for several reasons. First, the Court upheld the distinction between, on the one hand, withholding or withdrawing treatment, and, on the other hand, physician-assisted suicide. In doing so, the Court clarified its ruling in the Cruzan case, noting that the right to *refuse treatment* is based on the right to maintain one's bodily integrity, not on a right to *hasten death*. When treatment is withheld or withdrawn, the Court said, the intent is to honor the patient's wishes, not cause death, unlike PAS, where the patient is "killed" by the lethal medication. Second, the Court affirmed the rights of states to craft policy concerning physician-assisted suicide, prohibiting it, as most states now do, or permitting it under some regulatory system, as is now happening in Oregon.

Oregon is currently the only state where PAS is permitted. The Death with Dignity Act, a ballot initiative, was passed by Oregon voters in 1994 and, after surviving judicial challenges, was reaffirmed in 1997. The Oregon Death with Dignity Act allows physicians to prescribe lethal medication to terminally ill patients.[15] Doctors who are opposed to aid-in-dying can refuse to participate, and the provisions of the law are available only to individuals who are legal residents of Oregon. In March 1998, an elderly woman with breast cancer became the first known person to die under the law, taking a lethal dose of barbiturates prescribed by her doctor. During its first two years of implementation, 42 people were reported to have legally committed suicide with the assistance of physicians.[16] These patients exhibited strong beliefs in personal autonomy and determination to control the end of their lives. The decision to request a prescription for lethal medication was associated mainly with concerns about loss of autonomy and control. Specific quality-of-life concerns included decreasing ability to participate in activities that make life enjoyable, losing control of bodily functions, and physical suffering.

A third finding of importance in the Supreme Court's 1997 rulings about physician-assisted suicide relates to the concept of *double effect* in the medical management of pain. The doctrine of double effect states that a harmful effect of treatment, even if it results in death, is permissible if the harm is not intended and occurs as a side effect of a beneficial action.[17] Sometimes the dosages of medication needed to relieve a patient's pain (especially at the end-stage of some diseases) must be increased to levels that can cause respiratory depression, resulting in the patient's death, a practice sometimes termed "terminal sedation."[18] Thus, the relief of suffering (the intended good effect) may have a potential bad effect, which is foreseen but is not the primary intention. The Court said that such medication for pain, even if it hastens death, is not physician-assisted suicide if the intent is to relieve pain.

"Before we try assisted suicide, Mrs. Rose, let's give the aspirin a chance."

In commenting on the 1997 U.S. Supreme Court decisions, Chief Justice William Rehnquist said, "Throughout the nation, Americans are engaged in an earnest and profound debate about the morality, legality, and practicality of physician-assisted suicide. Our [decision] permits this debate to continue, as it should in a democratic society."[19]

Ira Byock, a hospice and palliative care physician, welcomed the Supreme Court's decision but expressed concern that "the legalization of physician-assisted suicide is a particularly dangerous proposition unless fundamental changes are made in the care of the dying."[20] He emphasized the pressing need for physicians and other caregivers to become more competent in pain management and other aspects of palliative medicine. Others—including former executive director of the Hemlock Society, John Pridonoff—believe that hospice care and aid-in-dying are not necessarily incompatible; that they can be complementary aspects of a comprehensive approach to end-of-life decisions.[21]

Although the trend over the past few decades has been toward greater freedom for individuals to choose when and how they will die, questions about physician-assisted suicide continue to be debated. As this book goes to press, a bill proposed in the United States Congress seeks to ban the use of lethal drugs for physician-assisted suicide. If successfully passed, it would effectively invalidate the program of physician-assisted suicide practiced in Oregon.

Death Certification

The official registration of death is considered the most important legal procedure following a death. A death certificate constitutes legal proof of death, and death certificates are required by all jurisdictions in the United States. Although death certificates vary somewhat from state to state, most follow the format outlined by the United States Standard Certificate of Death.

Death certificates reflect both a private and a public function. On the face of it, the document used to certify the facts of death is quite straightforward, a concise summary of the pertinent data regarding the deceased and the mode and place of death. However, this seemingly simple document has broader implications than one might imagine. Besides its value and purpose as a legal document that affects disposition of property rights, life insurance benefits, pension payments, and so on, the utility of the death certificate extends to such diverse matters as aiding in crime detection, tracing genealogy, and gaining knowledge about the incidence of disease and other aspects of physical and psychological health.

The typical death certificate (see Figure 9-4) provides for noting four different *modes* of death: accidental, suicidal, homicidal, and natural. As Edwin Shneidman points out, however, the *cause* of death isn't necessarily the same as the *mode* of death.[22] For example, if a death were caused by asphyxiation due to drowning, should such a death be classified as an accident, a suicide, or a homicide? Any of these modes might apply.

Underlying the distinction between mode and cause is the more complex issue of intentions and subconscious factors, the states of mind and actions, that may have contributed, directly or indirectly, to the death. For instance, if an intoxicated person jumps into a swimming pool with no one else present and drowns, is the death accidental or suicidal? Does it make a difference whether the alcohol abuse was related to emotional distress and despondency? Or what is the mode of death if the cocktails were served by a too-generous host? What if the person serving excessive alcohol were also an heir of the person who dies?

Obviously, intentions and subconscious factors can be more complex than allowed for by the relatively elementary distinctions concerning mode and cause of death now listed on most death certificates. A study done in Marin County, California, to assess the conventional classifications of mode of death as well as the lethality of the deceased's intention revealed that some deaths classified as natural, accidental, and homicidal were also precipitated by the deceased's own actions; the deceased had lethal intentions against himself or

CERTIFICATE OF DEATH
STATE OF CALIFORNIA
USE BLACK INK ONLY/NO ERASURES, WHITEOUTS OR ALTERATIONS
VS-11 (REV. 1/00)

STATE FILE NUMBER   LOCAL REGISTRATION NUMBER

DECEDENT PERSONAL DATA

1. NAME OF DECEDENT—FIRST (GIVEN)   2. MIDDLE   3. LAST (FAMILY)

4. DATE OF BIRTH M M / D D / C C Y Y   5. AGE YRS.   IF UNDER 1 YEAR (MONTHS / DAYS)   IF UNDER 24 HOURS (HOURS / MINUTES)   6. SEX   7. DATE OF DEATH M M / D D / C C Y Y   8. HOUR

9. STATE OF BIRTH   10. SOCIAL SECURITY NO.   11. MILITARY SERVICE YES / NO / UNK   12. MARITAL STATUS   13. EDUCATION—YEARS COMPLETED

14. RACE   15. HISPANIC—SPECIFY YES ____ No   16. USUAL EMPLOYER

17. OCCUPATION   18. KIND OF BUSINESS   19. YEARS IN OCCUPATION

USUAL RESIDENCE

20. RESIDENCE—(STREET AND NUMBER OR LOCATION)

21. CITY   22. COUNTY   23. ZIP CODE   24. YRS IN COUNTY   25. STATE OR FOREIGN COUNTRY

INFORMANT

26. NAME, RELATIONSHIP   27. MAILING ADDRESS (STREET AND NUMBER OR RURAL ROUTE NUMBER, CITY OR TOWN, STATE, ZIP)

SPOUSE AND PARENT INFORMATION

28. NAME OF SURVIVING SPOUSE—FIRST   29. MIDDLE   30. LAST (MAIDEN NAME)

31. NAME OF FATHER—FIRST   32. MIDDLE   33. LAST   34. BIRTH STATE

35. NAME OF MOTHER—FIRST   36. MIDDLE   37. LAST (MAIDEN)   38. BIRTH STATE

DISPOSITION(S)

39. DATE M M / D D / C C Y Y   40. PLACE OF FINAL DISPOSITION

FUNERAL DIRECTOR AND LOCAL REGISTRAR

41. TYPE OF DISPOSITION(S)   42. SIGNATURE OF EMBALMER   43. LICENSE NO.

44. NAME OF FUNERAL DIRECTOR   45. LICENSE NO.   46. SIGNATURE OF LOCAL REGISTRAR   47. DATE M M / D D / C C Y Y

PLACE OF DEATH

101. PLACE OF DEATH   102. IF HOSPITAL, SPECIFY ONE: IP / ER/OP / DOA   103. FACILITY OTHER THAN HOSPITAL: CONV. HOSP. / RES. CARE / OTHER   104. COUNTY

105. STREET ADDRESS—(STREET AND NUMBER OR LOCATION)   106. CITY

CAUSE OF DEATH

107. DEATH WAS CAUSED BY: (ENTER ONLY ONE CAUSE PER LINE FOR A, B, C, AND D)   TIME INTERVAL BETWEEN ONSET AND DEATH

IMMEDIATE CAUSE (A)

DUE TO (B)

DUE TO (C)

DUE TO (D)

108. DEATH REPORTED TO CORONER YES / NO REFERRAL NUMBER

109. BIOPSY PERFORMED YES / NO

110. AUTOPSY PERFORMED YES / NO

111. USED IN DETERMINING CAUSE YES / NO

112. OTHER SIGNIFICANT CONDITIONS CONTRIBUTING TO DEATH BUT NOT RELATED TO CAUSE GIVEN IN 107

113. WAS OPERATION PERFORMED FOR ANY CONDITION IN ITEM 107 OR 112? IF YES, LIST TYPE OF OPERATION AND DATE.

PHYSICIAN'S CERTIFICATION

114. I CERTIFY THAT TO THE BEST OF MY KNOWLEDGE DEATH OCCURRED AT THE HOUR, DATE AND PLACE STATED FROM THE CAUSES STATED. DECEDENT ATTENDED SINCE M M / D D / C C Y Y | DECEDENT LAST SEEN ALIVE M M / D D / C C Y Y

115. SIGNATURE AND TITLE OF CERTIFIER   116. LICENSE NO.   117. DATE M M / D D / C C Y Y

118. TYPE ATTENDING PHYSICIAN'S NAME, MAILING ADDRESS, ZIP

CORONER'S USE ONLY

I CERTIFY THAT IN MY OPINION DEATH OCCURRED AT THE HOUR, DATE AND PLACE STATED FROM THE CAUSES STATED.

119. MANNER OF DEATH NATURAL / SUICIDE / HOMICIDE / ACCIDENT / PENDING INVESTIGATION / COULD NOT BE DETERMINED

120. INJURY AT WORK YES / No   121. INJURY DATE M M / D D / C C Y Y   122. HOUR   123. PLACE OF INJURY

124. DESCRIBE HOW INJURY OCCURRED (EVENTS WHICH RESULTED IN INJURY)

125. LOCATION (STREET AND NUMBER OR LOCATION AND CITY, ZIP)

126. SIGNATURE OF CORONER OR DEPUTY CORONER   127. DATE M M / D D / C C Y Y   128. TYPED NAME, TITLE OF CORONER OR DEPUTY CORONER

STATE REGISTRAR A B C D E F G H FAX AUTH. # CENSUS TRACT

Figure 9-4 *Certificate of Death in Use in California*

© Carol A. Foote

When death occurs under suspicious or uncertain circumstances, the coroner or medical examiner usually directs an investigation to determine the cause of death. If foul play is suspected, a police or sheriff's department investigation is undertaken.

herself. The use of a *psychological autopsy* as an investigative tool for reconstructing the intentions and factors leading up to a death is discussed in Chapter 12.

The Coroner and the Medical Examiner

Most deaths in the United States result from disease. The physician attending the patient at the time of death completes and signs the death certificate. However, when death occurs in suspicious circumstances or is sudden and there is no physician to sign the death certificate, the cause of death must be determined by a coroner or medical examiner. Besides suspected homicides and suicides, other circumstances of death that require investigation include accidents; deaths that occur on the job, in jails, and in other government institutions; deaths that occur in hospitals or other health care facilities when negligence is suspected or the death was unexpected; and deaths that occur at home when there is no attending physician who can sign a death certificate attesting to the cause of death.

Cause of death is determined by use of various scientific procedures, possibly including an autopsy (described in the following section), toxicology and bacteriology tests, chemical analyses, and other studies that are needed to arrive at adequate findings. Unlike autopsies performed as part of medical training or at a family's request, those done as part of an investigation conducted by a coroner or medical examiner are required by law. The results of such postmortem examination can play a crucial role in court cases and insurance settlements. The outcome of such proceedings may be important not only to law enforcement agencies but also to the families involved: The mode of death—whether it is due to foul play, negligence, suicide, accident, or natural causes—can have a significant emotional effect on survivors. It may also have an economic effect; for example, some life insurance policies cover only accidental death, whereas others pay twice the face value of the contract in case of accidental death (double indemnity).

Coroners are usually elected officials; medical examiners are usually appointed. The main difference between the two positions, however, has to do with training. Whereas coroners may not possess any special background or training, medical examiners are qualified medical doctors, generally with advanced training and certification in *forensic pathology* (the application of medical knowledge to questions of law). Besides their responsibilities for investigating the cause of death in questionable circumstances, medical examiners often play a key role in community health programs such as suicide prevention and drug abuse education.

Autopsies

An autopsy (from the Greek *autopsia,* meaning "seeing with one's own eyes") is a medical examination of a body after death to determine cause of death or to investigate the extent and nature of changes caused by disease. Autopsies involve detailed examination of both the exterior and interior of the body. Once the abdominal cavity is exposed, organs are removed for examination of their internal structure, and small samples may be taken for later analysis. After the autopsy is completed, organs not needed for further study are replaced in the body cavity and all incisions are closed.

An autopsy may be performed for legal or official reasons (as mentioned in the previous section in connection with the role of the coroner or medical examiner), or as part of a hospital's teaching or research program. Sometimes, the deceased's family will request an autopsy to determine whether genetic or infectious conditions led to death or to help resolve questions about possible malpractice. Except when required by law, an autopsy can be performed only after the next of kin's consent is obtained or when the deceased has donated his or her body for autopsy under the provisions of the Uniform Anatomical Gift Act.

Forensic science has achieved noteworthy results in investigating human rights violations. In Argentina, for example, a team of forensic scientists helped to identify remains of the *desaparecidos,* the "disappeared," who had been buried in mass graves during a period of military rule and terrorism in that country. The families of the disappeared had often been helpless in their attempts to determine the fate of loved ones. Aided by the techniques of forensic science, including the use of autopsies to determine the cause of death, many families were able to learn the fate of their missing loved ones and to give them a proper burial. Furthermore, during the ensuing trials of several former military leaders, forensic scientists presented expert testimony that helped convict those responsible for the deaths.

Similar techniques for identifying remains are used by the Army Central Identification Laboratory at Hickam Air Force Base in Hawaii (CILHI). With nearly 150 staff members, CILHI is the only organization of its kind in the U.S. military, with responsibility for searching for, recovering, and identifying service members killed or listed as missing.[23] It investigates cases from World War II, the Korean War, and the Vietnam War, as well as recent military and civilian cases. As part of a joint task force charged with resolving cases of Americans missing as a result of the Vietnam War, CILHI has investigated nearly 700 cases and inspected more than 360 crash or gravesites in Vietnam, Cambodia, and Laos.

Organized into three sections, CILHI includes teams devoted to search and recovery, casualty data analysis, and the lab itself. The analysis section focuses on the medical and dental records of individuals whose remains have not been recovered. In the lab, recovered remains and other evidence are examined by physical anthropologists and other experts. Remains arrive at Hickam in flag-draped caskets with full military honors. Although CILHI does not expect to be able to recover or identify all of the roughly 2250 individuals unaccounted for from the Vietnam War, its perseverance in this task confirms the emotional importance that human beings attach to psychological closure when death occurs.

As a method of conclusively establishing the cause of death, autopsies serve a number of important purposes in law and medicine. As a tool of medical investigation, autopsies are used to confirm diagnoses, train doctors, and conduct research. In this way, autopsies increase the understanding of disease, thereby leading to improved treatment and life-saving interventions. Because they are *required* in just a few circumstances, the percentage of autopsies performed in the United States is now about 5 percent of all hospital deaths, down from a peak of 42 percent in 1965. At one time, agencies that accredit hospitals required a minimum number of autopsies, but since this requirement was dropped, many hospitals no longer have full autopsy facilities. Valuable data regarding health and disease may go missing because autopsies are not performed with their prior frequency. A recent study, which included 1000 autopsies, found that the presumed cause of death was contradicted in about one-third of the cases.[24] John Lantos, a physician, says, "Postmortem examinations have long been recognized as one of the best teaching tools in medicine. They are the final check on whether what we did and what we thought we ought to be doing were correct or whether we missed something."[25] Recently, a number of private autopsy services have gone into business to conduct autopsies on behalf of hospitals and individual clients, many of whom are family members seeking information about hereditary diseases

© Carol A. Foote

When a coroner's preliminary investigation reveals the need to scientifically determine the cause of death, the corpse is brought to the morgue, where it is held until an autopsy can be performed.

The autopsy, or medical examination to determine the cause of death, is conducted under the coroner's direction when the circumstances of a death are violent, suspicious, or unexplained, or when a death is medically unattended and a doctor is unable to certify the cause of death. All homicides, accidents, and suicides come under the coroner's or medical examiner's jurisdiction.

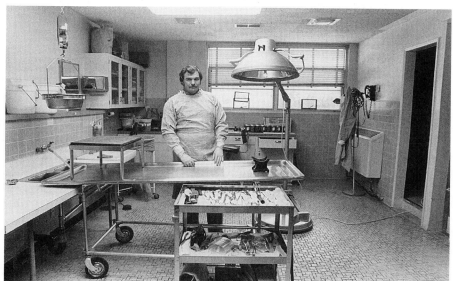

© Carol A. Foote

or who suspect malpractice and want evidence that may be obtained through an autopsy. The pathologists who operate such services note that, quite often, "what families really want from an autopsy is some attention," which they do not receive from the medical establishment because conversations about death are not encouraged. The freelance autopsy services, in contrast, take time to explain the cause of death in terms that families can understand.[26]

Wills and Inheritance

A *will* is a legal instrument expressing a person's intentions and wishes for the disposition of his or her property after death. It is a declaration of how a person's *estate*—that is, money, property, and other possessions—will be distributed upon that person's death. The will is a valuable tool for planning one's estate and for conveying property to one's heirs and beneficiaries. Conferring a kind of immortality on the *testator* (the person making the will), a will can be thought of as the deceased's last words. During the life of the testator, a will can be changed, replaced, or revoked. Upon the testator's death, it becomes a legal instrument that governs the distribution of his or her estate. (A glossary of terms relating to wills and inheritance is provided in Table 9-1.)

A will can evoke powerful emotions, embodying as it does the testator's feelings and intentions toward his or her survivors. The legalities associated with wills and inheritance may have either a beneficial or adverse effect on survivors, possibly affecting the intensity or course of grief.[27] People usually think of the will as simply a tool for estate planning, perhaps overlooking its comforting, and possibly even therapeutic, effects for both the testator and his or her survivors.

Terminally ill patients and their families often turn to counselors and other mental health professionals to help explore their fears, uncertainties, and conflicts, as well as devise a plan to meet the prospects that lie ahead; an attorney can be an important part of that team.[28] The death of a major breadwinner can be devastating. Estate planning not only optimizes survivors' financial security, but also helps ensure peace of mind both for the bereaved and the terminally ill person, who is confident that his or her affairs have been put in order. In addition, the services of an attorney may help ensure that the dying person's wishes about organ donation or advance directives for medical care are carried out.

Barton Bernstein outlines three basic legal stages that apply in cases of terminal illness when death follows expected medical probabilities.[29] The *first* stage involves long-range planning, in which the terminally ill person arranges

When it comes to divide an estate, the politest men quarrel.

Ralph Waldo Emerson, *Journals* (1863)

T A B L E *9-1*   *Terms Related to Wills and Inheritance*

Administrator: A person appointed by the court (in the absence of a will, or if no executor is named in one) to carry out the steps necessary to settling an estate. When an administrator is to be appointed, state law requires the drawing up of a preferential list of candidates. Assuming that the necessary qualifications are met, the order of preference typically begins with the spouse of the deceased and continues successively through the deceased's children, grandchildren, parents, siblings, more distant next of kin, and a public administrator.

Attestation clause: A statement signed by the persons who witness the testator's making of the will.

Codicil: An amendment to a will.

Conditional will: A type of formally executed will that states that certain actions will take place provided that a specified future event occurs. For example, suppose a testator wishes to bequeath money or property to a potential beneficiary who is incapable of self-care but who has a reasonable chance of recovery. With a conditional will, the money or property could be held in trust for that person until the conditions specified in the will (e.g., recovery) have been satisfied. A problem of conditional wills lies in the difficulty of stipulating with exactitude the nature of events and circumstances that might occur in the future.

Executor: A person named by the testator in his or her will to see that the provisions in the will are carried out properly.

Holographic will: A will written entirely by the hand of the person signing it. Some states do not recognize holographic wills as valid, and those that do generally have stringent conditions for such a document to be deemed valid. Not considered a substitute for a formally executed will.

Intestate: The condition of having made no valid will.

Mutual will: A type of formally executed will that contains reciprocal provisions. May be used by husbands and wives who wish to leave everything to the other spouse with no restrictions, although it limits the range of choices that are available when a will is executed individually.

Nuncupative will: A will made orally. Many states do not recognize a nuncupative will, or do so only under extremely limited circumstances. A few states admit an oral will if the person makes it in fear of imminent death or expectation of receiving mortal injuries, and the peril does result in death. A nuncupative will may also be valid when made by a soldier or sailor engaged in military service or by a mariner at sea; in these instances, the individual need not be in immediate peril. Generally, an oral will must be witnessed by at least two persons who attest that the will is indeed a statement of the testator's wishes.

Probate: The process by which an estate is settled and the property distributed. This process generally occupies an average of nine to twelve months, though it may be longer or shorter depending on circumstances and the complexity of the estate.

his or her legal and financial affairs for the eventuality of death. During the *second* stage, which occurs shortly before death, the survivors gather pertinent legal papers, obtain sufficient funds to cover immediate expenses, and notify the attorney and insurance representative so they will be ready to make a smooth transition of the deceased's legal and financial affairs. Also at this time,

"What would you like for breakfast, Jack?" I asked my son-in-law on Sunday, the day after the funeral.

"A fried egg, over," he replied.

Such a simple thing. Yet, I'd never fried an egg.

Oh, we often had them on weekends; but my husband was the breakfast cook, while I dashed up and down the steps putting clothes in the washer, running the vacuum, and all the other tasks always awaiting a working wife.

I stook there, the frying pan in one hand, the egg in the other.

How many times in the future would I find myself standing the same way? How many things had I never done? How many things had I taken for granted?

Maxine Dowd Jensen, *The Warming of Winter*

if the dying person intends to make an anatomical gift, the appropriate medical personnel are alerted.

In the *third* stage of legal activity, which follows the death, the will is delivered to an attorney for probate (the process of settling an estate). The effort that went into planning is now rewarded in the survivors' greater sense of security and certainty that affairs have not been left to chance. The survivors can confront their loss without the distraction and worry of complex legal and financial entanglements.

Definitions and Elements of Wills

The right to make a will is an acknowledgment of the rights of private property rather than communal ownership. In early legal systems, property belonged to the family, clan, or tribe. The right or privilege of determining how one's property will be distributed following death is not available in all societies, nor is it without limitations. In some countries, the government automatically assumes control over the settlement of a person's affairs; in the United States and most other modern societies, a person has considerable liberty in determining how property will be distributed. Still, depending on the laws of a particular state, enforcing and carrying out the provisions of a will may be constrained by circumstances affecting one's heirs. For example, someone may try to avoid willing anything to his or her spouse, but, if the will is contested, a court may overturn it. State statutes usually stipulate that a surviving spouse cannot be disinherited. Some statutes require that dependent children be provided for in the will. As a rule of thumb, anything that conflicts with ordinary standards of social conduct may be abrogated or made invalid if the will is contested.

The person who makes a will must have the mental capacity to understand the nature of the document and the consequences of signing it. He or she must understand the nature and extent of the property being bequeathed by the will and be able to identify the persons who, by convention, ought to be considered when making a will, whether or not they actually become beneficiaries. Given these conditions, and in the absence of any significant delusions, the testator is said to be of sound mind, capable of executing a legal will. State laws generally specify a minimum age at which a person can make a legal will—usually eighteen, though in several states as young as fourteen—and various other requirements, such as the presence of witnesses and execution of the document in a proper form.

In addition to standard information such as the testator's identification and a declaration that the document constitutes the person's last will and testament (along with a statement revoking previous wills, if applicable), a will may include information regarding the property to be distributed, the names of children and other heirs, specific bequests and allocations of property, as well as information concerning the establishment of trusts, the granting of powers to a trustee and/or guardian, other provisions for disposition of property, and payment of taxes, debts, and expenses of administration. Not all these items are necessarily part of every will, nor is a will limited to the items listed here.

In making a will, it is generally advisable to involve close family members, or at least one's spouse, to prevent problems that can arise when actions are taken without the knowledge of those who will be affected. When survivors discover that things are not as expected, it may add to the burden of grief. There is no requirement, however, that one's mate be involved in the making of a will. In loving families, it is usually important for everyone to have at least some idea of what is going to happen with the estate when the will becomes effective. There may be valid reasons for not disclosing the details of a will. But the *testator* can tell his or her survivors something like, "Call Rick, my attorney; he knows where my will is and can help you in handling my estate." Some experts suggest that there ought to be some kind of governmental or administrative program whereby wills, as well as other important documents such as advance directives, could be registered ahead of time and be readily available when they are needed.

The Formally Executed Will

The *formally executed will* is the conventional document used for specifying a person's wishes for the distribution of his or her estate after death (see Figure 9-5). If carefully prepared, it not only has sufficient clarity of purpose and expression to withstand a court's scrutiny, but can help ease the burden and stress on survivors while demonstrating the testator's affection for those who were close during life.

In making a formally executed will, most people find it beneficial to consult an attorney. A comprehensive review of an estate requires that legal records and other information be gathered. Several meetings may be required to carefully determine the nature of the property and the testator's wishes for its distribution. Once the will's content is determined and its provisions set, the attorney has it typed and an appointment is made for its formal execution. On that occasion, two (in some states, three) disinterested persons are brought in to serve as witnesses, the will is reviewed, and the testator

Will of Tomás Antonio Yorba

In the name of the Holy Trinity, Father, Son, and the Holy Ghost, three distinct persons and one true God, Amen.

1st Clause. Know all [men] who may read this my last will and testament: that I—Tomás Antonio Yorba, native born resident of this department of California, legitimate son of Antonio Yorba and Josefa Grijalva—being sick, but, by divine mercy, in the full enjoyment of my reason, memory and understanding, believing, as I firmly do, in all the mysteries of our holy Catholic faith, which faith is natural to me, since I have lived in it from my infancy and I declare that I want to live in it as a faithful Christian and true Catholic, trusting that, for this reason, his divine Majesty will have mercy on me and will pardon all my sins, through the mysteries of our Lord Jesus Christ and the intercession of his most holy mother, who is my protector and benefactress in these my last moments, so that together with my guardian angel, with St. Joseph, my own name's saint, and all the other saints of my devotion and all the other hosts of heaven, they will assist me before the grand tribunal of God, before which all mortals must render account of their actions—make and decree this my last will and testament as follows, in ordinary paper because of lack of stamped paper.

2nd Clause. Firstly, I commend my soul to God who created it, and my body to the earth, from whence it was fashioned, and it is my wish that I be buried in the church of the Mission of San Gabriel in the shroud of our father St. Francis, the funeral to be according to what my executors and heirs consider that I deserve and is befitting.

3rd Clause. Item: In regard to the expense of the funeral and masses, these should be drawn from the fifth of my estate, according to the disposition of my executors, and I leave the residue of this fifth to my son Juan.

4th Clause. I declare that with respect to my debts, my heirs and executors should collect and pay any legal claims that may turn up or be due according to law. Item: I declare to have been married to Doña Vicenta Sepúlveda, legitimate daughter of Don Francisco Sepúlveda and Doña Ramona Sepúlveda, of this neighborhood, by which marriage I had five children named: (1) Juan; (2) Guadalupe, deceased; (3) José Antonio; (4) Josefa; (5) Ramona. The first being 10 years old, the second died at the age of three, the third six years old, the fourth four years old, and the fifth two years old. Item: I declare to have given my wife jewels of some value as a wedding present, but I do not remember how many nor their value; but they must be in her possession, since I gave them to her. Item: According to my reckoning I have about 2,000 head of cattle, 900 ewes and their respective males, three herds of about 100 mares and their stallions, and three donkeys; about 21 tame horses, 7 tame and 12 unbroken mules; and lastly, whatever cattle, horses or mules may turn up with my brand which may not have been legally sold. Item: I declare to have the right—through inheritance from my father—to part of Middle Santa Ana and Lower Santana, known to be of the Yorbas. I have in Middle Santa Ana an adobe house, its roof being part timber and part thatched, consisting of 18 rooms, including the soap-house. Item: I declare that I have two vineyards with wooden fences which are now planted with bearing vines and some fruit trees; also a section of enclosed land.

5th Clause. I declare that it is my wish to name as executors and guardians of my estate, first, my brother, Don Bernardo Yorba, and second, Don Raimundo Yorba, by joint approval, to whom I give all my vested power, as much as may be necessary, to go in and examine my property for the benefit of my heirs in carrying out this will, and I grant them the power to procure another associate [executor] to expedite its due execution, whom I consider appointed as a matter of course, granting him the same authority as those previously named.

6th Clause. I name as my heirs my children and my wife, in the form and manner indicated by the law, following the necessary inventory.

7th Clause. In this my last will, I annul and void whatever will or wills, codicil or codicils, I may have previously made, so that they may stand nullified with or without judicial process, now and forever, since I definitely desire that the present testamentary disposition be my last will, codicil, and final wish, in the manner and form most legally valid. To this effect I beg Don Vicente Sanchez, Judge of 1st *instancia,* to exercise his authority in probating this will.

To which I, the citizen Vicente Sanchez, 1st constitutional Alcalde and Judge of the 1st *instancia* of the city of Los Angeles, certify; and I affirm that the present testamentary disposition was made in my presence, and that the testator, Don Tomás Antonio Yorba, although ill, finds himself in the full command of his faculties and natural understanding, and, to attest it, I do this before the assistant witnesses—the citizens Ramon Aguilar and Ignacio Coronel—the other instrumental witnesses being the citizens Bautista Mutriel and Mariano Martinez; on the 28th day of the month of January, 1845. The testator did not sign because of physical inability, but Don Juan Bandini signed for him.

Figure 9-5 *Historical Will*
Social custom plays a significant part in the making of a will. The will of Don Tomás Antonio Yorba, dating from the period of Mexican rule in California, presents an illuminating contrast to the modern will with its emphasis on the distribution of the testator's property. Although Yorba's estate was among the largest of the time—consisting of a Spanish land grant of 62,000 acres known as the Rancho Santiago de Santa Ana in Southern California— only a small fraction of his will relates to matters affecting the distribution of the estate to his heirs.

acknowledges that the document accurately reflects his or her wishes and signs it. Although preparation of the will may involve weeks or even months of thoughtful consideration and planning, the actual signing can take less than five minutes.

Amending or Revoking a Will

A will is not cast in stone; it can be changed as the testator's situation changes. A will can be revoked and replaced by an entirely new will, or only certain parts of it can be amended. Amending a will is a means of adding new provisions without having to rewrite it entirely. A testator who, after the will has been executed, acquires valuable property, such as an art collection, might want to make a specific provision for the new property without disturbing other parts of his or her estate plan. A *codicil,* which is executed in much the same manner as a will, accomplishes that objective. All wills should be reviewed periodically to determine if changed circumstances call for revision.

When the addition of codicils makes a will unwieldy or potentially confusing, it is time to review the entire will and make a new one. States vary in their

© Carol A. Foote

*Many of the legal issues surrounding death can be clarified with the help of a
competent attorney who is versed in the options available to clients.*

requirements for legally revoking a will. Generally, the testator's intent to
revoke the will must be demonstrated; the accidental burning of a will, for
instance, does not imply revocation. However, if someone turns up with an
earlier will, it may be difficult to prove that it was revoked if a subsequent will
does not explicitly say so. When in doubt about the validity of a will, seek
competent legal advice.

Probate

The period of *probate* allows time for the deceased's affairs to be resolved, debts
and taxes paid, and arrangements made to receive funds that were owed to
the deceased. During the course of probate, the validity of the will is proved;
an executor or administrator of the estate is appointed; the necessary matters
for settling the estate are carried out; and, with the probate court's approval,
the decedent's property is distributed to beneficiaries. If the deceased left a
valid will, property is distributed in accordance with its terms. When a person
dies *intestate*—that is, without having left a valid will—property is distributed
according to rules set up by the state.

The Duties of the Executor or Administrator

Someone has to be responsible for carrying out all the steps necessary to
settling an estate through probate. Whether an *executor* named in the will or
an *administrator* appointed by the court, this person generally must meet cer-

tain requirements stipulated by the law of the state in which probate occurs. Whereas an executor named by the testator is permitted to act more or less independently in the management of the estate provided that he or she acts prudently, the court-appointed administrator may be required to obtain the court's approval before proceeding with sensible and necessary decisions.

The executor's or administrator's first duty is to notify interested parties of the testator's death. This is generally accomplished in two ways. First, parties who are likely to be interested in the settlement of the estate are notified of the deceased's death by mail and, if they request it, are sent a copy of the will. Second, a legal notification of the death is published in appropriate newspapers (see Figure 9-6). This notice serves three purposes in the probate process: (1) It announces that someone is ready to prove the will of the decedent; (2) it acknowledges that someone is petitioning to be appointed by the court to begin probate; and (3) it gives notice of the death to creditors so that outstanding claims against the decedent can be submitted for settlement.

The estate is inventoried, including all personal and real property owned by the decedent. When a surviving spouse is the estate's primary or sole heir, the inventory of personal and household goods can be less meticulous, though items that have significant worth, such as paintings, jewelry, and antiques, are specified. Important papers are gathered, including insurance policies, Social

---

**NOTICE OF DEATH OF
LEE D. WILLIAMS
AND OF PETITION TO
ADMINISTER ESTATE
Case Number: 11111**

To all heirs, beneficiaries, creditors, contingent creditors, and persons who may be otherwise interested in the will or estate of LEE D. WILLIAMS.

A petition has been filed by JANE DOE, in the Superior Court of Santa Cruz County requesting that JANE DOE be appointed as personal representative to administer the estate of the decedent.

A hearing on the petition will be held on March 22, 1982, at 8:30 a.m. in Dept III, located at 701 Ocean Street, Santa Cruz, California 95060.

IF YOU OBJECT to the granting of the petition, you should either appear at the hearing and state your objections or file written objections with the court before the hearing. Your appearance may be in person or by your attorney.

IF YOU ARE A CREDITOR or a contingent creditor of the deceased, you must file your claim with the court or present it to the personal representative appointed by the court within four months from the date of first issuance of letters as provided in section 700 of the California Probate Code. The time for filing claims will not expire prior to four months from the date of the hearing noticed above.

YOU MAY EXAMINE the file kept by the court. If you are a person interested in the estate, you may file a request with the court to receive special notice of the filing of the inventory of estate assets and of the petitions, accounts and reports described in section 1200 of the California Probate Code.

s/ JOHN P. SMITH
Attorney for the Petitioner

JOHN P. SMITH
9999 Pacific Avenue
Santa Cruz, CA 95060
March 7, 9, 14

Figure *9-6 Newspaper Notice to Creditors*

© Chronicle Features, 1984

"The Far Side," drawing by Gary Larson, Creators Syndicate

3-9 Larson

"Aaaaaaaa! . . . It's George! He's taking it with him!"

Security and pension information, military service records, and other documents that require review and possibly action.

The executor is responsible for properly managing the estate pending its final disbursement to heirs. Tax returns may need to be filed on behalf of the decedent and the estate. The executor may be charged with paying an allowance to the spouse or to minor children for their support during the period of probate. If the decedent was in business or was a stockholder in a corporation, the executor must manage a smooth transition that benefits the estate. An executor or administrator who is not knowledgeable in the law usually enlists the aid of an attorney to make certain that legal requirements are satisfied.

Finally, an accounting and schedule for distributing the estate's property to the beneficiaries is prepared and submitted for the approval of the probate court. Once the court's approval is obtained, the property is distributed and receipts are obtained to certify that the distribution has been made correctly. Assuming that everything has been carried out properly, the court then discharges the executor or administrator. The estate is settled.

Avoiding Probate

Because probate involves delays and can sometimes be expensive, many people take sensible, legal steps to avoid or minimize it. For example, a husband and wife may own their house and other assets in joint tenancy, a form of property ownership that allows a spouse to take full legal possession of the property upon the other's death, without probate. Some approaches to avoiding probate, however, have serious pitfalls, particularly the do-it-yourself approach that is taken without obtaining qualified legal counsel. For example, placing a minor's name on a deed may seem like a good way to avoid probate; but, if circumstances change, it can require going into court to request that a legal guardian be appointed to act on the minor's behalf, thus complicating, rather than simplifying, things.

Living trusts can minimize the costs of passing one's estate to heirs, and they can avoid the publicity about an estate that accompanies public proceedings. In fact, they can be a substitute for engaging in the more complicated process of making a will and going through probate. In addition, living trusts may be used to avoid or minimize inheritance taxes that would otherwise have to be paid on the value of an estate. Of course, all decisions about wills and probate should always be carefully considered and, in most cases, it is wise to have the advice of an attorney who is well-versed in such matters.

Laws of Intestate Succession

Statistics indicate that seven out of ten Americans die without leaving a will. Perhaps the failure to plan ahead for death by making a will is attributable to the discomfort many people feel about their own mortality. Or perhaps, overwhelmed by busyness, we neglect this aspect of planning ahead with the questionable excuse that we are not yet at an age when death is statistically probable. Whatever the reason, dying without having made a will can lead to unnecessary hardships for our survivors, even when an estate is modest in size.

The failure to execute a will may result in a distribution of property that is not compatible with a person's wishes nor best suited to the interests and needs of heirs.

 And in a decade or two or more when death taps at the door, your estate may be far larger than you now envisage. It may be so already. One tends to think in terms of a few principal segments of one's estate. For purposes of planning, your "estate" includes everything of monetary value: your home and other real estate; all bank and savings accounts; usables including *objets d'art* and hobbies, such as a stamp collection; your carefully planned investment portfolio; life insurance; rights under a pension plan, if you enjoy that umbrella; as well as growing protection from social security. All must be arranged so as to afford maximum benefit to the beneficiaries.

Paul P. Ashley, *You and Your Will*

One of the chief reasons for making a will is to ensure that property will be disbursed according to one's wishes. In the absence of a will, property is distributed according to guidelines established in state law. The state generally tries to accomplish what it believes the deceased would have done had he or she actually made a will. Nevertheless, the laws that dictate the disbursement of property, the care of minor children, and all the matters that pertain to settling the estate reflect society's ideas of fair play and justice. Thus, the values of society, rather than the deceased's personal values, determine the outcome.

Although the laws of intestate succession differ among states, some general patterns prevail. In community property states, for example, all community property goes to the surviving spouse. In separate property or non–community property states, when there is only one child, an estate is generally divided equally between child and surviving spouse. If there is more than one child, usually one-third of the estate goes to the surviving spouse and the remaining two-thirds is divided equally among the children.

If there is no surviving spouse, property is divided among the children; if no children, disbursement is made to the deceased's parents; if they are not living, property is likely to be divided among the deceased's surviving siblings; if there are none, the estate may be divided among the deceased's siblings' children. In attempting to settle an estate, the court will make a determined effort to locate surviving heirs. If none can be found, the proceeds from the estate go to the state.

Life Insurance and Death Benefits

In the United States, the first life insurance company was established in 1759 by the Presbyterian Synod of Philadelphia for Presbyterian ministers. Although life insurance did not become common until the middle of the nineteenth century, it is now a huge industry. Most American households include at least one member who owns some form of life insurance.

Depending on a person's age and health, life insurance can provide a convenient and relatively inexpensive way of leaving at least a basic estate for

Inheritance

When I was ten years old, my father died. And at that time, of course, I thought my father was the best and finest man there ever was. And some years later when I was eighteen and I began to mingle in the adult community, I introduced myself to strangers and they would ask me if John Estrada was my father. When I said yes, they would say, "Well, let me shake your hand. He was a fine man and a good friend of mine." And then they would tell me wonderful stories about him. Since that time, I have hoped that when I am gone, some people might meet my children and say to them that I was a good man and a good friend. To me that is a finer inheritance than any material possession.

Fred Estrada

our beneficiaries after we die. It may represent a small portion of a large estate or the major portion of a smaller estate. Insurance plans can be designed in a number of ways and to suit many purposes. Some policies are part of a total investment portfolio that can be drawn upon during the insured's lifetime. Other policies provide benefit payments only after the death of the insured.

Those who favor including insurance as part of estate planning argue that life insurance offers some advantages not available with other investments. For example, life insurance benefits that are payable to a named beneficiary (not the decedent's estate) are not subject to attachment by the decedent's creditors. Also, unlike assets that must be processed through probate, insurance benefits usually become available immediately following death. These benefits can have important psychological and emotional value, possibly providing relief and a sense of security to a surviving spouse or other dependents in the period soon after bereavement. Knowing that money is available to cover anticipated expenses may help to reduce stress. However, a hasty or ill-informed decision concerning how insurance benefits are spent may ultimately increase the survivor's stress rather than alleviating it. Issues like this, so important for the well-being of one's survivors, should be considered in devising a comprehensive estate plan.

A recent development in the insurance business allows patients with terminal illness to sell their life insurance policies to "viatical settlement companies" so that they can pay medical bills, travel, or purchase things they want to enjoy before dying. A viatical settlement allows an individual with terminal illness to sell his or her life insurance policy before death for a lump-sum settlement. Viatical settlement companies typically pay about 70 percent of the full face value of the policy, and the policy is cashed in for its full value

Burial in a national cemetery, such as the Black Hills National Cemetery in South Dakota, is a benefit made available to veterans who have served in American military forces during wartime. Such cemeteries have been established across the United States. Other death benefits for veterans include a lump-sum payment to help defray burial expenses and, under certain circumstances, direct payments to survivors.

Death of a Son

"I'm not happy because I no more my son already. . . . I miss him. Even if I get my money, I no more my loved one, my son. I'm not interested in money. Every day, after work, even if I feel tired, I no miss to go visit my boy. Sometimes I cry. Sometimes I give food [for his grave]. Soda. His favorite—Kentucky Fried Chicken. Sometimes fried saimin. Then I give an orange. Ice cream. . . . One day after the crash, my boy, he come my house in spirit. He tell me, 'Daddy, I miss you. I no more hands. I no more eyes.' Ho, I cry."

Figure 9-7 *Death of a Son*
Jovencio Ruiz of Molokai, responding to a question about a six-figure insurance settlement in the death of his 14-year-old son, Jovencio Jr., in an air crash.

after the policyholder's death. For example, on a policy with a face value of $100,000, the settlement company might pay $70,000 to the policyholder. Patients with less than a year to live usually receive a higher percentage of face value than those who are expected to live longer. When the patient dies and the policy is cashed in, the settlement company pockets the difference between what was paid to the policyholder and the face amount of the policy, less its operating expenses. Some mainstream insurers offer similar options, allowing the policyholder to do business with the same company that he or she purchased the policy from. As with any area of financial planning, it is wise to compare the available choices before entering into a deal.

Many survivors qualify for benefits from government programs and institutions such as Social Security and the Veterans Administration. To obtain current information about such death-benefit programs, one can call or write the government bureau administering them. A person entitled to benefits under one or more of these programs may not receive them unless a claim is filed. Moreover, delays in filing may result in a loss of benefits. An adequate estate plan includes consideration of benefits that may accrue from government programs, as well as those related to employee or union pension programs.

When death results from accident or negligence, insurance settlements or other death benefits may become payable to survivors. Such benefits sometimes result from court cases that involve the attempt to place a "value" on the deceased person's life and what that loss represents to his or her survivors. Although settlements of this kind may indeed be helpful to survivors, the monetary amount of a settlement, no matter how large, is poor compensation for the loss of a loved one (see Figure 9-7).

Dealing with the varied legal issues surrounding dying and death can be a heavy burden when a person is grieving the death of a loved one or coping with the impending death of a family member with a terminal illness. Yet crucial and perhaps irrevocable decisions about financial matters often must be made at difficult times like these. To the extent it can be accomplished, adequate preparation can help to ease the burden somewhat. Although it is not possible to plan for every contingency, it is feasible to recognize the range of legalities that may impinge on our experiences of death and dying, and, acting out of that recognition, take appropriate steps to prepare ourselves for the likely or inevitable eventualities.

Further Readings

George J. Annas. *The Rights of Patients: The Basic ACLU Guide to Patient Rights.* 2d ed. Clifton, N.J.: Humana Press, 1991.

Joseph M. Belth. *Life Insurance: A Consumer's Handbook.* 2d ed. Bloomington: Indiana University Press, 1985.

Tony Blanche and Brad Schreiber. *Death in Paradise: An Illustrated History of the Los Angeles County Department of Coroner.* Los Angeles: General Publishing Group, 1998.

Denis Clifford and Cora Jordan. *Plan Your Estate.* 5th ed. Berkeley, Calif.: Nolo Press, 2000.

Thane Josef Messinger. "A Gentle and Easy Death: From Ancient Greece to Beyond Cruzan Toward a Reasoned Legal Response to the Societal Dilemma of Euthanasia." *Denver University Law Review* 71, no. 1 (1993): 175–251.

Carole Shammas, Marylynn Salmon, and Michel Dahlin. *Inheritance in America from Colonial Times to the Present.* New Brunswick, N.J.: Rutgers University Press, 1987.

Carol Buchalter Stapp. *Afro-Americans in Antebellum Boston: An Analysis of Probate Records.* New York: Garland, 1993.

Cyril Wecht. *Cause of Death.* New York: Dutton, 1993.

*A child feels the death of a parent or other close family member or friend as
deeply as do adult survivors of a close death. This young girl finds solace and
a means of coming to terms with the death of her father by bringing a favorite
drawing to the gravesite and spending some time alone with her thoughts
and memories of her father and what his loss represents in her life.*

CHAPTER 10

Death in the Lives of Children and Adolescents

Change is pervasive in the lives of children and adolescents. Families move. Children leave familiar playmates and friends, their neighborhood, school, and the people and places they have come to know and to which they feel attached. A parent may say, "But, dear, it's only for a year," or, "We'll come back to visit next summer." To a child, however, a year or next summer can seem a very long time indeed. Change can bring a very real loss.

Changes in family relationships—divorce or separation, for instance—may be experienced as a kind of death. The child senses that the known relationship has changed, but exactly what the future holds is uncertain and possibly bewildering. Even though such changes do not have the finality that adults reserve for death, children can experience a lingering uncertainty, a kind of "little death."

Change is experienced as older brothers and sisters grow up and move away from home. As the composition of the family shifts, a child is faced with the need to adjust to new and unfamiliar situations. Perhaps the child delights in the change because it means he or she now enjoys the thrill of having one's own room. However, with the departure of an older sibling, the child may lose an advocate or a confidant who provided support and understanding. Change can bring both gains and losses.

An addition to the family, a new baby brother or sister, can give rise to both excitement and anxiety. The new family member can represent an intrusion upon the child's

Small boy. "Where do animals go when they die?"
Small girl. "All good animals go to heaven, but the bad ones
    go to the Natural History Museum."

Caption to drawing by E. H. Shepard, *Punch,* 1929

place in the family, a loss of attention from parents and other family members. Yet the child may also enjoy the adventure and the more mature responsibilities that accompany change. Change requires readjustments.

In addition, children and adolescents may experience significant losses: the death of a brother or sister, a parent, or a friend; or confrontation with an illness that threatens his or her own life. As much as we may wish it were otherwise, children are exposed to events of change and loss, experiences of bereavement and grief.

Early Childhood Encounters With Death

When does a child first become aware of death? By the time children are four or five, death-related thoughts and experiences are usually evident in their songs, their play, and their questions. The infant's experience of the difference between sleep and wakefulness may involve a perception of the distinction between being and nonbeing.[1] Children begin to experiment with this difference at a very early age, as in the "peekaboo" game, for instance. The infant's experience of having a cloth thrown over her face, shutting out sensory awareness of the environment, is analogous to death. The "boo," when the cloth is removed, is like being alive again. Thus, death may be experienced in games of this kind as separation, disappearance, and return.

The ability to distinguish between the animate and the inanimate is among the child's earliest encounters with death. The child perceives whether or not something has life. The following story illustrates how this may occur in quite ordinary circumstances. An eighteen-month-old boy was out walking with his father when the father inadvertently stepped on a caterpillar. The child kneeled down, looked at the dead caterpillar lying on the sidewalk, and said, "No more!" That is the typical genesis of a child's awareness of death: *No more.*

Similar experiences may produce quite different responses in different children. Encountering a dead caterpillar or dead bird may set off a reaction in one child that lasts for several days, during which time the child is eager to find answers. Another child may pay such an encounter little heed, apparently without a moment's reflection about an event that the first child found provocative and mysterious. Some theorists believe that much of the behavior shown by infants and very young children is *protothanatic*—that is, preparation for concepts about life and death that will eventually emerge in the child's later interactions with the environment.

For older children, play activities can help them deal with evolving concerns about death. Games like cowboys and Indians and cops and robbers reflect, in part, a child's efforts to reach some understanding about the place of death in his or her world. Play can be a means of exorcising fears, trying out roles, making decisions, investigating consequences of actions, experimenting with value judgments, and finding a comfortable self-image.

Death-Experienced Children, Ages One to Three

A study conducted by Mark Speece to investigate the impact of death experiences on children ages one to three suggests that very young children make efforts to come to terms with death-related experiences.[2] Speece says, "It seems safe to conclude that death experiences occur in the lives of a sizable proportion of children of this age and that those children who do have such experiences attempt to deal with and integrate their specific death experiences into their understanding of the world in general."

Speece found that slightly over half of the children he studied had some experience with death: in some cases, a human death (for example, a grandmother, a cousin, a neighbor); in others, a nonhuman death, such as that of a pet (most often birds, dogs, and fish). Speece found that these young children responded to death in observable ways. One child became angry when a pet bird that had died would not come back to life. Some actively looked for the deceased pet or person. They questioned the immobility of the deceased and what happens after death, and expressed concern about the welfare of the living.

The Very Young Child and Death: An Example

So, how does one answer the question: When does the understanding of death begin, and what governs its development? The dialogue between a twenty-seven-month-old child and his psychologist father provides an illuminating and suggestive case study.[3] (Note how the father's professional skills in

---

Death has a different emotional meaning to young children. In the game of Cowboys and Indians death is not final; the game must continue. The common threat when angered may be, "I'll kill you." One can readily see that the concept of killing is not viewed as final and that there is no association of pain with killing. Perhaps the following example will best prove the point. Upon arriving home from a business trip, a young child's father brought her a gun ahd holster set. After buckling on her new present she took out the gun, pointed it at her father and said, "Bang, bang, you're dead! I killed you." Her father replied, "Don't hurt me." His daughter's innocent answer was, "Oh, Daddy, I won't hurt you, I just killed you." To many children death is seen only as something in the distant future; "only old people die."

Dan Leviton and Eileen C. Forman,
"Death Education for Children and Youth"

listening and his sensitivity to his child's behavior helped him engage in this kind of conversation.)

For two months the child had been waking several times each night and screaming hysterically for a bottle of sugar water. The father describes getting up one night, for the second or third time, and deciding with his wife to use firmness in refusing to meet the child's demand. He went into his son's room and told him that he was too old to have a bottle and would have to go back to sleep without it. The father, his mind made up that enough was enough, started to leave the room.

But then he heard a frightened cry, one of desperation that sounded like the fear of death. Wondering what could be causing the child such alarm, the father turned back into the room, took his son out of the crib, and asked, "What will happen if you don't get your bottle?" The child, no longer hysterical, but very tearful and sniffling, said, "I can't make contact!" The father asked, "What does that mean, 'you can't make contact'?" His son replied, "If I run out of gas, I can't make contact—my engine won't go. You know!"

The father then remembered several family excursions during the previous summer, when vehicles had run out of gas. "What are you afraid will happen if you run out of gas?" Still crying, the child replied, "My motor won't run and then I'll die." At that point, the father recalled another incident his son had witnessed. Some time earlier, when they were selling an old car, the prospective buyer had tried to start the engine, but the battery was dead and the engine wouldn't turn over. The child had heard remarks like, "It's probably *not making contact*," "the *motor died*," and "I guess *the battery's dead*."

With this incident in mind, the father asked, "Are you afraid that your bottle is like gasoline and, just like when the car runs out of gas, the car dies; so, if you run out of food, you'll die?" The child nodded his head, "Yes." The father explained, "Well, that's not the same thing at all. You see, when you eat food, your body stores up energy so that you have enough to last you all night. You eat three times a day; we only fill up the car with gas once a week. When the car runs out of gas, it doesn't have any saved up for an emergency. But with people it isn't anything like that at all. You can go maybe two or three days without eating. And, even if you got hungry, you still wouldn't die. People aren't anything like cars."

This explanation seemed to do little toward alleviating the child's anxiety, so the father tried a different tack. "You're worried that you have a motor, just like a car, right?" The child nodded, "Yes." "So," continued the father, "you're worried that if you run out of gas or run out of food you'll die, just like the motor of a car, right?" Again, the child nodded yes. "Ah, but the car has a key, right? We can turn it on and off anytime we want, right?"

Now the child's body began to relax. "But where is your key?" The father poked around the boy's belly button: "Is this your key?" The child laughed. "Can I turn your motor off and on? See, you're really nothing like a car at all. Nobody can turn you on and off. Once your motor is on, you don't have to worry about it dying. You can sleep through the whole night and your motor will keep running without you ever having to fill it up with gas. Do you know what I mean?" The child said, "Yes."

"Peanuts," drawing by Charles Schultz, © 1995 United Features Syndicate, Inc.

"Okay. Now you can sleep without worrying. When you wake in the morning, your motor will still be running. Okay?" Never again did the child wake up in the middle of the night asking for a bottle of warm sugar water.

Think of the impressive reasoning that goes on in a child's mind—the way of stringing together concepts. In this case, the father speculates that two experiences contributed to his child's understanding: First, the child had decided that sugar water would give him gas because he had overheard his parents saying that a younger sibling had "gas" from drinking sugar water; second, when the child's parakeet died, his question "What happened to it?" was answered by his father: "Every animal has a motor inside that keeps it going. When a thing dies, it is like when a motor stops running. Its motor just won't run anymore."

A child's understanding of death is composed of a series of concepts, strung together like beads in a strand that is worked with until it eventually becomes a necklace, a coherent understanding of death. The description of this twenty-seven-month-old's complex associations of language and death demonstrates that children are capable of formulating an elementary understanding of death very early in life.

Development of the Understanding of Death

The evolving understanding of death is a process of continuous adjustments and refinements. This process is often quite rapid; a child's understanding of death can change dramatically in a very brief time. By observing and questioning to gather information, and then analyzing the data, researchers identify characteristic patterns of childhood development. (You have probably done this yourself by observing the changes that occur in children with whom you have frequent contact. For example, the kinds of play activities that engross a child change over time; the toys that elicited great excitement at one age become uninteresting at a later time.) By observing children's behavior, developmental psychologists devise models to describe the characteristic concerns and interests of children at various ages. These models are like maps that describe the main features of the territory of childhood at different stages of development. The models are useful for describing the characteristics of a

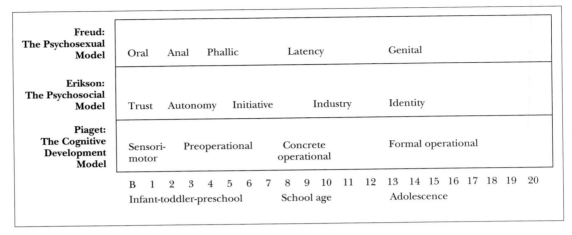

Figure 10-1 *Comparison of Major Developmental Models, or Theories, Concerning Childhood Phases of Development*

typical child at, say, age two or age seven. They give a general picture of each stage of development. But the map should not be mistaken for the territory.

Models of human development are abstractions, representations, interpretations of the actual territory (see Figure 10-1). Such maps can be helpful in guiding one's way, locating certain landmarks, and sharing knowledge with others, but the particular features of the landscape always possess a uniqueness that cannot be fully described by a map. Children vary in individual rates of development—not only physically, but also emotionally and cognitively, or intellectually. Thus, with respect to a child's understanding of death, as with other human traits, developmental levels do not correspond neatly to chronological age.

The child's concerns and behaviors change over time due to the interplay between experiences and the level of maturity brought to understanding them. Or, put another way, the child's understanding of death usually fits with his or her model of the world at each stage of development.[4] Thus, an adult could give a young child a lengthy, detailed explanation of the concept of death as adults understand it, yet the child will grasp its components only as he or she is developmentally ready to understand. However, a child's cognitive and emotional readiness to understand is not simply a matter of age: Experience plays an important role. A child who has had firsthand encounters with death may arrive at an understanding of death beyond what is typical of other children of the same age.

Until recently, few studies of children's development focused specifically on how children learn about death. A study done in the early 1940s by Sylvia Anthony in England and another done by Maria Nagy in Hungary a bit later are two notable exceptions.[5] Early theoretical models proposed a series of

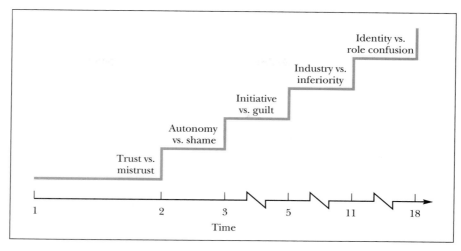

Figure *10-2* *Five Stages of Preadult Psychosocial Development Proposed by Erikson*
Source: Based on Erik H. Erikson, *Childhood and Society,* 2d ed. (New York: Norton, 1964),
pp. 247–274.

stages with more or less fixed corresponding ages within which certain death-related conceptual developments occurred. As some of the blanks in developmental studies are filled in by current research, the picture drawn by earlier theorists is being refined.[6] It is increasingly clear, for example, that emphasizing developmental *sequence* is more reliable than correlating stages of understanding to *age.*

In tracing the development of the death concept in children, it is useful to have a theoretical framework within which to place the distinctive attitudes and behaviors that pertain to various phases of childhood. In the discussion that follows, we use two theories of development—namely, those devised by Erik Erikson and Jean Piaget.

The model of human development devised by psychologist Erik Erikson focuses on the *stages of psychosocial development,* or psychosocial milestones, that occur successively throughout a person's life (see Figure 10-2).[7] In Erikson's model, psychosocial development depends significantly on the environment and is linked to the individual's *relationships* with others. Each stage of development involves a turning point, or crisis, that requires a response from the individual.

Jean Piaget is considered to have been the world's foremost child psychologist, a profound theorist as well as an astute observer of children's behavior. Piaget's focus was on the *cognitive transformations* that occur during childhood (see Table 10-1).[8] In Piaget's view, an individual's mode of understanding the world changes in sequential stages from infancy to adulthood. Accordingly, four different periods of cognitive, or intellectual, development can be distinguished. These developmental stages are based on the characteristic ways in

TABLE 10-1   *Piaget's Model of Cognitive Development*

Age (approximate)	Developmental Period	Characteristics
Birth–2 years	Sensorimotor	Focused on senses and motor abilities; learns object exists even when not observable (object permanence) and begins to remember and imagine ideas and experiences (mental representation).
2–7 years	Preoperational	Development of symbolic thinking and language to understand the world. (2–4 years) *Preconceptual subperiod:* sense of magical omnipotence; self as center of world; egocentric thought; all natural objects have feelings and intention (will). (4–6 years) *Prelogical subperiod:* beginning problem solving; seeing is believing; trial and error; understanding of other points of view; more socialized speech; gradual decentering of self and discovery of correct relationships.
7–12 years	Concrete operational	Applies logical abilities to understanding concrete ideas; organizes and classifies information; manipulates ideas and experiences symbolically; able to think backwards and forwards; notion of reversibility; can think logically about things experienced.
12+ years	Formal operational	Reasons logically about abstract ideas and experiences; can think hypothetically about things never experienced; deductive and inductive reasoning; complexity of knowledge; many answers to questions; interest in ethics, politics, social sciences.

which individuals organize their experience of the world: *sensorimotor, preoperational, concrete operational,* and *formal operational.*

All children move through these periods in the same order, although each child's rate of cognitive development is unique. Thus, Piaget's theory emphasizes *sequence,* not a direct age–stage correlation. Although particular cognitive abilities are associated with a specific age range, these abilities develop earlier in some children and later in others. Thus, when statements about age are made in discussing children's development, they should be understood as approximations, not as norms.

Infancy and Toddlerhood

According to the model devised by Erikson, infancy is characterized by the development of a sense of *trust* concerning the environment. If the infant's needs are not met, the result may be distrust. Thus, other people in the environment—typically, parents—play an important part in the infant's psychosocial development as he or she acquires a sense of self and others as reliable and nurturant.

During Erikson's second stage, toddlerhood (roughly one to three years of age), the child begins to grapple with the issues of *autonomy* versus shame and doubt. As the toddler explores the environment and develops greater independence, there is usually a clash between what the child wants to do and what others want the child to do. Toilet training typically occurs during this time. In both physical and psychosocial development, this is a period of "letting go" and "holding on."

Turning our attention to Piaget's cognitive model, we find that the first two years of life are characterized as the *sensorimotor* period. The child develops and strengthens sensory and motor abilities, becoming acquainted with the body and learning about the environment. Because the child has not yet acquired the ability to name objects, this is not considered to be a period of conceptual development. A parent who leaves the room has simply vanished from the scene; there is no thought, "My parent is in the other room." Piaget says, "As long as there is no subject, that is, as long as the child does not recognize itself as the origin of its own actions, it also does not recognize the permanency of objects other than itself."[9] As the child accumulates experiences of the flow of events in the environment, he or she gradually begins to perceive patterns that become generalized into what Piaget terms "schemes." These schemes tie together the common features of actions occurring at different times. About this stage of development, Piaget says, "a Copernican revolution takes place," with the result that "at the end of this sensory-motor evolution, there are permanent objects, constituting a universe within which the child's own body exists also."

Early Childhood

During the years of preschool and kindergarten (roughly three to five or six years of age), a child's psychosocial development involves issues of *initiative* versus guilt. The child increasingly seeks his or her own purpose and direction, yet is also concerned about how parents (and other significant adults) perceive these tentative efforts to express initiative and individuality. The egocentric orientation of the infant gives way to the socially integrated self of the older child, which assumes its place as one among many. This transition involves situations that induce feelings of guilt. For instance, a child who has fantasies of doing away with a parent—expressed perhaps by the frustrated scream, "I wish you were dead!"—may feel guilty about having such thoughts. How others respond to this conflict affects whether the crisis is resolved positively. This period marks the beginning of the child's moral sense, the ability to function within socially sanctioned modes of behavior. Reflecting the child's emerging communication skills, the concept of death expands quite rapidly during the preschool years.

Among the fears that may manifest during this period is that of bodily mutilation. Children at this age are racing around on tricycles, learning to cut small pieces of paper very precisely, making their muscles work for them,

Figure *10-3 Accident Drawing by a Five-Year-Old*
In this drawing by a five-year-old who witnessed his younger brother's accidental death, the surviving child is depicted as riding a "big wheel" on the
left side of the truck that ran over his brother. The four wheels of the truck
are shown, and the younger brother's head is drawn next to the wheel far-
thest to the right. This drawing is similar to one drawn by the child on the
night of the fatal accident, when he told his parents, "I can't sleep because
I can't get the pictures out of my head." The act of externalizing these disturbing images by making a drawing had therapeutic value for this child in
coming to terms with the traumatic experience of his sibling's death.

gaining greater control over their bodies. Thus, the body is important to the
child's self-image. This preoccupation with the body can be illustrated: A five-
year-old witnessed the death of his younger brother, who was killed when the
wheel of a truck rolled over his head. The parents, who were considering
having a wake in their home, asked the surviving son how he might feel if his
younger brother's body was brought into the house for a wake. His question
was, "Does he look hurt?" This child's concern about bodily disfigurement is
characteristic of this stage of psychosocial development (see Figure 10-3).

In Piaget's model, the years of early childhood are characterized as the
preoperational period. The child's cognitive development centers on learning
to use language and symbols to represent objects. Vocabulary develops at an
astounding rate. During this period, the child's primary task is to explore and
appraise his or her situation in the world. Whereas during the sensorimotor
period the child perceives the subjective and objective worlds as more or less
fused into a single reality, now the child seeks causes and explanations.

How does Piaget's model of cognitive development apply to children's
concepts of death? A partial answer is supplied by a study conducted by Gerald
Koocher.[10] After being tested to determine which of Piaget's periods he or she
fit into, each child was asked four questions about death. You might want to
answer each of these questions for yourself.

The first question was, "What makes things die?" Children in the preoperational stage used fantasy reasoning, magical thinking, and realistic causes of death (sometimes expressed in egocentric terms). Here are sample responses:

- Nancy: "When they eat bad things, like if you went with a stranger and they gave you a candy bar with poison on it. [*The researcher asks, "Anything else?"*] Yes, you can die if you swallow a dirty bug."
- Carol: "They eat poison and stuff, pills. You'd better wait until your Mom gives them to you. [*Anything else?*] Drinking poison water and stuff like going swimming alone."
- David: "A bird might get real sick and die if you catch it. [*Anything else?*] They could eat the wrong foods like aluminum foil. That's all I can think of."

These findings received corroboration in a study done by Helen Swain.[11] When the concept of finality was investigated, most of the children in Swain's study expressed the notion that death was reversible. They attributed the return of life to the good effects of ambulances, hospitals, or doctors, whose participation is often summoned magically, as if a dead person could ring up the hospital and say, "Will you send me an ambulance over here? I'm dead and I need you to fix me up." About two-thirds of Swain's study group said that death is unlikely or avoidable, or is brought on only by unusual events such as an accident or catastrophe. About one-third expressed disbelief that death could happen to them or to their families. Nearly half were uncertain whether they would ever die or else thought they would die only in the remote future.

The Middle Years of Childhood

In Erikson's model, the years from about six to eleven correspond to the stage of *industry* versus inferiority. This is a time when the child is busy in school, interacting with peers in a variety of ways. As the child's efforts begin to gain recognition and bring satisfaction, there may be anxieties about those areas in which the child senses a failure to measure up. Overcoming feelings of inadequacy or inferiority becomes the major task of this psychosocial stage. Encouragement from others is crucial to the child's well-being.

In Piaget's framework, this period is denoted by the term *concrete operations*. The child begins to use logic to solve problems and to think logically about things without having to have their relationships demonstrated directly. The ability to do arithmetic, for instance, requires the recognition that

I was astonished to hear a highly intelligent boy of ten remark after the sudden death of his father: "I know father's dead, but what I can't understand is why he doesn't come home to supper."

Sigmund Freud, *The Interpretation of Dreams*

numbers are symbols for quantities. Children at this stage are able to manipulate concepts in a logical fashion, although they are typically unable to engage in abstract thinking. That is, the ability to think logically can be applied to objects, but not yet to hypotheses, which require the ability to carry out operations on operations. Thus, the characteristic mode of thought in this period emphasizes concreteness and the logic of *things*. Children can think forward and backward in time, and they demonstrate an appreciation of time as "passing," although their comprehension does not yet allow them to manipulate such concepts with the flexibility or abstraction that comes with the ability to engage in formal operations of thought.

During this period of development, children tend to name both intentional and unintentional means by which a person may die. The child is familiar with a wide range of causes of death. Here are some responses from the children in Koocher's study when asked about causes of death:

- Todd: "Knife, arrow, guns, and lots of stuff. You want me to tell you all of them? [*As many as you want.*] Hatchets and animals, and fires and explosions, too."
- Kenny: "Cancer, heart attacks, poison, guns, bullets, or if someone drops a boulder on you."
- Deborah: "Accidents, cars, guns, or a knife. Old age, sickness, taking dope, or drowning."

Adolescence

In Erikson's model of psychosocial development, adolescence is marked by the milestone of establishing an individual *identity*. A bridge is established between the past—the years of childhood and dependency—and the future— the years of adulthood and independence. Thus, adolescence is an important time of personality development, a period of integration as well as separation. The central question addressed by adolescents is: "Who am I as an emotional, thinking, physical, and sexual being?"[12]

Remember what it's like being a teenager? Becoming more your own person? Striving to express your own ideas and beliefs? Sorting out the unbelievable tangle of all that's happening to you? Deciding what you want for your life? These years can be confusing and challenging. With the desire for a greater sense of one's identity—an answer to the question "Who am I?"—there may also be anxieties about framing an adequate answer. The achievement of their goals and dreams seems nearly within their grasp. Death threatens that achievement.

In Piaget's theory of cognitive development, adolescence is characterized by the use of *formal operations*. The fourth and final phase in Piaget's theory, this period begins at about the age of eleven or twelve and extends into adulthood, although a person's fundamental way of seeing the world is thought to be fairly well established by about the age of fifteen. With the arrival of formal operational thinking, the child is able to "think about thinking"—that is, to formulate concepts that are abstract or symbolic. Relations of correspondence or implication between complex sets of statements can be perceived, analogies recognized, and assumptions or deductions made. It becomes possible to predict outcomes without having to try them in the real world. In a chess game, for example, formal operations of thought allow the player to consider a number of complicated strategies and to predict the likely result of each move, without having to touch a single piece on the board.

Although in Koocher's study most of the children who used formal operations of thought were twelve or older, some were as young as nine or ten. In fact, more recent research tends to indicate that most children have acquired a mature concept of death around the age of nine or ten.[13] The children interviewed by Koocher reflected a mature understanding of death in their responses to the question "What makes things die?"

- Ed: "You mean death in a physical sense? [*Yes.*] Destruction of a vital organ or life force within us."
- George: "They get old and their body gets all worn out, and their organs don't work as well as they used to."
- Paula: "When the heart stops, blood stops circulating. You stop breathing, and that's it. [*Anything else?*] Well, there's lots of ways it can get started, but that's what really happens."

Although adolescents typically demonstrate a mature understanding of death, this does not necessarily mean that there are no differences in the ways adolescents and adults understand and cope with death. For example, an adolescent's understanding of the universality of death may be modified by a sense of his or her invulnerability ("It can't happen to me"). Similarly, adolescents tend to engage in more risk taking of the kind that tests the limits between physically existing and not existing. An exaggerated preoccupation with their own lives may cause adolescents to think they are "beyond death." The concept of personal death, "even as one thread in the larger totality of the life cycle," may not be easily accepted. In forging a sense of one's own identity, the adolescent is confronted by the need to "reconcile that identity with ultimate disintegration and not being."[14]

The Evolution of a Mature Concept of Death

Through successive periods of development, children progress toward a mature understanding of death and exhibit characteristic responses to loss. We have already examined children's responses to the question "What makes things die?" Their answers to other questions posed by Koocher also corresponded to varied developmental stages—preoperational, concrete operational, and formal operational. Asked "How do you make dead things come back to life?" children who conceived of death as reversible gave answers like: "You can help them; give them hot food and keep them healthy so it won't happen again." Another child said, "No one ever taught me about that, but maybe you could give them some kind of medicine and take them to the hospital to get better." Children in later developmental stages recognized death as permanent: "If it was a tree, you could water it. If it's a person, you

George Willard became possessed of a madness to lift the sheet from the body of his mother and look at her face. The thought that had come into his mind gripped him terribly. He became convinced that not his mother but someone else lay in the bed before him. The conviction was so real that it was almost unbearable. The body under the sheets was long and in death looked young and graceful. To the boy, held by some strange fancy, it was unspeakably lovely. The feeling that the body before him was alive, that in another moment a lovely woman would spring out of the bed and confront him, became so overpowering that he could not bear the suspense. Again and again he put out his hand. Once he touched and half lifted the white sheet that covered her, but his courage failed and he, like Doctor Reefy, turned and went out of the room. In the hallway outside the door he stopped and trembled so that he had to put a hand against the wall to support himself. "That's not my mother. That's not my mother in there," he whispered to himself and again his body shook with fright and uncertainty. When Aunt Elizabeth Swift, who had come to watch over the body, came out of an adjoining room he put his hand into hers and began to sob, shaking his head from side to side, half blind with grief. "My mother is dead," he said. . . .

Sherwood Anderson, *Winesburg, Ohio*

could rush them to the emergency room, but it would do no good if they were dead already." Another child said, "Maybe some day we'll be able to do it, but not now. Scientists are working on that problem."

Asked "When will you die?" children in the preoperational period provided answers ranging from "When I'm seven" (from a six-year-old) to "Three hundred years." In contrast, older children expected to live out a statistically correct lifespan, or a bit more; the usual age at which death was expected was about eighty.

In answer to the researchers' question, "What will happen when you die?" one nine-and-a-half-year-old said, "They'll help me come back alive." The researcher asked, "Who?" "My father, my mother, and my grandfather," the child responded. "They'll keep me in bed and feed me and keep me away from rat poison and stuff." According to some early developmental models of how children learn about death, a child of nine would understand that none of those measures would work. Thus, this example illustrates the point that age-and-stage correlations provide, at best, a rule of thumb concerning how children develop. As with any *model* of human behavior, the age–stage developmental framework is indicative, not rigorously descriptive.

In answer to the same question, an eight-and-a-half-year-old replied, "You go to heaven and all that will be left of you will be a skeleton. My friend has some fossils of people. A fossil is just a skeleton." Notice how the child makes use of comparison to help interpret what happens when death occurs. An eleven-year-old said, "I'll feel dizzy and tired and pass out, and then they'll bury me and I'll rot away. You just disintegrate and only your bones will be left."

A twelve-year-old said, "I'll have a nice funeral and be buried and leave all my money to my son." One ten-year-old said, "If I tell you, you'll laugh." The researcher assured the child, "No, I won't. I want to know what you really think." Thus encouraged, the child continued, "I think I'm going to be reincarnated as a plant or animal, whatever they need at that particular time." The ability to imagine what things might be like in the future is seen in this child's response.

Children With Life-Threatening Illnesses

Seriously ill children need "mental first aid" to help them cope with their thoughts and feelings. This may mean simply comforting the child and being supportive through a difficult or painful procedure, or it may require more substantive intervention to deal with anxiety, guilt, anger, or other conflicting or unresolved emotions. Caring for children requires a flexible approach. A child who feels unsupported or unsure about what is happening may have fantasies that are more frightening than the truth. A supportive atmosphere in which the child feels free to express his or her fears diminishes feelings of separation and loneliness.

Parents and other adults may find it painful to respond to a child's questions about a serious disease and its prognosis. Such questions can evoke uncertainty and may be met with silence or other forms of avoidance. Is it ethical, or even possible, to withhold information about a serious or life-threatening illness from a child? This question poses a dilemma for those who might wish to keep troubling news from a child. William Bartholome observes that "[t]he most daunting problem facing parents and caregivers who are caring for a terminally ill child is that the person they are caring for lives in a different reality."[15]

The Child's Perception of Serious Illness

Based on a study of children in a leukemia ward, Myra Bluebond-Langner observed that seriously ill children are usually able to guess their condition by interpreting how people behave toward them.[16] Crying or avoidance behaviors are interpreted as indicating the serious nature of the disease and the likelihood of dying. The children in the leukemia ward, most of whom were between the ages of three and nine, were able to accurately assess the seriousness of their illness even though the adults in their lives had not shared this information with them. Although they sometimes discussed their illnesses with their peers, these children refrained from doing so with adults. Recognizing that such conversations made adults uncomfortable, the children talked about the taboo topics among themselves, much as children discuss other forbidden topics, out of range of an adult's hearing.

Over time, the children's interpretations of their conditions changed. At first, the illness was seen as acute, then chronic, and finally fatal. Similarly, medications were first "healing agents," then "something that prolongs life." As their perception of the drugs changed from being "always effective" to "effective sometimes" to "not really effective at all," their behaviors toward taking medication likewise changed. Generally, the children on this leukemia ward knew a great deal about the world of the hospital, its staff and procedures, and the experiences of other leukemic children, making comments like "Jeffrey's in his first relapse" and noticing when other children died. Although the children did not always know the exact name of the disease afflicting them, they typically displayed considerable knowledge about its treatment and prognosis.

Development of the concept of death during childhood is reflected in the sequence of major concerns experienced by seriously ill children. For example, children under five years old tend to be most distressed by separation from the mother. Children in the middle group, roughly ages five to nine, tend to be most concerned about the discomforting and possibly disfiguring effects of the disease and related medical procedures. Older children tend to be anxious in response to other children's deaths. These findings are consistent with the developmental models discussed earlier in this chapter: Separation anxiety is typical of the young child; a personification of death, with accompanying fears about mutilation and pain, predominates during the middle years of childhood; and anxiety related to the deaths of other children is commonly experienced by older children and adolescents. The way a child copes with such concerns is influenced significantly by his or her perception of the meaning and likely consequences of an illness.

The Child's Coping Mechanisms

Seriously ill children are not passive participants in the medical and social events that occur because of their illness. How a child perceives the illness and the manner in which he or she responds to it depends on age, the nature of the illness and its treatment, family relationships, and the child's own personal history. A child's illness can result in absences from school, changes in family patterns, increased dependency on others, and financial or emotional strain on the child's family. Other sources of stress and grief include medical concerns, such as the presence of pain and, possibly, the visible effects of the disease or treatment, which may have symbolic significance depending on the child's age and the part of the body affected.

To cope with the anxiety and confusion that accompany serious or life-threatening illness, children use various coping mechanisms. Even very young children exhibit a wide range of coping mechanisms, although the child's stage of development influences his or her capacity for drawing on both internal and external resources. Some children use distancing strategies to limit the number of people with whom they have close relationships, thus reducing the number of opportunities for a distressing interaction. In this way, a child selects from the whole situation just those aspects or those people that seem least threatening. This coping mechanism allows the child to construct as safe and secure an environment as possible given the circumstances.

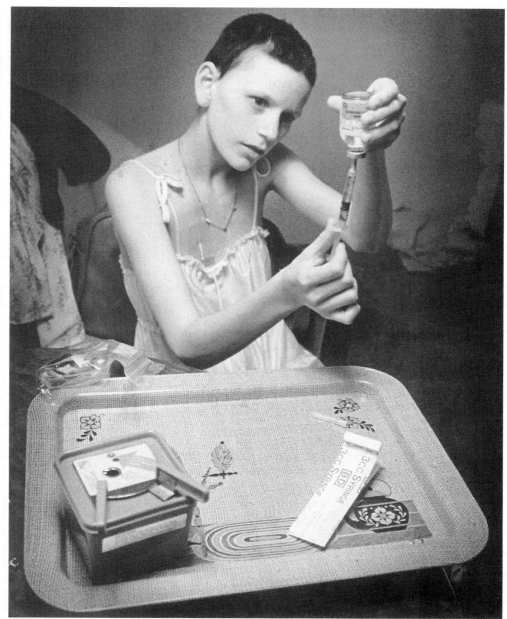

Adolescents and older children with life-threatening illnesses may take on increasing responsibilities for their daily treatment regimes. Here, a young cancer patient flushes her venous access catheter, the route used to administer chemotherapy, which must be cleaned nightly.

Children may cope with a painful medical procedure by making a deal that allows some desire to be fulfilled once the pain is endured: "After I get my shot, can I play with my toys?" In dealing with an overwhelming situation, sick children may regress to behavior patterns that recall a less demanding, more comfortable time in their lives. Children may revert to baby talk or "forget" their toilet training during stressful times. A child whose illness prevents him or her from engaging in a competitive sport may cope by using sublimation, perhaps finding a substitute for the desired activity by playing board games in a highly competitive way. One might envision scenes of sick children racing through the hospital corridors, IV bottles swinging from their wheelchairs, in a spontaneous competition. As with adults, children use varied coping mechanisms as they confront uncomfortable and frightening aspects of a potentially life-threatening illness.

Caring for a Seriously Ill Child

Serious illness separates children from their familiar surroundings and the people they love. The sick child is thrust into a more or less alien world of hospitals and medical paraphernalia. Even as a child becomes accustomed to the rhythms of life in and out of hospital, new therapies or unfamiliar medical settings or personnel can make everything again seem out of whack and be upsetting. Such changes in routine often add to the child's anxieties and fears.[17] "Each time a child returns to the hospital he is literally a different person. He is at a wholly new stage of development with correspondingly different fears and expectations."[18] Some children are quite resilient in their response to the stressors of treatment, debilitating side effects, and the day-to-day experience of living with serious illness; others have difficulty coping with all the varied acute and chronic stressors that accompany illnesses like childhood cancer.[19] Caregivers and parents should try to minimize such stressors and make the child as comfortable as possible.

The participation of family members in some aspects of care can be comforting to a child. Although professionals are usually better equipped to care for a child's medical needs, parents have special expertise in the nontechnical aspects of child care. Parents can be involved in activities like bathing the child, assisting at mealtimes, tucking the child in at night, and generally giving the child emotional support. However, parents should carefully consider whether it is in the child's best interest for them to be involved in performing medical procedures that might cause the child pain. Parents who do so may be seen by the child as causing or intensifying pain. Generally speaking, parents should focus on their parenting role, rather than trying to play the role of a nurse. Depending on the circumstances, however, there may be occasions when parents are asked to provide more than emotional support by taking on responsibilities for the child's physical care that might otherwise be provided by professional caregivers.

Hospice and home-based palliative care programs are an important option in the care of terminally ill children.[20] Ida Martinson, a nurse-educator who helped pioneer such home and hospice care, observes:

> The greatest barrier [to providing effective care to dying children and their families] is the difficulty in accepting the reality of the dying child by the parents and physicians as well as the nurses. No one wants a child to die, so continued treatment goes beyond what is desirable and useful for the child.[21]

Martinson adds: "Parents may have difficulty in realizing that the care they are providing their child in the home is as good—and most likely better—than what we health care professionals could provide in the hospital." Whatever the setting—hospital, hospice, or home—families who are coping with a child's serious illness and impending death should have access to appropriate professional and community support.

Children As Survivors of a Close Death

Nearly all parents would wish to spare their children the pain of bereavement. When a loss occurs in a child's life, attempts are often made to minimize its effects. The death of a pet, for example, may be swiftly followed by its replacement with another animal. At best, such a course of action has limited usefulness. Death is a fact of life that eventually cannot be ignored. A more constructive approach is to help the child explore his or her feelings about death and develop an appropriate understanding of it.

The Bereaved Child's Experience of Grief

Children are capable of experiencing grief. A bereaved child can experience physical and emotional symptoms similar to those experienced by adults, including lack of appetite, insomnia, nightmares, and nausea. This does not mean that the grief of children and adults is exactly the same. Children differ from adults in their cognitive abilities, coping styles, need for identification figures, and their dependence on adults for support.[22] Although children tend to be quite resilient in coping with tragedy, adults can guide a child through grief by listening to the child's concerns and communicating support for the child's well-being.

A child's response to loss reflects the influence of such factors as age, stage of mental and emotional development, the patterns of interaction and communication within his or her family, the relationship with the person who has died, and previous experiences with death. As with adults, deaths that are sudden and unexpected or that result from suicide or homicide may complicate the issues that the child faces in coming to terms with loss.

Even among children of the same age, significant differences can be observed with respect to their ability to comprehend death and cope with its effects. Whereas one five-year-old might seem devastated by the death of a parent, another might seem comparatively unaffected. The first child may put forth intense effort in dealing with the loss; the second may appear satisfied with the explanation that "Daddy's gone and he won't ever be coming back." Which of these children do you believe exhibits the healthier response to loss?

As you may have guessed, such a question is inappropriate because not enough is known about each child to allow framing an adequate reply.

The classmates of a murdered child carry his coffin to the grave. The rituals and ceremonies surrounding death can provide an avenue for children and adolescents to express their grief and to begin the process of coming to terms with loss.

Suppose, however, that the first child's pattern of coping involves a period of acute grief, followed by acceptance and integration of the loss. Suppose, further, that the second child's apparent indifference is only transitory, a temporary state of mind that is followed by a protracted and painful process of coming to terms with the death, a process that may continue into adolescence or even adulthood before the loss is satisfactorily resolved. As this example suggests, it is not always possible to rely on appearances to assess how a child is coping with loss.

If a child feels that he or she played a role in the events that led to the death of a relative or friend, guilt might predominate among the emotions experienced after the loss. In such cases, unless the circumstances of the death are openly discussed and the child given opportunities to work through his or her grief, the traumatic effects can linger into adulthood. To illustrate, in one situation, involving three brothers playing with a loaded gun, the youngest pushed the oldest, who held the gun, as the bullet was discharged, killing the third sibling. "I have always struggled with myself about whether my brother would have died if I hadn't tried to push my other brother away," said a thirty-year-old man, recalling events that had taken place more than a quarter of a century earlier. "I always thought I did the right thing, but no one ever told me or even talked with me about my feelings. For years, I cried myself to sleep alone in my bed at night." Even when a child clearly has no responsibility for a death, he or she should be encouraged to share his or her perceptions about how the death occurred. The child's experience may be different from that of the adults in his or her environment.

Children sometimes cope with loss by selectively forgetting, or by reconstructing reality in a more desirable and comfortable way. For example, a child may not recall how frightened he was by the sight of a sibling lying in a hospital bed surrounded by awesome medical paraphernalia; or a protracted illness with long stays in the hospital may be remembered as if the sibling were away from home briefly for a few tests. The forgotten details or reconstructed images allow the child to cope with the experience without being overwhelmed by painful memories. Although age and cognitive development affect a child's response to loss, many other variables are at work, not least of which are the attitudes exhibited by the significant adults in the child's life.

The Death of a Pet

When a child's pet dies, adults may wonder how best to help him or her cope with the loss. Should one minimize the loss? Or should the death be seen as a natural opportunity to help the child consider what death means and explore his or her feelings about the loss?

One mother described the responses of her daughters to the deaths of a new litter of baby rabbits.[23] Upon learning the news, the seven-year-old burst into tears and howled, "I don't want them dead." The five-year-old at first stood silently and then asked to call her father at work. She told him, "If you had been here, Daddy, you could have been the rabbits' doctor," reflecting a belief, appropriate for her age, that it should have been possible somehow to

Jack Delano, FSA Collection, Library of Congress

Children can feel strong attachment to their pets. Involving a child in the experience of a pet's death through ritual or discussion provides a means of coping with the loss.

save the baby rabbits or restore them to life. Later, when the children began to dig a grave to bury the dead rabbits, the seven-year-old stopped crying for the first time since learning the news, while the five-year-old kept repeating, "The baby rabbits are dead, the baby rabbits are dead," in a monotone.

In the days following the rabbits' deaths, the girls asked many questions. The seven-year-old was particularly interested in questioning a family friend who was a widow about her dead husband. How often did she think about him and why did people have to be taken away from those who loved them, she wanted to know. The five-year-old, meanwhile, continued to mourn silently until her mother encouraged her to express her feelings. Then she began to sob. Finally, she said, "I'm glad I'm only five; you only die when you're old."

The younger child's first concern was for herself, the fear that she herself could die. The older child worried about the durability of relationships. Although each child had a distinctive response to the loss, both children showed a need to be close to their parents during the days following the deaths of the rabbits, and they told the story of the rabbits' deaths again and again as they dealt with their experience.

Of course, it is not just children who are affected by the death of a pet. A woman described the reaction of her husband to the death of Iggy, a desert iguana.[24] When the iguana died, her husband "cried throughout the shoebox burial in the backyard." He later said that he was crying "for every pet he had ever loved and lost." The death of a pet can evoke numbness and disbelief, preoccupation with the loss, being drawn toward reminders of the pet, anger, depression, and the whole range of mental and emotional qualities associated with grief following a significant loss. Rather than viewing a pet as a possession, many people feel that a pet is not only a companion, but "part of the family."[25]

Attachments between humans and pets can be very strong. Yet mourning the loss of a pet sometimes elicits ridicule. Some may say that the bereaved pet owner is overreacting. After all "it was only an animal, a mere pet." However, as Allan Kellehear and Jan Fook point out, "Despite the popular tendency in some quarters to trivialize such loss, the general literature on pet–human relations portrays bereaved owners as every bit as beset with the same power and range of emotions as for other kinds of human loss."[26]

Those who counsel individuals who are grieving over the loss of a pet emphasize that feelings should be expressed by adults as well as children. As for replacing a pet, sufficient time should be allowed to mourn the loss before a new animal is acquired. This may take weeks or months, perhaps longer. The bonds of attachment to the pet that has died may jeopardize a healthy transition of affections to another animal if the natural process of grief has been prematurely curtailed or ignored. When the bond between a pet and its owner is broken by death, the significance of that loss is increasingly recognized as a natural occasion for mourning.[27] Indeed, as Avery Weisman observes, "The depth of a human–animal bond often exceeds that between a person and close kith and kin."[28] Thus, mourning for a dead pet should be considered a normal experience for adults as well as children.

The Death of a Parent

Of all the deaths that may be experienced in childhood, the most affecting is likely to be the death of a parent.[29] A parent's death is perceived as a loss of security, nurture, and affection—a loss of the emotional and psychological support upon which the child could formerly rely. Based on data obtained

The Lesson

'Your father's gone,' my bald headmaster said.
His shiny dome and brown tobacco jar
Splintered at once in tears. It wasn't grief.
I cried for knowledge which was bitterer
Than any grief. For there and then I knew
That grief has uses—that a father dead
Could bind the bully's fist a week or two;
And then I cried for shame, then for relief.

I was a month past ten when I learnt this:
I still remember how the noise was stilled
In school-assembly when my grief came in.
Some goldfish in a bowl quietly sculled
Around their shining prison on its shelf.
They were indifferent. All the other eyes
Were turned towards me. Somewhere in myself
Pride, like a goldfish, flashed a sudden fin.

Edward Lucie-Smith

from the Child Bereavement Study, Phyllis Silverman and her colleagues conclude that children who have lost a parent typically establish a set of memories, feelings, and actions that the child draws on in "reconstructing" an image of the dead parent.[30] This involves building an "inner representation" that allows the child to sustain his or her relationship with the deceased parent, and "this relationship changes as the child matures and as the intensity of grief lessens." The child negotiates and renegotiates the meaning of the loss over time. The loss is permanent and unchanging; the process of coping with it changes.

When the death of a parent occurs when a child is very young, an important component of grief may involve mourning the years of relationship that were lost as a result of the parent's premature death. There can be a lingering sense of "never having known" the deceased parent. Consider, for example, the situation of a parent who dies as a result of war. Powerful emotions may lie buried for years until some stimulus—perhaps the discovery of the parent's military papers or a visit to a war memorial—brings the loss to the surface. Sharing the loss with others can aid healing. Some children who lost a parent during the Vietnam War find solace by joining together in a national support organization, Sons and Daughters in Touch, where they share a common bond.[31] Their attempts to understand the loss include talking to other veterans, which allows them to fill in the picture of a deceased parent they were not able to fully know.

Children may feel guilty if they imagine themselves as somehow contributing to a parent's death. For example, a child whose parent died of a terminal illness might remember times when she was noisy and her parent needed to

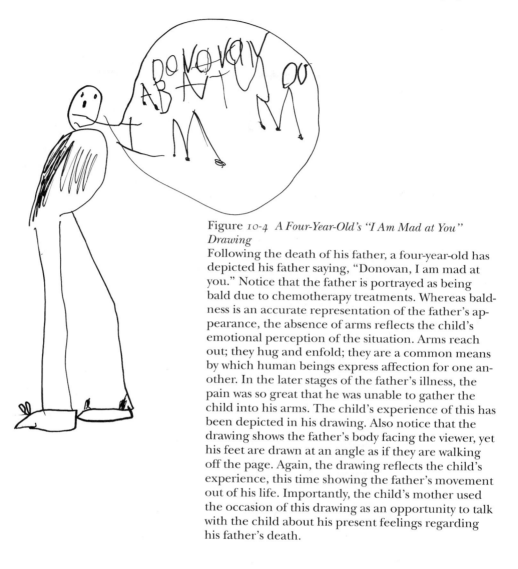

Figure *10-4 A Four-Year-Old's "I Am Mad at You" Drawing*

Following the death of his father, a four-year-old has depicted his father saying, "Donovan, I am mad at you." Notice that the father is portrayed as being bald due to chemotherapy treatments. Whereas baldness is an accurate representation of the father's appearance, the absence of arms reflects the child's emotional perception of the situation. Arms reach out; they hug and enfold; they are a common means by which human beings express affection for one another. In the later stages of the father's illness, the pain was so great that he was unable to gather the child into his arms. The child's experience of this has been depicted in his drawing. Also notice that the drawing shows the father's body facing the viewer, yet his feet are drawn at an angle as if they are walking off the page. Again, the drawing reflects the child's experience, this time showing the father's movement out of his life. Importantly, the child's mother used the occasion of this drawing as an opportunity to talk with the child about his present feelings regarding his father's death.

rest. "Perhaps if I had been less noisy," the child thinks, "Mom would have gotten well." Children may assume responsibility as they try to understand a close death. A drawing made by a four-year-old whose father had died of leukemia illustrates this (see Figure 10-4). Some time after his father's death, as the child was playing with pencils and drawing paper, he asked his mother how to spell various words. Attracted by the child's activity, his mother noticed that he had drawn a picture of his father. In the drawing the father was saying to the child, "I am mad at you!" Surprised at this depiction of her husband's anger toward her son, the mother asked, "Why should your father have been mad at you?" The child explained, "Because you and I can still play together and Dad isn't with us anymore." Amid the confusing feelings resulting from his father's death, the child was attempting to come to terms with the fact of his survivorship.

Now, in working with this child as a survivor, his mother did a very wise thing. She said, "Tell me about this picture." In other words, she asked open-ended questions to elicit information about the child's feelings. This allowed her to respond directly to the child's concerns. Spontaneous drawings and other forms of art therapy are excellent methods for working with young children; they help them explore and express feelings that otherwise might remain hidden, yet be disturbing to them.[32] Using art with bereaved children helps them to work through grief by providing a safe, focused environment for expressing their concerns and feelings.[33]

The Death of a Sibling

Unlike a parent's death, a sibling's death rarely represents a loss of security for the surviving child. Yet, the effect of such a close death may increase the surviving child's sense of vulnerability to death, especially when siblings are close in age. Betty Davies points out that relatively little attention has been devoted to sibling bereavement.[34] When a child dies, most of the attention is focused on the parents, rather than on the dead child's surviving siblings. Yet, in countries like the United States, where families tend to be small in size, the death of a sibling can make the surviving child an *only* child. Losing a brother or sister can be a lonely experience. As one child said, "It was like my mom and dad had each other, and I had no one." The brother or sister may have been a protector or caregiver, as well as a playmate. The surviving child may be grieving the loss of this unique relationship, worried that the protection and care given by the sibling is no longer available, and yet relieved or even pleased that, with the sibling's absence, he or she is now more the center of attention in the family. This mixture of emotions can produce guilt and confusion as a child comes to terms with the sibling's death.

For adolescents bereaved by a sibling's death, their efforts to cope with the loss may be intertwined with the developmental task of formulating a personal sense of the meaning of life, a task that usually includes intense questioning about the value of religious beliefs and the existence of God. David Balk points out that the death of a sibling shatters "trust in a benign, innocent universe" and "questions about the nature of life and death, about good and evil, and about the meaning of life become personal."[35] Coping with a sibling's death can bring about a greater maturity in cognitive development, social reasoning, moral judgment, identity formation, and religious understanding. Indeed, bereaved young people often cite religion as an important resource for coping with loss, a source of meaning that provides solace as they search for significance in the aftermath of tragedy. A sense of the "ongoing presence" of the sibling bond is also reported by bereaved adolescents, as they continue the "conversation" with a deceased brother or sister and take time to "catch up" on things that have been going on in their lives.[36]

Children typically look to their parents for help in understanding the significance of a sibling's death and in coping with its effects on the family.

© Karen Saltzman

Siblings enjoy a special relationship, one conjoining both rivalries and mutual affection and love. The death of a brother or sister thus severs a unique human relationship. The surviving child may feel the loss more intensely because of an identification with the deceased brother or sister. The surviving child recognizes that he or she is also not immune to dying at an early age.

The parents' methods of coping can be an important determinant of how the child copes. Sometimes the parents' response to a sibling's death sets into motion dysfunctional family patterns that impair the surviving child's ability to cope. Such dysfunctional responses range from overt resentment of the surviving child to attempts to re-create in that child some of the qualities of the deceased child. Parental responses like these may be present to a lesser extent even in families that appear to be coping successfully. As parents try to come to terms with a child's death, they may unintentionally minimize contact with the surviving child. The living child can be a painful reminder of the child now lost. Conversely, parents may become overprotective of the surviving child.

The bereaved child must be given opportunities to acknowledge and express his or her grief. If a child talks about feeling guilty, one can ask, "What would it take to forgive yourself?" Feelings of guilt are often related to normal sibling rivalry. The sister at whom I angrily yell, "I hate you!" in the morning may be lying dead at the morgue in the afternoon, the victim of a bicycle accident. To a young child, anger directed toward a person and that person's subsequent death might be viewed as a cause-and-effect relationship.

This assumption of responsibility is sometimes displayed as a preoccupation with the "should haves." One five-year-old whose younger brother was run over by a truck while they were outside playing told his mother later, "I should have . . . I should have." He saw himself as his younger brother's protector, responsible for his safety. His mother asked him, "You should have what?" He replied, "I just should have!"

His mother then asked, "What do you mean, you 'should have'?" The boy answered, "I should have looked, I should have known, I should have . . .": a flood of "should haves" about being his brother's guardian and protector. Taking the child into her arms, his mother said, "I understand, honey. Daddy's got the 'should haves.' Mommy's got the 'should haves.' We all have them. It's okay to have them. And it's okay to know that everybody could have done something differently, and that they *would* have if they'd had a choice."

Allowing a child to be a participant in the family's experience helps the child cope with crisis, as we see exemplified in a drawing by the five-year-old who saw his younger brother killed (see Figure 10-5). The drawing represents "the day my brother was killed"; the point of greatest stress is shown to be the period of time when he was left at a neighbor's house while his parents were at the hospital. Even more frightening than seeing the wheel of the truck roll over his brother's head was the feeling of being left alone, separated from the rest of his family, not knowing what was happening with his parents and his younger brother.

This child's parents not only encouraged the child to express his feelings, they also sought out community resources as additional support for coping with the tragedy. Just as the child's work with spontaneous drawings helped bring to light his anger at being left out, the parents received support by sharing their experience with others who had survived similar experiences and by calling on therapeutic resources in their community. In studies of

Figure *10-5 A Five-Year-Old's "Crooked Day" Drawing*
In this drawing of "The Crooked Day," a five-year-old boy depicts his experience of the events that transpired on the day his brother received fatal injuries in an accident. Contrary to what might be assumed about this drawing, the places on the line where the greatest stress is indicated occurred after the accident itself. The sharp dip in the line at the left-hand side of the drawing represents the accident; the point at which the line crosses back on itself denotes the time when the surviving child was left with a neighbor while his parents were at the hospital with his brother. This was a period of uncertainty and confusion, and the child was angry about not being with the other members of his family. The point at which his parents returned and informed him of his brother's death is indicated by the vertical slash marks, which were literally stabbed onto the paper. The jagged line connoting the remainder of the day represents the emotional upheaval that occurred as the child and his parents together focused their attention on coping with the initial shock of their loss. Importantly, the drawing ends with an upward slanting line that is indicative of an essentially positive attitude—the child's ability to deal constructively with his experience of loss. This drawing demonstrates that even a simple artistic expression, such as a line depicting the chronology of events, can reveal a wealth of detail about a child's experience of a traumatic event such as death.

adolescent sibling bereavement, the support considered most helpful by the bereaved teenagers was perceived as "people being there for me."[37]

Helping Children Cope With Change and Loss

How can a parent—or any caring person—help a child come to terms with the experience of loss? How do family patterns and styles of communication influence a child's ability to cope with death? In the aftermath of bereavement, what assistance can be offered to a child?

Children usually cope more easily with their feelings about a close death or serious illness of a family member when they feel that they are included as participants in the unfolding experience. If they are excluded, or when their questions go unanswered, uncertainty in the child's mind creates more anxiety and confusion. When an adult is also struggling to cope with a traumatic experience, it is difficult to explain these painful circumstances to a child.

Because of the nature of the crisis, perhaps coupled with notions about a child's limited ability to understand, the child's feelings and concerns may be dismissed or ignored. Even when adults agree with the notion that children have a right to know the truth, they may feel uncomfortable about exposing them to painful and disturbing news. They may ask themselves: Would knowing the truth cause the child more harm than good? In most instances, the child's natural curiosity effectively eliminates the option of withholding such information.

Guidelines for Sharing Information

Responding to a child's natural inquisitiveness and concern does not mean that one should carelessly overwhelm the child with excessive detail, nor does it mean "talking down" to the child, as if he or she were incapable of any comprehension. Nevertheless, a child's manner of perceiving, experiencing, and coping with change needs to be considered by parents and others who wish to be helpful to children in crisis. This implies responding to the child's questions and concerns on the basis of his or her ability to understand. As a general guideline for discussing death with a child, it is important to keep the explanation simple, stick to basic facts, and verify what the child has understood.

Discussing Death Before a Crisis Occurs

However tempered children may be by the influence of peers and by what is learned in the classroom and elsewhere outside the home, parental attitudes are a significant influence on their attitude toward death. Thus, parents have natural concerns about what to tell their children about it. What can the child understand? How should I start the discussion? We have seen that children develop their own concepts about death, whether or not they receive parental instruction, even when the topic is considered taboo. Children want to know about death, just as they want to learn about all of the things they encounter in their lives. One child wrote, "Dear God, what's it like when you die? Nobody will tell me. I just want to know. I don't want to do it."

In explaining death to children, honesty is foremost. Be aware, however, that a parent who sets a ground rule that it's okay to be open and honest in talking about death may find that there are times when the child wants to initiate a discussion and the parent is tired or would rather avoid the subject. If talking about death is part of normal life and not a reaction to crisis, choosing a good time is more of a possibility.

Second, don't put off introducing the topic of death. When a close death precedes the discussion, the parent is faced with the need to provide an explanation in the midst of crisis. This unfortunate situation arises when a parent puts off discussing death "because it's not really going to happen," only to find that "it's happening right now and my child has to be told something." In these circumstances, the explanation to the child is likely to be charged with all the emotions the parent is dealing with, making the aim of clear communication more difficult to attain. Thus, it is a good idea to make use of "teachable moments," occasions that come up in everyday activities, for talking with children about death (see discussion in Chapter 3).[38]

© Lawrence Migdale

Exemplifying the age-old oral tradition of elders transmitting culture to the young, this Native American grandmother shares memories and stories as her grandson learns about his deceased grandfather and his place in the family's heritage. Occasions for discussing death with children arise naturally out of our interactions; the most important contribution an adult can make in talking with a child about death is often simply to be a good listener.

Third, set the explanation to the child's level of understanding. By using as a guide the child's interest and ability to understand, the parent can provide an explanation that is appropriate to the child's particular circumstances.

When talking with children about death, it is important to verify what it is they think you've told them. Have them tell you what they learned or heard you saying about death. Children tend to generalize from known concepts to make new experiences fit. This sometimes leads to a very literal-minded interpretation of new information, especially among young children, who tend to emphasize the concreteness of things. Recognizing this, strive to keep your communication free of associations that could be confusing. Metaphorical explanations about death may help you draw a child-sized picture as an aid to understanding, but unless fact and fancy are clearly distinguished, the child may grasp the fanciful details instead of the underlying facts the analogy was meant to convey. This is illustrated in the following story: A girl of age five was told that her grandfather's cancer was like a seed that grew in his body; it grew and grew until he couldn't live in his body anymore and he died. Her parents didn't notice that ever afterward, all through childhood, she never ate another seed. Not one. Not a cucumber seed, watermelon seed, no seeds. Finally, at age twenty-one, she was asked, "Why are you avoiding the seeds? Isn't that a little bizarre? What's wrong with the seeds?" Her automatic response was, "You swallow them and you die." After all those years, she saw the fallacy of her compulsion to avoid eating seeds. It would have been useful if someone had asked her when she was five, "What will happen if you swallow that seed?"

When a Family Member Is Seriously Ill

When a member of a child's family is seriously ill, family routine is disrupted. If the child is kept from learning the truth about a parent's or sibling's illness, he or she may become confused about the reasons for changes in the family's usual pattern of interactions. The child may feel rejected, left out of family activities, or ignored for no apparent reason: "Why are my parents so nice to my sister, but they ignore me all the time!" or "Geez, I get into trouble about every little thing while my brother gets off scot-free no matter what he does!" Siblings of a child with cancer may be alarmed by changes in the appearance of the sick child caused by the disease as well as by side effects of treatment.[39] For children who have a sibling afflicted with human immunodeficiency virus (HIV), there are often multiple losses that must be endured and mourned, possibly including the death of other family members, unpredictable living arrangements, and changes of school, as well as issues involving stigma, secrecy, and shame.[40]

Although open communication is important in helping a child cope with the crisis, explanations must be suited to the child's cognitive capacity. A very young child whose parent is seriously ill might be told simply that "Mommy has an ouch in her tummy which the doctors are trying to fix." A school-age child could be given a more complex explanation—perhaps that the parent needs medical treatment because something is growing in her stomach that doesn't belong there.

Anxiety about a parent's or sibling's illness may be manifest in varied ways. A child may be angry because "Mommy isn't here," yet feel guilty because he or she imagines somehow "causing the illness." To balance these conflicting feelings, the child can be encouraged to participate in caring for the sick family member in appropriate ways. For example, a child might pick a bouquet or make a small drawing as a gift. Such activities allow the child to express his or her feelings of love and kindness.

Children may feel neglected and resent adjustments they must make in their own lives. To counteract these feelings, help the child feel that he or she is a fully participating member of the family. Encourage the child to be part of the process of dealing with the illness. Including the child helps promote normalcy in family communication styles and routines.[41] Although children cannot be protected from the reality of death, their experiences of it can be made less difficult if they have sensitive, caring support from those closest to them.

In the Aftermath of Loss

We tend to assume that others share our experience of the world. In fact, each of us perceives the world uniquely. Understanding another person's ex-

Suddenly the feeling that this was all just a dream ended. Christopher was angry. It wasn't fair. Why did that dumb man have to hit Bodger?

"I ought to run *him* over with a truck."

"Oh, honey, Bodger ran right in front of him. The man didn't have time to stop."

They took Christopher home to bed where he relived the accident over and over in his mind. He tried to pretend that the truck had missed the dog, or that he hadn't called and Bodger had stayed on the other side. Or he pretended that they hadn't left the dirt road where there were hardly ever any cars. Or that they had stayed home and waited.

But the bad dream always rolled on out of his control until the moment when Bodger was lying in the road.

Carol and Donald Carrick, *The Accident*

perience requires the art of listening. The aim is to discover what the other person thinks, feels, and believes: What does he or she find important? What are his or her concerns, fears, hopes? If a need for support or assistance is being expressed, what kind of help is he or she asking for? Questions of this kind are especially important in helping children cope with loss. We need to be willing *to listen and to accept the reality of the child's experience.*

When death disrupts familiar patterns of living, the result can be confusion and conflict, creating a tangle of emotions and thoughts that are hard to sort out. In the midst of this, children may be asked to remain "unseen and unheard," thus thwarting their natural tendencies to explore and grapple with the emotions and thoughts generated by change. Paying attention to a child's behavior is useful for gathering information about his or her experience of crisis. Crying, for instance, is a natural response to the loss of someone significant. Admonishing a child to "Be brave!" or "Be a little man and buck up!" denies the validity of the child's spontaneous human emotion.

In helping children cope with loss, adults must strive to *answer the child's questions honestly and directly.* Explanations should be truthful to the facts and should be as concrete as possible. Telling a child that her goldfish "went to heaven" may cause her to make an elaborate picture of the pearly gates and different sections of heaven: Here is goldfish heaven, cat heaven, and over here is people heaven—a very logical concept that makes sense to a child. We need to be careful that the concepts we convey to a child don't turn out to be dysfunctional.

One woman recalled that when she was three or four a favorite old black dog had to "go away for a long sleep." It wasn't until she was about seven years old that she realized that the dog wasn't just away napping someplace, at the puppy farm having a nice long sleep. If Rover was just "off somewhere to sleep," then a casual goodbye was fine. But, when she realized that in fact her beloved dog was dead, she felt angry and upset that she hadn't had the opportunity to give it a proper farewell.

Similarly, religious beliefs are an important part of how death is understood in many families. In such families, parents usually want to share these beliefs with their children when coping with the death of a family member or friend. Children may indeed be comforted by such beliefs, but they deserve to be told that these are *beliefs*. Care should be taken to talk about such beliefs in a way that avoids confusing the child. For example, a parent's concept of an afterlife may be quite different from what a child is able to understand. A child who is told that "God took Daddy to be with him in heaven" may not feel very kindly toward a being who could be so capricious and inconsiderate of the child's feelings.

For the same reason, fairy tales, metaphors, and the like should be avoided or used with care because children may take such explanations of death literally. Consider the case of a four-year-old whose brother (nine) told him that daddy had gone to heaven. The four-year-old promptly went and told his mother, "My daddy's on the roof!" She said, "What? Who told you that?" He said, "Andrew did." The older brother then explained, "We were looking out the window and I told him that daddy was in heaven up there." To the four-year-old, the highest "up there" was up on the roof. If you tell a four-year-old that someone who has died is "up there" and you also say that Santa Claus lands on the roof on Christmas Eve, he may decide that Santa Claus and the person who has died are great buddies. He might make up stories about how they work together, making toys, feeding the reindeer, and so on.

The concreteness of a young child's concepts about death is also illustrated in the experience of a woman whose first experience with death occurred when she was three-and-a-half and her mother died. It seemed that her mother had just disappeared; she didn't know what had happened to her. Some time later, she began to realize that her mother had died and she started asking questions. Some people told her that her mother had been buried, and her thought was, "Why don't they dig her up?" Others said that her mother had gone to heaven, so she kept looking at the sky, watching for her. With both of these concepts running through her young mind, she did her best to figure out, "How can my mother be buried in heaven?"

When asked about their experiences involving a close death, children often say that the most difficult times were when they did not know what was happening. A child whose diagnosis of serious illness was withheld from her by her family said later, "We'd always done everything with each other knowing what was going on. Suddenly, it was different. That scared me more than what was happening to my body. It felt like my family was becoming strangers."[42] Sudden change in family communication patterns can be alarming to a child, actually heightening anxiety about the crisis. A child who is kept away from the funeral of a close friend or relative may feel anxious about not being included in an activity that had obvious importance to the significant adults in his or her life. Some young children may choose not to attend a funeral. Those who do attend, however, tend to report that participating in the funeral helped them acknowledge the death, provided an occasion for honoring the deceased person, and made it possible for them to receive social support and comfort.[43]

He lived a long way from here
Lew's mother explained.
You never asked
so I never told you
Grandpa died.

I want him to come back.
I miss him, Lewis said.
I have been waiting for him
and I miss him especially tonight.

I do too
said Lew's mother.
But you made him come back
for me tonight
by telling me what you remember.

Charlotte Zolotow, *My Grandson Lew*

The crisis of a child's illness can lead to a serious breakdown in communication. A young girl told a hospital staffer, "I know I'm going to die. I want to talk to Mother, but she won't let me. I know she's hurting, but I'm the one who's dying." When told of this conversation by the staff member, the girl's mother replied angrily, "She wouldn't be thinking of dying if you hadn't made her talk about it."

The communication between mother and daughter went from bad to worse. Still refusing to discuss her daughter's feelings, the mother's style of communication degenerated into baby talk: "Her doesn't feel goody today . . . her doesn't want to talk." A lack of openness was hampering satisfaction of normal human needs for affection and reassurance.

The best gauge of a child's readiness to be informed about a potentially painful situation is the child's own interest, usually expressed through questions. Using these questions as a guide, caregivers can give straightforward answers without burdening the child with facts irrelevant to his or her understanding of the situation. Above all, children in crisis situations need to be reassured that they are loved.

Children are apt to point out any inconsistencies in what we tell them about death. When one three-year-old's playmate was killed, his mother explained to him that Jesus had come and taken his friend to heaven. His response was, "Well, that's an awful thing to do; I want to play with him. Jesus isn't very nice if he comes down here and takes my friend from me." In discussing death with a child, it is crucial to consider the child's belief system, the kind of thought processes he or she uses to understand the world. Then, from your very first statement, ask yourself: "If I explain death in this way, how will it be understood by the child?"

Using Books As Tools for Coping

Bibliotherapy—that is, using books as an aid to coping—facilitates discussion between adults and children and creates opportunities for sharing feelings. Most bookshops are well stocked with a variety of children's books about dying, death, and bereavement. Fiction and nonfiction books are regularly published on such topics as the deaths of parents, grandparents, siblings, and other relatives and friends, as well as pets. A four-year-old whose father has died might view a picture book such as *Everett Anderson's Good-Bye,* which depicts a young boy's feelings about his father's death, and be encouraged to talk about his or her own feelings. An adult might ask, "What else do you think someone like Everett might do or say when feeling angry about his father's death?" An appropriate book can give adults and children an opportunity to begin talking about each other's experiences (see Figure 10-6).[44]

Support Groups for Children

Community support is an important addition to the family's own internal support system. Many organizations that offer support during the crises of serious illness and bereavement emphasize caring for all members of a family, including children. Organizations such as The Compassionate Friends and the Bereaved Families of Ontario not only serve bereaved parents, but conduct programs to help children and adolescents cope with loss. In Maryland, the Hospice of Frederick County offers an innovative outreach program in which bereaved children ages six to fourteen are paired with a group of caring adults, many of whom are recovering from losses.[45] Named after a young hospice patient who died before his third birthday, Camp Jamie provides children with "a haven to learn about coping with grief." In the context of a weekend camp in an idyllic mountain setting, participants enjoy recreational activities and also have opportunities to explore their losses in a safe environment among peers and "big buddies."

Other groups provide social support to seriously ill children. An organization called HUGS: Help, Understanding, and Group Support for Hawaii's Seriously Ill Children and Their Families, which was founded in 1982, offers a wide range of services, which are provided free of charge. These include 24-hour crisis support, hospital and home visits, transportation to medical appointments, recreational activities, and respite care. Children and their families can avail themselves of counseling to learn how to cope with fear, anger, and heartache. Bereavement support is provided when a child dies. Organized around a professional staff and a network of trained volunteers, HUGS provides services "to help families stay together in the face of overwhelming adversity."[46]

Care for seriously ill children is also supported by foundations that provide financial aid to make hospice care more widely available to children. The Loewen Children's Foundation, for example, is a founding patron of Canuck Place, the first free-standing hospice in North America designed specifically for pediatric hospice care, and of StarShine Hospice, which is affiliated with Children's Hospital Medical Center in Ohio.[47]

Telephone-oriented support groups are another type of organized social support that has been effectively used with varied populations, including children. The telephone was first used as a method of outreach for suicide prevention by the Samaritans in London in 1953.[48] Recently, the Pediatric Branch of the National Cancer Institute created a telephone network to offer social support to HIV-infected children. The organizers found that the telephone offered "a sense of confidentiality not afforded in face-to-face groups," thus

Books for Children and Adolescents

Nicholas Allan. *Heaven*. New York: HarperFestival, 1997. When Dill the dog dies, he shares a whimsical view of heaven with his owner, Lily. Ages 4–up.

T. A. Barron. *Where Is Grandpa?* Illustrations by Chris K. Soentpiet. New York: Philomel Books, 2000. A young boy copes with his feelings and thoughts about the death of his grandfather. Memories of the past show him where grandpa lives. Ages 4–6.

Arno Bohlmeijer. *Something Very Sorry*. New York: Putnam, 1997. Based on a true story about a girl whose whole family is in a serious car crash, this novel describes with loving sensitivity how Rosemyn and her family cope with the accident's aftermath, including the mother's death after being removed from life-support. Ages 8–12.

Laurie Krasny Brown and Marc Brown. *When Dinosaurs Die: A Guide to Understanding Death*. Boston: Little, Brown, 1996. Offers comfort and reassurance to children by addressing their fears about death and explaining in simple language the feelings people may have when a loved one dies and ways of remembering someone who has died. Ages 3–8.

Eve Bunting. *The Happy Funeral*. New York: Harper and Row, 1982. The funeral of a child's Chinese-American grandfather. Ages 3–6.

Leo Buscaglia. *The Fall of Freddie the Leaf: A Story of Life for All Ages*. Thorofare, N.J.: Charles B. Slack, 1982. The passage of a leaf through the seasons. Ages 3–6.

Carol Carrick. *The Accident*. Illustrations by Donald Carrick. New York: Seabury/Clarion, 1976. A young child copes with the death of a pet. Ages 3–8.

Lucile Clifton. *Everett Anderson's Good-Bye*. Illustrated by Ann Grifalconi. New York: Holt, Rinehart and Winston, 1983. A young boy explores his feelings about the death of his father. Ages 3–8.

John B. Coburn. *Anne and the Sand Dobbies: A Story About Death for Children and Their Parents*. New York: Seabury Press, 1964. This classic tells how a father answers the question of his son who has lost both his dog and his younger sister. Ages 3–8.

Eleanor Coerr. *Sadako and the Thousand Paper Cranes*. Illustrations by Ronald Himler. New York: Putnam, 1977. The story of a Japanese girl's illness and death from leukemia resulting from the Hiroshima bomb, her courage, and the memorial to her by her classmates and community. Ages 7–10.

Miriam Cohen. *Jim's Dog Muffins*. Illustrations by Lillian Hoban. New York: Greenwillow, 1984. A friend and a teacher help a boy cope with the loss of his dog. Ages 3–8.

Janice Cohn. *I Had a Friend Named Peter: Talking to Children About the Death of a Friend*. New York: Morrow, 1987. When Betsy's playmate dies from an accident while chasing a ball into the street, her parents help her cope with the loss and describe the coming funeral and burial, inviting her to attend if she wants to; includes two sections, one for parents and one for children. Ages 4–7.

Janice Cohn. *Molly's Rosebush: A Concept Book*. Morton Grove, Ill.: Albert Whitman, 1994. Through the story of Molly, whose mother suffers a miscarriage, this book offers guidance to parents about how children are affected by such a loss and provides a way of explaining the loss to young children. Ages 3–6.

Penny Colman. *Corpses, Coffins, and Crypts: A History of Burial*. New York: Henry Holt, 1997. Ranging from ancient Chinese history and the embalming of soldiers during the Civil War to today's Internet memorial parks and e-mail tributes, this book describes how diverse cultures and religions honor their dead, allowing readers to view death as a universal experience that connects them to others. Ages 9–up.

(continued)

Figure *10-6 Books for Helping Children Cope With Loss*

Books for Children and Adolescents (continued)

Tomie DePaola. *Nana Upstairs and Nana Downstairs.* New York: Penguin, 1978. A boy learns to face the eventual deaths of his grandmother and great-grandmother. Ages 3–8.

Paula Fox. *The Eagle Kite.* New York: Dell/Laurel-Leaf, 1996. When Liam, a high school freshman, learns that his father is dying of AIDS, he experiences feelings of shame and betrayal heightened by family secrets as he reckons with the truth and ultimately finds a healing in his relationship with his father. Ages 11–14.

Jason Gaes. *My Book for Kids with Cansur: A Child's Autobiography of Hope.* Aberdeen, S.D.: Melius and Peterson, 1987. A boy's gift to other children with cancer. Ages 6–up.

Mordicai Gerstein. *The Mountains of Tibet.* New York: Harper and Row, 1987. Inspired by the Tibetan Book of the Dead, this illustrated tale uses the theme of reincarnation to tell the story of a Tibetan woodcutter who, after dying, is given the choice of going to paradise or living another life anywhere in the universe. Ages 3–up.

Barbara Snow Gilbert. *Stone Water.* Arden, N.C.: Front Street, 1996. After Grandpa Hughes suffers a massive stroke and lies unconscious in a nursing home bed, 14-year-old Grant is sure that his grandfather is ready to die and struggles with his decision to take matters into his own hands in this story of assisted suicide. Ages 10–up.

Charlotte Graeber. *Mustard.* Illustrations by Donna Diamond. New York: Macmillan, 1982. A young boy deals with the increasing infirmity and eventual death of a cat that had been part of the family since before he was born. Ages 3–6.

Earl Grollman. *Talking About Death: A Dialogue Between Parent and Child.* 3d ed. Boston: Beacon Press, 1990. A nonfiction explanation about death.

Kevin Henkes. *Sun & Spoon.* New York: Greenwillow, 1997. A ten-year-old boy wrestles with grief during the first summer since his beloved grandmother's death and finds the healing power of remembering a deceased loved one. Ages 6–9.

Lyn Littlefield Hoopes. *Nana.* New York: Harper and Row, 1981. A grandmother's death. Ages 3–8.

Davida Wills Hurwin. *A Time for Dancing.* New York: Puffin, 1997. In this novel about how terminal illness affects the lives of friends and those around them, two teenage girls who have been best friends since childhood face mortality when one of them is diagnosed with histiocytic lymphoma, a deadly form of cancer. Ages 12–up.

Hadley Irwin. *So Long at the Fair.* New York: McElderry-Macmillan, 1988. Joel Logan, a high school senior, finds that he must remember and work through the past to come to terms with the suicidal death of his girlfriend. Ages 12–up.

Jill Krementz. *How It Feels When a Parent Dies.* New York: Knopf, 1981. A photographic essay with children's descriptions of their experiences. Ages 10–up.

Madeleine L'Engle. *A Ring of Endless Light.* New York: Farrar, Straus & Giroux, 1980. A teenage girl copes with the experience of loss, grief, and terminal illness by discovering underlying spiritual and moral dimensions. Ages 10–up.

Joyce McDonald. *Swallowing Stones.* New York: Delacorte, 1997. A bizarre Fourth of July accident, which leaves an innocent man dead, draws together four teens, whose lives are drastically changed as they deal with guilt, anxiety, and grief. Ages 12–up.

Gloria H. McLendon. *My Brother Joey Died.* Photographs by Harvey Kelman. New York: Simon & Schuster, 1982. The issues surrounding a sibling's death as told from the perspective of a nine-year-old. Ages 8–up.

Miska Miles. *Annie and the Old One.* Illustrations by Peter Parnall. Boston: Little, Brown, 1971. The story of a Navajo girl's efforts to prevent the inevitable by unraveling each day's weaving on a rug whose completion she fears will bring her grandmother's death. Ages 3–8.

Jane Mobley. *The Star Husband.* Illustrations by Anna Vojtech. New York: Doubleday, 1979. This adaptation of a Native American myth affirms the natural cycle of life, death, and rebirth. Ages 3–8.

Walter Dean Myers. *Fallen Angels.* New York: Scholastic, 1988. The gritty and heartrending story of Richie Perry, just out of high school, who enlists in the Army and spends a devastating year in Vietnam. Ages 12–up.

Donna Jo Napoli. *Stones in Water.* New York: Dutton, 1997. Based on the life of a survivor and told from the point of view of a young Venetian boy forced into the war by the Nazis, this story leads readers through a gradual unfolding of events until they come face to face with the scope of the atrocities that occurred in Europe during World War II. Ages 10–up.

Lesléa Newman. *Too Far Away to Touch.* New York: Clarion, 1995. This illustrated story of a girl whose uncle has AIDS is presented in a way that will be meaningful to all children who have lost a beloved relative to any illness, but especially to AIDS. Ages 5–9.

Ann Novac. *The Beautiful Days of My Youth: My Six Months in Auschwitz and Plaszow.* New York: Henry Holt, 1997. A memoir of the Holocaust that poignantly describes life, death, and survival in Hitler's camps. Ages 12–up.

Linda Peavy. *Allison's Grandfather.* Illustrations by Ronald Himler. New York: Charles Schribner's Sons, 1981. A young child reflects upon her friend's grandfather's death. Ages 3–8.

Barbra Ann Porte. *Harry's Mom.* Illustrations by Yossi Abolafia. New York: Greenwillow/Morrow, 1985. A story for young children about a mother's death. Ages 3–8.

Elizabeth Richter. *Losing Someone You Love: When a Brother or Sister Dies.* New York: G. P. Putnam's Sons, 1986. The experience of sibling loss as related in interviews with young people. Ages 10–up.

Freg Rogers. *When a Pet Dies.* New York: G. P. Putnam's Sons, 1988. Portrays a family whose dog dies and another family whose cat dies; the grieving children ask questions of their parents and adjust to their losses. Ages 3–8.

Gary D. Schmidt. *The Sin Eater.* New York: Dutton, 1996. After his mother's death from cancer and the subsequent suicide of his father, Cole's grandfather guides him in exploring the immediate and enduring benefits of preserving family history and helps him recognize how the past holds keys to the present and how stories can keep loved ones alive. Ages 10–14.

Maria Shriver. *What's Heaven?* Illustrations by Sandra Sperdel. New York: St. Martin's Press, 1999. Story about Kate, a little girl whose great-grandmother has just died. Kate seeks answers, and her mother helps her learn about heaven. The many questions in this book came from Shriver's own children when her grandmother Rose Fitzgerald Kennedy died. Ages 4–6.

Sara Bonnett Stein. *About Dying: An Open Family Book for Parents and Children Together.* New York: Walker and Company, 1974. A story about death composed of parallel texts providing basic information for children and supplemental information for adults. Ages 3–6.

Yukio Tsuchiya. *Faithful Elephants: A True Story of Animals, People, and War.* Boston: Houghton Mifflin, 1988. A poignant story of the horror of war and its effect on animals and people. Ages 5–9.

Susan Varley. *Badger's Parting Gifts.* New York: Lothrop, Lee and Shepard, 1984. The story of an old animal's dying and the grieving of those who loved him, Ages 5–9.

(continued)

Books for Children and Adolescents (continued)

Judith Viorst. *The Tenth Good Thing About Barney.* Illustrations by Erik Blegvad. New York: Atheneum, 1971. A boy thinks of the ten best things about his pet cat, who has died. Ages 3–8.

E. B. White. *Charlott'e Web.* Illustrations by Garth Williams. New York: Harper and Row, 1952. This classic story describes the grief experienced at the death of a close friend—Charlotte, a spider—and the continuing of life through her offspring. Ages 3–up.

Kazumi Yumoto. *The Friends.* Translated by Cathy Hirano. New York: Farrar, Straus & Giroux, 1996. In this story that is both universal and rooted in the country and culture from which it comes, three youngs boys' fascination with death leads them to form an unexpected friendship with an old man through which they confront their fears and learn to accept the inevitable with a sense of joy in life. Ages 10–up.

Charlotte Zolotow. *If You Listen.* New York: Harper and Row, 1980. A mother reassures a child of her father's love. Ages 3–6.

Charlotte Zolotow. *My Grandson Lew.* New York: Harper and Row, 1974. Lew learns the value of memories of his deceased grandfather. Ages 3–6.

providing "a creative and therapeutic way to help HIV-infected children and their family members cope with the impact this disease had on their lives." Interactions among participants included a great deal of self-disclosure and sharing of mutual fears and concerns.

Yet another type of social support for seriously ill children can be found in organizations that exist to grant the wishes of children who have been given a limited or uncertain prognosis. The Sunshine Foundation, founded in 1976, and the Starlight Foundation, founded in 1983, are two examples.[49] Through the efforts of such groups, seriously ill children and their families are able to take a vacation together or fulfill some other wish that seems impossible without outside help.

Adults often tend to worry about children in their encounters with death. Are they doing all right? Will they be okay? Is death going to be too hard for them to handle? Can they survive this particular loss? In general, children do remarkably well. As Erik Erikson said, "Healthy children will not fear life if their parents have the integrity not to fear death."[50]

Further Readings

David W. Adams and Eleanor J. Deveau. *Beyond the Innocence of Childhood.* 3 vols. Amityville, N.Y.: Baywood, 1995.

Myra Bluebond-Langner. *In the Shadow of Illness: Parents and Siblings of the Chronically Ill Child.* Princeton, N.J.: Princeton University Press, 1996.

Charles A. Corr and David E. Balk, eds. *Handbook of Adolescent Death and Bereavement.* New York: Springer, 1996.

Charles A. Corr and Donna M. Corr, eds. *Handbook of Childhood Death and Bereavement.* New York: Springer, 1996.

Betty Davies. *Shadows in the Sun: The Experience of Sibling Bereavement in Childhood.* Washington, D.C.: Taylor & Francis, 1998.

Kenneth J. Doka, ed. *Children Mourning, Mourning Children.* Washington, D.C.: Hospice Foundation of America, 1995.

Linda Goldman. *Life & Loss.* 2d ed. Philadelphia: Taylor & Francis, 1999.

Anne Hunsaker Hawkins. *A Small, Good Thing: Stories of Children with HIV and Those Who Care for Them.* New York: W. W. Norton, 2000.

Phyllis Rolfe Silverman. *Never Too Young to Know: Death in Children's Lives.* New York: Oxford University Press, 2000.

Barbara M. Sourkes. *Armfuls of Time: The Psychological Experience of the Child with a Life-Threatening Illness.* Pittsburgh: University of Pittsburgh Press, 1996.

J. William Worden. *Children and Grief: When a Parent Dies.* New York: Guilford Press, 1996.

Holding their dead baby, this Harlem couple finds comfort in the sharing of their memories and their grief as they acknowledge the death of their firstborn child. Of all the losses that can be experienced during adult life, most people feel that the death of a child is the most painful.

C H A P T E R *11*

Death in the Lives of Adults

*J*ust as human development does not stop with childhood's end, so the patterns of coping with loss continue to evolve throughout a person's lifespan. Just as we can associate distinct developmental tasks and abilities with children of varying ages, so too we can distinguish distinctive phases and transitions during adult life. In the previous chapter, we discussed the first five stages of psychosocial development proposed by Erik Erikson—namely, those pertaining to the years of childhood and adolescence. The last three stages of psychosocial development, according to this model, occur during adulthood. As in childhood, each stage of adult life requires a particular developmental response, and each stage builds on previous ones.

Young adulthood is represented by the conflict between intimacy and isolation. This stage involves various forms of commitment and interaction, including sex, friendship, cooperation, partnership, and affiliation. Because mature love takes the risk of commitment, the death of a loved one may be most devastating during this stage and the next.[1]

The next psychosocial stage, according to Erikson, is *adulthood,* which involves the crisis of generativity versus stagnation. This stage is characterized by a widening commitment to take care of the people, things, and ideas one has learned to care for. This emphasis on care helps explain why the death of a child is so painful. Symbolically and actually, a child's death is opposed to the nurturant psychosocial task of adulthood.

383

When we reach the stage of *maturity*, the eighth and final stage of the life cycle, the turning point or crisis to be resolved is that of integrity versus despair. Viewing all the developmental phases as connected, each building on the ones before, the crisis of this stage is especially powerful. It is marked by the end of our "one given course of life." Successfully negotiating this developmental task gives us the strength of wisdom, which Erikson describes as "informed and detached concern with life itself in the face of death itself."[2]

You may find it useful to consider the losses that have occurred in your own life, both as a child and as an adult. How have they differed, and in what ways are they similar? Notice how your orientation to loss changed as you got older. Have others responded to your experiences of loss in supportive ways? What coping mechanisms were you able to bring into play to move through the experience successfully? Questions of this kind can form a framework for examining typical losses in adult life.

Parental Bereavement

What makes the loss of a child a high-grief death? To most people, the death of a child represents the unfinished, the untimely loss of a potential future. We expect that a child will outlive his or her parents. Death may be viewed as appropriate in old age, but a child's death underscores the truth that no one is immune to death. These attitudes about the death of a child are very much related to advances in health care that have greatly reduced infant and child mortality during the past century. In earlier times, and in parts of the world today, a newborn or infant child is not really viewed as a "person" until he or she has lived long enough to exhibit a strong likelihood of ongoing viability. In the cultural context of modern societies, however, the death of a child is generally considered the least natural of deaths.[3]

Parents envision their children playing on the local youth soccer team, graduating from school, getting married, raising their own children—all the various milestones and occasions that comprise a sense of continuity into the future. Death brings an end to the plans and hopes for a child's life. A child carries something of the parent into the future, even after the parent's death. A child's very existence grants a kind of immortality to the parent; this is taken away when the child dies.

The interdependency between parent and child makes the death of a child a deep experience of loss.[4] Grief may focus on issues of parental responsibility. Parenting is generally defined as protecting and nurturing a child until he or she can act independently in the world. Thus, the death of a child may be experienced as the ultimate lack of protection and nurture, the ultimate breakdown and failure in being a "good parent." Among the Cree of North America, infants were given "ghost-protective" moccasins to wear. Holes were cut in the bottom of the moccasins to safeguard the baby from death. If the spirit of an ancestor appeared and beckoned, the infant could refuse to go, pointing out that his or her moccasins "needed mending."[5] Such feelings about the parental role of safeguarding a child are universal.

Many issues of parental bereavement span the adult life cycle. They are present for thirty-year-old parents and eighty-year-old parents. They are experienced by parents of grown children as well as by parents of infants. A parent's fantasies and plans can be as strong for an unborn infant as for an older child. A sixty-five-year-old divorced or widowed mother may feel considerable loss of security when her thirty-five-year-old child dies suddenly. One such woman said: "He was going to take care of me when I got old; now I have no one." Whether or not her son would have indeed taken on the responsibility she envisioned, his death represented the loss of *her* imagined future.

Parental bereavement is a powerful experience that relates to both socio-biological and psychological explanations of grief. Studies of human bonding and the psychodynamics of family systems contribute to a comprehensive model of parental grief. Bereaved parents often maintain an inner representation of the dead child that is sustained through memories and religious beliefs.[6] It is in appreciating the uniqueness of the parent–child relationship that we begin to understand the grief evoked by the death of a child.

Coping With Parental Bereavement As a Couple

In counseling bereaved parents, clinicians sometimes note the presence of a kind of "general chaos," a pervasive sense that the parents have been robbed of a past and a future. With such a traumatic event, parents expect, and are expected, to support each other. But the energy expended by each partner in coping with his or her own grief can deplete the emotional resources necessary for mutual support. Some bereaved parents report that, in addition to losing a child, they felt they had lost their spouse for a time. Studies indicate that the death of a child has the potential to either improve or worsen a marital relationship.[7] A child's death may have the paradoxical effect of creating a feeling of estrangement and a strong bond between parents at the same time.[8]

Even though they share the same loss, parents typically have different grieving styles, which can leave each of them feeling isolated and unsupported by the only other person who shares the magnitude of the loss. Individual differences in values, beliefs, and expectations may cause conflicts in coping styles, thereby reducing the sense of "commonality" in a couple's grief experience.[9] Although husbands and wives do not always or necessarily grieve in an asynchronous or "roller coaster" pattern, it is not uncommon for bereaved parents to find themselves grieving "out of synch" with one another at times.[10]

The sense of commonality in a couple's grief is also affected by their view of themselves as a *couple*. They may have difficulty reaching agreement about the best way to regain a sense of stability and meaning in life after their child's death. Despite each partner's desire and expectation to "go through grief" together, differences in grieving styles may create conflict about whether one's partner is behaving appropriately.

Conflict can arise out of each partner's *interpretation* of the other's behavior. A husband who contains his grief so that he can "be there" for his wife may be perceived by the spouse as cold and unfeeling. His desire to be caring and protective may be misinterpreted, resulting in conflict rather than comfort. Disagreement or misunderstanding can also relate to issues about what constitutes "proper" mourning behavior, the couple's "public face" of grief.

Reducing conflict and promoting positive interactions between grieving partners requires the willingness of each to engage in open and honest communication. In this way, each partner's emotional expression of loss helps validate the reality of the other's perceptions. Simply crying together can be helpful in resolving conflict and working through the loss. A characteristic of couples who report little conflict is their positive view of each other and their relationship. Accepting differences and being flexible about roles also contribute to sharing grief.

Coming to terms with a grieving spouse's behavior is enhanced by the ability of partners to *reframe* each other's behavior in a positive way. For example, a husband who views his wife's sobbing as "breaking down" can alter his perception so that the crying is seen as emotionally cleansing and therefore valuable. Reframing a spouse's behavior makes it possible to explain the behavior in positive terms, rather than judging it as inappropriate or dysfunctional. When previously unsettling behavior is seen as providing emotional release, it allows a mate to support the expression instead of trying to curtail it by urging the spouse to "get it together." As always, it is often the "little things" spouses do that cause their partners to feel supported and loved.

Childbearing Losses

Pregnancy usually represents a major life transition for adults. The normally expected result is the birth of a viable, healthy baby. Miscarriage, stillbirth, or neonatal death is not the anticipated outcome. Yet, in a recent year, 63,153 fetal and infant deaths were recorded in the United States, with about 45 percent of these deaths having been stillbirths, another 34 percent neonatal deaths, and the remaining 21 percent postneonatal deaths.[11] The grief experienced after a perinatal loss can be as devastating as the loss of an older child.[12]

According to medical definition, *stillbirth* refers to fetal death occurring between the twentieth week of gestation (pregnancy) and the time of birth, resulting in the delivery of a dead child. *Neonatal* deaths are those occurring during the first four weeks following birth. In the statistics just given, *postneonatal* deaths include those that occur after the first four weeks and up to eleven months following birth.

The statistics given do not include deaths from *miscarriage,* which occurs prior to the twentieth week of pregnancy. Miscarriage, also termed *spontaneous abortion,* is defined as "loss of the products of conception before the fetus is viable."[13] The distinction between miscarriage and stillbirth is based on the logic that most fetuses are viable—that is, able to survive outside the mother's body—after the twentieth week of pregnancy. It is estimated that about 20 percent of all pregnancies end in miscarriage, with about three-fourths of these ending before twelve weeks.[14] In contrast to spontaneous abortion, which occurs naturally, *induced abortion* (sometimes called artificial or therapeutic abor-

Käthe Kollwitz, Library of Congress

The overwhelming grief of parental bereavement is expressed in the soft-ground etching
Überfahren *(Passing Over), by Käthe Kollwitz, whose art became a means of working through her own sorrow following the death of a child. The dead child is carried
by adults bent with the burden of grief; other children look on.*

tion) is brought about intentionally with the aim of ending a pregnancy by
mechanical means or drugs.

Broadly considered, reproductive loss also includes losses resulting from
infertility and sterility. Whereas *infertility* refers to "diminished or absent capacity to produce offspring," *sterility* denotes "complete inability to produce
offspring," due either to inability to conceive (female) or to induce conception (male).[15] Although most couples are able to produce children without
undue difficulty, it is sadly true that "some manage only after years of disappointment and some not at all."[16] Despite advances in medical treatment for
infertility, many couples ultimately remain childless, their biological and social
urges to reproduce thwarted by forces beyond their control.

Another example of reproductive loss involves giving up a child for *adoption.* Although this might not initially be thought of as a childbearing loss
because adoption usually results from choice, grief may nonetheless accompany such decisions. Psychologists point out,

> In a society that defines women as mothers, mothers-to-be, or childless, the
> woman who has given birth and then relinquished her child for adoption is an

enigma. Having signed away her legal claim to the child, she is often perceived as the most unnatural of women, a rejecting mother. [But] the maternal experience does not end with the signing of surrender papers.[17]

Although the grief following adoption is often unrecognized, unsupported, and unresolved, it can nonetheless have deep emotional effects on the birth parents.[18] Seeing a child at play or walking down the street can spur the reaction of wondering what one's own child might be like at that age.

A comprehensive view of childbearing losses also includes the losses that ensue when a child is born with severe disabilities, such as congenital deformities or mental retardation. Parents may have difficulty accepting the reality that their child is not as they had wished for and dreamed about; they may grieve the loss of the "perfect" or "wished-for" child.[19] These lost expectations need to be acknowledged and mourned.

All these varied childbearing losses involve grief for unlived lives. Judith Savage says, "Childbearing losses are mourned not only for what was, but also for what might have been."[20] Grief is felt not only for the physical loss, but also for symbolic losses. Parents mourn "the child of the imagination, that part of themselves which seems now to have no possibility of embodiment in the world." Writing from the perspective of a Jungian psychologist who by age 33 had experienced multiple losses (her adoptive and biological parents, her two brothers, and her infant son), Savage says:

> By unraveling the mystery of the imaginative relationship, that is, the projections of the self onto the unborn child, it becomes clear that primary relationships are not composed merely of interchangeable functional attributes and roles but are uniquely personal bonds that are generated from deep within and are as much a reflection of the individual soul as they are an accurate reflection of the other.[21]

It is important to be aware of two distinct yet related realities: the *actual* relationship and the *symbolic* nature of the parent–child bond. Grieving parents often talk about lost companionship, lost dreams—all the ways in which the child would have enriched their lives. Such discussion is concerned with the actual loss. The symbolic loss relates to the meaning attached to the relationship, as when an individual, by parenting a child, becomes a nurturing, supportive guide. A bereaved father said, "Not only have I lost a son who might follow in my footsteps, but, without him, I have no feet." It was important for this father to acknowledge and mourn both the loss of his son and the loss of meaning and purpose in his own life. The image of the lost child activates powerful associations, which become part of a natural process guiding the bereaved parent's journey toward wholeness.

With a childbearing loss, blame can be turned inward as well as directed outward. A parent may ask, "Didn't I want this baby enough?" Questions about the cause of the tragic outcome abound: Was it that glass of wine, the aspirin, or, as one mother asked in desperation, "Was it the nutmeg I put on my oatmeal?" Even inconsequential actions may be scrutinized.

Anger may be focused on the dead child, resulting in confusing and tangled emotions. After all, what kind of person could be angry at an innocent

Small Son

They have gone.
The last mourner,
the last comfort,
last cliche.

I wrap a pillow
in your blanket.
Lie burying my face
to hold your fading
milk sweet smell.

The silence swells.

    I run

to where the stand
of saplings wait
for clearing.

Chopping, slashing,
small limbs
dragged and pulled
and piled for burning.

I turn away
consumed,
the taste of ashes
in my mouth.

             Maude Meehan

infant? Yet anger is a natural response to loss. As one woman said of her stillborn daughter, "Why did she just drop in and out of my life? Why did she bother coming at all?" Emotional responses may be accompanied by auditory or kinesthetic hallucinations: A baby cries in the night, waking parents from sleep; the baby kicks inside the womb, yet there is no pregnancy, no live child.

Absent a baby, the mother may be confronted by physical reminders of the loss, such as the onset of lactation. One bereaved mother said, "I wanted to go to the cemetery and let my milk flow onto my daughter's grave." Meanwhile, the father may feel culturally constrained to "be brave" so that he can support the mother, who is recuperating physically as well as emotionally. As a result, the father's need to grieve may go unmet, his emotions pushed below the surface.

Grief following a childbearing loss is also potentially influenced by the parents' perceptions that the loss is neither understood nor acknowledged by others. Bereaved parents report hearing insensitive comments, such as, "It must be easier since you didn't get too attached." Well-intentioned family members and friends may attempt to minimize the death in an effort to console the bereaved parent. They may say, "You're young; you can have another baby," unaware that such a comment, though possibly true, is inappropriate: No other baby will replace the one who has just died. Advice such as this is especially difficult for couples who postponed having children—they may feel an added constraint of time that compounds the experience of loss.

Perinatal bereavement care is important. The program sponsored by the Reuben Center for Women and Children at Toledo Hospital in Ohio is a positive example of support for parents who have suffered a childbearing loss.[22] The program has a variety of bereavement protocols, including guidelines for bereavement support, photographic techniques (photos are taken of all deceased infants and are given to parents either at the time of the death or at whatever time they want them), use of hospital chaplains and trained support group volunteers, distribution of printed materials on bereavement and grief (including a brochure written expressly to educate relatives and friends of the bereaved about what they can do), various funeral and memorialization options, and the availability of support groups for families who do not live near the hospital. Educational programs and mutual support are also provided for staff members who care for newly bereaved families. In this way, comprehensive support for perinatal loss is provided to families, staff, and the community.

As always, it is important to keep in mind that there is considerable individual variation in the expression and, indeed, experience of grief. This may be especially true of childbearing losses. Irving Leon points out that:

> Not long ago the death of a baby was an unspeakable event in a hospital. Hushed silence greeted the delivery of a stillborn. The baby was whisked away before parents could see and hold their child. They were told to forget what happened and have another baby as soon as possible. The mother was given tranquilizers if she became too upset, if she "lost it" (meaning that she was grieving over what she *had* lost).[23]

Today, in most hospitals, the situation is very much the opposite; grief for perinatal loss is respected, and even expected. We must remember, however, that people are different, as are their attachments to their newborn and unborn children. Bereaved parents should not be expected or forced to "follow a script" or enact some "right way" to grieve. Caregivers, as well as supportive friends and relatives, must distinguish between an approach that merely encourages a "canned," programmed interaction and one that promotes genuine empathy.

Miscarriage

Many people assume that the loss of a baby during the early stages of pregnancy evokes feelings of disappointment, but not grief. To parents who have dreamed about the baby even before its conception, however, miscarriage evokes pain and confusion. Parents may be told that the loss is simply "Nature's way" of weeding out genetic anomalies. Such a remark offers little or no consolation to grieving parents; it was *their* baby that Nature decided to sort. Platitudes that minimize or deny the loss are unhelpful. When parents experience a series of miscarriages, loss is compounded upon loss.

Parents may have difficulty identifying their loss precisely or making sense of what has happened. After a miscarriage, one young mother's grief was complicated because she had no remains to be buried. "I didn't know where my baby was," she said. Even though a miscarriage may have occurred many years ago, grief for an unborn baby can recur with other significant life events—for example, at the birth of a subsequent child or the onset of menopause. A particular marker, such as reaching age forty or age sixty-five, can reawaken feelings of grief.

Induced Abortion

In the United States, slightly less than one-fourth of all pregnancies are terminated by induced abortion, a total of about 1.4 million abortions annually.[24] Although induced abortion is also termed "elective" abortion, in many cases it is less a choice than a medical necessity. Some people assume that women who *elect* to terminate a pregnancy do not experience a significant grief reaction, but this notion is not always true. The grief reaction to elective abortion can be substantially the same as grief after involuntary fetal or infant loss.[25] Much depends on the person's perception of the pregnancy: Does she perceive herself as simply pregnant, or as a potential mother? Similar questions apply to men who participate in decisions about elective abortion.

The emotional reaction to induced abortion varies. In some cases, the repercussions are not felt until much later. One woman, who had chosen to abort a pregnancy as a young adult because she and her husband felt their relationship couldn't withstand the pressures of raising a child at that time, experienced great remorse when she and her husband later found themselves unable to have other children. "That may have been our only chance," she lamented. Subsequent pregnancy loss may be experienced as "retribution" for an earlier abortion. In addition, personal and social attitudes toward abortion can affect the resolution of grief. When social support is lacking, people have fewer opportunities to express their feelings about a loss.

When the decision for an abortion is made because of adverse information about the baby's health, the inherent conflict about the choice may add to parents' grief. Many genetic diseases are identified by tests during the early stages of pregnancy; and, when the results are unfavorable, terminating the pregnancy may seem the best or only choice. Some tests can be done only well into the pregnancy, after the mother has already felt the baby moving. Parents who decide in favor of a therapeutic abortion may worry that no one will understand their "choice" and that they will be judged harshly. Furthermore, in this situation, couples may face not only the loss of a particular baby, but also the possibility of a childless future; biological considerations or genetic risk may preclude the choice to conceive again.

In Japan, at places like Hase Temple in Kamakura and Shiun Jizo Temple north of Tokyo, thousands of tiny stone statues called *mizuko* represent children conceived but never born.[26] Some of these "water children" wear bibs and stocking caps. Placed alongside them are toy milk bottles, dolls, and twirling pinwheels, along with memorials written by their sponsors—women who chose to have an abortion rather than give birth. The statues, each one costing several hundred dollars, are erected as repositories for the souls of unborn babies. At Hase Temple, the more than 50,000 *mizuko* are watched over by a thirty-foot-tall wooden statue of the "Goddess of Mercy," who is also the patroness of safe birth. Even though abortion is common in Japan, "mizuko worship" bears witness to an intense desire to acknowledge the unborn fetus.

Kenneth Doka points out that contemporary views about abortion may place the bereaved in a dilemma: Those who believe a loss occurred may not sanction the act, whereas those who sanction the act may not recognize that grief in response to the perceived loss needs to be expressed and legitimized. Difficulties in grieving may be exacerbated when customary sources of solace and social support are not readily available.[27]

Stillbirth

"Instead of giving birth, I gave death," said a mother whose daughter died in childbirth. Instead of a cradle, there is a grave; instead of a receiving blanket, there are burial clothes; instead of a birth certificate, there is a death certificate. After a stillbirth, "a family's wishes and hopes and dreams—the individuals' illusions about what life *ought* to be—are quickly shattered by the reality of what life really *is*."[28] Those who counsel newly bereaved parents of a stillborn baby emphasize the importance of acknowledging the child's birth. Rather than whisking away the stillborn infant as quickly as possible, hospital staff can encourage parents to see and hold their baby. Acknowledging the reality of the baby's life and death facilitates healthy grief. A postmortem photograph of the child may assist in the process of grieving.[29] Parents may hold a memorial service for the stillborn baby, a choice that not only acknowledges the reality of what has happened, but that provides an opportunity to find meaning and solace by sharing grief with others.

Some hospitals give bereaved parents an information packet that includes a "Certificate of Stillbirth," which acknowledges the birth as well as the death of the child. Linking objects, such as a lock of hair, a photograph, and the receiving blanket can be comforting to parents. Nearly 90 percent of the parents included in a study by John De Frain named their stillborn baby, thereby recognizing that it was indeed part of the family, no matter how briefly: "Naming seemed to help show others that the baby really existed and was important, not just something to be thrown away and forgotten."[30] The hurt may fade as time passes, the memories do not.

Neonatal Death

When a baby is born alive but with life-threatening disabilities due to prematurity or congenital defects, the ensuing period of uncertainty about the baby's survival can be a nightmare for parents. Parents may experience an overwhelming sense of frustration and futility as medical interventions are discussed, attempted, and perhaps fail. Sometimes a baby born with one or more life-threatening conditions embarks on a life-or-death struggle that lasts weeks. During this time, parents may have to make difficult ethical choices that determine whether the baby lives or dies. Meanwhile the costs incurred in keeping the baby alive continue to mount. If the baby does die, parents may resent the medical institution and its personnel, feeling as if they survived a painful and futile ordeal only to be billed later for the experience.

In circumstances involving a critically ill newborn, *any* decision may haunt parents as they repeatedly ask themselves if they made the right choice. Caregivers who appreciate the heart-wrenching ethical dilemmas that occur in the context of neonatal intensive care are in a position to provide sensitive care

When we bury the old, we bury the known past, the past we imagine sometimes better than it was, but the past all the same, a portion of which we inhabited. Memory is the overwhelming theme, the eventual comfort.

But burying infants, we bury the future, unwieldy and unknown, full of promise and possibilities, outcomes punctuated by our rosy hopes. The grief has no borders, no limits, no known ends, and the little infant graves that edge the corners and fencerows of every cemetery are never quite big enough to contain that grief. Some sadnesses are permanent. Dead babies do not give us memories. They give us dreams.

Thomas Lynch,
The Undertaking: Life Studies from the Dismal Trade

and support to parents facing the prospect of making and living with these difficult decisions. When the life of a critically ill infant is being sustained by extraordinary medical means, the decision to terminate the artificial support ought to be handled with as much grace as circumstances allow. The choices made in the context of neonatal care can be troubling for medical practitioners as well as parents. As one young neonatologist remarked, "One of the most difficult and important things for me to learn was to hand over the baby to the parents so it could die in their arms."

Sudden Infant Death Syndrome

In terms of parental bereavement, sudden infant death syndrome (SIDS) has many of the same characteristics and consequences as the other types of childbearing loss already discussed. SIDS is defined as "the sudden and unexpected death of any infant or young child in which a thorough postmortem examination fails to show an adequate cause."[31] It is the most common cause of death for infants between two weeks and one year of age, accounting for about 30 percent of all deaths in this age group.[32] The unexpected nature of the death, age of the child and of the parents (who are generally young and possibly experiencing an intimate death for the first time), and uncertainty about the cause of death combine to make SIDS deaths a difficult loss for the whole family.[33]

Because of uncertainty about the cause of death, the parents may be subject to a criminal investigation. Concerns about the possibility of child abuse prompt law enforcement officials to question whether the parents are responsible. It is a tragic fact that parents do sometimes murder their own infants and try to pass the deaths off as natural or accidental.[34] Ascertaining a cause of death in SIDS cases is often fraught with ambiguity, even for experts. Because of this ambiguity, many investigators try to handle apparent SIDS cases with sensitivity. This has come about partly as a result of information disseminated by parent support groups concerned about the effects of misdirected questioning and accusations on grieving parents. Even so, the parents may

The items placed around the grave of this infant in Hawaii—balloons, flowers, and jars of baby food—bespeak the parents' loss and acknowledge the enduring bonds of even a short-lived relationship.

question themselves just as sternly: Was the death in any way due to something they did or left undone? Could it have been prevented? The unexplained nature of SIDS deaths can lead survivors to embark on a quest for answers that may not be available. Peer support provided by other parents who have dealt with SIDS can be a source of reliable information as well as emotional comfort through grief.

The Death of an Older Child

Many of the issues discussed in the preceding section pertain as well to parents' grief following the death of an older child or adolescent. The meaning of such a death is usually more complex, however, because the relationship between parent and child has been of longer duration, with a correspondingly larger store of memories. A child represents many things to a parent. As Beverly Raphael reminds us, a child is "a part of the self, and of the loved partner; a representation of generations past; the genes of the forebears; the hope of the future; a source of love, pleasure, even narcissistic delight; a tie or a burden; and sometimes a symbol of the worst parts of the self and others."[35] As experiences are shared, the bond between parent and child takes on increasing complexity.

Among the major causes of death among children between the ages of five and fourteen, accidents top the list (with a death rate of 8.3 per 100,000), followed by cancer (3.5), homicide (2.6), congenital anomalies (0.9), heart disease (0.8), suicide (0.8), chronic obstructive pulmonary disease (0.4), and pneumonia and influenza (0.3).[36] Of the deaths resulting from accidents in this age group, over half involved motor vehicles. As the most prominent cause of death during the first half of the human lifespan, injury is characterized as "the last major plague of the young."[37] As these statistics show, children also die from violent, sudden deaths related to homicide and suicide. Suicide among the young is discussed in Chapter 12, and factors influencing bereavement in cases of sudden or violent death are discussed in Chapter 7.

Although many more children and adolescents die from injuries received in accidents than from the effects of disease, the situation confronting the child with a life-threatening illness is one of special poignancy. Perhaps we feel, justifiably or not, that an accident is something that just "happens" and is, therefore, not preventable, whereas we expect medicine to provide a cure for disease.

When a child's life is threatened by serious illness, it affects the whole fabric of family life. Parents and siblings, along with other relatives, are all involved in coping with the illness. Witnessing the disintegration caused by disease can be very painful, especially as the child draws nearer to death. This sometimes results in a kind of psychic separation, a distancing from the child, as parents and others in the child's life try to avoid situations that elicit painful

Last year, a fourteen-year-old boy who suddenly collapsed on the street was rushed to our hospital emergency room. Even though there were no clinical signs of life, at least six physicians frantically attempted resuscitative measures. In the hallway outside the emergency room, I came upon two stunned parents who were standing absolutely alone. None of the physicians wanted to leave the dramatic scene to obtain a history, let alone provide any solace. I did not want to either, the boy was dead (possibly from a cardiac conduction defect—even the autopsy later was unrevealing); but I forced myself to sit down in an adjoining room and listen while they talked of their hopes and their son's aspirations. I am used to talking with parents whose children die of sudden infant death syndrome; this was different and I was overwhelmed. Afterward, I went to my office and cried. I later thought that I should have let my interns and residents witness me cry to learn that professionalism does not preclude expression of human feeling.

Abraham B. Bergman, "Psychological Aspects of Sudden Unexpected Death in Infants and Children" feelings. This can lead to parents creating excuses for absences from the child's room when the situation becomes too painful.

Few families are able to sustain total openness to the reality of a child's terminal illness throughout what may be a long process from diagnosis of the disease to the child's death. At times, the sick child may function quite normally, and the routine of medical care becomes just another aspect of family life. At other times, the disease requires parents and other family members to deal intensely with changes in the child's condition. It is a tremendous challenge to try to adjust to fluctuations between hope for recovery and acceptance of terminality, all while trying to support the child in the best way possible.

Parents seem to have a somewhat easier time coping when they do not derive their personal identities solely from their role as parents. In other words, although parenting is an important part of their lives, it is not the totality of their self-image, which encompasses other accomplishments and values as well. Some parents not only manage to cope and survive the devastating loss of a child, but grow from the experience. Jerome Schulman observes that such parents are able to "respond to a [child's] severe illness by making a more mature reevaluation of their lives and achieving a truer vision of what counts. Their lives become more significant, more basic, more meaningful. They live one day at a time . . . but they learn to make each new day more enriching."[38]

The Death of an Adult Child

For a young or middle-aged adult to die while his or her parents live on seems unnatural. It is a death "out of sequence." A study of parents who had lost an adult son during military service found that the parents felt an "existential vacuum," which was expressed through lack of meaning and purpose in life.[39] Thus, even though there is likely to be a degree of separation between an adult child and his or her parent, the parent's grief is not necessarily correspondingly less intense. With the death of an only child, the resulting "loss of motherhood" may be accompanied by a kind of "perpetual bereavement," in which a struggle to understand the "meaning" of the child's death continues all through life.[40]

The older parent who survives the death of a middle-aged child may also be losing a caregiver. The adult child may represent a source of comfort and security that is now gone. Parental bereavement can be complicated by the sense of "competing" with the deceased's spouse or children for the role of "most bereaved." Who has priority in receiving care and comfort? Sometimes the death of an adult child involves circumstances that require parents to assume care of their grandchildren, a result that may be emotionally as well as economically disruptive.

Parents who suffer the death of a child already grown to adulthood may find themselves virtually alone in coping with their grief. In contrast to the situation of parents who lose younger children or individuals who survive the death of a spouse, comparatively few social support resources are available to

We had waited, agonizing through the nights and days without sleep, startled by nearly any sound, unable to eat, simply staring at our meals. Suddenly in a few seconds of radio time it was over. My first son, whose birth had brought me so much joy that I jumped up in a hall outside the room where he was born and touched the ceiling—the child, the scholar, the preacher, the boy singing and smiling, the son— all of it was gone. And Ebenezer was so quiet. All through the church as the staff learned what had happened, the tears flowed, but almost completely in silence.

Martin Luther King, Sr.

help parents cope with the death of an adult child. Perhaps because this type of bereavement is an anomaly, it has not been studied extensively. Yet, the death of a child—at whatever age—is always a major loss.

Social Support in Parental Bereavement

A variety of support groups exist to offer information and help to parents who are coping with the serious illness or death of a child. Some of these groups are for all types of parental bereavement; others have more specific agendas. The Compassionate Friends, for example, offers support to bereaved parents in a broad range of losses. This group was founded in England in 1969, and the first chapter in the United States was established in 1972. Since then, more than 400 chapters have been organized throughout the nation.[41] Another group, The Candlelighters Childhood Cancer Foundation, focuses more specifically on providing support for parents of children with cancer. From a child's initial diagnosis with cancer, through his or her treatment, and to long-term survival or death, there are specific programs for the child, his or her parents, and other family members.

Some support organizations for bereaved parents engage in political advocacy designed to remedy the situation that precipitated the child's death— for example, Mothers Against Drunk Driving and Parents of Murdered Children. Deaths that result from violence or drunk driving involve issues that may complicate grief for bereaved parents. In such cases, there may be intrusions on the parents' grief because of coverage by the media and by subsequent criminal investigation and judicial proceedings. Organizations of bereaved parents who have experienced similar losses constitute what some have called "communities of feeling" within which grief can be shared.[42]

Friends and relatives can find many ways to offer support to bereaved parents, including simply listening, sending cards or letters of condolence, bringing food, doing housework or other chores, caring for other children in the family, sharing their own grief over the loss, giving the parents time to be alone, and so on. People who are open to talking about the issues of grief in the wake of a child's death can be a great source of support to bereaved parents.

Death of a Parent

The death of a parent typically represents the loss of a long-term relationship characterized by nurture and unconditional support. Parents are often described as "always there when the chips are really down, no matter what." The death of a parent generally brings on a period of upheaval and transition. A parent's death is an important symbolic event for midlife adults. Most people report that the death of a parent changes their outlook on life, often spurring them on to examine their lives more closely, to begin changing what they don't like, and to appreciate more fully their ongoing relationships.[43]

Any death reminds us of our own mortality, but the death of a parent forces a person to realize, perhaps for the first time, that he or she has become an adult. The death of a parent can result in a "developmental push," which may effect a "more mature stance in parentally bereaved adults who no longer think of themselves as children."[44] When both parents have died, there is a role change for the adult child, who no longer has his or her parents to "fall back on," even if only in the imagination. When parents are alive, they may be a source of moral support; there is a sense that if real trouble comes a child

You Don't Miss Your Water

At home, my mother wakes up and spends some of her day talking back to my father's empty chair.

In Florida, my sister experiences the occasional dream in which my father returns; they chat.

He's been dead and gone for a little over a year. How it would please me to hear his unrecorded voice again, now alive only in the minds of those who remember him.

If I could, if as in the old spiritual, I could actually get a direct phone link to the other side, I could call him up, tell him about this small prize of a week I've had teaching poetry at a ski resort a few miles from Lake Tahoe, imagination jackpot, brief paradise of letters.

How could I make him believe that I have gotten all of this, this modern apartment, this pond in front of my window, all from the writing of a few good lines of verse, my father, who distrusted anything he couldn't get his hands on?

Most likely, he would listen, then ask me, as he always did, just for safety's sake, if my wife still had her good paying job.

And I can't tell you why, but this afternoon, I wouldn't become hot and stuffy from his concern, think "old fool" and gripe back *Of course I'm still teaching college. It's summer, you know?*

This afternoon, I miss his difficult waters, and when he'd ask, as he always would, *how're they treating you?* I'd love to answer back, *fine, daddy. They're paying me to write about your life.*

Cornelius Eady

can call on his or her parents. When a parent dies, that sense of security is diminished. The bereaved child may feel there is no one left to answer a call for help unconditionally. After the deaths of both her parents, one woman said that, although she knew friends and other relatives loved and cared about her, she felt that the love from her parents had been unique, unconditional, and irreplaceable. Adjusting to the death of one's parents can involve both "holding on" and "letting go," as the bereaved child simultaneously recognizes the reality of death and treasures comforting memories of the deceased.[45]

Even when a parent has lived in a nursing home for a considerable time before death, many adult children say that losing a parent is one of the hardest things they have ever dealt with in their lives. The ensuing grief may encompass sadness over the loss; relief at the ending of the parent's suffering; anxiety because the "protection against death" formerly provided by a parent is gone; as well as persistent memories, painful as well as comforting, of the deceased parent.[46]

Many people consider the death of a mother a harder loss to sustain than the death of a father. This may be due partly to a mother's traditional status as primary nurturing caregiver. Another reason may be the fact that, statistically, fathers tend to die before mothers. In such cases, the death of a mother represents the loss of having "parents," as the bereaved adult child experiences reactive grief over the death of the other parent as well.

When a family relationship has been dysfunctional, the death of a parent brings to an end the hope of creating a better, more functional relationship. Upon the death of her alcoholic mother, one middle-aged woman lamented, "With her death, dead also is the dream that she would eventually go into treatment and that we would finally heal the wounds our family has suffered. I'm relieved that I can no longer be hurt by her drinking, but I wish it could have turned out differently."

As a general rule, for adults, the death of a parent is likely to evoke less intense grief than, say, the death of a child. This phenomenon is probably related to the fact that an adult child is involved in his or her own life; feelings of attachment to parents have been redirected to some extent toward others, such as spouse and children. Still, marriages can become strained when the person whose parent has died feels that his or her partner is not offering as much emotional support as needed or expected, or does not understand the impact of the loss.[47] Relationships with parents have unique symbolic importance for adult children, and a parent's death can have a long-term impact, as the bereaved child mourns the loss of the special relationship that had existed with the deceased parent.

Spousal Bereavement

The ties between two persons in a paired relationship are usually so closely interwoven that, as Beverly Raphael says, the death of one partner may "cut across the very meaning of the other's existence."[48] We may recognize the

When a man to whom you have been married for more than thirty years dies, a piece of you that you will never know again goes out the door with him. Sitting dry-eyed in a chair watching the rescue-squad men load him onto the stretcher and strap him in, I was mercifully numb. Yes, I said obediently, I would await a call from the coroner; yes, his doctor could be reached at the hospital; yes, I would be all right alone.

And then they were wheeling him out the door, casting uneasy backward glances at me. Thirty years of being us was suddenly transformed into just me.

Elizabeth C. Mooney, *Alone: Surviving as a Widow*

likelihood that one spouse will die before the other and that the survivor will be left to carry on alone, but such thoughts are usually kept in the background. The pressing activities of daily life occupy our attention until one day the possibility becomes a reality that can't be ignored.

The aftermath of a mate's death has been described as follows: "Everyday occurrences underscore the absence of your mate. Sitting down to breakfast, or dinner, opening mail, hearing a special song, going to bed, all become sources of pain when they were formerly sources of pleasure. Each day is full of challenges and heartbreaks."[49] Think of all the sensory stimuli—thermal, olfactory, and tactile—that are associated with an intimate, lifelong relationship.[50] A spouse's death requires an adjustment from being a couple to being single, a transition that is especially hard for the survivor who is also a parent. With children to care for, there is the added burden of single parenthood. As with all other types of bereavement, there is great variability in the way people adapt to the death of a mate. The way a particular person copes with the role of a "newly widowed person" depends on a host of sociocultural, personal, and circumstantial factors.[51]

Factors Influencing Spousal Bereavement

Although the loss of a spouse is the most intensively studied of all loss experiences during adulthood, most research has focused on a brief time span immediately after bereavement; there are few studies of the enduring effects of spousal loss.[52] It is also noteworthy that studies of spousal, or conjugal, bereavement focus on heterosexually paired relationships, mostly ignoring homosexual couples who make a lifelong commitment to each other. Grief following the death of a partner in a same-sex relationship is acknowledged only minimally. Such grief may be exacerbated by conflict with a mate's parents who never made peace with their son's or daughter's life style. "If I was effectively nonexistent to them before," one surviving mate said, "I really vanished after my partner died. For years, they denied our commitment to each other; now they acted as if they could completely erase me! They claimed everything: the body, our home, and, seemingly, my right to grieve." The reality of grief over the loss of a mate is independent of legal or social sanctions about the nature of relationships.

Jack Delano, FSA Collection, Library of Congress

Mr. and Mrs. Andrew Lyman, Polish tobacco farmers living near Windsor Locks, Connecticut, exemplify some of the qualities that contribute to a close relationship. When such a bond is severed by death, the effect is felt in every area of the survivor's life.

The patterns of intimacy and interaction between spouses are an important determinant of how the loss of a partner will be experienced by a survivor. One couple derives primary satisfaction from shared activities; another prefers a higher degree of separateness. In some relationships, the focus is on children; in others, the adult partners take precedence. The patterns of any relationship are in flux as circumstances change over time.

Consider the difference in outlook between a young couple, together only a short time, and an older couple, who have shared their lives over many years. Spousal bereavement in old age typically follows a lifetime of mutual commitment and shared experiences. In contrast, a young couple is just setting out to build a world together. When a partner dies, the survivor is left alone to reconstitute previously shared aims. During the years from youth to old age, a person's standard of living and overall quality of life are also likely to change, thus affecting the meaning and reality of loss.

Although bereaved spouses of all ages report depressive symptoms during the first year of bereavement, younger people seem to experience more physical distress and tend to rely more on drugs to counter this distress than do older people. However, older people may have health problems that were neglected while caring for an ailing spouse. In the first year following the loss of a mate, there are increases in the morbidity and mortality rates of widows and widowers, with aged people particularly at risk. Also, while caring for a dying spouse, the survivor's ties to the outside world may have lessened, thus increasing feelings of loneliness following bereavement.

Relief following the death of a spouse, although little discussed, is an emotion experienced by many people who have cared for an ailing spouse over a long period of time. Death may be viewed as ending further suffering for an ailing loved one. Less socially accepted, or acknowledged, is relief experienced when a mate's death is the welcomed end to an unsatisfactory relationship.

Spousal bereavement also elicits distinct behaviors related to culturally sanctioned gender roles. In one culture, a widower might avoid crying publicly because doing so would be viewed as "weak" and shameful. A widower in another culture, conversely, might express his grief through many tears and loud crying because not doing so would suggest a "weakness" in ability to love.

Individuals who have lived out traditional sex roles may find the transition to widowhood especially hard. Learning to manage unfamiliar role responsibilities in the midst of grief can be a formidable task, intensifying feelings of helplessness. The widow who has never written a check or the widower who has never prepared dinner is confronted not only with grief at losing a loved one, but also with major role readjustments. New skills must be learned to manage the needs of daily life. Widowed persons whose life styles include multiple roles—such as parent; employee; friend; student; hobbyist; or participant in community, political, and religious organizations—seem to experience a better adjustment to bereavement than do those with fewer role involvements.

Adverse effects of spousal death appear to be more prevalent among widowers, perhaps because men with conventional gender roles find it more difficult to manage domestic matters that were once left to the now-deceased spouse. Widowers also may be less likely than widows to seek help from others, again a trait of "self-reliance" that may be associated with a gender role. As Judith Stillion points out, men who care for an ailing partner over an extended period of time may be at a disadvantage in coping with the onset of normal physical and psychological problems of bereavement if "their socialization prohibits them from asking for help, showing strain, or even, in some instances, recognizing and discussing their feelings with helping professionals."[53]

Because women statistically live longer than men, it is estimated that three out of every four married women will be widowed at one time or another. Of the 13.6 million widowed people living in the United States, 11 million are widows.[54] Widows who want to remarry face not only social pressures, but also a situation wherein there are few eligible men. However, it has been suggested that widowhood is less difficult for women than retirement is for men. This is because there are many other widows with whom to share leisure time and activities; thus, a woman's status may increase with widowhood, whereas a man's status usually decreases at retirement.

Social Support for Bereaved Spouses

The death of a mate results in the loss of a primary source of social interactions and alters a person's social role in the community. The availability of a stable social support network is a crucial factor in determining how bereaved spouses adjust to their changed status.[55] A good social support network can be important in adjusting to loss and alleviating disruptions caused by a role change after the death of a spouse.

Maintaining relationships with nonrelatives appears to be especially important because friendships are based on common interests and life styles. Indeed, participation in leisure activities with friends may help widowed people cope with role transitions and maintain a sense of resiliency and positive morale despite difficult life changes.[56] Family relationships, in contrast, may pose a potential psychological threat to the widowed elderly because they contain elements of "role reversal" between the adult child and the aging parent that suggest or demand dependency from the aged widow or widower. Furthermore, an adult child's experience of the loss differs from that of the bereaved spouse, who is likely to value the loss as more significant than does the child and to feel the effects of the loss more intensely with respect to physical and emotional health.[57]

Cultural practices influence the type of support a widowed person may receive. A study of widows in western Nigeria found that difficulty in grieving often occurred when in-laws acted to dispossess the widow and her children of property (under the traditional rule in African societies that a woman has no rights of inheritance in her deceased husband's estate).[58] One observer at an African funeral said, "When a widow cries uncontrollably at her husband's

your hair is falling out,   and
you are not so beautiful:
your eyes have dark shadows
your body is bloated;   arms covered with
        bruises and needlemarks;
legs swollen and useless . . .
                your body and spirit
are weakened with toxic chemicals
urine smells like antibiotics,
                even the sweat
that bathes your whole body
        in the early hours of morning
reeks of dicloxacillin   and methotrexate.

                you are nauseous all the time
i am afraid to move on the bed
for fear of waking you   to moan
and lean over the edge
        vomiting into the bag

        i curl up fetally
                withdraw into my dreams
with a frightened back to you . . .
                and i'm scared
                and i'm hiding
but i love you so much;

burial, she is not crying only for the loss, but for herself, because of the ordeal ahead of her." Indeed, it is a common saying that widowhood should not be wished even for an enemy.

One of the most valuable resources for the recently widowed is contact with peers—that is, other bereaved people who have lost a mate and who can serve as role models during the subsequent period of adjustment. The person acting as role model does not minimize the painful or difficult feelings of grief. Exposed to the helper's accepting attitude, the newly widowed person learns to live with these feelings and gain perspective on them.

The Widowed Persons Service (WPS), whose parent organization is the American Association of Retired Persons (AARP), began implementing a concept of mutual help to widowed individuals in 1973, following on the pioneering work of Phyllis Silverman at Harvard University Medical School.[59] As a one-to-one outreach program of peer support, WPS offers help to newly widowed people by trained volunteers who themselves have been widowed. Individuals who participate in support groups such as those offered by the Widowed Persons Service report that such help is beneficial in helping them work through grief and achieve a positive resolution of the loss.

> this truth does not change . . .
> 　　　　　　　　years ago,
> when i met you, as we were falling in love,
> your beauty attracted me:
> 　　　long, golden-brown hair
> clear and peaceful green eyes
> high cheekbones　　and long smooth muscles
> 　　　but you know—and this is true—
> i fell in love with your soul
> 　　　the real essence of you
> and this cannot grow less beautiful . . .
>
> 　　　　　sometimes　　these days
> even your soul is cloudy
> 　　　i still recognize you
>
> we may be frightened
> 　　　　　be hiding our sorrow
> it may take a little longer
> to acknowledge the truth,
> but i would not want to be　　anywhere else
> 　　　i am here　　with you
> you can grow less beautiful to the world
> 　　you are safe
> 　　　　i will always love you.
>
> Christine Longaker

Death of a Friend

The death of a close friend is a significant loss that evokes grief much the same as would be experienced following the death of a relative.[60] Yet there are few opportunities to openly mourn the death of a friend. Whereas most employers provide at least some type of bereavement leave when death occurs in an employee's family, such leave is unlikely to be provided when a close friend dies, even when the mourner and the deceased have been "best friends" for years. We tend to believe that the most important human relationships are found within families. But friendship involves similar bonds. Because of changes in family structure, social and geographical mobility, and other psychological or cultural factors, friendship ties are increasingly important for many people.

The term "friend" encompasses many different kinds of relationships. Most people have casual friends, close friends, and best friend(s), as well as special-purpose friends such as colleagues, associates, and acquaintances. Many people identify a spouse as their best friend; when death ends the marital relationship, it packs a double whammy because it also means the loss of the surviving partner's best friend. Some friends do not see each other often, but, when they get together, their friendship "picks up where we left off."

What Personnel Handbooks Never Tell You

They leave a lot out of the personnel handbooks.
Dying, for instance.
You can find funeral leave
but you can't find dying.
You can't find what to do
when a guy you've worked with since you both
     were pups
looks you in the eye
and says something about hope and chemotherapy.
No phrases,
no triplicate forms,
no rating systems.
Seminars won't do it
and it's too late for a new policy on sabbaticals.

They don't tell you about eye contact
and how easily it slips away
when a woman who lost a breast
says, "They didn't get it all."
You can find essays on motivation
but the business schools
don't teach what the good manager says
to keep people taking up the slack
while someone steals a little more time
at the hospital.
There's no help from those tapes
you pop into the player
while you drive or jog.
They'd never get the voice right.

And this poem won't help either.
You just have to figure it out for yourself,
and don't ever expect to do it well.

        James A. Autry

For older adults, friendships are sometimes more important than family relationships. For example, despite the fact that many older women live alone, they often say that they are not lonely because of the mutually supportive relationships they have developed and maintained with a circle of friends.[61]

At any age, however, friendships are important to people. When a friend dies, grief should be acknowledged. Even when society tends to disenfranchise such grief, it is nonetheless important to make time to mourn the death of a friend.

BLOOM COUNTY. by Berke Breathed

"Bloom County," drawing by Berke Breathed, © 1984 by Washington Post Writers Group

Aging and the Aged

Aging doesn't begin at fifty, or sixty-five, or eighty-five. At this moment, we are all aging. A person festively celebrating his or her thirtieth or fortieth birthday may find that these milestones of life also bring sobering reflections about the meaning of growing older and the lost opportunities that occur in taking one particular path in life rather than another.[62] Interestingly, the expectations most people have about aging or being old differ from the actual experience. Young adults typically expect problems among older people to be more serious than they actually are for those who experience them. Bernice Neugarten reports that when she first developed a course on Adult Development and Aging "it was generally assumed that you reached a plateau simply called adulthood and you lived on that plateau until you went over the cliff at age sixty-five."[63]

The stereotyped image of an aged person is marked by such outward signs as dry and wrinkled skin, graying hair, baldness, failing eyesight, loss of hearing, stiff joints, and general physical debility. Indeed, the physical signs of *senescence,* or the process of becoming old, are rightly associated with the aging of the human organism. (Senescence can be thought of in terms of vulnerability; the risk that an illness or an injury will prove fatal increases with age.[64]) Many illnesses and disabilities—with accompanying losses in many areas of life—occur most commonly among people in the seventh or eighth decade of life or older. (However, age alone is a poor predictor of outcome for a particular individual.[65]) As we age, we not only experience with increasing frequency the deaths of others, we also come closer to our own death. Some of the reasons given by aged people for preferring death to continued existence are found in Table 11-1.

In developed societies, there is a public health push toward improving the quality of life while "compressing" morbidity and extending "active" life expectancy.[66] Making the period of debilitating illness briefer enables people to stay active until quite near the end of their lives. Indeed, most individuals in modern societies enjoy relatively good health until close to the time of death.

TABLE *11-1*   *Some Reasons Given by Aged People for Accepting Death*

Death is preferable to inactivity.
Death is preferable to the loss of the ability to be useful.
Death is preferable to becoming a burden.
Death is preferable to loss of mental faculties.
Death is preferable to living with progressively deteriorating physical health and concomitant physical discomfort.

Source: Adapted from Victor W. Marshall, *Last Chapters: A Sociology of Aging and Dying* (Monterey, Calif.: Brooks/Cole, 1980), pp. 169–177.

Historically, the family has been a haven for ill and aged relatives, and families continue to provide the major portion of care for these relatives. Some individuals and cultural groups put a high value on keeping an older person within the family unit as opposed to placing him or her in an institutional care setting. However, some aged people require more assistance than relatives or friends can realistically provide. Professional care in a nursing home may be needed to manage symptoms associated with debility in old age. Such care can have a significant impact on families as well as on the older person. In listening to people talk about care of the chronically ill older adult, notice how the need for care may be described in language like this: "She couldn't live by herself so her son took her in" or "He was failing and had to be put in a nursing home." When round-the-clock care is needed, the best outcome ensues when adequate information is gathered before a decision is made about a particular nursing facility (see Table 11-2). Questions about how best to provide appropriate, as well as cost-effective, care for the aged continue to be of public concern.

The changing status of older adults is acknowledged in the National Council on Aging's use of the terms "young-old" for people ages 60 to 75, "middle-old" for those 75 to 85, and "old-old" for those over the age of 85. This last group is the fastest growing segment of the aged population. As a "highly selected" group of survivors, they tend not to match stereotypes of advanced age as a time of fragility and dependency.[67]

TABLE *11-2*   *Steps in Choosing a Nursing Care Facility*

1. Make a list of local facilities offering the type of services needed.
2. Find out whether the facilities are licensed and certified.
3. Visit the facilities.
4. Prepare a checklist of desirable features and evaluate each facility in light of the needs of the person who would be moving in.
5. Determine the costs.
6. Make your decision.

Source: Adapted from Colette Browne and Roberta Onzuka-Anderson, eds., *Our Aging Parents: A Practical Guide to Eldercare* (Honolulu: University of Hawaii Press, 1985), pp. 204–209.

While There Is Time

I carry the folding chair
for my mother
I carry the shawl
the large straw hat
to shield her from the glare
She leans her small weight
on my arm   Frail legs unsteady
feet now cramped with pain

Each day we sit for hours
at the ocean   The sun is hot
but she is wrapped and swathed
her hands are icy cold
they hide their ache
beneath the blanket

Her eyes follow the
movement that surrounds us
the romp of children
flight of gulls
the strong young surfers
challenging the sea

When the visit is ended
when my mother leaves
I will burst from the house
run empty-handed to the beach
hold out my arms
and swoop like a bird
my hands will tag children
as I pass

I will run and run
until I fall
and weep
for the crushed feet
the gnarled fingers
for her longing
I will run for both of us

Maude Meehan

In contrast to their stereotypical image, old people tend to be more individually distinct than any other segment of the population: They have had more years to create unique life histories. Neugarten says, "People are 'open systems,' interacting with the people around them. All their experiences leave traces."[68] Mutual respect, faith, communion with others, and concern with existential issues of life are essential to the well-being of the aged.[69]

As a society, we provide for the physical care of older people through programs like Social Security and Medicare. We appear to be less interested, however, in providing a "place" for the aged in society. The societal wish seems to be only that the old "age gracefully." As Daniel Callahan observes, the impulse to rid ourselves of stereotypes about old age may have the ironic effect of leading us "away from fruitful and valid generalizations about the elderly and fresh efforts to understand the place of old age in the life cycle."[70] While acknowledging individual *differences* among the aged, says Callahan, we should also appreciate the "*shared* features of old age, the features that make it meaningful to talk about the aged as a group and about old age as an inherent part of individual life." In seeking what Callahan terms a "public meaning" of aging, important questions need to be discussed:

1. Aging is often accompanied by "private suffering" caused by physical and psychological losses—how can such suffering become a meaningful and significant part of life?

2. What moral virtues (for example, patience, cultivation of wisdom, courage in the face of change) should properly be associated with preparing for and living old age?
3. What are the characteristic moral and social obligations of the elderly? Is old age a time for devoting one's life to pleasure and well-being, or is it a time for active involvement in the civic life of society?
4. What medical and social entitlements are due to the elderly? If we cannot meet every medical need or pursue every possible line of medical research, how can we arrive at an equitable level of support?

As Callahan suggests, our answers to such questions need to reflect both "what kind of elderly person we want ourselves to be and what ideal character traits we would like to promote and support." In considering one's own future status as an elder, it is worth noting that attempts to meet *all* the "needs" of the elderly must inevitably fail, especially if those needs are defined as the

© Carol A. Foote

Of America's more than 1 million nursing home patients, women outnumber men by about three to one. The majority are white, widowed, and disabled. Few have visitors and only about 20 percent return home; the vast majority will die in the nursing home.

avoidance of disease and frailty. The obvious truth, says Callahan, is that "it will *always* be impossible to meet such needs" despite an implicit social ideology that apparently "seeks to neutralize any inevitability about the process of aging and decline."

The positive images and meanings of growing old are eroded when we regard old age as a pathological state or as an avoidable affliction. In some societies, the aged hold special status as the "elders" of a community. Elderly women in the African-American community, for example, continue to occupy a special place as they continue the oral traditions of passing on cultural meanings to succeeding generations.[71] This kind of respect for elders is also found among Native American peoples.[72]

Growing old is not essentially a "medical problem." Robert Butler says, "None of us knows whether we have already had the best years of our lives or whether the best are yet to come. But the greatest of human possibilities remain to the very end of life—the possibilities for love and feeling, reconciliation and resolution."[73] As the culminating phase of human life, the period of old age or maturity is an appropriate time to focus on the tasks specific to that part of the human journey. Butler says:

> After one has lived a life of meaning, death may lose much of its terror. For what we fear most is not really death but a meaningless and absurd life. I believe most human beings can accept the basic fairness of each generation's taking its turn on the face of the planet if they are not cheated out of the full measure of their turn.[74]

Further Readings

Robert C. DiGiulio. *Beyond Widowhood: From Bereavement to Emergence and Hope.* New York: Free Press, 1989.

Kathleen R. Gilbert and Laura S. Smart. *Coping with Infant or Fetal Loss: The Couple's Healing Process.* New York: Brunner/Mazel, 1992.

Sharon R. Kaufman. *The Ageless Self: Sources of Meaning in Later Life.* Madison: University of Wisconsin Press, 1995.

Dennis Klass. *Parental Grief: Solace and Resolution.* New York: Springer, 1988.

Dennis Klass. *The Spiritual Lives of Bereaved Parents.* Philadelphia: Brunner/Mazel, 1999.

Helena Znaniecka Lopata. *Current Widowhood: Myths and Realities.* Thousand Oaks, Calif.: Sage Publications, 1996.

Therese A. Rando, ed. *Parental Loss of a Child.* Champaign, Ill.: Research Press, 1986.

Paul C. Rosenblatt. *Parent Grief: Narratives of Loss and Relationship.* Philadelphia: Brunner/Mazel, 2000.

Catherine M. Sanders. *Grief, The Mourning After: Dealing with Adult Bereavement.* New York: John Wiley and Sons, 1989.

Jay Sokolovsky, ed. *The Cultural Context of Aging: Worldwide Perspectives.* New York: Bergin & Garvey, 1990.

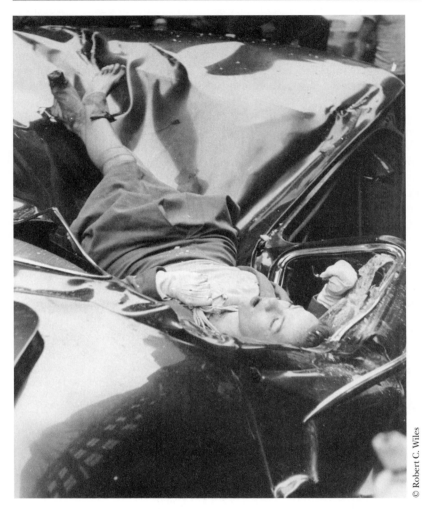

After plummeting eighty-six floors from the observation deck of the Empire State Building—visible in the metallic reflection at lower left—this young woman lies dead, the victim of suicide.

CHAPTER 12

Suicide

Suicide, the intentional taking of one's own life, encompasses a variety of motives and behaviors. Although suicide has been characterized by some as a "disease of civilization," suicide is found in virtually all societies. It is influenced by personality and culture as well as by the unique circumstances of an individual's situation. Judith Stillion observes that "suicide is arguably the most complex and the least understood of all human behaviors, although it has been documented throughout recorded history."[1] Altruistic suicide—that is, a person giving up his or her life for others or for a greater good—has likely existed since human beings first banded together in clans. We can imagine situations in which one individual volunteers to draw the attention of a herd of animals to himself, thereby allowing other members of a hunting party to trap the animals more easily. Although the probability of surviving the onrushing herd was low, the reward for the clan was survival. Nomadic peoples accepted suicide among the elderly or infirm to maintain the mobility needed for the survival of the group. Indeed, honor was given to the person who, recognizing that the end of life was near, willingly left the community for certain death. In much the same way, suicide has been seen as a way of expressing the ultimate commitment to a moral or philosophical principle. The self-inflicted death of Socrates has stood for twenty-four hundred years as a symbol of dying for one's principles.

The contemporary context of suicide is quite different. In modern societies, especially those that have developed out of the Western European tradition, suicide is generally not a socially approved act. Instead, suicide and other forms of self-destructive behavior are seen as involving such factors as depression, low self-esteem, negative life experiences, and chronic physical pain.

Comprehending Suicide

The subject of suicide may be dealt with by forced humor, uneasy laughter, or a way of thinking that distances us from the real threat of mortality. We mask our discomfort at the awesome fact that each of us has the power to choose whether or not we continue to exist. Death is usually conceived of as something that "happens" to an individual. "Why," it is asked, "would someone willingly end his or her own life?"

Most people have at some time in their lives fantasized about the possibility of committing suicide. Such thoughts are not uncommon during childhood and adolescence, and they may crop up from time to time in later life as well. Thoughts like these occur as a kind of "trying out" or "testing" of the notion rather than as a serious consideration of suicidal behavior. In considering what might influence a person to commit suicide, you may find yourself thinking, "There's nothing that could cause me to think seriously about ending my own life." To those who believe they have the resources to deal effectively with the demands of life, suicide seems a radical solution indeed. Yet suicide is a complex human behavior, one involving diverse motives and intentions. Thus, the first step toward understanding suicide must be to develop a working definition that provides a framework for organizing this complexity into manageable form.

In thinking about the reasons why a person would elect to end his or her own life, it soon becomes evident that suicide can be studied on the basis of the apparent cause or purpose of the suicidal act, the individual and cultural meanings attached to suicidal behaviors, and the specific populations affected by suicide. The definitions of suicide given in Table 12-1 can help establish a working definition that is useful for all of these approaches.

Notice that each definition emphasizes certain aspects of suicidal intention and behavior. The basic dictionary definition is a good starting point for understanding suicide, but it is vague. As you review the definitions, pay particular attention to how each explains the dynamics of suicide. Ask yourself: What kinds of human behavior does the definition include? Is suicide a specific act, or is it a behavioral process? What is the context of suicide?

For example, Ronald Maris's definition focuses on the cause or rationale for suicide. French social scientist Jean Baechler's definition emphasizes suicide as a means of resolving problems. Notice that suicide is defined as a behavior rather than as a specific act. Notice also that suicidal behavior may be immediate or long term. Thus, alcohol abuse can be considered as suicidal behavior inasmuch as it reflects the attempt to solve an existential problem by making use of something that, over time, can have fatal consequences. Finally,

T A B L E *12-1* *Four Definitions of Suicide*

Suicide is . . .

The act or an instance of taking one's own life voluntarily and intentionally, especially by a person of years of discretion and of sound mind. (*Webster's New Collegiate Dictionary*)[a]

Self-killing deriving from one's inability or refusal to accept the terms of the human condition. (Ronald W. Maris)[b]

All behavior that seeks and finds the solution to an existential problem by making an attempt on the life of the subject. (Jean Baechler)[c]

The human act of self-inflicted, self-intentioned cessation. (Edwin Shneidman)[d]

---

[a]Used by permission. From *Webster's Ninth New Collegiate Dictionary*, © 1986 by Merriam-Webster Inc. Publishers of the Merriam-Webster® Dictionaries.

[b]Ronald W. Maris, *Pathways to Suicide: A Survey of Self-Destructive Behaviors* (Baltimore: Johns Hopkins University Press, 1981), p. 290.

[c]Jean Baechler, *Suicides* (New York: Basic Books, 1979), p. 11.

[d]Edwin S. Shneidman, ed., *Death: Current Perspectives*, 2d ed. (Mountain View, Calif.: Mayfield, 1980), p. 416.

Edwin Shneidman's definition emphasizes intention and action, along with the concept of ending one's conscious existence. From your perusal of these definitions, you can see that suicide involves the mental intention to cause one's own death as well as actions to carry out that intention.

Statistical Issues

About 30,000 people end their lives by suicide each year in the United States.[2] Although females attempt suicide more frequently than males, males are more likely to die, partly because they generally use more violent methods. About 66 percent of men kill themselves with guns, compared with 40 percent of women. Alcohol abuse, a risk factor for suicide, is also more widespread among men. The suicide rate among whites is twice that of blacks, and white males have the highest suicide rate. Attempted suicides account for about 20 percent of emergency medical admissions in the United States and 10 percent of all medical admissions.[3]

Suicide is commonly viewed as representing failure—on the part of the individual who commits suicide, his or her family and friends, and society as a whole. Open discussion about suicide remains largely taboo. There is general agreement that official counts of suicide understate the actual number of suicides, perhaps by as much as half. A death is unlikely to be classified as a suicide unless the coroner or medical examiner suspects such a possibility due to the deceased's history of suicidal tendencies or acts of self-injury, or because the deceased left a suicide note, or because the circumstances of death so clearly point to suicide.

If the circumstances of a death are equivocal (meaning that the causes are uncertain or unclear) and there is a question about whether the death was a suicide or an accident, it is likely to be classified as accidental. Many automobile accidents, for example, are believed to be suicides in disguise. Some

Richard Cory

Whenever Richard Cory went down town,
　We people on the pavement looked at him:
He was a gentleman from sole to crown,
　Clean favored, and imperially slim.

And he was always quietly arrayed,
　And he was always human when he talked;
But still he fluttered pulses when he said,
　"Good-morning," and he glittered when he walked.

And he was rich—yes, richer than a king—
　And admirably schooled in every grace:
In fine, we thought that he was everything
　To make us wish that we were in his place.

So on we worked, and waited for the light,
　And went without the meat, and cursed the bread;
And Richard Cory, one calm summer night,
　Went home and put a bullet through his head.

Edwin Arlington Robinson

---

authorities believe that if these "autocides" were added to the known statistics, it would make suicide the number one killer of young people.

Victim-precipitated homicide may also mask an individual's suicidal intentions. The homicide victim who deliberately provokes others by flashing a knife or wielding a gun, or by goading others with threats of violence, may be attempting to gain the unwitting help of others in causing his or her own death. Such deaths are rarely included in suicide statistics, however, because victim-precipitated deaths tend to be classified as homicides unless further investigation reveals otherwise. Individuals may create violent situations in which they are likely to be killed, thereby "dying as heroes."[4]

In summarizing the problems in compiling suicide statistics, Edwin Shneidman says, "Because of religious and bureaucratic prejudices, family sensitivity, differences in the proceedings of coroner's hearings and postmortem examinations, and the shadowy distinctions between suicides and accidents—in short, the unwillingness to recognize the act for what it is—knowledge of the extent to which suicide pervades modern society is diminished and distorted."[5]

The Psychological Autopsy

The investigative methods of the psychological autopsy improve the accuracy of death classification, particularly when the cause of death is uncertain and potentially related to suicidal intent. Developed in 1961—primarily by Norman Farberow, Edwin Shneidman, and Robert Litman—the psychological autopsy is an investigative technique used by behavioral scientists in cases of equivocal death.[6] It attempts to recreate the personality and life style of the deceased and the known circumstances of his or her death. Information gathered from interviews, documents, and other materials is used to make a determination concerning the mode of death: natural, accident, suicide, or homicide. With this information in hand, "The historical gestalt that emerges from the data can clarify the most probable mode of death."[7]

Of particular importance is the information pieced together from interviews with the victim's friends and relatives, as well as other members of the community. This involves learning about current and previous stresses, psychiatric and medical histories, and the general life style of the victim, as well as any communication about suicidal intent. The deceased's routine in the days and hours before death is carefully considered as investigators attempt to create a picture of the person's character, personality, and state of mind. Based on an assessment of all the data gathered, a judgment is made about the mode of death (see Table 12-2).

In 1989, an explosion aboard the USS *Iowa*, which killed forty-seven sailors, brought increased public attention to the use of psychological autopsies.[8] Based on an "equivocal death analysis" conducted by the FBI, the U.S. Navy attributed the tragedy to alleged suicidal acts by Gunners Mate Clayton Hartwig, a decision viewed in some quarters as a preemptive strike against wrongful death suits filed against the Navy by families of some of the dead sailors. Because of questions about the investigation, the House Armed Services Committee convened a panel of distinguished psychologists to conduct a peer review of the FBI's report and the Navy's subsequent conclusion. After weighing the evidence, the Committee rejected the Navy's allegation that Hartwig intentionally caused the explosion and characterized its inquiry as an "investigative failure," particularly with respect to the FBI's analysis. Later tests indicated that the blast may have been due to mechanical error, and the Navy recanted its allegations of Hartwig's responsibility; in 1991, the Chief of Naval Operations issued a formal apology to Hartwig's family.

T A B L E   *12-2   Four Purposes of the Psychological Autopsy*

---

1. To help clarify the mode of death: natural, accident, suicide, or homicide (a classification system known by the acronym NASH). Note that *mode* of death differs from *cause* of death. The mode of death may be uncertain while the cause is clear.
2. To determine why a death occurred at a particular time; in other words, to examine the possible connection between the individual's psychology or state of mind and the timing of his or her death.
3. To gain data that may prove useful in predicting suicide and assessing the lethality of the suicidal person, thus helping clinicians and others identify trends in suicidal behavior and high-risk groups.
4. To obtain information that can be of therapeutic value to survivors in resolving emotional turmoil and questions that follow upon a loved one's death by suicide.

Source: Adapted from Thomas J. Young, "Procedures and Problems in Conducting a Psychological Autopsy," *International Journal of Offender Therapy and Comparative Criminology* 36, no. 1 (Spring 1992): 43–52.

TABLE 12-3   *Limitations of the Psychological Autopsy*

1. *Lack of standardized procedures.* Several guidelines for conducting a psychological autopsy have been proposed, but a set of standardized procedures does not exist. Thus, critics question the reliability and validity of psychological autopsies. Proponents, on the other hand, argue that wide latitude is needed to accommodate unique situations.
2. *Retrospective nature.* Examiners are required to offer observations or opinions about a person's past mental state.
3. *Third-party informants may distort representations of the decedent for a variety of reasons.* Everyone who participates in a psychological autopsy has some stake in its outcome. Information from friends or relatives may be biased; public agencies may shape the story to fit certain preconceived parameters.
4. *The individual of interest is not available for examination,* a fact that makes this the greatest limitation of the psychological autopsy.
5. *There are few studies examining the reliability and validity of data obtained by psychological autopsies.*

Source: Adapted from James R. P. Ogloff and Randy K. Otto, "Psychological Autopsy: Clinical and Legal Perspectives," *Saint Louis University Law Journal* 37, no. 3 (Spring 1993): 610–614; and Thomas J. Young, "Procedures and Problems in Conducting a Psychological Autopsy," *International Journal of Offender Therapy and Comparative Criminology* 36, no. 1 (Spring 1992): 47–48.

In commenting about the case, the Committee's psychologists cited several limitations of reconstructive psychological procedures, such as the FBI's equivocal death analysis and psychological autopsies (see Table 12-3). They concluded that such psychological reconstruction should not result in an assertion of "categorical conclusions about the precise mental state or actions suspected of the actor at the time of his or her demise."[9] At present, the judicial system appears to be undecided about the admissibility of psychological autopsies as evidence: Some courts admit them into evidence whereas others exclude them.

The Hartwig case demonstrates that a lack of scientific precision may lead investigators to erroneous conclusions about the data collected through the use of psychological autopsies. However, as proponents of such investigative techniques point out, even *medical* autopsies are not perfect—yet they are viewed as having the potential to clarify circumstances surrounding death.

Despite its limitations, the psychological autopsy has proved to be a useful tool in assessing risk factors for suicide. It has been especially helpful in increasing the understanding of factors that place young people at risk.[10] As both an investigative approach and a research tool, the psychological autopsy deepens our understanding of suicide and suicidal behavior.

Explanatory Theories of Suicide

The study of suicide has mainly followed two lines of theoretical investigation: (1) the sociological model, which has its foundation in the work of nineteenth-century French sociologist Emile Durkheim; and (2) the psychological model, based on the work of Viennese psychoanalyst Sigmund Freud. Contemporary scholars usually seek an integrated approach to understanding suicide, one that combines sociological and psychological insights (see Figure 12-1).

The Social Context of Suicide

The sociological model, as its name implies, focuses on the relationship between the individual and society. Individual behavior is considered in its social setting and within the context of group dynamics. According to Durkheim, these social forces are manifested in the degree of regulation and integration present in a given society.[11]

Degree of Social Regulation

When a society is loosely regulated, individuals experience a sense of chaos and confusion, as well as a loss of traditional values and social mores. Rules, customs, and traditions cannot be relied on as a definitive guide to behavior. Such circumstances are characterized by *anomie* (meaning "lawlessness"). Individuals experience anxiety, disorientation, isolation, and loneliness. When there is insufficient social regulation, *anomic* suicides result. The classic example of this phenomenon occurs in societies that are losing their traditional moorings under the pressures of rapid modernization. The sense of identity with the social group may be shaken, leaving individuals feeling confused and anxious. Among the Aboriginal people of Australia, for example, the rapid pace of social change relative to their traditional life style has been accompanied by signs of behavioral distress, including suicide.[12]

Sudden trauma or catastrophe can also shatter the relationship between an individual and society. The loss of a job, the amputation of a limb, the death of a close friend or family member—any of these losses can be an anomic event. Indeed, any disruptive change—whether it is perceived as positive or negative—can precipitate a state of anomie. Sudden wealth may lead to suicidal behavior if the person is unable to cope with his or her changed status.

At the other extreme of regulation we find a society characterized by repressive constraints. Lack of freedom and absence of choice produce what Durkheim termed *fatalistic* suicide. The inability to openly express one's individuality leads to a sense of fatalism, a feeling that one has nowhere to turn. The high rate of suicides in jails is due at least partly to the rigid regulation found in such environments.

Degree of Social Integration

Turning to the effect of social integration, at one end we find situations in which the individual feels alienated, separate from the significant institutions and traditions in his or her society. In this instance, the person is not integrated into society but is instead dependent on his or her own resources and devices. Durkheim termed suicides in this type of social environment *egoistic*. An individual's mental energies are concentrated on the self to such an extent that social sanctions against suicide are ineffective. People who are disenfranchised or who live at the fringes of society may feel no compulsion to heed

> Thurs July 10
> 1·35PM
>
> My Darling Wife.
>
>   This afternoon I am going to make a 3rd attempt at bringing my turbulent life to an end. I hope that it is successful.
>
>   I dont know what I want from this world of ours, but you see I am due to go soon anyway. My Mother died at 60 ish as did her brothers and father. Also Alf has gone now.
>
>   Please dont get Margaret to come over here. – but you go as planned It will do you good. Put the Bungalow on the market and have a sale of the chattels. Then buy a smaller one.
>
>   The field will have vacant pos in Nov if you want to sell that
>
>   The wills are in the safe.
>
> My love to you, Margaret, Michael and Janice.
>
>   I love you all & you have been so good to me
>
>   Tommy
>
>   X.X.X.X.X.
>   XX.X.X.X.X.
>
> Dial Police   999
> Also Bill   891459.
>
>
> IT IS NOW 2.00 PM
>   TOMMY xx.

Figure 12-1 *Suicide Note and Report of Death*
Even when a newspaper account is as detailed as this British report (*facing page*), the facts of suicide as described in the newspaper may reveal very little of the intense human factors—the personal and social dynamics—that precipitated the suicidal act.

Retired man's suicide

A HYTHE man aged 64 killed himself because he could not stand old age, an inquest heard yesterday.

Retired maintenance engineer Aubrey Heathfield Aylmore, who lived at Forest Front, Hythe, was found dead in his car by his wife.

The inquest heard that Mrs. Heathfield Aylmore had been to a WI meeting and returned home an hour later than planned.

She found her husband's body in the garage with a length of hose pipe running from the exhaust into the car.

A note was found in which Mr. Heathfield Aylmore said that this was his third suicide attempt and that he wanted to "put an end to my turbulent life."

Dr. Richard Goodbody, consultant pathologist, said cause of death was asphyxia due to carbon monoxide poisoning.

Coroner Mr. Harry Roe said that Mr. Heathfield Aylmore had been depressed at the thought of growing old.

life-affirming values because they do not experience themselves as meaningfully related to the wider community. In this sense, anomie (lack of regulation) and egoism (lack of integration) reinforce each other. In Durkheim's view, when a person is detached from social life, individual personality takes precedence over collective personality. Thus, egoistic suicide is "the special type of suicide springing from excessive individualism."[13]

Conversely, in the case of *altruistic* or institutional suicide, excessive identification with the values or causes of society produces such a strong sense of integration with the social group that the individual loses his or her own personal identity. The group's values predominate over the individual's.

In feudal Japanese society, when samurai warriors sacrificed their lives to maintain the honor or reputation of their lords, their suicide was viewed as heroic. Ritual disembowelment, called *seppuku* or *hara-kiri,* was culturally accepted, and expected, in certain circumstances. *Seppuku* might have been the only socially acceptable choice if one were disgraced in battle. *Seppuku* was also used to show devotion to a superior, frequently being enacted by a samurai on the death of his lord. *Seppuku* could also be an honorable way for a samurai to make a public statement of disagreement with a superior. In traditional Japan, ritual suicide was considered an honorable act, and it was accompanied by a particular etiquette.[14] In the Durkheimian perspective, a highly integrated society like Japan encourages altruistic and fatalistic suicide.[15]

Similarly, until modern times, certain castes in India were expected to practice *suttee,* which called for the wife to throw herself upon her husband's

Malcolm Brown, AP/Wide World Photos

Flames engulf the body of a Buddhist monk, Quang Duc, whose self-immolation before thousands of onlookers in downtown Saigon was a protest against alleged persecution of Buddhists by the government of South Vietnam.

cremation pyre. Such self-immolation was condoned by the prevailing religious and cultural beliefs. A widow's reluctance to enact such ritual suicide was met with social disapproval. Indeed, a reluctant widow might be "helped" onto the burning pyre.

To these well-known examples of *seppuku* and *suttee* could be added the deaths of kamikaze pilots in Japan's air attack corps during World War II and the example of the dedicated captain who goes down with the ship. In these examples, suicide is "the self-destruction demanded by a society . . . as a price for being a member of that society."[16] As with the samurai warriors in feudal Japan who committed *seppuku* to express disagreement, suicide as protest came to public attention during the Vietnam War, when Buddhist monks died by self-immolation to protest governmental policies.

Mass suicide usually takes place within social dynamics that characterize altruistic suicide. On November 20, 1978, in Jonestown, Guyana, more than 900 persons met their death in what is considered the largest mass suicide in history.[17] At a previously little-noticed jungle clearing, which had been the communal settlement of the followers of the Reverend Jim Jones, many of the

For more than 900 Americans who left their home to join a religious fanatic called the Reverend Jim Jones, death came in the jungles of Guyana with these comforting words from the man who engineered the largest mass suicide the world has witnessed:

> What's going to happen here in a matter of a few minutes is that one of those people in the plane is going to shoot the pilot. . . . So you be kind to the children and be kind to seniors, and take the potion like they used to in Ancient Greece, and step over quietly, because we are not committing suicide—it's a revolutionary act.
>
> Everybody dies. I haven't seen anybody yet didn't die. And I like to choose my own kind of death for a change. I'm tired of being tormented to hell. Tired of it. (Applause)

A few cultists protested. Some women screamed. Children cried. Armed guards took up positions around the camp to keep anyone from escaping:

> Let the little children in and reassure them. . . . They're not crying from pain, it's just a little bitter-tasting. . . . Death is a million times more preferable to spend more days in this life. If you knew what was ahead of you, you'd be glad to be stepping over to-night . . . quickly, quickly, no more pain. . . . This world was not your home. . . .

Here the tape runs out. The sound stops before the report of the pistol that killed Jim Jones, presumably fired by his own hand.

Robert Ramsey and Randall Toye, *The Goodbye Book*

victims drank cyanide-laced fruit punch, and families died together in one another's arms. In hypnotic tones, from his throne above the crowd, Jones urged community members to drink the poison. The customs of the social group influenced the individual's decision to commit suicide. The same phenomenon can be seen in the more recent suicides of the "Heaven's Gate" group in Rancho Santa Fe, California.

From the social perspective, then, suicide is seen to be the result of a disturbance in the ties between the individual and society. When there is imbalance or upset with respect to this relationship, the potential for suicide is heightened. Each form of suicide—anomic, fatalistic, egoistic, altruistic—is related to a particular kind of interplay between society and the individual.

The Psychodynamics of Suicide

Drawing on theories proposed by Sigmund Freud, the psychodynamic model of suicide focuses on an individual's mental and emotional life. This model incorporates both affective and cognitive components, and it encompasses conscious as well as unconscious motives.[18] It assumes that a person's behavior is determined by both past experience and current reality. Unlike the Durkheimian view, which seeks an explanation for suicide in external events, the psychodynamic model focuses on the processes occurring within the mind or personality of the individual.

Among the insights developed from the psychological model of suicide are the following:

1. The *acute* suicidal crisis is of relatively brief duration; that is, it lasts hours or days rather than weeks or months—though it may recur.
2. The suicidal person is likely to be *ambivalent* about ending his or her life. Plans for self-destruction are generally accompanied by fantasies that rescue or intervention will occur before the fatal act is completed.
3. Most suicidal events are *dyadic*: They involve both the victim and a significant other in some way.

The psychodynamics of suicide can be understood more completely by looking in greater detail at two of its aspects: aggression and ambivalence.

Aggression

According to the psychodynamic model, suicide involves strong, unconscious hostility combined with a lack of capacity to love others. Under conditions of enormous stress, the intrapsychic pressures impelling a person toward self-destruction increase to the point that they overwhelm the defense mechanisms of the ego, or self. This results in regression to more primitive ego states, which involve powerful forces of aggression. Whereas murder is aggression turned upon another, suicide is aggression turned upon oneself. That is, suicide is murder in the 180th degree.

Ambivalence

Even with the aggressive forces mobilized, however, the urge toward self-preservation works against the self's acquiescence in its own death. Thus, another psychodynamic process comes into play: *ambivalence*. Analysis of suicidal behavior often reveals conflicting forces that compete for the greater share of the person's mental energies. At issue is the will to live versus the will to die. Erwin Stengel says, "Most people who commit acts of self-damage with more or less conscious self-destructive intent do not want either to live or to die, but to do both at the same time."[19]

Ambivalence, as it applies to suicidal behavior, can be considered in several ways. First, the person contemplating suicide is likely to harbor simultaneously a wish to live and a wish to die. The balance between these opposing polarities may be delicate, with an otherwise minor incident tipping the scales

---

 ### Suicide Note Written by a Divorced Woman, Age 61

You cops will want to know why I did it, well just let us say that I lived 61 years too many.

People have always put obstacles in my way. One of the great ones is leaving this world when you want to and have nothing to live for.

I am not insane. My mind was never more clear. It has been a long day. The motor got so hot it would not run so I just had to sit here and wait. The breaks were against me to the very last.

The sun is leaving the hill now so hope nothing else happens.

Suicide Note Written by a Married Man, Age 45

My darling,

May her guts rot in hell—I loved her so much.

Henry

one way or the other. Ambivalence also refers to situations in which, although one of these forces is stronger than the other, the weaker one nevertheless continues to affect the person's behavior. Stengel says, "Most suicidal acts are manifestations of risk-taking behavior. They are gambles. The danger to life depends on the relationships between self-destructive and life-preserving, contact seeking tendencies, and on a variety of other factors, some of which are outside the control of the individual."

Toward an Integrated Understanding of Suicide

Each of the two major theories of suicide contributes to increased understanding of suicidal behavior. Although each model has its roots in a particular methodology, current theories of suicide draw upon both to form a comprehensive understanding. Consider how a disrupted or disturbed home environment (the social context) might be conjoined with feelings of abandonment, low self-esteem, and ambivalence about the future (psychodynamics), so that the two explanations, social and psychodynamic, interact in an integrated fashion.

These explanations are crucial to a comprehensive understanding of suicide and suicidal behavior. Yet we must be careful about overanalyzing so much that we fail to see the forest for the trees. After a lifetime studying suicide, Edwin Shneidman distilled his learning into five words: *Suicide is caused by psychache.*[20] In using the term *psychache,* Shneidman refers to intolerable and unbearable pain related to blocked needs, of whatever kind. Suicide is the act of reducing the tension of this pain. In adopting this perspective on suicide, we do not lose sight of the fact that suicidal events are multidimensional and multifaceted; and that they have concomitant biological, sociological, psychological, epidemiological, and philosophical elements. But, in Shneidman's view, the key element is the pain of psychache. Remedying a person's suicidal state involves identifying and ameliorating the "vital frustrated needs" that are causing psychache. Suicidal gestures and attempts represent communications about the intensity of experienced despair.

Shneidman's template for understanding the key element in suicide and suicidal behavior should be kept in mind as you read through the topics discussed in this chapter. All of these topics—suicide types, risk factors, lifespan perspectives, orders of lethality, and so on—are necessary for developing a comprehensive understanding of suicide. Yet, in the end, our attention must rest on the person who is hurting.

T A B L E *12-4*   *Meanings of Suicide*

Some Cultural Meanings of Suicide

Suicide is sinful: A crime against nature, a revolt against the preordained order of the universe.

Suicide is criminal: It violates the ties that exist, the social contract between persons in a society.

Suicide is weakness or madness: It reflects limitations or deviancy ("He must have been crazy" or "He couldn't take it").

Suicide is the Great Death, as in *seppuku, suttee,* and other culturally approved forms of ritual suicide.

Suicide is the rational alternative: The outcome of a "balance-sheet" approach that sizes up the situation and determines the best option.

Some Individual Meanings of Suicide

Suicide is reunion with a lost loved one, a way to "join the deceased."

Suicide is rest and refuge: A way out of a burdensome and depressing situation.

Suicide is getting back: A way of expressing resentment and revenge at being rejected or hurt.

Suicide is the penalty for failure: A response to disappointment and frustration at not meeting self-expectations or the expectations of others.

Suicide is a mistake: The attempt was made as a cry for help and was not intended to be fatal, but there was no rescue or intervention and the outcome was death.

Source: Adapted from Robert Kastenbaum, *Death, Society, and Human Experience,* 2d ed. (St. Louis, Mo.: C. V. Mosby, 1981), pp. 239–255.

Some Types of Suicide

Many classification schemes have been applied to suicide in attempts to better comprehend its personal and social meanings (see Table 12-4). In this section, to provide a more complete picture of self-destructive behavior, we examine more closely some of the "types" of suicide.

Suicide As Escape

Suicide is often seen as a means of escape or release from some physical pain or mental anguish. For example, a person with a painful or terminal illness may perceive suicide as a way out of suffering.[21] Ending one's life in such a circumstance is sometimes termed "rational suicide" because the reasoning used—death will bring release from pain—conforms to normal logic. This type of suicide, which is also termed "euthanasia," may be regarded as a benevolent act, one stemming from a decision made by the patient and perhaps enacted with the consent of loved ones. The impact of AIDS has brought renewed attention to the question of rational suicide as a response to life-threatening illness.[22]

Other forms of seeking escape through suicide result from a destructive logic. In these cases, the victim's self-concept or sense of identity is confused. When this confusion is coupled with problems in relating to others, it can lead to the victim's self-perception as a failure. Suicides of this type are sometimes termed "referred," bringing to mind the analogy of physical pain that is experienced at some distance from its source. An inflammation of the liver may be experienced as pain in the shoulder. Just as this physical phenomenon is characterized as referred pain, so the root causes of referred suicide are likewise only indirectly related to the end result—namely, suicide. The decision to end one's life is not based on a dispassionate assessment of the situation, but instead results from an overwhelming sense of anguish and confusion about one's options.

Not performing up to expectations or according to certain role definitions may provoke a crisis of self-concept that ultimately leads to the desire to escape the unsatisfactory situation. Expectations may be related to something outside the individual ("If I can't be a good enough daughter to please my parents, I give up!"), or they may be related to inward feelings of frustration ("Everybody thinks I'm doing okay, but I feel rotten").

The desire to escape may arise from the loss of meaning in one's life. Despite significant accomplishments, a person may come to feel, "Now what?" The accumulation of successes one after another may seem a Sisyphean effort, a continual struggle for achievement without a corresponding sense of accomplishment. Like Alexander the Great, after "conquering the world," there seems nothing more to strive for, no reason to live. Conversely, success may be accompanied by feelings of ennui—"If this is what success is all about, it's not worth the effort." Stress, competition, aggressiveness, and inability to balance conflicting demands can be overwhelming. The causal chain begins with events that fall short of standards and expectations.[23] A sense of inadequacy and failure makes self-awareness painful, and the individual seeks to escape from this negative sense of self. Drastic measures seem acceptable, with suicide becoming the ultimate step in the effort to find release.

Psychotic Suicide and Depression

Psychotic suicide is associated with the impaired logic of a delusional state of mind related to clinically diagnosed schizophrenia or manic-depressive psychosis. There is no conscious intention to die, but the victim wishes to eradicate the psychic malignancy or punish himself or herself by self-destruction. Treatment of the suicidal impulses requires that one first treat the psychosis.

Depression is a major risk factor for suicide. People who are depressed may act out their depression in harmful, disruptive, or illegal ways, often involving alcohol or drug abuse. Major depression is a syndrome that can be triggered by a wide variety of physical and psychosocial factors, and it is a suicide warning sign that should not be ignored.[24] Family members or friends often do not realize the depth of an individual's depression or do not wish to admit to its seriousness. Differences in family patterns of responding to a person's depression may help explain why some depressed people attempt suicide while most do not.[25] The key aspect of depression in relation to suicide is the sense of *hopelessness*.

Subintentional and Chronic Suicide

As defined by Edwin Shneidman, a subintentional death is "one in which the person plays some partial, covert, subliminal, or unconscious role in

Suicide Note Written by a Single Man, Age 51

Sunday 4:45 PM   Here goes

To who it may concern

Though I am about to kick the bucket I am as happy as ever. I am tired of this life so am going over to see the other side.

Good luck to all.

Benjamin P.

hastening his own demise."[26] Some fatalities reported as accidents result from the victim's choosing to take unnecessary and unwise risks. Such behavior might be called careless or imprudent. A deeper probing into causes, however, shows that accidents are sometimes the end result of a self-destructive pattern of behavior. Similarly, homicide investigations sometimes turn up evidence that points to subintentional factors that result in a victim's behaving in ways that provoke his or her death at another's hands.

Besides subintentioned death, Shneidman delineates two other patterns of death-related behaviors: intentioned and unintentioned. Table 12-5 presents an outline of these three patterns. Notice that within each of these categories a person might exhibit a variety of attitudes and behaviors regarding death. As you review this table, ask yourself: Where do I stand on this list? What does that say about my own regard for life and death?

The term *chronic suicide,* coined by Karl Menninger, refers to individuals who choose to destroy themselves by means of drugs, alcohol, smoking, reckless living, and the like. This type of suicide is also termed "characterological suicide." These individuals may consciously find the idea of suicide repugnant or unacceptable, but an analysis of their life styles typically reveals the presence of a "death wish."[27]

Cry for Help

Considered as a *cry for help,* suicide aims to force a change. The suicidal person's situation is such that he or she no longer wishes to continue living in it. Generally, the goal is not death but the elimination of some problem; suicide is perceived as a means of accomplishing that goal. Thus, suicidal behavior is a message to the effect that "something has to change in my life; I can't go on living this way." Much suicidal behavior among young people is of this type. Cutting one's wrist or taking a drug overdose may be done to express frustration or gain attention, with the inherent danger of the act not fully recognized or admitted to oneself. Whatever the motive, the outcome can be deadly.

The "cry for help" is associated with persons who threaten or attempt suicide as opposed to those who actually kill themselves. There is often no

TABLE *12-5* *Patterns of Death-Related Behavior and Attitudes*

Intentioned Death: Death resulting from the suicide's direct, conscious behavior to bring it about. A variety of attitudes or motives may be operative:

The *death seeker* wishes to end consciousness and commits the suicidal act in such a way that rescue is unlikely.

The *death initiator* expects to die in the near future and wants to choose the time and circumstances of death.

The *death ignorer* believes that death ends only physical existence and that the person continues to exist in another manner.

The *death darer* gambles with death, or, as Shneidman says, "bets his life on a relatively low objective probability that he will survive" (such as by playing Russian roulette).

Subintentioned Death: Death resulting from a person's patterns of management or style of living, although death was not the conscious, direct aim of the person's actions:

The *death chancer,* although in many ways like the death darer, may want higher odds of survival.

The *death hastener* may expedite his or her death by substance abuse (drugs, alcohol, and the like) or by failing to safeguard well-being (for example, by inadequate nutrition or precautions against disease or disregard of available treatments).

The *death facilitator* gives little resistance to death, making it easy for death to occur, as in the deaths of patients whose energies, or "will to live," are low because of their illness.

The *death capitulator* is one who, usually out of a great fear of death, plays a subintentional role in his or her own death, as may a person upon whom a so-called voodoo death has been put, or as may a person who believes that someone admitted to a hospital is bound to die.

The *death experimenter* does not consciously wish to die, but lives on the brink, usually in a "befogged state of consciousness" that may be related to taking drugs in such ways that the person may become comatose or even die with little concern.

Unintentioned Death: Death in which the decedent plays no significant causative role. However, various attitudes toward death may shape the experience of dying:

The *death welcomer,* though not hastening death, looks forward to it (as might an aged person who feels unable to manage adequately or satisfactorily).

The *death accepter* is resigned to his or her fate; the style of acceptance may be passive, philosophical, resigned, heroic, realistic, or mature.

The *death postponer* hopes to put death off for as long as possible.

The *death disdainer* feels, in Shneidman's words, "above any involvement in the stopping of the vital processes."

The *death fearer* is fearful, and possibly phobic, about anything related to death; death is something to be fought and hated.

The *death feigner* pretends to be in mortal danger or pretends to perform a suicidal act without being in actual danger, possibly in an attempt to gain attention or to manipulate others.

Source: Adapted from Edwin S. Shneidman, *Deaths of Man* (New York: Quadrangle Books, 1973), pp. 82–90.

history of suicidal behavior, and the lethality of the attempt is generally low. The aim of the behavior is to communicate to significant others how desperate or unhappy the person feels. A suicide attempt says, in effect: "I am deadly serious, and you'd better pay attention!" This message may be directed inwardly to oneself as well as outwardly to others.

When low-lethality suicidal behavior is met with defensive hostility or with attempts to minimize its seriousness, the suicide risk increases, along with the possibility that the next attempt will be lethal. In responding to the cry for help, it is important to recognize that a problem exists and take steps toward increasing communication and proposing remedies.

It is useful to make a distinction between *attempted* suicide and the *fait accompli*. According to Glen Evans and Norman Farberow, attempted suicide "refers to behavior directed against the self which results in injury or self-harm, or has strong potential for injury. Intention in the behavior may or may not be to die, or may or may not be to inflict injury or pain on oneself."[28] There may be two fairly distinct populations of individuals who engage in suicidal behavior: (1) *attempters* (who tend toward repeated, but not lethal, attempts) and (2) *completers* (whose first attempt typically results in death). In this view, attempters and completers may have quite different aims with regard to their suicidal acts.[29] Indeed, the suggestion has been made that the study of suicide should focus on attempted suicide as the norm, while viewing completed suicide as a failed behavior in which the individual inappropriately died.[30]

It should never be assumed that a suicide attempt was meant only as a gesture, a cry for help. Suicidal behavior is life-threatening. Psychological autopsies of some suicide victims indicate that they thought the attempt would be stopped short of death, but help did not arrive in time.

Attempted suicides outnumber completed suicides by a significant margin. For the population as a whole, it is estimated that, for every eight suicide attempts, one is lethal. In all age groups above age fourteen, females *attempt* suicide more often than do males, while males *kill themselves* more often than do females.[31] (Among children younger than age fourteen, males both attempt and complete suicide more often than do females.) This gender difference may be explained partly by the methods used, with males using more lethal methods. Females tend to take pills or slash wrists; males tend to use less equivocal means, such as guns. Perhaps males consider a failed attempt to be cowardly or unmasculine and thus make a special effort to be successful. In addition to the "suicidal success syndrome" that afflicts males, there is evidence that males are less likely than females to report suicidal thoughts or seek help (such as from crisis intervention centers). By hiding feelings of depression or hopelessness, males hinder efforts at intervention.

Some people who survive a suicide attempt look on their continued existence as a second chance or "bonus life." If this opportunity is used well, the individual may discover himself or herself anew and find a way to transcend the pain that led to the attempt.[32] When this is done, the suicide attempt becomes an opportunity for growth. By altering the mindset and

---

 Suicide Note Written by a Married Man, Age 74

What is a few short years to live in hell. That is all I get around here.

No more I will pay the bills.

No more I will drive the car.

No more I will wash, iron, & mend any clothes.

No more I will have to eat the leftover articles that was cooked the day before.

This is no way to live.

Either is it any way to die.

Her grub I can not eat.

At night I can not sleep.

I married the wrong nag-nag-nag and I lost my life.

W.S.

To the undertaker

We have got plenty money to give me a decent burial. Don't let my wife kid you by saying she has not got any money.

Give this note to the cops.

Give me liberty or give me death.

W.S.

---

circumstances that nearly resulted in death, the person can begin the process of healing.

Risk Factors Influencing Suicide

Another way to increase our understanding of suicide involves examining the risk factors that influence suicidal behaviors. Generally speaking, these risk factors encompass four broad areas: culture, personality, the individual situation, and biological factors. These risk factors typically are found to overlap to varying degrees in particular instances of suicidal behavior.

Culture

Cultural messages about the acceptability of various suicidal behaviors influence the kinds of behavior engaged in by members of a social group. For example, in American society, suicide intended to end physical suffering related to terminal disease appears to be more acceptable than suicide related o escaping the mental pain of other life problems.[33]

Cultural disruption and associated stress appear to play a part in the prevalence of suicide among Native Americans.[34] Forced onto reservations, their cultures undermined, the native peoples of North America have undergone severe dislocations. Conflicts between the traditional ways and the ways of contemporary white society can lead to feelings of powerlessness and anxiety. An added burden is experienced by those Native Americans who live in large cities, where support systems, such as family ties and traditional customs, are lacking. These stresses, sometimes combined with dysfunctional behaviors such as alcohol and drug abuse, can make suicide seem the only way out.

Kathleen Erwin has examined the social factors that influence gay and lesbian suicide.[35] A relatively high rate of psychological distress and suicide among homosexual populations has long been recognized, although explanations have been sought mostly in theories centering on individual psychology. More recently, however, the antecedents of gay and lesbian suicide have been located in terms of a sociocultural model focusing on the impact of social forces that have historically been intolerant and oppressive with respect to homosexuals. Thus, the focus on individual psychology is being balanced by the recognition that social factors are important, if not crucial, in the incidence of homosexual suicide.

Within African-American communities, many young people consider suicide a weak, cowardly way out of their problems, a view that is also held by many of their elders. The rate of suicide among African Americans is lower than among white Americans, a phenomenon due at least partly to a common perception among African Americans that suicide is a "white thing." In their study of attitudes toward suicide expressed by African Americans, Kevin Early and Ronald Akers observed that religion and family play important roles in "buffering" social forces that might otherwise promote suicide among African Americans. Early and Akers found that suicide is typically viewed as "inherently contradictory to the black experience and a complete denial of black identity and culture."[36]

The acceptability of violence as a solution to problems is another cultural factor that increases suicide risk. The availability of lethal weapons as well as the prevalence of violence in the media contribute to a sense that violence is an acceptable alternative when the going gets rough. Easy access to guns is an important factor in suicide among children and young adults. Dr. Alex Crosby of the U.S. Centers for Disease Control (CDC) notes that children and adolescents are increasingly using guns to end their lives instead of methods that might fail. According to the CDC, among persons under age 25 who kill themselves, more than half do so with a gun.[37] The apparent acceptance of violence in our lives can change posturing into deadly deeds.[38]

The idea that suicide is contagious has a long history. Following the publication of Johann Wolfgang von Goethe's *The Sorrows of Young Werther* in 1774, an epidemic of suicide among young people was attributed to the book's influence. The influence of "suggestion" on suicidal behavior has been termed the "Werther effect." The question of whether such an imitative effect actually exists in suicidal behavior remains controversial.[39] What is clear is the fact that the social environment does exert a significant influence on the incidence of suicide.

Cultural factors relative to suicide are highlighted in what Brian Barry calls "the balance between pro-life and pro-death forces operating at any given time."[40] Pro-life forces include (1) the belief that problems can promote growth, (2) a perceived ability to solve life problems, (3) a willingness to struggle and suffer if necessary, and (4) a healthy fear of death and its aftermath. In contrast, pro-death forces include (1) the belief that problems are intolerable, (2) a perception that life problems are intractable or unyielding, (3) a sense of entitlement to a rewarding life, and (4) a philosophical stance that sees suicide as a means of obtaining relief. In Barry's view, people in modern societies have accepted two fundamental assumptions about life that no previous generation has embraced so thoroughly: first, the belief that we deserve significant fulfillment in our jobs, marriages, and overall lives; and second, the belief that, rather than accepting unalterable circumstances, we must live and die on our own terms. We not only aspire to a good life, but we have convinced ourselves that we are entitled to it. When this sense of entitlement is not actualized to our satisfaction, we feel that it's appropriate to remove ourselves from the intolerable situation. An emphasis on individual freedom includes the freedom to make costly choices, even when the outcome is death.

Personality

Some people have a "basic optimism," whereas others have a "basic pessimism"—a phenomenon that can be a deciding factor in some suicides.[41] The way people relate to others, as well as how they relate to their own problems in life, influences the onset of suicidal thoughts.

The way in which individuals relate to fears of death may influence suicidal behavior. In nonsuicidal individuals, fear of death inhibits suicidal behavior; suicidal individuals, in contrast, tend to perceive death as "an attractive state and as a continuation of life under improved conditions in which long-standing wishes may come true."[42] The psychic maneuver of reducing the fear of death appears to facilitate suicidal behavior. Thus, the meanings attributed to death influence the way individuals experience and evaluate the possibility of suicide.

An individual's fascination with the "mystique" of death, especially self-willed death, may increase suicide risk. Some suicidal behaviors appear to be related to a "poetic" or "romantic" attraction to death. Following the example of Thomas Chatterton, who killed himself in 1770 at the age of 17, the Romantics thought of death as "the great inspirer" and "great consoler." Death may be seen as a lover to be courted. The poet Sylvia Plath wrote: "I will marry dark death, the thief of the daytime."[43] Do the suicides of such writers as Ernest Hemingway, Anne Sexton, Plath herself, and, more recently, musician Kurt Cobain, reflect a conscious desire to embrace the mystery of death? Or are they the result of commonplace human experiences? Failure to find meaning in life and relationship problems are common threads.[44] As someone said: "The death of love evokes the love of death." Low self-esteem; difficulties with intimate relationships; lack of coping skills; hopelessness; and feelings of stagnation, loneliness, and despair are among the personality factors that contribute to suicidal thoughts and behaviors.

The Individual Situation

The intersection of culture and personality creates a unique situation experienced by a particular individual. Every person is subject to a constellation of environmental factors that involve varying degrees of suicide risk. These include the social forces existing within society as a whole, as well as the particular characteristics associated with an individual's family, economic situation, and so on.

Stressful life events are associated with suicidal behaviors.[45] For example, individuals who have been bereaved as a result of suicide may be vulnerable to an increased risk of committing suicide themselves.[46] In *crisis suicide,* the typical pattern is that of an adolescent who experiences traumatic change in his or her life, such as the loss of a loved one or the threatened loss of status in school. In a study of Korean adolescents, academic stress was associated with suicidal behaviors.[47]

The influence of peers can also affect an individual's suicide risk, especially among adolescents and young adults. A study of suicide among Micronesian males confirmed the occurrence of an "epidemic-like" increase during a twenty-year period.[48] This period was marked by rapid sociocultural transformation, as traditional styles of living gave way to reliance on a capitalist economy and modern forms of education, employment, health services, and technology. Investigators found links among the suicides, with several occurring among a small circle of friends over several months. There were also cases of self-destructive behavior in reaction to the suicide of a friend or relative, as well as "suicide pacts" between two or more people. Taken together, these phenomena pointed to the existence of a "suicide subculture" wherein suicide begat suicide. In an environment characterized by a general familiarity with and acceptance of the *idea* of suicide, suicide had become a culturally patterned and partly collective response to personal dilemmas and problems.

Romeo and Juliet also embody another popular misconception: that of the great suicidal passion. It seems that those who die for love usually do so by mistake and ill-luck. It is said that the London police can always distinguish, among the corpses fished out of the Thames, between those who have drowned themselves because of unhappy love affairs and those drowned for debt. The fingers of the lovers are almost invariably lacerated by their attempts to save themselves by clinging to the piers of the bridges. In contrast, the debtors apparently go down like slabs of concrete, apparently without struggle and without afterthought.

A. Alvarez, *The Savage God*

Suicide Note Written by a Married Man, Age 45

Dear Claudia,

You win, I can't take it any longer. I know you have been waiting for this to happen. I hope it makes you very happy, this is not an easy thing to do, but I've got to the point where there is nothing to live for, a little bit of kindness from you would of made everything so different, but all that ever interested you was the *dollar.*

It is pretty hard for me to do anything when you are so greedy even with this house you couldn't even be fair with that, well it's all yours now and you won't have to see the Lawyer anymore.

I wish you would give my personal things to Danny, you couldn't get much from selling them anyway, you still have my insurance, it isn't much but it will be enough to take care of my debts and still have a few bucks left.

You always told me that I was the one that made Sharon take her life, in fact you said I killed her, but you know down deep in your heart it was you that made her do what she did, and now you have two deaths to your credit, it should make you feel very proud.

Good By Kid

P.S. Disregard all the mean things I've said in this letter, I have said a lot of things to you I didn't really mean and I hope you get well and wish you the best of everything.

Cathy—don't come in.

Call your mother, she will know what to do.

Love,
Daddy

Cathy don't go in the bedroom.

Biological Factors

Recent studies indicate the presence of altered brain neurochemistry in some people who commit suicide.[49] Specifically, biochemical studies of suicide victims and attempters indicate that low levels of serotonin (5-HT) or its neurotransmitter metabolite (5-HIAA) appear to be correlated with suicidal behavior. Genetics may also play a role.[50] Biological markers appear to have promise in assessing suicide risk. In some way, not yet completely understood, a person's serotonin levels seem to be related to vulnerability to suicide. As the role of such biological markers becomes clearer, it may be possible to reduce suicide risk by appropriate pharmacological therapies. At present, however, such neurochemical correlates do not fully explain the timing and type of suicidal behavior, nor do they explain why some aggression is directed outward toward others and some is directed toward the self. Still, the research done to date supports the idea that the "biology of suicide" may become an important part of assessment and intervention.

Lifespan Perspectives on Suicide

The risks and motives for suicide change through the lifespan as human beings encounter changing circumstances related to different periods of human development. The usual causes of suicide among adolescents, for example, tend to be distinct from those common to people in old age. In studying the various risks that pertain to different segments of the lifespan, notice which factors affect people of all ages and which factors tend to exert a particular influence on people in specific age groups.

Childhood

Although suicide is relatively rare in young children, suicidal thoughts and attempts are more frequent. Many researchers and clinicians believe that suicidal behavior is found among even very young children. Between 1980 and 1996, the suicide rate doubled among children ages ten to fourteen.[51] Because suicide risk is higher among those who have made an earlier attempt, young children with a history of suicide ideation or attempt are at risk for multiple recurrence of suicidal ideas or acts.[52]

Researchers believe that the rate of suicide among children would be higher if childhood accidents were examined more carefully for intent. Some of the childhood deaths resulting from running in front of cars or plastic bag suffocation are probably intentional rather than accidental. Although young children usually do not have access to the means of self-destruction, as do people at older ages, they nevertheless engage in acts of self-harm, and some kill themselves. In the case of young children, however, labeling a death as suicide may be problematic because of questions about whether a child possesses a mature concept of death and, thus, is fully aware of the consequences of his or her actions.[53] Recall the discussion of childhood development in Chapter 10; there is evidence that children who attempt suicide, especially those on the cusp between childhood and adolescence, tend to be at the edge of a transition between concrete operational and formal operational thought, a period that possibly involves heightened vulnerability to suicidal ideation and behaviors.[54]

Adolescence and Young Adulthood

Suicide is the third leading cause of death for people ages fifteen to twenty-four in the United States.[55] Among countries reporting data to the World Health Organization, higher suicide rates worldwide are due largely to increases in suicide among young people.[56] Adolescent suicide begins to appear in the age group of ten- to fourteen-year-olds, and it increases dramatically among older adolescents and young adults, which suggests that developmental changes play a role, possibly related to cognitive development and the conceptualization of death, as well as to dissatisfaction with life.[57]

Social disruption is an important factor in self-destructive behaviors among the young (see Table 12-6). Psychiatric diagnosis, dysfunctional personality traits, and psychosocial problems also increase the risk of suicide.[58]

Unable to earn a living by writing and too proud to accept food offered to him by his landlady, this seventeen-year-old killed himself by taking poison. Painted in 1856 by Henry Wallis, The Death of Chatterton *depicts an adolescent suicide that was precipitated by crisis arising out of the developmental transition from child to adult.*

Henry Wallis, Tate Gallery, London

Suicidal adolescents are linked with interpersonal conflict (with parents as well as boy- or girlfriends), interpersonal losses (including disruption of a romantic attachment, as well as other separations), and "external" stressors (most notably, legal or disciplinary problems, which are often related to tendencies to engage in impulsive violence).[59]

Family problems pose a significant risk. Suicidal young people tend to be exposed to family violence, disengaged families and deficient family support, physical abuse, parental suicidal behavior, instability in their living situation, and other acute and chronic stressors related to family life.[60] The young person's response to such turmoil may bring together a number of affective and cognitive states, including rage, hopelessness, despair, guilt, revenge, self-punishment, and retaliatory abandonment.[61] Substance abuse is a common theme, both in families and among young suicide-prone individuals. Active substance abuse, combined with depression and the availability of a handgun, is potentially lethal.[62]

Upheavals in family life—and in contemporary life styles generally—add to the pressures experienced by young people. Suicide may be seen as a way to impose some control over confusing and upsetting events, or to escape them. As Paulina Kernberg points out,

TABLE 12-6   *Risk Factors in Youthful Suicide*

1. Early separation from one's parents
2. Family dissolution, economic hardship, and increased mobility
3. Effect of highly conflicted families or families who are unresponsive to the young person's needs, or who are anomic (not accepting of the usual standards of social conduct) or depressed, alcoholic, and so on
4. Increased social isolation as compared to the support previously provided by the extended family, church, and community
5. Rapidly changing sex roles
6. Increase in relative proportion of young people in the total population, and corresponding increase in competition because of the large youthful cohort population
7. Pressure for achievement and success, perhaps resulting from parental expectations
8. Impact of peer suicides and role models of popular entertainers in terms of "copy cat" suicide
9. Media attention given to suicide, and the influence of self-destructive themes in popular culture, especially in popular song lyrics
10. Sense of lack of control over one's life
11. Low self-esteem and poor self-image
12. Devaluing of emotional expression
13. Lack of effective relationships with peers
14. Easy access to drugs and alcohol

Source: Adapted from William C. Fish and Edith Waldhart-Letzel, "Suicide and Children," *Death Education* 5 (1981): 217–220; Michael Peck, "Youth Suicide," *Death Education* 6 (1982): 29–47; and Judith M. Stillion, Eugene E. McDowell, and Jacque H. May, *Suicide Across the Life Span: Premature Exits* (New York: Hempisphere, 1989), pp. 95–100.

> An important meaning of suicide is that it can serve as an act of mastery, of ultimate control, of competency in individuals who are suffering loss of a sense of control over themselves and their lives. It is, as it were, the ultimate "locus of control."[63]

Substance abuse, delinquency, and suicide are linked on a continuum of "escape behaviors" that young people engage in to avoid feelings of depression and hopelessness. Engaging in risk-taking behavior may represent a "way out" for the individual who no longer cares whether he or she lives or dies. Flirting with death, as in "playing chicken," may be engaged in lackadaisically, with little concern for the outcome. When substance abuse and increasingly risky behaviors no longer provide sufficient distraction from the painfulness of their lives, young people may opt for suicide to provide the ultimate numbness.[64]

Adolescents and young adults may be susceptible to a kind of "contagion," whereby one person's suicide triggers another. So-called *cluster suicides* typically take place within the same locale, are closely related in time, and involve the same method.[65] (Mass suicide can be considered as a special form of clustering.) The term "copycat suicide" is also used to describe cluster suicides, especially when such imitation occurs in connection with the depiction of a suicide in the media. In a study of two Texas clusters, researchers concluded that exposure to reports of suicides may affect individuals who are already at risk. Sensational or romanticized media coverage may foster an affinity with those who commit suicide and confer an aura of celebrity on them. In suicide-susceptible individuals, this could evoke the impression that suicide is a "powerful act" that will claim special—albeit posthumous—attention from their family and peers.[66]

Suicide pacts are a similar phenomenon in that they relate to an arrangement between two or more people who determine to kill themselves at the same time and usually in the same place.[67] Four teenagers in New Jersey, two boys and two girls, decided to commit suicide together by sitting in a car with the motor running inside a locked garage. Reportedly, they were distraught over the death of a friend. They were discovered dead the next morning. Two days later, another suicide pact took the lives of two teenage girls in Illinois, who killed themselves in similar fashion.

Another instance of adolescents entering into a suicide pact involved a boy and girl who reportedly became obsessed with the possibility of reincarnation. They crashed their car into their old junior high school building, causing the boy to be killed instantly. The girl, who apparently had last-second doubts about reincarnation, barely survived by diving under the car's dashboard.

An unusual, and "one-sided," version of a suicide pact occurs in the phenomenon of graveside suicides, in which a pathological grief reaction leads to a bereaved person killing himself or herself at the grave of a deceased loved one. Cemeteries are symbolic of the reunion of the living and the dead, and graveside suicides are analogous to a death pact between two persons in which the second death occurs as a reaction to the first, and without the knowledge of the first.[68] As with the "epidemic" suicides among young people in Micronesia, suicide clusters and suicide pacts can be a deadly influence on individuals who are vulnerable to suicidal intentions.

Whereas the motives for suicide among adolescents often involve issues relating to family and relationships with peers, for young adults the major issues tend to involve academic achievement, courtship, family formation, and career. A desire for perfection, whether self-imposed or socially demanded, can also lead to suicide ideation when accomplishments fall short of ideals.[69]

At present, the most promising approaches for reducing suicide among young people appear to be in two major areas: first, providing treatment for disorders that increase the risk of suicide, such as depression, substance abuse, and family conflict; and, second, targeting prevention efforts at high-risk groups, such as affectively disordered young men who exhibit substance abuse and other antisocial behavior.[70]

Middle Adulthood

Middle age, the period roughly between ages thirty-five and sixty-five, has been called the "terra incognita" of the human lifespan. This is a period of "generativity," of giving back to society some of the gifts of nurture and sustenance received during earlier periods of life. It is a time of shifting from

Suicide Note Written by a Single Woman, Age 21

My dearest Andrew,

It seems as if I have been spending all my life apologizing to you for things that happened whether they were my fault or not.

I am enclosing your pin because I want you to think of what you took from me every time you see it.

I don't want you to think I would kill myself over you because you're not worth any emotion at all. It is what you cost me that hurts and nothing can replace it.

valuing physical capabilities to valuing wisdom, of building new relationships as old ones are lost or altered, and of gaining greater flexibility in life. This part of the lifespan has also been characterized as "middlescence," suggesting that middle age may be as turbulent for many adults as the period of adolescence.

This is also a time of coping with the loss of dreams and ambitions, coming to terms with the realization that one may not reach the goal of being a great artist or writer, a company president, or whatever visionary goal one had for oneself earlier in life. It may not be possible to achieve the aim of attaining a perfect marriage or raising perfect children.

The motive for suicidal behavior may be related to difficulties in an individual's career or marriage. In some cases, the nature of the career itself has a particular impact on suicidal behavior, as seems to be the case with the comparatively high incidence of suicide among police officers.[71] The major factors influencing suicide among the middle-aged often include an accumulation of negative life events; affective disorders, especially major depression; and alcoholism.

Late Adulthood

Although teenage suicide attracts more media attention, elderly people are at higher risk for suicide than any other age group. This is especially true of elderly white males, particularly widowers.[72] Some of the reasons given for suicide among those in later adulthood (generally defined as people over age sixty-five) are given in Table 12-7. Major risk factors include being divorced or widowed, living alone, and psychiatric or physical illness.[73] Older people are less likely to have expressed suicidal ideation or to have made a previous attempt than people in younger age groups.[74] Researchers seem to agree that elderly people who attempt suicide genuinely want to die, unlike younger people, whose attempts are often a "cry for help."[75] For some older people, suicide is seen as a rational choice that offers release from severe illness or other hardships of old age. Old age can be a period of increased life satisfaction and ego integrity, or one of dissatisfaction, despair, and disgust.

Double suicides (a type of suicide pact) occur with greatest frequency among the elderly. The typical double suicide involves an older couple with

T A B L E *12-7* *Risk Factors in Late-Adulthood Suicide*

1. Social isolation and loneliness
2. Boredom, depression, sense of uselessness
3. Loss of purpose and meaning in life after retirement and separation from family and friends
4. Financial hardship
5. Multiple losses of loved ones
6. Chronic illness, pain, incapacitation
7. Alcohol abuse and drug dependence
8. Desire to avoid being a "burden" to others or to end one's life with "dignity"

one or both partners physically ill. Heavy alcohol use by one or both partners is also common. Such couples tend to be dependent on each other and isolated from external sources of support. There seems to be a "special chemistry" between couples who commit suicide together, with the more suicidal partner dominant and the more ambivalent partner passive in the relationship.[76]

Contemplating Suicide

Imagine for a moment the progression of thoughts of someone considering suicide. Assume first that in an untenable situation suicide seems the only recourse, or at least an option to be considered further. The next step might involve formulating some means of killing oneself. At this point the means have not actually been acquired, but various possibilities are considered.

Many people have reached this stage—perhaps through mere fantasizing, or perhaps with serious intentions. For some, the shock of recognizing that one is harboring such thoughts is enough to force a decision toward a more life-affirming alternative. For others, the next step toward suicide is taken, a step that greatly increases the level of lethality with regard to suicidal intention.

This stage involves acquiring the means to kill oneself, thereby setting into motion the logistics that make suicide a real possibility. A change of mind is still possible; a different solution can be sought. Otherwise, the final step in the suicidal progression comes into play: actually using the means that have been acquired to commit the suicidal act.

These steps toward lethality have been described as occurring in a definite sequence, but to the person involved they may be experienced as anything but logical and orderly. Suicide typically involves a complex array of conflicting thoughts and emotions. Still, recognizing the particular steps that must be taken to carry out the suicidal act is useful for understanding both the amount of sustained effort involved and the many decision points at which a change of mind or outside intervention is possible.

Once a decision is made to commit suicide, a choice must be made concerning the means to be used (see Figure 12-2). Sometimes a particular

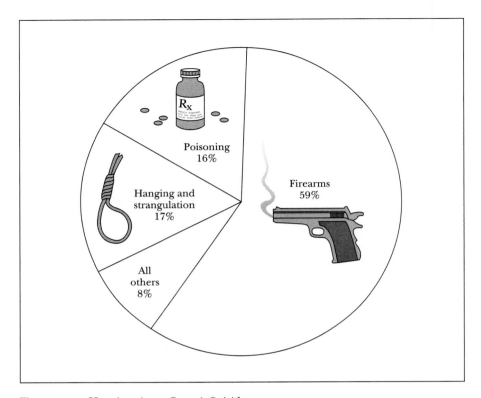

Figure *12-2* *How Americans Commit Suicide*
Source: U.S. Census Bureau, *Statistical Abstract of the United States: 1999,* p. 108.

method is chosen because of the image it represents to the suicidal individual. One might imagine drowning as a dreamy kind of death, a merging back into the universe. Or one might associate an overdose of sleeping pills with the death of a movie star. Whatever one's image of a particular method, the reality is likely to be quite different. Some people who overdose on drugs do so expecting a quiet or peaceful death. The actual effects of a suicidal drug overdose are usually far from peaceful or serene.

Sometimes a particular method of suicide is chosen for its anticipated impact on survivors. A study of suicide notes found that people using "active" methods of suicide more often communicated that rejection was a critical factor in the decision for self-injury.[77] An individual who wants survivors to "really pay for all the grief they caused me" might select a method of suicide that graphically communicates this rage. Someone who did not want to "make a scene" might choose a method imagined as being less shocking or disturbing to one's survivors.

Experience and familiarity also influence the choice of suicidal method. For example, an experienced hunter, well acquainted with rifles, might be inclined to turn to such a weapon for suicide because of its accessibility and

Resume

Razors pain you;
Rivers are damp;
Acids stain you;
And drugs cause cramp.
Guns aren't lawful;
Nooses give;
Gas smells awful;
You might as well live.

Dorothy Parker

familiarity. Someone who understands the effects of various drugs might use them to concoct a fatal overdose. In short, the choice of suicidal method reflects the experience and state of mind of the person choosing it. It may be a spontaneous choice, with the person using whatever lethal devices are readily at hand, or it may be the outcome of deliberate thought and even research.

Choosing a method of killing oneself can be likened to making travel arrangements for a cross-country trip. A person wanting to travel from the West Coast to the East Coast must consider the kinds of transportation available—automobile, train, airplane, and so on. Some of these are quite rapid; others are relatively slow and deliberate. For example, once you board an airplane and it lifts off the runway, there is no opportunity to change your mind and disembark before reaching the destination. However, someone bicycling from coast to coast has innumerable opportunities to decide on a different destination.

Similarly, some methods of committing suicide offer little hope of changing one's mind after the lethal act is initiated. Once the trigger is pulled on a revolver placed next to one's skull, there's virtually no possibility of altering the likelihood of a fatal outcome. However, the would-be suicide who cuts his or her wrists or takes an overdose of drugs *might* have time to alter an otherwise fatal outcome by seeking medical help. If help is not forthcoming, the likelihood of dying may be as great as with a gunshot wound to the head, but there is a chance of intervention. Among methods used in the suicidal act, then, there is an order of lethality.

Suicide Notes

Suicide notes have been called "cryptic maps of ill-advised journeys."[78] Such notes are usually written in the minutes or hours immediately preceding suicide. Although it is often assumed that nearly all suicides leave notes behind for their survivors, in fact only about one-fourth of suicides write a final message. As a partial record of the mental state of suicides, such notes are of immense interest to scholars and helping professionals, not to mention the bereaved families. Imagine yourself in circumstances that would lead to your writing a suicide note. What kinds of things would you want to say in your last words to your survivors?

Actual suicide notes display a variety of messages and intentions. Some notes explain to survivors the decision to commit suicide. Others express anger or blame. Conversely, some notes emphasize that the writer's suicide is "no one's fault." The messages in suicide notes range from sweeping statements of the writer's philosophy or credo regarding suicide to detailed listings of practical chores that will require attention after the writer's death. For example, one note instructs survivors, "The cat needs to go to the vet next Tuesday; don't miss the appointment or you'll be charged double. The car is due for servicing a week from Friday." Suicide notes represent the writer's "last chance to take care of business, decide who gets what, or to make funeral wishes known."[79]

Suicide notes may include expressions of love, hate, shame, disgrace, fear of insanity, self-abnegation; feelings of rejection; explanations for the suicidal act or defense of the right to take one's life; disavowal of any survivor's responsibility for the suicide; instructions for distributing the suicide's property and possessions. They typically display dichotomies of logic, hostility toward others mixed with self-blame, the use of particular names and specific instructions to survivors, and a sense of decisiveness about suicide. Many suicide notes convey an intense love-hate ambivalence toward survivors, as expressed succinctly in the following note:

> Dear Betty:
>   I hate you.
>   Love,
>   George

This example of ambivalence also points up the dyadic nature of suicide— here involving husband and wife. Suicide notes provide clues about the intentions and emotions that lead a person to suicide, but they rarely tell the whole story—and they often raise more questions than they answer. The message in a suicide note may come as a surprise to survivors who had no hint of the person's feelings. Suicide notes can have a significant effect on survivors. Whether the final message is one of affection or blame, survivors have no opportunity to respond. In this sense, suicide represents the ultimate last word.

Suicide Prevention, Intervention, and Postvention

The Los Angeles Suicide Prevention Center, founded in 1958 by Norman L. Farberow and Edwin S. Shneidman, became the prototype for prevention and crisis centers not only in the United States but throughout the world.[80]

> The importance of the Los Angeles Suicide Prevention Center cannot be overstated in any history of suicide. The work begun in that center by Shneidman and his associates, and expanded upon later when Shneidman became director of the Suicide Center in the National Institute of Mental Health, changed the nation's

Graffiti

I find a snapshot
buried in my father's drawer.
A picture of the grandfather I never knew.
Small, stooped yet dignified he stands
beside my brother's wicker pram
surrounded by his family.
My mother tells the story, hidden in the past
of the last time she saw him.
She was big with child, and so allowed to sit
while his two daughters served the sons
who gathered at the table.
Grandma who reigned as always at the head
arranged the seating of those sons
not in the order of their age
but of the weekly wage they earned
and without question brought to her.

I learn that you, mild gentle man
never at home in the new language, the new land,
subdued by failure, each passing year withdrew
further into old world memories, and silence.
Rising that evening from the table, as usual
scarcely noticed as you went to lie down
on your narrow bed, there was no sign, no signal.
Only that as you passed, you bent
with a shy unaccustomed show of tenderness
to murmur "*Liebchen*" and to kiss my mother's head.
She tells me that I leaped and struggled in her womb
when from your room you shattered silence
with a shot. Your life exploding
sudden messages across blank walls in bursts of red.

Maude Meehan

view of suicide and suicidal behavior. The most important change was a shift away from seeing suicide as an act committed by an insane person to seeing it as an act committed by a person who felt overwhelming ambivalence toward life.[81]

The ensuing decades have seen a dramatic increase in the number of suicide crisis centers, coupled with the rise of telephone hotlines focusing on suicide prevention. The typical suicide prevention center operates as a telephone-answering center with around-the-clock availability to people in crisis. The services provided are mainly designed to serve as a short-term resource for people contemplating suicide. The caller's anonymity is respected, and the caller's expressed need for help is accepted unquestioningly. Staff members—some of them professionals, many of them volunteers who receive special training—use crisis intervention strategies to reduce the suicidal caller's stress.

Like other public health services, suicide crisis centers vary in their standards of professionalism; overall, however, they have a positive impact on countless people.[82]

Some suicide intervention centers have expanded their services to encompass treatment for a broad range of self-destructive behaviors. For example, the Los Angeles Suicide Prevention Center offers counseling and community services. Low-cost counseling is available for potential suicide victims, as well as for survivors of a friend's or relative's suicide. Clinics provide treatment for depression and drug abuse. Community-based programs for troubled youths have been implemented to help individuals overcome destructive behaviors. The activities of the Los Angeles Suicide Prevention Center exemplify the understanding of suicide as a subset of a larger class of self-destructive behaviors, all of which require attention.

Prevention

There is little reason to be optimistic about the prospect of preventing suicide, at least in the sense of eliminating it from the repertory of human behaviors. To do so, the causes of human unhappiness and dissatisfaction would have to be eliminated. Efforts to create a social utopia inevitably fall short of perfection. This is not to say that efforts to relieve human suffering are not worth pursuing, only that they are inherently limited.

Still, much can be done to reduce suicide risk.[83] Education is an essential element in any program of suicide prevention. The lessons to be learned can be applied across the lifespan and include the following key points: First, it is crucial to acknowledge the reality that life is complex and that all of us will inevitably have experiences of disappointment, failure, and loss in our lives. Second, we can learn to deal with such experiences by developing appropriate coping techniques, including the skills of critical thinking. Individuals "who form a habit early of analyzing situations from a variety of perspectives, of asking appropriate questions, and of testing the reality of their own thinking are far less likely to settle easily into the cognitive inflexibility that focuses on suicide as *the* solution."[84] A corollary of such coping skills involves the cultivation of a sense of humor, especially the ability to laugh at oneself and at life's problems, to see the humor in situations. Finally, it is important to learn how to set appropriate and attainable goals. Good self-esteem is a preventative against suicide.

Suicide prevention programs are being expanded to reach populations at greatest risk. One native Ojibway/Cree community in Ontario, Canada, for example, the Muskrat Dam community, has organized a group known as Helping Hands to confront suicide.[85] Patterning its program on traditional Native American spiritual values, the Helping Hands project has several primary objectives: (1) instilling a sense of value within the general community population; (2) rebuilding the lives of disturbed youth, thereby enabling them to proceed with direction and purpose; (3) restoring pride and a sense of well-being to members of the community; (4) motivating young people to lead constructive and productive lives; (5) providing life-skills training that can be

Despair, a common component of many suicides, is starkly depicted in this lithograph, Nachdenkende Frau, *by Käthe Kollwitz. If the potential victim's warning signals are observed by persons who take steps to provide crisis intervention, the suicidal impulse may be thwarted.*

applied within the family and community; and (6) helping individuals develop good mechanisms for coping with mental health problems. Programs like this, which are sensitive to the needs of a particular community or risk-prone segment of the population, are a crucial supplement to conventional methods of suicide prevention.

Another strategy for preventing suicides involves setting up physical barriers in places where suicides are likely to occur. In Washington, D.C., the number-one jump site historically has been the Duke Ellington Bridge, a three-arch concrete structure with pedestrian lookouts. In 1985, after three suicides from the bridge within a ten-day period, authorities ordered the construction of an eight-foot-high fence. This was opposed by neighborhood groups and by the National Trust for Historic Preservation because the fence would block scenic views and diminish the architectural aesthetics of the structure. Further, it was argued, such protective fences do not prevent suicides. The barrier was installed, however, and only one suicide occurred from the Ellington Bridge during the period 1986–1990. This is in comparison with ten suicides from the nearby Taft Bridge, which had no fence.[86] It would seem, then, that the barriers did prevent some suicides. Nevertheless, there are too many variables and unknowns to allow a confident conclusion. It is possible that individuals who would have jumped from the Ellington Bridge simply found other ways to kill themselves. To a suicide-prone individual, one researcher asked, what is the true meaning of a bridge barrier? Could it solve the issues, or at least alleviate the sense of crisis that drove an individual to that point of action? These questions are difficult to answer with certainty. It is known, however, that appropriate intervention during a suicidal crisis can reduce its lethality and give the would-be suicide another chance to assess a painful situation and perhaps find a more constructive and healthier solution.

Intervention

Suicide intervention programs emphasize short-term care and treatment of persons who are actively experiencing a suicidal crisis. Their aim is to reduce the lethality of the crisis. Although many suicide intervention programs are actually named "suicide prevention centers," such programs generally use theories and techniques common to crisis intervention. Antoon Leenaars notes:

> Suicide intervention is optimally practiced in cooperation with a number of colleagues, representing various disciplines, and even individuals outside the helping professions. . . . The treatment of a suicidal person should reflect the learning and response of individuals with different points of view.[87]

The cardinal rule in suicide intervention is to *do something*. Thus, suicide intervention involves: (1) taking threats seriously; (2) watching for clues to suicidal intentions and behaviors; (3) answering cries for help by offering support, understanding, and compassion; (4) confronting the problem by asking questions and being unafraid to discuss suicide with the person in crisis; (5) obtaining professional help to manage the crisis; and (6) offering constructive alternatives to suicide. A key theme of suicide intervention is that talking is a positive step toward resolving the crisis. In cases where family support is inadequate, other sources of support must be sought out and provided.

Postvention

Suicide *postvention,* a term coined by Edwin Shneidman, refers to the assistance given to *all* survivors of suicide, including those who attempt suicide as well as the families, friends, and associates of those who commit suicide. As a therapeutic activity directed to the "survivor victims" of suicide, postvention

> When I was thirteen months old, my mother killed herself. So I eventually learned, as I learned her maiden name, Georgia Saphronia Collier, and where she was born, Sulphur Springs, Arkansas, and how old she was when she ended her life, twenty-nine. (And good lord, writing these words now, all these years afterward, for the first time in memory my eyes have filled with tears of mourning for her. What impenetrable vessel preserved them?) I didn't know my mother, except as infants know. At the beginning of my life the world acquired a hole. That's what I knew, that there was a hole in the world. For me there still is. It's a singularity. In and out of a hole like that, anything goes.
>
> Richard Rhodes, *A Hole in the World: An American Boyhood*

"aims to alleviate the distress of affected individuals, reduce the risk of interactive suicidal behavior, and promote the healthy recovery of the affected community."[88] The bereaved survivors of suicide have special needs, for they often experience feelings of guilt and self-blame that need to be confronted. When these feelings are not dealt with or are mismanaged, it can lead to dysfunctional relationships and emotional problems in the lives of survivors. Survivors who actually witnessed someone commit suicide may face a particularly challenging time.[89] (Some issues for survivors bereaved by suicide are discussed in Chapter 7.)

Cases of "railway suicide" present an important example of postvention for unwitting survivor-victims of someone's suicide. In some cities, there are dozens of cases each year where people jump in front of trains in apparent attempts to kill themselves.[90] For the drivers of these trains, these cases are unexpected and violent events, and they often cause a severe posttraumatic stress reaction.[91] In the aftermath, postvention can involve not only debriefing and counseling sessions for the affected train drivers, but also preventive efforts designed to reduce the incidence of such suicides. Thus, postvention efforts often play an important role in suicide prevention.

Helping a Person Who Is in Suicidal Crisis

Warnings that an individual is considering suicide may be communicated in a variety of ways. Evans and Farberow point out that suicidal intent may be expressed in four main ways: (1) *verbal direct* ("I will shoot myself if you leave me"), (2) *verbal indirect* ("A life without love is a life without meaning"), (3) *behavioral direct* (for example, a chronically ill person hoarding pills), and (4) *behavioral indirect*.[92] Among the warning signs that fall under this last category, Evans and Farberow mention:

1. Giving away prized possessions, making a will, or attending to other "final" arrangements
2. Sudden and extreme changes in eating habits or sleep patterns
3. Withdrawal from friends or family, or other major behavioral changes accompanied by depression

TABLE 12-8   Myths and Facts About Suicide

Myth: People who talk about suicide don't commit suicide.
  Fact: This fallacy has been called the "grand old myth of suicide," one that excuses the failure to respond to another person's cry for help. Most people who attempt suicide communicate their intentions to others, as hints, direct threats, or self-destructive actions or preparations for suicide. Unfortunately, these cries for help often go unheeded by friends, family members, coworkers, or health care personnel.
Myth: Improvement in a suicidal person means the risk of suicide has passed.
  Fact: Improvement may be necessary before a severely depressed person can take the steps necessary to carry out the suicidal intention. Many suicides occur within three to six months following apparent improvement. Thus, an apparently positive change in mood can be a danger signal: Making the decision to carry out the suicidal act can be exhilarating and freeing; the person feels, "Now that I've made the decision, I no longer have to agonize about what I'm going to do." This relief is subject to misinterpretation by others, who may believe the crisis has passed.
Myth: Once a suicide risk, always a suicide risk.
  Fact: The peak of suicidal crisis is generally brief. The simultaneous conjunction of the thought of killing oneself, possession of the means to complete the act, and the lack of help or internvention is a more-or-less unusual set of circumstances. If intervention occurs, the suicidal person may well be able to put suicidal thoughts behind and lead a productive life.
Myth: Suicide is inherited.
  Fact: Although this fallacy gives suicidal behavior an aura of biological fate, the fact is that suicide does not "run in families," in the sense of being a genetically inherited trait. However, dysfunctional family patterns with respect to problem solving or surviving the suicide of a loved one may create beliefs about suicide that influence a person's subsequent behavior. The fear that one has a greater potential for suicide may create a self-fulfilling prophecy. In this sense, the

4. Changes in school or job performance
5. Personality changes, such as nervousness, outbursts of anger, or apathy about health or appearance
6. Use of drugs or alcohol

The recent suicide of a friend or relative, or a history of previous suicide attempts, should also be seen as a warning sign of suicide risk.

A number of commonly held beliefs, or myths, have grown up about suicide and about the kind of person who is likely to commit suicide. Unfortunately, many of these beliefs—being false—are harmful, for they have the effect of depriving the suicidal person of needed help. As you review the listing of fallacies about suicide given in Table 12-8, notice which ones you may have believed or unconsciously incorporated into your assumptions about suicide. It is important to separate fact from fallacy if we wish to understand suicide.

If a person says, "I feel like killing myself," that statement should not be taken lightly or brushed aside with the quick response, "Oh, well, you'll prob-

T A B L E *12-8* *(continued)*

---

suicide of a family member may provide an excuse, or make it easier, to contemplate suicide as a means of escape from a difficult situation.

Myth: Suicide affects only a specific group or class of people.

Fact: Suicide is not the "curse of the poor" or "disease of the rich." It occurs among all socioeconomic groups and affects individuals with widely divergent life styles. Social integration is a more important determinant of suicidal bebhavior than socioeconomic class.

Myth: Suicidal individuals are insane.

Fact: Although it is true that some suicides are mentally ill, the planning and carrying out of suicide usually requires careful reasoning and deliberate judgment. Many suicide notes reveal not only ambivalence, but also considerable lucidity about the writer's intentions. Despite its devastating effect on the individual's physical being, suicide can be considered as a defensive act or problem-solving technique to preserve the integrity of the self.

Myth: Suicidal individuals are fully intent on dying.

Fact: Actually, most suicides are undecided about continuing to live or ending their lives. In their ambivalence, they may gamble with death, leaving the possibility of rescue to fate. Although some attempters do ultimately commit suicide after previously uncompleted attempts, the majority do not. Thus, a suicide attempt may signal that a person's psychological or interpersonal needs are not being satisfactorily met and a change is desired; it does not necessarily indicate that he or she wants to die.

Myth: The motive for a particular suicide is clearly evident.

Fact: People often try to establish a quick "cause" for suicide, attributing it to economic hardship, disappointment in love, or some other immediate condition. Deeper analysis usually uncovers a lengthy sequence of self-destructive behaviors leading up to the act of suicide. The apparent "cause" may be simply the final step of a complex pattern of self-destructive acts.

---

ably feel better tomorrow." To the person in crisis, there may seem little hope of a "tomorrow" at all. Pay attention to the message being communicated.

Similarly, responding to a suicidal statement with a provocation—"You wouldn't be capable of committing suicide!"—or with a tone of moral superiority—"I don't want to hear such unhealthy talk!"—can worsen rather than ease the crisis. A response that provides only a litany of the "good reasons" why the person should not commit suicide may also offer little practical assistance to a person in crisis.

More helpful is listening carefully to exactly what the person is communicating; the tone and context of statements should reveal to the sensitive listener something about the communicator's real intent. Often, remarks about suicide are made in an offhand manner: "If I don't get that job, I'll kill myself!" Perhaps the remark is intended as a figure of speech, much as in the joking threat, "I'll kill you for that!" There is a tendency to discount such statements in a culture where "talk is cheap," and "actions speak louder than

Stanley Forman, *Boston Herald American*

Once a person is this close to the suicidal act, the chance of a successful intervention is usually slight. Fortunately, in this dramatic instance intervention was successful.

words."[93] Suicidal threats should be taken seriously. To do otherwise is to fall prey to the myth that "talking about suicide means the person will not really go through with it." Knowing the patterns of suicidal behavior can help distinguish facts from fallacies. It is also helpful to become acquainted with the crisis intervention resources available in your own community.

Lastly, it is important to recognize that no one can take *ultimate* responsibility for another human being's decision to end his or her life. This may go against one's inclination to preserve life, yet only so much can be done to assist another person in crisis. In the short term, it may be feasible to keep someone from taking his or her life. Constant vigilance or custodial care can prevent suicide during an acute suicidal crisis. Over the longer term, however, taking responsibility for preventing someone else's suicide is likely to be unsuccessful. A terminally ill man dying in great pain said to his wife: "You'd better keep my medication out of reach, because I don't want to keep up this struggle any longer." The wife had to decide whether she could take responsibility for whether he would continue to live with pain or end his life by an overdose. After much soul searching, she concluded that, although she had great compassion for his predicament, she could not take responsibility for safeguarding his medication, doling out one pill at a time, constantly fearful that he might locate the drugs and attempt suicide anyway.

Not taking responsibility does not mean that one must go to the opposite extreme: "Well, if you're going to kill yourself, then get it over with!" Although there are limits to how much one person can *protect* another, it is always possible to offer life-affirming support and compassion. A person who seems intent on suicide may nonetheless be hoping for some intervention. It is important to sustain or stimulate that person's desire to live. Plans for self-destruction are likely to proceed apace with fantasies of rescue. The person who is cast in the role of helper in such a drama can affirm the fact that there are choices other than suicide.

One way to help people in crisis is to help them discover what about themselves *can* matter, however small or insignificant it may seem. It is important to find something that matters *to the person*. What are the possibilities of sustaining that value into the present? Asking the person what is useful, what he or she needs in order to feel valuable and worthwhile, may be a matter of survival. In the short term, external support can help to ensure survival during the height of crisis. But one should be skeptical of the notion that anyone can sustain, over the long term, another person's will to live.

Suicidal thoughts and behaviors indicate a critical loss of a person's belief that he or she is someone who matters. The feeling that nothing matters, in the sense that one's life is in complete disarray, is by itself the stimulus for suicide. More important to suicidal thoughts and behaviors is the person's belief that "*I* don't matter." Those two streams of thought in combination—the sense that the external situation is unsatisfactory and that one does not matter enough to improve it—can lead to death by suicide. As has been well stated, "Suicide is a permanent solution to what is most likely a temporary problem."[94]

Further Readings

Fred Cutter. *Art and the Wish to Die*. Chicago: Nelson-Hall, 1983.

Kevin E. Early. *Religion and Suicide in the African-American Community*. Westport, Conn.: Greenwood, 1992.

Norman L. Farberow, ed. *Suicide in Different Cultures*. Baltimore: University Park Press, 1975.

Keith Hawton and Kees van Heeringen, eds. *The International Handbook of Suicide and Attempted Suicide*. New York: Wiley, 2000.

Kay Redfield Jamison. *Night Falls Fast: Understanding Suicide*. New York: Alfred A. Knopf, 1999.

Antoon A. Leenaars, ed. *Suicidology: Essays in Honor of Edwin Shneidman*. Northvale, N.J.: Jason Aronson, 1993.

Edwin S. Shneidman. *The Suicidal Mind*. New York: Oxford University Press, 1996.

Judith Stillion, Eugene McDowell, and Jacque May. *Suicide Across the Life Span: Premature Exits*, 2d ed. Washington, D.C.: Taylor & Francis, 1996.

Charles C. Thompson, II. *A Glimpse of Hell: The Explosion of the USS Iowa and Its Cover-Up*. New York: W. W. Norton, 1999.

Calling attention to the threat posed by AIDS and other modern encounters with death, this drawing depicts victims embraced by Azrael, the angel of death.

CHAPTER 13

Risks of Death
in the Modern World

The essayist E. B. White said, "To confront death, in any guise, is to identify with the victim and face what is unsettling and sobering."[1] Though we in modern societies tend to be insulated from firsthand experiences of death, we nevertheless encounter it in many guises. Our environment furnishes us with opportunities for encountering death at almost every turn. The mass media—newspapers, television, movies—as well as art, literature, and music all present images that influence our attitudes toward death. We also risk subtle, and sometimes dramatic, encounters with death as we engage in our life's pursuits—on our jobs and in our recreational activities. Occasionally, the risk of death is evident in the form of natural disasters, violence, or war. The possibility of violent death, for example, threatens us not only as individuals but also as a society, overshadowing and influencing our plans and activities.

In 1721, the novelist Daniel Defoe wrote *A Journal of the Plague Year*, a fictional account of the Great Plague that had devastated London in 1665. Drawing on published accounts and his recollection of tales heard during childhood, he vividly depicted a plague-stricken city and the terror of its helpless citizens, confronted by a horror they could not comprehend. What prompted Defoe to write about a plague that had taken place two generations earlier? Defoe knew that a plague again threatened to sweep across Europe, a plague that could potentially cause death and destruction on the scale of the Great Plague of 1665.

He wrote to alert a largely indifferent populace to the threat so that precautions could be taken to avert catastrophe.

Today we no longer fear the Black Death. Yet in a subtle though pervasive way, we are confronted by a multidimensioned "plague" that is no less threatening than the more easily distinguishable plague of Defoe's time. Indifference to the risks of death that now plague us—accidents, violence, war, natural and industrial catastrophe, and emerging diseases like AIDS—only increases the possibility of a disastrous encounter with death.[2]

Risk Taking

All life involves risks. However, the degree of risk we assume is often subject to our own choices about how we live our lives. Our willingness to take risks is influenced by the images communicated in the media and popular culture. Risks frequently accompany our activities in pursuit of the "good life." Think about your own life. What risks do you face in connection with your job, leisure activities, and overall life style? Are any of these risks potentially life-threatening? Do some risks seem to be unavoidable? Do you take "calculated" risks? In some cases, we can exercise considerable choice about the nature and degree of risk to which we are exposed. Smoking, drinking, taking drugs, and driving habits involve risks that can be controlled. We are also in a position to exercise choice in our occupational and recreational activities.

The risks associated with some jobs can be quite dramatic, involving dangers that most people, if given a choice, would avoid. Examples of such occupations come readily to mind: explosives expert, high-rise window washer, movie stuntperson, test pilot, as well as police officer and fire fighter, to name a few representative examples.[3] Such a list could be continued almost indefinitely. We could add scientists who handle hazardous materials, mine workers, electricians, heavy-equipment operators, and farm workers using toxic pesticides. As you add your own examples to this list, notice whether they involve the risk of sudden death (as from an explosion or a fall from a high-rise building) or long-term exposure to hazardous materials or conditions. Sometimes risks are identified only after years of exposure to a hazardous condition.[4] At other times, individuals accept risks as something that "comes with the territory," as in the case of the hazards encountered in professional sports like football.[5]

In Japan, occupational stress reportedly claims the lives of more than 10,000 victims a year.[6] Mostly men in their prime working years, these victims of *karōshi*, or sudden death from overwork, are found in virtually every occupational category. *Karōshi* is characterized as a buildup of fatigue caused by "long hours of work that clearly exceed all normal physiological limitations," disruptions in an individual's normal daily rhythms (often related to travel or lengthy commutes to and from the job), and other job-related strains placed on workers. In some occupations, the rise of global markets (with their corresponding time differences) has forced workers to conduct business far into the night after the normal day's work has been completed. The incidence of *karōshi* in Japan has been accompanied by a growing recognition that exhaustion induced by chronic overwork can aggravate preexisting health problems

I stared in a horrified trance as a figure appeared, frozen in the air for the briefest moment, its arms outstretched above its head as if in utterly hopeless supplication. Then it continued its relaxed, cart-wheeling descent, with only the thundering crashes attesting to its frightening impacts on the rock. It disappeared into a gully.

"Don't look!" I screamed to my wife, who was, of course, as helplessly transfixed as I was. And the sounds continued. After a time, the figure came into view at the base of the gully and continued down the pile of rubble below. My last view of it is frozen in time. The figure's arm was curled easily over its head, and its posture was one of relaxation, of napping. It drifted down that last boulder field like an autumn leaf down a rippling brook. Then it disappeared under the trees, and only the pebbles continued to clatter down the rock. Suddenly it was very, very still.

I looked down to Debby and had to articulate the obvious: "That was a man," I said quietly, numbly.

William G. Higgins, "Groundfall"

and harm even the healthiest person—sometimes causing a life-threatening crisis that ends in death.

The threat of death may also be found in our recreational activities: mountain climbing, parachuting, scuba diving, motorcycle racing, and the like. Activities like these are sometimes characterized as thrill seeking, although this term suggests motives that some participants in these activities would not necessarily ascribe to themselves. Activities of this kind present opportunities to test our limits and develop confidence. They can help us learn to deal positively with fear. Mountain climbers, for instance, accept certain risks because climbing provides physical conditioning as well as the pleasure of reaching the heights and surveying the expanse of uncluttered nature.

Although mountain climbing involves obvious risks, two different climbers can relate to these risks in different ways. One climber displays an attitude of abandon that could only be called foolhardy or death defying. The other devotes many hours to obtaining instruction, preparing equipment, conditioning for the climb, and asking advice from more experienced climbers before deciding to set foot on a mountain. In short, risk can be minimized. An activity may be attractive to some individuals *because* of its inherent risk; other people accept the risk as inseparable from other attractive features of the activity. When behavior involves doing dangerous things simply for the thrill of it, or as a way to "laugh in the face of death," it may reflect an individual's attempt to deny death or to deny a fear of death.[7]

No one is immune to risks. At home, on the job, or at play, the risk of death confronts us in varied ways. After a classroom discussion about the risks involved in various activities, one student said, "It seems we're coming around to the point that everything we do involves risks. You could even stab yourself with your knitting needle!" Perhaps, but usually when we consider activities involving risk, we think of pursuits about which there is a direct acknowledgment of the risk. The possibility of falling backward from a rocking

To keep from tumbling through space at 125 miles per hour, this mile-high skydiver spreads his arms and legs to control his freefall before opening his parachute. Although risks are ever present in our lives, we expose ourselves to many of them by personal choice.

chair while knitting strikes most people as less risky than, say, driving a formula race car or heading out on expedition to the Himalayas.

Sometimes the risks we face are not known. More often, however, we have choices that allow us to control or manage the element of risk. What automobile driver has not chosen at some time to drive just a bit faster in order to arrive at the destination sooner? Accident statistics, as well as common sense, tell us that speeding is risky. Yet we make a trade-off; the added risk is exchanged for the expected benefit of arriving at the destination sooner.

A death resulting from a high-risk sport or similar activity may have a special impact on others engaged in the same activity. In addition to its effect on those who are most immediately involved (for example, people who had rented equipment or given instruction to the deceased), the death affects the wider community of those who participate in the sport. It challenges "the underlying assumption of the sport that careful, cautious practice insures safety."[8] To cope with the challenge presented by the death, rumors may circulate that the deceased failed to take necessary precautions or followed an unwise or ill-considered course of action. These rumors represent an attempt to fit what has happened into a manageable scheme and perhaps to mitigate feelings of guilt about having been unable to prevent the death. As a means of coping with such a death, "blaming the victim" may allow other participants to feel comfortable continuing the activity despite the risks.

Accidents

Do accidents happen by chance or because of "fate" or "bad luck"? If so, it follows that little if anything can be done to prevent them. However, the definition of an accident as an event that occurs "by chance or from unknown causes" can be refined to encompass the understanding that an accident may be due to "carelessness, unawareness, or ignorance." Most accidents are events over which individuals do have varying degrees of control. Suppose a gun is brought into a person's household. The presence of the gun increases from zero the chance that there may be an accidental firing of the weapon. Of course, such an accident may never happen. But if a gun were *not* in the home, there would be *no* chance of an accidental firing.

The choices we make affect the probabilities of various kinds of accidents. It is an established fact that drivers who have been drinking tend to take greater risks than do sober drivers. It is also a fact that a driver's judgment and performance are inversely related to the amount of alcohol consumed, whereas a driver's tendency to overrate his or her driving abilities is directly related to the amount imbibed. About half of the drivers involved in accidents are under the influence of alcohol. Are such accidents due to mere "chance" or "fate"? When we view accidents as chance events, it lessens the probability that steps will be taken to prevent their occurrence.

Sometimes—often jokingly—we call a person *accident-prone* because he or she seems to be involved in accidents more often than others. There may be no scientific way to describe a personality type as accident-prone, but certain known factors can affect the probability that an individual will be involved in an accident. In this sense, "accident-proneness" is usually based on factors such as age and experience. When accidents of all types are considered, adolescent and young adult males are statistically at the greatest risk. Is this due to cultural attitudes that tend to encourage males more than females to engage in risky activities? In studies of young children, researchers find that boys and girls see risk differently.[9] Whereas boys tend to evaluate whether the benefit is worth the risk (while at the same time underestimating the risks), girls tend to base their decisions on whether they could be hurt at all. One researcher reported that boys won't consider avoiding a risky situation unless they think there is a strong potential for injury, whereas girls will consider avoiding it if there is any such potential. Injury appears to be more a negative event for girls than boys.

So far we have emphasized intrinsic factors that influence accidents—that is, factors having to do with a person's own physical and mental qualities. Another set of factors—extrinsic factors, or conditions that exist within the environment—also influence the occurrence of accidents. Unsafe conditions present in the environment are sometimes called "accidents waiting to happen." Such conditions may be due to negligence or ignorance about the

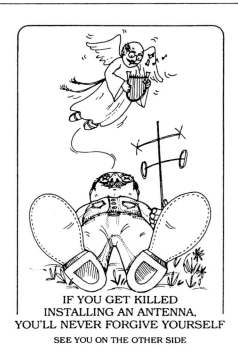

WHEN YOU'RE INSTALLING YOUR
CB BASE STATION OR TV ANTENNA,
TAKE THIS ADVICE OR YOU COULD
BE IN FOR THE SHOCK OF YOUR LIFE!

1.
When raising any antenna —
either CB or television —
make certain that the antenna
and its support cables or guy wires
cannot fall into or contact power lines.

2.
Never place your ladder next to
electric wires leading to your home.

3.
If you're installing a rotor,
be sure that it won't turn the antenna
around into nearby power lines.
Make sure the power lead is grounded.

4.
Support cables should be
well secured at both ends and
should be insulated according to
manufacturer's instructions.

PG and E

IF YOU GET KILLED
INSTALLING AN ANTENNA,
YOU'LL NEVER FORGIVE YOURSELF

SEE YOU ON THE OTHER SIDE

Figure *13-1 Antenna Hazard Warning*
The threat of death may be used to warn consumers and employees of risks to
safety. Here, the threat of death is presented with a touch of humor, being represented as a transition to an angelic state complete with stereotypical harp.

threat they pose to safety. Consider the situation of a swimming pool left
unattended and easily accessible to young children; if a toddler happens by,
falls into the pool, and is drowned, the owner of the pool and the child's
guardians may be judged negligent.

Unsafe conditions in the environment frequently are related to the attitudes and value systems of the person or group responsible, or of society as a
whole. For example, accidents caused by drunk driving occur because of
choices made by both the drinking driver and society. Similarly, fire safety is a
serious problem in the United States, even though action could be taken to
correct unsafe conditions. Despite such threats to life and health, individuals
and society as a whole often fail to take adequate steps to alleviate these problems.[10] It is, of course, naive to think that the risks we encounter in our lives
can be totally eliminated. Still, in most cases, risk can be minimized (see Figure 13-1). Lack of attention—or lack of resolve—to take the necessary action
toward correcting unsafe conditions prompts the question: "How negligent
must a society be before 'accidental' deaths are tantamount to homicide?"[11]

Disasters

Disaster is defined as a life-threatening event that affects many people within a relatively brief period of time, bringing sudden and great misfortune. Disasters result from natural phenomena—floods, earthquakes, and other "acts of God"—as well as from human activities. Included in the latter category would be fires, airplane crashes, chemical spills, and nuclear contamination.

In the United States, the incidence of disaster has increased in recent years. One reason for this increase is that more than half the U.S. population now lives within fifty miles of the coastline, an area that, in the West, is vulnerable to fires, floods, earthquakes, and landslides, and, in the Southeast, is prey to storms, hurricanes, and tornadoes. Population growth and industrialization increase our exposure to disasters related to human activities—for example, fires, explosions, and chemical pollution.

When a nuclear power plant at Chernobyl in the Ukraine failed in 1986, it released radioactivity across a large area of eastern and northern Europe. Dangerous levels of radiation contaminated the area around the plant, causing injury and death as well as damaging food supplies.[12] Risk theorists point out that modern technological systems are complex and may fail in ways that cannot be anticipated, with minor events unexpectedly interacting to produce a major problem, a phenomenon that Charles Perrow calls a "normal accident."[13] As one writer concludes: "We have constructed a world in which the potential for high-tech catastrophe is embedded in the fabric of day-to-day life."[14] The presence of hazardous technologies requires not only that steps be taken to prevent catastrophe, but also that effective systems of evacuation and disaster relief be in place if preventive efforts prove inadequate.

Reducing the Impact of Disasters

Communities can decrease the risk of injury and death by implementing measures designed to lessen the impact of a potential disaster. In Japan, for example, where the Great Kanto earthquake of 1923 killed more than 100,000 people, some 8 million people nationwide have participated in emergency exercises to prepare for a major earthquake that officials say could occur at any time.[15] Still, it is difficult to anticipate all the effects of a potential disaster. In September 1985, a devastating earthquake hit Mexico City, without warning, killing almost 10,000 people. Earlier, city officials had enacted building codes based on the possibility of low-frequency earthquake waves, which are associated with the ancient lake beds on which Mexico City is built. Despite this effort to ward off disaster, however, the codes did not include specifications for the number of shaking cycles buildings should be constructed to withstand, a factor that experts later determined contributed to the large number of fatalities.

People often subject themselves to the possibility of experiencing a disaster because of considerations that make the risk acceptable. Employment opportunities, for example, may be the deciding factor. People who live in areas where disasters are a common occurrence—earthquake or hurricane country,

Yanker Poster Collection, Library of Congress

for example—may rationalize the danger, if they give it any thought at all, as "playing the percentages."

Adequate warnings of an impending disaster can save lives. Yet necessary information may be withheld due to greed, political expediency, uncertainty about the nature and extent of the threat, or because of concerns about causing panic. The tragedy that followed the eruption in 1902 of the Mount Pelee volcano, on the island of Martinique in the West Indies, is instructive of how information that could warn potential disaster victims is sometimes mismanaged, with disastrous consequences. The officials of the nearby community of St. Pierre were alerted to the likelihood that the volcano would erupt. But, concerned that the population would panic if notified and thus thwart their plans for an upcoming local election, officials withheld any warning of the danger from the populace. As a result, almost the entire population of the small community was incinerated. The May 1980 eruption of Mount St. Helens provides an instructive comparison. Even though this eruption was larger, only sixty lives were lost compared with 30,000 casualties resulting from the eruption of Mount Pelee. This dramatic difference is attributable in part to adequate warnings of the hazard and timely establishment of a restricted zone of access.[16]

Even with an adequate warning system and a reliable, efficient information network, however, people do not always respond to threats in a prudent fashion. Just as the risks associated with smoking or drug abuse may be ignored, some people feel they are immune to disaster. Predictions of potential disasters are often met with the response: "I've never been affected before. Why should I worry now?" This is the apparent attitude of people who, when they learn of a chemical spill, travel to the disaster area for a closer look and of those who, hearing about an incoming tsunami, head for the ocean.[17] Philip Sarre says, "It seems that most people deliberately underestimate the risks to themselves."[18] Because preventive efforts are inherently limited, he says, "the best prospect seems to be for more effective systems of evacuation and disaster relief."

Coping With the Aftermath of Disaster

What can be done when disaster strikes? What kind of help is needed in its aftermath? Imagine the situation: People are injured, some are missing, others are dead. Survivors are likely to be in a state of shock, uncertain about the whereabouts of loved ones and about the future.[19] In the wake of a disaster, the survivors may experience an "existential crisis" that is marked by a profound sense of emptiness and despair.[20]

Meeting the immediate needs of survivors—providing food and shelter, caring for medical needs, and restoring vital community services—is essential. Yet even as attention is given to physical needs, the emotional needs of survivors should be addressed as well (see Figure 13-2). Ministering to these needs might include forming a missing persons group to help alleviate the anxieties of survivors worried about the safety of relatives. Locating and caring for the dead is another important aspect of helping survivors cope with the trauma of disaster. The comment of one relief agency worker, "It doesn't really make too much sense to dig up the dead and then go and bury them again," reveals an unfortunate ignorance of the human emotions that surround disposition of the dead. Perhaps what survivors of a disaster need most is compassion. Although efforts directed toward coping with disaster tend to be focused on the emergency period, the return to financial and emotional stability may take years. Unfortunately, the therapeutic community that comes together to assist in recovery from disaster is usually designed to function for only a brief time; it rapidly dissolves with the end of the emergency period.

Those who come to the aid of the survivors of a disaster may also become "survivors" in the sense that their work involves an intense encounter with human suffering and tragedy. Consider the experience of a Kansas City doctor who arrived at the scene of the Hyatt Regency Hotel disaster to find, among the debris left when a balcony collapsed onto the lobby below, bodies chopped in half, decapitated, and maimed. He watched as a critically injured man's leg, trapped under a fallen beam, was amputated with a chain saw. He worked sensitively and professionally as one of the first caregivers to force his way to

Unocal
425 First Street
San Francisco, California 94105-2681
Telephone (415) 362-7600

UNOCAL⑦⑥

October 27, 1989

We sincerely hope that you and your family were not
seriously affected by the recent earthquake in your
area.

We would like to assist our credit card customers
whose daily routine has been disrupted by this
disaster, by offering additional time to pay their
credit card account, if needed.

If we can assist you with special arrangements, just
drop us a note in the enclosed postage paid envelope
or call toll-free on 1-800-652-1520 and ask for
D. Enomoto.

C. B. Evans
General Manager
Credit Card Operations

Figure 13-2 *Disaster Letter from Unocal*
Even a computerized corporate response to the disruption of normal living
patterns can assist and comfort survivors as they cope with the devastation
wrought by a natural disaster.

where the victims were trapped. In the aftermath of the disaster, when things
returned more or less to normal, he told officials that he felt the need to
spend some time away from reminders of the disaster to cope with his own
experience as a survivor. Often, those who provide care and support are themselves given little support for their own coping needs. The provision of effective care for the survivors of critical incidents or disasters requires a
comprehensive approach that includes "predisaster preparedness, early intervention using psychological first aid, and postdisaster treatment" using a
range of counseling and therapeutic resources.[21]
    When a storm dumped twenty inches of rain in one night on a coastal
community in California, residents awoke the next morning to the news that
twenty-two people had been killed, more than a hundred families had lost
their homes, and another 3000 homes had been severely damaged. Within a

Al Diaz, AP/Wide World Photos

Shared support can help the bereaved cope with the traumatic impact of a disaster. Here, survivors embrace during the funeral services for passengers and crew of ValuJet Flight 592, which crashed in the Florida Everglades in May 1996.

few days, an impromptu organization was set up to help survivors deal with the psychological trauma of their losses. Known as Project COPE (Counseling Ordinary People in Emergencies), it provided immediate counseling to disaster victims and coordinated the services of more than a hundred mental health professionals.[22] Counselors found that people who had lost loved ones or property were experiencing grief reactions heightened by the sudden, capricious nature of their losses. Some who had lost only material possessions felt guilty for mourning the loss of property when others had lost family members. Some felt guilty for surviving the disaster. Those made homeless by the storm felt isolated and alone. Bureaucratic delay and uncooperative insurance companies and government agencies caused people to feel angry and frustrated. Many victims felt anxious, vulnerable, and depressed. For some, old problems related to personal or relationship issues reemerged in the aftermath of the disaster.

COPE set up programs to respond to each of these problems. Survivors were reassured that their reactions were normal and their grief legitimate. Counselors helped them sort out their priorities so they could begin to solve problems created by the disaster. Emergency crews and relief workers were included in these efforts to provide critical incident stress debriefing. Individuals who come to the aid of victims (including those who counsel the victims) are also vulnerable to the emotional impact of a disaster. Although we cannot eliminate the encounter with death that accompanies disaster, steps can be taken to reduce its impact, preserve life, and demonstrate compassion for survivors.

Violence

Violence is one of the most potent of our encounters with death. It can affect our thoughts and actions even when we have not been victimized ourselves. Potentially, anyone may become its unsuspecting victim. Interpersonal violence is now officially recognized as a public health problem. In 1997, 15,839 murders occurred in the United States; roughly half of the victims were under thirty years old.[23] About 30 percent of these murders were related to arguments—over money, property, "romantic" situations, or other issues—whereas about 19 percent were related to the commission of a felony. In about two-thirds of all murders, guns were used as the murder weapon.[24] In some urban areas, emergency room physicians report being "besieged with patients whose injuries are identical to wounds incurred by soldiers in Vietnam."[25] These wounds result from semi-automatic "assault weapons" that fire dozens of bullets per minute at several times the velocity of an ordinary pistol: "Organs that would have been merely grazed or even cleanly pierced by a handgun bullet are exploded by assault weapon fire, requiring massive transfusions of blood."

Young people are disproportionately represented among victims of violence.[26] According to a government report comparing the rates of homicide in twenty-six countries, young people in the United States kill themselves or are murdered at higher rates than young people in any other country in the industrialized world. Between 1950 and 1993, murder rates tripled among U.S. children under fifteen, and children were twelve times more likely to die from a gun than in all the other countries combined. One commentator remarked that "Being a child in America can be deadly."[27] Among the most troubling aspects of handgun violence, says a report by the American Medical Association, "is the fact that children very often are the victims of fatal gunshot wounds, self-inflicted either intentionally or accidentally, or received as innocent bystanders in scenes of domestic or street violence."[28] Rap musician Ice-T has drawn attention to the troubled condition of his hometown, South Central Los Angeles. Gang warfare, he says, is comparable to other wars: Members of gangs are like "veterans from war," and "thousands of people have died on each side of this bloody battlefield."[29] In Los Angeles County, more than 40 percent of the murders are gang-related.[30] Violence resulting from gang warfare has even intruded upon the serene setting of the cemetery. In Anaheim, California, two Vietnamese men died of multiple gunshot wounds they received while visiting the graves of two fellow Vietnamese gang members who had been murdered the previous year.[31] In Detroit, a mother whose sixteen-year-old son had been shot while walking to a neighborhood store with friends told a reporter that shooting occurred in her neighborhood every night. "They shoot like it's their job or something," she said. "All I want to do is move to someplace safe," she added. "Someplace where there's no shooting

Kevin Higley, AP/Wide World Photos

On April 20, 1999, at Columbine High School in Littleton, Colorado, distraught students grieve the violent deaths of friends in the aftermath of a shooting rampage carried out by two schoolmates who murdered 13 and wounded 23 before killing themselves.

on your block or the next block over. That's all. That's good enough. Just two safe blocks."[32]

Among the factors correlated with youth violence are poverty, repeated exposure to violence, drugs, easy access to firearms, unstable family life and family violence, delinquent peer groups, and media violence.[33] In 1995, the results of the federal government's first nationwide survey of schoolyard violence were released, revealing that more than one in ten of the nation's high school students said they had carried a weapon on school property.[34] Weapon-related violence is a major public health problem in the United States.[35] For some, guns are more than just weapons; they are symbols of power and energy. One young man said:

> When you are carrying a gun, I think other people can tell. Some kind of way a gun makes you light up. If you don't have a gun on you, a dude might mug you down. People don't mug you if you've got your gun on. They can detect something about you that wasn't there before.[36]

In advocating educational programs to promote the use of conflict resolution skills among at-risk school-age males, Joseph Giuliano says that the "ubiquity of violence in our cities [is] leading to the death of an entire generation of youth."[37]

Children who witness violence have been called "silent victims"; they appear physically unharmed, but are nevertheless emotionally affected as they hear gunshots outside their homes, witness shootings on the playground, or have a family member (often an older sibling) involved with violence.[38] Some children and adolescents, particularly those who live in urban environments, are exposed to high levels of violence throughout their lives. In describing a community-based approach to violence prevention in Richmond, California, Larry Cohen and Susan Swift remark:

> Interpersonal violence, although most concentrated among youth in densely populated, low-income communities, affects everyone in the United States. An awareness of violence permeates the environment, determining where people prefer to live, where they shop, how they respond to strangers on the streets, where they walk and drive, and how late at night they stay outside of their homes. Unlike any other environmental threat, violence has turned into a public health epidemic.[39]

The most threatening of violent acts are those that occur without apparent cause, when the victim is selected seemingly at random, thus heightening anxiety at the possibility that violence could unexpectedly confront anyone. A few years ago, in California, a number of murders were committed by someone whom the police dubbed the Trailside Killer because the killings occurred along several popular woodland trails. A woman who usually jogged every morning along one of these trails expressed feelings of being personally threatened because these violent acts had taken place "so close to home." In an area where she had previously felt safe and secure, she now felt fearful. Although she had no direct experience of the killings, she was nevertheless victimized by the violence because it occurred in her own familiar environment.

James Finley, AP/Wide World Photos

Eight days after a terrorist car bombing killed more than 160 people, the search for victims continues at the Alfred P. Murrah Federal Building in downtown Oklahoma City. The April 1995 bombing focused national attention on deadly violence, as Americans across the country engaged in ceremonies of mourning for victims and their families.

One woman described a potential encounter with death that began innocently enough when she answered a knock on her door. Recognizing a former schoolmate whom she hadn't seen in a long time, she invited him in and they began to chat. She began to feel uneasy, although she couldn't say why. About two months later, she heard on the news that her visitor had been arrested and was subsequently convicted for the brutal murders of several young women. The murders had been committed around the time of his unexpected visit. Recalling the experience, this woman commented, "I sometimes wonder how close we may be to death at times and just not realize it. It seems we really never know." In reviewing the motivations of serial killers, Dana DeHart and John Mahoney conclude that "One of the more disturbing aspects of serial murder is that virtually everyone is at some risk. Even cautious and circumspect persons are not safe from a serial killer; the victims need not provoke or even be acquainted with the killer."[40]

Some people say that violence is endemic in the United States. With few legal restraints during the great westward expansion, there arose attitudes that promoted arbitrary justice and encouraged people to do whatever it took to ensure survival, be it inside or outside the law. Some people argue that "Americans are obsessively devoted to the autonomy and the liberty of the individual, and are correspondingly indifferent to the needs—or even the idea—of the community."[41] Others conclude that, unwittingly or not, Americans have fostered the notion that violence can solve one's problems, and, in support of this thesis, these researchers cite the record of violence against Native Americans and African Americans, as well as analyses of present-day violence. In fact, the use of violence in pursuit of personal or political ends is a phenomenon found worldwide. Consider, for example, the effects of terrorism.[42] Terrorist acts occur outside the boundaries of social sanctions that have been erected to regulate conduct between individuals and between groups. In this respect, terrorism is comparable to other homicidal acts that take place between strangers.

Assessing the Homicidal Act

Community standards of justice play a major role in determining how the act of killing is assessed by a society and by its legal-political-judicial system. As Figure 13-3 illustrates, *homicide*—the killing of one human being by another— is separated into two main categories: criminal and noncriminal, and these categories encompass additional distinctions. For example, an act of homicide is considered excusable or justifiable when a person who kills another is found to have acted within certain legal rights, such as that of self-defense, or when the killing is judged an accident involving no gross negligence.

Thus, although a murder is necessarily a homicide, a homicide is not always a murder. The law has traditionally recognized two main distinctions within the category of *criminal* homicide: murder and manslaughter. Murder is associated with acts carried out with deliberate intention ("malice aforethought"), and the category of first-degree murder is used to designate killings that are carefully planned or that take place in conjunction with other serious crimes, such as rape. Manslaughter, however, is defined as wrongful, unplanned killing, done without malice. An example of *voluntary* manslaughter is that of a person who, after being provoked, kills another person in a fight. Such a person is said to have acted in the heat of passion, without considering the consequences. When homicide results from criminal carelessness but is unintentional, it is termed an act of *involuntary* manslaughter, as in the case of a fatal automobile accident caused by reckless driving or a death caused by gross negligence.

The circumstances surrounding a particular killing, the relationship between the killer and the victim, and the killer's motivation and intention are all considered in determining how an act of homicide is assessed within the American judicial system. In a study by Henry Lundsgaarde of more than 300 killings that occurred in a major American city, it was found that more than half of the suspects were released before reaching trial.[43] To understand why some homicide cases are not brought to trial, it is necessary to look at how the circumstances of a homicidal act influence its investigation and how the judicial processes determine whether an accused killer is brought to trial.

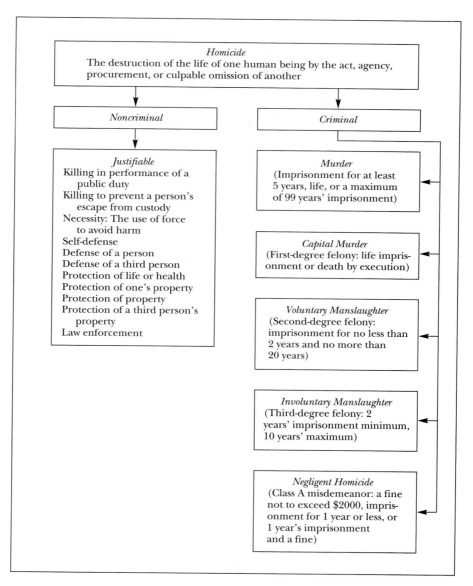

Figure *13-3 Schematic View of Texas Homicide Statutes*
Source: Vernon's Texas Codes Annotated: Penal Code, 1974. From Henry
Lundsgaard, *Murder in Space City: A Cultural Analysis of Houston Homicide Patterns* (New York: Oxford University Press, 1977), p. 213.

The medical-legal investigation of an act of homicide generally includes
three components: (1) an autopsy to determine the official cause of death;
(2) a police investigation to ascertain the facts and gather evidence pertinent
to the killing; and (3) various judicial and quasi-judicial procedures, carried

out by the district attorney's office and the court system, to determine whether there is sufficient cause to bring a case to trial.

Fundamental to this investigation is the acknowledgment that homicide is an interpersonal act. That is, it involves a relationship between the killer and the victim: They may have had close domestic ties, being members of the same family or otherwise related; they may have been friends or associates; or they may have been strangers. In the study conducted by Lundsgaarde, it was found that "the closer, or more intimate, the relationship is between a killer and his victim, the less likely it is that the killer will be severely punished for his act." In other words, killing a stranger was more likely to result in a stiff penalty than was killing a friend or family member.

The response of the criminal justice system to homicide reflects cultural attitudes about killing. Lundsgaarde says, "What appears so shocking, or understandable, as the case may be, about many killings depends upon our personal understandings of and assumptions about the rules that 'should' and 'ought' to govern a particular kind of relationship." Basing its standards on cultural attitudes, the criminal justice system in a community sets about its task of determining whether an act of homicide is lawful or unlawful. If lawful, the killer is released and the case is closed. If unlawful, a further determination is made as to whether the killing in question was an act of murder, manslaughter, or negligent homicide—and there are various degrees of criminal intent within each of these categories as well. In making these determinations, the criminal justice system, including the police investigation, takes into account the intention, motivation, and circumstances surrounding the homicide.

What are the cultural assumptions by which an act of homicide is judged? Lundsgaarde's research showed that the legal outcome for a person who kills his wife's lover is quite different from the outcome for a person who combines killing with theft, robbery, or similar criminal or antisocial acts. An extensive investigation conducted by the *Los Angeles Times* found that people who killed strangers were more likely to get tough treatment from the criminal justice system than those who killed lovers, relatives, or other people they knew. One police investigator said, when "innocent victims, God-fearing people, end up murdered," other cases "take a back seat" because such killing causes neighborhood terror and therefore must be resolved quickly. However, he added, "When 'Snoopy' kills 'Chilly Willie,' nobody cares."[44]

Society is usually reluctant to become involved in matters that fall within the domain of the family. This appears to be true even in cases of family homicide involving a child victim. Although child homicide typically evokes great public anger, situational elements within the family often result in a more tempered view by the criminal justice system, with lesser penalties being imposed on the basis of statutes defining manslaughter or child abuse rather than murder.[45] A close relationship is believed to involve its own set of mutual responsibilities and obligations—its own "code of justice," if you will—that provides social sanctions for acts that occur within the relationship. In contrast, says Lundsgaarde, "The killer who chooses a stranger as his victim overtly threatens the preservation of the social order."

When death is unreal, violence also becomes unreal, and human life has no value in and of itself.

Vine Deloria, Jr.

To put it another way, an individual who kills a stranger is not likely to be constrained by personal concern for the victim. Thus, society devotes its attention to acts of homicide that threaten the preservation of law and order within the larger society. Killings that occur within the family unit or between persons who know one another tend to be viewed as less of a threat to society at large.

Capital Punishment

Some people believe that violence is "contagious" in modern American society. This reasoning can be developed along several lines: First, it may be that a violent society creates an environment in which disturbed individuals are encouraged to act out their antisocial behaviors in more harmful ways than they might if other ways of releasing such violent tendencies were available. Second, each violent incident may spawn others, thus spreading the contagion of violence. Third, some believe that if an act of violence is not properly resolved, it will be repeated. With regard to this last point, a "proper resolution," according to Fredrick Wertham, is "for society to make clear what it wants. Society must say, *No, this we will not tolerate,*" and this must be affirmed and upheld by a judicial process that emphasizes accountability for one's acts.[46]

Is capital punishment, then, the strong statement that is needed? In theory, capital punishment, which has been termed "planned, timed dying," serves a twofold purpose: (1) It punishes the offender and (2) deters other potential offenders. Hanging, electrocution, the gas chamber, and lethal injection have all been used to carry out executions at various times in the United States. Figures compiled by law professor Victor Streib indicate that, although one out of every eight murder suspects arrested is a woman, forty-nine out of fifty death sentences are imposed on men. What accounts for this apparent discrepancy? Women commit fewer of the types of murder generally punished with death. In two-thirds of the murders committed by women, the victim is an intimate, and almost half of the murders of intimates each year are committed by women.[47] Society does not take violent domestic crimes as seriously as it does crimes against strangers. The vast majority of murderers who receive the death penalty are involved in intraracial offenses—that is, cases of whites killing whites or blacks killing blacks.[48]

During 1997, seventy-four people were executed in the United States, all for murder, and, at year's end, about 3300 people were under sentence of death.[49] Herb Haines observes that "executions have become highly ritualized affairs," as death-row prisoners are moved to special cells for their final visits

The deepest grave on earth can never contain the violent death of a single decent soul.

John Nichols, *American Blood*

and last meals, and then transferred from one prison staffer to another as they are taken to the place where the death sentence is carried out.[50] Haines says: "The modern orchestration of death lends assurance that everything is in order, everything is humane and civilized and that we aren't, after all, barbarians."

Although the death penalty has been applied to various offenses since ancient times, many people argue that it is needlessly cruel and overrated as a deterrent to murder. According to Glenn Vernon,

> Investigations into the ineffectiveness of the death penalty as a deterrent to murder revealed that some murderers were so busy with other things during the events preceding the murder that they simply did not think of the death penalty, and that others were interacting with their victims in such an extremely emotional manner that the consequences of their murderous acts were not even taken into account.[51]

By the mid-nineteenth century, reforms of the death penalty began to occur in various countries. In the United States, most statutes require that a sentence of death be imposed only after evidence is submitted to establish that "aggravating" or "mitigating" factors were present in the crime. If "aggravating" factors are found and the sentence is death, then the case is reviewed by an appellate court. Apart from certain crimes on which the Supreme Court has not ruled (the most notable being treason), the only capital crime in the United States today is murder.[52] Public opinion surveys indicate that fewer people favor capital punishment when "life without parole" is an option.[53] Also, whereas some call for a "man-sized punishment for a man-sized crime," few people are willing to impose capital punishment on juveniles who commit murder.[54] As capital punishment has been removed from public arenas and secreted away in prisons, capital *trials* have taken on special significance. Robert Emerson says that such trials have become "the public ceremonial drama of capital punishment," allowing "the modern state to segregate and sanitize its violence."[55]

Is it inconsistent for society to try to eradicate or prevent murder by itself engaging in killing? Does capital punishment reinforce the idea that violence solves problems? Citing evidence from psychology and behavioral therapy, which emphasizes the effects of positive reinforcement, Kastenbaum and Aisenberg say "there is little evidence to suggest that imposing massive punishment on one individual will 'improve' the behavior of others"; on the contrary, it may reinforce hostile fantasies and murderous tendencies.[56] The greatest risk for a potential murderer, they contend, is not the risk of execution, "but the risk of being killed by the police, the intended victim, or some bystander."

If capital punishment is not an effective deterrent to murder, are there other options? Comparing our present-day system with early Anglo-Saxon and English law and with many non-Western legal systems as well, Lundsgaarde says, "Modern criminal law has completely transformed the ancient view of homicide as a wrong against a victim and his family to its modern version that views homicide as an offense against the state."[57] In short, the modern tendency is to view crime as a social problem. The separation of civil and criminal law—or, more specifically, the separation of personal obligation and criminal liability—eliminates the killer's liability to the *victim as person*. Instead, the violent act is viewed as having been committed against the public at large.

Steps Toward Reducing Violence

The term *psychic maneuvers* has been used to describe the factors that facilitate murder and other homicidal acts (see Table 13-1). You may find it interesting to review this list three times. First, consider how each of these psychic maneuvers might function in your own life. Notice that they do violence to ourselves and others even when they function far more subtly than the overt act of homicide. Second, note how these psychic maneuvers function within society, how they contribute to violence between individuals and between groups. The third time, consider how each of these psychic maneuvers may be a dysfunctional strategy found in conflicts between nations.

T A B L E   *13-1*   *Factors Favoring Violence*

Anything that physically or psychologically separates the potential killer from the victim. For example, the use of a gun leads to a concentration on the means (pulling the trigger) rather than the end result (the death of a person). Psychological separation occurs when the victim is perceived as fundamentally different from oneself.

Anything that permits the killer to define murder as something else, such as "making an example of the victim," "making the world safe for democracy," "implementing the final solution," or "exterminating the terrorists."

Anything that fosters perceiving people as objects or as less than human. This happens when victims become "cases," "subjects," or "numbers," as well as when the killing occurs from a distance as with high-altitude bombing or submarine warfare.

Anything that permits one to escape responsibility by blaming someone else: "I was just carrying out orders."

Anything that encourages seeing oneself as debased or worthless: "If I'm treated like a rat, I might as well act like one. What have I got to lose?"

Anything that reduces self-control or that is believed to have this effect: alcohol, mind-altering drugs, hypnotism, mass frenzy, and the like.

Anything that forces a hasty decision or that does not permit time for "cooling off." That is, a situation may force one to decide to shoot or not to shoot with no opportunity for deliberation.

Anything that encourages a person to feel above or outside the law: The notion that rank, prestige, wealth, or the like makes it possible for one to "get away with murder."

Source: Adapted from Robert Kastenbaum and Ruth Aisenberg, *The Psychology of Death: Concise Edition* (New York: Springer, 1976), pp. 291–294.

Victims sometimes play a role in encouraging violent acts against themselves. Homicide investigators have found that victims are not always as innocent as might initially be assumed. Consider the example of a husband who has been repeatedly threatened by his angry wife wielding a loaded revolver. His response to this threat is, "Go ahead, you might just as well kill me." What can be said about his role as a victim in such circumstances? Or consider another such incident: A daughter, overhearing her parents arguing, tries to intercede but is told by her mother, "Never mind, honey, let him kill me." After the daughter leaves the house to seek assistance, her father obtains a revolver from another room and shoots and kills the girl's mother.

Investigators note that, during domestic strife, wives have made statements like, "What are you going to do, big man, kill me?" coupled with dares like, "You haven't got the guts." Such statements combine "elements of seduction and lethality."[58] In some instances, there are indications that the victim not only seemed to be "asking for it," but was the one actually responsible for escalating the conflict to the level of physical violence.

While recognizing that victims do sometimes help to bring violence on themselves, we should be cautious about placing a stigma of blame on victims indiscriminately. Lula Redmond underscores the fact that labeling victims as bad, careless, seductive, "with the wrong crowd," or as somehow "asking for it" denies the reality that everyone is vulnerable to victimization.[59] Blaming the victim is a convenient, albeit erroneous, way to overcome one's own sense of vulnerability and thereby regain a sense of personal security. If suitable "explanations" can be found to account for the victim's demise, they offer convincing evidence that a similar encounter *could never* happen in one's own life.

Far more effective than blaming the victim is to understand the factors that favor violence and take action to reduce their presence in our own lives and in society as a whole. Studies show that violence is reduced when the residents of a community work together to create a safe and orderly environment and when neighbors themselves take a measure of responsibility for maintaining social order.[60] In addition, the sense of social isolation that helps breed violence is counteracted when families take seriously their role in communicating positive community values.[61] Cohen and Swift argue that "stopping the momentum of violence requires a 'critical mass' of people who are willing to speak out and to work together to change the structures and policies that frame the way we live."[62] In seeking ways to reduce the level of violence, it is useful to consider the factors that tend to *prevent* violent behaviors (see Table 13-2).

War

Within the context of ordinary human interaction, our moral and legal codes stand in strict opposition to killing. In war, however, killing is not only accepted, but possibly heroic. War abrogates the conventional sanctions against killing by substituting a different set of conventions and rules about moral conduct. The expectation that one will kill and, if necessary, die for one's

T A B L E *13-2*   *Guidelines for Lessening the Potential for Violence*

1. Avoid the use of prejudicial, dehumanizing, or derogatory labels, whether applied to oneself or to others.
2. Avoid or eliminate conditions that underlie dehumanizing perceptions of oneself or others.
3. Promote communication and contact between potential adversaries, emphasizing similarities and common goals rather than differences.
4. Refrain from using physical punishment as the primary means of discipline.
5. Champion the good guys.
6. Teach children that violence is not fun, cute, or smart. Emphasize that they are responsible for their behavior.
7. Identify and foster the human resources that can provide alternatives to violence. For example, promote sharing among children, and encourage them to think before engaging in impulsive and possibly hostile actions against others.
8. Reduce the attractiveness of violence in the mass media.

Source: Adapted from Robert Kastenbaum and Ruth Aisenberg, *The Psychology of Death: Concise Edition* (New York: Springer, 1976), pp. 296–297.

country is a concomitant of war. As Arnold Toynbee says, "The fundamental postulate of war is that, in war, killing is not murder."[63]

In Dalton Trumbo's classic antiwar novel, *Johnny Got His Gun,* we find a veteran "without arms legs ears eyes nose mouth" who devises a means of communicating with the outside world by "tapping out" messages on his pillow with his head.[64] He asks to be taken outside, where he can become an "educational exhibit" to teach people "all there was to know about war." He thinks to himself, "That would be a great thing to concentrate war in one stump of a body and to show it to people so they could see the difference between a war that's in newspaper headlines and liberty loan drives and a war that is fought out lonesomely in the mud somewhere, a war between a man and a high explosive shell."

The last century saw not only two major world wars and an unprecedented buildup of arms during the "cold war," but also innumerable regional conflicts. Historians believe that 7.5 million Russian troops may have perished during World War II. In more recent decades, 58,000 Americans died in Vietnam, and over 400,000 North Vietnamese and Viet Cong died in that conflict. During the Persian Gulf War, whereas American casualties were few, estimates place the number of Iraqi troops killed at from 40,000 to 100,000. In addition to the death and injury directly related to war, a continuing emphasis on "militarism" around the world has been singled out as having a variety of deleterious health effects, including poverty, environmental damage, social unrest, political instability, national debt, and military oppression.[65]

Genocide, defined as the effort to destroy an entire nation or human group, was practiced with dire results during the last century.[66] Between 1941 and 1945, Nazi Germany exterminated 6 million Jews in the Holocaust and killed another 5 million people deemed to be political opponents, mentally ill, retarded, or somehow "genetically inferior." With the coming to power of the Khmer Rouge in Cambodia during the mid-1970s, about 2 million Cam-

At Buchenwald, near Weimar, Germany, a few of the dead are piled in a yard awaiting burial following the invasion by the Allies. Starvation and disease due to unsanitary living conditions, as well as the incessant torture of prisoners, caused an average of two hundred deaths each day at this infamous Nazi concentration camp.

bodians died from execution and starvation, an example of "autogenicide," a group killing its own people. Also during the 1970s, the infamous "disappearances" carried out by the military in Argentina resulted in the deaths of as many as 30,000 people. In the aftermath of the Persian Gulf War, the regime led by Saddam Hussein may have killed tens of thousands of indigenous Kurds in northern Iraq, while causing another 2 million to flee their homes. Following the assassination of the president of Rwanda in 1994, up to a million people, mainly members of the Tutsi tribe, were massacred in an attempt to exterminate them. Colin Murray Parkes suggests that, among the factors contributing to the genocide, the repression of grief in the wake of traumatic bereavement may perpetuate a cycle of violence focused on revenge. Parkes says, "It is not unreasonable to hope that any action to encourage people to grieve and express their discontent in controlled and safe ways might reduce the risk of uncontrolled violence."[67]

Chivalrous notions of combat, with mounted men-at-arms meeting gallantly to do battle on an uninhabited hill or plain, have been replaced in modern times by the reality of mass technological warfare. Explosive land mines kill or maim more than 15,000 people each year, most of them innocent civilians and many of them children, yet thousands of them are still being planted every day.[68] According to the International Red Cross, nine out of ten casualties in modern warfare are civilians—men, women, and children who simply "got in the way of somebody's war."[69] In the so-called postwar period since 1945, at least 20 million people have died in over one hundred conflicts, and another 60 million have been wounded, imprisoned, separated from their families, and forced to flee their homes or their countries. This human misery goes on even as you read these words.

Technological Alienation

When we recall the epic battles of Achilles and Agamemnon, or of the legendary King Arthur and the Knights of the Round Table, or of the samurai in medieval Japan, we encounter a view of warfare as heroic. The enemy is seen as a worthy opponent with whom one is engaged in a "metaphysic of struggle" or a "ritual of purification."[70] This sense of chivalry is now largely absent from warfare, leaving "only the abstract virtue of obedience to duty," a change due in significant measure to technological advances in weaponry. Instead of individual initiative and courage, modern warfare emphasizes bureaucratic cooperation and calculation.

"Technological alienation" has been termed the "most characteristic feature of the modern war machine."[71] Not until World War I did warfare begin to involve civilians on a large scale. During the Spanish Civil War, the world was horrified by the German aerial bombing of the Basque town of Guernica, indiscriminately slaughtering civilians of both sexes and of all ages. In tallying the dead of World War II, civilian victims outnumbered military casualties. In modern warfare, distinctions between combatants and noncombatants have been blurred, if not erased.

Early warfare had limits: the bow and arrow, the bullet from the gun, the artillery shell. The conventional limits of warfare were radically altered with the advent of the atomic bomb, unleashed on Hiroshima on August 6, 1945. Gil Elliot says:

> By the time we reach the atom bomb, the ease of access to target and the instant nature of macroimpact [large-scale destruction] mean that both the choice of city and the identity of the victim have become completely randomized, and human technology has reached a final platform of self-destructiveness. . . . At Hiroshima and Nagasaki, the "city of the dead" is finally transformed from a metaphor into a literal reality.[72]

The characteristic human response to such carnage is one of *psychic numbing*. Exposed to mass death, our self-protective psychological response is to become insensitive and unfeeling. Robert Lifton and Eric Olson observe that "jet pilots who cooly drop bombs on people they never see tend not to feel

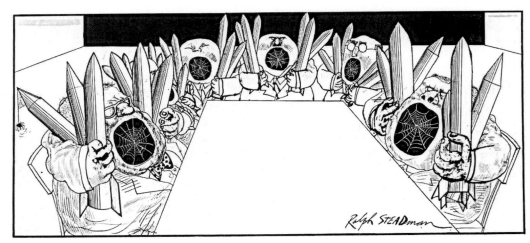

"Disarmament Talks," © 1987 Ralph Steadman, Swann Collection, Library of Congress

what goes on at the receiving end."[73] They add that "those of us who watch such bombing on TV undergo a different though not unrelated desensitization." Confronted by the death-dealing potential of modern weaponry, it is worth remembering the story of Dalton Trumbo's veteran, who wanted to be a living exhibit of the ravaging, destructive effects of war. His request was denied, the story explains, because "he was a perfect picture of the future and they were afraid to let anyone see what the future was like."

Think for a moment about your responses when you hear or read about war. What kinds of images are evoked when you think about combat, the atomic bomb, the Nazi Holocaust, Hiroshima, Vietnam, or the Persian Gulf War? Reflect on your own personal experiences and the experiences of those close to you. What makes the encounter with death in times of war different from other encounters with death? Glenn Vernon observes that "confrontation with wartime killing may be one of the most difficult experiences of those who have been taught to avoid killing."[74]

The Conversion of the Warrior

War activates a special set of conventions that make it psychologically possible for individuals to go against the grain of what they have learned about right and wrong—to put aside the ordinary rules of moral conduct. As long as the combatant "keeps more or less faithfully to the recognized rules," Toynbee says, "most of humankind have been willing to alter their moral sense in such a way as to regard the killer in war as 'being righteous.'"[75] One of the conventions of warfare, Toynbee points out, is to dress the part. The psychological effect of the soldier's uniform is that it "symbolizes the abrogation of the normal taboo on killing fellow human beings: it replaces this taboo by a duty to kill them."

Joel Baruch, a Vietnam veteran, writing about his combat experiences, says, "Changes in personality and mood are rooted in the special climate of

The third plane came in, skimming the treetops, engine screeching. Two napalm canisters spun down from the Skyhawk's bomb rack into the tree line, and the plane pulled into a barrel-rolling climb as the red-orange napalm bloomed like an enormous poppy.

"Beautiful! Beautiful!" I said excitely. "They were right on 'em."

The napalm rolled and boiled up out of the trees, dirty smoke cresting the ball of flame. The enemy mortar fire stopped. Just then, three Viet Cong broke out of the tree line. They ran one behind another down a dike, making for the cover of another tree line nearby. "Get 'em! Get those people. Kill 'em!" I yelled at my machine-gunners, firing my carbine at the running, dark-uniformed figures two hundred yards away. The gunners opened up, walking their fire toward the VC. The bullets made a line of spurts in the rice paddy, then were splattering all around the first enemy soldier, who fell to his knees. Letting out a war whoop, I swung my carbine toward the second man just as a stream of machine-gun tracers slammed into him. I saw him crumple as the first Viet Cong, still on his knees, toppled stiffly over the dike, behind which the third man had taken cover. We could see only the top of his back as he crawled behind the dike. What happened next happened very quickly, but in memory I see it happening with an agonizing slowness. It is a ballet of death between a lone, naked man and a remorseless machine. We are ranging in on the enemy soldier, but cease firing when one of the Skyhawks comes in to strafe the tree line. The nose of the plane is pointing down at a slight angle and there is an orange twinkling as it fires its mini-gun, an aerial cannon that fires explosive 20-mm bullets so rapidly that it sounds like a buzz saw. The rounds, smashing into the tree line and the rice paddy at the incredible rate of one hundred per second, raise a translucent curtain of smoke and spraying water. Through this curtain, we see the Viet Cong behind the dike sitting up with his arms outstretched, in the pose of a man beseeching God. He seems to be pleading for mercy from the screaming mass of technology that is flying no more than one hundred feet above him. But the plane swoops down on him, fires its cannon once more, and blasts him to shreds. As the plane climbs away, I look at the dead men through my binoculars. All that remains of the third Viet Cong are a few scattered piles of bloody rags.

Philip Caputo, *A Rumor of War*

the combat zone. These mutations evolve in such a wily fashion that the person who undergoes them is not aware of the alterations himself."[76] The conventions of war are mind- and personality-altering. Here is Baruch's account of his first encounter with death on the battlefield:

Stone dead, he was. Eyes wide open, staring at nothing. A thin veneer of blood curling at the corner of his lips. Two gaping holes in his chest. Right leg half gone. My first combat fatality. A lifeless body where only moments before a heart beat its customary seventy pumps in one orbit of the minute hand. It is one thing to hear about death; to watch it happen is quite another. I went over to the nearest tree and vomited my guts out.

By his next experience of combat death, however, Baruch began to question whether he was becoming callous and unfeeling: "I was becoming

> To despise another human being, to wound another human being, to open another human being's body in the name of proving a belief, requires denying those other human beings' essential humanity. Otherwise the wellsprings of compassion, of our profound and bodily identification with one another—all mothers, all fathers, all brothers and sisters and daughters and sons, all lovers and neighbors and friends—would flood the mechanism of alienation that cleaves us apart.
>
> We distance those whom we fear, and we fear them more for their distance. We distance them psychologically by reducing them to epithets: Hun, kike, Jap, kulak, gook, nigger, fascist, liberal, communist, Sandinista, enemy of the people, queer. We distance them physically by refusing to acknowledge their common humanity or to attend their suffering. Only then can we bear to injure or destroy them.
>
> Technology amplifies this effect. Destruction at a distance with projectiles and bombs short-circuits the identification with similarly embodied beings . . . that might otherwise stay our hand.
>
> Richard Rhodes

impervious to the death of my fellow soldiers, and, in addition, I was negating the possibility of my own . . . demise." Another Vietnam veteran explains:

> Social context is much more important than most people realize. We pretty much live within the boundaries of one social context. If you lived in a different society, you would consider a different set of behaviors as normal. What's bewildering and frightening in the combat situation is how quickly "normal" can change.[77]

Each of us experiences differences in our behavior according to the social context. How we behave among our relatives is likely to be different from how we behave among strangers or business associates. Usually, such differences are subtle and rarely meet head on. The contradictory values that exist for the soldier in combat, however, require what the veteran just quoted calls

> . . . a much more total "schizophrenia." When you're there you don't really remember what it's like to come back into the social context of a society where killing is abhorrent. And, when you come back home, you don't really remember the context of the combat situation, except perhaps in your nightmares.

When societies reflect on their participation in war, they often speak in terms of patriotism, the heroism of fighting for one's country, the need to defend the things that are held dear. When we listen to the words of those who have experienced combat, however, we hear a very different value system at work. We hear about individuals fighting for their lives. Heroic intentions and patriotic feelings may be the rationale for donning the uniform, but in combat the emphasis is likely to be on survival.[78]

Coping With the Aftermath of War

Veterans do not necessarily resolve their losses merely by leaving the combat zone or being discharged from military service. In the aftermath of war, many experience symptoms such as numbness, irritability, depression, difficulties in relationships, and guilt at having survived when others did not. Some experience nightmares and flashbacks to traumatic scenes. Although some veterans avoid intrusive reminders of a stressful past, others "experience positive excitement when reviving memories of mortal risk and killing."[79] The tension and hyper-alertness of being in combat can produce a "high" that is virtually addictive. The term *posttraumatic stress disorder* (PTSD) has been used to describe such symptoms, although such reactions could also be termed "delayed grief syndrome" or "posttraumatic grief disorder."[80] Known as "shell shock" during World War I and "battle fatigue" during World War II, PTSD became prominent in the 1970s in the aftermath of the war in Vietnam.

Psychiatrist Jonathan Shay finds parallels between the grief and rage experienced by modern combat veterans and the description in Homer's *Iliad* of similar symptoms experienced by warriors who fought in the Trojan Wars 3000 years ago.[81] Shay says, "There have been technological changes, but there have been no changes to the human mind and heart and soul." The chilling atrocities committed by Achilles in a berserk rage following the battlefield death of his friend Patroclus are echoed in episodes of grief-driven combat violence such as the My Lai massacre during the Vietnam War. One of the lessons to be learned from Homer's *Iliad,* says Shay, is that soldiers should be allowed to grieve: "Snatching bodies off the battlefield in black bags and spiriting them back to stateside mortuaries without permitting comrades to mourn the fallen is profoundly damaging to survivors."

Although psychotherapy, support groups, and other such approaches to healing have been at the center of efforts to treat PTSD, some veterans achieve solace and renewed self-respect through innovative means of coming to terms with their experiences.[82] On Memorial Day, 1990, a group of Vietnam veterans began a 700-mile walk from Angel Fire, New Mexico, to the Pine Ridge Indian Reservation in South Dakota. At the end of their journey, the veterans (who called themselves "The Last Patrol") were welcomed by several hundred Oglala Sioux and invited to participate in traditional ceremonies for returning warriors. After participating in the honoring dances, sweat-lodge rituals, and smoking the sacred pipe of the Oglala Sioux, one veteran had one of his few nights of restful sleep after years of nightmares and said, "This is a new life for many of us. . . . [This] was an opportunity to eliminate the things that have tortured us." Other veterans participated in retreats led by the Vietnamese Buddhist monk Thich Nhat Hanh. The Buddhist walking meditation reminded some veterans of "walking point" in Vietnam. Traumatic memories surfaced and were discussed during group sessions. One veteran said that the hours of silent meditation with the Vietnamese Buddhists "dissolved his mistrust of the 'enemy.'"

In contrast to the war in Vietnam, the Persian Gulf War was brief, supported at home, and hailed as a victory. Yet, regardless of its outcome, combat leaves haunting memories. After the shooting stops, the mind must "sort out and file the almost incomprehensible facts of war."[83] One helicopter door gunner during the Persian Gulf War told his friends to stop boasting about high

Rites of Passage

. . . As a psychiatrist who has worked with Vietnam veterans, I know all too well the long-term effects of wartime traumas. Ten and fifteen years after the events, there remain nightmares, fears, depression and, most fundamentally, failures of loving in veterans of combat. The timelessness of the unconscious does not bend to political realities. National treaties mark the beginning, not the end, of the psychic work of mastery.

Primitive societies intuitively knew the value of cultural ceremonies that marked the end of hostilities. Rites of passage were provided for the soldiers and the society to make the transition from the regression of combat to the structure of integrated living. These rituals acknowledged and sanctioned the otherwise forbidden acts of war. They thanked the soldier for his protection, forgave him his crimes and welcomed him back to life.

Our failure to provide such a cleansing for our warriors and ourselves has left our culture struggling for closure. It has as well made the task of intrapsychic mastery so much more difficult for the individual soldier.

Harvey J. Schwartz, M.D.

Iraqi casualties after he saw dead Iraqi troops for the first time. "It's different when you see their faces, with blood coming out of their wounds," he said.

Since its dedication in 1982, the Vietnam Veterans Memorial has become a "wailing wall" for the families and friends of the more than 58,000 whose names are engraved there, as well as for those who served and survived. Many visitors have left mementos, ranging from a pair of old cowboy boots found at the base of the Memorial shortly after its dedication, to teddy bears, baseball caps, newspaper clippings, diaries, and tear-stained letters. One of the first letters was placed by the mother of an Army sergeant whose death had occurred nearly fifteen years before her visit to the Memorial. In the letter, she described finding her son's name for the first time:

> We had been looking for about a half-hour when your father quietly said, "Honey, here it is." As I looked to where his hand was touching the black wall, I saw your name, William R. Stock.
>
> My heart seemed to stop. I felt as though I couldn't breathe. It was like a bad dream. I felt as though I was freezing. My teeth chattered. God, how it hurt.[84]

The sacrifices made by the families of men and women in the military have often gone unnoticed. In recalling her odyssey as the wife of a Marine Corps officer who served in Vietnam, Marian Novak says: "I watched my husband train for war; I waited thirteen months for him to return from it; and then I waited another fifteen years for him to truly come home."[85] Warfare creates a "phantom army" that is composed of the spouses, children, parents, and friends who serve invisibly at home. In this sense, the euphemistic term "collateral damage" encompasses not only the civilian deaths that occur in a war zone, but also the grief experienced by individuals and families whose lives are disrupted by the loss of loved ones serving in the armed forces.

Among the most poignant losses that can be experienced in adult life are those related to war. The Vietnam Veterans Memorial in Washington, D.C., is a focal point for coping with the grief of individual as well as national losses. For many who fought the war, as well as for other survivors, the effects are pervasive and felt daily. Here, visitors reflect on the names of the individuals engraved on the face of the black wall of the Memorial, following its official dedication in November 1982.

TABLE 13-3   *Motives and Needs That Promote Aggression*

1. To gain power or wealth.
2. To gain territory or physical dominance, or to get others to adopt one's ideals and values
3. To defend or elevate personal and societal self-concept, self-esteem, or sense of identity
4. To retaliate and do harm after being provoked
5. To achieve personal or national glory
6. To respond to a sense of injustice
7. To act in self-defense
8. To fulfill a sense of duty or responsibility
9. To encourage a sense of personal competence and gain personal power
10. To gain hope for control over events and renewed faith in the future
11. To restore or revitalize the comprehension of self and world following chaos, disorder, or other sudden profound changes
12. To gain a sense of positive social identity by adopting shared ideologies

Source: Adapted from Ervin Staub, *The Roots of Evil: The Origins of Genocide and Other Group Violence* (New York: Cambridge University Press, 1989), pp. 36–43, 249–250.

Making War, Making Peace

The causes of war have been sought in natural human aggression, as well as in the role of special interest groups in society.[86] According to Karl von Clausewitz, a nineteenth-century military writer whose *On War* is considered a classic study, war is the continuation of political policy by other means. Generally speaking, war is defined as a condition of hostile conflict between opposing forces, each of which believes its vital interests are at stake and thus seeks to impose control on the opposing side through the use of force. Why do nations resort to war as a means of solving problems? A number of motives and needs may be related to its onset (see Table 13-3). Joining together against a common enemy often creates a sense of connectedness and community within a warring group—qualities that represent yet another need that may be satisfied by going to war. It may be that human beings have an innate tendency to divide the world into "us" and "them." Sam Keen says:

> In the beginning we create the enemy. Before the weapon comes the image. We *think* others to death and then invent the battle-axe or the ballistic missiles with which to actually kill them. Propaganda precedes technology. . . . It seems unlikely that we will have any considerable success in controlling warfare unless we come to understand the logic of political paranoia, and the process of creating propaganda that justifies our hostility.[87]

The role of media reports in generating public support for war while facilitating denial of death is borne out in research conducted by Debra Umberson and Kristin Henderson. Their analysis of news stories about the Gulf War revealed four major themes: (1) rhetorical devices that distance the reader from death and encourage denial of death in the war, (2) official denial of responsibility for war-related deaths and reassurance to the public that death

TABLE *13-4*   *Faces of the Enemy*

- The enemy as stranger. "Us" versus "Them."
- The enemy as aggressor. "Good" versus "Evil."
- The faceless enemy. "Human beings" versus "Dehumanized barbarians."
- The enemy as enemy of God; war as applied theology. "Holy" versus "Unholy."
- The enemy as barbarian (threat to culture, heathen, pagan).
- The greedy enemy (appetite for empire).
- The enemy as criminal, as committer of atrocities, as torturer (anarchists, terrorists, outlaws).
- The enemy as torturer or sadist.
- The enemy as rapist, desecrator of women and children. ("Woman as bait and trophy.")
- The enemy as beast, reptile, insect, germ. (Gives sanctions for extermination.)
- The enemy as death. ("The ultimate threat.")
- The enemy as worthy opponent. ("Heroic warfare or chivalry.") Examples: The epic battles of Achilles and Agamemnon, King Arthur and the Knights of the Round Table, the samurai in medieval Japan.

Source: Adapted from Sam Keen, *Faces of the Enemy: Reflections of the Hostile Imagination* (San Francisco: Harper and Row, 1986).

would be "minimal," (3) rhetoric that prepares the public for death in war and to view the deaths as just, and (4) ambiguity and uncertainty about the actual death toll from the war.[88]

If we come to see other human beings as hostile, their ambiguous actions may then be perceived as threatening. When we act to defend ourselves against this perceived threat, their reaction confirms our initial assumption (see Table 13-4). It is important to recognize, however, that sometimes our images of the enemy are accurate. Keen says, "Short of utopia there are real enemies. It is a luxury of the naive and sheltered to think that right thinking, good intentions, and better communication techniques will turn all enemies into friends."[89] There are times when maintaining freedom depends on choosing between killing and surrendering our humanity.

Viewed symbolically, war allows us to ritually affirm our own deathlessness by killing the enemy who *is* Death. This idea is reflected in the promise made by some religions that warriors who fall in battle go directly to Valhalla or Paradise. "War as the bringer of death," says Keen, "wears the face of horror, but also of ecstasy."[90] In determining the steps that can be taken to civilize hostilities, we must consider both the individual psyche and social institutions (see Table 13-5).

The Nuclear Threat

The watershed moment for any discussion of the nuclear threat is the bombing of Hiroshima at 8:15 A.M. on August 6, 1945. The bomb fell near the center of the city, and its explosive force, heat, and radiation engulfed all of Hiroshima. A soldier who viewed the city the next day left this description:

> . . . I could find nothing but a wide stretch of burned ruins with a lot of debris. Where had the former city of Hiroshima gone? . . . The seven rivers that ran

T A B L E   *13-5*   *Steps Toward Civilizing Hostilities*

1. Replace dehumanizing language with metaphors that dignify the enemy.
2. Become aware of individual and group processes that cause biased perceptions about others, and learn to test perceptions before acting.
3. Create and use strategies to resolve conflict peacefully.
4. Counteract the human tendency to create us/them distinctions by creating "cross-cutting" relations among groups within society and between nations.
5. Limit armaments to reduce the risk of war.
6. Establish mechanisms for dealing with crisis.
7. Exercise restraint about supplying arms or intervening in regional conflicts.
8. Bridge the knowledge gap between adversaries by encouraging exchange programs, tourism, and other forms of direct communication.
9. View war as an "optional" social institution and work toward eliminating the factors—social injustice, poverty, ignorance—that contribute to conflict.
10. Accept responsibility, for better or worse, for the conduct engaged in by one's community or nation.
11. Be aware of the tendency to glorify past wars.
12. Replace the ancient reverence for the warrior and for heroic sacrifice in war with a new ideal of the kindly, compassionate human.
13. Remember that the human species is young and that the past may not be an adequate mirror in which to find an accurate reflection of human possibilities.
14. Keep in mind that the real enemy is the war system itself, which includes both the political and social institutions through which we educate ourselves and our own psychological defense mechanisms.
15. Go beyond the mind-set that convinces us *a priori* that war is inevitable and that any hope of a world without war is utopian.
16. Explore options other than war for bringing about the qualities of companionship, bravery, devotion to a worthy cause, and honor.
17. Find positive ways of fulfilling the human potential for transcendence.
18. Implement, as a first necessity, a new vision, a new sense of possibility.

Source: Adapted from Sam Keen, *Faces of the Enemy: Reflections of the Hostile Imagination* (San Francisco: Harper and Row, 1986), pp. 157–168; and Ervin Staub, *The Roots of Evil: The Origins of Genocide and Other Group Violence* (New York: Cambridge University Press, 1989), pp. 255–274.

through the city were full of corpses, soot, smoke, and charred driftwood, stretching like black lines through Hiroshima, which was reduced to ashes.[91]

The growth of the nuclear weapons arsenal has brought about the possibility of an encounter with death of unprecedented proportions. The fact that nuclear weapons might be used, with little or no warning, has shaped our lives in ways both subtle and dramatic.

Modern weapons technology has progressed to the point where a missile can carry its strategic nuclear warhead a distance of 6000 miles in less than half an hour and hit within a few hundred feet of its target. The hydrogen bomb in today's arsenals is a thousand times more powerful than the atomic bomb, which itself produces an explosion about a million times more powerful than comparably sized bombs with conventional explosives such as TNT. The impact of even a small or limited nuclear attack would be enormous. Yet, it is estimated that existing nuclear weapons represent 18,000 megatons of

I grew up during the Depression; everything in the country had stopped; there was no work, the factories were cold and empty. People daydreamed about what this country was going to be like when it got going again—the kind of houses people would live in, the kind of cars they would drive, the kind of vacations they'd take, the kind of clothes they'd wear, and all that—and it was a dream for their descendants. I don't find anybody now who gives a damn about what kind of world their grandchildren are going to inherit . . .

All the ads tell you that your own life is short, enjoy it while you can: buy this right now, start drinking really good wines, just take a really swell vacation, drive a really fast car, do it right now. I think it's much more absorbing to plan a world for our grandchildren, but there are no ads that invite you to do that. In a way, the threat of the Bomb may be a boon to wine merchants, restaurateurs, manufacturers of fancy automobiles, salesmen of condos in Aspen. It's all going to blow up—that's part of the sales message.

Kurt Vonnegut, quoted in *Publishers Weekly*

explosive power, the equivalent of 3.5 tons of TNT for every person on the planet.[92] Robert Lifton and Eric Olson write:

Nuclearism is a peculiar, twentieth-century disease of power. We would do well to specify it, trace its roots, and see its connection with other forms of religious and immortalizing expression. It yields a grandiose vision of man's power at a historical time when man's precarious sense of his own immortality makes him particularly vulnerable to such aberrations.[93]

Political and military conflicts around the world, combined with poor economic conditions in many countries, continue to make peace an elusive quarry. In the past few decades, few areas of the world have escaped the impact of war, and the nuclear threat to survival has amounted to a more or less constant encounter with death for more than five decades.

AIDS and Other Emerging Diseases

Although most people living in modern societies have become complacent about the threat of infectious diseases over the last half-century, the AIDS epidemic is a wake-up call and possible harbinger of other emerging diseases that scientists believe may threaten the health of human beings worldwide in coming decades. This threat is highlighted in publications like Richard Preston's *The Hot Zone* and Laurie Garrett's *The Coming Plague*. If the history of AIDS (acquired immune deficiency syndrome) is representative, the social and personal costs of newly emerging diseases will have devastating consequences for both individuals and societies.

The Response to AIDS

What images and feelings do you become aware of as you think about AIDS? For many people, AIDS is synonymous with death: a dread disease, contagious and epidemic, a modern plague. According to Robert Kastenbaum, the symbolism of AIDS embodies the stigma of earlier forms of catastrophic dying: disfiguration, dementia, and skeletonization. It conveys multiple meanings about human vanity and pride, divine punishment, attack by an enemy from within, the terror of life in death and the despair of death in life, and the romantic exit of brilliant and beautiful doomed youth.[94]

The first cases of AIDS, a disease that destroys the body's natural defenses against infection, were reported in 1981; by early 1982, researchers believed that AIDS was caused by an infectious agent. Discovery of HIV (human immunodeficiency virus) as the likely cause of AIDS was confirmed in January 1984 by Luc Montagnier at the Pasteur Institute in Paris and by Robert Gallo at the U.S. National Institutes of Health. Late in 1985, the genetic sequence of the virus had been determined and a blood test devised to detect antibodies to HIV.

The main epicenters of the AIDS pandemic have been the United States and sub-Saharan Africa.[95] The virus has also made rapid inroads in Asia, mainly in India, Burma, and Thailand. According to a United Nations report, more than 30 million people worldwide are living with the AIDS virus and about 16,000 are newly infected every day.[96] Peter Piot, director general of UNAIDS, says, "The main message of our report is that the AIDS epidemic is far from over. In fact, it's far worse."[97] In the developing world, AIDS is wiping out gains in life expectancy that had been made in recent decades. The disease is overwhelmingly concentrated in the developing world, where more than 90 percent of HIV-infected people now live. In the United States, AIDS predominantly affects intravenous (IV) drug users, hemophiliacs, and recipients of blood transfusions, as well as the sexual partners of individuals infected with the virus. In other parts of the world, the AIDS virus is transmitted mainly through heterosexual contact. On a personal level, AIDS causes massive suffering. Many survivors—the friends, neighbors, business associates, and relatives of people who died from AIDS—have experienced multiple losses.

In the initial response to AIDS, with very little reliable information available, health care workers were concerned about their own vulnerability to the virus. At first, some caregivers distanced themselves from patients with AIDS, and a few refused to treat them. As more was learned about the disease, however, evidence accumulated that AIDS could be transmitted through only three primary routes, all requiring contact with body fluids: (1) sexual intercourse (vaginal or anal) with an infected person, (2) exposure to infected blood or blood products, and (3) transmission from an infected mother to her child before or during birth.

The social and political response to AIDS has been mixed.[98] From the first inklings that AIDS was a new and challenging disease, debate began about how to mobilize and allocate economic, medical, and social resources. Some communities responded with a variety of health and public service programs. Others reacted by hampering humanitarian efforts to help individuals affected by AIDS. When Elisabeth Kübler-Ross proposed a hospice for infants with AIDS in rural Virginia, the local community denied the necessary permits. Fear of contagion overruled the wish to help sick and dying infants. In Africa, years into the pandemic, most governments and media ignored the crisis, attributing victims' deaths to anything but AIDS.[99] Poverty has been a factor in getting the word out about AIDS and mounting an effective response.[100]

At a cultural level, AIDS has challenged our notions of how family is defined and who constitutes a family, with persons other than kin often playing important roles in caring for persons with AIDS.[101] Efforts to cope with AIDS have stimulated interest in palliative treatment and hospice care. A hospice model of caregiving usually with home care as a major component has been widely adopted in caring for AIDS patients. From 1983 to 1991, the percentage of AIDS deaths occurring in hospitals dropped from 92 percent to 57 percent, with corresponding increases in the percentages of AIDS deaths occurring in nursing homes and hospices and at home.[102] Nevertheless, as Ronald Barrett points out, the self-initiated isolation and social withdrawal of people dying from AIDS still occurs.[103] People who display this behavior have been termed "elephant people," a reference to the belief that dying elephants remove themselves from their herd and go away to a remote elephant burial ground to die.

Society still seems uncertain about how to respond to AIDS. In California, the Department of Motor Vehicles (DMV) refused to provide a customized license plate requested by a registered nurse who specializes in AIDS care.[104] The plate, reading "AIDS RN," was requested by Steve Lee, who said he wanted the new plate on his Thunderbird to show pride in his work and AIDS awareness. After the DMV deemed the plate offensive and turned down the request, Lee said, "What [DMV] is kind of saying is the way the general society wants to deal with AIDS—they don't want to deal with it." The DMV eventually reversed itself, but it reported that some AIDS groups had told the DMV they didn't want plates issued bearing the words "AIDS" or "HIV" because they would be reminders for people with the virus. Meanwhile, the clinical supervisor of an AIDS project said the DMV's rejection of Lee's plate was the "ultimate in political incorrectness." As a commentary on attitudes toward AIDS, this saga of a license plate exemplifies the conflicting and confusing responses elicited by the disease.

AIDS reminds us that infectious diseases remain a threat and that human beings remain uncertain about how to respond to epidemic disease. Viewing AIDS in historical perspective, Charles Rosenberg says:

> Mortality is built into our bodies, into our modes of behavior, and into our place in the planet's ecology. Like other epidemics, AIDS has served well to remind us, finally, of these ultimate realities.[105]

When confronted by a new disease with an unknown mode of transmission, people become anxious and fearful. In this regard, the social response to the outbreak of AIDS tended to resemble patterns of response to epidemics historically. Eventually, panic recedes and more thoughtful measures are implemented.

© Carolyn Jones, from *Living Proof, Courage in the Face of AIDS*

Zoë Lorenz and her daughter Candice are among the many people affected by AIDS. Zoë saw her father die from AIDS, plagued not only by the disease but by the humiliation and shame so often associated with it. Now afflicted with the virus herself, Zoë says, "I have a beautiful four-year-old daughter who has beat the odds and remains HIV negative. So many people have the attitude that I should go off and die somewhere alone. They don't see the tragedy of this child losing her mommy. I don't need to be proud that I have AIDS, but I won't be ashamed that I do. I don't want to feel that I have to tell people I've got cancer or some other acceptable disease."

Living With AIDS

Acquired immune deficiency syndrome (AIDS) impairs the body's immune system.[106] It affects the body's ability to fight disease, making it more vulnerable to opportunistic infections. It is important to distinguish between AIDS and human immunodeficiency virus (HIV), which causes AIDS. Medically defined, HIV infection is caused by one of two related retroviruses that become incorporated into host cell DNA, progressively destroying white blood cells called lymphocytes and causing AIDS and other diseases that result from impaired immunity. Of the two AIDS-producing viruses, HIV-1 is most common in the Western Hemisphere, Europe, Asia, and in Central, South, and East Africa; HIV-2 is most common in West Africa. HIV infection results in a wide range of clinical presentations, varying from asymptomatic "carrier states" to debilitating and fatal disorders. People infected with HIV lose helper T lymphocytes (CD4+ cells) in three phases, which occur over the course of months or years.

During the first phase, lasting about six months, the CD4+ count typically decreases by 40 to 50 percent as the body fights the virus, although it is unable to clear up the infection. Because individuals usually do not have visible symptoms of the illness, this phase is characterized as one of *asymptomatic HIV infection*. However, some people do experience relatively mild symptoms such as fever, rashes, swollen lymph nodes, and general discomfort lasting from a few days to two weeks. The incubation period before the onset of AIDS can be from eight to eleven years, perhaps longer. People infected with the virus are usually not aware of it until symptoms become evident years later. A blood test (called the ELISA test) can be used to screen people for HIV infection. Although the pattern of progression from HIV infection to AIDS is not entirely clear, the consensus has been that almost all HIV-infected persons eventually develop AIDS. Newly developed drugs may improve this prognosis.

In the one to two years before recognizable AIDS develops, the CD4+ lymphocyte count drops more rapidly, ushering in a period of *symptomatic HIV infection*. The symptoms occurring during this phase were formerly referred to as "AIDS-related complex" (ARC), but now the main focus is on falling CD4+ cell counts, which increase a person's vulnerability to infection. The clinical signs at this phase of HIV infection can include fever, recurring diarrhea, severe weight loss or "wasting syndrome" (called "slim disease" in Africa), swollen lymph nodes, fatigue, and general malaise.

By definition, *AIDS*—the third phase of HIV infection—begins with a low CD4+ lymphocyte count (less than 200 cells per microliter of blood) or the development of opportunistic infections, such as pneumonia caused by the fungus *Pneumocystis carinii*. Cancers such as Kaposi's sarcoma and non-Hodgkin's lymphoma may develop, as well as infections of the brain, spinal cord, and nervous system, which can lead to dementia, paralysis, and blindness. Thus, both the HIV infection and the opportunistic infections and cancers produce the symptoms associated with AIDS. Opportunistic infections are the usual cause of death in AIDS patients.

Despite ongoing efforts by laboratories around the world, no cure or preventive vaccine for AIDS yet exists. However, the prognosis for AIDS patients is much improved, as new drugs have become available. New treatments can often slow or decrease replication of the virus and result in at least a temporary increase in CD4+ cell counts. Combination drug therapies frequently reduce the virus in the blood to undetectable levels. Besides new drugs, there are advances in understanding the biology of HIV infectivity and the role of natural chemicals called chemokines in suppressing HIV's ability to infect cells.[107]

One year ago today, I told my colleagues that I was dying of AIDS. I had been fighting it for years—the illness and the telling. . . . But now I was gaunt, tired, and rather sure I was losing the battle.

I was happily dying—and about to go on a Mexican vacation. I felt I had made my peace with death and, in a way, was looking forward to it. I had blown my mother's estate, about $180,000, on living for the moment, eating in the best restaurants and taking three or four foreign vacations a year. There was no time to lose, and I was determined to go out in style.

What has happened in the past year, at least for me, is a miracle that couldn't have taken place at any other moment. The year 1996 is when everything changed, and very quickly, for people with AIDS.

Thanks to the arrival of the new drugs called protease inhibitors, I am probably more likely to be hit by a truck than to die of AIDS.

I stopped the presses on my obituary. Oddly enough, the return from my near-death experience was at first very annoying. I had a few adjustments to make. I had to start thinking again about my bills. . . . We had to start living within our means. . . . I have had to re-energize myself for the daily grind. I'm even thinking about cleaning the basement.

But I'm not out of the woods.

Some HIV-negative men are guilt-ridden when they see so many of their friends dying. I feel guilty that I am getting the best possible medical care, because it is unavailable to most of the world's AIDS sufferers, and to the poor and uninsured in this country.

Figure 13-4 *Back to a Future*

With new treatment options, the focus is changing from "dying with AIDS" to "living with HIV and AIDS."[108] Patients who have depleted their financial resources for care or for travel and other extravagances at what had seemed the end of their lives are now confronted by the need to reappraise their planning for "last days" and reconstruct their lives so as to include a future that didn't seem likely until quite recently (see Figure 13-4). To make this future a reality, however, they must also cope with the fact that the new therapies are expensive, often limited in availability, involve various side effects, and may need to be taken over a long period of time to promote continuing improvement.

Unfortunately, many people with HIV or AIDS are not able to take advantage of the new therapies, which are accessible only to a comparatively elite group. For patients who lack financial resources or access to sophisticated health care—a group that includes not only a significant portion of patients in the United States, but the majority of patients in many other countries—the future is bleaker. In recent years, the greatest impact of AIDS in the United States has been among African Americans and Hispanics.

Despite the fact that many questions remain, AIDS is increasingly being viewed as a treatable disease. Still, researchers agree that "keeping HIV at bay, even with the most potent three-drug cocktails now available, remains a daunting challenge."[109] If replication of the virus is not completely suppressed, drug-resistant mutants are given a chance to appear. Furthermore, the new drugs are not effective with all patients, and some have trouble complying with a regimen that requires daily doses of dozens of pills, many with serious side effects. AIDS researcher David Ho says, "We must dutifully avoid unwarranted triumphalism [as well as] the undue pessimism that prevails in some circles. The state of HIV treatment is neither black nor white. We must paint the situation in the proper shade of gray."[110]

The Threat of Emerging Diseases

If AIDS does turn out to be a harbinger of things to come, what are some of the lessons that we need to learn? Three of the most important involve (1) early identification of people who are at risk for disease, (2) a shift to community and public health perspectives, and (3) the need to address health problems on a global scale.[111] Confronted by AIDS, most North American and Western European countries valued their individual citizens' privacy more highly than society's interest in controlling the disease. Thus, rather than forgoing patient confidentiality in order to promote public health efforts designed to prevent the spread of the virus, the decision was made to guard the privacy of HIV-infected individuals. In the case of AIDS, this approach was deemed appropriate because the virus is not transmitted by ordinary contact with infected individuals, and the carrier of HIV represents no risk to others in normal social and commercial life. This is not true of all viruses, however. The epidemiology and mode of infection of a given disease are crucial in determining the ways in which societies cope with it.[112]

In recent years, there have been localized epidemics of a number of emerging diseases, including hemorrhagic fever viruses such as the Marburg, Ebola, Lassa, and hantaviruses, as well as yellow fever, swine flu, Legionnaires' disease (*Legionella*), and cholera.[113] Bernard Le Guenno of the Pasteur Institute in Paris says:

> Hemorrhagic fever viruses are among the most threatening examples of what are commonly termed emerging pathogens. They are not really new. Mutations or genetic recombinations between existing viruses can increase virulence, but what appears to be novel viruses are generally viruses that have existed for millions of years and merely come to light when environmental conditions change. The changes allow the virus to multiply and spread in host organisms. New illnesses may then sometimes become apparent.[114]

Most outbreaks of hemorrhagic fevers result from disruption of the environment due to human activities. With expansion of the human population, forest clearing and other agricultural activities disturb previously stable ecosystems, thereby facilitating contact with pathogenic viruses that threaten life and health.

Patrick Olson, an epidemiologist at the Naval Medical Center in San Diego, theorizes that the plague that struck the Greek city of Athens in 430 B.C., which was reported by the Athenian general and historian Thucydides, was actually caused by the deadly Ebola virus (which is named after a river in the

Congo, where it was first detected in 1976).[115] Olson finds many parallels between the ancient and modern accounts. Fever, diarrhea, and severe weakness are prominent symptoms. As with the Athenian plague, Ebola claims almost all of its victims, and quickly, with most people who are infected dying within two weeks. Ebola outbreaks usually last only a few weeks because its victims die faster than they are able to spread the virus, which then disappears for a time, only to reemerge later. The most recent major outbreak of Ebola was in the Congo in 1995, where it killed 245 people. Since then, other outbreaks have occurred in Gabon, Sudan, the Ivory Coast, and northern Uganda.[116]

The worst infectious disease episode in modern times was the 1918 pandemic caused by an influenza virus that killed more than 20 million people worldwide. In the United States, a quarter of the population had the flu and more than half a million people died. Many of the thousands of young men crammed onto World War I troop ships were just developing the flu as they left the United States. After a week's crossing of the Atlantic, the ships arrived in France with hundreds of sick servicemen, many of whom died. Experts believe that many flu viruses reside harmlessly in birds and occasionally infect pigs, where they are changed into a new form of the virus that can affect humans.[117] Similar mechanisms involving "species jumping" have been suggested for AIDS and other emerging viruses.

In studying how newly emerging diseases like AIDS are disseminated in urban societies, Rodrick and Deborah Wallace conclude that physical and social disruption intensifies the pathological behaviors and conditions that promote the rapid spread of infectious diseases.[118] Political abandonment of inner-city areas results in what the Wallaces term "urban desertification" or "social thanatology."[119] The devastation and disintegration in some urban areas is characterized as "unprecedented in a modern industrialized state short of the aftermath of total war."[120] Among disadvantaged populations, a lack of crucial municipal services leads to what Richard Rothenberg of the U.S. Centers for Disease Control and Prevention calls "the metastasis of dangerous behavior."[121] For some marginalized individuals, the view of AIDS is quite different from the view held in society's mainstream: AIDS appears to be a form of race or class warfare, "a virus created in a government or CIA laboratory in an attempt to 'clean up' a seemingly dirty population."[122] The fact that such a view exists is itself evidence of the gap between the haves and have-nots of American society.

Since the advent of penicillin, most people have become complacent about infectious diseases, believing that epidemics are no longer a threat. But the pandemic of AIDS shows that complacency is ill-advised. In addition to newly emerging diseases, some diseases that had seemed conquered are reemerging as a threat. For example, drug-resistant strains of tuberculosis are spreading, even in wealthy countries, due to migration as well as international business and tourist travel.[123] This upswing in a disease believed to be under control since the 1940s, when effective drugs were introduced, has been blamed on "worldwide medical chaos," which results in TB being pushed into the poorer sections of society, particularly among inner-city dwellers and the homeless. Malaria, which was subjected to a global eradication effort during the 1970s, has also staged a comeback, with as many as 500 million people in 90 countries affected each year.[124] The most ominous reason for this comeback, researchers say, is the ability of the mosquito-borne parasite, the plasmodium protozoa, to develop resistance to antimalaria drugs. Very little money is invested in surveillance efforts to combat the threat of emerging and reemerging infectious diseases like malaria, tuberculosis, dengue fever, Ebola, and other plagues.

Coping With Risks

Daniel Leviton uses the term *horrendous death* to describe categories of death that affect large numbers of people.[125] The typical horrendous-type death has its origins in human activity and often involves the motivation to kill, maim, injure, or destroy another human being. Homicide, terrorism, assassination, and genocide are examples of horrendous-type deaths. The first step in eliminating, or at least reducing, such deaths involves confronting the wish to deny the reality of such deaths. Sometimes horrendous-type deaths are treated as an aberration, an anomaly. Yet they involve enormous costs for present as well as future generations. Risks of various kinds—accidents, disasters, violence, war, epidemic diseases—affect us to varying degrees as we go about our daily lives. Sometimes the encounter is subtle; at other times it is overt, calling into action our ability to cope with threat. The failure to find adequate means of coping with these encounters with death represents a threat to the survival of society as well as the individual.

Further Readings

Roy F. Baumeister. *Evil: Inside Human Violence and Cruelty.* New York: W. H. Freeman, 1997.

Kenneth J. Doka. *AIDS, Fear, and Society: Challenging the Dreaded Disease.* Washington, D.C.: Taylor & Francis, 1997.

Kai Erikson. *A New Species of Trouble: Explorations in Disaster, Trauma, and Community.* New York: W. W. Norton, 1994.

Laurie Garrett. *The Coming Plague: Newly Emerging Diseases in a World out of Balance.* New York: Farrar, Straus and Giroux, 1994.

Dave Grossman. *On Killing: The Psychological Cost of Learning to Kill in War and Society.* Boston: Little, Brown, 1995.

Albert R. Jonsen and Jeff Stryker, eds. *The Social Impact of AIDS.* Washington, D.C.: National Academy Press, 1993.

Walter Laqueur. *The New Terrorism: Fanaticism and the Arms of Mass Destruction.* New York: Oxford University Press, 1999.

Ann Larabee. *Decade of Disaster.* Urbana: University of Illinois Press, 2000.

Albert J. Reiss, Jr., and Jeffrey A. Roth, eds. *Understanding and Preventing Violence.* Washington, D.C.: National Academy Press, 1993.

Fred Turner. *Echoes of Combat: The Vietnam War in American Memory.* New York: Anchor-Doubleday, 1996.

The corpse placed on the funeral pyre, these men prepare to light the cremation fire. Cremation has been a traditional practice in India, where Hindus believe that "even as the person casts off worn-out clothes and puts on others that are new, so the embodied Self casts off worn-out bodies and enters into others that are new."

CHAPTER 14

Beyond Death/After Life

*D*eath—and then what?

Some people have a ready answer to this question: "When you're dead, you're dead—that's it!" or "You go through a transition and take birth in another body," or "After you die you go to heaven." Each of these responses reflects a particular understanding of the meaning of human existence. Beliefs about life after death occupy a broad spectrum, from the notion that death spells the end, to the notion that the "soul" or "self" lives on after death in some fashion. Answering the question, "What happens after I die?" has occupied the attention of human beings since the dawn of consciousness.

Concern with immortality—that is, survival after physical death—is cut from the same cloth as questions about the meaning of life and the corollary, "How, then, should one live?" Responses to these questions reflect a person's values and beliefs about human experience and the nature of reality. Andrew Greeley says: "We are born with two incurable diseases: life, from which we die, and hope, which says maybe death isn't the end."[1] Our philosophy of life influences our philosophy of death. Conversely, our understanding of death and its meaning affects the way we live.

According to Socrates, "the unexamined life is not worth living." Such self-investigation includes discovery of what one believes about the consequences of death. Ambivalence about belief in survival after death is aptly described in an anecdote related by

> Every time an earth mother smiles over the birth of a child, a spirit mother weeps over the loss of a child.
>
> Ashanti saying

Bertrand Russell: A woman whose daughter had recently died was asked what she thought had become of her daughter's soul. She replied, "Oh, well, I suppose she is enjoying eternal bliss, but I wish you wouldn't talk about such unpleasant subjects."[2]

Exploring your beliefs about immortality may not result in an easier acceptance of death—nor should it necessarily. After all, the prospect of immortality is not always looked upon favorably.[3] Nevertheless, such an exploration can lead to a more coherent philosophy of life and death, making possible a congruence between hopes and perceptions. Even when we are firmly settled upon a particular belief system, exposure to other views can both broaden our understanding of different responses to mortality and enhance appreciation of our own beliefs. In this chapter we explore the meaning of mortality by investigating some of the ways that cultures ancient and modern, Eastern and Western, have answered the question, "What happens after death?" These answers provide grist for the mill of our own contemplation about this ultimate human concern.

Traditional Concepts About Life After Death

The notion that life continues in some form after death is one of the oldest concepts held by human beings. In some of the earliest known graves, archaeologists have uncovered skeletons that were bound by hands and feet into a fetal position, perhaps indicating beliefs about "rebirth" into other forms of existence following death. We know that in traditional societies death represents a change of status for the deceased, a transition from the land of the living to the land of the dead.

Some form of judgment is a key feature of many beliefs about what follows death. Among the various concepts of afterlife among traditional Hawaiians, for example, was the belief that a person who had offended a god or who had harmed others would suffer eternal punishment.[4] Such an unworthy soul became a wandering spirit, "forever homeless, forever hungry." The ancestor-gods had the power to punish or reward the released spirit, or even send it back to the body. Misfortune could result when a person had neither loving relatives to care for the corpse nor the guardianship of family ancestor-gods, who help souls find their way to the world of spirits. Thus, those who had lived worthily were welcomed into eternity, whereas those who had done misdeeds in life, without repenting for or correcting them, were punished. The reward for a good life was reunion with those closest to the family-loving Hawaiian: one's own ancestors.

William Hodges, Bishop Museum

The platform burial of a Tahitian chief is depicted in this drawing by William Hodges, made during Captain Cook's second voyage to the South Pacific in the 1770s.

In a world populated by unseen spirits who could exert their influence for good or evil upon the living, the death of a chief or other important person occasioned a spectacular display of grief, which was presided over by a chief mourner (right). Usually a priest or close relative of the deceased, the chief mourner wore an elaborate costume of pearl shells and the feathers of tropic birds. Rattling a pearl shell clapper and brandishing a long wooden weapon inset with sharks' teeth, the chief mourner was accompanied by other weapon-carrying men who could strike anyone in their way, thus helping ensure that funeral rites were carried out in a manner that would offend neither the living nor the dead.

Bishop Museum

To understand the consciousness from which such a view of immortality arises, the notions of selfhood in Western cultures must be put aside momentarily. Against an emphasis on individual identity and the self, imagine a mentality in which group identity is all-encompassing. The family, the clan, the people—these social groups represent the loci of communal consciousness within which the thoughts and actions of the individual are subsumed. Thus, traditional beliefs are less concerned with individual survival than with continuation of the community and its common heritage. Having shared in the life of the group, the individual is part of its ultimate destiny, a destiny that transcends death.

Jewish Beliefs About Death and Resurrection

The Bible does not present a systematic theology of death or the afterlife. Death is not ignored, but biblical literature about it reflects a progression of ideas over a long period of time. The biblical story describes a people focused on their communal destiny. Individuals are actors in an unfolding drama; its denouement foretold in the promises made by Yahweh. The characteristic theme emphasizes faith—faith in the people of Israel as a community with a common destiny and faith in Yahweh, whose promises will be realized in the unfolding of the divine plan. As the patriarch Abraham lay dying, his last thoughts involved hope for the survival of his progeny so that these promises could be realized. Abraham's vision is reiterated by biblical heroes in one circumstance after another, as they affirm Israel's destiny. By contributing to this common destiny, the righteous person never ceases to be part of the continuing story of the people as a whole.

As Judaic thought developed over time, there were corresponding changes in how mortality and its meaning were understood. In the story of Job's en-

"There is always hope for a tree:
    when felled, it can start its life again;
    its shoots continue to sprout.
Its roots may be decayed in the earth,
    its stump withering in the soil,
but let it scent the water, and it buds,
    and puts out branches like a plant new set.
But man? He dies, and lifeless he remains;
    man breathes his last, and then where is he?
The waters of the sea may disappear,
    all the rivers may run dry or drain away;
but man, once in his resting place, will never rise again.
    The heavens will wear away before he wakes,
    before he rises from his sleep."

Job 14:7–12, *The Jerusalem Bible*

counter with adversity and death, the human situation is described bleakly: "As a cloud fades away and disappears, so a person who goes down to the grave will not come up from it."[5] Resignation toward death is echoed in the other Wisdom books—including Proverbs, Ecclesiastes, and some of the Psalms—which present the thought of the ancient Hebrew sages on the question of human destiny. Righteous conduct is advised because it leads to harmony in the present life, not because it guarantees future rewards for the individual.

Between the time of Job and the later prophets there was a gradual change from resignation to hopefulness in the face of death. In the apocalyptic, or visionary, writings of prophets such as Daniel and Ezekiel, we find the strands of thought that are eventually woven together in ideas about the resurrection of the body. Daniel envisions a future in which the "sleeping" dead will awaken, "some to everlasting life, some to everlasting disgrace."[6] This is an important development in Hebrew thought, and it greatly influenced Christian theology. Stated succinctly, this development "consists in the belief that, at the end of time, the bodies of the dead will be resurrected from the grave and reconstituted."[7]

Hints of this change are also evident in the meanings ascribed over time to the Hebrew word *She'ol,* which in early usage is generally defined as the underworld of all the dead, a shadowy realm of ghostly, disembodied souls (much like the *Hades* of Greek mythology). An old story gives an account of necromancy in which King Saul requests the witch of En-dor to summon the spirit of the dead prophet Samuel. Asked by Saul to describe what she sees, the witch of En-dor replies, "I see a ghost [*elohim* = superhuman being] rising

---

 I knew my former father-in-law from the time I was thirteen. Although I had divorced many years ago, he remained a second father to me. Kurt was born in Germany. He left for Holland on the day of Kristallnacht. He arrived here penniless and went on to become an extremely successful business man. In coming to this country, he left his entire family. With the exception of an uncle, they all died in the Holocaust. He remained an observant Jew and did not talk much about the Holocaust until the last two years of his life. Since he never knew when his parents, sisters, and other loved ones died, he observed the *yahrzeit* (anniversary of their deaths) on Yom Kippur (the day of atonement).

Just before Rosh Hashanah two years ago, he became very ill and was hospitalized. Following an old European tradition, in the synagogue on Rosh Hashanah he was given a new Hebrew name (so that when the angel of death came looking for him, he wouldn't find him). I went to visit him in the hospital that day. He was in and out of consciousness. I doubt that he consciously knew who I was, and I'm sure was not aware of the day. When he did speak, he was speaking only in German. I said my good-bye to him and left. He remained alive for the entire ten-day period (often referred to as the Days of Awe) and (I believe) went to be with his loved ones on Yom Kippur.

Barbara J. Paul

up from the earth [*She'ol*]." Later, with further refinement of these concepts, the shadowy underworld of *She'ol* is divided into two distinct realms: *Gehinom* (hell) and *Pardes* (heaven or paradise).[8]

In the main, the references to resurrection of the body found in the Jewish prophets did not alter the essential understanding of the human person as an undivided psychophysical entity. Wheeler Robinson says, "The Hebrew idea of personality is an animated body, and not an incarnated soul."[9] In other words, it is not as if the soul *takes* a body, but rather that the body *has* life. In this understanding of personhood, such concepts as body or soul cannot be abstracted from the essential integrity of the human person.

The consensus expressed by the biblical writers seems to be: "Our present existence is of God; if there is life hereafter, it will also be God's gift. Why be anxious about death? What matters is to live righteously." The enduring concern is that one should not lose sight of the tasks at hand. God appears to be mainly concerned with the living, not the dead. The communal faith of Israel is sustained through customs like the *Minyan,* which requires a minimum number of individuals to carry out a complete prayer service, and the reciting of *Kaddish,* the Jewish prayer for the dead, as well as in the practice of *Shivah,* the period of formal mourning after a person has been buried. An Aramaic prayer for the dead, the *Kaddish* is essentially a "pledge from the living to dedicate one's life to the God of Life." It is recited by mourners during the first eleven months after death and then on the anniversary, or *yahrzeit,* of the death. In Judaism, the customary mourning rituals help the bereaved face the reality of death, give honor to the deceased, and engage in a reaffirmation of *life.*[10]

Hellenistic Concepts of Immortality

Among the ancient Greeks, or Hellenes, there were various views about what might follow the death of the body. Generally, however, the afterworld was not an attractive prospect. *Hades,* the realm of the dead, was typically pictured as a shadowy place inhabited by bloodless phantoms, an image that could evoke despair. The heroes in Greek drama are often portrayed as raging against death.[11]

In the Athenian democracy, what mattered was the survival of the *polis,* the corporate existence of the city-state. Personal immortality was important only to the extent that it affected the survival of the community. Within this context, a person could achieve social immortality by fulfilling the responsibil-

For the whole world is the sepulchre of famous men, and it is not the epitaph upon monuments set up in their own land that alone commemorates them, but also in lands not their own there abides in each breast an unwritten memorial of them, planted in the heart rather than graven on stone.

Thucydides, *The Peloponnesian War*

Speak not smoothly of death, I beseech you, O famous Odysseus. Better by far to remain on earth the thrall of another . . . rather than reign sole king in the realm of bodyless phantoms.

Homer, *The Odyssey*

ities of citizenship—that is, by performing actions directed toward the common good. Because the community remembers heroic acts, the hero achieves a renown that extends beyond his or her lifetime.

For those who sought more than symbolic immortality, assurances of happiness beyond death were obtained by participating in one of the mystery religions, cults whose origins are clouded in the mists of prehistory. By dedicating themselves to the rites prescribed by the priests of the mystery cult, they exchanged the dire picture of bloodless phantoms in the afterworld for the more promising one of an idyllic future in paradise.

Among the early Greek philosophers, most thought of life and death as aspects of an ever-changing, eternal flux. Although they believed that the soul was a vital principle that continued in some fashion after death, they generally did not imagine it surviving as a distinct entity. If some quality of "soul" continued beyond death, it merged with the stuff of the universe.

Somewhat later, Pythagoras taught that one's conduct during life determined the destiny of the soul after death. Thus, with discipline and purification, one could influence the transmigration—successive rounds of births and deaths—of the soul that led to eventual union with the Divine or Universal Absolute. These beliefs drew upon the Orphic mystery religions of ancient Greece, which went back to the cult of Dionysus. The notion that a person's conduct in this life somehow influenced existence in the afterlife contrasted with the predominant view of an indistinct immortality in which all human beings participated regardless of their actions. Nevertheless, the ideas expressed by Pythagoras and his followers were eventually adopted in a somewhat altered form during the pre-Christian era, and the relationship between righteous conduct and immortality would be further refined during the early centuries of Christianity.

. . . he who has lived as a true philosopher has reason to be of good cheer when he is about to die, and that after death he may hope to receive the greatest good in the other world. . . . For I deem that the true disciple of philosophy . . . is ever pursuing death and dying; and if this is true, why, having had the desire of death all his life long, should he repine at the arrival of that which he has been always pursuing and desiring?

Plato, *Phaedo*

Become accustomed to the belief that death is nothing to us. For all good and evil consists in sensation, but death is deprivation of sensation. And therefore a right understanding that death is nothing to us makes the mortality of life enjoyable, not because it adds to an infinite span of time, but because it takes away the craving for immortality. For there is nothing terrible in life for the man who has truly comprehended that there is nothing terrible in not living.

Epicurus, *Letter to Menoeceus*

With Socrates, there are signs of a shift from a social immortality predicated on the life of the community to the possibility of personal survival after death. Precisely what Socrates believed in this regard is unclear, although he apparently favored the notion that the soul survives the death of the body. On his deathbed, he describes a sense of anticipation at the prospect of communion with the spirits of the great in the afterworld. But, in the *Apology*, he describes death as *either* eternal bliss *or* dreamless sleep.

In the *Phaedo*, Plato advanced a number of "proofs" that the soul is eternal and is released from the body at death. The dualism of body and soul is emphasized, and their respective fates are distinguished: Because it is mortal, the body is subject to corruption; the soul, however, is immortal and therefore not subject to death.

Among Plato's successors, the fact of death as the common fate of all humankind became a worthy reminder of the importance of choosing wisely how to live in the present life. The Roman Stoic, Marcus Aurelius, who lived in the second century of the present era, echoes these thoughts. "The constant recollection of death," he said, "is the test of human conduct."[12]

Christian Beliefs About the Afterlife

Jesus spoke of the "kingdom of heaven" as a place of eternal reward with "many dwelling places." The central insight of both Jewish and Christian thought has two main premises: first, "that human beings are creatures, composites of dust and God's animating breath; and [second] that they are created in the image and likeness of God, with a destiny—a royal dignity—that overtakes their finite status."[13] For early Christians like the Apostle Paul, death was vanquished by Christ's resurrection. William Barclay says: "As Paul sees it, the Christian certainty of the life to come comes from the fact that the Christian's Saviour is one who was dead and is alive again."[14] The life, death, and resurrection of Jesus is the model of ultimate reality for Christians. In effect, Jesus is the prototype of salvation from death, a salvation available to all who, by faith, share in his resurrection.

With Jesus no longer in their midst, the growing band of Christians began to reframe their expectations about the chronology of the Kingdom of God and their understanding of resurrection. The Apostle Paul attempts to resolve some of the problems of death, afterlife, and the events foretold for the end of time. For Paul, resurrection is a special kind of bodily existence, but it also has a symbolic or spiritual meaning.

Hellenistic notions of cosmic dualism were a persistent influence on early Christian thought. In this dualistic understanding of soul and body, the soul was viewed as immortal, a part of the human person that existed in a disembodied state after death. During the formative period of Christianity, there was constant interplay between the Hebrew traditions and the philosophical heritage of classical culture. Milton Gatch says about this period:

> The notion of resurrection and of the restoration of an elect people continued to be prominent. But the idea of a disembodied afterlife for the soul was also current and led to the conception of some sort of afterlife between the separation and the reunion of soul and body. From a picture of death as the inauguration of a sleep which would last until the divinely instituted resurrection, there emerged a picture of death as the beginning of quiescence for the body and of a continued life for the soul, the nature of which remained more or less undefined.[15]

And so gradually there developed a greater emphasis on the destiny of the individual soul and increasing concern about the consequences of an individual's conduct during life. Church doctrine began to accommodate the idea that punishment for misconduct could take place during an intermediate period between death and resurrection.[16] An intermediate state, which came to be known as *purgatory*, offered an opportunity for purification to eliminate any remaining personal obstacles to the full enjoyment of eternal union with God.[17]

In the writings of Dante and Thomas Aquinas, earlier concepts of death, which focused on eventual resurrection of the body, are subordinated to a more pronounced emphasis on the soul's immortality after death. Nevertheless, both of these ideas are present within Christianity:

> The classical Christian view, expressed in countless catechisms and confessions, is that upon death the souls of the blessed enter immediately into the divine presence, where they enjoy the unmediated vision of God, join in the angelic liturgy, and attend to the needs of the living who turn to them for intercession. . . . They await the return of Christ, the resurrection of the dead, and the renewal of all creation. Their bliss is perfect after its kind; but until the soul regains its body, and the whole body of Christ is complete in all its members, this perfection is, paradoxically, an unfinished work.[18]

Behold, I show you a mystery; We shall not all sleep, but we shall all be changed. In a moment, in the twinkling of an eye, at the last trump: for the trumpet shall sound, and the dead shall be raised incorruptible, and we shall be changed. For this corruptible must put on incorruption, and this mortal must put on immortality. So when this corruptible shall have put on incorruption, and this mortal shall have put on immortality, then shall be brought to pass the saying that is written, Death is swallowed up in victory. O death, where is thy sting? O grave, where is thy victory?

I Corinthians, 15

This scene from Dante's Divine Comedy *shows the guide Charon ferrying worthy souls up the River Styx toward Paradise. Unable to reach the heavenly kingdom, the unworthy, immersed in the river, struggle in despair.*

Go Down, Death—A Funeral Sermon

Weep not, weep not,
She is not dead;
She's resting in the bosom of Jesus.
Heart-broken husband—weep no more;
Grief-stricken son—weep no more;
Left-lonesome daughter—weep no more;
She's only just gone home.

James Weldon Johnson

The interplay between the concepts of resurrection and immortality is illustrated by two tombstone inscriptions from the American colonial period found in a cemetery in New Haven, Connecticut.[19] On the first tombstone, the inscription reads, "Sleeping, but will someday meet her maker." The second is inscribed, "Gone to his eternal reward." Whereas the first inscription reflects the view that resurrection of the body is an event that will occur in the future, the second inscription is based on the concept of the immortality of the soul, which continues to exist even though the body dies. The contrast between these inscriptions is particularly incongruous when you consider that these two individuals were married to each other and are buried side by side in this New England cemetery. Yet, one of them is "sleeping," while the other is "gone." In these tombstone inscriptions we see a curious example of how contrasting ideas about the afterlife can coexist in time.

The Afterlife in Islamic Tradition

The third of the great religious traditions stemming from the patriarch Abraham is Islam. Like Judaism and Christianity, Islam shares the Semitic religious heritage of monotheism, God's revelation through the prophets, ethical responsibility, and accountability for one's actions at the Day of Judgment. *Islam* means "peace" or "submission" (peace comes from submission to transcendent reality, the Divine). Thus, a *Muslim* is one who has submitted and therefore is at peace with God. Muslims are those who have accepted Islam as a way of life, an approach to transcendent reality, which embraces both this world and "the other life."[20]

The Islamic message came through Muhammad, who received his call to be a prophet in 610 when he was about forty, and was recorded in the Qur'an (meaning "readings," and perhaps more familiarly spelled phonetically as "Koran" in the West). According to Muslims, the Qur'an "does not abrogate or nullify, but rather corrects the scriptures preserved by the Jewish and Christian communities."[21] Frithjof Schuon notes that the doctrine of Islam hangs on two statements: First, "There is no divinity (or reality) outside the only Divinity (or Absolute)" and, second, "Muhammad is the Envoy (the mouthpiece, intermediary, or manifestation)."[22]

> The happiness of the drop is to
> die in the river.
>
> Ghazal of Ghalib

A basic premise of Qur'anic teaching about death is that God determines the span of a person's life: "He creates man and also causes him to die."[23] After death, Allah judges a person's conduct. The Book of Deeds, wherein are recorded good and bad actions, will be opened and each person will be consigned either to everlasting bliss or everlasting torment. Huston Smith says, "For the Muslim, life on earth is the seedbed of an eternal future."[24]

The Islamic vision of the afterlife is both spiritual and physical. "Since the Last Day will be accompanied by bodily resurrection," says John Esposito, "the pleasures of heaven and the pain of hell will be fully experienced."[25] Heaven is a paradise of "perpetual peace and bliss with flowing rivers, beautiful gardens, and the enjoyment of one's spouses (multiple marriage partners are permitted in Islam) and beautiful, dark-eyed female companions (*houris*)." The terrors of hell are described in equally physical terms.

Some Muslims believe that, after a person dies, "two black-faced, blue-eyed angels named Munkar and Nakir visit the grave and interrogate the deceased about his beliefs and deeds in life." Depending on the answers, the deceased is comforted or punished. Thus, "At a Muslim funeral a mourner may approach a corpse as it is about to be laid in the tomb and whisper instructions for answering these questions."[26] It is also believed by some that "no one should precede the corpse in the funeral procession because the angels of death go before it."[27]

When death nears, passages from the Qur'an may be read to the dying person to help ensure a righteous state of mind and facilitate an easy release. Following death, a ritual washing, or ablution, is done—except in the case of a martyr, in which case washing is not done "in order not to remove traces of blood which are the hallmark of his martyrdom."[28] According to tradition, the funeral should be conducted without elaborate ceremony with the body wrapped in white cloth and laid in a simple, unmarked grave. There is no coffin to come between the body and the earth to which it returns. Some believe the grave should be deep enough for the dead person to sit up without his or her head appearing above ground when it comes time to answer questions at the Last Judgment. The grave is laid out in a north-south axis, with the deceased's face turned toward the East—that is, toward Mecca—so that it is symbolically in a state of prayer. It is important that burial follow as soon as possible after death. On hearing of someone's death, it is customary to say, "Allah Karim": From God we came and to him we shall return.[29] For believers, the goal is to die in the knowledge that one has submitted to the transcendent reality and has passed the test of this life. The moment of death is a call to prayer.

Death and Immortality in Asian Religions

Western thought typically makes distinctions, points up contrasts, establishes differences. Experiences are analyzed as being *either* this *or* that. Within this context, life is opposed to death, death is the enemy of life; life represents affirmation, death negation; death is "evil," life "good." In Asian cultures, the characteristic mode of thought emphasizes the integrity of the whole rather than distinctions between constituent parts. Whereas Western thought distinguishes between "either/or," Eastern thought subsumes such distinctions within a holistic "both/and" approach.

This view of reality is reflected in many of the sacred texts of the East. In Chinese tradition, for example, the *I Ching,* or *Book of Changes,* postulates a world of experience that is constantly being transformed. Life and death are manifestations of a constantly changing reality. Like the symbol of the *Tao,* these contrasting aspects of reality interpenetrate one another. Death and life are not seen as mutually exclusive opposites, but as complementary facets of an underlying process revealed in the inexorable cycles of birth, decay, and death. Like a pendulum moving through its arc, the completion of one cycle heralds the beginning of another. The Chinese sage Chuang Tzu expresses the traditional Chinese attitude toward death as follows:

> Life and death are fated—constant as the succession of dark and dawn, a matter of Heaven. I received life because the time had come; I will lose it because the order of things passes on.[30]

By observing this process, the philosophers of the East developed the concept of reincarnation, or transmigration. Some people understand reincarnation as a physical reality: "I will take birth in another body following the death of my present body." Others shun a materialist understanding of reincarnation, saying that there is, in fact, no "I" to be reborn. In the constant arising and passing away of experience, something is carried over from one state to the next, but this "something" is impersonal, essentially formless, and ineffable.

Hindu Theologies of Death and Rebirth

In Hinduism, death is defined as "the personification of time (*mahakala*) and the very foundation of the cosmo-moral order (*dharma*)."[31] Among the distinguishing features of Hindu tradition is belief in the transmigration of the soul—that is, the passing at death of the soul from one body or being to another. This process is termed *samsara,* which refers to "journeying" or

Though it will die soon
The voice of the cicada
Shows no sign of this.

Bashō

"passing through" a series of incarnational experiences. What links these experiences together is *karma,* which can be roughly defined as the moral law of cause and effect. The thoughts and actions of the past determine the present state of being; and, in turn, present choices influence future states. This karmic process pertains to the ever-changing flow of moment-to-moment experience, as well as to successive rounds of deaths and rebirths. As each moment conditions the next, karma governs the reincarnational flow of being. In the *Bhagavad-Gita,* Krishna tells Arjuna:

> For death is a certainty for him who has been born,
> and birth is a certainty for him who has died.
> Therefore, for what is unavoidable thou shouldst not grieve.

In his commentary on this passage, Nikhilananda adds, "It is not proper to grieve for beings which are mere combinations of cause and effect."[32]

According to Hinduism, behind the apparent separateness of individual beings is a unitary reality. Just as the ocean is composed of innumerable drops of water, undifferentiated being manifests itself in human experience as apparently separate selves. Huston Smith expresses the Hindu perception this way: "Underlying man's personality and animating it is a reservoir of being that never dies, is never exhausted, and is without limit in awareness and bliss. This infinite center of life, this hidden self or *Atman,* is no less than *Brahman,* the Godhead."[33]

Hinduism teaches that we can be free of the illusion of separate selfhood, with its attendant pain. Our attachment to, or identification with, the concept of "self" as separate and distinct causes us suffering in our present life and perpetuates the endless wheel of births and deaths, the wheel of *karma.* Liberation (*moksha*) from one's fate and the cycles of history involves the recognition that life and death are beyond such mistaken notions of self-identity. "The one who has attained *moksha* can see the eternal in the temporal and the temporal in the eternal."[34] The *Bhagavad-Gita* says:

> Worn-out garments are shed by the body:
> Worn-out bodies are shed by the dweller.

Nikhilananda says: "In the act of giving up the old body or entering into the new body, the real Self does not undergo any change whatsoever. . . . Brahman, through Its inscrutable *maya* (illusion), creates a body, identifies Itself with it, and regards Itself as an individual, or embodied, soul."[35]

Death is inescapable, a natural corollary of conditioned existence. What is born passes away. Yet, for the person "whose consciousness has become stabilized by the insight that it is the very nature of things to come-to-be and pass-away," there is no "occasion either for rejoicing over birth or grieving over death."[36] To be free of death means letting go of attachments to the phenomenal world.

To loosen the bonds of attachment, Hinduism offers various aids in the form of rites and practices that assist in the awakening to truth. For example, one practice involves paying close attention to the transitory and ever-changing nature of one's own being—its transformation, moment to moment.

Los Angeles County Museum of Art

The cosmic dance of the Hindu deity Shiva, an ever-changing flow of creation and dissolution, embodies the fundamental equilibrium between life and death, the underlying reality behind appearances. As the Lord of the Dance, Shiva is portrayed with one foot on the demon of ignorance and poised for the next step.

Another practice involves imagining one's own death and the ultimate fate of the body, its return to elemental matter in the grave or on the funeral pyre. Other practices involve meditation in the presence of a dead body or at burial or cremation grounds. By confronting mortality, one becomes reoriented toward the transcendent dimensions of reality. The death of the separate self is the letting go of conditioned existence, "the death that conquers death."[37]

The Buddhist Understanding of Death

Zen master Dōgen, founder of the Soto Zen sect in Japan, said, "The thorough clarification of the meaning of birth and death—this is the most important problem of all for Buddhists."[38] Although there is considerable variety in Buddhist practices and beliefs—as there is in the Hinduism that served as the background of Siddhartha Gautama's experience of awakening to become the Buddha—death holds a central place in the teachings of Buddhism. The ultimate aim is *nirvana*, which literally means "extinction," as when a flame goes out when deprived of fuel. According to Philip Kapleau, *nirvana* is the "unconditioned state beyond birth and death that is reached after all ignorance and craving have been extinguished and all karma, which is the cause of rebirth, has been dissolved."[39]

In this view, there is no "self" to survive after death or be reborn. Everything is transitory and impermanent (*anicca*), in continual unease and unrest (*dukkha*), and substanceless (*anatta*). In the Buddhist view, *karma* is seen as the universal principle of causality that underlies the stream of "psychophysical" events. Dōgen says, "Life constantly changes, moment by moment, in each of its stages, whether we want it to or not. Without even a moment's pause our karma causes us to transmigrate continuously."[40]

This transmigration can be likened to impressing a seal onto wax, or to transferring energy in a game of billiards when the cue ball strikes the cluster of balls, creating new energy events. Philip Kapleau says: "Rebirth does not involve the transfer of a substance, but the continuation of a process."[41] From the Buddhist perspective, it could be said that there are two kinds of death: continuous and regular. Continuous death is the "passing show" of phenomenal experience, constantly arising and passing away, moment by moment. Regular, or corporeal, death is the physical cessation of vital body functions at the end of a lifetime.

Like Hinduism, Buddhism teaches that it is necessary to renounce the desires and cravings that maintain the delusion of a separate self. When all

Thus shall you think of all this fleeting world:
A star at dawn, a bubble in a stream;
A flash of lightning in a summer cloud.
A phantom, an illusion, a dream.

Buddha,
The Diamond Sutra

attachments are dropped, the wheel of *karma,* the incessant round of birth-decay-death, is given no further fuel. How does one awaken to this reality, to *nirvana?* Dōgen says, "Simply understand that birth and death are in themselves *nirvana,* there being no birth-death to be hated or *nirvana* to be desired. Then, for the first time you will be freed from birth and death."[42]

The paradox of Dōgen's statement about birth-death and the importance of using death as a means of awakening to truth is echoed in the words of Hakuin, who is known as the reviver of the Rinzai sect, the other great Zen Buddhist lineage in Japan.[43] For those who wish to investigate their true nature, Hakuin advised meditation on the word *shi,* the character for death. To do this, he suggested a *koan* (a teaching question): "After you are dead and cremated, where has the main character [the chief actor or one's "original face"] gone?" Hakuin wrote:

> Among all the teaching and instructions, the word *death* has the most unpleasant and disgusting connotations. Yet if you once suddenly penetrate this "death" koan, you will find that there is no more felicitous teaching than this instruction that serves as the key to the realm in which birth and death are transcended, where the place in which you stand is the Diamond indestructible, and where you have become a divine immortal, unaging and undying. The word *death* is the vital essential that the warrior must first determine for himself.

The period immediately following death is considered to be an especially opportune time for gaining insight. The priest at a Buddhist funeral, for example, speaks directly to the deceased, expounding on the teachings that can awaken the intermediate being to the true nature of existence. Philip Kapleau says, "The funeral and subsequent services thus represent literally a 'once in a lifetime' opportunity to awaken the deceased and thereby liberate him from the binding chain of birth-and-death."[44] (A similar practice occurs in the Hindu tradition, with the *Bhagavad-Gita* being read as a person is dying.)

After-Death States in Tibetan Buddhism

According to W. Y. Evans-Wentz, "Buddhists and Hindus alike believe that the last thought at the moment of death determines the character of the next incarnation."[45] On this point, the Buddha said: "Rebirth arises from two causes: the last thought of the previous life as its governing principle and the actions of the previous life as its basis. The stopping of the last thought is known as decease; the appearance of the first thought as rebirth."[46] Scriptures like the *Bardo Thödol,* or *The Tibetan Book of the Dead,* as it is better known in the West, are intended to influence the thoughts of the dying person during the transitional period of life-death-rebirth. Indeed, the *Bardo Thödol* is also known as "The Book of Natural Liberation."

The term *bardo* can be translated as "gap" or "interval of suspension." Although *bardo* is usually interpreted as an intermediate or transitional state between death and rebirth, Chögyam Trungpa suggests that the term refers not only to the interval after death, but also to "suspension within the living situation."[47] The *Bardo Thödol* and similar texts are commonly read as a person experiences the process of dying, but they have a broader application. Such

© Albert Lee Strickland

In the Japanese section of this cemetery on the island of Oahu, graves holding the ashes of deceased members of the community are ornamented with Buddhist symbols of the Wheel of Dharma and the Lotus.

texts can serve as a guide for the living as well as the dying. Chögyam Trungpa says: The *Bardo Thödol* deals with "the principle of birth and death recurring constantly in this life." Indeed, in this view, "the bardo experience is part of our basic psychological make-up."

As to the states described in *The Tibetan Book of the Dead*, they are intermediate states of consciousness. The *Bardo Thödol* offers counsel on how to use these experiences—some terrifying, some benign—to awaken to a more enlightened incarnation. Although acknowledging that these experiences are likely to appear quite real to the *bardo* traveler, the text emphasizes that the deities or demons encountered are simply apparitions, the experiencer's own projections. They do not represent ultimate or transcendent perfection but rather steps on the way. (Some scholars believe, as Christopher Carr argues, that modern near-death experiences, or NDEs, "describe, at most, the beginning of death processes, whereas the Tibetan books of the dead describe entire death processes."[48])

Secular Concepts of Immortality

In modern technology-oriented and economics-driven societies—both East and West—traditional religious and philosophical beliefs about the purpose

Before we were born we had no feeling; we were one with the universe. This is called "mind-only," or "essence of mind," or "big mind." After we are separated by birth from this oneness, as the water falling from the waterfall is separated by the wind and rocks, then we have feeling. You have difficulty because you have feeling. You attach to the feeling you have without knowing just how this kind of feeling is created. When you do not realize that you are one with the river, or one with the universe, you have fear. Whether it is separated into drops or not, water is water. Our life and death are the same thing. When we realize this fact we have no fear of death anymore, and we have no actual difficulty in our life.

Shunryu Suzuki, *Zen Mind, Beginner's Mind*

of life or the nature of death no longer enjoy the universal acceptance they had when societies and communities were more cohesive. *Secularization* is "the process in modern societies whereby religious ideas, practice, and organizations lose their influence in the face of scientific and other knowledge."[49] For many people today, death has been divorced from its religious and mythic connotations. Traditional beliefs no longer carry the same weight in a social milieu that emphasizes rationalism and scientific method. Theological or philosophical discussions about the afterlife may seem to resemble the famous debate about the number of dancing angels that will fit on the head of a pin. Yet vestiges of traditional concepts about death and the afterlife remain part of our modern consciousness.

The Abrahamic religious traditions—Judaism, Christianity, and Islam—present a linear picture of human history, one that describes a progression of events that begins with creation and eventuates in the resolution of the cosmic story at the end of time. Such an orientation leads to an interest in *eschatologies*—that is, pictures of the ultimate state, doctrines of the last things. From the wellsprings of the Judeo-Christian tradition and Hellenistic thought, people in Western culture have predominantly framed their beliefs about the afterlife in a historical context oriented toward the future. The predominant viewpoint in Western culture is that human beings live a single life; that the soul survives death, perhaps in a disembodied state; that at some future time each soul will be judged; and that, depending on one's conduct during earthly existence, the aftermath will be either hellish torment or heavenly bliss. This view is challenged by modern ways of thinking about human existence and death.

Among the most influential secular alternatives to religious orientations are humanism and positivism. *Humanism* (from the Latin *humanus*, meaning "centered on human beings") emphasizes human intellectual and cultural achievements rather than divine intervention and the supernaturalism of religion.[50] In stressing scientific rationalism, it tends to reflect an antireligious, even atheistic, stance in which human beings are the measure of all things. *Positivism*, a school of thought associated with science, reflects the belief that

British Museum

The Egyptian papyrus of Hunefer depicts the Hall of Judgment and the Great Balance, where the deceased's soul is weighed against the feather of truth. Beneath the scales, the Devourer of Souls awaits the unjust while Horus is ready to lead the just to Osiris, the lord of the underworld, and to a pleasurable afterlife.

religious or metaphysical modes of knowing are imperfect and that "positive knowledge" is based on what can be directly observed in nature and in human activities. The intellectual and artistic movement known as *existentialism* also influences secular attitudes about life and death. In its inquiry into the meaning of human experience, this movement disavows the comforting answers offered by religion or social convention. Instead, it focuses squarely on our individual responsibility for making choices that define who we are and what we will become. The "human predicament" is that we cannot shirk our responsibility for making the difficult, but crucial, choices that shape our existence.

> We are self-creating creatures: we can choose what we want to be, and choose to be it. The moment of choice, the leap into existence, comes between two fixed points: the nothingness from which we come and the nothingness to which we return after we die. Our glory is the self-defining choice; our agony is that we need to make it.[51]

It is not unusual for a person to hold several competing worldviews at the same time, perhaps combining elements of religious faith carried over from childhood with elements of the viewpoints and attitudes represented by the secular alternatives just discussed.

The absolute certainty that death is a complete and definitive and irrevocable annihilation of personal consciousness, a certainty of the same order as our certainty that the three angles of a triangle are equal to two right angles, or contrariwise, the absolute certainty that our personal consciousness continues beyond death in whatever condition (including in such a concept the strange and adventitious additional notion of eternal reward or punishment)—either of these certainties would make our life equally impossible. In the most secret recess of the spirit of the man who believes that death will put an end to his personal consciousness and even to his memory forever, in that inner recess, even without his knowing it perhaps, a shadow hovers, a vague shadow lurks, a shadow of the shadow of uncertainty, and, while he tells himself: "There's nothing for it but to live this passing life, for there is no other!" at the same time he hears, in this most secret recess, his own doubt murmur: "Who knows? . . ." He is not sure he hears aright, but he hears. Likewise, in some recess of the soul of the true believer who has faith in a future life, a muffled voice, the voice of uncertainty, murmurs in his spirit's ear: "Who knows? . . ." Perhaps these voices are no louder than the buzzing of mosquitoes when the wind roars through the trees in the woods; we scarcely make out the humming, and yet, mingled in the uproar of the storm, it can be heard. How, without this uncertainty, could we ever live?

Miguel de Unamuno, *The Tragic Sense of Life*

Secular, or nonreligious, responses to questions about survival after death often reflect ideas about some kind of *symbolic immortality*.[52] These ideas include the biological continuity that results from having children who sustain a person's genetic legacy through succeeding generations, thus conferring a kind of personal immortality. Other "children" that symbolically convey personal immortality include those produced through creative works of art, contributions to a field of knowledge, and even heroic or helpful deeds. A person who has arranged for his or her body to be donated after death for the purpose of medical research gains a kind of "medical immortality" through training new physicians or advancing medical science in other ways. The fact that we are all members of one human race means that the good things we do and our contributions to the welfare of others extend beyond our deaths, thereby conferring a kind of "communal immortality" as our good deeds continue to resonate with a positive influence on humankind.

Today, despite the option of unbelief, most Americans affirm belief in God. Nearly 80 percent say they believe in life after death.[53] Researchers note that images of what the afterlife might be like generally involve union with God, peace and tranquility, and reunion with relatives.[54] It is apparent that religious ideas continue to play a role in both personal and social thought.

Although the assurances of religion are comforting to believers, a contrasting view is expressed by Simone Weil:

Not to believe in the immortality of the soul, but to look upon the whole of life as destined to prepare for the moment of death; not to believe in God, but to love the universe, always, even in the throes of anguish, as a home—there lies the road toward faith by way of atheism. This is the same faith as that which shines resplendent in religious symbols.[55]

Questions about immortality and "life after death" continue to engage our thoughts. When religious answers do not suffice, a search for scientific proof of "something beyond" ensues. The search for satisfying answers about what lies beyond death is illustrated by widespread interest in near-death experiences.

Near-Death Experiences: At the Threshold of Death

Stories of travel to another world can be found in virtually all cultures. The traveler may be a hero, shaman, prophet, king, or even an ordinary mortal who passes through the gates of death and returns with a message for the living. Examples of such journeys include the heavenly ascent of the prophet Muhammad and the heavenly visions of Enoch and the Apostle Paul, as well as Odysseus's and Gilgamesh's epic adventures to the underworld, and the descent of the goddess Inanna. Carol Zaleski identifies three forms of the *otherworld* journey: (1) the journey to the underworld, (2) the ascent to higher worlds, and (3) the fantastic voyage.[56] The common thread of all such journeys, says Zaleski, is the "story," which is shaped not only by what appear to be universal laws of symbolic experience, but also by the particular experiences of a given culture. Belief in a future life was historically based on religious experience; today, near-death experiences are often cited by people as a reason for such belief.[57] *Near-death experiences (NDEs)* are defined as "profound psychological events with transcendental and mystical elements, typically occurring to individuals close to death or in situations of intense physical or emotional danger."[58]

The publication in 1975 of Raymond Moody's *Life After Life* sparked the current interest in otherworld journeys and, more specifically, in near-death experiences. These accounts by individuals who have come back from the edge of death provide fascinating glimpses into a paranormal, or scientifically unexplainable, order of existence that seemingly transcends the limits of biological life. Some people view near-death experiences as proof that the human personality survives death. Others assign more materialistic psychological or neurophysiological causes to NDEs, describing them as naturalistic responses to the stress of facing a life-threatening danger. What are the components of a typical near-death experience?

NDEs: A Composite Picture

Although researchers differ in their interpretations of near-death experiences, their studies provide a very similar picture of such phenomena. Suppose, in a horrific accident or acute medical crisis, you find yourself suddenly faced by an overwhelming encounter with death. Perhaps, almost beyond awareness, you begin to realize you're not going to make it, you're going to die.

Palace of the Doges, Venice

In Hieronymous Bosch's portrayal of the Ascent into the Empyrean—the highest heaven in medieval cosmology—the soul, purged of its impurities, approaches the end of its long journey and union with the Divine.

It's like a dream; yet the experience seems more real than ordinary waking consciousness. Your vision and hearing are extremely acute. Sensory perceptions are heightened, and your thought processes are vividly clear, rational. Somehow, you are no longer bound to your body. Becoming aware of this feeling of disconnectedness, you realize that you are, in fact, separate from the body, floating free, as you look down at the mangled or suffering body and recognize it as your own.

Perhaps you feel a little lonely, drifting in space, although there is a pervasive sense of calm, a serenity that was rarely if ever experienced in the body. The constraints of time and space seem irrelevant, unreal. As you move away from the once-familiar world of the now-dead body, you enter a darkness, a tunnel, a transitional stage in your journey.

Now you notice a light, more brilliant than could have been imagined during your earthly existence. It beckons, drawing you onward, its golden hues heralding your approach to the other side. The whole of your life is experienced in a nearly instantaneous matrix of flashbacks, impressions of your prior life, events, places, people: your life reviewed and projected on the transparent screen of consciousness.

As you begin to enter the light, you glimpse a world of unimaginable and unspeakable brilliance and beauty. Someone is greeting you, perhaps a loved one, or perhaps you become aware of Jesus or Moses or another being of ineffable grace. But now you realize that you cannot enter fully into the light, not yet, not this time.

Dimensions of Near-Death Experiences

Many people emerge from a near-death experience with a greater appreciation of life, a determination to make better use of the opportunities presented to them. Often, they are more self-confident, more able to cope with the difficulties of life. Relationships become more important and material comforts less important. Psychologist and NDE researcher Kenneth Ring says that the typical near-death experiencer "has achieved a sense of what is important in life and strives to live in accordance with his understanding of what matters."[59] People who experience NDEs share many features with the "conversion" stories associated with life-changing religious experiences. Furthermore, near-death experiencers typically report reduced fear of death and lessened death anxiety after their near-death experience.[60]

In outline, our imaginary near-death experience is typical of reports by those who have actually had such experiences. Four core elements have been identified as characteristic of NDEs—namely, the person (1) hears the news of his or her death; (2) departs from the body; (3) encounters significant others; and (4) returns to the body. However, this "typical" NDE is experienced variously by different individuals. In one sample, only about 33 percent of the respondents experienced themselves as separate from their bodies, 23 percent experienced the entry into a dark tunnel or transitional stage, 16 percent experienced seeing a bright light, and 10 percent experienced themselves as actually entering the light (though only for a "peek" into the

"Calvin and Hobbes," drawing by Bill Watterson, © 1990 Universal Press Syndicate

unearthly surroundings). Ring found that NDEs resulting from illness were more likely to be complete—to have all of these characteristic core elements— than were NDEs resulting from accidents. Over half of the NDEs related to accidents, however, included an experience of panoramic memory, or life review, compared to only 16 percent of those whose NDE was related to illness or attempted suicide.

Panoramic life review, in itself a fascinating feature of NDEs, usually consists of vivid and almost instantaneous visions of the person's whole life or "selected highlights" of it.[61] The life review may appear in an orderly sequence, or it may happen "all at once." Either way, it apparently occurs without any conscious control or effort on the part of the experiencer. Sometimes, life review includes visions of the future, with experiencers visualizing their death, the reactions of friends and relatives, and events at the funeral.

The encounter with a presence—a feature of NDEs typically related to the "tunnel" experience—usually involves the experiencer seeing deceased relatives or friends, or sensing a religious figure. This presence has often been understood as a representation of the "higher self," but this is not always the case.[62] William Serdahely describes an eight-year-old boy who was "comforted by two of his family's pets who had died prior to the incident."[63] These encounters with a presence are sometimes linked to the decision to return, to terminate the NDE. Some experiencers believe that the decision to return to earthly life is made for them; others report that they arrived at this decision themselves. Usually, the decision to return relates in some way to unfinished business or to responsibilities that the person must attend to before his or her death.

The majority of NDEs are characterized by feelings of joy, peace, and cosmic unity, but some are distressing and frightening.[64] These "hellish" NDEs may include imagery and sounds of torment, as well as demonic beings. An initial period of terror is, in some instances, followed by peaceful resolution. In other cases, the aftermath of the NDE brings a sense of emptiness and despair. In yet other instances, a benevolent guide accompanies the experiencer through the disconcerting experience. Some scholars think that hellish

NDEs may be a truncated version of the typically radiant NDE; that is, hellish NDEs are *incomplete* NDEs. Another explanation highlights the fact that many saintly persons and mystics—St. Teresa of Avila and St. John of the Cross, to name two examples—reported frightening visions while engaged in deep prayer or meditation. A hellish NDE could therefore be a "purification experience," a kind of "dark night of the soul," as St. John of the Cross described his distressing religious experiences. What are we to make of near-death experiences? How should they be interpreted?

Interpreting Near-Death Experiences

Near-death experiences are fascinating. To some they suggest (or confirm) hoped-for possibilities of an afterlife or immortality. Others view near-death experiences as some sort of psychological phenomenon that may tell us something about the nature of human consciousness. To yet others, NDEs are related to psychodynamic processes that occur when the self is threatened by annihilation. NDEs are precipitated by the belief that one is dying—whether or not one is in fact close to death.[65] Some of the theories devised to explain near-death experiences are listed in Table 14-1.[66]

For early Hawaiians, their observations of *apparent* death, or persons who had "left the body prematurely," were interpreted in accordance with beliefs about the ancestor-gods.[67] On each island, there was a special promontory overlooking the sea; this was the *leina,* or leaping place, of the soul or spirit on its journey to the realm of the ancestors. If, on its way to the *leina,* a soul was met by an ancestor-god and sent back, the body would revive. Otherwise the ancestor-god would lead it safely to and over the *leina;* once beyond that hurdle, the soul was safe with the ancestors.

For various reasons (often, though not always, having to do with a person's behavior), an ancestor-god might delay a soul's acceptance into eternity. For instance, if a person died before his or her earthly work was done, the ancestor-god conducted the soul back to the body. "Sometimes when it is not yet time to die," reports Mary Pukui, "the relatives [ancestors] stand in the road and make you go back. Then the breath returns to the body with a crowing sound, *o'o-a-moa.*"[68]

Albert Heim, a Swiss geologist and mountain climber, is thought to have been the first to systematically gather data on near-death experiences.[69] During the early part of the twentieth century, Heim interviewed some thirty skiers and climbers who had been involved in accidents resulting in paranormal experiences. Heim's subjects experienced such phenomena as detachment from their bodies and panoramic memory, or life review.

The data compiled by Heim were subsequently reviewed by psychoanalytic pioneer Oskar Pfister, who explained NDEs as being caused by shock and depersonalization in the face of impending death. In other words, when a person's life is threatened, psychological defense mechanisms may come into play, giving rise to the phenomena associated with NDEs. Pfister's interpretation continues to be elaborated by present-day researchers who think that

TABLE 14-1   *Theories of the Near-Death Experience*

1. Neuropsychological theories:
   A. *Temporal lobe paroxysm,* or limbic lobe syndrome: Seizurelike neural discharges in the temporal lobe or, more generally, in the limbic system
   B. *Cerebral anoxia,* or oxygen deprivation: Shortage of oxygen in the brain
   C. *Endorphin release:* Release of certain neurotransmitters associated with analgesic (pain-killing) effects and a sense of psychological well-being
   D. *Massive cortical disinhibition:* Loss of control over the random activity of the central nervous system
   E. *False sight:* Hallucinatory imagery arising from structures in the brain and nervous system
   F. *Drugs:* Side-effects
   G. *Sensory deprivation*
2. Psychological theories:
   A. *Depersonalization:* Psychological detachment from one's body; in this case, a defensive reaction to the perceived threat of death. May be accompanied by hyperalertness
   B. *Motivated fantasy:* A type of "defensive" fantasy that basically proposes that experiencers have an impression of surviving death because they desire to survive death
   C. *Archetypes:* Images associated with various elements of the near-death experience are "wired" into the brain as mythological archetypes of our common humanity.
3. Metaphysical theories:
   A. *Soul travel:* Transitional journey of the soul or spirit to another mode of existence or realm of reality (e.g., "heaven"); proof of life after death
   B. *Psychic vision:* Glimpses into another mode of reality, though not necessarily providing proof of soul-survival after death

NDEs can be explained satisfactorily without resorting to the hypothesis that they prove life after death.

According to Russell Noyes and Roy Kletti, when the self is confronted by mortal danger, defensive reactions may result in a sense of depersonalization.[70] Their model, which may be the most comprehensive psychological explanation of NDEs offered thus far, distinguishes three stages in the typical near-death experience: (1) resistance, (2) life review, and (3) transcendence. The first stage, *resistance,* includes the processes of recognizing the danger, struggling against it, and finally accepting death as imminent. Such acceptance, or surrender, marks the beginning of the second stage, which is characterized by *life review.* As the self detaches from its bodily representation, panoramic memories occur and appear to encompass a person's whole life. The experience of life review is often accompanied by affirmation of the meaning of one's existence and its integration into the universal order of things. The third stage, *transcendence,* occurs as there is further detachment from one's individual existence. It is characterized by an increasingly transcendental, or cosmic, consciousness that replaces limited ego- or self-identity.

Calm detachment, heightened sensory awareness, life review or panoramic memory, and mystical consciousness are all phenomena associated with the ego's protective response to the possibility of its own demise. In other words, the threat of death stimulates various psychological processes that allow the ego, or experiencing self, to "escape" the threat. Because these processes dissociate the experiencing self from the body, death is perceived as a threat only to the *body,* not to the perceiving "self." It is important to point out that a psychological interpretation of NDEs does not necessarily invalidate any possible spiritual meaning that may be associated with NDEs.

In seeking the meaning of NDEs, some researchers follow the lines of inquiry founded in the late nineteenth century by parapsychologists. To adequately understand NDEs, these researchers say, one must go beyond the usual boundaries of scientific inquiry. In short, we must be prepared to accept the possibility, which is not scientifically verifiable, that NDEs are in fact what they seem to be—that is, valid experiences of states of consciousness that transcend the death of the body. In this view, NDEs teach us that the *appearance* of death is not the same as the *experience* of death. In conducting cross-cultural studies of near-death experiences, Karlis Osis and Erlendur Haraldsson concluded that the evidence strongly suggests life after death.[71] They reported that "Neither medical, nor psychological, nor cultural conditioning can explain away deathbed visions." Supporting this conclusion is the observation that in some deathbed visions there are apparitions that are contrary to the experiencer's expectations, such as "apparitions of persons the person thought were still living, but who in fact were dead," as well as apparitions that do not conform to cultural stereotypes, as with dying children who are "surprised to see 'angels' without wings." The belief that NDEs strongly suggest, or even prove, that there is life after death seems to resonate with many people. In national surveys, most Americans answer yes to the question, "Do you believe in life after death?"[72]

In summary, then, two distinct explanations have been offered to explain near-death experiences. In the first, NDEs offer proof of survival after death. Death is seen as a transition to another mode of existence. NDEs are what they appear to be: experiences of life after death. This is the explanation that appears to have captured most of the interest in NDEs by the general public.[73] In the second explanation, NDEs are a response to the threat of death and the destruction of the self. This response is related to the brain or nervous system and results from the ego's defensive reaction to a life-threatening situation.

Each explanation offers a model, or representation, of "how the world works." Louis Appleby, writing in the *British Medical Journal,* says that the explanations put forward to explain NDEs share one attribute: Each requires a form of faith.[74] The explanation that best suits your own perception of how things work is likely to be accepted most readily. There remains, however, another approach to interpreting the significance of near-death experiences. Perhaps both of the explanations are valid: There is life after death and there is also a psychological phenomenon involving various defense mechanisms whereby the personality is radically altered as the transition from one state to the next is negotiated. In Carol Zaleski's view, "We need to find a middle path between the extremes of dismissing near-death experience as 'nothing but' and embracing it as 'proof.'"[75]

Raymond Moody, who coined the term *near-death experiences*, now prefers to characterize NDEs as part of a "paranormal death syndrome," which includes apparitions of "death-bed escorts" frequently reported by individuals who are near death.[76] Concerning the way his findings about NDEs have been interpreted over the years, Moody is disturbed when people discuss NDEs as if they provide scientific evidence or proof of life after death. The prospect of finding scientific proof of life after death is, he says, "unthinkable." To Moody, NDEs represent a "wading out collectively into a domain of experience that has been closed for the most part to us until the past few decades and which is now opening up due to the developments and techniques of cardiopulmonary resuscitation." People who have experienced NDEs and shared their stories are enabling us all "to move across a frontier of consciousness." On the subject of how best to interpret NDEs, Herman Feifel's remarks are also pertinent:

> What is somewhat disquieting is the claim by some that near-death experiences are evidence for and proof of the existence of an after-life. There may well be life after death, but jumping to that conclusion from reported near-death experiences reflects more a leap of faith than judicious scientific assessment. This in no way minimizes the reality of these occurrences for the people who declare them. I just think that in weighing the evidence in this area we have less far-fetched and more parsimonious interpretations within the canons of science that can explain these phenomena. What strikes me about many of these out-of-body reports is the hunger for meaning and purpose they suggest in this age of faltering faith.[77]

Robert Kastenbaum cautions that we should be careful about readily accepting the "fantastic voyage" implied by most life-after-death accounts.[78] He says:

> The happily-ever-after theme threatens to draw attention away from the actual situations of the dying persons, their loved ones, and their care givers over the days, weeks, and months preceding death. What happens up to the point of the fabulous transition from life to death recedes into the background. This could not be more unfortunate. The background, after all, is where these people are actually living until death comes.

Finally, we should consider three points expressed by Charles Garfield, who has worked extensively with dying patients:[79]

1. Not everyone dies a blissful, accepting death.
2. Context is a powerful variable in altered-state experiences. A supportive environment for the dying person may be an important factor in determining whether the outcome is a positive altered-state experience for the dying.
3. The "happily ever after" stance toward death may represent a form of denial when what is really needed by the dying person is a demonstration of real concern and real caring in his or her present experience.

Whatever the beliefs that one may hold about life after death, Garfield says, "Let us have the courage to realize that death often will be a bitter pill to swallow."

Death Themes in Dreams and Psychedelic Experiences

Besides the intimations about what may follow physical death associated with "classic" near-death experiences, fascinating hints about afterlife possibilities have also been communicated through "death dreams" and experiences borne from the use of psychedelic or mind-altering drugs.

Based on an extensive study of death dreams from a Jungian perspective, Marie-Louise von Franz says that, in comparison with near-death experiences, which tend to be schematic and more specifically culture-bound, the death imagery in dreams is richer in graphic detail and more subtle.[80] Among older people, dreams often appear to be psychically preparing them for impending death by symbolically indicating "the end of bodily life and the explicit continuation of psychic life after death." Using the medium of dreams, the unconscious communicates a comforting message—namely, that there *is* an afterlife. Franz argues that such dreams cannot simply be interpreted as "wish-fulfillment" because they also predict the end of physical existence, sometimes quite brutally and unequivocally:

> All of the dreams of people who are facing death indicate that the unconscious . . . prepares consciousness not for a definite end but for a profound transformation and for a kind of continuation of the life process which, however, is unimaginable to everyday consciousness.[81]

Death dreams incorporate a great variety of alchemical and mythological motifs, including themes associated with the growth of vegetation or flowering plants; the divine marriage of the soul with the cosmos; travel through a dark, narrow passageway, or through fire or water, to new birth; sacrifice or transformation of the old body; shifting ego- or soul-identity; and resurrection.

The journey through a dark passageway toward "a light at the end of the tunnel" is a common motif not only in dreams and NDEs, but in numerous mythological traditions. Among the Egyptians, for example, the sun was viewed as the goal of the soul's journey along the pathway of the dead. Indeed, many mythologies embody a comparison of the sun's path with the mystery of life and death. Interpreted psychologically, says von Franz, the sun symbolizes the source of *awareness,* of becoming conscious. "This meaning of life," she says, "also lies behind the widespread custom of lighting candles and letting them burn in mortuary rooms and on tombs and graves," which is a form of "analogy magic through which new life and an awakening to new consciousness is granted to the deceased."[82]

 It is wonderful that five thousand years have now elapsed since the creation of the world, and still it is undecided whether or not there has ever been an instance of the spirit of any person appearing after death. All argument is against it; but all belief is for it.

James Boswell, *Life of Johnson*

Turning to death imagery in connection with the use of psychedelic drugs, it is interesting to note that, although LSD (lysergic acid diethylamide) was first synthesized in 1938 by the Swiss chemist Albert Hoffman, its biochemical action on the brain is still not completely understood.[83] Nevertheless, its amplifying and catalyzing effects on the mind are well documented. From the earliest studies of LSD, researchers noticed that it activated "unconscious material from various deep levels of the personality."[84] Most notably, it seemed to inaugurate a "shattering encounter" with certain critical aspects of human existence: birth, decay, and death.

This encounter often evokes a profound emotional and philosophical crisis, causing the person taking the drug to question the meaning of existence and his or her values in life. It seems to open up areas of religious and spiritual experience that are intrinsic to the human personality but independent of a person's cultural or religious background.

In the early 1960s, Eric Kast of the Chicago Medical School began studies of the pain-relieving effects of LSD and other psychedelic substances on patients suffering intense pain.[85] Besides relieving the symptoms of physical pain and discomfort, LSD therapy also diminished emotional symptoms, such as depression, anxiety, tension, insomnia, and psychological withdrawal. LSD seemed to accomplish these results by altering the patient's learned response to pain—that is, the patient's anticipation of pain based on past experiences. By becoming free of this conditioning, the patient was more oriented to the present and thus able to respond to sensations as they were actually experienced rather than to an image of pain that had grown more and more discomforting over time. Noting that pain is a composite phenomenon that has both a neurophysiological component (the pain sensation) and a psychological component (the pain affect), Stanislav Grof and Joan Halifax conclude that the primary influence of psychedelic therapy seems to be in modifying the psychological component.

Perhaps even more significant than the diminution of pain was the change of attitude toward death and dying among patients. After the psychedelic session, patients typically displayed a diminished fear of death and less anxiety about the life-threatening implications of the illness. According to Grof and Halifax, "Dying persons who had transcendental experiences developed a deep belief in the ultimate unity of all creation; they often experienced themselves as integral parts of it, including their disease and the often painful situations they were facing."[86]

Many patients exhibited a greater responsiveness to their families and their environment. Self-respect and morale were enhanced, and they showed a greater appreciation of the subtleties of everyday life. The fact that LSD induced such transcendental experiences in randomly selected subjects was considered to be strong evidence that "matrices for such experiences exist in the unconscious as a normal constituent of the human personality."[87]

As with the phenomena discussed in connection with near-death experiences, the psychedelic experience typically includes phenomena that are not scientifically explainable. Grof and Halifax point out that persons

> *Now Let the Weeping Cease (Hymn)*
>
> Now let the weeping cease
> Let no one mourn again
> The love of God will bring you
>   peace
> There is no end
>
> *The Gospel at Colonus*

"unsophisticated in anthropology and mythology experience images, episodes, and even entire thematic sequences that bear a striking resemblance to the descriptions of the posthumous journey of the soul and the death-rebirth mysteries of various cultures."[88] As with near-death experiences, the result is usually a significantly altered outlook with respect to the meaning of life and death. The evidence accumulated through reports of near-death experiences, as well as psychedelic experiences, has led some researchers to the view that modern science should broaden its perspective on the nature of human consciousness. Stanislav Grof says, "Reality is always larger and more complex than the most elaborate and encompassing theory."[89]

Beliefs About Death: A Wall or a Door?

In the final analysis, then, what shall we believe about personal immortality or the afterlife? Is death's aftermath the joyful and ultimately fulfilling experience it seems to be from reports of near-death experiences? Or are these experiences psychological projections, wish-fulfilling fantasies that mask the terror of confronting one's own demise? Furthermore, what shall we say about traditional religious understandings? Do their various concepts of the afterlife have some basis in reality? Or should we adopt a strictly scientific approach to such questions? The two basic philosophical perspectives regarding death and the afterlife can be summarized as follows: Death is either a *wall* or it is a *door*.[90]

We can imagine many variations on these two basic positions regarding what happens at death. Indeed, the doctrines of various religions and the explanations offered for paranormal experiences of death are just such variations. For example, stating the Christian perspective, we could say that death appears to be a wall, but at some time in the future—at the Resurrection—it turns out to have been a door. The Hindu concept of reincarnation would suggest that death is a door, not a wall. Buddhists might respond that death is both a door and a wall, and is neither. The conventional psychological explanation of NDEs might seem an argument in favor of the position that death is a wall that is experienced as a door. The transpersonal and parapsychological explanation, however, might suggest that the door and the wall are simply alternative ways of experiencing the same reality.

As emphasized by the International Work Group on Death, Dying and Bereavement, "Dying is more than a biological occurrence. It is a human, social, and spiritual event, [but] too often the spiritual dimension of patients is neglected."[91] A close relationship between religion and health has existed since ancient times. Caregivers need to recognize and acknowledge the spiritual component of patient care. Appropriate resources should be offered to those who wish them. In carrying out these objectives, each person's spiritual beliefs and preferences must be respected.[92]

What we believe about death and the afterlife can influence the actions taken when we or others near death. If we have a materialist view, seeing death as a wall, we may insist that life-sustaining efforts be carried out to the end. Conversely, if we believe in continued existence after death, we may prefer to spend our final hours on earth in preparation for a transition into another mode of existence. Similarly, a bereaved person may find solace in his or her belief about what lies beyond death. The person who views death as the end may be reassured that the suffering of a loved one truly ends at death. Another person finds similar comfort in believing that the personality survives physical death. By understanding our own beliefs about death, we are able to "care more adequately for each other when death—wall or door—comes to those we love."[93]

Further Readings

Paul Badham and Linda Badham, eds. *Death and Immortality in the Religions of the World.* New York: Paragon House, 1987.

John Bowker. *The Meanings of Death.* New York: Cambridge University Press, 1991.

Neil Gillman. *The Death of Death: Resurrection and Immortality in Jewish Thought.* Woodstock, Vt.: Jewish Lights, 1997.

Murray J. Harris. *Raised Immortal: Resurrection and Immortality in the New Testament.* Grand Rapids, Mich.: Eerdmans, 1985.

Allan Kellehear. *Experiences Near Death: Beyond Medicine and Religion.* New York: Oxford University Press, 1996.

Kenneth Kramer. *The Sacred Art of Dying: How World Religions Understand Death.* Mahwah, N.J.: Paulist Press, 1988.

Christine Longaker. *Facing Death and Finding Hope: A Guide to the Emotional and Spiritual Care of the Dying.* New York: Doubleday, 1997.

Geddes MacGregor. *Images of Afterlife: Beliefs from Antiquity to Modern Times.* New York: Paragon House, 1992.

Jack Riemer, ed. *Wrestling with an Angel: Jewish Insights on Death and Mourning.* New York: Schocken, 1995.

Kenneth Ring and Evelyn Elsaesser. *Lessons from the Light: What We Can Learn from the Near-Death Experience.* New York: Plenum/Insight, 1998.

Jeffrey Burton Russell. *A History of Heaven: The Singing Silence.* Princeton, N.J.: Princeton University Press, 1997.

J. I. Smith and Y. Haddad. *The Islamic Understanding of Death and Resurrection.* Albany: State University of New York Press, 1981.

Photojournalist W. Eugene Smith's children appear in his 1946 photograph, "The Walk to Paradise Garden," the first taken by Smith after two years of inactivity and numerous operations to make him sound again after multiple wounds received in the Pacific during World War II. Smith said he was determined that his first frame successfully "speak of a gentle moment of spirited purity in contrast to the depraved savagery I had raged against with my war photographs."

C H A P T E R 15

The Path Ahead: Personal and Social Choices

*D*eath may be devalued, even denied for a time, but it cannot be eluded. In telling the story, "The Mortal King," a Chinese folk tale, Allan Chinen draws attention to the fact that the desire for immortality has its own pitfalls.[1] Surveying his realm one day, a King is struck by the awesome thought that someday he will die and lose it all. "I wish we could live forever!" the King exclaims. "That would be wonderful!" Encouraged by his friends, the King fantasizes how great it would be if they were never to grow old and die. Of all his companions, only one refrained from delighting in this prospect. Instead, he bowed to the King and explained, "If we all lived forever as you suggest, why, then, all the great heroes of history would still live among us; compared to them, we would be fit only to plow the fields or be clerks in the provinces."

In our complex relationship with death, we are both survivors and experiencers. In previous chapters we have seen that there can be many different attitudes toward death and dying. Death may be seen as a threat or as a catalyst provoking us to greater awareness and creativity in life. Death may seem the ignominious end to even the best of human accomplishment, or it may be seen as a welcome respite from life's sufferings. Death holds many meanings.

One student in a death and dying class said, "Confronting death has put me in touch with life." Acknowledging the impact of death in our lives awakens us to the

I say, "Why should a spirited mortal feel proud, when like a swift, fleet meteor or fast-flying cloud, man passes through life to his rest in the grave?" They've asked me, "How do I feel?" I told them that there's nothing to it; you do things the way they ought to be done. I don't see anything to be proud about. It's pretty difficult for a man to feel proud when knowing as he does the short space of time he's here and all paths, even those of our greatest glory, lead but to the grave. So it is very difficult to feel proud when Death says this. You're here today and gone sometimes today.

"A Very Long Conversation with
James Van Der Zee at the Age of Ninety-One,"
in *The Harlem Book of the Dead*

preciousness of life. This insight can lead to a greater appreciation of the relationships in one's life. Learning about death can also bring insights concerning the death of old notions of self, as one grows beyond limiting concepts of "who I am."

Death is inseparable from the whole of human experience. The study of death and dying touches on the past, the present, and the future. It takes account of individual acts as well as customs of entire societies. The study of death and dying leads naturally to the arena of political decision, and it ultimately brings us to choices of an emphatically personal nature. Death education is germane to the sphere of social relationships, as well as to the confrontation with mortality that comes in the most private, personal moments of solitude and introspection.

Think about your own relationship to death. What place does death have in your life? What kinds of meanings does death hold for you? Are death and dying compartmentalized in a category all their own, or are they woven into the fabric of human experience?

In this chapter we touch on some of the ways in which what we learn about death impinges on individual and social experience. Rather than providing answers, our aim will be to stimulate inquiry, to raise questions, to speculate about the path ahead.

The Value of Exploring Death and Dying

Taking a course or reading a book about death and dying offers an opportunity to take death "out of the closet" and examine it from many perspectives. Possibly you are making new choices in your life as a result of your personal exploration of death. Reflecting on the study of death and dying, one student remarked, "The thought of death had always created a lot of fear; now I find that there's something very fascinating about exploring my own feelings about death and the way that society relates to death." Often, the study of death brings insights into past experiences in one's life. One woman said, "I see now what a big part denial and mutual pretense played in my family's experience of death; the subject of death had really been taboo." Another said, "I was surprised to find how many events in my own life had carried the same kind of emotional impact as a death. Divorce, separation, illness, disappointment— all meant coping with grief, loneliness, fear, and sadness in much the same way as when dealing with a death."

As you think about the various topics covered in this book, what do you notice concerning your understanding of death? Has learning about death and dying expanded your perspective or altered your attitude toward death? Do the terms *death* and *dying* elicit the same patterns of thought and emotion as when you began your study?

"When I used to think about my own death," a student remarked, "I used to slam the door, thinking of all the things I still wanted to do in my lifetime. Now, I've become a bit more calm, a bit more balanced about it." Another said, "Before I got involved in studying death, I was really uptight about death and dying, especially my own death, even though I haven't had many personal encounters with death. Now I feel that facing my own death is not as difficult, really, as being a survivor of other people's deaths." For some, investigation of death and dying allows a more accurate perception of what one can do to protect or be responsible for another. A parent said, "I've learned something about letting go where my children are concerned. No matter how much you might wish it were otherwise, you can never shield your loved ones from everything."

 ### The Illusion of Order

The world is not an ordered place. It is a chaotic place and random events occur in this chaotic world all the time. We fool ourselves into thinking that the world is an ordered place. That's how we get up in morning and how we go to bed at night, because we are ordering the world in some fashion and it is just an illusion, an illusion that keeps us going. If we didn't pretend that's the way it is, we wouldn't be able to function. We created a nice little world that we work in; we sleep from night to morning and we eat three meals a day. We know about gravity, and we know about the elements, but in fact we don't know anything. The world is just a massive pile of molecules zipping around, knocking into each other. At any time, one of these random events can occur. Earthquakes and floods and other acts of God, being symbols of all that, that all our houses with all of their roofs can be blown off, airplanes could crash into apartment buildings, babies can be taken away from their mothers. A baby that you've waited six years to conceive can go completely wrong inside. It's very, very difficult to go back to an ordered, normal life after this because my illusion of order has been shattered.

Julia

Responding to this awareness, one student said, "I learned how important it is to appreciate people while you've got them." Becoming aware of death can focus attention on the importance in relationships of taking care of unfinished business, saying the things that need to be said, and not being anxious about those things that do not. As one student expressed it, her study of death and dying had impressed upon her a sense of "the precariousness of life."

Recognizing that the preciousness of the human situation is revealed not only in major changes—such as those brought about by death—but also in the less noticed changes experienced in daily life, one can choose to be attentive to the things and people that are most highly valued. As Thomas Attig points out, coming to terms with our own finiteness and mortality can be understood as a grieving process.[2] Such self-mourning is really a lifelong process of coming to terms with impermanence, uncertainty, and vulnerability—qualities that are inherent in being mortal.

As more people willingly confront issues surrounding death and dying and examine options for themselves, changes are occurring throughout society. Examples are the establishment of hospices and suicide intervention programs, as well as support groups that aid individuals and families in crisis. As death is subjected to less fearful scrutiny, there is movement—both individually and as a society—toward gaining knowledge that can be helpful in dealing with death intelligently and compassionately. Think about the personal and social implications of death and dying. Have your previous opinions on such issues as euthanasia, funerals and body disposition, and war, among others, been confirmed? Or have they changed as a result of your studies?

For some, the close examination of death brings insights that help dissipate or resolve long-held feelings of guilt or blame about a loved one's death. The encounter with death that comes through study can open up new and creative possibilities that result in an easier, more comfortable relationship with others and with life itself. The study of death and dying can help to put previously unsettling experiences into perspective.

The notions that may be present at the beginning of a personal exploration of death and dying are expressed in the following statement:

> When I first began to recognize the seriousness of death and dying, I fled from it in fear, although I didn't realize what I was doing. Emotionally, it was harder than I had expected. But I learned that people do survive their losses, and I now know why they are called "survivors." I also learned a lot about myself, not all pleasant. A lot of my learning occurred amidst avoidance and trepidation. I thought about things that I had neglected for a long time . . . all my old concepts of death, shadowed in images of hells and old horror movies.

For one man who had felt frustrated, resentful, and guilty about his brother's death twenty years earlier, the study of death provided an opportunity to open up unexpressed and unresolved grief about a number of close family deaths. As the "stored tears" began to be expressed, he summed up the benefit of his exploration of death: "It feels so good to get rid of that ache."

For some, the study of death and dying brings benefits related to professional concerns. One nurse said: "When death occurs on the ward, people

I attended your Dealing with Death and Dying class May 10 and 11. You excused me at 1:00, May 11, so that I could go to a function that I needed to attend. I agreed to write notes on an article on cancer to compensate for the class time that I'd miss.

At the same time I was driving home from the class, my Mother was admitted to a Midwestern hospital for internal bleeding due to her accelerated cancerous condition. I left the Bay Area soon after and arrived in Iowa to deal with the reality of death.

Comments on the article don't seem as important to me, now, as some other comments I'd like to make. They concern the necessity of dealing with death and dying.

Had it not been for your class, I would have had more severe problems dealing with all the things death causes us to deal with. The openness of the people in class helped me work through some of the pain I was experiencing as I knew that my Mother didn't have long to live. The class helped me during the time the mortician sat with us and helped us work out the business details, and it helped me through the Midwestern Protestant wake. I was helped as I remembered to make sure that we got what we wanted and were allowed to say our good-byes in ways we wanted. I was able to help my family think clearly about the needs they had so that after Mother was removed from us, we would not say "if only."

A student in a Death and Dying class

often think, 'Oh, well, you're a nurse; it shouldn't bother you.' But it does. . . . I really miss the patient; it's a real loss." A ward clerk in a hospital emergency room described the new and more helpful choices she could use in relating to survivors:

> My desk is in the same area with the survivors of an ER [emergency room] death. I used to feel a pain right in the pit of my stomach, wondering what to say to them. I thought I should be able to comfort them in some way, that I should somehow offer them words of wisdom. But now I don't feel that way. I've learned how important it is to simply listen, to be supportive just by being there, instead of trying to find some words that will magically make it all go away.

Others find the study of death and dying academically intriguing. The avenues of exploration into other cultures or into one's own society opened up through such study can be a rapid means of gaining insight into what is essential about a society's values and concepts. Learning about the meaning of death in feudal Japan, for example, provides the student of Japanese culture an appreciation that goes beyond the usual aesthetic or historic approach to cross-cultural understanding. Concepts about what constitutes a "good" death or about immortality reveal a great deal about the tenor and form of a culture's daily life as well as its highest achievements.

Cultural attitudes toward death are reflected in a society's programs for the aged and its care of the dying. The willingness of a society to engage in activities that pose risks for the well-being of its citizens also reveals something

© Carol A. Foote

*Culture and individual personality shape our attitudes toward death. What we under-
stand of death and what meanings we ascribe to it become significant to the extent
that we construct a meaningful relationship with the experience of death and dying in
our lives. This grave marker expresses a memorialization that is consonant with the
life styles of both the deceased and her survivors.*

of the social consensus with regard to the value of human life. Funeral customs
reflect a society's attitudes toward death and intimate relationships. Investigating a society's relationship with death makes available a wealth of information
to the person with an inquiring mind and an interest in discerning the larger
patterns of belief and behavior.

New Directions in Death Education

Death education is still a relatively new field of study. A clear sense of continuity and common tradition is being developed, and the curricula of death education are being defined. The question of accountability in death education has been difficult to address, partly because such education takes place in a variety of settings, often with differing methodologies and goals. Should the aim of death education be to *alleviate* discomfort and anxiety about dying and death? If acceptance of death is thought to be superior to denial, then the validity of that notion needs to be investigated.[3] As with this example, further research is needed to address the fundamental concerns of thanatology, or death studies.

As Robert Fulton pointed out some years ago, there seems to be a fixation on nineteenth-century hydrostatic models of grief, which postulate a certain volume of grief that must be poured out.[4] The "work" of mourning, Fulton said, is generally conceived of in linear terms, as a step-by-step progression, rather than as a dynamic process of "unraveling the skein of grief." Since Fulton made these points, theorists and scholars have suggested alternatives to the linear, hydrostatic model of grief, but these newer understandings frequently are not known by caregivers and counselors who work with the bereaved or terminally ill in the local community. Thus, part of the mission of death education is to expand its reach so that information can reach those on the front lines, as well as reaching their clients and patients.

In striving to improve care of the dying and the bereaved, paternalism may replace sensitivity if answers are proposed before the necessary questions have been asked. We need to be alert to presuppositions that originate in a caregiver's personal preferences rather than from unbiased and informed study and appraisal. A caregiver who places a high value on resolving conflicts as part of preparing for endings may unintentionally demand, expect, or wish that his or her clients or patients do the same. Our understanding of dying and death can grow only when we take into account the interplay between theory and application in constructing an adequate knowledge base.

Ethnic groups and other minorities are underrepresented in the resource materials commonly used in death education courses. Although this situation has improved somewhat over the last decade or so, many of the "lessons taught" are still based on studies of a predominantly middle-class, white population. Responding to this state of affairs, Darrell Crase asks the rhetorical question, "Black people do die, don't they?"[5] In today's multicultural and pluralistic social environment, this question should be understood as applying to people from many diverse backgrounds. Indeed, some of the most insightful research findings and theories of the last decade have resulted from the willingness of scholars and clinicians to take a broad cross-cultural view of dying, death, and bereavement.

Much of the research in thanatology has been concerned with the measurement of attitudes toward death, and, more particularly, toward *death anxiety,* with its related concepts of fear, threat, and concern in the face of one's

Zen Questions

Men who have seen life and death as . . . an unbroken continuum, the swingings of an eternal pendulum, have been able to move as freely into death as they walked through life.

The Zen masters were so intimately involved with the *whole* of existence that they found overinvolvement with any of its parts, death included, to be a misplaced concern, saying to people who ask about an afterlife, "Why do you want to know what will happen to you after you die? Find out who you are now!"

Philip Kapleau

own death. Death anxiety research has been characterized as "the largest area of empirical study in the field of thanatology."[6] Almost all of this research has made use of questionnaires to gather data on death anxiety, and a number of "death anxiety" and "fear of death" scales have been proposed by various researchers. Those developed by Donald Templer, David Lester, and Robert Neimeyer are among noteworthy examples.[7]

Generally speaking, the findings from this research indicate that death anxiety tends to be higher among females than among males, higher among blacks than among whites, and higher among youth and middle-aged adults than among older people. Religious belief appears to be inversely related to death anxiety; that is, people who characterize themselves as "religious" tend to report less death anxiety than those who do not characterize themselves this way. Individuals who report a greater degree of self-actualization and sense of internal control also report less death anxiety than their counterparts. This finding also applies to people whose orientation to life is one of "living in the present," rather than looking to the past or the future.

Despite a great deal of accumulated data from numerous studies, there are significant questions about death anxiety research. Robert Neimeyer summarizes these questions as follows:[8] First, what definition of death is implied by the various testing instruments? Second, what are the strengths and limitations of the various instruments that have been used in death anxiety research? Third, based on the answer to the first two questions, what are the implications for future research? And, finally, reviewing the data gathered up to now, what do we really know?

Reviewing the status of research and practice in thanatology, Herman Feifel said:

> Fear of death is not a unitary or monolithic variable. . . . In the face of personal death, the human mind ostensibly operates simultaneously on various levels of reality, or finite provinces of meaning, each of which can be somewhat autonomous. We, therefore, need to be circumspect in accepting at face value the degree of fear of death affirmed at the conscious level.[9]

Robert Kastenbaum has characterized research into death anxiety as "thanatology's own assembly line."[10] Part of the appeal of death anxiety re-

It's a matter of honor, death. It's your white page, do you see? Or your shame. Either you're worthy of it or you ain't. To accept it, to face it with honor and respect and goodwill, to *earn* it, that is to be brave.

N. Scott Momaday, *The Ancient Child*

search, Kastenbaum says, lies in the fact that it "allows the researcher (and the readers, if they so choose) to enjoy the illusion that death has really been studied." How the data from such research ought to be applied to practical issues in death education, counseling, and care is still mostly uncertain. If we could reliably state, for example, that physicians with a high degree of death anxiety do less well in relating to dying patients, then that lesson could possibly be applied constructively in health care settings. With few exceptions, however, we are not yet in a position to adequately gauge the effects of death anxiety on real-world issues. Consider the fact that a number of studies show that women have higher death anxiety scores than do men. Does this resulting gender difference mean that women are *too anxious* about death, or that men are *not anxious enough*?[11] This question is representative of the difficulties with death anxiety research that remain to be satisfactorily addressed.

In any event, there are few signs that practitioners have made much use of either research or theory in their work with patients or with the bereaved. It appears, says Robert Kastenbaum, "that many practitioners in the area of terminal care and bereavement have neither an up-to-date mastery of thanatological research nor a secure grasp of the historical and theoretical dimensions." In providing a contemporary portrait of thanatological research, theory, and practice, Kastenbaum concludes that,

> at the worst, perhaps, we have sketched a picture of practitioners who fail to read a literature that wouldn't help them very much anyway. The academicians continue to tread their mills . . . with only each other to amuse, while the practitioners base their services on individual experiences and a grab-bag of unexamined assumptions and "facts" whose veridicality has seldom been tested, let alone established.[12]

Echoing such thoughts, Myra Bluebond-Langner observes that, "while the quantity of research has increased, what more do we actually know? Has progress in thanatology kept pace with publication? What differences have our efforts made in the care of dying patients and their families, and in our own responses to death and impending disasters?"[13]

In a similar vein, Herman Feifel calls attention to the need to "integrate existing knowledge concerning death and grief into our communal and public institutions."[14] People who are involved in death education, counseling, and care must participate in the work of formulating public policies that impinge on those areas of concern. Acknowledging that the still-young field of thanatology (and, by extension, the so-called death awareness movement) has many

During an annual cremation ceremony in Bali, young men carry a papier-mâché tiger containing the remains of a villager through the center of town to a temple outside the village, where the actual cremation takes place. On the way, they run, halt abruptly, shout and make noise, and turn the palanquin around and around to confuse the spirit so that it leaves the earthly realm and journeys to the afterworld.

tasks facing it, Feifel says that it can already be credited with a number of significant contributions to our collective well-being:

> The [death] movement has been a major force in broadening our grasp of the phenomenology of illness, in helping humanize medical relationships and health care, and in advancing the rights of the dying. It is highpointing values that undergird the vitality of human response to catastrophe and loss. Furthermore, it is contributing to reconstituting the integrity of our splintered wholeness. More important, perhaps, it is sensitizing us to our common humanity, which is all too eroded in the present world. It may be somewhat hyperbolic, but I believe that how we regard death and how we treat the dying and survivors are prime indications of a civilization's intention and target.[15]

In commenting on the message of palliative care put forward by Elisabeth Kübler-Ross, Dame Cicely Saunders, and Mother Teresa of Calcutta, Robert Fulton and Greg Owen note that this message is also about "essential religious and spiritual values that extend beyond the immediate goal of care for the dying."[16] They point out that death awareness fosters "compassionate acts of service" that are founded on recognition of the identity and worth of each human being.

As the disciplines of death education and thanatology continue to evolve, there has been a persistent call for a global perspective. Although personal experiences related to dying and death are indeed central concerns of thanatology and death education, the global dimensions of death—war, violence, environmental catastrophe—are important as well. Daniel Leviton and William Wendt offer a conceptual framework that focuses on the reality of death to help improve the quality of civilized life.[17] In this model, death education not only aids individuals in their personal confrontations with death, but also helps ameliorate the causes of large-scale deaths that are human-caused and unnecessary. The term *horrendous death* describes such confrontations with death, a term that Leviton and Wendt define as

> a form of premature death which is ugly, fashioned by man, without any trace of grace, totally unnecessary, and, as they say of pornography, lacking any redeeming social value. It is that death which is caused by war, homicide, holocaust, terrorism, starvation, and poisoning of the environment.

The comprehensive concerns that are intrinsically part of death education have been aptly summarized in a document formulated by the International Work Group on Death, Dying, and Bereavement:

> Death, dying, and bereavement are fundamental and pervasive aspects of the human experience. Individuals and societies achieve fullness of living by understanding and appreciating these realities. The absence of such understanding and appreciation may result in unnecessary suffering, loss of dignity, alienation, and diminished quality of living. Therefore, education about death, dying, and bereavement, both formal and informal, is an essential component of the educational process at all levels.[18]

Death in the Future

Imagine the social patterns of death and dying fifty years from now. Think about the key issues discussed in previous chapters, and consider present realities and current possibilities. What speculations can you make about how our relationship with death and dying will change by the middle years of the twenty-first century? Looking into the future, what do you see as the questions about death and dying that will demand attention from individuals and societies? Consider the effects of an older population. In the United States, it is estimated that the number of people age sixty-five and over will grow from about 35 million in 2000 to 62 million by the year 2025.[19] Will care of the dying become "big business," as corporations expand their role as surrogate caregivers for the aged and dying?

Imagine the kinds of rituals or ceremonies surrounding the dead several decades from now. Writing about the rapid pace of social change among societies in the South Pacific, Ron Crocombe comments on the trend of reducing the time devoted to funerals, marriages, births, and other such occasions of community celebration.[20] Increasingly, such community events are diverted from day to night and weekday to weekend. "Most traditional social rituals took more time than can be spared today," he says, "both because there are

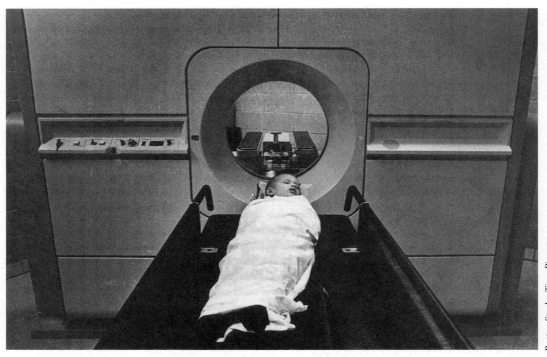

Extrapolating from current medical technologies, we can foresee only faintly the questions and decisions about death and dying that children of the future will face.

Burton Steele, *Times-Picayune*

I've finally realised that my mother and father were right when they used to say, life is too short. At 20, 30, or 35, you don't understand. But it's so true. When you get to my age, 72, and look back, you realise that life has flown by. It's awe-inspiring.

I get the feeling I've only been around for a few weeks, that I've just arrived, and already I've got to leave. It's absurd. So tell me, why am I here? To continue the species, as they say? To reproduce, have children? That's wonderful, but it would be even better to be able to look after them, watch them for two or three hundred years. See what they're going to do, them, and their children, and my grandchildren's granchildren. Then life would be beautiful.

Marcello Mastroianni,
"A Last Interview with the Legendary Actor"

many more things to do, and because each person is doing different things."[21] Although our own values and judgments play a role in determining how we spend our time, such decisions are rarely made independently of social norms and practices. If our work schedule conflicts with a midweek funeral, for example, we may be reluctant to insist on having time off unless the deceased is a close relative. As notions about community rituals and the use of time change, what kinds of funeral practices and services might evolve in response to such changes?

Consider, too, how changing circumstances may affect traditional patterns for disposition of the dead. Will there be enough land to continue the practice of burials? Or might we see a substitution of high-rise cemeteries, cities of the dead towering above the landscape of the living? In fact, this is already happening in Japan, where burial space in large cities like Tokyo is at a premium. Our current funeral practices are not likely to disappear altogether within the foreseeable future, but changes in methods of arranging for and carrying out last rites undoubtedly will occur as people exercise evolving choices. Changes are already occurring in some areas of the country, where discount casket dealers have set up shop to make their wares available to the public independently of conventional funeral establishments.

What types of social services for help in coping with the death of a loved one will be available in the years to come? Just a few decades ago, few could have foreseen the advent of specialized support and advocacy groups like Parents of Murdered Children and Mothers Against Drunk Driving, to name but two organizations that offer a forum for issues resulting from particular types of bereavement. In recent years, innovative forms of social support—as well as resources for learning about death, dying, and bereavement—have become available on the Internet and World Wide Web.[22] What other developments in bereavement, grief, and mourning may take place in the coming years?

In addition to support groups, recent decades have also seen increased emphasis on counseling or therapy following bereavement. In the future, might there be "grief clinics" available on call for emergencies? Would these clinics—much like present health institutions—send out reminders for individuals to come in for a bereavement checkup before the anniversary date of a significant death? Along with greater openness in talking about death and acknowledging its place in our lives, perhaps the time is not far off when some kind of professional assistance in coping with grief is the norm. In fact, efforts are already underway to create diagnostic classifications for "symptoms" that are generally considered part of normal grief.

If life-threatening diseases such as cancer and heart disease become matters of routine prevention or cure in the future, what diseases will endanger our survival? Given the rapid pace of medical innovation, what change do you imagine will occur within even as short a time as the next decade? The prognosis for a given disease may change from very poor to exceptionally good within the span of a few years. At the same time, diseases that were previously unknown may present new threats. As a case in point: Who could have foreseen the frightening implications of AIDS? Yet it quickly assumed proportions comparable to the great plagues of the Middle Ages in terms of public fear and uncertainty. Will novel diseases and threats, as yet undescribed and unknown, cause similar distress in the future?

It is difficult to imagine a time when *no* disease or illness will be life-threatening. Yet we have already lived through many technological advances that make possible the sustaining of life beyond any measure conceivable by earlier generations. What medical technologies will become commonplace for sustaining life in coming decades? Perhaps "off-the-shelf" replaceable body parts will sustain life when conventional methods prove futile. Organ substitution may replace organ transplantation. If it turns out that there is a "bionic" human in our future, what values should guide the use of such technologies, and who will decide? In Damon Knight's science fiction story, "Masks," a man who has suffered physically devastating injuries is repaired with functional artificial body parts.[23] But his mechanically sustained life causes him to question what constitutes a living human being.

Will medical scientists develop techniques for more accurately predicting the time of a person's death? This theme is explored in Clifford Simak's "Death Scene" and in Robert Heinlein's "Life-Line."[24] Both stories appear to suggest that the moment of one's death may be better left unknown. Although such explorations in speculative fiction are typically located in the future, in a setting different from our own, and often incorporate elements of fantasy, the

 I was sitting by myself. The hotel had cleared. A little old lady came in, so I asked her to sit with me. And she told me her life. She had lived for twelve years in hotels. All she had was in this one little room. She had a daughter. She said her daughter wrote twice a week, but her daughter lived at a distance. She went into quite some detail, and I think it hit me then, harder than it ever had, that some day that might be me!

A student in a Death and Dying class

The contemplation of death and its meaning will determine how we and our children think about and behave toward death in the decades ahead.

themes investigated bear on present possibilities and on current dilemmas of ethical choice.

What changes are likely to occur in the health care system? What will be the quality of life—and of dying? In the story "Golden Acres," Kit Reed envisions a future in which the administrators of an institution for the aged make life-or-death decisions about the inmates in order to make room for new arrivals.[25] Golden Acres provides everything for its residents except the possibility of living out their lives in the ways they wish. Reed's story focuses on a resident who refuses to acquiesce in society's neglect of its aged members. As the protagonist describes it, Golden Acres is "a vast boneyard." Will that bleak description apply to the prospects facing aged members of our own communities?

In learning from our encounters with dying and death that life is precious and precarious, we must also consider how the insights we've gained can be compassionately applied to the life of the planet as a whole. The poet Gary Snyder writes:

> The extinction of a species, each one a pilgrim of four billion years of evolution, is an irreversible loss. The ending of the lines of so many creatures with whom we have traveled this far is an occasion of profound sorrow and grief. Death can be accepted and to some degree transformed. But the loss of lineages and

all their future young is not something to accept. It must be rigorously and intelligently resisted.[26]

Living With Death and Dying

As you think about the varied perspectives covered in your study of death and dying, take a moment to assess the areas that seem of particular value to you. What insights did you gain by examining how death is seen in other cultures? How does your study of children's responses to death relate to your own experiences as a child, or as an adult? What have you learned about your risk-taking behaviors? What choices would you now make regarding funeral ritual, terminal care, life-sustaining medical technologies? In sum, ask yourself: What have I learned that can be helpful to me as a survivor of others' deaths—and in confronting my own death? Have you become more comfortable in thinking about death and discussing it with others?

Recently, an advertisement in several high-fashion magazines used death imagery to showcase the desirable qualities of the product being promoted (see Figure 15-1). In "pushing the envelope" of advertising design, however, the manufacturer, ad agency, and others involved in the project received letters from disgruntled readers who found the use of death imagery "offensive and tasteless." Do you suppose this reaction might have been different if the letter writers were more comfortable with thinking about dying and death?

In considering the personal value derived from thinking about and exploring the meanings of death, notice how the study of death and dying engages both your mental faculties and your emotions. You may also notice that your exploration of death has a rippling effect, extending outward to your social milieu and relationships with others. Has a greater awareness of death had an impact on the quality of your relationships with family members and friends, or with the person down the street or at the neighborhood shop? Has your awareness of "the precious precariousness of life" elicited greater sensitivity toward your own and others' needs or greater compassion for the suffering of others? On this topic, Alfred Killilea says, "Rather than threatening to deprive life of all meaning, death deepens an appreciation of life and the capacity of every person to give life to others."[27]

Humanizing Death and Dying

Many people are encouraged by what appears to be the increasing openness about and humanizing of death in North American society. There are signs that the circumstances surrounding death are being brought back into the personal control of the individuals and families who are closest to a particular death. Traditional customs and practices are being revived in new ways.

It is appropriate, however, to question whether this apparent openness toward death is somewhat illusory. When death becomes just another topic of casual (or sensational) discussion on television talk shows, does it reflect a kind of minimizing or devaluing of death? Is "openness" about death always to be applauded? Or does it sometimes reflect a nervous effort to achieve

Obsessively shoe obsessed   Madeline
                                 www.madelineshoes.com

Figure 15-1 *Death imagery in advertising design*

The Angel of Death

The Angel of Death is always with me—
the hard wild flowers of his teeth,
his body like cigar smoke
swaying through a small town jail.

He is the wind that scrapes through our months,
the train wheels grinding over our syllables.
He is the footstep continually pacing through our chests,
the small wound in the soul,
the meteor puncturing the atmosphere.
And sometimes he is merely a quiet between the start of an act
and its completion,
a silence so loud
it shakes you like a tree.

It is only then you look up from the wars,
from the kisses,
from the signing of the business agreements;
It is only then you observe the dimensions
housed in the air of each day,
each moment;

only then you hear the old caressing the cold rims of their sleep,
hear the middle-aged women in love with their pillows
weeping into the gray expanse of each dawn,
where young men, dozing in alleys,
envision their loneliness to be a beautiful girl
and do not know they are part of a young girl's dream,
as she does not know that she is the dream in the sleep
of middle-aged women and old men,
and that all are contained in a gray wind
that scrapes through our months.

"death without regrets"? The urge to humanize death and dying, to accept death, is laudable, but can it sometimes result in a more subtle form of denial? Death is not necessarily fully described or contained by rosy-colored projections and fantasies about the good death.

In a sense, no one is really able to "humanize" death. Death is already an intensely human experience. What we can do is work to balance our fears with openness, our anxieties with trust. We can try to understand the dynamics of grief, to make room for loss and change in our lives and in the lives of others. Death need not always be seen as something foreign to our nature, a foe to be vanquished or fought to the bitter end.

While developing an easier familiarity with death, however, we should beware of becoming merely casual. Otherwise, we may find we have con-

But soon we forget that the dead sleep in buried cities,
that our hearts contain them in ripe vaults,
We forget that beautiful women dry into parchment
and ball players collapse into ash;
that geography wrinkles and smoothes like the expressions on a face,
and that not even children
can pick the white fruit from the night sky.

And how *could* we laugh while looking at the face
that falls apart like wet tobacco?
How could we wake each morning
to hear the muffled gong beating inside us,
our mouths full of shadows, our rooms filled with a black dust?

Still,
it is humiliating to be born a bottle:
to be filled with air, emptied, filled again;
to be filled with water, emptied, filled again;
and, finally, to be filled with earth.

And yet I am glad that The Angel of Death is always with me:
his footsteps quicken my own,
his silence makes me speak,
his wind freshens the weather of my day.
And it is because of him
I no longer think
that with each beat
my heart
is a planet drowning from within
but an ocean filling for the first time.

Morton Marcus

fronted only our *image* of death, not death itself. An increased casualness toward death is very evident in modern society. Consider, for example, the growing number of death notices that bear the announcement: "No services are planned." Yet few people die without survivors who are affected by the loss. Is death a solitary or a communal event? Can I truly say that my death is "my own"? Or is death an event whose significance ripples outward to touch the lives not only of friends and loved ones, but also the lives of casual acquaintances and even strangers in ways little understood?

Defining the Good Death

There is no single definition of what constitutes a *good* death. In ancient Greece, to die young, in the fullness of one's creative energies, was considered to be exceptional luck. In our society, death at a young age is considered a misfortune. The death of a young person just embarking on an independent life or of someone in the prime of life seems a great tragedy.

The good death can be defined in many ways. The main feature of a religious concept of a good death, for example, is "one in which the person dies in a properly sanctified state."[28] How might you define a good death? Consider all of the factors—age, mode of death, surroundings, and so on— that would enter into your concept of a good death. Is your concept of a good death the same for yourself and for others? Some may question whether there can be any such thing as a good death. "Death is never good," they might say. "It can only cause pain and sadness."

More useful, perhaps, is the concept of an *appropriate* death. What makes some deaths seem more appropriate than others? Our answers are influenced by cultural values and by the social context of death. Avery Weisman describes some of the conditions that comprise the definition of appropriate death in contemporary societies.[29]

First, an appropriate death is relatively pain free; suffering is kept to a minimum. The social and emotional needs of the dying person are met to the fullest extent possible. There is no impoverishment of crucial human resources. Within the limits imposed by disabilities, the dying person is free to operate effectively as an individual and to enjoy mobility and independence. In addition, the dying person is able to recognize and resolve, as far as possible, any residual personal and social conflicts. The person is allowed to satisfy his or her wishes in ways that are consistent with the situation and with his or her self-identity and self-esteem.

My Death

"Death is our eternal companion,"
Don Juan said with a most serious
air. "It is always to our left, at
an arm's length. . . . It has always been
watching you. It always will until
the day it taps you."

Carlos Castenada

My death
looks exactly like me,
She lives to my left,
at exactly an arm's length.
She has my face, hair, hands;
she ages
as I grow older.

Sometimes, at night,
my death awakens me

or else appears in dreams
I did not write.
Sometimes a sudden wind
blows from nowhere,
& I look left
& see my death.
Alive, I write
with my right hand only.
When I am dead,
I shall write with my left.

But later I will have to write
through others.
I may appear
to future poets
as their deaths.

Erica Jong

Jerry Soloway, UPI/Corbis-Bettmann Newsphotos

Death can be viewed as a burden or as a blessing. Its meaning changes as circumstances change and as our understanding evolves toward new recognitions of its place in our lives.

As death approaches, the dying person is allowed to freely choose to relinquish control over various aspects of his or her life, turning over control to people in whom confidence and trust have been placed. The dying person also may choose to seek out or to relinquish relationships with significant others. In other words, the person chooses a comfortable level of social interaction.

Weisman emphasizes that to achieve an appropriate death we must first rid ourselves of the notion that death is *never* appropriate. Such a belief acts as a self-fulfilling prophecy. It stops us from creating the possibility of a more appropriate death.

For an appropriate death to become possible, the dying person must be protected from needless, dehumanizing, and demeaning procedures. The person's preferences about pain control and consciousness, and about the extent of solitude or gregarious interaction desired, should be respected. "An appropriate death," Weisman says, "is a death that someone might choose for himself—had he a choice."

The death of Charles Lindbergh has many of the features of an appropriate death as defined by Weisman.[30] Lindbergh was diagnosed in 1972 as having lymphoma. Until he died two years later, he continued living an active life, traveling and promoting the cause of conservation. When chemotherapy became ineffective, Lindbergh made arrangements for eventual burial on his beloved island of Maui. As his condition grew worse, Lindbergh was hospitalized for several months, but the best efforts of his physicians could not alter the consequences or course of the disease. Lindbergh then asked that a cabin on Maui be obtained, and he was flown "home to Maui," where, with two nurses, his physician, and his family, he spent the last eight days of his life in the environment he loved.

During these last days, Lindbergh gave instructions for the construction of his grave and conduct of his funeral, requesting that people attend in their work clothes. As Dr. Milton Howell, one of Lindbergh's physicians, describes this period, "There was time for reminiscing, time for discussion, and time for laughter."

Finally, Lindbergh lapsed into a coma and died twelve hours later. In accordance with his wishes, there had been no medical heroics. Dr. Howell says: "Death was another event in his life, as natural as his birth had been in Minnesota more than seventy-two years before."

Postscript and Farewell

Death education sometimes has immediate, practical consequences. At the conclusion of a course on death and dying, a student said, "It has helped me and my family in dealing with my mother's serious illness." For others, the practical application may be less immediate. Yet, as one student said, "I've gained a lot of useful information which may not be applicable to my life right now, but I know now that information and help is available and I didn't know that before."

Many people who complete a course in death and dying find that their explorations have consequences for their life that had not been foreseen when they first signed up for the course. One student said, "To me, this study has focused on more than just death and dying; it has dealt with ideas and with living, like a class on philosophy." Another student expressed the value of her death explorations as having "expanded my faith in the resilience of the human spirit." After describing how several individuals faced the prospect of dying, Sandra Bertman concluded that a common thread was the sense of "connectedness, affinity with all mankind: past, present, alive, dead."[31]

The study of death and dying includes components of information and data, but it also embraces a wisdom that arises out of the human encounter with death. This wisdom involves "a different kind of knowing, an integrative approach that refuses to look aside from the real human situation of uncer-

© P. S. Mueller

tainty and ultimate death."[32] To be sure, death education does pertain to practical aspects of the individual and social encounter with death. But it offers more than that. Awareness of death and dying brings an added dimension to the moment-to-moment experience of living. It brings us into the present and serves as a reminder of the precious precariousness of life and the value of compassion through the ordinary as well as extraordinary circumstances of human experience.

Further Readings

Daniel Callahan. *The Troubled Dream of Life: Living with Mortality.* New York: Simon & Schuster, 1993.

Lynne Ann DeSpelder. "Developing Cultural Competency." In *Living with Grief: Who We Are, How We Grieve,* edited by Kenneth J. Doka and Joyce D. Davidson, pp. 97–106. Washington, D.C.: Hospice Foundation of America, 1998.

F. Gonzalez-Crussi. *The Day of the Dead and Other Mortal Reflections.* New York: Harcourt, Brace, 1993.

J. Krishnamurti. *On Living and Dying.* San Francisco: HarperCollins, 1992.

Richard John Neuhaus, ed. *The Eternal Pity: Reflections on Dying.* Notre Dame, Ind.: University of Notre Dame Press, 2000.

Irvin D. Yalom. "Life, Death, and Anxiety." In *Existential Psychotherapy.* New York: Basic Books, 1980. Chapter 2.

E P I L O G U E

It's late. I wonder what Death will look like? A drooling ogre? Perhaps an unblinking skull, the Grim Reaper? A veiled mistress with beckoning arms? The standard forms. Or maybe Death will be a polished young man in a three-piece suit, all smiles and sincerity and confidence. What a disappointment that would be. No, I prefer the scythe—no ambiguity, no surrender . . . no dickering. What's that? . . . I hear him. He's here.

"May I come in?"

I nod. It's the young man who left me two days ago to knock on the doors of his neighbors' homes. "Well . . . ?" My breath is shorter than I thought.

He smiles, looks down at his hands, then at me. "Well, I did as you said. It didn't take long before I realized that I wasn't going to find a household that hadn't been touched by death."

"How many did you go to?"

He covers his mouth with his hand a moment, trying to hide his pride, I guess. "All of them."

"All?"

"Every house . . . I'm very stubborn."

We both smile. My wheezing is worse, and he notices. He shows his concern, and I can see that he understands what is happening.

"You're dying, aren't you, old man?"

I close my eyes in answer. When I open them again, he is at my side.

"Is there someone I should get for you? Your family?"

"Gone."

"Some friend?"

"Gone. All gone . . . except for you." The young man nods, then pulls his chair over next to my own. He takes my hand. I rest a moment. "There is something you must do for me," I wheeze. "When I'm dead, burn this house and everything in it, including me."

"Leave nothing behind?"

"This is only a filthy old shack. I'm leaving behind the only thing that anyone really can leave behind . . . the difference I've made in the lives of the people I've met." I squeeze his hand as best I can. He squeezes back. "Oh . . . and this." I try to lift the book in my lap—my book. He sees me struggling, and picks it up for me. "You take this. It's yours." His eyes widen.

"But I don't deserve—"

"There isn't time for that now!" He nods, and lays the book on his lap. Good, that's done. Moments pass. It gets quieter. . . . I must close my eyes. I witness again the glory of ten thousand mornings, ten thousand afternoons, ten thousand nights . . . then they, too, fade. All that's left is the sound of our breathing, and the wind. Time slows. Time changes. Where is the scythe? The young man's hand leaves mine and I hear his footsteps recede . . . stop . . . return. He sits down and I feel his hand on mine. He opens my fingers and lays something cool and light in my palm, all lace and limbs . . . the ballerina.

Now I can go.

David Gordon

N O T E S

CHAPTER 1

1. See Tony Walter, "Modern Death: Taboo or Not Taboo?" *Sociology* 25 (May 1991): 293–310.

2. Joseph J. Fins, "Death and Dying in the 1990s: Intimations of Reality and Immortality," *Generations: Journal of the American Society on Aging* 23, no. 1 (1999): 81–86.

3. Talcott Parsons, "Death in American Society: A Brief Working Paper," *American Behavioral Scientist* 6, no. 9 (1963): 61–65.

4. Philip A. Mellor and Chris Shilling, "Modernity, Self-Identity and the Sequestration of Death," *Sociology: The Journal of the British Sociological Association* 27, no. 3 (1993): 411–431.

5. See James J. Farrell, *Inventing the American Way of Death, 1830–1920* (Philadelphia: Temple University Press, 1980).

6. "Expectation of Life at Birth," *Statistical Abstract of the United States: 1999,* 119th ed. (Washington, D.C.: Government Printing Office, 1999), p. 93. All of the statistics cited reflect the latest available data at the time this textbook was published.

7. On the relationship between life expectancy and the maximum human lifespan, see David W. E. Smith, "Why Do We Live So Long?" *Omega: Journal of Death and Dying* 31, no. 2 (1995): 143–150; and Levin Santos, "Dead Man's Curve: Animals and People Follow the Same Mortal Trajectory," *The Sciences* 37, no. 1 (January–February 1997): 10.

8. "Deaths by Selected Causes and Characteristics," *Statistical Abstract of the United States: 1999,* p. 101.

9. "Deaths and Death Rates," *Statistical Abstract of the United States: 1999,* p. 95.

10. Jörg Vögele, "Urbanization and the Urban Mortality Change in Imperial Germany," *Health & Place* 6, no. 1 (2000): 41–55.

11. Jennie Benford, "Victorian Mourning at the Frick," *The Forum: Newsletter of the Association for Death Education and Counseling* 22, no. 1 (January–February 1996): 7–8.

12. S. Jay Olshansky and A. Brian Ault, "The Fourth Stage of the Epidemiologic Transition: The Age of Delayed Degenerative Diseases," *Milbank Quarterly* 64, no. 3 (1986): 355–391; see also David L. Streiner and Geoffrey R. Norman, *PDQ Epidemiology* (St. Louis: Mosby, 1996), pp. 3–4.

13. "Resident Population by Age: 1900 to 1997" and "Deaths by Age and Leading Cause," *Statistical Abstract of the United States: 1999,* pp. 102, 869.

14. "Mobility Status of the Population," *Statistical Abstract of the United States: 1999,* p. 31.

15. Sue Shellenbarger, "An Anguishing Flaw in Many Benefit Plans: Bereavement Leaves," *Wall Street Journal,* 23 February 2000, p. B1.

16. Daniel Callahan, "Frustrated Mastery: The Cultural Context of Death in America—Caring for Patients at the End of Life," *Western Journal of Medicine* 163, no. 3 (1995): 226–230.

17. Marsha McGee, "Faith, Fantasy, and Flowers: A Content Analysis of the American Sympathy Card," *Omega: Journal of Death and Dying* 11, no. 1 (1980–1981): 27, 29.

18. Kemi Adamolekun, "Bereavement Salutations Among the Yorubas of Southwestern Nigeria," *Omega: Journal of Death and Dying* 39, no. 4 (1999): 277–285.

19. Mike Antonucci, "Hallmark Sends Suicide Solace," *San Jose Mercury News,* 2 March 1998, p. 1A.

20. Alynn Day Harvey, "Evidence of a Tense Shift in Personal Experience Narratives," *Empirical Studies of the Arts* 4, no. 2 (1986): 151–162.

21. Mary N. Hall, "Laughing As We Go" (paper presented at the annual meeting of the Forum for Death Education and Counseling, Philadelphia, April 1985); see also Mary N. Hall and Paula T. Rappe, "Humor and Critical Incident Stress," in *The Path Ahead: Readings in Death and Dying,* ed. Lynne Ann DeSpelder and Albert Lee Strickland (Mountain View, Calif.: Mayfield, 1995), pp. 289–294.

22. Graeme Galloway and Arthur Cropley, "Benefits of Humor for Mental Health: Empirical Findings and Directions for Further Research," *Humor: International Journal of Humor Research* 12, no. 3 (1999): 301–314.

23. Carmen C. Moran and Margaret M. Massam, "Differential Influences of Coping Humor and Humor Bias on Mood," *Behavioral Medicine* 25, no. 1 (1999): 36–42.

24. William E. Loges, "Canaries in the Coal Mine: Perceptions of Threat and Media System Dependency Relations," *Communications Research* 21, no. 1 (February 1994): 5–23.

25. Robert Kastenbaum, *Death, Society, and Human Experience* (St. Louis: C. V. Mosby, 1977), p. 93.

26. For recent studies of obituaries, see Bill Bytheway and Julia Johnson, "Valuing Lives? Obituaries and the Life Course," *Mortality* 1, no. 2 (1996): 219–234; Alan Marks and Tommy Piggee, "Obituary Analysis and Describing a Life Lived: The Impact of Race, Gender, Age, and Economic Status," *Omega: Journal of Death and Dying* 38, no. 1 (1998): 37–57; and Karol K. Maybury, "Invisible Lives: Women, Men, and Obituaries," *Omega: Journal of Death and Dying* 32, no. 1 (1995–1996): 27–37.

27. Jack Lule, "News Strategies and the Death of Huey Newton," in *The Path Ahead,* ed. DeSpelder and Strickland, pp. 33–40.

28. Staff article, "Why Do They React? Readers Assail Publication of Funeral, Accident Photos," *News Photographer* 36, no. 3 (March 1981): 20–23. See also, in the same issue, John L. Huffman, "Putting Grief in Perspective," pp. 21–22.

29. Robert M. Sapolsky, "On Human Nature: Primate Peekaboo," *The Sciences* 35, no. 2 (March–April 1995): 18.

30. G. Pascal Zachary, "Junk History: It's Bigger Than Big; It's More Than News: It's a Defining Moment," *Wall Street Journal,* 19 September 1997, pp. A1, A6.

31. Robert Fulton and Greg Owen, "Death and Society in Twentieth Century America," *Omega: Journal of Death and Dying* 18, no. 4 (1987–1988): 379–395.

32. "Utilization of Selected Media," *Statistical Abstract of the United States: 1999,* p. 581.

33. George Comstock and Victor C. Strasburger, "Media Violence: Q & A," *Adolescent Medicine* 4, no. 3 (October 1993): 495–509.

34. George Gerbner, "Death in Prime Time: Notes on the Symbolic Functions of Dying in the Mass Media," *Annals of the American Academy of Political and Social Science* 447 (January 1980): 64–70; see also George Gerbner and others, "Television's Mean World: Violence Profile No. 14–15," Annenberg School of Communications, University of Pennsylvania (September 1986).

35. Jessica M. Fishman, "The Populace and the Police: Models of Social Control in Reality-Based Crime Television," *Critical Studies in Mass Communication* 16, no. 3 (1999): 268–288.

36. Travis L. Dixon and Daniel Linz, "Overrepresentation and Underrepresentation of African Americans and Latinos As Lawbreakers on Television News," *Journal of Communication* 50, no. 2 (2000): 131–154.

37. Gene Rowe, Lynn Frewer, and Lennart Sjöberg, "Newspaper Reporting of Hazards in the UK and Sweden," *Public Understanding of Science* 9, no. 1 (2000): 59–78.

38. Carolyn Marvin, "On Violence in Media," *Journal of Communication* 50, no. 1 (2000): 142–149.

39. Roger Ebert, film critic of the Chicago *Sun-Times,* "At the Movies," NBC-TV, 8 September 1985.

40. Fred Molitor and Barry S. Sapolsky, "Sex, Violence, and Victimization in Slasher Films," *Journal of Broadcasting and Electronic Media* 37, no. 2 (1993): 233–242; see also Mary Beth Oliver, "Contributions of Sexual Portrayals to Viewers' Responses to Graphic Horror," *Journal of Broadcasting and Electronic Media* 38, no. 1 (1994): 1–17.

41. Evan Gahr, "Gore for Sale: Computer Games at a Store Near You," *Wall Street Journal,* 30 April 1999, p. W13.

42. Michael A. Glueck and Robert J. Cihak, "Oregon's Suicide Video," *Western Journal of Medicine* 172 (2000): 234.

43. For more information on this series, access the "On Our Own Terms" web site at www.pbs.org/onourownterms.

44. Frederic B. Tate, "Impoverishment of Death Symbolism: The Negative Consequences," *Death Studies* 13, no. 3 (1989): 305–317.

45. Joseph Moreno, "Orpheus in Hell: Music and Therapy in the Holocaust," *Arts in Psychotherapy* 26, no. 1 (1999): 3–14.

46. Wilfred Dolfsma, "The Consumption of Music and the Expression of Values: A Social Economic Explanation for the Advent of Pop Music," *American Journal of Economics and Sociology* 58, no. 4 (1999): 1019–1046.

47. Adrian C. North, David J. Hargreaves, and Susan A. O'Neill, "The Importance of Music to Adolescents," *British Journal of Educational Psychology* 70 (2000): 255–272.

48. On death and dying themes in the folk songs of central Appalachia, see James K. Crissman, *Death and Dying in Central Appalachia: Changing Attitudes and Practices* (Urbana: University of Illinois Press, 1994), pp. 156–182.

49. Bruce L. Plopper and M. Ernest Ness, "Death As Portrayed to Adolescents Through Top 40 Rock and Roll Music," *Adolescence* 28, no. 112 (Winter 1993): 793–807; see also Robert Marrone, "Rock 'n' Roll 'n' Death," *The Forum: Newsletter of the Association for Death Education and Counseling* 21, no. 4 (July–August 1995): 1, 20–22.

50. Steven Stack, Jim Gundlach, and Jimmie L. Reeves, "The Heavy Metal Subculture and Suicide," *Suicide and Life-Threatening Behavior* 24, no. 1 (Spring 1994): 15–23. See also Steven Stack, "Heavy Metal, Religiosity, and Suicide Acceptability," *Suicide and Life-Threatening Behavior* 28, no. 4 (1998): 388–394.

51. See Richard A. Pacholski, "Death Themes in Music: Resources and Research Opportunities for Death Educators," *Death Studies* 10, no. 3 (1986): 239–263.

52. John Corigliano, program notes, John F. Kennedy Center for the Performing Arts, Washington, D.C., November 1995; and Tim Page, "A Sweet, Sorrowful Symphony for the Times," *Washington Post,* 10 November 1995, pp. F1, F5.

53. See Michael Herzfeld, "In Defiance of Destiny: The Management of Time and Gender at a Cretan Funeral," *American Ethnologist* 20, no. 2 (1993): 241–255.

54. George S. Kanahele, ed., *Hawaiian Music and Musicians* (Honolulu: University Press of Hawaii, 1979), pp. 53, 56.

55. Marguerite K. Ashford, Bishop Museum, Honolulu, personal communication.

56. See Terrence Des Pres, *The Survivor: An Anatomy of Life in the Death Camps* (New York: Oxford University Press, 1976); Lawrence L. Langer, *Versions of Survival: The Holocaust and the Human Spirit* (Albany: State University of New York Press, 1982) and *Holocaust Testimonies: The Ruins of Memory* (New Haven, Conn.: Yale University Press, 1991); and Alvin H. Rosenfeld, *A Double Dying: Reflections on Holocaust Literature* (Bloomington: Indiana University Press, 1980).

57. William Ruehlmann, *Saint with a Gun: The Unlawful American Private Eye* (New York: New York University Press, 1984), p. 9.

58. Frederick J. Hoffman, *The Mortal No: Death and the Modern Imagination* (Princeton, N.J.: Princeton University Press, 1964).

59. This theme is explored by Lawrence Langer in *The Age of Atrocity: Death in Modern Literature* (Boston: Beacon Press, 1978).

60. Jahan Ramazani, *Poetry of Mourning: The Modern Elegy from Hardy to Heaney* (Chicago: University of Chicago Press, 1994); quoted material from pp. 1, 361.

61. On the use of dramatic literature in college courses on death and dying, see Lawrence J. Hill and Judith M. Stillion, "An Interdisciplinary Undergraduate Seminar: Death and Dying in Psychology and Theater," *Death Studies* 19, no. 4 (1995): 365–378; and Gina K. Hart and Steffany M. LaBree, "Two White Roses," in the same issue, pp. 379–389.

62. See Richard A. Pacholski, "Death Themes in the Visual Arts: Resources and Research Opportunities for Death Educators," *Death Studies* 10, no. 1 (1986): 59–74.

63. Fritz Eichenberg, *Dance of Death: A Graphic Commentary on the Danse Macabre Through the Centuries* (New York: Abbeville, 1983).

64. See Vivian Alpert Thompson, *A Mission in Art: Recent Holocaust Works in America* (Macon, Ga.: Mercer University Press, 1988).

65. Kirk Varnedoe, "Dreams of a Summer Night," *Portfolio* (November–December 1982), p. 93.

66. See Martha V. Pike and Janice Gray Armstrong, *A Time to Mourn: Expressions of Grief in Nineteenth Century America* (Stony Brook, N.Y.: The Museums at Stony Brook, 1980); and Anita Schorsch, *Mourning Becomes America: Mourning Art in the New Nation* (Philadelphia: Main Street Press, 1976).

67. Cindy Ruskin, *The Quilt: Stories from the Names Project* (New York: Pocket Books, 1988).

68. See Christopher Stephen Knaus and Erica Weintraub Austin, "The AIDS Memorial Quilt As Preventative Education: A Developmental Analysis of the Quilt," *AIDS Education and Prevention* 11, no. 6 (1999): 525–540; and Christopher Stephen Knaus, Bruce E. Pinkleton, and Erica Weintraub Austin, "The Ability of the AIDS Quilt to Motivate Information Seeking, Personal Discussion, and Preventative Behavior As a Health Communication Intervention," *Health Communication* 12, no. 3 (2000): 301–316.

69. Maxine Borowsky Junge, "Mourning, Memory and Life Itself: The AIDS Quilt and the Vietnam Veterans' Memorial Wall," *Arts in Psychotherapy* 26, no. 3 (1999): 195–203. For a minority view on the value of the AIDS Quilt, see Daniel Harris, "Making Kitsch From AIDS," *Harper's Magazine* (July 1994), pp. 55–60.

70. Michael Franklin, "AIDS Iconography and Cultural Transformation: Visual and Artistic Responses to the AIDS Crisis," *The Arts in Psychotherapy* 20, no. 4 (1993): 299–316.

71. David E. Stannard, *The Puritan Way of Death: A Study in Religion, Culture, and Social Change* (New York: Oxford University Press, 1977).

72. Robert Kastenbaum, "Reconstructing Death in Postmodern Society," in *The Path Ahead,* ed. DeSpelder and Strickland, p. 8.

73. Octavio Paz, *The Labyrinth of Solitude: Life and Thought in Mexico* (New York: Grove Press, 1961), p. 60.

74. Herman Feifel, "Psychology and Death: Meaningful Rediscovery," in *The Path Ahead,* ed. DeSpelder and Strickland, pp. 19–28.

75. A useful example and entry point is "Kearl's Guide to Social Thanatology," which can be accessed on-line at http://www.trinity.edu/~mkearl/death.html.

76. Patrick Vernon Dean, "Is Death Education a 'Nasty Little Secret'? A Call to Break the Alleged Silence," in *The Path Ahead,* ed. DeSpelder and Strickland, pp. 323–326.

77. Buck Wolf, *Burial at Sea* on-line (retrieved 22 July 1999; http://abcnews.go.com/sections/us/DailyNews/kennedycrash990722.html).

78. Vanderlyn R. Pine, "A Socio-Historical Portrait of Death Education," *Death Education* 1, no. 1 (1977): 57–84; see also, by Pine, "The Age of Maturity for Death Education: A Socio-Historical Portrait of the Era 1976–1985," *Death Studies* 10, no. 3 (1986): 209–231; and Dan Leviton, "The Scope of Death Education," *Death Education* 1, no. 1 (1977): 41–56.

79. Darrell Crase, "Death Education: Its Diversity and Multidisciplinary Focus," *Death Studies* 13, no. 1 (1989): 25–29.

80. Thomas Attig, "Person-Centered Death Education," *Death Studies* 16, no. 4 (1992): 357–370.

81. See, for example, Delese Wear, "Toward Qualitative Understandings of Health Phenomena or a Pedagogical Epiphany From a Long-Time Medical Humanities Professor Who Thought She Was on the Right Track," *Qualitative Health Research* 10, no. 2 (2000): 277–283.

82. See Darrell Crase and Dan Leviton, "Forum for Death Education and Counseling: Its History, Impact, and Future," *Death Studies* 11, no. 5 (1987): 345–359; and Judith M. Stillion, "Association for Death Education and Counseling: An Organization for Our Times and for Our Future," *Death Studies* 13, no. 2 (1989): 191–201.

83. International Work Group on Death, Dying, and Bereavement, "Education about Death, Dying, and Bereavement," in *Statements on Death, Dying, and Bereavement* (London, Ont.: IWG, 1994), pp. 73–92.

84. See Tracy L. Smith and Bruce J. Walz, "Death Education in Paramedic Programs: A Nationwide Assessment," *Death Studies* 19, no. 3 (1995): 256–267; and Duane Weeks, "Death Education for Aspiring Physicians, Teachers, and Funeral Directors," *Death Studies* 13, no. 1 (1989): 17–24.

85. Hannelore Wass, "Visions in Death Education," in *The Path Ahead,* ed. DeSpelder and Strickland, pp. 327–334.

86. Robert E. Kavanaugh, *Facing Death* (Los Angeles: Nash, 1972).

87. Paul Duro and others, "Postmodernism," in *Key Ideas in Human Thought,* ed. Kenneth McLeish (New York: Facts on File, 1993), pp. 584–585. See also William Simon, C. Allen Haney, and Russell Buenteo, "The Postmodernization of Death and Dying," *Symbolic Interaction* 16, no. 4 (1993): 411–426.

88. Kathleen B. Bryer, "The Amish Way of Death: A Study of Family Support Systems," *American Psychologist* 34, no. 3 (March 1979): 255–261.

89. For more information, see the following web sites: "Project on Death in America" at http://www.soros.org/death.html and "Last Acts Program" at http://www.lastacts.org.

90. Lisa Miller, "Boomers Begin to Look Beyond the Good Life to the 'Good Death,'" *Wall Street Journal,* 25 February 2000, p. A1.

91. Andrew S. Ziner, Department of Sociology, University of North Dakota, personal communication, May 1994.

CHAPTER 2

1. Richard Tipping, "'Ritual' Floral Tributes in the Scottish Bronze Age: Palynological Evidence," *Journal of Archaeological Science* 21 (1994): 133–139.

2. The use of blood-red oxide to decorate corpses is likely the earliest widespread funeral custom. Red ochre was mined in Africa by the earliest *Homo sapiens sapiens;* it appeared in Europe in Neanderthal funeral practices and was used in burials throughout Europe, Africa, Asia, Australia, and the Americas. If we imagine the earth as a living organism, hematite is analogous to the blood of Mother Earth.

3. Joseph Campbell, "Mythological Themes in Creative Literature and Art," in *Myths, Dreams, and Religion,* ed. Joseph Campbell (Dallas, Tex.: Spring Publications, 1970, 1988), pp. 138–175; see also, by Campbell, *Historical Atlas of World Mythology,* 5 vols. (New York: Harper and Row, 1988, 1989).

4. See Hans Abrahamson, *The Origin of Death: Studies in African Mythology* (New York: Arno Press, 1977); Joseph Campbell, *The Masks of God: Primitive Mythology* (New York: Viking Press, 1959); and Jacques Choron, *Death and Western Thought* (New York: Macmillan, 1963).

5. Anita J. Glaze, *Art and Death in a Senufo Village* (Bloomington: Indiana University Press, 1981), pp. 150–151.

6. See Ndolamb Ngokwey, "Pluralistic Etiological Systems in Their Social Context: A Brazilian Case Study," *Social Science & Medicine* 26, no. 8 (1988): 793–802; and Paul Katz and Faris R. Kirkland, "Traditional Thought and Modern Western Surgery," *Social Science & Medicine* 26, no. 12 (1988): 1175–1181.

7. Ninian Smart, *The Long Search* (Boston: Little, Brown, 1977), p. 231.

8. Carol Warren, "Disrupted Death Ceremonies: Popular Culture and the Ethnography of Bali," *Oceania* 64. no. 1 (September 1993): 36–56.

9. See Neville Drury, *The Elements of Shamanism* (Dorset: Element Books, 1989); David Riches, "Shamanism: The Key to Religion," *The Journal of the Royal Anthropological Institute* 29, no. 2 (1994): 381–405; and Lyle B. Steadman and Craig T. Palmer, "Visiting

Dead Ancestors: Shamans As Interpreters of Religious Traditions," *Zygon: Journal of Religion and Science* 29, no. 2 (1994): 173–189.

10. Kenneth McLeish, "Necromancy," in *Key Ideas in Human Thought,* ed. McLeish (New York: Facts on File, 1993), pp. 508–509.

11. Mary Kawena Pukui, E. W. Haertig, and Catherine A. Lee, *Nana I Ke Kumu (Look to the Source),* 2 vols. (Honolulu: Hui Hanai; Queen Lili'uokalani Children's Center, 1972). A study conducted in the 1930s found families still tracing their lineage from ancestors who were viewed as spiritual guardians of their descendants and who often interceded in very practical ways. See E. S. Craighill Handy and Mary Kawena Pukui, *The Polynesian Family System in Ka-'u, Hawai'i* (Rutland, Vt.: Charles E. Tuttle, 1972).

12. J. Peter Brosius, "Father Dead, Mother Dead: Bereavement and Fictive Death in Penan Geng Society," *Omega: Journal of Death and Dying* 32, no. 3 (1995–1996): 197–226.

13. T. H. Gaster, in James Frazer, *The New Golden Bough* (New York: New American Library, 1964), p. 241.

14. Handy and Pukui, *Polynesian Family System in Ka-'u, Hawai'i,* pp. 98–101.

15. Important studies include Philippe Ariès, *Western Attitudes Toward Death: From the Middle Ages to the Present* (Baltimore: Johns Hopkins University Press, 1974), *The Hour of Our Death* (New York: Alfred A. Knopf, 1981), and *Images of Man and Death* (Cambridge, Mass.: Harvard University Press, 1985); T. S. R. Boase, *Death in the Middle Ages: Mortality, Judgment and Remembrance* (New York: McGraw-Hill, 1972); Jacques Choron, *Death and Western Thought* (New York: Macmillan, 1963); John Cohen, "Death and the Danse Macabre," *History Today* (August 1982): 35–40; and Ian Gentles, "Funeral Customs in Historical Context," *Journal of Palliative Care* 4, no. 3 (1988): 16–20. Except where otherwise noted, quoted material is from Ariès's works.

16. See, for example, Claire LaMont, "The Romantic Period," in *The Oxford Illustrated History of English Literature,* ed. Pat Rogers (New York: Oxford University Press, 1994), pp. 274–325.

17. See Elisabeth Darby and Nicola Smith, *The Cult of the Prince Consort* (New Haven, Conn.: Yale University Press, 1983); and John Morley, *Death, Heaven, and the Victorians* (Pittsburgh: University of Pittsburgh Press, 1971).

18. See, for example, Philip A. Mellor and Chris Schilling, "Modernity, Self-Identity, and the Sequestration of Death," *Sociology* 27, no. 3 (August 1993): 411–431; and Charles O. Jackson, "Death Shall Have No Dominion: The Passing of the World of the Dead in America," in *Death and Dying: Views from Many Cultures,* ed. Richard A. Kalish (New York: Baywood, 1980), pp. 47–55.

19. Elizabeth A. Hallam, "Turning the Hourglass: Gender Relations at the Deathbed in Early Modern Canterbury," *Mortality* 1, no. 1 (1996): 61–82.

20. Valerie M. Hope, "Constructing Roman Identity: Funerary Monuments and Social Structure in the Roman World," *Mortality* 2, no. 2 (1997): 103–121.

21. See Peter Brown, *The Cult of the Saints: Its Rise and Function in Latin Christianity* (Chicago: University of Chicago Press, 1981); and Patrick J. Geary, *Living with the Dead in the Middle Ages* (Ithaca, N.Y.: Cornell University Press, 1994).

22. Rob Kay, *Santa Cruz Sentinel,* 20 March 1983.

23. Richard A. Etlin, *The Architecture of Death: The Transformation of the Cemetery in Eighteenth-Century Paris* (Cambridge, Mass.: MIT Press, 1984).

24. See Diana Williams Combs, *Early Gravestone Art in Georgia and South Carolina* (Athens: University of Georgia Press, 1986); James J. Farrell, *Inventing the American Way of Death, 1830–1920* (Philadelphia: Temple University Press, 1980) and "The Dying of Death: Historical Perspectives," *Death Education* 6, no. 2 (1982): 105–123; Gordon E.

Geddes, *Welcome Joy: Death in Puritan New England* (Ann Arbor: UMI Research Press, 1981); David E. Stannard, *The Puritan Way of Death: A Study in Religion, Culture, and Social Change* (New York: Oxford University Press, 1977) and "Calm Dwellings: The Brief, Sentimental Age of the Rural Cemetery," *American Heritage* 30, no. 5 (August/September 1979): 42–55, and, edited by Stannard, *Death in America* (Philadelphia: University of Pennsylvania Press, 1975); Michael Vovelle, "A Century and One-Half of American Epitaphs: Toward the Study of Collective Attitudes About Death," *Comparative Studies in Society and History* 22, no. 4 (October 1980): 534–547.

25. James Stevens Curl, *A Celebration of Death: An Introduction to Some of the Buildings, Monuments, and Settings of Funerary Architecture in the Western European Tradition* (New York: Charles Scribner's Sons, 1980), p. 367.

26. See Georges Bataille, *Death and Sensuality: A Study of Eroticism and the Taboo* (New York: Walker and Company, 1962).

27. Frank Gonzalez-Crussi, "Anatomy and Old Lace: An Eighteenth-Century Attitude Toward Death," *The Sciences* (January–February 1988): 48–49.

28. On the anthropology of death, see Maurice Bloch and Jonathan Perry, eds., *Death and the Regeneration of Life* (New York: Cambridge University Press, 1982); Loring M. Danforth, *The Death Rituals of Rural Greece* (Princeton, N.J.: Princeton University Press, 1982); Richard Huntington and Peter Metcalf, *Celebrations of Death: The Anthropology of Mortuary Ritual* (New York: Cambridge University Press, 1979); and Johannes Fabian, "How Others Die: Reflections on the Anthropology of Death," *Social Research* 39 (1972): 543–567.

29. Louise B. Halfe, "The Circle: Death and Dying from a Native Perspective," *Journal of Palliative Care* 5, no. 1 (1989): 37–41. See also Paul Radin, *The Road of Life and Death: A Ritual Drama of the American Indians* (Princeton, N.J.: Princeton University Press, 1973).

30. Richard J. Preston and Sarah C. Preston, "Death and Grieving Among Northern Forest Hunters: An East Cree Example," in *Coping with the Final Tragedy: Cultural Variation in Dying and Grieving,* ed. David R. Counts and Dorothy A. Counts (Amityville, N.Y.: Baywood, 1991), pp. 135–155.

31. Jamake Highwater, *The Primal Mind: Vision and Reality in Indian America* (New York: Harper and Row, 1981), p. 165.

32. Åke Hultkrantz, *Native Religions of North America: The Power of Visions and Fertility* (New York: Harper and Row, 1987); see also, by Hultkrantz, *The Religions of the American Indians* (Berkeley: University of California Press, 1979) and *The Study of American Indian Religions* (New York: Crossroad, 1983).

33. John Witthoft, "Cherokee Beliefs Concerning Death," *Journal of Cherokee Studies* 8, no. 2 (Fall 1983): 68–72.

34. Joseph E. Trimble and Candace M. Fleming, "Providing Counseling Services for Native American Indians: Client, Counselor, and Community Characteristics," in *Counseling Across Cultures*, 3d ed., ed. Paul B. Pedersen, Juris G. Dragus, Walter J. Lonner, and Joseph E. Trimble (Honolulu: University of Hawaii Press, 1989), pp. 177–204.

35. See, for example, C. E. Schorer, "Two Centuries of Miami Indian Death Customs," *Omega: Journal of Death and Dying* 20, no. 1 (1989–1990): 75–79; and Carl Waldman, *Atlas of the North American Indian* (New York: Facts on File, 1985).

36. Quoted in Vine Deloria, Jr., *God Is Red* (New York: Dell, 1973), pp. 176–177.

37. Malcolm Margolin, *The Ohlone Way: Indian Life in the San Francisco Monterey Bay Area* (Berkeley, Calif.: Heyday Books, 1978), pp. 145–149.

38. Concern for the proper disposition of human remains is a major issue for indigenous peoples. See "Human Remains: Contemporary Issues," in *Death Studies* 14, no. 6 (1990), ed. Glen W. Davidson and Larry W. Zimmerman.

39. Robson Bonnichsen and Alan L. Schneider, "Battle of the Bones," *The Sciences* 40, no. 4 (2000): 40–46.

40. Gerry R. Cox, "Native American Spirituality, Illness, Dying, and Death" (paper presented at the annual meeting of the Midwest Sociological Society, Chicago, 1995); see also Gerry R. Cox and Ronald J. Fundis, "Native American Burial Practices," in *Personal Care in an Impersonal World: A Multidimensional Look at Bereavement,* ed. John D. Morgan (Amityville, N.Y.: Baywood, 1993), pp. 191–203.

41. David G. Mandelbaum, "Social Uses of Funeral Rites," in *The Meaning of Death,* ed. Herman Feifel (New York: McGraw-Hill, 1959), pp. 189–217.

42. Noel Q. King, *Religions of Africa: A Pilgrimage into Traditional Religions* (New York: Harper and Row, 1970), pp. 13–14; see also, by King, *Christian and Muslim in Africa* (New York: Harper and Row, 1971), p. 95.

43. King, *Religions of Africa,* p. 68.

44. Kofi Asare Opoku, "African Perspectives on Death and Dying," in *Perspectives on Death and Dying: Cross-Cultural and Multidisciplinary Views,* ed. Arthur Berger and others (Philadelphia: The Charles Press, 1989), pp. 14–23. See also Dominique Zahan, *The Religion, Spirituality, and Thought of Traditional Africa* (Chicago: University of Chicago Press, 1979).

45. Francis Bebey, *African Music: A People's Art* (Brooklyn, N.Y.: Lawrence Hill, 1975), p. 126.

46. Kwasi Wiredu, "Death and the Afterlife in African Culture," in *Perspectives on Death and Dying,* ed. Berger and others, pp. 24–37.

47. John E. Reinhardt, *Life . . . Afterlife: African Funerary Sculpture* (Washington, D.C.: National Museum of African Art, 1982). For a systematic account of African religions, see John S. Mbiti, *African Religions and Philosophy* (Garden City, N.Y.: Anchor/ Doubleday, 1970).

48. From a story by Robert Dvorchak, *Los Angeles Times,* 8 July 1990.

47. Jack Goody, *Death, Property, and the Ancestors: A Study of the Mortuary Customs of the LoDagaa of West Africa* (Stanford, Calif.: Stanford University Press, 1962). The complex ritual associated with African funeral ceremonies has also been recently addressed by Pamilla C. Morales, "Death Rituals and Funeral Ceremonies of Four Major Ugandan Tribes of East Africa" (paper presented at the annual meeting of the Association for Death Education and Counseling, Chicago, 1998).

50. Gillian Feeley-Harnik, "The Political Economy of Death: Communication and Change in Malagasy Colonial History," *American Ethnologist* 11, no. 1 (1984): 1–19.

51. J. F. Ade Ajayi, "On the Politics of Being Mortal," *Transition,* no. 59 (1993): 32–44, esp. pp. 38–42.

52. Olatunde Bayo Lawuyi, "Obituary and Ancestral Worship: Analysis of a Contemporary Cultural Form in Nigeria," *Sociological Analysis* 48, no. 4 (1988): 372–379; see also A. Odasuo Alali, "Management of Death and Grief in Obituary and in Memoriam Pages of Nigerian Newspapers," *Psychological Reports* 73 (1993): 835–842.

53. See Linda M. Chatters, Robert Joseph Taylor, and Karen D. Lincoln, "African American Religious Participation: A Multi-Sample Comparison," *Journal for the Scientific Study of Religion* 38, no. 1 (1999): 132–145.

54. John F. Toth, Jr., "Power and Paradox in an African American Congregation," *Review of Religious Research* 40, no. 3 (1999): 213–229.

55. Mary Abrums, "Death and Meaning in a Storefront Church," *Public Health Nursing* 17, no. 2 (2000): 132–142.

56. Stefania Capone, "Gods on the Net: The Rise of Religions of African Origin in the United States," *Homme,* no. 151 (1999): 47–74.

57. Miguel León-Portilla, "Those Made Worthy by Divine Sacrifice: The Faith of Ancient Mexico," in *South and Meso-American Native Spirituality: From the Cult of the Feathered Serpent to the Theology of Liberation*, ed. Gary H. Gossen (New York: Crossroad, 1993), pp. 41–64. See also, in the same volume, Louise M. Burkhart, "The Cult of the Virgin of Guadalupe in Mexico," pp. 198–227.

58. See Ignacio Aguilar and Virginia N. Wood, "Therapy Through a Death Ritual," in *Death and Dying: Theory, Research, and Practice*, ed. Larry Bugen (Dubuque, Iowa: William C. Brown, 1979), pp. 131–141; Barbara Brodman, *The Mexican Cult of Death in Myth and Literature* (Gainesville: University of Florida Press, 1976); Patricia Fernández Kelly, "Death in Mexican Folk Culture," *American Quarterly* 26, no. 5 (December 1974): 516–535; Oscar Lewis, *A Death in the Sanchez Family* (New York: Vintage Books, 1970); Joan Moore, "The Death Culture of Mexico and Mexican Americans," in *Death and Dying: Views from Many Cultures*, ed. Kalish, pp. 72–91; Patricia Osuna and David K. Reynolds, "A Funeral in Mexico: Description and Analysis," *Omega: Journal of Death and Dying* 1, no. 3 (1970): 249–269.

59. León-Portilla, "Those Made Worthy," p. 56.

60. Jose Antonio Burciaga, "A Day to Laugh at Death," *San Jose Mercury News*, 1 November 1985. In "El Día de los Muertos: The Day of the Dead in Mexican Tradition" (paper presented at the annual meeting of the Association for Death Education and Counseling, Chicago, 1998), Pamilla C. Morales notes that Posada's cavorting skeletons in modern dress are very much part of the popular imagery of Mexico's celebration of the Day of the Dead.

61. Octavio Paz, *The Labyrinth of Solitude: Life and Thought in Mexico* (New York: Grove Press, 1961).

62. See Robert Childs and Patricia B. Altman, *Vive tu Recuerdo: Living Traditions of the Mexican Days of the Dead* (Los Angeles: Museum of Cultural History, UCLA, 1982); Douglas Day, "A Day with the Dead," *Natural History* (October 1990): 67–73; Frank Gonzalez-Crussi, *The Day of the Dead and Other Mortal Reflections* (New York: Harcourt Brace, 1993); and Judith Strupp Green, "The Days of the Dead in Oaxaca, Mexico: An Historical Inquiry," in *Death and Dying: Views from Many Cultures*, ed. Kalish, pp. 56–71.

63. Glenn Whitney, "Mexico's Day of the Dead Is Actually Very Lively," United Press International story in the *Honolulu Star-Bulletin & Advertiser*, 1 November 1987.

64. Quoted in Whitney, "Mexico's Day of the Dead."

65. Paz, *Labyrinth of Solitude*.

66. References consulted in preparing this section include: Momoo Yamaguchi and Setsuko Kojima, eds., *A Cultural Dictionary of Japan* (Tokyo: The Japan Times, 1979); H. Byron Earhart, "Religions of Japan: Many Traditions Within One Sacred Way," in *Religious Traditions of the World*, ed. Earhart (San Francisco: HarperCollins, 1992); Takashi Ishikawa, *Kokoro: The Soul of Japan* (Tokyo: The East Publications, 1986); Hajime Nakamura, *Ways of Thinking of Eastern Peoples: India, China, Tibet, Japan*, trans. and ed. Philip P. Wiener (Honolulu: University of Hawaii Press, 1964); Sokyo Ono, *Shinto: The Kami Way* (Rutland, Vt.: Charles E. Tuttle, 1962); Daniel L. Overmyer, "Religions of China: The World As a Living System," in *Religious Traditions of the World*, ed. Earhart; Ian Reader, *Religion in Contemporary Japan* (Honolulu: University of Hawaii Press, 1991); Robert J. Smith, *Ancestor Worship in Contemporary Japan* (Stanford, Calif.: Stanford University Press, 1974); Laurence G. Thompson, *Chinese Religion: An Introduction*, 4th ed. (Belmont, Calif.: Wadsworth, 1989); and Yamaori Tetsuo, "The Metamorphosis of Ancestors," *Japan Quarterly* 33, no. 1 (January–March 1986): 50–53.

67. Inge Rösch-Rhomberg, "Hierarchical Opposition and the Concept of *um-yang* (*yin-yang*): A Reevaluation of Values in the Light of the Symbolism of Korean Rituals for the Dead," *Anthropos* 89 (1994): 471–491.

68. Dennis Klass, "Ancestor Worship in Japan: Dependence and the Resolution of Grief," *Omega: Journal of Death and Dying* 33, no. 4 (1996): 279–302; see also Dennis Klass and Amy Olwen Heath, "Grief and Abortion: *Mizuko Kuyo,* the Japanese Ritual Resolution," *Omega: Journal of Death and Dying* 34, no. 1 (1996–1997): 1–14.

69. Roberta Halporn, *Gods, Ghosts, and Ancestors: The Ching Ming Festival in America* (Brooklyn, N.Y.: Center for Thanatological Research and Education, 1994), and "Chinese Americans in Loss and Grief," *The Forum: Newsletter of the Association for Death Education and Counseling* 17, no. 6 (November–December 1992): 1, 16–20.

70. Johannes Fabian, "How Others Die: Reflections on the Anthropology of Death," *Social Research* 39 (1972): 543–567.

CHAPTER 3

1. Mark W. Speece and Sandor B. Brent, "The Development of Children's Understanding of Death," in *Handbook of Childhood Death and Bereavement,* ed. Charles A. Corr and Donna M. Corr (New York: Springer, 1996).

2. See Sandor B. Brent and Mark W. Speece, " 'Adult' Conceptualization of Irreversibility: Implications for the Development of the Concept of Death," *Death Studies* 17, no. 3 (1993): 203–224.

3. Kwok-Fai Ting and Catherine C. H. Chiu, "Materialistic Values in Hong Kong and Guangzhou: A Comparative Analysis of Two Chinese Societies," *Sociological Spectrum* 20, no. 1 (2000): 15–40.

4. Norman Goodman, *Introduction to Sociology* (New York: HarperCollins, 1992), p. 42.

5. Gordon Marshall, ed., *The Concise Oxford Dictionary of Sociology* (New York: Oxford University Press, 1994), p. 104.

6. Ralph LaRossa and others, "The Changing Culture of Fatherhood in Comic-Strip Families: A Six-Decade Analysis," *Journal of Marriage and the Family* 62, no. 2 (2000): 375–387.

7. Hannelore Wass, "Death Education for Children," in *A Challenge for Living: Dying, Death and Bereavement,* ed. Inge B. Corless, Barbara B. Germino, and Mary A. Pittman (Boston: Jones and Bartlett, 1995), pp. 335–350; quote, p. 337.

8. Goodman, *Introduction to Sociology,* pp. 84–85. See also Amitai Etzioni, "Toward a Theory of Public Ritual," *Sociological Theory* 18, no. 1 (2000): 44–59.

9. See, for example, Phyllis Silverman, *Widow to Widow* (New York: Springer, 1986); and Scott Campbell and Phyllis Silverman, *Widower: When Men Are Left Alone* (New York: Prentice-Hall, 1987).

10. Mark A. Mesler, "Negotiating Life for the Dying: Hospice and the Strategy of Tactical Socialization," *Death Studies* 19, no. 3 (1995): 235–255.

11. Linda J. Waite, "The Family As a Social Organization: Key Ideas for the Twenty-First Century," *Contemporary Sociology* 29, no. 3 (2000): 463–469.

12. Lynn Okagaki and Denise K. Moore, "Ethnic Identity Beliefs of Young Adults and Their Parents in Families of Mexican Descent," *Hispanic Journal of Behavioral Sciences* 22, no. 2 (2000): 139–162.

13. Reed Larson, "Youth Organizations, Hobbies, and Sports As Developmental Contexts," in *Adolescence in Context: The Interplay of Family, School, Peers, and Work in*

Adjustment, ed. Rainer K. Silbereisen and Eberhard Todt (New York: Springer-Verlag, 1993), pp. 46–65.

14. A. Cordell Perkes and Roberta Schildt, "Death-Related Attitudes of Adolescent Males and Females," *Death Education* 2, no. 4 (1979): 359–368. For gender differences in adults as well as children, see Judith M. Stillion, *Death and the Sexes: An Examination of Differential Longevity, Attitudes, Behaviors, and Coping Skills* (Washington, D.C.: Hemisphere, 1985).

15. Martha Wolfenstein and Gilbert Kliman, eds., *Children and the Death of a President: Multi-Disciplinary Studies* (Garden City, N.Y.: Anchor Press/Doubleday, 1965), especially pp. 217–239.

16. "First Graders Paint a Happy Ending," Associated Press story, 31 January 1986; and other newspaper sources.

17. Elizabeth P. Lamers, "Children, Death, and Fairy Tales," *Omega: Journal of Death and Dying* 31, no. 2 (1995): 151–167.

18. Carolyn Marvin, "On Violence in Media," *Journal of Communication* 50, no. 1 (2000): 142–149.

19. See, for example, Eve Morel, ed., *Fairy Tales and Fables* (New York: Grosset & Dunlap, 1970), pp. 11–13.

20. Ed Young, trans., *Lon Po Po: A Red-Riding Hood Story from China* (New York: Philomel Books, 1989).

21. Kalle Achte and others, "Themes of Death and Violence in Lullabies of Different Countries," *Omega: Journal of Death and Dying* 20, no. 3 (1989–1990): 193–204.

22. Adrienne M. L. Rock, Laurel J. Trainor, and Tami L. Addison, "Distinctive Messages in Infant-Directed Lullabies and Play Songs," *Developmental Psychology* 35, no. 2 (1999): 527–534.

23. Reported by Richard Lonetto, *Children's Conceptions of Death* (New York: Springer, 1980), p. 9.

24. Robert A. Emmons, "Religion in the Psychology of Personality: An Introduction," *Journal of Personality* 67, no. 6 (1999): 873–888.

25. Justin L. Barrett, "Cognitive Constraints on Hindu Concepts of the Divine," *Journal for the Scientific Study of Religion* 37, no. 4 (1998): 608–619.

26. Davina A. Allen and others, "Religion," in *Key Ideas in Human Thought,* ed. Kenneth McLeish (New York: Facts on File, 1993), pp. 626–627.

27. David E. Balk and Nancy S. Hogan, "Religion, Spirituality, and Bereaved Adolescents," in *Beyond the Innocence of Childhood: Helping Children and Adolescents Cope with Death and Bereavement,* ed. David W. Adams and Elanor J. Deveau (Amityville, N.Y.: Baywood, 1995), pp. 61–88.

28. Vernon Reynolds and Ralph Tanner, *The Social Ecology of Religion* (New York: Oxford University Press, 1995), p. 211.

29. Michael E. McCullough and others, "Religious Involvement and Mortality: A Meta-Analytic Review," *Health Psychology* 19, no. 3 (2000): 211–222.

30. Andrew J. Weaver and others, "Research on Religious Variables in Five Major Adolescent Research Journals: 1992 to 1996," *Journal of Nervous and Mental Disease* 188, no. 1 (2000): 36–44.

31. Goodman, *Introduction to Sociology,* p. 215.

32. Lynne Ann DeSpelder and Albert Lee Strickland, "Using Life Experiences As a Way of Helping Children Understand Death," in *Beyond the Innocence of Childhood: Factors Influencing Children and Adolescents' Perceptions and Attitudes Toward Death,* ed. David W. Adams and Eleanor J. Deveau (Amityville, N.Y.: Baywood, 1995), pp. 45–54.

33. Lynne Ann DeSpelder and Nathalie Prettyman, *A Guidebook for Teaching Family Living* (Boston: Allyn and Bacon, 1980), pp. 130–134.

34. See Mary Anne Sedney, "Children's Grief Narratives in Popular Films," *Omega: Journal of Death and Dying* 39, no. 4 (1999): 315–324.

35. For a comprehensive survey of death anxiety research, see Robert A. Neimeyer, ed., *Death Anxiety Handbook: Research, Instrumentation, and Application* (Washington, D.C.: Taylor & Francis, 1993).

36. *Newsweek,* 5 May 1980; see also Roger Rosenblatt, *Children of War* (New York: Anchor/Doubleday, 1983); Claudine Vegh, *I Didn't Say Goodbye: Interviews with the Children of the Holocaust* (New York: E. P. Dutton, 1985); and Robert Westall, *Children of the Blitz: Memories of Wartime Childhood* (New York: Viking, 1986).

37. James Garbarino, "Challenges We Face in Understanding Children and War: A Personal Essay," in *The Path Ahead: Readings in Death and Dying,* ed. Lynne Ann DeSpelder and Albert Lee Strickland (Mountain View, Calif.: Mayfield, 1995), pp. 169–174.

38. Zlata Filipovic, "Zlata's Diary: A Child's Life in Sarajevo," in *The Path Ahead,* ed. DeSpelder and Strickland, pp. 175–178.

39. Ice T, "The Killing Fields," in *The Path Ahead,* ed. DeSpelder and Strickland, pp. 179–181.

40. Ronald Keith Barrett and Lynne Ann DeSpelder, "Ways People Die: The Influence of Environment on a Child's View of Death" (paper presented at the annual meeting of the Association for Death Education and Counseling, Washington, D.C., 26 June 1997).

41. Nancy Scheper-Hughes, "Death Without Weeping: The Violence of Everyday Life in Brazil," in *The Path Ahead,* ed. DeSpelder and Strickland, pp. 41–58.

42. Kathy Charmaz, "Conceptual Approaches to the Study of Death," *Death and Identity,* 3d ed., ed. Robert Fulton and Robert Bendiksen (Philadelphia: The Charles Press, 1993), pp. 44–45.

43. Robert Blauner, "Death and Social Structure," in *Death and Identity,* rev. ed., ed. Robert Fulton (Bowie, Md.: The Charles Press, 1976), pp. 35–59.

44. Robert Bendiksen, "The Sociology of Death," in *Death and Identity,* rev. ed., ed. Fulton, pp. 59–81.

45. Robert Kastenbaum and Beatrice Kastenbaum, *Encyclopedia of Death* (Phoenix, Ariz.: Oryx Press, 1989), pp. 90–93.

46. Robert Kastenbaum, *Death, Society, and Human Experience,* 5th ed. (Boston: Allyn and Bacon, 1995), p. 53.

47. Robert Kastenbaum, "A World Without Death? First and Second Thoughts," *Mortality* 1, no. 1 (1996): 111–121.

48. Davina A. Allen, "Social Construction of Reality," in *Key Ideas in Human Thought,* ed. McLeish, pp. 725–726.

49. Robert Fulton and Robert Bendiksen, "Introduction," in *Death and Identity,* 3d ed., ed. Fulton and Bendiksen, p. 7.

50. Myra Bluebond-Langner, *The Private Worlds of Dying Children* (Princeton, N.J.: Princeton University Press, 1978), p. 5.

51. Joseph M. Kaufert and John D. O'Neil, "Cultural Mediation of Dying and Grieving Among Native Canadian Patients in Urban Hospitals," in *The Path Ahead,* ed. DeSpelder and Strickland, pp. 59–74.

52. Goodman, *Introduction to Sociology,* p. 93.

53. Fulton and Bendiksen, "Introduction," p. 7.

54. Wolfgang Stroebe and Margaret Stroebe, "Is Grief Universal? Cultural Variations in the Emotional Reaction to Loss," in *Death and Identity,* 3d ed., ed. Fulton and Bendiksen, p. 181.

55. Greg Owen, Robert Fulton, and Eric Marcusen, "Death at a Distance: A Study of Family Bereavement," in *Death and Identity,* 3d ed., ed. Fulton and Bendiksen, p. 241.

56. Stroebe and Stroebe, "Is Grief Universal?" p. 197.

57. Christopher L. Hayes and Richard A. Kalish, "Death-Related Experiences and Funerary Practices of the Hmong Refugee in the United States," in *The Path Ahead,* ed. DeSpelder and Strickland, pp. 75–79.

58. Gerdien Jonker, "The Knife's Edge: Muslim Burial in the Diaspora," *Mortality* 1, no. 1 (1996): 27–43.

59. Pittu Laungani, "Death and Bereavement in India and England: A Comparative Analysis," *Mortality* 1, no. 2 (1996): 191–212.

60. Ronald L. Akers, *Deviant Behavior: A Social Learning Approach,* 3d ed. (Belmont, Calif.: Wadsworth, 1985), p. 57.

61. Ibid., p. 5.

62. Davina A. Allen and Catherine McDermott, "Subculture," in *Key Ideas in Human Thought,* ed. McLeish, pp. 718–719.

63. Goodman, *Introduction to Sociology,* p. 37.

64. David Clark, ed., *The Sociology of Death: Theory, Culture, Practice* (Cambridge, Mass.: Blackwell, 1993), p. 3.

65. David H. Olson and John DeFrain, *Marriage and Family: Diversity and Strengths* (Mountain View, Calif.: Mayfield, 1994), p. 37.

66. Stroebe and Stroebe, "Is Grief Universal?" p. 201; see also M. Eisenbruch, "Cross-Cultural Aspects of Bereavement: Ethnic and Cultural Variations in the Development of Bereavement Practices," *Culture, Medicine, and Psychiatry* 8 (1984): 315–347.

67. Ronald Keith Barrett, "Contemporary African-American Funeral Rites and Traditions," in *The Path Ahead,* ed. DeSpelder and Strickland, pp. 80–92; and "Psychocultural Influences on African-American Attitudes Toward Death, Dying, and Funeral Rites," in *Personal Care in an Impersonal World: A Multidimensional Look at Bereavement,* ed. John D. Morgan (Amityville, N.Y.: Baywood, 1995), pp. 213–230.

68. David R. Roediger, "And Die in Dixie: Funerals, Death & Heaven in the Slave Community, 1700–1865," *The Massachusetts Review* 22, no. 1 (Spring 1981): 163–183.

69. Alvin O. Korte, "*Despedidas* As Reflections of Death in Hispanic New Mexico," *Omega: Journal of Death and Dying* 32, no. 4 (1995–1996): 245–267.

70. See Philip A. Mellor, "Death in High Modernity: The Contemporary Presence and Absence of Death," in *The Sociology of Death,* ed. Clark, pp. 11–30 (especially pp. 12–13, 18–19); and, in the same volume, Jane Littlewood, "The Denial of Death and Rites of Passage in Contemporary Societies," pp. 69–84; see also Philip A. Mellor and Chris Schilling, "Modernity, Self-Identity and the Sequestration of Death," *Sociology* 27, no. 3 (1993): 411–431.

71. Eleanor C. Nordyke, *The Peopling of Hawai'i,* 2d ed. (Honolulu: University of Hawaii Press, 1989), p. 1.

72. Patrick Vinton Kirch, *Feathered Gods and Fishhooks: An Introduction to Hawaiian Archeology and Prehistory* (Honolulu: University of Hawaii Press, 1985), p. 298.

73. The term "Asian American" is rarely used in Hawaii; instead, people identify themselves as Chinese, Japanese, or Filipino, or whatever, while at the same time employing the panethnic identity of being a local. Jonathan Okamura says that the notion of "local" represents "the common identity of people of Hawaii and their shared ap-

preciation of the land, peoples, and cultures of the islands." See Jonathan Y. Okamura, "Why There Are No Asian Americans in Hawai'i: The Continuing Significance of Local Identity," *Social Process in Hawaii* 35 (1994): 161–178.

74. Colette Browne, a specialist in aging at the University of Hawaii School of Social Work, quoted in John Griffin, "If You Have to Grow Old, Hawaii's a Good Place for It," *Star-Bulletin & Advertiser,* 23 July 1989.

75. See Benjamin B. C. Young, "The Hawaiians," in *People and Cultures of Hawaii: A Psychocultural Profile,* ed. John F. McDermott, Jr., Wen-Shing Tseng, and Thomas W. Maretzki (Honolulu: John A. Burns School of Medicine and University of Hawaii Press, 1980), pp. 5–24.

76. George Hu'eu Sanford Kanahele, *Ku Kanaka, Stand Tall: A Search for Hawaiian Values* (Honolulu: University of Hawaii Press, 1986), p. 182. On the soul after death and realms of the spirits of the dead, see also Donald D. Kilolani Mitchell, *Resource Units in Hawaiian Culture* (Honolulu: The Kamehameha Schools Press, 1982), pp. 84–86.

77. Bob Krauss, "Wails and Prayers for Missing Bones," *Honolulu Advertiser,* 6 March 1994, p. A1.

78. Nordyke, *The Peopling of Hawai'i,* p. 52; see also Walter F. Char and others, "The Chinese," in *People and Cultures of Hawaii,* ed. McDermott, Tseng, and Maretzki, pp. 53–72.

79. This discussion of contemporary Chinese funeral customs in Hawaii is based on interviews by the authors with Anna Ordenstein and Ken Ordenstein who, along with their Chinese-Hawaiian-Jewish-Portuguese forebears, have provided funeral services to residents of Hawaii over the course of five generations. We are grateful for their assistance.

80. Terence Rogers and Satoru Izutsu, "The Japanese," in *People and Cultures of Hawaii,* ed. McDermott, Tseng, and Maretzki, pp. 73–99; see especially pp. 87ff.

81. John F. McDermott, Jr., "Toward an Interethnic Society," in *People and Cultures of Hawaii,* ed. McDermott, Tseng, and Maretzki, p. 231; see also Wayne S. Wooden, *What Price Paradise? Changing Social Patterns in Hawaii* (Washington: University Press of America, 1981).

82. McDermott, "Toward an Interethnic Society," pp. 229–230; see also Elvi Whittaker, *The Mainland Haole: The White Experience in Hawaii* (New York: Columbia University Press, 1986).

83. Mary Kawena Pukui and Samuel H. Elbert, *Hawaiian Dictionary,* rev. ed. (Honolulu: University of Hawaii Press, 1986), p. 34.

84. McDermott, "Toward an Interethnic Society," p. 225.

85. Ibid., p. 231.

86. Paul Spickard, quoted in Susan Yim, "Hapa in Hawai'i," *Honolulu* (December 1994), pp. 44–47, 90, 92.

87. Sandor B. Brent and Mark W. Speece, "'Adult' Conceptualization of Irreversibility: Implications for the Development of the Concept of Death," *Death Studies* 17, no. 3 (1993): 203–224.

88. Sandor B. Brent and others, "The Development of the Concept of Death Among Chinese and U.S. Children 3–17 Years of Age: From Binary to 'Fuzzy' Concepts?" *Omega: Journal of Death and Dying* 33, no. 1 (1996): 67–83.

89. David W. Plath, "Resistance at Forty-Eight: Old-Age Brinksmanship and Japanese Life Course Pathways," in *Aging and Life Course Transitions: An Interdisciplinary Perspective,* ed. Tamara K. Hareven and Kathleen J. Adams (New York: Guilford Press, 1982), pp. 109–125.

90. Alberta M. Gloria, Traci R. Rieckmann, and Jeffrey D. Rush, "Issues and Recommendations for Teaching an Ethnic/Culture-Based Course," *Teaching of Psychology* 27, no. 2 (2000): 102–107.

91. Pamela Balls Organista, Kevin M. Chun, and Gerardo Marin, "Teaching an Undergraduate Course on Ethnic Diversity," *Teaching of Psychology* 27, no. 1 (2000): 12–17.

92. Charles Waddell and Beverly McNamara, "The Stereotypical Fallacy: A Comparison of Anglo and Chinese Australians' Thoughts About Facing Death," *Mortality* 2, no. 2 (1997): 149–161.

93. Rhonda S. Fair, "Becoming the White Man's Indian: An Examination of Native American Tribal Web Sites," *Plains Anthropologist* 45, no. 172 (2000): 203–213.

94. Jeanne L. Tsai, Yu-Wen Ying, and Peter A. Lee, "The Meaning of 'Being Chinese' and 'Being American': Variation Among Chinese American Young Adults," *Journal of Cross-Cultural Psychology* 31, no. 3 (2000): 302–332.

95. Richard A. Kalish and David K. Reynolds, *Death and Ethnicity: A Psychocultural Study* (Los Angeles: Ethel Percy Andrus Gerontological Center, University of Southern California, 1976).

CHAPTER 4

1. James C. Robinson, "The Changing Boundaries of the American Hospital," *The Milbank Quarterly* 72, no. 2 (1994): 259–275.

2. V. David Schwantes, "Hospital Resource Allocation: The Real Story," *Hospitals & Health Networks* 68, no. 11 (5 June 1994): 80.

3. Celia S. Gabrel, "An Overview of Nursing Home Facilities: Data from the 1997 National Nursing Home Survey," *Advance Data from Vital and Health Statistics,* no. 311 (Hyattsville, Md.: National Center for Health Statistics, 2000).

4. Joshua Hauser and John Lantos, "Stories of Caring and Connection," *Hastings Center Report* 30, no. 2 (2000): 44–47.

5. See Margaretta K. Bowers and others, *Counseling the Dying* (New York: Thomas Nelson & Sons, 1964).

6. Charles E. Rosenberg, "Institutionalized Ambiguity: Conflict and Continuity in the American Hospital," *Second Opinion* 12 (November 1989): 63–73; see also by Rosenberg, *The Care of Strangers: The Rise of America's Hospital System* (New York: Basic Books, 1987).

7. "National Health Expenditures," *Health, United States: 1999* (Hyattsville, Md.: National Center for Health Statistics, 1999), p. 11.

8. Alastair Gray, "International Patterns of Health Care, 1960 to the 1990s," in *Caring for Health: History and Diversity,* ed. Charles Webster, Health and Disease Series, Book 6 (Buckingham, U.K.: Open University Press, 1994), p. 174.

9. Larry R. Churchill, "The United States Health Care System Under Managed Care: How the Commodification of Health Care Distorts Ethics and Threatens Equity," *Health Care Analysis* 7, no. 4 (1999): 393–411. See also Richard Epstein, "Managed Care Under Siege," *Journal of Medicine and Philosophy* 24, no. 5 (1999): 434–460; and Jonathan E. Fielding, "Public Health in the Twentieth Century: Advances and Challenges," *Annual Review of Public Health* 20 (1999): xiii–xxx.

10. D. Lupton, "Consumerism, Reflexivity, and the Medical Encounter," *Social Science & Medicine* 45, no. 3 (1997): 373–381.

11. See Annetine Gelijns and Nathan Rosenberg, "The Dynamics of Technological Change in Medicine," *Health Affairs* 13, no. 3 (1994): 29–46.

12. Howard M. Spiro, "Too Many Specialists or Too Many Generalists?" *Science & Medicine* 3, no. 4 (July–August 1996): 4–5.

13. Howard M. Spiro, "If It Ain't Broke," *Science & Medicine* 3, no. 6 (November–December 1996): 4–5.

14. Donna M. Wilson, "End-of-Life Care Preferences of Canadian Senior Citizens with Caregiving Experience," *Journal of Advanced Nursing* 31, no. 6 (2000): 1416–1421.

15. Samuel W. Levitt, "Quality of Care and Investment in Property, Plant, and Equipment in Hospitals," *Health Services Research* 28, no. 6 (1994): 713–727.

16. Peter P. M. Harteloh and Frank W. S. M. Verheggen, "Quality Assurance in Health Care: From a Traditional Towards a Modern Approach," *Health Policy* 27, no. 3 (1994): 261–270.

17. See P. A. Ubel and S. Goold, "Recognizing Bedside Rationing: Clear Cases and Tough Calls," *Annals of Internal Medicine* 126, no. 1 (1997): 74–80.

18. Daniel P. Sulmasy, "Physicians, Cost Control, and Ethics," *Annals of Internal Medicine* 116, no. 11 (1 June 1992): 920–926; see also Wendy K. Mariner, "Patients' Rights After Health Care Reform: Who Decides What Is Medically Necessary?" *American Journal of Public Health* 84, no. 9 (1994): 1515–1520.

19. Daniel Callahan, "The Limits of Medical Progress: A Principle of Symmetry," in *The Path Ahead: Readings in Death and Dying*, ed. Lynne Ann DeSpelder and Albert Lee Strickland (Mountain View, Calif.: Mayfield, 1995), pp. 103–105.

20. See Susan M. Wolf, "Quality Assessment of Ethics in Health Care: The Accountability Revolution," *American Journal of Law and Medicine* 20, nos. 1–2 (1994): 105–125.

21. See Graham Loomes and Lynda McKenzie, "The Use of QALYs in Health Care Decision Making," *Social Science & Medicine* 28 (1989): 299–308; Erik Nord, "The QALY: A Measure of Social Value Rather Than Individual Utility?" *Health Economics* 3 (1993): 89–93, and "The Trade-Off Between Severity of Illness and Treatment Effect in Cost-Value Analysis of Health Care," *Health Policy* 24 (1993): 227–238. See also Colin Burrows and Kaye Brown, "QALYs for Resource Allocation: Probably Not and Certainly Not Now," *Australian Journal of Public Health* 17, no. 3 (1993): 278–286.

22. Michael D. Fetters and Howard Brody, "The Epidemiology of Bioethics," *Journal of Clinical Ethics* 10, no. 2 (1999): 107–115.

23. C. D. Bessinger, "Doctoring: The Philosophic Milieu," *Southern Medical Journal* 81, no. 12 (1988): 1558–1562. See also William Campbell Felch, *The Secret(s) of Good Patient Care: Thoughts on Medicine in the 21st Century* (Westport, Conn.: Praeger, 1996); and Edmund D. Pellegrino and David C. Thomasma, *A Philosophical Basis for Medical Practice: Towards a Philosophy and Ethic of the Healing Professions* (New York: Oxford University Press, 1981).

24. Stanley Joel Reiser, "The Era of the Patient: Using the Experience of Illness in Shaping the Missions of Health Care," in *The Path Ahead*, ed. DeSpelder and Strickland, pp. 106–115.

25. See J. Balint and W. Shelton, "Regaining the Initiative: Forging a New Model of the Patient–Physician Relationship," *Journal of the American Medical Association* 275, no. 11 (1996): 887–891; Christine K. Cassel, "The Patient–Physician Covenant: An Affirmation of Asklepios," *Annals of Internal Medicine* 124 (1996): 604–606; C. Charles, A. Gafni, and T. Whelan, "Shared Decision-Making in the Medical Encounter: What Does It Mean? (Or, It Takes At Least Two to Tango)," *Social Science & Medicine* 44, no. 5 (1997): 681–692; and M. Sirmon and R. Kreisberg, "Clinical Problem Solving: The Invisible Patient," *New England Journal of Medicine* 334, no. 14 (1996): 908–911. See also

Dan W. Brock, "The Ideal of Shared Decision Making Between Physicians and Patients," *Kennedy Institute of Ethics Journal* (March 1991): 28–47.

26. Joan L. Bottorff and others, "Facilitating Day-to-Day Decision Making in Palliative Care," *Cancer Nursing* 23, no. 2 (2000): 141–150.

27. See Robert Berkow, ed., *The Merck Manual of Medical Information: Home Edition* (Whitehouse Station, N.J.: Merck Research Laboratories, 1997), pp. 16–17.

28. See, for example, Salim M. Adib and Ghassan N. Hamadeh, "Attitudes of the Lebanese Public Regarding Disclosure of Serious Illness," *Journal of Medical Ethics* 25, no. 5 (1999): 399–403; and Fetters and Brody, "The Epidemiology of Bioethics."

29. Mei-che Samantha Pang, "Protective Truthfulness: The Chinese Way of Safeguarding Patients in Informed Treatment Decisions," *Journal of Medical Ethics* 25, no. 3 (1999): 247–253.

30. Karen Lutfey and Douglas W. Maynard, "Bad News in Oncology: How Physician and Patient Talk About Death and Dying Without Using Those Words," *Social Psychology Quarterly* 61, no. 4 (1998): 321–341.

31. Geoffrey H. Gordon, Sandra K. Joos, and Jennifer Byrne, "Physician Expressions of Uncertainty During Patient Encounters," *Patient Education and Counseling* 40, no. 1 (2000): 59–65.

32. For a model of such discussion, see Ernest Rosenbaum, "Oncology/Hematology and Psychosocial Support of the Cancer Patient," in *Psychosocial Care of the Dying Patient,* ed. Charles A. Garfield, (New York: McGraw-Hill, 1978), pp. 169–184.

33. M. E. Carlsson and P. M. Strang, "How Patients with Gynecological Cancer Experience the Information Process," *Journal of Psychosomatic Obstetrics and Gynecology* 19, no. 4 (1998): 192–201.

34. Virginia Teas Gill, "Doing Attributions in Medical Interaction: Patients' Explanations for Illness and Doctors' Responses," *Social Psychology Quarterly* 61, no. 4 (1998): 342–360.

35. Candace West, *Routine Complications: Troubles with Talk Between Doctors and Patients* (Bloomington: Indiana University Press, 1984).

36. Sandra L. Bertman, Michael D. Wertheimer, and H. Brownell Wheeler, "Humanities in Surgery, a Life-Threatening Situation: Communicating the Diagnosis," *Death Studies* 10, no. 5 (1986): 431–439.

37. Richard S. Sandor, "On Death and Coding," in *The Path Ahead,* ed. DeSpelder and Strickland, pp. 144–147.

38. Eugene A. Stead, Jr., *A Way of Thinking: A Primer on the Art of Being a Doctor* (Durham, N.C.: Carolina Academic Press, 1995), p. 126.

39. Albert Lee Strickland and Lynne Ann DeSpelder, "Communicating About Death and Dying," in *A Challenge for Living: Dying, Death, and Bereavement,* ed. Inge B. Corless, Barbara B. Germino, and Mary A. Pittman (Boston: Jones and Bartlett, 1995), pp. 37–51.

40. S. M. Johnson and M. E. Kurtz, "Name Usage in Clinical Practice: Ethnic and Gender Disparities," *Humane Medicine* 11, no. 3 (1995): 106–109.

41. Jeanne Quint Benoliel, "Health Care Providers and Dying Patients: Critical Issues in Terminal Care," *Omega: Journal of Death and Dying* 18, no. 4 (1987–1988): 341–363.

42. "Tapping Human Potential: An Interview with Norman Cousins," *Second Opinion* 14 (July 1990): 57–71.

43. See Balfour Mount, "Whole Person Care: Beyond Psychosocial and Physical Needs," *American Journal of Hospice and Palliative Care* 10, no. 1 (January–February 1993): 28–37.

44. Marilee Ivars Donovan and Sandra Girton Pierce, *Cancer Care Nursing* (New York: Appleton-Century-Crofts, 1976), p. 32.

45. Betty Davies and others, *Fading Away: The Experience of Transition in Families with Terminal Illness* (Amityville, N.Y.: Baywood, 1996).

46. Andrea O. Baumann and others, "Who Cares? Who Cures? The Ongoing Debate in the Provision of Health Care," *Journal of Advanced Nursing* 28, no. 5 (1998): 1040–1045.

47. See David A. Alexander, "'Stressors' and Difficulties in Dealing with the Terminal Patient," *Journal of Palliative Care* 6, no. 3 (1990): 28–33.

48. Donald M. Sledz, "Nursing an Old Wound in Medicine," *Wall Street Journal,* 6 February 1997, p. A14.

49. See Egilde P. Seravalli, "The Dying Patient, the Physician, and the Fear of Death," *New England Journal of Medicine* 319 (29 December 1988): 1728–1730.

50. Lesley Spencer, "How Do Nurses Deal with Their Own Grief When a Patient Dies on an Intensive Care Unit, and What Help Can Be Given to Enable Them to Overcome Their Grief Effectively?" *Journal of Advanced Nursing* 19 (1994): 1141–1150. See also Emilie Beck, "When Nurses Take Risks," *Second Opinion* 18, no. 1 (July 1992): 100–103.

51. Elisabeth Kübler-Ross, *On Death and Dying* (New York: Macmillan, 1969), p. 249. For a biographical account of Kübler-Ross's experiences, see Elisabeth Kübler-Ross, *The Wheel of Life: A Memoir of Living and Dying* (New York: Scribner, 1997).

52. Balfour M. Mount, "Keeping the Mission," in *The Path Ahead,* ed. DeSpelder and Strickland, pp. 125–132.

53. *Facts and Figures on Hospice Care in America* on-line (retrieved September 2000; http://www.nhpco.org).

54. Quoted in Sanchia Aranda, "Global Perspectives on Palliative Care," *Cancer Nursing* 22, no. 1 (1999): 33–39.

55. David S. Greer, Vincent Mor, and Robert Kastenbaum, "Concepts, Questions, and Research Priorities," in *The Hospice Experiment,* ed. Vincent Mor, David S. Greer, and Robert Kastenbaum (Baltimore: Johns Hopkins University Press, 1988), p. 249.

56. See Rien M. J. P. A. Janssens, Zbigniew Zylicz, and Henk A. M. J. Ten Have, "Articulating the Concept of Palliative Care: Philosophical and Theological Perspectives," *Journal of Palliative Care* 15, no. 2 (1999): 38–44.

57. Inge B. Corless, "Dying Well: Symptom Control Within Hospice Care," in *Annual Review of Nursing Research* 12, eds. J. J. Fitzpatrick and J. S. Stevenson (New York: Springer, 1994), pp. 125–146.

58. S. Kay Toombs, "Chronic Illness and the Goals of Medicine," *Second Opinion* 21, no. 1 (July 1995): 11–19.

59. Inge B. Corless, "Settings for Terminal Care," *Omega: Journal of Death and Dying* 18, no. 4 (1987–1988): 319–340.

60. See, for example, Avery D. Weisman, "Appropriate Death and the Hospice Program," *Hospice Journal* 4, no. 1 (1988): 65–77.

61. Ira Byock, "Palliative Care," in *On Our Own Terms: Moyers on Dying,* ed. Public Affairs Television (New York: WNET, 2000), pp. 10–11.

62. See William E. Phipps, "The Origin of Hospices / Hospitals," *Death Studies* 12, no. 2 (1988): 91–99; Susan Lynn Sloan, "The Hospice Movement: A Study in the Diffusion of Innovative Palliative Care," *American Journal of Hospice and Palliative Care* (May–June 1992): 24–31; and Sandol Stoddard, "Hospice in the United States: An Overview," *Journal of Palliative Care* 5, no. 3 (1989): 10–19.

63. James Luther Adams, "Palliative Care in the Light of Early Christian Concepts," *Journal of Palliative Care* 5, no. 3 (1989): 5–8.

64. See Thelma Ingles, "St. Christopher's Hospice" in *A Hospice Handbook: A New Way to Care for the Dying,* ed. Michael P. Hamilton and Helen F. Reid (Grand Rapids, Mich.: Eerdmans, 1980), pp. 45–56. See also Cicely Saunders, "The Evolution of Palliative Care," *Patient Education and Counseling* 41, no. 1 (2000): 7–13.

65. Cicely Saunders, personal communication.

66. Quoted in Constance Holden, "Hospices for the Dying, Relief from Pain and Fear," in *Hospice Handbook,* ed. Hamilton and Reid, p. 61.

67. Geoffrey W. Hanks, "Hospital Palliative Care Teams and the Disadvantaged Dying," *European Journal of Palliative Care* 1, no. 3 (1994): 112.

68. William M. Lamers, Jr., "Hospice: Enhancing the Quality of Life," in *The Path Ahead,* ed. DeSpelder and Strickland, pp. 116–124.

69. Robert Berkow, ed., *The Merck Manual of Diagnosis and Therapy,* 16th ed. (Rahway, N.J.: Merck Research Laboratories, 1992), p. 2571.

70. See F. Ackerman, "Goldilocks and Mrs. Ilych: A Critical Look at the 'Philosophy of Hospice,'" *Cambridge Quarterly of Healthcare Ethics* 6, no. 3 (1997): 314–324.

71. See Katherine Froggatt, "Rites of Passage and the Hospice Culture," *Mortality* 2, no. 2 (1997): 123–136.

72. Val Robb, "The Hotel Project: A Community Approach to Persons with AIDS," *Nursing Clinics of North America* 29, no. 3 (1994): 521–531.

73. V. David Schwantes and Margaret Ann Smith, *Resource Allocation: The Key to Better Hospital Cost Management* (Minneapolis: Health Initiatives Press, 1994), p. 10.

74. Clive F. Seale, "What Happens in Hospices: A Review of Research Evidence," *Social Science & Medicine* 28, no. 6 (1989): 551–559.

75. Debbie Ward, "Women and the Work of Caring," *Second Opinion* 19, no. 2 (October 1993): 11–25.

76. Claudette Varricchio, "Human and Indirect Costs of Home Care," *Nursing Outlook* 42, no. 4 (1994): 151–157.

77. See Pamela J. Miller and Paula B. Mike, "The Medicare Hospice Benefit: Ten Years of Federal Policy for the Terminally Ill," *Death Studies* 19, no. 6 (1995): 531–542.

78. Miller and Mike, "Medicare Hospice Benefit."

79. George Anders, "U.S. Cracks Down on Hospices Treating Patients Who Aren't on Brink of Death," *Wall Street Journal,* 8 January 1997, p. B8.

80. Lucette Lagnado, "Medicare Head Tackles Criticism on Hospice Care," *Wall Street Journal,* 15 September 2000, pp. B1, B4; and Nancy-Ann Min DeParle, Administrator, Health Care Financing Administration, "Letter to Medicare Hospices" (12 September 2000). For more information about the Medicare Hospice Benefit, access the web site *medicare.gov* or call (800) MEDICARE.

81. Charles A. Corr and Donna M. Corr, "Children's Hospice Care," *Death Studies* 16, no. 5 (1992): 431–439.

82. *Facts and Figures on Hospice Care in America.*

83. Sandol Stoddard, quoted in Sloan, "The Hospice Movement."

84. Ronald K. Barrett, "Blacks, Death, Dying, and Funerals: Things You've Wondered About but Thought It Politically Incorrect to Ask" (keynote presentation, King's College 15th International Conference on Death & Bereavement, London, Ontario, 12 May 1997).

85. See, for example, Harold P. Freeman and Richard Payne, "Racial Injustice in Health Care," *New England Journal of Medicine* 342, no. 14 (6 April 2000): 1045–1047;

and Harold P. Freeman, Richard Payne, and Louis W. Sullivan, "Racial Injustice in Health Care: How Should It Be Addressed?" *Medical Crossfire* 2, no. 8 (2000): 31–33.

86. Richard Payne, "At the End of Life, Color Still Divides," *Washington Post,* 15 February 2000. See also Ann Alpers and Bernard Lo, "Avoiding Family Feuds: Responding to Surrogate Demands for Life-Sustaining Interventions," *Journal of Law Medicine & Ethics* 27, no. 1 (1999): 74–80; Leslie J. Blackhall and others, "Ethnicity and Attitudes Towards Life Sustaining Technology," *Social Science & Medicine* 48, no. 12 (1999): 1779–1789; and Eric W. Mebane and others, "The Influence of Physician Race, Age, and Gender on Physician Attitudes Toward Advance Care Directives and Preferences for End-of-Life Decision-Making," *Journal of the American Geriatrics Society* 47, no. 5 (1999): 579–591.

87. Roy Cain, "Community-Based AIDS Services: Formalization and Depoliticization," *International Journal of Health Services* 23, no. 4 (1993): 665–684.

88. Inge B. Corless, "Hospice and Hope: An Incompatible Duo," *American Journal of Hospice and Palliative Care* (May–June 1992): 10–12.

89. Nicky James and David Field, "The Routinization of Hospice: Charisma and Bureaucratization," *Social Science & Medicine* 34, no. 12 (1992): 1363–1375.

90. Corless, "Settings for Terminal Care," p. 331. See also Josefina B. Magno, "The Hospice Concept of Care: Facing the 1990s," *Death Studies* 14, no. 2 (1990): 109–119.

91. Betty Ferrell, Rose Virani, and Marcia Grant, "Analysis of End-of-Life Content in Nursing Textbooks," *Oncology Nursing Forum* 26, no. 5 (1999): 869–876; and Betty Ferrell, Rose Virani, Marcia Grant, and Tami Borneman, "Analysis of Content Regarding Death and Bereavement in Nursing Texts," *Psycho-Oncology* 8, no. 6 (1999): 500–510.

92. William M. Lamers, Jr., "How Patient Deaths Affect Health Professionals: A Plea for More Open Communication," *Journal of Pharmaceutical Care in Pain & Symptom Control* 5, no. 3 (1997): 59–71.

93. Patricia Anstett, "State Plans to Boost Care for the Dying," *Detroit Free Press,* 25 January 2000, pp. 1A, 3A.

94. William M. Lamers, Jr., "Hospice Care and Its Effect on the Grieving Process," in *Living with Grief When Illness Is Prolonged,* eds. Kenneth J. Doka and Joyce Davidson (Washington, D.C.: Hospice Foundation of America, 1997), pp. 67–82.

95. Richard Smith, "A Good Death," *British Medical Journal* 320 (15 January 2000): 129–130.

96. Nicholas A. Christakis and Theodore J. Iwashyna, "Impact of Individual and Market Factors on the Timing of Initiation of Hospice Terminal Care," *Medical Care* 38, no. 5 (2000): 528–541.

97. Frances M. Weaver and others, "The Involvement of Physicians in VA Home Care: Results from a National Survey," *Journal of the American Geriatrics Society* 48, no. 6 (2000): 677–681.

98. Stephanie M. Schim and others, "Knowledge and Attitudes of Home Care Nurses Toward Hospice Referral," *Journal of Nursing Administration* 30, no. 5 (2000): 273–277.

99. Huda Huijer Abu-Saad, "Palliative Care: An International View," *Patient Education and Counseling* 41, no. 1 (2000): 15–22.

100. Marilyn F. Jackson, "Discharge Planning: Issues and Challenges for Gerontological Nursing," *Journal of Advanced Nursing* 19 (1994): 492–502.

101. Bart Collopy, Nancy Dubler, and Connie Zuckerman, "The Ethics of Home Care: Autonomy and Accommodation," *Hastings Center Report* (March/April 1990): Supplement. See also Ruth McCorkle and Jeannie V. Pasacreta, "Enhancing Caregiver

Outcomes in Palliative Care," *Cancer Control: Journal of the Moffitt Cancer Center* 8, no. 1 (2001): 36–45.

102. Pam Brown, Betty Davies, and Nola Martens, "Families in Supportive Care—Part II: Palliative Care at Home: A Viable Care Setting," *Journal of Palliative Care* 6, no. 3 (1990): 21–27.

103. Heather A. Turner, Joseph A. Catania, and John Gagnon, "The Prevalence of Informal Caregiving to Persons with AIDS in the United States: Caregiver Characteristics and Their Implications," *Social Science & Medicine* 38, no. 11 (1994): 1543–1552.

104. See, for example, Randy H. Magen and Myra Glajchen, "Cancer Support Groups: Client Outcome and the Context of Group Process," *Research on Social Work Practice* 9, no. 5 (1999): 541–554.

105. Information provided by Frank Ostaseski, director of Zen Hospice Project, and based on the Project's "Mission Statement" and "At a Glance" fact sheet.

106. Frank Ostaseski, "Stories of Lives Lived and Now Ending," *Inquiring Mind: A Journal of the Vipassana Community* 10, no. 2 (Spring 1994): 14–16.

107. Donald D. Trunkey, "Impact of Violence on the Nation's Trauma Care," *Health Affairs* 12, no. 4 (1993): 162–170.

108. Seth B. Golbey, "Critical Cares: Life-Saving Aeromedical Helicopter Services," *AOPA Pilot* 30, no. 4 (April 1987): 39–46, and, also by Golbey, "Dust Off," pp. 46–48.

109. "Deaths and Death Rates by Selected Causes," *Statistical Abstract of the United States: 1999,* 119th ed. (Washington, D.C.: Government Printing Office, 1999), p. 99.

110. Trunkey, "Impact of Violence on the Nation's Trauma Care."

111. John Grossman, "Emergency! Emergency!" *Health* 21, no. 7 (July 1989): 76–94.

112. C. A. J. McLauchlan, "Handling Distressed Relatives and Breaking Bad News," *British Medical Journal* 301 (17 November 1990): 1145–1149.

113. Quoted by Marilyn Chase, "Tending to Patients with AIDS Teaches Valuable Lessons," *Wall Street Journal,* 22 July 1996, p. B1.

114. Jeanette Pickrel, "'Tell Me Your Story': Using Life Review in Counseling the Terminally Ill," *Death Studies* 13, no. 2 (1989): 127–135.

115. Tenshin Reb Anderson, from a talk to volunteers at the San Francisco Zen Hospice Project, quoted by Ostaseski, "Stories of Lives Lived and Now Ending," p. 29.

116. Janmarie Silvera, "Crossing the Border," in *The Path Ahead,* ed. DeSpelder and Strickland, pp. 301–302.

CHAPTER 5

1. Cassandra Lorius, "Taboo," in *Key Ideas in Human Thought,* ed. Kenneth McLeish (New York: Facts on File, 1993), p. 731.

2. S. Kay Toombs, "Chronic Illness and the Goals of Medicine," *Second Opinion* 21, no. 1 (July 1995): 11–19.

3. Marjorie Kagawa-Singer, "Redefining Health: Living with Cancer," *Social Science & Medicine* 37, no. 3 (1993): 295–304.

4. Linda J. Kristjanson and Terri Ashcroft, "The Family's Cancer Journey: A Literature Review," *Cancer Nursing* 17, no. 1 (1994): 1–17.

5. Betsy L. Fife, "The Conceptualization of Meaning in Illness," *Social Science & Medicine* 38, no. 2 (1994): 309–316.

6. Peter Conrad, "Wellness As Virtue: Morality and the Pursuit of Health," *Culture, Medicine, and Psychiatry* 18 (1994): 385–401.

7. G. P. Sholevar and R. Perkel, "Family Systems Intervention and Physical Illness," *General Hospital Psychiatry* 12 (1990): 363–372. See also Margaret I. Fitch, Terry Bunston, and Mary Elliot, "When Mom's Sick: Changes in a Mother's Role and in the Family After Her Diagnosis of Cancer," *Cancer Nursing* 22, no. 1 (1999): 58–63.

8. See Charles A. Garfield, *Stress and Survival: The Emotional Realities of Life-Threatening Illness* (St. Louis: C. V. Mosby, 1979); and Lon G. Nungusser and William D. Bullock, *Notes on Living Until We Say Goodbye: A Personal Guide* (New York: St. Martin's Press, 1988).

9. Arthur Kleinman, *The Illness Narratives: Suffering, Healing, and the Human Condition* (New York: Basic Books, 1988), pp. 3–6.

10. Carl May, "Disclosure of Terminal Prognosis in a General Hospital: The Nurse's View," *Journal of Advanced Nursing* 18 (1993): 1362–1368.

11. Quoted in Marilyn M. Rawnsley, "Recurrence of Cancer: A Crisis of Courage," *Cancer Nursing* 17, no. 4 (1994): 342–347.

12. Arthur W. Frank, "The Pedagogy of Suffering: Moral Dimensions of Psychological Therapy and Research with the Ill," *Theory & Psychology* 2, no. 4 (1992): 467–485.

13. See Eva Benzein, Astrid Norberg, and Britt-Inger Saveman, "Hope: Future Imagined Reality—The Meaning of Hope As Described by a Group of Healthy Pentecostalists," *Journal of Advanced Nursing* 28, no. 5 (1998): 1063–1070.

14. Clifford H. Swensen, Steffen Fuller, and Richard Clements, "Stage of Religious Faith and Reactions to Terminal Cancer," *Journal of Psychology and Theology* 21, no. 3 (1993): 238–245.

15. Jeffrey S. Levin, "Religion and Health: Is There an Association, Is It Valid, and Is It Causal?" *Social Science & Medicine* 38, no. 11 (1994): 1475–1482.

16. Ana Wong-McDonald and Richard L. Gorsuch, "Surrender to God: An Additional Coping Style?" *Journal of Psychology and Theology* 28, no. 2 (2000): 149–161.

17. Susan M. Heidrich, Cynthia A. Forsthoff, and Sandra E. Ward, "Psychological Adjustment in Adults with Cancer: The Self As Mediator," *Health Psychology* 13, no. 4 (1994): 346–353.

18. Barney G. Glaser and Anselm L. Strauss, *Awareness of Dying* (Chicago: Aldine, 1965).

19. L. J. Muzzin and others, "The Experience of Cancer," *Social Science & Medicine* 38, no. 9 (1994): 1201–1208. See also E. Mansell Pattison, *The Experience of Dying* (Englewood Cliffs, N.J.: Prentice-Hall, 1977); and "The Living-Dying Process," in *Psychological Care of the Dying,* ed. Charles Garfield (New York: McGraw-Hill, 1978), pp. 163–168.

20. Avery D. Weisman, *On Dying and Denying: A Psychiatric Study of Terminality* (New York: Behavioral Publications, 1972).

21. Elisabeth Kübler-Ross, *On Death and Dying* (New York: Macmillan, 1969).

22. Harold Brodkey, "To My Readers," in *The Path Ahead: Readings in Death and Dying,* ed. Lynne Ann DeSpelder and Albert Lee Strickland (Mountain View, Calif.: Mayfield, 1995), pp. 295–300.

23. Philip R. Muskin and others, "Maladaptive Denial of Physical Illness: A Useful New 'Diagnosis'." *International Journal of Psychiatry in Medicine* 28, no. 4 (1998): 463–477.

24. Lucille A. Joel, "Deferring to the Dying," *American Journal of Nursing* 94, no. 2 (1994): 7.

25. Herman Feifel, "Psychology and Death: Meaningful Rediscovery," in *The Path Ahead,* ed. DeSpelder and Strickland, pp. 19–28.

26. Tone Rustøen and Ingela Wiklund, "Hope in Newly Diagnosed Patients with Cancer," *Cancer Nursing* 23, no. 3 (2000): 214–219.

27. Charles A. Corr, "A Task-Based Approach to Coping with Dying," *Omega: Journal of Death and Dying* 24, no. 2 (1991–1992): 81–94; and "Coping with Dying: Lessons That We Should and Should Not Learn from the Work of Elisabeth Kübler-Ross," *Death Studies* 17, no. 1 (1993): 69–83.

28. Avery D. Weisman, *The Coping Capacity: On the Nature of Being Mortal* (New York: Human Sciences Press, 1986).

29. Weisman, *On Dying and Denying*; see also by Weisman, *Coping with Cancer* (New York: McGraw-Hill, 1979); and "Thanatology," in *Comprehensive Textbook of Psychiatry*, ed. O. Kaplan (Baltimore: Williams & Wilkins, 1980).

30. Therese A. Rando, *Grief, Dying, and Death: Clinical Interventions for Caregivers* (Lexington, Mass.: Lexington Books, 1993).

31. Kenneth J. Doka, "Coping with Life-Threatening Illness: A Task Model," *Omega: Journal of Death and Dying* 32, no. 2 (1995–1996): 111–122; see also Charles A. Corr and Kenneth J. Doka, "Current Models of Death, Dying, and Bereavement," *Critical Care Nursing Clinics of North America* 6, no. 3 (1994): 545–552.

32. Doka, "Coping with Life-Threatening Illness," p. 120.

33. Robert Kastenbaum and Sharon Thuell, "Cookies Baking, Coffee Brewing: Toward a Contextual Theory of Dying," *Omega: Journal of Death and Dying* 31, no. 3 (1995): 175–187.

34. Ibid., p. 186. See also Robert Kastenbaum, "'How Far Can an Intellectual Effort Diminish Pain?' William McDougall's Journal As a Model for Facing Death," *Omega: Journal of Death and Dying* 32, no. 2 (1995–1996): 123–164.

35. Joel, "Deferring to the Dying."

36. Susan Folkman and Steven Greer, "Promoting Psychological Well-Being in the Face of Serious Illness: When Theory, Research and Practice Inform Each Other," *Psycho-Oncology* 9, no. 1 (2000): 11–19.

37. Michael Kusch and others, "Structuring Psychosocial Care in Pediatric Oncology," *Patient Education and Counseling* 40, no. 3 (2000): 231–245.

38. See Phoebe Cramer, "Coping and Defense Mechanisms: What's the Difference?" *Journal of Personality* 66, no. 6 (1998): 919–946; and "Defense Mechanisms in Psychology Today: Further Processes for Adaptation," *American Psychologist* 55, no. 6 (2000): 637–646.

39. Russell Noyes, Jr., and others, "Illness Fears in the General Population," *Psychosomatic Medicine* 62, no. 3 (2000): 318–325.

40. See Susan Folkman, "Positive Psychological States and Coping with Severe Stress," *Social Science & Medicine* 45, no. 8 (1997): 1207–1221; and Susan Folkman and Judith Tedlie Moskowitz, "Positive Affect and the Other Side of Coping," *American Psychologist* 55, no. 6 (2000): 647–654.

41. Mark R. Somerfield and Robert R. McCrae, "Stress and Coping Research: Methodological Challenges, Theoretical Advances, and Clinical Applications," *American Psychologist* 55, no. 6 (2000): 620–625.

42. Richard S. Lazarus, "Toward Better Research on Stress and Coping," *American Psychologist* 55, no. 6 (2000): 665–673.

43. Kusch and others, "Structuring Psychosocial Care."

44. Folkman and Greer, "Promoting Psychological Well-Being in the Face of Serious Illness."

45. Betsy L. Fife, "The Measurement of Meaning in Illness," *Social Science & Medicine* 40, no. 8 (1995): 1021–1028.

46. See Debra Wood, "Postponing Death: How Strong Is the Will to Live?" on-line (retrieved August 2000; healthgate.com).

47. Mary-Jo Del Vecchio Good and others, "Oncology and Narrative Time," *Social Science & Medicine* 38, no. 6 (1994): 855–862.

48. Robert L. Wrenn, Dan Levinson, and Danai Papadatou, *End of Life Decisions: Guidelines for the Health Care Provider* (Tucson: University of Arizona Health Sciences Center, 1996), p. 20.

49. Orville Kelly, "Making Today Count," in *Death and Dying: Theory/Research/Practice,* ed. Larry A. Bugen (Dubuque, Iowa: William C. Brown, 1979), pp. 277–283; see also, by Kelly, *Until Tomorrow Comes* (New York: Everest House, 1979).

50. Mickey S. Eisenberg and others, "Sudden Cardiac Death," *Scientific American* 254, no. 5 (May 1986): 37–43. See also Hendrika Meischke, John Finnegan, and Mickey Eisenberg, "What Can You Teach About Cardiopulmonary Resuscitation (CPR) in 30 Seconds? Evaluation of a Television Campaign," *Evaluation & the Health Professions* 22, no. 1 (1999): 44–59.

51. Robert Berkow, ed., *The Merck Manual of Medical Information: Home Edition* (Whitehouse Station, N.J.: Merck Research Laboratories, 1997), p. 126.

52. Arthur Selzer, *Understanding Heart Disease* (Berkeley: University of California Press, 1992), p. 114.

53. Paolo Venies, "Definition and Classification of Cancer: Monothetic or Polythetic?" *Theoretical Medicine* 14 (1993): 249–256.

54. Linda J. Kristjanson and Terri Ashcroft, "The Family's Cancer Journey: A Literature Review," *Cancer Nursing* 17, no. 1 (1994): 1–17.

55. Robert Berkow, ed. *The Merck Manual of Diagnosis and Therapy,* 16th ed. (Rahway, N.J.: Merck Research Laboratories, 1992), p. 1275.

56. See Lesley F. Degner, "Treatment Decision Making," in *A Challenge for Living: Dying, Death, and Bereavement,* ed. Inge B. Corless, Barbara B. Germino, and Mary A. Pittman (Boston: Jones and Bartlett, 1995), pp. 3–16.

57. Berkow, ed., *Merck Manual of Diagnosis and Therapy,* 16th ed., p. 1275.

58. R. A. Hope and others, *Oxford Handbook of Clinical Medicine,* 3d ed. (New York: Oxford University Press, 1994), p. 768.

59. This section on radiation draws on data presented in Berkow, ed., *Merck Manual of Diagnosis and Therapy,* 16th ed., pp. 1276–1277; *Merck Manual: Home Edition,* p. 801; and Hope and others, *Oxford Handbook of Clinical Medicine,* p. 768.

60. See Samuel Hellman and Everett E. Vokes, "Advancing Current Treatments for Cancer," *Scientific American* 275, no. 3 (September 1996): 118–123.

61. This section on chemotherapy draws on data presented in Berkow, ed., *Merck Manual of Diagnosis and Therapy,* 16th ed., pp. 55, 1277, 1287; and *Merck Manual: Home Edition,* pp. 799, 802; and Hope and others, *Oxford Handbook of Clinical Medicine,* p. 768.

62. See *Alternative Medicine: Expanding Medical Horizons, A Report to the National Institutes of Health on Alternative Medical Systems and Practices in the United States* (Bethesda, Md.: National Institutes of Health, 1992). See also David Edelberg, "Making Room for Alternatives," *Second Opinion* 20, no. 1 (July 1994): 21–33; Robert C. Fuller, "The Turn to Alternative Medicine," *Second Opinion* 18, no. 1 (July 1992): 11–31; and Arthur Kleinman, *Patients and Healers in the Context of Culture* (Berkeley: University of California Press, 1980).

63. See Josep M. Comelles, "The Role of Local Knowledge in Medical Practice: A Trans-Historical Perspective," *Culture Medicine and Psychiatry* 24, no. 1 (2000): 41–75.

64. Lori Arviso Alvord and Elizabeth Cohen Van Pelt, *The Scalpel and the Silver Bear* (New York: Bantam, 1999).

65. Berkow, ed., *Merck Manual of Diagnosis and Therapy,* 16th ed., pp. 2593–2596.

66. Lisa L. Capps, "Change and Continuity in the Medical Culture of the Hmong in Kansas City," *Medical Anthropology Quarterly* 8, no. 2 (1994): 161–177.

67. Robert T. Trotter II, and Juan Antonio Chavira, *Curanderismo: Mexican-American Folk Healing,* 2d ed. (Athens: University of Georgia Press, 1997).

68. Kaja Finkler, "Sacred Healing and Biomedicine Compared," *Medical Anthropology Quarterly* 8, no. 2 (June 1994): 178–197.

69. Paul Trachtman, "NIH Looks at the Implausible and the Inexplicable," *Smithsonian* 25, no. 6 (September 1994): 110–123.

70. Adrian Furnham and Julie Forey, "The Attitudes, Behaviors and Beliefs of Patients of Conventional vs. Complementary (Alternative) Medicine," *Journal of Clinical Psychology* 50, no. 3 (1994): 458–469.

71. Berkow, ed., *Merck Manual of Diagnosis and Therapy,* 16th ed., p. 1263.

72. Lawrence J. Schneiderman, "Alternative Medicine or Alternatives to Medicine? A Physician's Perspective," *Cambridge Quarterly of Healthcare Ethics* 9, no. 1 (2000): 83–97.

73. David K. Reynolds, *A Thousand Waves: A Sensible Life Style for Sensitive People* (New York: Quill/Morrow, 1990).

74. Anson Shupe and Jeffrey K. Hadden, "Symbolic Healing," *Second Opinion* 12 (November 1989): 74–97.

75. Barrie R. Cassileth, "Complementary Therapy," *Science & Medicine* 3, no. 6 (November–December 1996): 8–9.

76. Doris M. Schoenhoff, *The Barefoot Expert: The Interface of Computerized Knowledge Systems and Indigenous Knowledge Systems* (Westport, Conn.: Greenwood Press, 1993), pp. 13–14.

77. Desmond Manderson, "Formalism and Narrative in Law and Medicine: The Debate over Medical Marijuana Use," *Journal of Drug Issues* 29, no. 1 (1999): 121–133.

78. Ross E. Gray and Brian D. Doan, "Heroic Self-healing and Cancer: Clinical Issues for the Health Professions," *Journal of Palliative Care* 6, no. 1 (1990): 32–41.

79. "Tapping Human Potential: An Interview with Norman Cousins," *Second Opinion* 14 (July 1990): 57–71. See also Norman Cousins, *Anatomy of an Illness As Perceived by the Patient: Reflections on Healing and Regeneration* (New York: W. W. Norton, 1979).

80. Michael H. Levy, "Pain Control Research in the Terminally Ill," *Omega: Journal of Death and Dying* 18, no. 4 (1987–1988): 265–279.

81. Marcia K. Merboth and Susan Barnason, "Managing Pain: The Fifth Vital Sign." *Nursing Clinics of North America* 35, no. 2 (2000): 375–383.

82. Paul J. Weithman, "Of Assisted Suicide and 'The Philosophers' Brief,'" *Ethics* 109, no. 3 (1999): 548–578.

83. Alison Twycross, "Education About Pain: A Neglected Area?" *Nurse Education Today* 20, no. 3 (2000): 244–253.

84. Berkow, ed., *Merck Manual of Diagnosis and Therapy,* 16th ed., p. 1409. See also Daniel B. Carr and others, *Acute Pain Management: Operative or Medical Procedures and Trauma.* Clinical Practice Guideline No. 1 (Rockville, Md.: Agency for Health Care Policy and Research, 1992).

85. *Dorland's Illustrated Medical Dictionary,* 26th ed. (Philadelphia: W. B. Saunders, 1985), p. 954.

86. Berkow, ed., *Merck Manual of Diagnosis and Therapy,* 16th ed., p. 1409, 1412. See also Fredrica Preson and Ruth McCorkle, "Philosophy, Principles, and Politics of Symptom Management for the Terminally Ill," in *A Challenge for Living,* ed. Corless, Germino, and Pittman, pp. 17–36.

87. See Ada Jacox and others, *Management of Cancer Pain, Clinical Practice Guideline No. 9*, (Rockville, Md.: Agency for Health Care Policy and Research, 1994).

88. Porter Storey, "Cancer Pain Management: How Are We Doing?" *American Journal of Hospice and Palliative Care* 9, no. 3 (1992): 6–7.

89. Joy Ufema, "Pain Control Survey Results: Not Good," *American Journal of Hospice and Palliative Care* 9, no. 1 (1992): 11–12.

90. Michael de Ridder, "Heroin: New Facts About an Old Myth," *Journal of Psychoactive Drugs* 26, no. 1 (1994): 65–68. See also Rita Carter, "Give a Drug a Bad Name . . . ," *New Scientist* 150 (6 April 1996): 14–15.

91. See Kathleen M. Foley, "Controlling the Pain of Cancer," *Scientific American* 275, no. 3 (September 1996): 164–165.

92. Judith A. Paice and Michelle M. Buck, "Intraspinal Devices for Pain Management," *Nursing Clinics of North America* 28, no. 4 (1993): 921–935.

93. Mary K. Sheehan, Philip G. Janicak, and Sheila Dowd, "The Role of Psychopharmacotherapy in the Dying Patient," *Psychiatric Annals* 24, no. 2 (1994): 98–103.

94. Linda C. Garro, "Culture, Pain and Cancer," *Journal of Palliative Care* 6, no. 3 (1990): 34–44. See also David B. Morris, *The Culture of Pain* (Berkeley: University of California Press, 1991).

95. Tim A. Ahles, "Cancer Pain: Research from Multidimensional and Illness Representation Models," *Motivation and Emotion* 17, no. 3 (1993): 225–243.

96. Robert Kastenbaum and Claude Normand, "Deathbed Scenes As Imagined by the Young and Experienced by the Old," *Death Studies* 14, no. 3 (1990): 201–217.

97. Barney G. Glaser and Anselm L. Strauss, *Time for Dying* (Chicago: Aldine, 1968). See also Kastenbaum and Thuell, "Cookies Baking, Coffee Brewing: Toward a Contextual Theory of Dying"; and Pattison, *The Experience of Dying*.

98. Anne Hunsaker Hawkins, "Constructing Death: Three Pathographies About Dying," *Omega: Journal of Death and Dying* 22, no. 4 (1990–1991): 301–317.

99. Berkow, ed., *Merck Manual: Home Edition*, p. 15.

100. Inge B. Corless, "Dying Well: Symptom Control Within Hospice Care," in *Annual Review of Nursing Research*, vol. 12, ed. J. J. Fitzpatrick and J. S. Stevenson (New York: Springer, 1994), pp. 125–146.

101. Berkow, ed., *Merck Manual: Home Edition*, pp. 18–20.

102. Eric J. Cassell, "Dying in a Technological Society," in *Death Inside Out: The Hastings Center Report*, ed. Peter Steinfels and Robert M. Veatch (New York: Harper and Row, 1974), pp. 43–48; see also, by Cassell, *The Nature of Suffering and the Goals of Medicine* (New York: Oxford University Press, 1991); Glaser and Strauss, *Awareness of Dying*; and David Sudnow, *Passing On: The Social Organization of Dying* (Englewood Cliffs, N.J.: Prentice-Hall, 1967).

103. For an example of such life review assessment, see Kastenbaum, "'How Far Can an Intellectual Effort Diminish Pain?' William McDougall's Journal As a Model for Facing Death."

104. Frank, "Pedagogy of Suffering"; see also, by Frank, "What Kind of Phoenix? Illness and Self-Knowledge," *Second Opinion* 18, no. 2 (October 1992): 31–41.

105. Kagawa-Singer, "Redefining Health: Living with Cancer."

106. Adrian Furnham, "Explaining Health and Illness: Lay Perceptions on Current and Future Health, The Causes of Illness, and the Nature of Recovery," *Social Science & Medicine* 39, no. 5 (1994): 715–725; see also Holly F. Mathews, Donald R. Lannin, and James P. Mitchell, "Coming to Terms with Advanced Breast Cancer: Black Women's Narratives from Eastern North Carolina," *Social Science & Medicine* 38, no. 6 (1994): 789–800.

107. Andrea Litva and John Eyles, "Health or Healthy: Why People Are Not Sick in a Southern Ontario Town," *Social Science & Medicine* 39, no. 8 (1994): 1083–1091.

108. Talcott Parsons, *The Social System* (New York: Free Press, 1951). See also Russell Noyes, Jr., and John Clancy, "The Dying Role: Its Relevance to Improved Patient Care," in *Psychiatry* 40 (February 1977): 41–47.

109. Robert J. Baugher and others, "A Comparison of Terminally Ill Persons at Various Time Periods to Death," *Omega: Journal of Death and Dying* 20, no. 2 (1989–1990): 103–155.

110. Allan Kellehear and Terry Lewin, "Farewells by the Dying: A Sociological Study," *Omega: Journal of Death and Dying* 19, no. 4 (1988–1989): 275–292.

111. Roderick Cosh, "Spiritual Care of the Dying," in *A Challenge for Living*, ed. Corless, Germino, and Pittman, pp. 131–143.

112. Cosh, "Spiritual Care of the Dying."

113. Makoto Ueda, *Modern Japanese Writers and the Nature of Literature* (Stanford, Calif.: Stanford University Press, 1976), p. 193.

CHAPTER 6

1. S. J. Diem and J. D. Lantos, "Cardiopulmonary Resuscitation on Television: Miracles and Misinformation," *New England Journal of Medicine* 334, no. 24 (1996): 1578–1582.

2. See Edmund D. Pellegrino and David C. Thomasma, *The Virtues in Medical Practice* (New York: Oxford University Press, 1993).

3. Alexander Morgan Capron, "The Burden of Decision," *Hastings Center Report* (May–June 1990): 36–41.

4. John D. Lantos, *Do We Still Need Doctors?* (New York: Routledge, 1997), pp. 47–48.

5. See L. J. Blackhall and others, "Ethnicity and Attitudes Toward Patient Autonomy," *Journal of the American Medical Association* 274, no. 10 (1995): 820–825; Larry O. Gostin, "Informed Consent, Cultural Sensitivity, and Respect for Persons," *Death Studies* 17, no. 3 (1993): 844–845; and, in the same issue, Marshall B. Kapp, "Living and Dying in the Jewish Way: Secular Rights and Religious Duties," pp. 267–276.

6. See Nancy S. Jecker, "The Role of Intimate Others in Medical Decision Making," *Gerontologist* (February 1990): 65–71.

7. Timothy E. Quill and Christine K. Cassel, "Nonabandonment: A Central Obligation for Physicians," *Annals of Internal Medicine* 122, no. 5 (1995): 368–374.

8. The President's Commission for the Study of Ethical Problems in Medicine and Biomedical and Behavioral Research, *Making Health Care Decisions: The Ethical and Legal Implications of Informed Consent in the Patient–Practitioner Relationship*, vol. 1, *Report*, and vol. 3, *Studies on the Foundations of Informed Consent* (Washington, D.C.: Government Printing Office, 1982). See also Jon F. Merz, "On a Decision-Making Paradigm of Medical Informed Consent," *Journal of Legal Medicine* 14 (1993): 231–264.

9. R. B. Deber and others, "What Role Do Patients Wish to Play in Treatment Decision Making?" *Archives of Internal Medicine* 156, no. 13 (1996): 1414–1420; and R. F. Nease and W. B. Brooks, "Patient Desire for Information and Decision Making in Health Care Decisions: The Autonomy Preference Index and the Health Opinion Survey," *Journal of General Internal Medicine* 10, no. 11 (1995): 539–600.

10. Donald Oken, "What to Tell Cancer Patients: A Study of Medical Attitudes," *Journal of the American Medical Association* 175 (1961): 1120–1128.

11. D. H. Novack and others, "Changes in Physician's Attitudes Toward Telling the Cancer Patient," *Journal of the American Medical Association* 241 (2 March 1979): 897–900.

12. D. H. Novack and others, "Physicians' Attitudes Toward Using Deception to Resolve Difficult Ethical Problems," *Journal of the American Medical Association* 261 (26 May 1989): 2980–2985.

13. Robert Berkow, ed., *The Merck Manual of Medical Information: Home Edition* (Whitehouse Station, N.J.: Merck Research Laboratories, 1997), p. 16.

14. *Steadman's Medical Dictionary,* 26th ed. (Baltimore: Williams & Wilkins, 1995), p. 1371.

15. David W. Towle, "Medical Ethics," *Academic American Encyclopedia* on-line (retrieved March 1991). See also Walter A. Brown, "The Placebo Effect," *Scientific American* 278, no. 1 (January 1998): 90–95.

16. Margot L. White and John C. Fletcher, "The Story of Mr. and Mrs. Doe: 'You Can't Tell My Husband He's Dying; It Will Kill Him,'" in *The Path Ahead: Readings in Death and Dying,* ed. Lynne Ann DeSpelder and Albert Lee Strickland (Mountain View, Calif.: Mayfield, 1995), pp. 148–153.

17. The SUPPORT Principal Investigators, "A Controlled Trial to Improve Care for Seriously Ill Hospitalized Patients: The Study to Understand Prognoses and Preferences for Outcomes and Risks of Treatment (SUPPORT)," *Journal of the American Medical Association* 274, no. 20 (1995): 1591–1598. See also in *Journal of the American Geriatrics Society* 48, no. 5 (2000): Russell S. Phillips and others, "Findings from SUPPORT and HELP: An Introduction" (S1–S5); Neil S. Wenger and others, "Physician Understanding of Patient Resuscitation Preferences: Insights and Clinical Implications" (S44–S51); and Carol E. Golin and others, "A Prospective Study of Patient–Physician Communication About Resuscitation" (S52–S60).

18. See C. H. Braddock and others, "How Doctors and Patients Discuss Routine Clinical Decisions: Informed Decision Making in the Outpatient Setting," *Journal of General Internal Medicine* 12, no. 6 (1997): 339–345; and, in the same issue, S. J. Diem, "How and When Should Physicians Discuss Clinical Decisions with Patients?" pp. 397–398; see also Jan C. Hoffman and others, "Patient Preferences for Communication with Physicians About End-of-Life Decisions," *Annals of Internal Medicine* 127, no. 1 (1997): 1–11.

19. See J. R. Curtis and others, "Use of the Medical Futility Rationale in Do-Not-Attempt-Resuscitation Orders," *Journal of the American Medical Association* 273, no. 2 (1995): 124–128; J. Chris Hackler and F. Charles Hiller, "Family Consent Orders Not to Resuscitate," *Journal of the American Medical Association* 264 (12 September 1990): 1281–1283; Robert A. Pearlman, Steven H. Miles, and Robert M. Arnold, "Contributions of Empirical Research to Medical Ethics," *Theoretical Medicine* 14 (1993): 197–210; Tom Tomlinson and Howard Brody, "Futility and the Ethics of Resuscitation," *Journal of the American Medical Association* 264 (12 September 1990): 1276–1280; and William Ventres and others, "Do-Not-Resuscitate Orders: A Qualitative Analysis," *Family Practice Research Journal* 12, no. 2 (1992): 157–169. See also Jessica H. Muller, "Shades of Blue: The Negotiation of Limited Codes by Medical Residents," *Social Science & Medicine* 34, no. 8 (1992): 885–898.

20. See Yvonne K. Scherer and Michael H. Ackerman, "Ethical and Legal Controversies in Critical Care Nursing," in *Nursing Issues for the Nineties and Beyond,* ed. B. Bullough and V. L. Bullough (New York: Springer, 1994), pp. 122–138.

21. Howard Brody and others, "Withdrawing Intensive Life-Sustaining Treatment:

Recommendations for Compassionate Clinical Management," *New England Journal of Medicine* 336, no. 9 (1997): 652–657.

22. See A. Halevy and B. A. Brody, "A Multi-Institutional Collaborative Policy on Medical Futility," *Journal of the American Medical Association* 276, no. 7 (1996): 571–574; A. U. Rivin, "Futile Care Policy: Lessons Learned from Three Years' Experience in a Community Hospital," *Western Journal of Medicine* 166, no. 6 (1997): 389–393. See also R. Tong, "Toward a Just, Courageous, and Honest Resolution of the Futility Debate," *Journal of Medicine and Philosophy* 20, no. 2 (1995): 165–189; T. Tomlinson and D. Czlonka, "Futility and Hospital Policy," *Hastings Center Report* 25, no. 3 (1995): 28–35; and V. A Sharpe and A. I. Faden, "Appropriateness in Patient Care: A New Conceptual Framework," *Milbank Quarterly* 74, no. 1 (1996): 115–138.

23. Berkow, ed., *Merck Manual of Medical Information: Home Edition*, p. 16.

24. President's Commission for the Study of Ethical Problems in Medicine and Biomedical and Behavioral Research, *Summing Up: Final Report on Studies of the Ethical and Legal Problems in Medicine and Biomedical and Behavioral Research* (Washington, D.C.: Government Printing Office, March 1983), p. 31. See also the companion volume, *Deciding to Forego Life-Sustaining Treatment: A Report on the Ethical, Medical, and Legal Issues in Treatment Decisions* (Washington, D.C.: Government Printing Office, March 1983).

25. See Choice in Dying, "Issues: Background on the Right to Die" on-line (retrieved 9 September 2000; http://www.choices.org/issues.htm).

26. Joseph Fletcher, "The Patient's Right to Die," in *Euthanasia and the Right to Die: The Case for Voluntary Euthanasia,* ed. A. B. Downing (London: Peter Owen Ltd., 1969), p. 30.

27. See Norman L. Cantor and George C. Thomas, III, "The Legal Bounds of Physician Conduct Hastening Death," *Buffalo Law Review* 48, no. 1 (2000): 83–173; and Philip Donald St. John and Malcolm Man-Son-Hing, "Physician-Assisted Suicide: The Physician As an Unwitting Accomplice," *Journal of Palliative Care* 15, no. 2 (1999): 56–58. See also Dan W. Brock, "A Critique of Three Objections to Physician-Assisted Suicide," *Ethics* 109, no. 3 (1999): 519–547.

28. *In the Matter of Karen Quinlan: The Complete Legal Briefs, Court Proceedings and Decisions in the Superior Court of New Jersey* (1975) and *In the Matter of Karen Quinlan, Volume 2: The Complete Briefs, Oral Arguments, and Opinion in the New Jersey Supreme Court* (1976; Arlington, Va.: University Publications of America).

29. Background to the Cruzan case and arguments on both sides of the issue can be found in *Hastings Center Report* (January–February 1990): 38–50. See also Ron Hamel, "The Supreme Court's Decision in the *Cruzan* Case: A Synopsis," *Bulletin of the Park Ridge Center* (September 1990): 18, 20.

30. Marshall B. Kapp, "Life-Sustaining Technologies: Value Issues," *Journal of Social Issues* 49, no. 2 (1993): 151–167.

31. See David Orentlicher, "The Alleged Distinction Between Euthanasia and the Withdrawal of Life-Sustaining Treatment: Conceptually Incoherent and Impossible to Maintain," *University of Illinois Law Review* (1998): 837–859.

32. Arthur S. Berger, *Dying & Death in Law & Medicine: A Forensic Primer for Health and Legal Professionals* (Westport, Conn.: Praeger, 1993), p. 48.

33. P. A. Singer and others, "Public Opinion Regarding End-of-Life Decisions: Influence of Prognosis, Practice, and Process," *Social Science & Medicine* 41, no. 11 (1995): 1517–1521.

34. See Howard Brody, "Assisted Death: A Compassionate Response to a Medical Failure," *New England Journal of Medicine* 327 (5 November 1992): 1384–1388; Eugenie

Anne Gifford, "*Artes Moriendi*: Active Euthanasia and the Art of Dying," *UCLA Law Review* 40 (1993): 1545–1585; Albert R. Jonsen, "Living with Euthanasia: A Futuristic Scenario," *Journal of Medicine and Philosophy* 18 (1993): 241–251; and Timothy Quill, "Care of the Hopelessly Ill: Proposed Clinical Criteria for Physician-Assisted Suicide," *New England Journal of Medicine* 327 (5 November 1992): 1380–1384.

35. "It's Over, Debbie," *Journal of the American Medical Association* 259 (8 January 1988): 272.

36. See Margaret P. Battin, "Euthanasia: The Way We Do It, The Way They Do It," *Journal of Pain and Symptom Management* 6, no. 5 (1991): 298–305; Herbert Hendin, "Seduced by Death: Doctors, Patients, and the Dutch Cure," *Issues in Law and Medicine* 10, no. 2 (1994): 123–168; Nancy S. Jecker, "Physician-Assisted Death in the Netherlands and the United States: Ethical and Cultural Aspects of Health Policy Development," *Journal of the American Geriatrics Society* 42 (1994): 672–678; Herman H. van der Kloot Meijburg, "How Health Care Institutions in the Netherlands Approach Physician-Assisted Death," *Omega: Journal of Death and Dying* 32, no. 3 (1995–1996): 179–196; Martien Muller, *Death on Request: Aspects of Euthanasia and Physician-Assisted Suicide with Special Regard to Dutch Nursing Homes* (Amsterdam: Thesis Publishers, 1996); David C. Thomasma, "The Ethics of Physician-Assisted Suicide," in *Physician-Assisted Death,* ed. James M. Humber, Robert F. Almeder, and Gregg A. Kasting (Totowa, N.J.: Humana Press, 1993), pp. 99–133; and G. Van der Wal and others, "Voluntary Active Euthanasia and Physician Assisted Suicide in Dutch Nursing Homes: Requests and Administration," *Journal of the American Geriatrics Society* 42 (1994): 620–623.

For data from a Dutch study on medical decisions at the end of life, see Paul J. van der Mass and others, "Euthanasia and Other Medical Decisions Concerning the End of Life," *The Lancet* 338 (14 September 1991): 669–674; Johannes J. M. van Delden, Loes Pijnenborg, and Paul J. van der Mass, "The Remmelink Study: Two Years Later," *Hastings Center Report* 23, no. 6 (1993): 24–27; and Loes Pijnenborg and others, "Nationwide Study of Decisions Concerning the End of Life in General Practice in the Netherlands," *British Medical Journal* 309 (5 November 1994): 1209–1212. For an update, see Paul J. van der Mass and others, "Euthanasia, Physician-Assisted Suicide, and Other Medical Practices Involving the End of Life in the Netherlands, 1990–1995," *New England Journal of Medicine* 335, no. 22 (1996): 1699–1711.

37. See Ann Alpers and Bernard Lo, "Avoiding Family Feuds: Responding to Surrogate Demands for Life-Sustaining Interventions," *Journal of Law Medicine & Ethics* 27, no. 1 (1999): 74–80; Leslie J. Blackhall and others, "Ethnicity and Attitudes Towards Life Sustaining Technology," *Social Science & Medicine* 48, no. 12 (1999): 1779–1789; and Eric W. Mebane and others, "The Influence of Physician Race, Age, and Gender on Physician Attitudes Toward Advance Care Directives and Preferences for End-of-Life Decision-Making," *Journal of the American Geriatrics Society* 47, no. 5 (1999): 579–591.

38. David J. Roy, "Euthanasia—Taking a Stand," *Journal of Palliative Care* 6, no. 1 (1990): 3–5. See also Richard M. Gula, "The Virtuous Response to Euthanasia," *Health Progress* 70 (December 1989): 24–27.

39. Dame Cicely Saunders, "A Response to Logue's 'Where Hospice Fails—The Limits of Palliative Care,'" *Omega: Journal of Death and Dying* 32, no. 1 (1995–1996): 1–5; quote from p. 2.

40. Charles J. Dougherty, "The Common Good, Terminal Illness, and Euthanasia," in *The Path Ahead,* ed. DeSpelder and Strickland, pp. 154–164.

41. Thomas Attig, "Can We Talk? On the Elusiveness of Dialogue," *Death Studies* 19, no. 1 (1995): 1–19.

42. R. J. Connelly, "The Sentiment Argument for Artificial Feeding of the Dying," *Omega: Journal of Death and Dying* 20, no. 3 (1989–1990): 229–237. See also Steven H. Miles, "Nourishment and the Ethics of Lament," *Linacre Quarterly* 56 (August 1989): 64–69; and J. Slomka, "What Do Apple Pie and Motherhood Have to Do with Feeding Tubes and Caring for the Patient?" *Archives of Internal Medicine* 155, no. 12 (1995): 1258–1263. For an opposing view, which emphasizes the "bond of human communion" that is maintained by artificially nourishing patients in a persistent vegetative state, see Germain Grisez and Kevin O'Rourke, "Should Nutrition and Hydration Be Provided to Permanently Unconscious and Other Mentally Disabled Persons," *Issues in Law and Medicine* 5 (1989): 165–196.

43. James J. McCartney and Jane Mary Trau, "Cessation of the Artificial Delivery of Food and Fluids: Defining Terminal Illness and Care," *Death Studies* 14, no. 5 (1990): 435–444.

44. Dena S. Davis, "Old and Thin," *Second Opinion* 15 (November 1990): 26–32; see also, in the same issue, Ronald M. Green, "Old and Thin: A Response," pp. 34–39.

45. Robert McCormick, "To Save or Let Die: The Dilemma of Modern Medicine," in *Ethical Issues in Death and Dying,* ed. Robert F. Weir (New York: Columbia University Press, 1977), pp. 173–184.

46. See Committee on Bioethics, American Academy of Pediatrics, "Ethics and the Care of Critically Ill Infants and Children," *Pediatrics* (1996): 149–152; A. G. M. Campbell and H. E. McHaffie, "Prolonging Life and Allowing Death: Infants," *Journal of Medical Ethics* 21, no. 6 (1995): 339–344; and W. J. E. Pinch and M. L. Spielman, "Ethics in the Neonatal Intensive Care Unit: Parental Perceptions at Four Years Postdischarge," *Advances in Nursing Science* 19, no. 1 (1996): 72–85.

47. President's Commission for the Study of Ethical Problems in Medicine, *Deciding to Forego Life-Sustaining Treatment,* p. 7.

48. Robert Berkow, ed. *The Merck Manual of Diagnosis and Therapy,* 16th ed. (Rahway, N.J.: Merck Research Laboratories, 1992), p. 346.

49. Leonard L. Bailey, "Organ Transplantation: A Paradigm of Medical Progress," *Hastings Center Report* (January–February 1990): 24–28; see also Susan L. Smith, "Progress in Clinical Organ Transplantation" on-line (retrieved 4 September 2000; http://www.medscape.com/medscape/transplantation/journal/2000/v/pnt-mt0406.smit.htm).

50. Berkow, ed., *Merck Manual of Diagnosis and Therapy,* 16th ed., pp. 346–347.

51. See Robert P. Lanza, David K. C. Cooper, and William L. Chick, "Xenotransplantation," *Scientific American* 277, no. 1 (July 1997): 54–59; and Jeffrey L. Platt, "Xenotransplantation," *Science & Medicine* 3, no. 4 (July–August 1996): 62–71. See also Frederick A. Murphy, "The Public Health Risk of Animal Organ and Tissue Transplantation into Humans," *Science* 273 (9 August 1996): 746–747.

52. See Health Resources and Services Administration, "Organ Donation" on-line (retrieved 9 September 2000; http://organdonor.gov).

53. See Charles J. Dougherty, "Our Bodies, Our Families: The Family's Role in Organ Donation," *Second Opinion* 19, no. 2 (October 1993): 59–67.

54. United Network for Organ Sharing, "The Critical Organ Shortage" on-line (retrieved 9 September 2000; http://www.unos.org/about/numone_main.htm).

55. Courtney S. Campbell, "The Selling of Organs, the Sharing of Self," *Second Opinion* 19, no. 2 (October 1993): 69–79. See also A. H. Barnett and David L. Kaserman, "The Shortage of Organs for Transplantation: Exploring the Alternatives," *Issues in Law and Medicine* 9, no. 2 (1993): 117–137; and Frank Th. de Charro, Hans E. M. Akveld, and Dick J. Hessing, "Systems of Donor Transfer," *Health Policy* 25 (1993): 199–212.

56. Douglas N. Walton, *On Defining Death: An Analytic Study of the Concept of Death in Philosophy and Medical Ethics* (Montreal: McGill-Queen's University Press, 1979).

57. On medical guidelines for PVS, see American Academy of Neurology, "Practice Parameters: Assessment and Management of Patients in the Persistent Vegetative State," *Neurology* 45, no. 5 (1995): 1015–1018.

58. Robert M. Veatch, *Death, Dying, and the Biological Revolution: Our Last Quest for Responsibility,* rev. ed. (New Haven: Yale University Press, 1989); see also, by Veatch, *A Theory of Medical Ethics* (New York: Basic Books, 1981).

59. Duncan MacDougall, "Hypothesis Concerning Soul Substance Together with Experimental Evidence of the Existence of Such Substance," *Journal of the American Society for Psychical Research* 1, no. 5 (May 1907): 237–244.

60. See Joseph C. Evers and Paul A. Byrne, "Brain Death: Still a Controversy," *The Pharos of Alpha Omega Alpha* 53, no. 4 (1990): 10–12; R. D. Truog, "Is It Time to Abandon Brain Death?" *Hastings Center Report* 27, no. 1 (1997): 29–37; and Robert M. Veatch, "The Impending Collapse of the Whole-Brain Definition of Death," *Hastings Center Report* 23, no. 4 (1993): 18–24.

61. Karen G. Gervais, "Advancing the Definition of Death: A Philosophical Essay," *Medical Humanities Review* 3 (July 1989): 7–19; and, by Gervais, *Redefining Death* (New Haven, Conn.: Yale University Press, 1986).

62. Robert M. Veatch, "What Counts As Basic Health Care? Private Values and Public Policy," *Hastings Center Report* 24, no. 3 (1994): 20–21.

63. This case study draws primarily on the following sources: Albert R. Jonsen, "Ethical Issues in Organ Transplantation," in *Medical Ethics,* 2d ed., ed. Robert M. Veatch (Boston: Jones and Bartlett, 1997), pp. 239–274; Rihito Kimura, "Organ Transplantation and Brain-Death in Japan: Cultural, Legal, and Bioethical Background," *Annals of Transplantation* 3, no. 3 (1998): 5–58; Masahiro Morioka, "Bioethics and Japanese Culture: Brain Death, Patients' Rights, and Cultural Factors," *Eubios Journal of Asian and International Bioethics* 5 (1995): 87–90; Emiko Ohnuki-Tierney, "Brain Death and Organ Transplantation: Cultural Bases of Medical Technology," *Current Anthropology* 35, no. 3 (1994): 233–254; and Mona Newsome Wicks, "Brain Death and Transplantation: The Japanese" on-line (retrieved 4 September 2000; http://www.medscape.com/medscape/ transplantation/journal/2000/v01/mt0425.wick.htm).

64. Leon R. Kass, "Practicing Ethics: Where's the Action?" *Hastings Center Report* (January–February 1990): 5–12.

65. Alexander Morgan Capron, "Why Law and the Life Sciences?" *Hastings Center Report* 24, no. 3 (1994): 42–44.

66. Lee LaTour, quoted in Andrew Solomon, "A Death of One's Own," *New Yorker* (22 May 1995), pp. 54–69.

CHAPTER 7

1. Elaine M. Blinde and Terese M. Stratta, "The 'Sport Career Death' of College Athletes: Involuntary and Unanticipated Sports Exits," *Journal of Sport Behavior* 15, no. 1 (1994): 3–20.

2. Bob Krizek, "Goodbye Old Friend: A Son's Farewell to Comiskey Park," *Omega: Journal of Death and Dying* 25, no. 2 (1992): 87–93.

3. See Jennifer Klapper, Sidney Moss, Miriam Moss, and Robert L. Rubinstein, "The Social Context of Grief Among Adult Daughters Who Have Lost a Parent," *Journal of Aging Studies* 8, no. 1 (1994): 29–43; and Paul C. Rosenblatt, "Grief: The Social Context of Private Feelings," *Journal of Social Issues* 44, no. 3 (1988): 67–78.

4. Mary Caroline Crawford, *Social Life in Old New England* (Boston: Little, Brown, 1914), p. 461.

5. Terry Tafoya, "The Widow As Butterfly: Treatment of Grief/Depression Among the Sahaptin," unpublished paper.

6. See Vernon Reynolds and Ralph Tanner, *The Social Ecology of Religion* (New York: Oxford University Press, 1995), p. 214.

7. Philippe Ariès, "The Reversal of Death: Changes in Attitudes Toward Death in Western Societies," in *Death in America,* ed. David E. Stannard (Philadelphia: University of Pennsylvania Press, 1975), pp. 134–158.

8. Stephen J. Fleming and Paul J. Robinson, "The Application of Cognitive Therapy to the Bereaved," in *The Challenge of Cognitive Therapy: Applications to Nontraditional Populations,* ed. T. M. Vallis, J. L. Howes, and P. C. Miller (New York: Plenum Press, 1991), pp. 135–158.

9. William M. Lamers, Jr., "On the Psychology of Loss," in *Grief and the Healing Arts: Creativity As Therapy,* ed. Sandra L. Bertman (Amityville, N.Y.: Baywood, 1998), pp. 1–18.

10. Paul J. Robinson and Stephen Fleming, "Differentiating Grief and Depression," *Hospice Journal* 5, no. 1 (1989): 77–88; and "Depressotypic Cognitive Patterns in Major Depression and Conjugal Bereavement," *Omega: Journal of Death and Dying* 25, no. 4 (1992): 291–305. See also B. Bower, "Grief Sometimes Heads Down a Grievous Path," *Science News* 147, no. 2 (14 January 1995): 22.

11. See Arthur S. Berger, "Quote the Raven: Bereavement and the Paranormal," *Omega: Journal of Death and Dying* 31, no. 1 (1995): 1–10; and, in the same issue, Torill Christine Lindström, "Experiencing the Presence of the Dead: Discrepancies in 'The Sensing Experience' and Their Psychological Concomitants," pp. 11–21.

12. Dennis Klass, "John Bowlby's Model of Grief and the Problem of Identification," *Omega: Journal of Death and Dying* 18, no. 1 (1987–1988): 13–32.

13. See Nancy Hogan, Janice M. Morse, and Maritza Cerdas Tasón, "Toward an Experiential Theory of Bereavement," *Omega: Journal of Death and Dying* 33, no. 1 (1996): 43–65.

14. See Liam Hyland and Janice M. Morse, "Orchestrating Comfort: The Role of Funeral Directors," *Death Studies* 19, no. 5 (1995): 453–474.

15. Sandra L. Bertman, Helen K. Sumpter, and Harry L. Green, "Bereavement and Grief," in *Introduction to Clinical Medicine,* ed. Harry L. Green (Philadelphia: B. C. Decker, 1991), p. 682.

16. Ibid.

17. See Hettie J. E. M. Janssen, Marian C. J. Cuisinier, and Kees A. L. Hoogduin, "A Critical Review of the Concept of Pathological Grief Following Pregnancy Loss," *Omega: Journal of Death and Dying* 33, no. 1 (1996): 21–42; and Beverly Raphael and Christine Minkov, "Abnormal Grief," *Current Opinion in Psychiatry* 12, no. 1 (1999): 99–102.

18. Sarah Brabant, "Old Pain or New Pain: A Social Psychological Approach to Recurrent Grief," *Omega: Journal of Death and Dying* 20, no. 4 (1989–1990): 273–279.

19. Ira O. Glick, Robert S. Weiss, and Colin Murray Parkes, *The First Year of Bereavement* (New York: John Wiley & Sons, 1974), p. viii; see also Colin Murray Parkes and Robert S. Weiss, *Recovery from Bereavement* (New York: Basic Books, 1983); and Robert S. Weiss, "Loss and Recovery," *Journal of Social Issues* 44, no. 3 (1988): 37–52.

20. Robinson and Fleming, "Differentiating Grief and Depression" and "Depressotypic Cognitive Patterns in Major Depression and Conjugal Bereavement." See also

Sidney Zisook and Lucy Lyons, "Bereavement and Unresolved Grief in Psychiatric Outpatients," *Omega: Journal of Death and Dying* 20, no. 4 (1989–1990): 307–322.

21. Therese A. Rando, "The Increasing Prevalence of Complicated Mourning: The Onslaught Is Just Beginning," *Omega: Journal of Death and Dying* 26, no. 1 (1992–1993): 43–59.

22. See Kjell Kallenberg and Björn Söderfeldt, "Three Years Later: Grief, View of Life, and a Personal Crisis After Death of a Family Member," *Journal of Palliative Care* 8, no. 4 (1992): 13–19; and Hans Stifoss-Hanssen and Kjell Kallenberg, *Existential Questions and Answers: Research Frontlines and Challenges* (Stockholm: Swedish Council for Planning and Coordination of Research, 1996), p. 54.

23. Holly G. Prigerson and others, "Consensus Criteria for Traumatic Grief: A Preliminary Empirical Test," *British Journal of Psychiatry* 174 (1999): 67–73.

24. W. D. Rees and S. G. Lutkins, "The Mortality of Bereavement," *British Medical Journal* 4 (1967): 13–16.

25. Arthur C. Carr and Bernard Schoenberg, "Object-Loss and Somatic Symptom Formation," in *Loss and Grief: Psychological Management in Medical Practice,* ed. Bernard Schoenberg and others (New York: Columbia University Press, 1970), pp. 36–47.

26. See Nicholas R. Hall and Allan L. Goldstein, "Thinking Well: The Chemical Links Between Emotions and Health," *The Sciences* 26, no. 2 (March/April 1986): 34–40. See also Jerome F. Fredrick, "Grief As a Disease Process," *Omega: Journal of Death and Dying* 7, no. 4 (1976–1977): 297–305; and Edgar N. Jackson, "The Physiology of Crisis," in his *Coping with the Crises of Your Life* (New York: Hawthorne Books, 1974), pp. 48–55.

27. For a review of these studies, see Colin Murray Parkes, "Research: Bereavement," *Omega: Journal of Death and Dying* 18, no. 4 (1987–1988): 365–377.

28. Hans Selye, *The Stress of Life,* rev. ed. (New York: McGraw-Hill, 1976).

29. George L. Engel, "Sudden and Rapid Death During Psychological Stress," *Annals of Internal Medicine* 74 (1971); see also, by Engel, "Emotional Stress and Sudden Death," *Psychology Today,* November 1977.

30. Colin Murray Parkes, "The Broken Heart," in his *Bereavement: Studies of Grief in Adult Life,* 2d ed. (Madison, Conn.: International Universities Press, 1987), p. 37. See also Gerald Epstein, Lawrence Weitz, Howard Roback, and Embry McKee, "Research on Bereavement: A Selective and Critical Review," *Comprehensive Psychiatry* 16 (1975): 537–546.

31. Quoted in Jerry E. Bishop, "Secrets of the Heart: Can It Be 'Broken'?" *Wall Street Journal,* 14 February 1994, pp. B1, B5.

32. Itzhak Levav, "Second Thoughts on the Lethal Aftermath of a Loss," *Omega: Journal of Death and Dying* 20, no. 2 (1989–1990): 81–90.

33. Margaret S. Stroebe, "The Broken Heart Phenomenon: An Examination of the Mortality of Bereavement," *Journal of Community & Applied Social Psychology* 4 (1994): 47–61.

34. See Robert M. Sapolsky, "The Solace of Patterns," *The Sciences* 34, no. 6 (November–December 1994): 14–16.

35. Sigmund Freud, "Mourning and Melancholia," *Collected Papers,* vol. 4 (New York: Basic Books, 1959), pp. 152–170. Originally published in 1917. See also Lorraine Siggins, "Mourning: A Critical Survey of the Literature," *International Journal of Psycho-Analysis* 47 (1966): 14–25.

36. Theresa A. Rando, "Grief and Mourning: Accommodating to Loss," in *Dying: Facing the Facts,* 3d ed., ed. Hannelore Wass and Robert A. Neimeyer (Washington, D.C.: Taylor & Francis, 1995), pp. 211–241.

37. See John Bowlby's three-volume work, *Attachment and Loss* (New York: Basic Books): vol. 1, *Attachment* (1969); vol. 2, *Separation: Anxiety and Anger* (1973); and vol. 3, *Loss: Sadness and Depression* (1982); and *The Making and Breaking of Affectional Bonds* (London: Tavistock, 1979). See also Dale Vincent Hardt, "An Investigation of the Stages of Bereavement," *Omega: Journal of Death and Dying* 9, no. 3 (1978–1979): 279–285; and Klass, "John Bowlby's Model of Grief and the Problem of Identification."

38. Attachments developed by animals may result in grief when events threaten or break these bonds; see Ute Carson, "Do Animals Grieve?" *Death Studies* 13, no. 1 (1989): 49–62.

39. Erich Lindemann, "The Symptomatology and Management of Acute Grief," *American Journal of Psychiatry* 101 (1944): 141–148.

40. Colin Murray Parkes, "Research: Bereavement,"

41. See Dennis Klass, "Developing a Cross-Cultural Model of Grief: The State of the Field," *Omega: Journal of Death and Dying* 39, no. 3 (1999): 153–178.

42. Margaret Stroebe, "Coping with Bereavement: A Review of the Grief Work Hypothesis," *Omega: Journal of Death and Dying* 26, no. 1 (1992–1993): 19–42.

43. Personal communication.

44. J. William Worden, *Grief Counseling and Grief Therapy: A Handbook for the Mental Health Practitioner,* 2d ed. (New York: Springer, 1991), pp. 10–18.

45. Therese A. Rando, *Treatment of Complicated Mourning* (Champaign, Ill.: Research Press, 1993).

46. Phyllis R. Silverman, "Helping the Bereaved Through Social Support and Mutual Help," in *A Challenge for Living: Dying, Death, and Bereavement,* ed. Inge B. Corless, Barbara B. Germino, and Mary A. Pittman (Boston: Jones and Bartlett, 1995), pp. 241–257.

47. Margaret Stroebe, Mary M. Gergen, Kenneth J. Gergen, and Wolfgang Stroebe, "Broken Hearts or Broken Bonds: Love and Death in Historical Perspective," in *The Path Ahead: Readings in Death and Dying,* ed. Lynne Ann DeSpelder and Albert Lee Strickland (Mountain View, Calif.: Mayfield, 1995), pp. 231–241.

48. See Dennis Klass and Robert Goss, "Spiritual Bonds to the Dead in Cross-Cultural and Historical Perspective: Comparative Religion and Modern Grief," *Death Studies* 23, no. 6 (1999): 547–567.

49. Sandra L. Bertman, "Communicating with the Dead: An Ongoing Experience As Expressed in Art, Literature, and Song," in *Between Life and Death,* ed. Robert J. Kastenbaum (New York: Springer, 1979), pp. 124–155.

50. Alexandra Hepburn, "What Do We Really Know About Grief Counseling? Exploring the Contemporary Challenges of Multiculturalism, Postmodernism, and Imaginal Psychology," *The Forum: Newsletter of the Association for Death Education and Counseling* 20, no. 6 (November–December 1994): 7–8, 13–14, 18. See also Simon Shimson Rubin, "Psychodynamic Therapy with the Bereaved: Listening for Conflict, Relationship, and Transference," *Omega: Journal of Death and Dying* 39, no. 2 (1999): 83–98.

51. Dennis Klass, "Solace and Immortality: Bereaved Parents' Continuing Bond with Their Children," in *The Path Ahead,* ed. DeSpelder and Strickland, pp. 246–259.

52. Dennis Klass, "The Inner Representation of the Dead Child and the Worldviews of Bereaved Parents," *Omega: Journal of Death and Dying* 26, no. 4 (1992–1993): 255–272.

53. Phyllis R. Silverman, Steven Nickman, and J. William Worden, "Detachment Revisited: The Child's Reconstruction of a Dead Parent," in *The Path Ahead,* ed. DeSpelder and Strickland, pp. 260–270.

54. David E. Balk and Nancy S. Hogan, "Religion, Spirituality, and Bereaved Adolescents," in *Loss, Threat to Life, and Bereavement: The Child's Perspective,* ed. David W. Adams and Ellie J. Deveau (Amityville, N.Y.: Baywood, in press). See also Nancy Hogan and Lydia DeSantis, "Adolescent Sibling Bereavement: An Ongoing Attachment," *Qualitative Health Research* 2 (1992): 159–177.

55. Rando, *Treatment of Complicated Mourning,* p. 53.

56. Lyn H. Lofland, "Loss and Human Connection: An Exploration into the Nature of the Social Bond," in *Personality, Roles, and Social Behavior,* ed. William Ickes and Eric S. Knowles (New York: Springer-Verlag, 1982), pp. 219–242. See also Kathy Charmaz, "Grief and Loss of Self," in *The Unknown Country: Death in Australia, Britain, and the USA,* ed. Kathy Charmaz, Glennys Howarth, and Allan Kellehear (London: Macmillan, 1997), pp. 229–241.

57. John D. Kelly, "Grief: Re-forming Life's Story," in *The Path Ahead,* ed. DeSpelder and Strickland, pp. 242–245.

58. Carolyn Ellis, " 'There Are Survivors': Telling a Story of Sudden Death," *Sociological Quarterly* 34, no. 4 (1993): 711–730.

59. Mary Anne Sedney, John E. Baker, and Esther Gross, " 'The Story' of a Death: Therapeutic Considerations with Bereaved Families," *Journal of Marital and Family Therapy* 20, no. 3 (1994): 287–296.

60. Tony Walter, "A New Model of Grief: Bereavement and Biography," *Mortality* 1, no. 1 (1996): 7–25; see also James A. Thorson, "Qualitative Thanatology," *Mortality* 1, no. 2 (1996): 177–190.

61. Fleming and Robinson, " Application of Cognitive Therapy to the Bereaved."

62. Nancy L. Moos, "An Integrative Model of Grief," *Death Studies* 19, no. 4 (1995): 337–364.

63. David W. Kissane and Sidney Bloch, "Family Grief," *British Journal of Psychiatry* 164 (1994): 728–740.

64. Terry L. Martin and Kenneth J. Doka, *Men Don't Cry . . . Women Do: Transcending Gender Stereotypes of Grief* (Philadelphia: Brunner/Mazel, 2000); see also, by Martin and Doka, "Revisiting Masculine Grief," in *Living with Grief: Who We Are, How We Grieve,* ed. Kenneth J. Doka and Joyce D. Davidson (Washington, D.C.: Hospice Foundation of America, 1998), pp. 133–142.

65. Margaret Stroebe and Henk Schut, "The Dual Process Model of Coping with Bereavement" (paper presented at the the Meeting of the International Work Group on Death, Dying, and Bereavement, Oxford England, June 1995).

66. Colin Murray Parkes, "Bereavement in Adult Life," *British Medical Journal* 316 (1998): 856–859; and "Facing Loss," *British Medical Journal* 316 (1998): 1521–1524.

67. Edgar N. Jackson, *Understanding Grief: Its Roots, Dynamics, and Treatment* (Nashville: Abingdon Press, 1957), p. 27; see also, by Jackson, *The Many Faces of Grief* (Nashville: Abingdon Press, 1977). In an interview with the authors, Dr. Jackson described how the death of his young son became the impetus for his studies of grief. In effect, his studies of grief were in part a mechanism for coping with, understanding, and coming to terms with the loss. This is an example of how an individual survivor's value system shapes the means of coping with a loss.

68. Karen S. Pfost, Michael J. Stevens, and Anne B. Wessels, "Relationship of Purpose in Life to Grief Experiences in Response to the Death of a Significant Other," *Death Studies* 13, no. 4 (1989): 371–378.

69. See Paul C. Rosenblatt, "Grief: The Social Context of Private Feelings," *Journal of Social Issues* 44, no. 3 (1988): 67–78. See also Richard A. Kalish and David K. Reynolds,

Death and Ethnicity: A Psychocultural Study (Los Angeles: Ethel Percy Andrus Gerontology Center, University of Southern California, 1976).

70. Unni Wikan, "Bereavement and Loss in Two Muslim Communities: Egypt and Bali Compared," *Social Science & Medicine* 27, no. 5 (1988): 451–460.

71. Fred Sklar and Shirley F. Hartley, "Close Friends As Survivors: Bereavement Patterns in a 'Hidden' Population," *Omega: Journal of Death and Dying* 21, no. 2 (1990): 103–112.

72. Larry A. Bugen, "Human Grief: A Model for Prediction and Intervention," *American Journal of Orthopsychiatry* 47, no. 2 (1977): 196–206. See also Sherry L. Chenell and Shirley A. Murphy, "Beliefs of Preventability of Death Among the Disaster Bereaved," *Western Journal of Nursing Research* 14, no. 5 (1992): 576–594; and Charles A. Guarnaccia, Bert Hayslip, and Lisa Pinkenburg Landry, "Influence of Perceived Preventability of the Death and Emotional Closeness to the Deceased: A Test of Bugen's Model," *Omega: Journal of Death and Dying* 39, no. 4 (1999): 261–276.

73. Robert J. Smith, John H. Lingle, and Timothy C. Brock, "Reactions to Death As a Function of Perceived Similarity to the Deceased," *Omega: Journal of Death and Dying* 9, no. 2 (1978–1979): 125–138.

74. See Robert L. Fulton, "Death, Grief, and Social Recuperation," *Omega: Journal of Death and Dying* 1, no. 1 (1970): 23–28; and Bruce J. Horacek, "A Heuristic Model of Grieving After High-Grief Death," *Death Studies* 19, no. 1 (1995): 21–31. See also Ruth Malkinson, Simon Shimson Rubin, and Eliezer Witzsum, eds., *Traumatic and Nontraumatic Loss and Bereavement: Clinical Theory and Practice* (Madison, Conn.: Psychosocial Press, in press).

75. Richard M. Leliaert, "Spiritual Side of 'Good Grief': What Happened to Holy Saturday?" *Death Studies* 13, no. 2 (1989): 103–117.

76. Arlene Sheskin and Samuel E. Wallace, "Differing Bereavements: Suicide, Natural, and Accidental Death," *Omega: Journal of Death and Dying* 7, no. 3 (1976): 229–242.

77. Therese A. Rando, *Loss and Anticipatory Grief* (Lexington, Mass.: Lexington Books, 1986), p. 24.

78. See Bernard Schoenberg, Arthur C. Carr, Austin H. Kutscher, David Peretz, and Ivan K. Goldberg, eds., *Anticipatory Grief* (New York: Columbia University Press, 1974), p. 4.

79. Sylvia Sherwood, Robert Kastenbaum, John N. Morris, and Susan M. Wright, "The First Months of Bereavement," in *The Hospice Experiment,* ed. Vincent Mor, David S. Greer, and Robert Kastenbaum (Baltimore: Johns Hopkins University Press, 1988), p. 150.

80. Yvonne K. Ameche, "A Story of Loss and Survivorship," *Death Studies* 14, no. 2 (1990): 185–198.

81. Lea Barinbaum, "Death of Young Sons and Husbands," *Omega: Journal of Death and Dying* 7, no. 2 (1976): 171–175.

82. See Marcia Williams and Bette Frangesch, "Developing Strategies to Assist Sudden-Death Families: A 10-Year Perspective," *Death Studies* 19, no. 5 (1995): 475–487.

83. Robert G. Dunn and Donna Morrish-Vidners, "The Psychological and Social Experience of Suicide Survivors," *Omega: Journal of Death and Dying* 18, no. 3 (1987–1988): 175–215; David E. Ness and Cynthia R. Pfeffer, "Sequelae of Bereavement Resulting from Suicide," *American Journal of Psychiatry* 147 (1990): 279–285; Lillian M. Range and Nathan M. Niss, "Long-Term Bereavement from Suicide, Homicide, Accidents, and Natural Deaths," *Death Studies* 14, no. 5 (1990): 423–433; and Jan Van der Wal, "The Aftermath of Suicide: A Review of Empirical Evidence," *Omega: Journal of Death and Dying* 20, no. 2 (1989–1990): 149–171.

84. Carol J. Van Dongen, "Social Context of Postsuicide Bereavement," *Death Studies* 17, no. 2 (1993): 125–141.

85. See Charles P. McDowell, Joseph M. Rothberg, and Ronald J. Koshes, "Witnessed Suicides," *Suicide and Life-Threatening Behavior* 24, no. 3 (1994): 213–223.

86. Francoise M. Reynolds and Peter Cimbolic, "Attitudes Toward Suicide Survivors As a Function of Survivors' Relationship to the Victim," *Omega: Journal of Death and Dying* 19, no. 2 (1988–1989): 125–133.

87. Gordon Thornton, Katherine D. Whittemore, and Donald U. Robertson, "Evaluation of People Bereaved by Suicide," *Death Studies* 13 (1989): 119–126.

88. Lula M. Redmond, *Surviving When Someone You Love Was Murdered: A Professional's Guide to Group Therapy for Families and Friends of Murder Victims* (Clearwater, Fla.: Psychological Consultation and Education Services, 1989), pp. 38–39, 46–49, 52–53.

89. James D. Sewell, "The Stress of Homicide Investigations," *Death Studies* 18, no. 6 (1994): 565–582.

90. See June S. Church, "The Buffalo Creek Disaster: Extent and Range of Emotional and Behavioral Problems," *Omega: Journal of Death and Dying* 5, no. 1 (1974): 61–63.

91. Terrence Des Pres, *The Survivor* (New York: Oxford University Press, 1976; Pocket Books, 1977); and Lawrence L. Langer, *Versions of Survival: The Holocaust and the Human Spirit* (Albany: State University of New York Press, 1982). See also Robert Jay Lifton, *Death in Life: Survivors of Hiroshima* (New York: Simon and Schuster, 1967).

92. Judith A. Libow, "Traumatized Children and the News Media: Clinical Considerations," *American Journal of Orthopsychiatry* 62, no. 3 (1992): 379–386.

93. Terry Tafoya, "Coyote, Chaos, and Crisis: Counseling the Native American Male," unpublished paper. See also David E. Stannard, *American Holocaust: Columbus and the Conquest of the New World* (New York: Oxford University Press, 1992).

94. See J. William Worden, "Grieving a Loss from AIDS," *Hospice Journal* 7 (1991): 143–150.

95. Ruben Schindler, "Mourning and Bereavement Among Jewish Religious Families: A Time for Reflection and Recovery," *Omega: Journal of Death and Dying* 33, no. 2 (1996): 121–129.

96. Kenneth J. Doka, "Disenfranchised Grief," in *The Path Ahead,* ed. DeSpelder and Strickland, pp. 271–275; and, edited by Doka, *Disenfranchised Grief: Recognizing Hidden Sorrow* (Lexington, Mass.: Lexington Books, 1989). See also Charles A. Corr, "Enhancing the Concept of Disenfranchised Grief," *Omega: Journal of Death and Dying* 38, no. 1 (1998): 1–20.

97. Darlene A. Kloeppel and Sheila Hollins, "Double Handicap: Mental Retardation and Death in the Family," *Death Studies* 13, no. 1 (1989): 31–38.

98. Kemi Adamolekun, "In-Laws Behavior As a Social Factor in Subsequent Temporary Upsurges of Grief in Western Nigeria," *Omega: Journal of Death and Dying* 31, no. 1 (1995): 23–34.

99. Glenn M. Vernon, *Sociology of Death: An Analysis of Death-Related Behavior* (New York: Ronald Press, 1970), p. 159.

100. Mary Kawena Pukui, E. W. Haertig, and Catherine A. Lee, *Nana I Ke Kumu (Look to the Source),* vol. 1 (Honolulu: Hui Hanai; Queen Lili'uokalani Children's Center, 1972), pp. 135–136, 141.

101. Nissan Rubin, "Social Networks and Mourning: A Comparative Approach," *Omega: Journal of Death and Dying* 21, no. 2 (1990): 113–127.

102. For more information, contact T.A.P.S., 2001 S Street NW, Suite 300, Washington, DC 20009; (800) 959–8277.

103. Stephen J. Fleming and Leslie Balmer, "Bereaved Families of Ontario: A Mutual-Help Model for Families Experiencing Death," in *The Path Ahead,* ed. DeSpelder and Strickland, pp. 281–288.

104. Giorgio Di Mola, Marcello Tamburini, and Claude Fusco, "The Role of Volunteers in Alleviating Grief," *Journal of Palliative Care* 6, no. 1 (1990): 6–10.

105. Onno van der Hart, *Coping with Loss: The Therapeutic Use of Leave-Taking Ritual* (New York: Irvington, 1988); and, also by van der Hart, "An Imaginary Leave-Taking Ritual in Mourning Therapy: A Brief Communication," *The International Journal of Clinical and Experimental Hypnosis* 36, no. 2 (1988): 63–69.

106. Nancy C. Reeves and Frederic J. Boersma, "The Therapeutic Use of Ritual in Maladaptive Grieving," *Omega: Journal of Death and Dying* 20, no. 4 (1989–1990): 281–291.

107. Vamik Volkan and C. R. Showalter, "Known Object Loss, Disturbance in Reality Testing, and 'Re-grief' Work As a Method of Brief Psychotherapy," *Psychiatric Quarterly* 42 (1968): 358–374; and Vamik Volkan, "A Study of a Patient's 'Re-grief' Work," *Psychiatric Quarterly* 45 (1971): 255–273.

108. John Schneider, *Stress, Loss, and Grief: Understanding Their Origins and Growth Potential* (Baltimore: University Park Press, 1984), pp. 66–76.

109. Lawrence G. Calhoun and Richard G. Tedeschi, "Positive Aspects of Critical Life Problems: Recollections of Grief," *Omega: Journal of Death and Dying* 20, no. 4 (1989–1990): 265–272.

110. Georges Bataille, "Sacrifice, the Festival, and the Principles of the Sacred World," *Theory of Religion,* trans. Robert Hurley (New York: Zone Books, 1992), p. 48.

111. Julie Fritsch with Sherokee Ilse, *The Anguish of Loss* (Maple Plain, Minn.: Wintergreen Press, 1988).

C H A P T E R 8

1. This account is based on the following sources: "Coffins and Sarcophagi," exhibition notes, Metropolitan Museum of Art, New York; Henri Frankfort, *Ancient Egyptian Religion: An Interpretation* (New York: Harper and Row, 1948, 1961); Manfred Lurker, *The Gods and Symbols of Ancient Egypt* (New York: Thames & Hudson, 1980); and Barbara Watterson, *The Gods of Ancient Egypt* (New York: Facts on File, 1984). See also Morris Bierbrier, *The Tomb-Builders of the Ancient Pharaohs* (New York: Charles Scribner's Sons, 1982); John Romer, *Ancient Lives: Daily Life in Egypt of the Pharaohs* (New York: Holt, Rinehart and Winston, 1984); and A. J. Spencer, *Death in Ancient Egypt* (New York: Penguin, 1982).

2. Vanderlyn R. Pine, "Funerals: Life's Final Ceremony," in *A Challenge for Living: Dying, Death, and Bereavement,* ed. Inge B. Corless, Barbara B. Germino, and Mary A. Pittman (Boston: Jones and Bartlett, 1995), pp. 159–171. See also Jenny Hockey, "Encountering the 'Reality of Death' Through Professional Discourse: The Matter of Materiality," *Mortality* 1, no. 1 (1996): 45–60.

3. Thomas Lynch, *The Undertaking: Life Studies from the Dismal Trade* (New York: W. W. Norton, 1997), p. 21.

4. David Sudnow, *Passing On: The Social Organization of Dying* (Englewood Cliffs, N.J.: Prentice-Hall, 1967), pp. 153–168.

5. Ronald K. Barrett, "Contemporary African-American Funeral Rites and Traditions," in *The Path Ahead: Readings in Death and Dying,* ed. Lynne Ann DeSpelder and Albert Lee Strickland (Mountain View, Calif.: Mayfield, 1995), pp. 80–92. See also, by Barrett, "The Legacy of Traditional African-American Funeral Rites," *Thanos*

16 (October 1994): 18–20; "Affirming and Reclaiming African-American Funeral Rites," *The Director* 66, no. 11 (October 1994): 36–40; and "Psychocultural Influences on African American Attitudes Toward Death, Dying, and Funeral Rites," in *Personal Care in an Impersonal World,* ed. John Morgan (Amityville, N.Y.: Baywood, 1993), pp. 213–230.

6. Ben H. Bagdikian, *The Information Machines: Their Impact on Men and the Media* (New York: Harper and Row, 1971), pp. 39, 59. Also see Bradley Greenberg, "Diffusion of News of the Kennedy Assassination," *Public Opinion Quarterly* 28, no. 2 (Summer 1964): 225–232.

7. J. Z. Young, *Programs of the Brain* (New York: Oxford University Press, 1978), p. 255.

8. Vernon Reynolds and Ralph Tanner, *The Social Ecology of Religion* (New York: Oxford University Press, 1995), p. 213.

9. John R. Elliott, "Funerary Artifacts in Contemporary America," *Death Studies* 14, no. 6 (1990): 601–612.

10. Federal Trade Commission, *Compliance Guidelines: Trade Regulation Rule on Funeral Industry Practices* (Washington, D.C., 1984).

11. O. Duane Weeks and Catherine Johnson, "Developing a Successful Aftercare Program," *The Director* 67, no. 12 (December 1995): 12–18.

12. Leroy Bowman, *The American Funeral: A Study in Guilt, Extravagance, and Sublimity* (Washington: Public Affairs Press, 1959).

13. Jessica Mitford, *The American Way of Death* (New York: Simon & Schuster, 1963), pp. 16–19.

14. D. van Vuure, "The Relatives Asked for a Duo-Committal for Their Parents," *Thanos* 22 (1996): 28–30.

15. Lynch, *The Undertaking,* p. 191.

16. National Funeral Directors Association, "Funeral Price Information" on-line (retrieved 9 September 2000; http://www.nfda.org/resources/99gpl.html).

17. "Service Industries—Annual Receipts," *Statistical Abstract of the United States: 1999,* 119th ed. (Washington, D.C.: Government Printing Office, 1999), p. 784.

18. Ronny E. Turner and Charles Edgley, "Death As Theatre: A Dramaturgical Analysis of the American Funeral," *Sociology and Social Research* 60, no. 4 (1976): 377–392. See also Liam Hyland and Janice M. Morse, "Orchestrating Comfort: The Role of Funeral Directors," *Death Studies* 19, no. 5 (1995): 453–474.

19. Kenneth V. Iserson, *Death to Dust: What Happens to Dead Bodies?* (Tucson, Ariz.: Galen Press, 1993), p. 185; see also pp. 197–214 for a detailed description of embalming and other body preparation procedures.

20. Edward C. Johnson and Melissa Johnson Williams, "Dr. Charles DeCosta Brown, Civil War Embalming Surgeon and the Masonic Order," *American Funeral Director* 120, no. 9 (September 1997): 74–78.

21. Vanderlyn Pine, "The Care of the Dead: A Historical Portrait," in *Death and Dying: Challenge and Change,* ed. Robert Fulton, Eric Markusen, Greg Owen, and Jane L. Scheiber (San Francisco: Boyd & Fraser, 1978), p. 276; see also, by Pine, *Caretaker of the Dead: The American Funeral Director* (New York: Irvington, 1985).

22. Briefly summarized, exceptions to this requirement occur when: (1) state or local law requires embalming; or (2) there are "exigent circumstances," such as: (a) when a family member or other authorized person cannot be contacted despite diligent efforts, and (b) there is no reason to believe the family does not want embalming, and (c) after the body has been embalmed, the family is notified that no fee will be charged if they choose a funeral that does not require embalming.

23. Casket Manufacturers Association of America, "Nationwide Summary—Estimate of Sales to Funeral Directors, Unit Volume (July–September 1985)."

24. Seth Lubove, "If You Gotta Go. . . . ," *Forbes* (4 January 1993), p. 16.

25. See Gordon Fairclough, "Casket Stores Offer Bargains to Die For," *Wall Street Journal* (19 February 1997), pp. B1, B8; and Matt Murray, "Casket Closeout Sales May Not Be Far Behind," *Wall Street Journal* (17 June 1994), p. B1.

26. *Thanos* 24 (1997): 9.

27. Reynolds and Tanner, *The Social Ecology of Religion*, p. 221.

28. Iserson, *Death to Dust*, p. 314.

29. See Niels Bonde and Arne Emil Christensen, "Dendrochronological Dating for the Viking Age Ship Burials at Oseberg, Gokstad, and Tune, Norway," *Antiquity* 67 (1993): 575–583.

30. See Bruce A. Iverson, "Bodies for Science," *Death Studies* 14, no. 6 (1990): 577–587; Robert D. Reece and Jesse H. Ziegler, "How a Medical School (Wright State University) Takes Leave of Human Remains," *Death Studies* 14, no. 6 (1990): 589–600; and Kathleen A. Schotzinger and Elizabeth Kirkley Best, "Closure and the Cadaver Experience: A Memorial Service for Deeded Bodies," *Omega: Journal of Death and Dying* 18, no. 3 (1987–1988): 217–227.

31. *Honolulu Star-Bulletin & Advertiser* (3 June 1984).

32. See Hali J. Weiss, "In the Long Run: Staying Relevant Amidst Cultural Change," *Cemetery Management* (January 1995): 14–16; and, also by Weiss, "Dust to Dust: Transforming the American Cemetery," *Tikkun* 10, no. 5 (1996): 21–25.

33. Jack Goody and Cesare Poppi, "Flowers and Bones: Approaches to the Dead in Anglo-American and Italian Cemeteries," *Comparative Studies in Society and History* 36, no. 1 (1994): 146–175.

34. See Diane O. Bennett, "Bury Me in Second Class: Contested Symbols in a Greek Cemetery," *Anthropological Quarterly* 67, no. 3 (1994): 122–134.

35. Douglas Keister, "A Brief History of the Community Mausoleum," *American Cemetery* 69, no. 9 (September 1997): 20–21, 50–52.

36. National Funeral Directors Association, "U.S. Cremation Statistics" on-line (retrieved 9 September 2000; http:///www.nfda.org/resources/cremationstats.html).

37. Sally Gribbin, "The Social Crisis Facing the Cremation Industry," *Cemetery Management* (January 1994), reprint.

38. Dan Morse, "Shirts for the Dead Are the New Rage in Some Inner Cities," *Wall Street Journal,* 4 February 1999, pp. A1, A16. For a related version of inner-city memorialization see Martha Cooper and Joseph Sciorra, *R.I.P.: Memorial Wall Art* (New York: Henry Holt, 1994).

39. Brochure, Leif Technologies, 1997.

40. William Lamers, Sr., quoted in *Concerning Death: A Practical Guide for the Living,* ed. Earl Grollman (Boston: Beacon Press, 1974), and in *Successful Funeral Service Practice,* ed. Howard C. Raether (Englewood Cliffs, N.J.: Prentice-Hall, 1971).

41. *Funeral Rites and Customs* (Dallas, Tx.: Professional Training Schools, 1991).

42. See, for example, Anne Brener, *Mourning and Mitzvah: A Guided Journal for Walking the Mourner's Path Through Grief to Healing* (Woodstock, Vt.: Jewish Lights Publishing, 1993); Paul Irion, *A Manual and Guide for Those Who Conduct a Humanist Funeral Service* (Baltimore: Waverly Press, 1971), and "Changing Patterns of Ritual Response to Death," *Omega: Journal of Death and Dying* 22, no. 3 (1990–1991): 159–172; Edgar N. Jackson, *The Christian Funeral: Its Meaning, Its Purpose, and Its Modern Practice* (New York: Channel Press, 1966); and Ernest Morgan. *Dealing Creatively with Death: A Manual of Death Education and Simple Burial,* 11th ed. (Burnsville, N.C.: Celo Press, 1988).

43. William M. Lamers, Jr., "Funerals Are Good for People: M.D.'s Included," *Medical Economics* (23 June 1969): 1–4.

44. Alan Wolfelt, "Understanding the Trend Toward Deritualization of the Funeral," *The Forum: Newsletter of the Association for Death Education and Counseling* 20, no. 6 (November–December 1994): 1, 15–17.

45. Sabine Bode and Fritz Roth, *Der Trauer Eine Heimat Geben: Für Einen Lebendigen Umgang mit dem Tod* [Giving Grief a Home] (Bergisch Gladbach: Gustav Lübbe Verlag, 1998).

46. See, for example, Andre Van Gemert, "The Digital Death," *Thanos* 21 (1996): 18–21; Lucette Lagnado, "Phone Eulogies, Cybermourners Make Funerals into Virtual Events," *Wall Street Journal* (21 August 1996), p. B1.

47. Brochure, The Virtual Memorial Company, 1997.

48. E. S. Craighill Handy and Mary Kawena Pukui, *The Polynesian Family System in Ka-'u, Hawai'i* (Rutland, Vt.: Charles E. Tuttle, 1972), p. 157; and Mary Kawena Pukui, E. W. Haertig, and Catherine A. Lee, *Nana I Ke Kumu (Look to the Source)*, vol. 1 (Honolulu: Hui Hanai; Queen Lili'uokalani Children's Center, 1972), p. 139.

C H A P T E R 9

1. The authors thank Richard G. Polse, Esq., for reviewing the material covered in this chapter and offering many helpful suggestions for this edition.

2. President's Commission for the Study of Ethical Problems in Medicine and Biomedical and Behavioral Research, *Defining Death: A Report on the Medical, Legal and Ethical Issues in the Determination of Death* (Washington, D.C.: Government Printing Office, 1981), p. 45.

3. Alexander M. Capron and Leon R. Kass, "A Statutory Definition of the Standards for Determining Human Death: An Appraisal and a Proposal," *University of Pennsylvania Law Review* 121 (1972): 87–118.

4. President's Commission, *Defining Death*.

5. Albert R. Jonsen, *The Birth of Bioethics* (New York: Oxford University Press, 1998), pp. 238–244.

6. Judi Lund Person, "Regulatory Issues," in *A Challenge for Living: Dying, Death, and Bereavement*, ed. Inge B. Corless, Barbara B. Germino, and Mary A. Pittman (Boston: Jones and Bartlett, 1995), p. 315.

7. Annalisa Pizzarello, "Policy and Attitudes on Advance Directives," *Bulletin of the Park Ridge Center* (May 1990): 42.

8. See Jane Foytack and Daniel J. West, "Physician Management Guidelines for Advance Directives with Patients," *Omega: Journal of Death and Dying* 29, no. 2 (1994): 165–175; Molly K. Hoffman, "Use of Advance Directives: A Social Work Perspective on the Myth Versus the Reality," *Death Studies* 18, no. 3 (1994): 229–241; and Joan M. Teno and others (SUPPORT investigators), "Do Formal Advance Directives Affect Resuscitation Decisions and the Use of Resources for Seriously Ill Patients?" *Journal of Clinical Ethics* 5, no. 1 (1994): 23–30.

9. Robert Berkow, ed., *The Merck Manual of Medical Information: Home Edition* (Whitehouse Station, N.J.: Merck Research Laboratories, 1997), p. 17.

10. See George J. Annas, "The Health Care Proxy and the Living Will," *New England Journal of Medicine* 324, no. 17 (1991): 1210–1213; Ezekiel J. Emanuel and Linda L. Emanuel, "Living Wills: Past, Present, and Future," *Journal of Clinical Ethics* 1, no. 1 (1990): 9–19; Linda L. Emanuel and others, "Advance Directives: Can Patients' Stated Treatment Choices Be Used to Infer Unstated Choices?" *Medical Care* 32, no. 2 (1994):

95–105; and Jim Stone, "Advance Directives, Autonomy, and Unintended Death," *Bioethics* 8, no. 3 (1994): 223–246. Example adapted from Wesley J. Smith, "The Living Will's Fatal Flaw," *Wall Street Journal* (4 May 1994).

11. The authors thank Senator John C. Danforth, sponsor of this measure, for providing information about its provisions. See also Elizabeth Leibold McCloskey, "The Patient Self-Determination Act," *Kennedy Institute of Ethics Journal* 1, no. 2 (1991): 163–169.

12. Person, "Regulatory Issues," p. 318.

13. Zelda Foster, "The Struggle to End My Father's Life," in *A Challenge for Living*, ed. Corless, Germino, and Pittman, pp. 327–334.

14. See James Bopp, Jr., and Richard E. Coleson, "Three Strikes: Is an Assisted Suicide Right Out?" *Issues in Law & Medicine* 15, no. 1 (1999): 3–86; Choice in Dying, "Physician-Assisted Suicide: Vacco v. Quill and Washington v. Glucksberg" on-line (retrieved 9 September 2000; http://www.choices.org/sctdec.htm); and Paul J. Weithman, "Of Assisted Suicide and 'the Philosophers' Brief,'" *Ethics* 109, no. 3 (1999): 548–578.

15. "Physician-Assisted Suicide Initiative Passes in Oregon," *Western Bioethics News*, no. 53 (January 1995): 2–3.

16. Oregon Health Division, "Oregon's Death with Dignity Act: The Second Year's Experience" on-line (retrieved 1 October 2000; http://www.ohd.hr.state.or.us/chs/pas/ar-smmry.htm); see also Arthur E. Chin and others, "Legalized Physician-Assisted Suicide in Oregon: The First Year's Experience," *New England Journal of Medicine* 340, no. 7 (1999): 577–583; and Christine Neylon O'Brien, Gerald A. Madek, and Gerald R. Ferrera, "Oregon's Guidelines for Physician-Assisted Suicide: A Legal and Ethical Analysis," *University of Pittsburgh Law Review* 61, no. 2 (2000): 329–365.

17. See Clare E. Kendall, "A Double Dose of Double Effect," *Journal of Medical Ethics* 26, no. 3 (2000): 204–205.

18. See J. A. Billings and S. D. Block, "Slow Euthanasia," *Journal of Palliative Care* 12, no. 4 (1996): 21–30; and Howard Brody, "Commentary on Billings and Block's 'Slow Euthanasia,'" in the same issue, pp. 38–41. See also P. Rousseau, "Terminal Sedation in the Care of Dying Patients," *Archives of Internal Medicine* 1556, no. 16 (1996): 1785–1786.

19. Richard Carelli, "Court: No Right to Assisted Suicide," *Associated Press Online* (26 June 1997). See also Thane Josef Messinger, "A Gentle and Easy Death: From Ancient Greece to Beyond Cruzan Toward a Reasoned Legal Response to the Societal Dilemma of Euthanasia," *Denver University Law Review* 71, no. 1 (1993): 175–251, especially pp. 229–237; Robert A. Sedler, "The Constitution and Hastening Inevitable Death," *Hastings Center Report* 23, no. 5 (September–October 1993): 20–25; and Raymond A. Whiting, "Natural Law and the 'Right to Die,'" *Omega: Journal of Death and Dying* 32, no. 1 (1995–1996): 11–26.

20. Ira Byock, "Dying: After the Court Ruling," *Wall Street Journal* (25 June 1997): A14.

21. John A. Pridonoff, "Introduction," in *Hospice and Hemlock: Retaining Dignity, Integrity, and Self-Respect in End-of-Life Decisions*, ed. Michele A. Trepkowski (Eugene, Ore.: The Hemlock Society, 1993).

22. Edwin S. Shneidman, *Deaths of Man* (New York: Quadrangle, 1973), pp. 121–130.

23. Jon Yoshishige, "Searching for Answers: Lab Identifies Remains of Soldiers, Civilians," *Honolulu Advertiser* (8 August 1993): A1, A2.

24. Jon Marcus, "Autopsy Decline Causes Concern," *Associated Press Online* (17 December 1996).

25. John D. Lantos, *Do We Still Need Doctors?* (New York: Routledge, 1997), pp. 129–130.

26. Greg Jaffe, "Need an Autopsy?" *Wall Street Journal* (2 July 1997): A1, A7.

27. See Kenneth J. Doka, "The Monkey's Paw: The Role of Inheritance in the Resolution of Grief," *Death Studies* 16, no. 1 (1992): 45–58.

28. Barton E. Bernstein, "Lawyer and Counselor As an Interdisciplinary Team: Interfacing for the Terminally Ill," *Death Education* 1, no. 3 (Fall 1977): 277–291; and, by Bernstein, "Lawyer and Therapist As an Interdisciplinary Team: Serving the Terminally Ill," *Death Education* 3, no. 1 (Spring 1979): 11–19.

29. Barton E. Bernstein, "Lawyer and Therapist As an Interdisciplinary Team: Serving the Survivors," *Death Education* 4, no. 2 (Summer 1980): 179–188.

C H A P T E R I O

1. Adah Maurer, "Maturation of Concepts of Death," *British Journal of Medicine and Psychology* 39 (1966): 35–41.

2. Mark W. Speece, "Very Young Children's Experiences with and Reactions to Death" (master's thesis, Wayne State University, 1983).

3. Sandor B. Brent, "Puns, Metaphors, and Misunderstandings in a Two-Year-Old's Conception of Death," *Omega: Journal of Death and Dying* 8, no. 4 (1977–1978): 285–293. The son, who is now an adult, has no recollection of this death-related experience. Dr. Brent believes that this indicates a successfully managed event. (Personal communication.)

4. See Linda J. Gudas, "Concepts of Death and Loss in Childhood and Adolescence," in *Children and Disasters,* ed. Conway E. Saylor (New York: Plenum Press, 1993), pp. 67–84.

5. Sylvia Anthony, *The Discovery of Death in Childhood and After* (New York: Basic Books, 1972), revised edition of *The Child's Discovery of Death: A Study in Child Psychology* (London: Kegan Paul, 1940); and Maria H. Nagy, "The Child's Theories Concerning Death," *Journal of Genetic Psychology* 73 (1948): 3–27.

6. See Mark W. Speece and Sandor B. Brent, "Children's Understanding of Death: A Review of Three Components of a Death Concept," *Child Development* 55, no. 5 (October 1984): 1671–1686; "The Acquisition of a Mature Understanding of Three Components of the Concept of Death," *Death Studies* 16, no. 3 (1992): 211–229; and "The Development of Children's Understanding of Death," in *Handbook of Childhood Death and Bereavement,* ed. Charles A. Corr and Donna M. Corr (New York: Springer, 1996).

7. Erik Erikson, *Childhood and Society* (New York: W. W. Norton, 1950).

8. Jean Piaget, *The Child and Reality: Problems of Genetic Psychology,* trans. Arnold Rosin (New York: Grossman Publishers, 1973), and *The Child's Conception of the World* (London: Routledge & Kegan Paul, 1929). See also Mary Ann Spencer Pulaski, *Understanding Piaget: An Introduction to Children's Cognitive Development* (New York: Harper and Row, 1980).

9. From a conversation with Jean Piaget in Richard I. Evans, *The Making of Psychology: Discussions with Creative Contributors* (New York: Alfred A. Knopf, 1976), p. 46.

10. Gerald P. Koocher, "Childhood, Death, and Cognitive Development," *Developmental Psychology* 9, no. 3 (1973): 369–375; "Talking with Children About Death," *American Journal of Orthopsychiatry* 44, no. 3 (April 1974): 404–411; and "Conversations with Children About Death," *Journal of Clinical Child Psychology* (Summer 1974): 19–21. Of the children in Koocher's study group, the mean age of those classified as preoperational

was 7.4 years; of those who used concrete operations, 10.4 years; and of those who used formal operations, 13.3 years.

11. Helen L. Swain, "Childhood Views of Death," *Death Education* 2, no. 4 (1979): 341–358.

12. Stephen J. Fleming and Rheba Adolph, "Helping Bereaved Adolescents: Needs and Responses," in *Adolescence and Death*, ed. Charles Corr and Joan McNeil (New York: Springer, 1986), pp. 97–118.

13. See, for example, Brian L. Mishara, "Conceptions of Death and Suicide in Children Ages 6–12 and Their Implications for Suicide Prevention," *Suicide and Life-Threatening Behavior* 29, no. 2 (1999): 105–118.

14. Lloyd D. Noppe and Illene C. Noppe, "Dialectical Themes in Adolescent Conceptions of Death," *Journal of Adolescent Research* 6, no. 1 (1991): 28–42.

15. William G. Bartholome, "Care of the Dying Child: The Demands of Ethics," in *The Path Ahead: Readings in Death and Dying*, ed. Lynne Ann DeSpelder and Albert Lee Strickland (Mountain View, Calif.: Mayfield, 1995), pp. 133–143.

16. Myra Bluebond-Langner, *The Private Worlds of Dying Children* (Princeton, N.J.: Princeton University Press, 1978), and, by Bluebond-Langner, "Worlds of Dying Children and Their Well Siblings," *Death Studies* 13, no. 1 (1989): 1–16.

17. Thesi Bergmann and Anna Freud, *Children in the Hospital* (New York: International Universities Press, 1965), pp. 27–28.

18. Donna Juenker, "Child's Perception of His Illness," in *Nursing Care of the Child with Long-Term Illness,* 2d ed., ed. Shirley Steele (New York: Appleton-Century-Crofts, 1977), p. 177. See also Jo-Eileen Gyulay, *The Dying Child* (New York: McGraw-Hill, 1978).

19. Marilyn Hockenberry-Eaton, Virginia Kemp, and Coleen Dilorio, "Cancer Stressors and Protective Factors: Predictors of Stress Experienced During Treatment for Childhood Cancer," *Research in Nursing and Health* 17 (1994): 351–361.

20. See Maurice Levy and others, "Home-Based Palliative Care for Children—Part 1: The Institution of a Program," *Journal of Palliative Care* 6, no. 1 (1990): 11–15; Ciaran M. Duffy and others, "Home-Based Palliative Care for Children—Part 2: The Benefits of an Established Program," *Journal of Palliative Care* 6, no. 2 (1990): 8–14; D. F. Dufour, "Home or Hospital Care for the Child with End-Stage Cancer: Effects on the Family," *Issues in Comprehensive Pediatric Nursing* 12 (1989): 371–383; Ida M. Martinson, "Impact of Childhood Cancer on Families at Home," in *Key Aspects of Caring for the Chronically Ill: Hospital and Home,* ed. Sandra G. Funk and others (New York: Springer, 1993), pp. 312–319; Ida M. Martinson, ed., *Home Care for the Dying Child: Professional and Family Perspectives* (Norwalk, Conn.: Appleton-Century-Crofts, 1976); Ida M. Martinson and others, "Home Care for Children Dying of Cancer," *Pediatrics* 62 (1978): 106–113; and D. Gay Moldow, Ida M. Martinson, and Arthur Kohrman, *Home Care for Seriously Ill Children: A Manual for Parents* (Alexandria, Va.: Children's Hospice of Virginia, 1984).

21. "Children's Hospice: An Omega Interview [by Robert Kastenbaum] with Ida M. Martinson," *Omega: Journal of Death and Dying* 31, no. 4 (1995): 253–261.

22. See John E. Baker, Mary Anne Sedney, and Esther Gross, "Psychological Tasks for Bereaved Children," *American Journal of Orthopsychiatry* 62, no. 1 (1992): 105–116; Cathy Krown Buirski and Peter Buirski, "The Therapeutic Mobilization of Mourning in a Young Child," *Bulletin of the Menninger Clinic* 58, no. 3 (1994): 339–354; and Stephen Fleming, "Children's Grief: Individual and Family Dynamics," in *Hospice Approaches to Care,* ed. Charles Corr and Donna Corr (New York: Springer, 1985), pp. 197–218.

23. Ute Carson, "A Child Loses a Pet," *Death Education* 3 (1980): 399–404.

24. Jane Brody, "When Your Pet Dies," *Honolulu Star-Bulletin & Advertiser,* 8 December 1985.

25. See John Archer and Gillian Winchester, "Bereavement Following the Death of a Pet," *British Journal of Psychology* 85 (1994): 259–271; Gerald H. Gosse and Michael J. Barnes, "Human Grief Resulting from the Death of a Pet," *Anthrozoös* 7, no. 2 (1994): 103–112; and Morris A. Wessel, "Loss of a Pet," in *A Challenge for Living: Dying, Death, and Bereavement,* ed. Inge B. Corless, Barbara B. Germino, and Mary A. Pittman (Boston: Jones and Bartlett, 1995), pp. 259–261.

26. Allan Kellehear and Jan Fook, "Lassie Come Home: A Study of 'Lost Pet' Notices," *Omega: Journal of Death and Dying* 34, no. 3 (1996–1997): 191–202; quote p. 192.

27. See William J. Kay, ed., *Pet Loss and Human Bereavement* (Ames: Iowa State University Press, 1984); and Wallace Sife, *The Loss of a Pet* (New York: Howell, 1993).

28. Avery D. Weisman, "Bereavement and Companion Animals," in *The Path Ahead,* ed. DeSpelder and Strickland, pp. 276–280.

29. See Erna Furman, *A Child's Parent Dies: Studies in Childhood Bereavement* (New Haven, Conn.: Yale University Press, 1974); and Robert A. Furman, "The Child's Reaction to Death in the Family," in *Loss and Grief: Psychological Management in Medical Practice,* ed. Bernard Schoenberg et al. (New York: Columbia University Press, 1970), pp. 70–86.

30. Phyllis R. Silverman, Steven Nickman, and J. William Worden, "Detachment Revisited: The Child's Reconstruction of a Dead Parent," in *The Path Ahead,* ed. DeSpelder and Strickland, pp. 260–270. See also Phyllis R. Silverman and J. William Worden, "Children's Reactions in the Early Months After the Death of a Parent," *American Journal of Orthopsychiatry* 62, no. 1 (January 1992): 93–104; and J. William Worden and Phyllis R. Silverman, "Parental Death and the Adjustment of School-Age Children," *Omega: Journal of Death and Dying* 32, no. 2 (1996): 91–102.

31. Al Santoli, "We Never Knew Our Fathers," *Parade* (27 May 1990), pp. 21–22. Sons and Daughters in Touch, c/o Friends of the Vietnam Veterans Memorial, 1350 Connecticut Avenue, N.W., Suite 300, Washington, DC 20036.

32. See Gregg M. Furth, *The Secret World of Drawings: Healing Through Art* (Boston: Sigo Press, 1988); and Maare E. Tamm and Anna Granqvist, "The Meaning of Death for Children and Adolescents: A Phenomenographic Study of Drawings," *Death Studies* 19, no. 3 (1995): 203–222.

33. Barbara Betker McIntyre, "Art Therapy with Bereaved Youth," *Journal of Palliative Care* 6, no. 1 (1990): 16–23.

34. Betty Davies, "Sibling Bereavement Research: State of the Art," in *A Challenge for Living,* ed. Corless, Germino, and Pittman, pp. 173–202. See also Darlene E. McCown and Betty Davies, "Patterns of Grief in Young Children Following the Death of a Sibling," *Death Studies* 19, no. 1 (1995): 41–53.

35. David E. Balk, "Sibling Death, Adolescent Bereavement, and Religion," *Death Studies* 15, no. 1 (1991): 1–20.

36. Nancy Hogan and Lydia DeSantis, "Adolescent Sibling Bereavement: An Ongoing Attachment," *Qualitative Health Research* 2, no. 2 (1992): 159–177. See also Nancy S. Hogan and David E. Balk, "Adolescent Reactions to Sibling Death: Perceptions of Mothers, Fathers, and Teenagers," *Nursing Research* 39, no. 2 (1990): 103–106; and Nancy S. Hogan and Daryl B. Greenfield, "Adolescent Sibling Bereavement: Symptomatology in a Large Community Sample," *Journal of Adolescent Research* 6, no. 1 (1991): 97–112.

37. Nancy S. Hogan and Lydia DeSantis, "Things That Help and Hinder Adolescent Sibling Bereavement," *Western Journal of Nursing Research* 16, no. 2 (1994): 132–153.

38. See Lynne Ann DeSpelder and Albert Lee Strickland, "Using Life Experiences As a Way of Helping Children Understand Death," in *Beyond the Innocence of Childhood: Factors Influencing Children and Adolescents' Perceptions and Attitudes Toward Death,* ed. David W. Adams and Eleanor J. Deveau (Amityville, N.Y.: Baywood, 1995), pp. 45–54.

39. See T. Havermans and C. Eiser, "Siblings of a Child with Cancer," *Child: Care, Health, and Development* 20 (1994): 309–322.

40. Joanna H. Fanos and Lori Wiener, "Tomorrow's Survivors: Siblings of Human Immunodeficiency Virus-Infected Children," *Developmental and Behavioral Pediatrics* 15, no. 3 (June 1994, Supplement): S43–S48.

41. See Myra Bluebond-Langner, *In the Shadow of Illness: Parents and Siblings of the Chronically Ill Child* (Princeton, N.J.: Princeton University Press, 1996), and, by Bluebond-Langner, "Worlds of Dying Children and Their Well Siblings," *Death Studies* 13, no. 1 (1989): 1–16; John Graham-Pole, Hannelore Wass, Sheila Eyberg, and Luis Chu, "Communicating with Dying Children and Their Siblings: A Retrospective Analysis," *Death Studies* 13, no. 5 (1989): 465–483. See also S. J. Bendor, "Preventing Psychosocial Impairment in Siblings of Terminally Ill Children," *Hospice Journal* 5 (1989): 151–163; and Linda K. Birenbaum and others, "The Response of Children to the Dying and Death of a Sibling," *Omega: Journal of Death and Dying* 20, no. 3 (1989–1990): 213–228.

42. This and the following anecdote from Gyulay, *The Dying Child,* pp. 17–18.

43. See Phyllis R. Silverman and J. William Worden, "Children's Understanding of Funeral Ritual," *Omega: Journal of Death and Dying* 25, no. 4 (1992): 319–331.

44. See Elizabeth P. Lamers, "Helping Children During Bereavement," in *A Challenge for Living,* ed. Corless, Germino, and Pittman, pp. 203–220.

45. Dana Cable, Laurel Cucchi, Faye Lopez, and Terry Martin, "Camp Jamie," *American Journal of Hospice and Palliative Care* 9, no. 5 (1992): 18–21.

46. *HUGS Fact Sheet.* For more information, contact HUGS (Help, Understanding, and Group Support for Hawaii's Seriously Ill Children and Their Families), 3636 Kilauea Avenue, Honolulu, HI 96816; tel. (800) 732-4846; www.hugslove.org.

47. *Loewen Children's Foundation: Supporting Hospice Care for Children,* brochure.

48. Lori S. Wiener and others, "National Telephone Support Groups: A New Avenue Toward Psychosocial Support for HIV-Infected Children and Their Families," *Social Work with Groups* 16, no. 3 (1993): 55–71.

49. Sunshine Foundation, 1041 Mill Creek Drive, Feasterville, PA 19052, Tel.: (215) 396-4770 or (800) 767-1976, www.sunshinefoundation.org; Starlight Children's Foundation International, 5900 Wilshire Blvd., Suite 2530, Los Angeles, CA 90036, Tel.: (323) 634-0080; www.starlight.org.

50. Erikson, *Childhood and Society,* p. 233.

CHAPTER 11

1. Charles W. Brice, "Mourning Throughout the Life Cycle," *American Journal of Psychoanalysis* 42, no. 4 (1982): 320–321; see also Kenneth J. Doka, "The Awareness of Mortality in Midlife: Implications for Later Life," *Gerontology Review* 2, no. 1 (1989): 19–28.

2. Erik H. Erikson, *The Life Cycle Completed: A Review* (New York: W. W. Norton, 1982), p. 67.

3. Laura S. Smart, "Parental Bereavement in Anglo American History," *Omega: Journal of Death and Dying* 28, no. 1 (1993–1994): 49–61; see also Nancy S. Jecker and Lawrence J. Schneiderman, "Is Dying Young Worse Than Dying Old?" *The Gerontologist* 34, no. 1 (1994): 66–72.

4. See Mildred J. Braun and Dale H. Berg, "Meaning Reconstruction in the Experience of Parental Bereavement," *Death Studies* 18, no. 2 (1994): 105–129; Brian DeVries, Rose Dalla Lana, and Vilma T. Falck, "Parental Bereavement over the Life Course: A Theoretical Intersection and Empirical Review," *Omega: Journal of Death and Dying* 29, no. 1 (1994): 47–69; and Harriett Sarnoff Schiff, *The Bereaved Parent* (New York: Crown, 1977).

5. Exhibition note, "Native Peoples," Glenbow Museum, Calgary, Alberta, Canada.

6. Dennis Klass, "Solace and Immortality: Bereaved Parents' Continuing Bond with Their Children," in *The Path Ahead: Readings in Death and Dying,* ed. Lynne Ann DeSpelder and Albert Lee Strickland (Mountain View, Calif.: Mayfield, 1995), pp. 246–259. See also Dennis Klass and Samuel J. Marwit, "Toward a Model of Parental Grief," *Omega: Journal of Death and Dying* 19 (1988–1989): 31–50.

7. Laura S. Smart, "The Marital Helping Relationship Following Pregnancy Loss and Infant Death," *Journal of Family Issues* 13, no. 1 (1992): 81–98.

8. Dennis Klass, *Parental Grief: Solace and Resolution* (New York: Springer, 1988).

9. Kathleen R. Gilbert, "Interactive Grief and Coping in the Marital Dyad," *Death Studies* 13, no. 6 (1989): 605–626.

10. See Cynthia Bach-Hughes and Judith Page-Lieberman, "Fathers Experiencing a Perinatal Loss," *Death Studies* 13, no. 6 (1989): 537–556; Judy Rollins Bohannon, "Grief Responses of Spouses Following the Death of a Child: A Longitudinal Study," *Omega: Journal of Death and Dying* 22, no. 2 (1990–1991): 109–121; Nancy Feeley and Laurie N. Gottlieb, "Parents' Coping and Communication Following Their Infant's Death," *Omega: Journal of Death and Dying* 19, no. 1 (1988–1989): 51–67; and Reiko Schwab, "Paternal and Maternal Coping with the Death of a Child," *Death Studies* 14, no. 5 (1990): 407–422.

11. "Fetal and Infant Deaths," *Statistical Abstract of the United States: 1999,* 119th ed. (Washington, D.C.: Government Printing Office, 1999), p. 97.

12. See Susan Borg and Judith Lasker, *When Pregnancy Fails* (Boston: Beacon Press, 1981); Rochelle Friedman and Bonnie Gradstein, *Surviving Pregnancy Loss* (Boston: Little, Brown, 1982); Hettie J. E. M. Janssen, Marian C. J. Cuisinier, and Kees A. L. Hoogduin, "A Critical Review of the Concept of Pathological Grief Following Pregnancy Loss," *Omega: Journal of Death and Dying* 33, no. 1 (1996): 21–42; J. A. Menke and R. E. McClead, "Perinatal Grief and Mourning," *Advances in Pediatrics* 37 (1990): 261–283; Philip G. Ney and others, "The Effects of Pregnancy Loss on Women's Health," *Social Science & Medicine* 38, no. 9 (1994): 1193–1200; and Anne C. Smith and Sherry B. Borgers, "Parental Grief Response to Perinatal Death," *Omega: Journal of Death and Dying* 19, no. 3 (1988–1989): 203–214.

13. *Dorland's Illustrated Medical Dictionary,* 26th ed. (Philadelphia: Saunders, 1985), p. 828.

14. Ellen Fish Lietar, "Miscarriage," in *Parental Loss of a Child,* ed. Therese A. Rando (Champaign, Ill.: Research Press, 1986), p. 122.

15. *Dorland's Illustrated Medical Dictionary,* 26th ed., pp. 664, 1251.

16. Peter Wingate, *The Penguin Medical Encyclopedia,* 2d ed. (New York: Penguin, 1976), p. 177; see also Gay Becker, "Metaphors in Disrupted Lives: Infertility and

Cultural Constructions of Continuity," *Medical Anthropology Quarterly* 8, no. 4 (1994): 383–410; and Gay Becker and Robert D. Nachtigall, "'Born to Be a Mother': The Cultural Construction of Risk in Infertility Treatment in the U.S.," *Social Science & Medicine* 39, no. 4 (1994): 507–518.

17. Leverett Millen and Samuel Roll, "Solomon's Mothers: A Special Case of Pathological Bereavement," *American Journal of Orthopsychiatry* 55, no. 3 (1985): 411–418.

18. See Phyllis R. Silverman, Lee Campbell, Patricia Patti, and Carolyn Briggs Style, "Reunions Between Adoptees and Birth Parents: The Birth Parents' Experience," *Social Work* 33, no. 6 (1988): 523–528; and, by Silverman, Patti, and Campbell, "Reunions Between Adoptees and Birth Parents: The Adoptive Parents' View," *Social Work* 39, no. 5 (1994): 542–548.

19. Glen W. Davidson, "Death of a Wished-for Child: A Case Study," *Death Education* 1, no. 3 (1977): 265–275.

20. Judith A. Savage, *Mourning Unlived Lives: A Psychological Study of Childbearing Loss* (Wilmette, Ill.: Chiron Publications, 1989).

21. Ibid., p. xiii.

22. Irwin J. Weinfeld, "An Expanded Perinatal Bereavement Support Committee: A Community-Wide Resource," *Death Studies* 14, no. 3 (1990): 241–252.

23. Irving G. Leon, "Perinatal Loss: Choreographing Grief on the Obstetric Unit," *American Journal of Orthopsychiatry* 62, no. 1 (1992): 7–8.

24. "Pregnancies: Number and Outcome," *Statistical Abstract of the United States: 1999*, p. 87.

25. Larry G. Peppers, "Grief and Elective Abortion: Breaking the Emotional Bond?" *Omega: Journal of Death and Dying* 18, no. 1 (1987–1988): 1–12.

26. See William R. LaFleur, *Liquid Life: Abortion and Buddhism in Japan* (Princeton, N.J.: Princeton University Press, 1992); Marie Okabe, "Japan Shrine Honors Infants Never Born," *Los Angeles Times* (13 November 1982); and Tom Ashbrook, "Japanese Temples Exploit Superstitions of Abortion," *Honolulu Star-Bulletin & Advertiser* (13 October 1985).

27. Kenneth J. Doka, "Disenfranchised Grief" (paper presented at the annual meeting of the Association for Death Education and Counseling, Atlanta, Spring 1986); and, edited by Doka, *Disenfranchised Grief—Recognizing Hidden Sorrow* (Lexington, Mass.: Lexington Books, 1989). See also Charles A. Corr, "Enhancing the Concept of Disenfranchised Grief," *Omega: Journal of Death and Dying* 38, no. 1 (1998): 1–20.

28. John DeFrain and others, "The Psychological Effects of a Stillbirth on Surviving Family Members," *Omega: Journal of Death and Dying* 22, no. 2 (1990–1991): 81–108; see also John DeFrain, "Learning About Grief from Normal Families: SIDS, Stillbirth, and Miscarriage," *Journal of Marital and Family Therapy* 17, no. 3 (1991): 215–232.

29. Jay Ruby, "Portraying the Dead," *Omega: Journal of Death and Dying* 19, no. 1 (1988–1989): 1–20; and Joy Johnson and S. Marvin Johnson, with James H. Cunningham and Irwin J. Weinfeld, *A Most Important Picture: A Very Tender Manual for Taking Pictures of Stillborn Babies and Infants Who Die* (Omaha: Centering Corp., 1985).

30. DeFrain and others, "Psychological Effects of a Stillbirth," p. 87.

31. Mark H. Beers and Robert Berkow, eds., *The Merck Manual of Diagnosis and Therapy*, 17th ed. (Whitehouse Station, N.J.: Merck Research Laboratories, 1999), p. 2196.

32. Ibid.

33. Claire J. Hutton and Benjamin Sylvester Bradley, "Effects of Sudden Infant Death on Bereaved Siblings: A Comparative Study," *Journal of Child Psychology and Psychiatry* 35, no. 4 (1994): 723–732.

34. Rebecca Zacks, "Sinister Science," *Scientific American* 277, no. 5 (November 1997): 118–119; see also Richard Firstman and Jamie Talan, *The Death of Innocents: A True Story of Murder, Medicine, and High-Stakes Science* (New York: Bantam, 1997).

35. Beverly Raphael, *The Anatomy of Bereavement* (New York: Basic Books, 1983), p. 229.

36. "Deaths and Death Rates for the 10 Leading Causes of Death in Specified Age Groups: United States, 1998," *Deaths: Final Data for 1998* (Hyattsville, Md.: National Center for Health Statistics, 2000), p. 26.

37. Committee on Trauma Research, National Research Council, *Injury in America: A Continuing Public Health Problem* (Washington, D.C.: National Academy Press, 1985).

38. Jerome L. Schulman, *Coping with Tragedy: Successfully Facing the Problem of a Seriously Ill Child* (Chicago: Follett, 1976), p. 335.

39. Victor Florian, "Meaning and Purpose in Life of Bereaved Parents Whose Son Fell During Active Military Service," *Omega: Journal of Death and Dying* 20, no. 2 (1989–1990): 91–102.

40. Kay Talbot, "Mothers Now Childless: Survival After the Death of an Only Child," *Omega: Journal of Death and Dying* 34, no. 3 (1996–1997): 177–189.

41. Inese Wheeler, "The Role of Meaning and Purpose in Life in Bereaved Parents Associated with a Self-Help Group: Compassionate Friends," *Omega: Journal of Death and Dying* 28, no. 4 (1994): 261–271.

42. Gordon Riches and Pam Dawson, "Communities of Feeling: The Culture of Bereaved Parents," *Mortality* 1, no. 2 (1996): 143–161.

43. Joan Delahanty Douglas, "Patterns of Change Following Parent Death in Midlife Adults," *Omega: Journal of Death and Dying* 22, no. 2 (1990–1991): 123–137; see also Rachel A. Pruchno and others, "Death of an Institutionalized Parent: Predictors of Bereavement," *Omega: Journal of Death and Dying* 31, no. 2 (1995): 99–119.

44. Marion Osterweis, Fredric Solomon, and Morris Green, eds. *Bereavement: Reactions, Consequences, and Care* (Washington: National Academy Press, 1984), p. 85; see also Andrew E. Scharlach and Karen I. Fredriksen, "Reactions to the Death of a Parent During Midlife," *Omega: Journal of Death and Dying* 27, no. 4 (1993): 307–319.

45. Miriam S. Moss, Sidney Z. Moss, Robert Rubinstein, and Nancy Resch, "Impact of Elderly Mother's Death on Middle Aged Daughters," *International Journal of Aging and Human Development* 37, no. 1 (1992–1993): 1–22; see also Jennifer Klapper, Sidney Moss, Miriam Moss, and Robert L. Rubinstein, "The Social Context of Grief Among Adult Daughters Who Have Lost a Parent," *Journal of Aging Studies* 8, no. 1 (1994): 29–43. On men's grief in response to the death of a father, see Sidney Z. Moss, Robert L. Rubinstein, and Miriam S. Moss, "Middle-Aged Son's Reactions to Father's Death," *Omega: Journal of Death and Dying* 34, no. 4 (1996–1997): 259–277.

46. Pruchno and others, "Death of an Institutionalized Parent."

47. Debra Umberson and Meichu D. Chen, "Effects of a Parent's Death on Adult Children: Relationship Salience and Reaction to Loss," *American Sociological Review* 59, no. 1 (1994): 152–168.

48. Raphael, *Anatomy of Bereavement,* p. 177.

49. Savine Gross Weizman and Phyllis Kamm, *About Mourning: Support and Guidance for the Bereaved* (New York: Human Sciences, 1985), p. 130. For a personal account of spousal bereavement, see Jill Truman, *Letter to My Husband: Notes About Mourning and Recovery* (New York: Viking Penguin, 1987).

50. Winifred Gallagher, "Motherless Child," *The Sciences* (July–August 1992): 12–15.

51. Leon H. Levy, Karen S. Martinkowski, and Joyce F. Derby, "Differences in Patterns of Adaptation in Conjugal Bereavement: Their Sources and Potential Significance," *Omega: Journal of Death and Dying* 29, no. 1 (1994): 71–87; see also Ariela Lowenstein, Ruth Landau, and Aron Rosen, "Adjustment to Loss of Spouse As a Multivariate Construct," *Omega: Journal of Death and Dying* 28, no. 3 (1993–1994): 229–245; and Hans Sande, "Palestinian Martyr Widowhood: Emotional Needs in Conflict with Role Expectations?" *Social Science & Medicine* 34, no. 6 (1992): 709–717.

52. Notable studies include Colin Murray Parkes, "The Effects of Bereavement on Physical and Mental Health: A Study of Medical Records of Widows," *British Medical Journal* 1 (1964): 272–279, and "Recent Bereavement As a Cause of Mental Illness," *British Journal of Psychiatry* 110 (1964): 198–204, as well as *Bereavement: Studies of Grief in Adult Life* (New York: International Universities Press, 1972); Ira O. Glick, Robert S. Weiss, and Colin Murray Parkes, *The First Year of Bereavement* (New York: Wiley, 1974), and its follow-up by Colin Murray Parkes and Robert S. Weiss, *Recovery from Bereavement* (New York: Basic Books, 1983); Helena Z. Lopata, *Widowhood in an American City* (Cambridge, Mass.: Schenkman, 1973) and *Women As Widows: Support Systems* (New York: Elsevier, 1979); Paula J. Clayton, "Mortality and Morbidity in the First Year of Widowhood," *Archives of General Psychiatry* 125 (1974): 747–750, and "The Sequelae and Non-Sequelae of Conjugal Bereavement," *American Journal of Psychiatry* 136 (1979): 1530–1543; Herbert H. Hyman, *Of Time and Widowhood: Nationwide Studies of Enduring Effects* (Durham, N.C.: Duke University Press, 1983). See also Kate Mary Bennett, "Widowhood in Elderly Women: The Medium- and Long-Term Effects on Mental and Physical Health," *Mortality* 2, no. 2 (1997): 137–148.

53. Judith M. Stillion, *Death and the Sexes: An Examination of Differential Longevity, Attitudes, Behaviors, and Coping Skills* (Washington: Hemisphere, 1985).

54. "Marital Status of the Population," *Statistical Abstract of the United States: 1999,* p. 57.

55. See Dale A. Lund, Michael S. Caserta, Jan Van Pelt, and Kathleen A. Gass, "Stability of Social Support Networks After Later-Life Spousal Bereavement," *Death Studies* 14, no. 1 (1990): 53–73.

56. Ian Patterson and Gaylene Carpenter, "Participation in Leisure Activities After the Death of a Spouse," *Leisure Sciences* 16 (1994): 105–117; see also Karen A. Roberto and Pat Ianni Stanis, "Reactions of Older Women to the Death of Their Close Friends," *Omega: Journal of Death and Dying* 29, no. 1 (1994): 17–27.

57. David M. Bass and others, "Losing an Aged Relative: Perceptual Differences Between Spouses and Adult Children," *Omega: Journal of Death and Dying* 21, no. 1 (1990): 21–40.

58. Kemi Adamolekun, "In-Laws Behavior As a Social Factor in Subsequent Temporary Upsurges of Grief in Western Nigeria," *Omega: Journal of Death and Dying* 31, no. 1 (1995): 23–34.

59. See Phyllis R. Silverman, *Widow to Widow* (New York: Springer, 1986); and, also by Silverman, "Widowhood As the Next Stage in the Life Cycle," in *Widows: North America,* ed. Helena Z. Lopata (Durham, N.C.: Duke University Press, 1987); and "The Widow-to-Widow Program: An Experiment in Preventive Intervention," *Mental Hygiene* 53, no. 3 (1969), a landmark report by Silverman on her work at Harvard Medical School's Laboratory of Community Psychiatry. On mutual support, see also Molly Hill Folken, "Moderating Grief of Widowed People in Talk Groups," *Death Studies* 14, no. 2 (1990): 171–176.

60. Harold Ivan Smith, *Friendgrief: An Absence Called Presence* (Amityville, N.Y.: Baywood, 2000).

61. See Sarah Greenberg and others, "Friendship Across the Life Cycle: A Support Group for Older Women," *Journal of Gerontological Social Work* 32, no. 4 (1999): 7–23.

62. See Stanley Brandes, *Forty: The Age and the Symbol* (Nashville: University of Tennessee Press, 1985).

63. Bernice L. Neugarten, "Growing As Long As We Live," *Second Opinion* 15 (November 1990): 42–51.

64. Robert M. Sapolsky and Caleb E. Finch, "On Growing Old," *The Sciences* 31 (March/April 1991): 30–38.

65. R. A. Hope and others, *Oxford Handbook of Clinical Medicine,* 3d ed. (Oxford: Oxford University Press, 1994), p. 64.

66. James F. Fries, Lawrence W. Green, and Sol Levine, "Health Promotion and the Compression of Morbidity," *Lancet* (4 March 1989): 481–483; see also, by Fries, "The Compression of Morbidity," *Milbank Memorial Fund Quarterly* 61 (1983): 397–419.

67. Iris Chi and James Lubben, "The California Preventive Health Care for the Aging Program: Differences Between the Younger Old and the Oldest Old," *Health Promotion International* 9, no. 3 (1994): 169–176; see also "Patterns of Aging: A Special Report," *Science* 273 (5 July 1996): 41–79; and Mark Snyder and Peter K. Miene, "Stereotyping of the Elderly: A Functional Approach," *British Journal of Social Psychology* 33 (1994): 63–82.

68. Neugarten, "Growing As Long As We Live."

69. Sandra L. Bertman, "Aging Grace: Treatment of the Aged in the Arts," *Death Studies* 13, no. 6 (1989): 517–535. See also Pamela T. Amoss and Steven Harrell, eds., *Other Ways of Growing Old: Anthropological Perspectives* (Palo Alto, Calif.: Stanford University Press, 1981); and M. Powell Lawton, Miriam Moss, and Allen Glicksman, "The Quality of the Last Year of Life of Older Persons," *Milbank Quarterly* 68 (1990): 1–28.

70. Daniel Callahan, "Can Old Age Be Given a Public Meaning?" *Second Opinion* 15 (November 1990): 12–23.

71. Jane W. Peterson, "Age of Wisdom: Elderly Black Women in Family and Church," in *The Cultural Context of Aging: Worldwide Perspectives,* ed. Jay Sokolovsky (New York: Bergin & Garvey, 1990), pp. 213–227.

72. See, for example, Cesare Marino, "Honor the Elders: Symbolic Associations with Old Age in Traditional Eastern Cherokee Culture," *Journal of Cherokee Studies* 13 (1988): 3–18.

73. Robert N. Butler, *Why Survive? Being Old in America* (New York: Harper and Row, 1975).

74. Butler, *Why Survive? Being Old in America*; see also Robert Kastenbaum, "Exit and Existence: Society's Unwritten Script for Old Age and Death," in *Aging, Death, and the Completion of Being,* ed. David D. Van Tassel (Philadelphia: University of Pennsylvania Press, 1979), pp. 69–94.

CHAPTER 12

1 Judith M. Stillion, "Premature Exits: Understanding Suicide," in *The Path Ahead: Readings in Death and Dying,* ed. Lynne Ann DeSpelder and Albert Lee Strickland (Mountain View, Calif.: Mayfield, 1995), pp. 182–197.

2. "Suicides by Race, Age, and Method," *Statistical Abstract of the United States: 1999,* 119th ed. (Washington, D.C.: Government Printing Office, 1999), p. 108.

3. Mark H. Beers and Robert Berkow, eds., *The Merck Manual of Diagnosis and Therapy,* 17th ed. (Whitehouse Station, N.J.: Merck Research Laboratories, 1999), p. 1545.

4. Glen Evans and Norman L. Farberow, *The Encyclopedia of Suicide* (New York: Facts on File, 1988), p. 268.

5. Edwin S. Shneidman, "Suicide," in *Death: Current Perspectives,* 2d ed., ed. Shneidman (Mountain View, Calif.: Mayfield, 1980), p. 432.

6. James R. P. Ogloff and Randy K. Otto, "Psychological Autopsy: Clinical and Legal Perspectives," *Saint Louis University Law Journal* 37, no. 3 (Spring 1993): 607–646. See also Edwin S. Shneidman, *Clues to Suicide* (New York: McGraw-Hill, 1957); and, by Avery D. Weisman, *The Psychological Autopsy* (New York: Human Sciences Press, 1968) and *The Realization of Death: A Guide for the Psychological Autopsy* (Northvale, N.J.: Aronson, 1974).

7. Thomas J. Young, "Procedures and Problems in Conducting a Psychological Autopsy," *International Journal of Offender Therapy and Comparative Criminology* 36, no. 1 (Spring 1992): 43–52.

8. See Norman Poythress and others, "APA's Expert Panel in the Congressional Review of the USS 'Iowa' Incident," *American Psychologist* 48, no. 1 (January 1993): 8–15; Randy K. Otto and others, "An Empirical Study of the Reports of APA's Peer Review Panel in the Congressional Review of the U.S.S. IOWA Incident," *Journal of Personality Assessment* 61, no. 3 (December 1993): 425–442; and Ogloff and Otto, "Psychological Autopsy: Clinical and Legal Perspectives."

9. Quoted material from Poythress and others, "APA's Expert Panel."

10. David A. Brent, "The Psychological Autopsy: Methodological Considerations for the Study of Adolescent Suicide," *Suicide and Life-Threatening Behavior* 19 (Spring 1989): 43–57. See also David Shaffer, "The Epidemiology of Teen Suicide: An Examination of Risk Factors," *Journal of Clinical Psychiatry* 49 (September 1988): Supplement, 36–41; and Mohammad Shafi and others, "Psychological Autopsy of Completed Suicide in Children and Adolescents," *American Journal of Psychiatry* 142 (1985): 1061–1064.

11. Emile Durkheim, *Suicide: A Study in Sociology* (New York: Free Press, 1951).

12. E. Hunter, "Using a Socio-Historical Frame to Analyze Aboriginal Self-Destructive Behavior," *Australian and New Zealand Journal of Psychiatry* 24 (1990): 191–198.

13. Durkheim, *Suicide,* p. 209.

14. Jack Seward, *Hara-Kiri: Japanese Ritual Suicide* (Rutland, Vt.: Charles E. Tuttle, 1968). See also Robert Jay Lifton, Shuichi Kato, and Michael R. Reich, *Six Lives, Six Deaths: Portraits from Modern Japan* (New Haven, Conn.: Yale University Press, 1979).

15. See Charles R. Chandler and Yung-Mei Tsai, "Suicide in Japan and the West: Evidence for Durkheim's Theory," *International Journal of Comparative Sociology* 34, nos. 3–4 (1993): 244–259.

16. Norman Farberow, "The History of Suicide," in Evans and Farberow, *Encyclopedia of Suicide,* p. viii.

17. See David Chidester, *Salvation and Suicide: An Interpretation of Jim Jones, the Peoples Temple, and Jonestown* (Bloomington: Indiana University Press, 1988); Jose I. Lasaga, "Death in Jonestown: Techniques of Political Control by a Paranoid Leader," *Suicide and Life-Threatening Behavior* 10, no. 4 (1980): 210–213; and Richard H. Seiden, "Reverend Jones on Suicide," *Suicide and Life-Threatening Behavior* 9, no. 2 (1979): 116–119.

18. See Herbert Hendin, "The Psychodynamics of Suicide," *International Review of Psychiatry* 4 (1992): 157–167.

19. Erwin Stengel, "A Matter of Communication," in *On the Nature of Suicide,* ed. Edwin S. Shneidman (San Francisco: Jossey-Bass, 1969), pp. 78–79.

20. Edwin S. Shneidman, "Suicide As Psychache," *Journal of Nervous and Mental Disease* 181, no. 3 (1993): 147–149, and "Some Controversies in Suicidology: Toward a Mentalistic Discipline," *Suicide and Life-Threatening Behavior* 23, no. 4 (1993): 292–298. See also Michael J. Kral, "Suicide As Social Logic," *Suicide and Life-Threatening Behavior* 24, no. 3 (1994): 245–255.

21. See Peter M. Marzuk, "Suicide and Terminal Illness," *Death Studies* 18, no. 5 (1994): 497–512.

22. See Nancy L. Beckerman, "Suicide in Relation to AIDS," *Death Studies* 19, no. 3 (1995): 223–234; and James L. Werth, Jr., "Rational Suicide Reconsidered: AIDS As an Impetus for Change," *Death Studies* 19, no. 1 (1995): 65–80.

23. Roy F. Baumeister, "Suicide As Escape from Self," *Psychological Review* 97 (1990): 90–113.

24. G. D. Tollefson, "Recognition and Treatment of Major Depression," *American Family Physician* 41 (1990): Supplement, 59–66; and A. T. Davis and C. Schrueder, "The Prediction of Suicide," *Medical Journal of Australia* 153 (1990): 552–554.

25. Gabor I. Keitner and Ivan W. Miller, "Family Functioning and Major Depression: An Overview," *American Journal of Psychiatry* 147 (1990): 1128–1137.

26. Edwin S. Shneidman, *Deaths of Man* (New York: Quadrangle Books, 1973), pp. 81–90.

27. M. A. Fine and R. A. Sansone, "Dilemmas in the Management of Suicidal Behavior in Individuals with Borderline Personality Disorder," *American Journal of Psychotherapy* 44 (1990): 160–171.

28. Evans and Farberow, *Encyclopedia of Suicide,* p. 21.

29. Ronald W. Maris, *Pathways to Suicide: A Survey of Self-Destructive Behaviors* (Baltimore: Johns Hopkins University Press, 1981), and *Understanding and Preventing Suicide* (New York: Guilford Press, 1988).

30. David Lester, "The Study of Suicide from a Feminist Perspective," *Crisis* 11 (May 1990): 38–43.

31. Judith M. Stillion, Eugene E. McDowell, and Jacque H. May, *Suicide Across the Life Span: Premature Exits* (New York: Hemisphere, 1989), p. 69. See also Silvia Sara Canetto, "She Died for Love and He for Glory: Gender Myths of Suicidal Behavior," *Omega: Journal of Death and Dying* 26, no. 1 (1992–1993): 1–17; and, also by Canetto, "Gender Issues in the Treatment of Suicidal Individuals," *Death Studies* 18, no. 5 (1994): 513–527; James Overholser, Steven Evans, and Anthony Spirito, "Sex Differences and Their Relevance to Primary Prevention of Adolescent Suicide," *Death Studies* 14, no. 4 (1990): 391–402;

32. Caryn Levington and Frank P. Gruba-McCallister, "Survival of Suicide As an Opportunity for Transcendence," *Journal of Humanistic Psychology* 33, no. 4 (1993): 75–88.

33. See Ellen Ingram and Jon B. Ellis, "Situational Analysis of Attitudes Toward Suicide Behavior," *Death Studies* 19, no. 3 (1995): 269–275; and, in the same issue, Lillian M. Range and Jerry R. Alliston, "Reacting to AIDS-Related Suicide: Does Time Since Diagnosis Matter?" pp. 277–282.

34. Philip A. May and Nancy Westlake Van Winkle, "Durkheim's Suicide Theory and Its Applicability to Contemporary American Indians and Alaska Natives," in *Emile Durkheim: Le Suicide 100 Years Later,* ed. David Lester (Philadelphia: Charles Press, 1994); see also Nancy Westlake Van Winkle and Philip A. May, "Native American Suicide in New Mexico: 1957–1979: A Comparative Study," *Human Organization* 45, no. 4 (1986): 296–309; and "An Update on American Indian Suicide in New Mexico, 1980–1987," *Human Organization* 52, no. 3 (1993): 304–315.

35. Kathleen Erwin, "Interpreting the Evidence: Competing Paradigms and the Emergence of Lesbian and Gay Suicide As a 'Social Fact,'" in *The Path Ahead*, ed. DeSpelder and Strickland, pp. 211–220.

36. Kevin E. Early and Ronald L. Akers, "'It's a White Thing'—An Exploration of Beliefs About Suicide in the African-American Community," in *The Path Ahead*, ed. DeSpelder and Strickland, pp. 198–210.

37. "Suicide Rates Up Among Young," *Associated Press Online* (20 April 1995).

38. Richard H. Seiden and Raymond P. Freitas, "Shifting Patterns of Deadly Violence," *Suicide and Life-Threatening Behavior* 10, no. 4 (Winter 1980): 209.

39. G. Sonneck, E. Etzersdorfer, and S. Nagel-Kuess, "Imitative Suicide on the Viennese Subway," *Social Science & Medicine* 38, no. 3 (1994): 453–457.

40. Brian Barry, "Suicide: The Ultimate Escape," *Death Studies* 13, no. 2 (1989): 185–190.

41. Jack D. Douglas, "Suicide," *Academic American Encyclopedia* on-line (March 1991).

42. Israel Orbach and others, "Fears of Death in Suicidal and Nonsuicidal Adolescents," *Journal of Abnormal Psychology* 102, no. 4 (1993): 553–558.

43. See Alfred Alvarez, *The Savage God: A Study of Suicide* (New York: Random House, 1971).

44. See, for example, Herbert Hendin, "The Suicide of Anne Sexton," *Suicide and Life-Threatening Behavior* 23, no. 3 (1993): 257–262; and Jeff Giles, "The Poet of Alienation (Kurt Cobain)," *Newsweek* (18 April 1994), pp. 46–47.

45. Dalia M. Adams, James C. Overholser, and Anthony Spirito, "Stressful Life Events Associated with Adolescent Suicide Attempts," *Canadian Journal of Psychiatry* 39, no. 1 (1994): 43–48.

46. D. E. Ness and C. R. Pfeffer, "Sequelae of Bereavement Resulting from Suicide," *American Journal of Psychiatry* 147 (March 1990): 279–285.

47. Hee-Soon Juon, Jung Ja Nam, and Margaret E. Ensminger, "Epidemiology of Suicidal Behavior Among Korean Adolescents," *Journal of Child Psychology and Psychiatry* 35, no. 4 (1994): 663–676.

48. Donald H. Rubinstein, "Epidemic Suicide Among Micronesian Adolescents," *Social Science & Medicine* 17 (1983): 657–665, and "Suicide in Micronesia," in *Culture, Youth and Suicide in the Pacific: Papers from an East-West Center Conference*, ed. Francis X. Hezel, Donald H. Rubinstein, and Geoffrey M. White (Honolulu: Pacific Islands Study Program, University of Hawaii, 1985), pp. 88–111.

49. K. Y. Little and D. L. Sparks, "Brain Markers and Suicide: Can a Relationship Be Found?" *Journal of Forensic Science* 35 (1990): 1393–1403; J. J. Mann, V. Arango, and M. D. Underwood, "Serotonin and Suicidal Behavior," *Annals of the New York Academy of Science* 600 (1990): 476–484; Lorna Cameron Ricci and Mary M. Wellman, "Monoamines: Biochemical Markers of Suicide?" *Journal of Clinical Psychology* 46 (1990): 106–116; Alec Roy, "Recent Biologic Studies on Suicide," *Suicide and Life-Threatening Behavior* 24, no. 1 (1994): 10–14; Andrew Edmund Slaby, "Psychopharmacotherapy of Suicide," *Death Studies* 18, no. 5 (1994): 483–495; and Michael Stanley and Barbara Stanley, "Postmortem Evidence for Serotonin's Role in Suicide," *Journal of Clinical Psychiatry* 51 (April 1990): Supplement, 22–28.

50. David A. Nielsen and others, "Suicidality and 5-Hydroxyindoleacetic Acid Concentration Associated with a Tryptophan Hydroxylase Polymorphism," *Archives of General Psychiatry* 51 (1994): 34–38.

51. "Suicides by Race, Age, and Method," *Statistical Abstract of the United States: 1999*, p. 108.

52. Cynthia R. Pfeffer and others, "Suicidal Children Grow Up: Suicidal Episodes and Effects of Treatment During Follow-Up," *Journal of the American Academy of Child and Adolescent Psychiatry* 33, no. 2 (1994): 225–230.

53. See Brian L. Mishara, "Conceptions of Death and Suicide in Children Ages 6–12 and Their Implications for Suicide Prevention," *Suicide and Life-Threatening Behavior* 29, no. 2 (1999): 105–118.

54. C. J. Lennings, "A Cognitive Understanding of Adolescent Suicide," *Genetic, Social, and General Psychology Monographs* 120, no. 3 (1994): 289–307.

55. "Deaths by Age and Leading Cause," *Statistical Abstract of the United States: 1999*, p. 102.

56. René F. W. Diekstra, "Suicidal Behavior and Depressive Disorders in Adolescents and Young Adults," *Neuropsychobiology* 22 (1989): 194–207.

57. C. Raymond Bingham and others, "An Analysis of Age, Gender, and Racial Differences in Recent National Trends of Youth Suicide," *Journal of Adolescence* 17 (1994): 53–71.

58. S. J. Blumenthal, "Youth Suicide: Risk Factors, Assessment, and Treatment of Adolescent and Young Adult Suicidal Patients," *Psychiatric Clinics of North America* 13 (1990): 511–556.

59. David A. Brent and others, "Stressful Life Events: Psychopathology and Adolescent Suicide: A Case Control Study," *Suicide and Life-Threatening Behavior* 23, no. 3 (1993): 179–187, and "Personality Disorder, Personality Traits, Impulsive Violence, and Completed Suicide in Adolescents," *Journal of the American Academy of Child and Adolescent Psychiatry* 33, no. 8 (1994): 1080–1086.

60. See, for example, David A. Brent and others, "Familiar Risk Factors for Adolescent Suicide: A Case-Control Study," *Acta Psychiatrica Scandinavica* 89 (1994): 52–58; E. J. De Wilde and others, "Social Support, Life Events, and Behavioral Characteristics of Psychologically Distressed Adolescents at High Risk for Attempting Suicide," *Adolescence* 29 (Spring 1994): 49–60; Mauri J. Marttunen and others, "Precipitant Stressors in Adolescent Suicide," *Journal of the American Academy of Child and Adolescent Psychiatry* 32, no. 6 (1993): 1178–1183; Christopher D. Morano and others, "Risk Factors for Adolescent Suicidal Behavior: Loss, Insufficient Familial Support, and Hopelessness," *Adolescence* 28 (Winter 1993): 851–865; and Mary B. Summerville and others, "Psychopathology, Family Functioning, and Cognitive Style in Urban Adolescents with Suicide Attempts," *Journal of Abnormal Child Psychology* 22, no. 2 (1994): 221–235.

61. Herbert Hendin, "Psychodynamics of Suicide, with Particular Reference to the Young," *American Journal of Psychiatry* 148, no. 9 (1991): 1150–1158.

62. O. G. Bukstein and others, "Risk Factors for Completed Suicide Among Adolescents with a Lifetime History of Substance Abuse: A Case-Control Study," *Acta Psychiatrica Scandanavica* 88 (1993): 403–408; and Frank E. Crumley, "Substance Abuse and Adolescent Suicidal Behavior," *Journal of the American Medical Association* 263 (1990): 3051–3056.

63. Paulina F. Kernberg, "Psychological Interventions for the Suicidal Adolescent," *American Journal of Psychotherapy* 48, no. 1 (1994): 52–63.

64. Lennings, "A Cognitive Understanding of Adolescent Suicide."

65. Philip Hazell, "Adolescent Suicide Clusters: Evidence, Mechanisms, and Prevention," *Australian and New Zealand Journal of Psychiatry* 27 (1993): 653–665; and M. S. Gould, S. Wallenstein, and L. Davidson, "Suicide Clusters: A Critical Review," *Suicide and Life-Threatening Behavior* 19 (Spring 1989): 17–29.

66. Rick Weis, "Teen Suicide Clusters: More Than Mimicry," *Science News* 136 (25 November 1989): 342.

67. See R. Milin and A. Turgay, "Adolescent Couple Suicide: Literature Review," *Canadian Journal of Psychiatry* 35 (March 1990): 183–186. Examples cited by Evans and Farberow, *Encyclopedia of Suicide,* pp. 26–27, 72, 254.

68. Bruce L. Danto, Mark L. Taff, and Lauren R. Boglioli, "Graveside Deaths," *Omega: Journal of Death and Dying* 33, no. 4 (1996): 265–278.

69. See Paul L. Hewitt, Gordon L. Flett, and Cathy Weber, "Dimensions of Perfectionism and Suicide Ideation," *Cognitive Therapy and Research* 18, no. 5 (1994): 439–460.

70. B. P. Low and S. F. Andrews, "Adolescent Suicide," *Medical Clinics of North America* 74 (1990): 1251–1264.

71. James Janik and Howard M. Kravitz, "Linking Work and Domestic Problems," *Suicide and Life-Threatening Behavior* 24, no. 3 (1994): 267–274.

72. On differences in suicide rates between elderly men and women, see Silvia Sara Canetto, "Elderly Women and Suicidal Behavior," in *Women and Suicidal Behavior,* eds. Silvia Sara Canetto and David Lester (New York: Springer, 1995), pp. 215–233.

73. Brian Draper, "Suicidal Behavior in the Elderly," *International Journal of Geriatric Psychiatry* 9 (1994): 655–661.

74. Susanne S. Carney and others, "Suicide over 60: The San Diego Study," *Journal of the American Geriatrics Society* 42 (1994): 174–180.

75. J. Conrad Glass, Jr., and Susan E. Reed, "To Live or Die: A Look at Elderly Suicide," *Educational Gerontology* 19 (1993): 767–778.

76. Stillion and others, *Suicide Across the Life Span,* pp. 180–181.

77. Antoon A. Leenaars and David Lester, "The Significance of the Method Chosen for Suicide in Understanding the Psychodynamics of the Suicidal Individual," *Omega: Journal of Death and Dying* 19, no. 4 (1988–1989): 311–314.

78. Edwin S. Shneidman, "Self-Destruction: Suicide Notes and Tragic Lives," in *Death: Current Perspectives,* 2d ed., ed. Shneidman, p. 467; and, by Shneidman, "A Bibliography of Suicide Notes: 1856–1979," in *Suicide and Life-Threatening Behavior* 9, no. 1 (Spring 1979): 57–59.

79. Stephen T. Black, "Comparing Genuine and Simulated Suicide Notes: A New Perspective," *Journal of Consulting and Clinical Psychology* 61, no. 4 (1993): 699–702.

80. Evans and Farberow, *Encyclopedia of Suicide,* p. 187.

81. Stillion and others, *Suicide Across the Life Span,* p. 13.

82. See C. James Frankish, "Crisis Centers and Their Role in Treatment: Suicide Prevention Versus Health Promotion," *Death Studies* 18, no. 4 (1994): 327–339.

83. See David Lester, "Challenges in Preventing Suicide," *Death Studies* 18, no. 6 (1994): 623–639.

84. Stillion and others, *Suicide Across the Life Span,* p. 194.

85. Stanley Beardy and Margaret Beardy, "Healing Native Communities Through 'Helping Hands'" (paper presented at the annual meeting of the Association for Death Education and Counseling, Duluth, Minnesota, April 1991).

86. Patrick W. O'Carroll, Morton M. Silverman, and Alan L. Berman, "Community Suicide Prevention: The Effectiveness of Bridge Barriers," *Suicide and Life-Threatening Behavior* 24, no. 1 (Spring 1994): 89–99.

87. Antoon A. Leenaars, "Crisis Intervention with Highly Lethal Suicidal People," *Death Studies* 18, no. 4 (1994): 341–360. See also, in the same issue, Alan L. Berman and David A. Jobes, "Treatment of the Suicidal Adolescent," pp. 375–389.

88. Philip Hazell and Terry Lewin, "An Evaluation of Postvention Following Adolescent Suicide," *Suicide and Life-Threatening Behavior* 23, no. 2 (1993): 101–109.

89. See Charles P. McDowell, Joseph M. Rothberg, and Ronald J. Koshes, "Witnessed Suicides," *Suicide and Life-Threatening Behavior* 24, no, 3 (1994): 213–223.

90. Richard Farmer, Ian O'Donnell, and Troy Tranah, "Suicide on the London Underground System," *International Journal of Epidemiology* 20, no. 3 (1991): 707–711; I. O'Donnell and R. D. T. Farmer, "Suicidal Acts on Metro Systems: An International Perspective," *Acta Psychiatrica Scandinavica* 86 (1992): 60–63; and A. Schmidtke, "Suicidal Behavior on Railways in the FRG," *Social Science & Medicine* 38, no. 3 (1994): 419–426.

91. Richard Farmer and others, "Railway Suicide: The Psychological Effects on Drivers," *Psychological Medicine* 22 (1992): 407–414; and T. Tranah and R. D. T. Farmer, "Psychological Reactions of Drivers to Railway Suicide," *Social Science & Medicine* 38, no. 3 (1994): 459–469.

92. Evans and Farberow, *Encyclopedia of Suicide,* pp. 58–59, 63.

93. Jack D. Douglas, *The Social Meanings of Suicide* (Princeton, N.J.: Princeton University Press, 1967), pp. 324ff.

94. Stillion and others, *Suicide Across the Life Span,* p. 24.

CHAPTER 13

1 From *Letters of E. B. White,* collected and edited by Dorothy Lobrano Guth (New York: Harper and Row, 1976), p. 558.

2. See Harvey M. Sapolsky, "The Politics of Risk," *Daedalus: Journal of the American Academy of Arts and Sciences* 119 (Fall 1990): 83–96.

3. See, for example, Robert J. Homant, Daniel B. Kennedy, and Jimmy D. Howton, "Risk Taking and Police Pursuit," *Journal of Social Psychology* 134, no. 2 (1994): 213–221.

4. See Frederica P. Perera, "Uncovering New Clues to Cancer Risk," *Scientific American* 274, no. 5 (May 1996): 54–62.

5. Kevin Young, "Violence, Risk, and Liability in Male Sports Culture," *Sociology of Sport Journal* 10 (1993): 373–396.

6. Kawahito Hiroshi, "Death and the Corporate Warrior," *Japan Quarterly* 38 (April–June 1991): 149–157.

7. James A. Thorson and F. C. Powell, "To Laugh in the Face of Death: The Games That Lethal People Play," *Omega: Journal of Death and Dying* 21, no. 3 (1990): 225–239.

8. Kenneth J. Doka, Eric C. Schwartz, and Catherine Schwarz, "Risky Business: Reactions to Death in Hazardous Sports" (paper presented at the annual meeting of the Association for Death Education and Counseling, Atlanta, 1986); see also, by the same authors, "Risky Business: Observations on the Nature of Death in Hazardous Sports," *Omega: Journal of Death and Dying* 21, no. 3 (1990): 215–223.

9. Ira Dreyfuss, "How Boys and Girls See Risk," *Associated Press Online* (17 February 1997). Studies cited were conducted by psychology professors Barbara Morrongiello of the University of Guelph in Ontario and Licette Peterson of the University of Missouri.

10. Michael C. Roberts, "Prevention/Promotion in America: Still Spitting on the Sidewalk (Lee Salk Distinguished Service Award Address)," *Journal of Pediatric Psychology* 19, no. 3 (June 1994): 267–281.

11. Robert Kastenbaum and Ruth Aisenberg, *The Psychology of Death: Concise Edition* (New York: Springer, 1976), p. 319. See also K. David Pijawka, Beverly A. Cuthbertson, and Richard S. Olson, "Coping with Extreme Hazard Events: Emerging Themes in Natural and Technological Disaster Research," *Omega: Journal of Death and Dying* 18, no. 4 (1987–1988): 281–297.

12. See "The Explosions That Shook the World" (Special Report, Chernobyl: 10 Years After), *Science* 272 (19 April 1996): 352–360; and Yuri M. Scherbak, "Ten Years of the Chornobyl Era," *Scientific American* 274, no. 4 (April 1996): 44–49.

13. Charles Perrow, *Normal Accidents: Living with High Risk Technology* (New York: Basic Books, 1984).

14. Malcolm Gladwell, "Blowup," *New Yorker* (22 January 1996): 32–36.

15. "Japan Braces for Major Earthquake," *Associated Press Online* (1 September 1997).

16. Robert I. Tilling, U.S. Geological Survey, *Eruptions of Mount St. Helens: Past, Present, and Future* (Washington, D.C.: Government Printing Office, n.d.).

17. See Gerard Fryer, "The Most Dangerous Wave," *The Sciences* 35, no. 4 (July–August 1995): 38–43.

18. Philip Sarre, "Natural Hazards," in *Key Ideas in Human Thought,* ed. Kenneth McLeish (New York: Facts on File, 1993), pp. 502–504.

19. See James W. Pennebaker and Kent D. Harber, "A Social Stage Model of Collective Coping: The Loma Prieta Earthquake and the Persian Gulf War," *Journal of Social Issues* 49, no. 4 (1993): 125–145; and Kathleen M. Wright and others, "The Shared Experience of Catastrophe: An Expanded Classification of the Disaster Community," *American Journal of Orthopsychiatry* 60, no. 1 (1990): 35–42.

20. Neil Thompson, "The Ontology of Disaster," *Death Studies* 19, no. 5 (1995): 501–510.

21. Gail Walker, "Crisis-Care in Critical Incident Debriefing," *Death Studies* 14, no. 2 (1990): 121–133.

22. Beverly McLeod, "In the Wake of Disaster," *Psychology Today* (October 1984), pp. 54–57.

23. "Murder Victims by Age, Sex, and Race," *Statistical Abstract of the United States: 1999,* 119th ed. (Washington, D.C.: Government Printing Office, 1999), p. 217.

24. "Murder—Circumstances and Weapons Used," *Statistical Abstract of the United States: 1999,* p. 217.

25. "'Vietnam Style' Triage Techniques Used to Treat Urban Assault Weapon Injuries," *Bulletin of the Park Ridge Center* (May 1989): 11–12. See also Wendy Max and Dorothy P. Rice, "Shooting in the Dark: Estimating the Cost of Firearm Injuries," *Health Affairs* 12, no. 4 (1993): 171–185.

26. See Ronald K. Barrett, "Urban Adolescent Homicidal Violence: An Emerging Public Health Concern," *Urban League Review* 16, no. 2 (1993): 67–75; Dewey G. Cornell, "Juvenile Homicide: A Growing National Problem," *Behavioral Sciences and the Law* 11 (1993): 389–396; Robert H. DuRant and others, "Factors Associated with the Use of Violence Among Urban Black Adolescents," *American Journal of Public Health* 84, no. 4 (1994): 612–617; and James A. Mercy, "Youth Violence As a Public Health Problem," *Spectrum* (Summer 1993): 26–30.

27. Tara Meyer, "Murder, Suicide Up for US Youth," *Associated Press Online* (6 February 1997). Based on data presented by Etienne Krug, medical epidemiologist at the U. S. Centers for Disease Control (CDC).

28. American Medical Association, Council on Scientific Affairs, "Firearms Injuries and Deaths: A Critical Public Health Issue," *Public Health Reports* 104 (1989): 111–120.

29. Ice T, "The Killing Fields," in *The Path Ahead: Readings in Death and Dying,* ed. Lynne Ann DeSpelder and Albert Lee Strickland (Mountain View, Calif.: Mayfield, 1995), pp. 178–181. See also John M. Hagedorn, "Homeboys, Dope Fiends, Legits, and New Jacks," *Criminology* 32, no. 2 (1994): 197–219; and Leland Ropp and others, "Death

in the City: An American Childhood Tragedy," *Journal of the American Medical Association* 267, no. 21 (1992): 2905–2910.

30. Ted Rohrlich and Fredric N. Tulsky, "Gang Killings Exceed 40% of L. A. Slayings," *Los Angeles Times* (5 December 1996): A1, A22–A23.

31. Bruce L. Danto, Mark L. Taff, and Lauren R. Boglioli, "Graveside Deaths," *Omega: Journal of Death and Dying* 33, no. 4 (1996): 265–278.

32. Mitch Albom, "Random Shooting Paralyzes Football Player," *Detroit Free Press* (28 December 1994): C1.

33. Hattie Ruttenberg, "The Limited Promise of Public Health Methodologies to Prevent Youth Violence," *The Yale Law Journal* 103, no. 7 (1994): 1885–1912.

34. "CDC: School a Hazardous Place," *Associated Press Online* (30 March 1995).

35. Charles M. Callahan and Frederick P. Rivara, "Urban High School Youth and Handguns: A School-Based Survey," *Journal of the American Medical Association* 267 (10 June 1992): 3038–3042; Arthur L. Kellerman, "Firearm-Related Violence: What We Don't Know Is Killing Us," *American Journal of Public Health* 84, no. 4 (1994): 541–542; and Daniel W. Webster, Patricia S. Gainer, and Howard R. Champion, "Weapon Carrying Among Inner-City Junior High School Students: Defensive Behavior vs. Aggressive Delinquency," *American Journal of Public Health* 83, no. 11 (1993): 1604–1608.

36. Quoted in Drew Leder, "Guns and Voices," *Second Opinion* 20, no. 2 (1994): 83–89.

37. Joseph D. Giuliano, "A Peer Education Program to Promote the Use of Conflict Resolution Skills Among At-Risk School Age Males," *Public Health Reports* 109, no. 2 (1994): 158–161.

38. Betsy McAlister Groves and others,"Silent Victims: Children Who Witness Violence," *Journal of the American Medical Association* 269, no. 2 (1993): 262–264. See also Sondra Burman and Paula Allen-Meares, "Neglected Victims of Murder: Children's Witness to Parental Homicide," *Social Work* 39, no. 1 (1994): 28–34; and Alice J. Hausman, Howard Spivak, and Deborah Prothrow-Stith, "Adolescents' Knowledge and Attitudes About and Experience with Violence," *Journal of Adolescent Health* 15 (1994): 400–406.

39. Larry Cohen and Susan Swift, "A Public Health Approach to the Violence Epidemic in the United States," *Environment and Urbanization* 5, no. 2 (1993): 50–66.

40. Dana D. DeHart and John M. Mahoney, "The Serial Murderer's Motivations: An Interdisciplinary Review," *Omega: Journal of Death and Dying* 29, no. 1 (1994): 29–45.

41. See Louis Menand, "The War of All Against All," *New Yorker* (14 March 1994), pp. 74–85.

42. Walter Laqueur, *The Age of Terrorism* (Boston: Little, Brown, 1987), p. 72.

43. Henry Lundsgaarde, *Murder in Space City: A Cultural Analysis of Houston Homicide Patterns* (New York: Oxford University Press, 1977).

44. Ted Rohrlich and Fredric N. Tulsky, "Not All L.A. Murder Cases Are Equal," *Los Angeles Times* (3 December 1995): A1, A14–A15.

45. See N. Prabha Unnithan, "The Processing of Homicide Cases with Child Victims: Systemic and Situational Contingencies," *Journal of Criminal Justice* 22, no. 1 (1994): 41–50, and "Children As Victims of Homicide: Making Claims, Formulating Categories, and Constructing Social Problems," *Deviant Behavior* 15, no. 1 (1994): 63–83.

46. Quoted in Kastenbaum and Aisenberg, *Psychology of Death,* pp. 269ff (italics in original).

47. Eric Felten, "The Death Penalty's Glass Ceiling," *Wall Street Journal* (24 January 1996): A15.

48. See Stanley Rothman and Stephen Powers, "Execution by Quota?" *The Public Interest* 116 (1994): 3–17.

49. "Movement of Prisoners Under Sentence of Death," *Statistical Abstract of the United States: 1999,* p. 234.

50. Herb Haines, "Flawed Executions, the Anti-Death Penalty Movement, and the Politics of Capital Punishment," *Social Problems* 39, no. 2 (1992): 125–138.

51. Glenn M. Vernon, *Sociology of Death: An Analysis of Death-Related Behavior* (New York: Ronald Press, 1970). See also Dennis J. Stevens, "The Death Sentence and Inmate Attitudes," *Crime & Delinquency* 38, no. 2 (1992): 272–279.

52. Hugo A. Bedau, "Capital Punishment," *Academic American Encyclopedia Online Edition* (March 1991).

53. Sally Costanzo and Mark Costanzo, "Life or Death Decisions: An Analysis of Capital Jury Decision Making Under the Special Issues Sentencing Framework," *Law and Human Behavior* 18, no. 2 (1994): 151–170. See also Robert M. Bohm and Ronald E. Vogel, "A Comparison of Factors Associated with Uninformed and Informed Death Penalty Opinions," *Journal of Criminal Justice* 22, no. 2 (1994): 125–143.

54. See Norman J. Finkel and others, "Killing Kids: the Juvenile Death Penalty and Community Sentiment," *Behavioral Sciences and the Law* 12 (1994): 5–20.

55. Robert M. Emerson, "Capital Trials and Representations of Violence," *Law & Society Review* 27, no. 1 (1993): 59–63.

56. Kastenbaum and Aisenberg, *Psychology of Death,* pp. 95–96, 284–285.

57. Lundsgaarde, *Murder in Space City,* p. 146.

58. Kastenbaum and Aisenberg, *Psychology of Death,* pp. 281–282.

59. Lula M. Redmond, *Surviving When Someone You Love Was Murdered: A Professional's Guide to Group Grief Therapy for Families and Friends of Murder Victims* (Clearwater, Fla.: Psychological Consultation and Education Services, 1989), p. 37. See also Charles Figley, *Helping Traumatized Families* (San Francisco: Jossey-Bass, 1989).

60. Robert J. Sampson, Stephen W. Raudenbush, and Felton Earls, "Neighborhoods and Violent Crime: A Multilevel Study of Collective Efficacy," *Science* 277 (15 August 1997): 918–923.

61. George B. Palermo and Douglas Simpson, "At the Roots of Violence: The Progressive Decline and Dissolution of the Family," *International Journal of Offender Therapy and Comparative Criminology* 38, no. 2 (1994): 105–116. See also George B. Palermo and others, "Modes of Defensive Behavior in a Violent Society," *International Journal of Offender Therapy and Comparative Criminology* 37, no. 3 (1993): 251–261.

62. Cohen and Swift, "A Public Health Approach to the Violence Epidemic in the United States."

63. Arnold Toynbee, "Death in War," in *Death and Dying: Challenge and Change,* ed. Robert Fulton and others (Reading, Mass.: Addison-Wesley, 1978), p. 367.

64. Dalton Trumbo, *Johnny Got His Gun* (New York: Bantam Books, 1970), pp. 214, 224.

65. Christie W. Kiefer, "Militarism and World Health," *Social Science & Medicine* 34, no. 7 (1992): 719–724.

66. Ervin Staub, *The Roots of Evil: The Origins of Genocide and Other Group Violence* (New York: Cambridge University Press, 1989). See also Norman Solkoff, "Children of Survivors of the Nazi Holocaust," *American Journal of Orthopsychiatry* 62, no. 3 (1992): 342–358.

67. Colin Murray Parkes, "Genocide in Rwanda: Personal Reflections," *Mortality* 1, no. 1 (1996): 95–110.

68. Gino Strada, "The Horror of Land Mines," *Scientific American* 274, no. 5 (May 1996): 40–45.

69. World Campaign for the Protection of Victims of War, International Red Cross and Red Crescent Movement. See also James Garbarino, "Challenges We Face in Understanding Children and War: A Personal Essay," in *The Path Ahead,* ed. DeSpelder and Strickland, pp. 169–174.

70. Sam Keen, *Faces of the Enemy: Reflections of the Hostile Imagination* (San Francisco: Harper and Row, 1986), p. 71.

71. Gil Elliot, "Agents of Death," in *Death: Current Perspectives,* ed. Edwin S. Shneidman, 3d ed. (Mountain View, Calif.: Mayfield, 1984), pp. 422–440.

72. Ibid.

73. Robert Jay Lifton and Eric Olson, *Living and Dying* (New York: Praeger, 1974), p. 32.

74. Vernon, *Sociology of Death,* p. 46.

75. Toynbee, "Death in War," p. 367.

76. Joel Baruch, "Combat Death," in *Death: Current Perspectives,* ed. Edwin S. Shneidman (Palo Alto, Calif.: Mayfield, 1976), pp. 92–93.

77. Personal communication.

78. See Harvey J. Schwartz, "Fear of the Dead: The Role of Social Ritual in Neutralizing Fantasies from Combat," in *Psychotherapy of the Combat Veteran,* ed. H. J. Schwartz (New York: SP Medical & Scientific Books, 1984), pp. 253–267. See also Robert Jay Lifton, *Home from the War: Vietnam Veterans, Neither Victims Nor Executioners* (New York: Basic Books, 1985).

79. Theodore Nadelson, "Attachment to Killing," *Journal of the American Academy of Psychoanalysis* 20, no. 1 (1992): 130–141.

80. See Harold A. Widdison and Howard G. Salisbury, "The Delayed Stress Syndrome: A Pathological Delayed Grief Reaction?" *Omega: Journal of Death and Dying* 20, no. 4 (1989–1990): 293–306.

81. Michael Browning, "Homer's 'Iliad' Has Lessons for Vietnam Nightmare," *Honolulu Advertiser* (12 February 1995): B1, B4. See also Jonathan Shay, *Achilles in Vietnam: Combat Trauma and the Undoing of Character* (New York: Atheneum, 1994).

82. The examples cited here of "The Lost Patrol" and the "walking meditation" are from Maja Beckstrom, "Vietnam Vets Find Peace in Healing Ceremonies: Rituals Help End the War Within," *Utne Reader* (March/April 1991): 34–35. See also Rod Kane, *Veteran's Day: A Vietnam Memoir* (New York: Crown, 1989), and Michael Norman, *These Good Men: Friendships Forged from War* (New York: Crown, 1989).

83. Paul Recer, "A Different Johnny," Associated Press wire story (3 March 1991).

84. From an account by Barbara Carton, Washington Park Service, in the *Honolulu Star-Bulletin & Advertiser* (11 August 1985).

85. Marian Faye Novak, *Lonely Girls with Burning Eyes: A Wife Recalls Her Husband's Journey Home from Vietnam* (Boston: Little, Brown, 1991), p. 3.

86. See, by Srdjan Vrcan, "The War in Ex-Yugoslavia and Religion," *Social Compass: International Review of Sociology of Religion* 41, no. 3 (1994): 413–422, and "Seven Theses on Religion and War in the Former Yugoslavia," *The Public* 1, nos. 1–2 (1994): 115–124; see also Thomas F. Homer-Dixon, "Environmental Scarcities and Violent Conflict," *International Security* 19, no. 1 (1994): 5–40.

87. Keen, *Faces of the Enemy,* pp. 10–14.

88. Debra Umberson and Kristin Henderson, "The Social Construction of Death in the Gulf War," *Omega: Journal of Death and Dying* 25, no. 1 (1992): 1–15.

89. Keen, *Faces of the Enemy,* pp. 180–181.

90. Ibid., p. 137.

91. Quoted in Shono Naomi, "Mute Reminders of Hiroshima's Atomic Bombing," *Japan Quarterly* (July–September 1993): 267–272. See also Robert Jay Lifton, "Psychological Effects of the Atomic Bomb in Hiroshima: The Theme of Death," in *The Threat of Impending Disaster: Contributions to the Psychology of Stress,* ed. George H. Grosser, Henry Wechsler, and Milton Greenblatt (Cambridge, Mass.: MIT Press, 1964), pp. 152–193.

92. Ruth Sivard, *World Military and Social Expenditures—1989,* 13th ed. (Washington, D.C.: World Priorities, 1989). See also Christine K. Cassel and Victor W. Sidel, "Prescribing Global Health," *Second Opinion* 10 (March 1989): 126–133.

93. Lifton and Olson, *Living and Dying,* p. 120. See also Thomas W. Keefe, "The Human Family and Its Children Under the Nuclear Addiction," *International Social Work* 35, no. 1 (1992): 65–77.

94. Robert Kastenbaum, "Reconstructing Death in Postmodern Society," in *The Path Ahead,* ed. DeSpelder and Strickland, pp. 7–18.

95. See John C. Caldwell and Pat Caldwell, "The African AIDS Epidemic," *Scientific American* 274, no. 3 (March 1996): 62–68.

96. Christopher Burns, "UN: More AIDS Cases Than Thought," *Associated Press Online* (26 November 1997). See also Renee Danziger, "The Social Impact of HIV/AIDS in Developing Countries," *Social Science & Medicine* 39, no. 7 (1994): 905–917.

97. Peter Piot, "AIDS: A Global Response," *Science* 272 (28 June 1996): 1855.

98. See Mary Catherine Bateson and Richard Goldsby, *Thinking AIDS: The Social Response to the Biological Threat* (Reading, Mass.: Addison-Wesley, 1988); Inge B. Corless and Mary Pittman-Lindeman, eds., *AIDS: Principles, Practices, and Politics* (New York: Hemisphere, 1989); Douglas Crimp, ed., *AIDS: Cultural Analysis, Cultural Activism* (Cambridge, Mass.: MIT Press, 1988); Eve K. Nichols, *Mobilizing Against AIDS,* rev. ed. (Cambridge, Mass.: Harvard University Press, 1989); and Randy Shilts, *And the Band Played On: Politics, People, and the AIDS Epidemic* (New York: Viking Penguin, 1988).

99. Malcolm D. Gibson, "AIDS and the African Press," *Media, Culture & Society* 16 (1994): 349–356.

100. See Donna M. Goldstein, "AIDS and Women in Brazil: The Emerging Problem," *Social Science & Medicine* 39, no. 7 (1994): 919–929.

101. Karen A. Bonuck, "AIDS and Families: Cultural, Psychosocial, and Functional Impacts," *Social Work in Health Care* 18, no. 2 (1993): 75–89.

102. Janet J. Kelly and others, "AIDS Deaths Shift from Hospital to Home," *American Journal of Public Health* 83, no. 10 (1993): 1433–1437.

103. Ronald Keith Barrett, "Elephant People: The Phenomena of Social Withdrawal and Self-Imposed Isolation of People Dying with AIDS," *AIDS Patient Care* (October 1995): 240–244.

104. "DMV Reverses AIDS Plate Denial," *Associated Press Online* (25 October 1994).

105. Charles E. Rosenberg, "What Is an Epidemic? AIDS in Historical Perspective," in *The Path Ahead,* ed. DeSpelder and Strickland, pp. 29–32.

106. This description of the diagnosis and treatment of HIV and AIDS is drawn primarily from the following sources: Robert Berkow, ed., *The Merck Manual of Diagnosis and Therapy,* 16th ed. (Rahway, N.J.: Merck Research Laboratories, 1992), pp. 55, 77, 83, 86; Robert Berkow, ed., *The Merck Manual of Medical Information: Home Edition,* (Whitehouse Station, N.J.: Merck Research Laboratories, 1997), pp. 926–932; and Virginia F. Sendor and Patrice M. O'Connor, *Hospice & Palliative Care: Questions and Answers* (Lanham, Md.: Scarecrow Press, 1997), pp. 46–47.

107. See Floyd E. Bloom, "Breakthroughs of the Year: 1996," *Science* 274 (20 December 1996): 1987; Jon Cohen, "Exploiting the HIV-Chemokine Nexus," *Science* 275 (28 February 1997): 1261–1264; and "The Pathogenesis of AIDS: A Special Report," *Science & Medicine* 4, no. 2 (March–April 1997): 6–13.

108. Jerry D. Durham, "The Changing HIV/AIDS Epidemic: Emerging Psychosocial Challenges for Nurses," *Nursing Clinics of North America* 29, no. 1 (1994): 9–18.

109. Jon Cohen, "The Daunting Challenge of Keeping HIV Suppressed," *Science* 277 (4 July 1997): 32–33.

110. Quoted in Jon Cohen, "Advances Painted in Shades of Gray at a D.C. Conference," *Science* 275 (31 January 1997): 615.

111. Margaret A. Chesney, "Health Psychology in the 21st Century: Acquired Immunodeficiency Syndrome As a Harbinger of Things to Come," *Health Psychology* 12, no. 4 (1993): 259–268.

112. John Harris and Soren Holm, "If Only AIDS Were Different," *Hastings Center Report* 23, no. 6 (1993): 6–12.

113. See Laurie Garrett, *The Coming Plague: Newly Emerging Diseases in a World out of Balance* (New York: Farrar, Straus and Giroux, 1994). See also Berkow, ed., *The Merck Manual of Diagnosis and Therapy,* pp. 211–220.

114. Bernard Le Guenno, "Emerging Viruses," *Scientific American* (October 1995): 56–64.

115. See Gunjan Sinha and Burkhard Bilger, "Skeletons in the Attic: Has the Scourge of Athens Returned to Haunt Us?" *The Sciences* 36, no. 5 (September–October 1996): 11; and Matt Crenson, "Researcher: Plague Sparked Ebola," *Associated Press Online* (20 January 1997).

116. Henry Wasswa, "Ebola Outbreaks in Northern Uganda," *Associated Press Online* (15 October 2000).

117. Paul Recer, "Origin of 1918 Flu Pandemic Found," *Associated Press Online* (20 March 1997).

118. Rodrick Wallace and Deborah Wallace, "Inner-City Disease and the Public Health of the Suburbs: The Sociogeographical Dispersion of Point-Source Infection," *Environment and Planning Abstracts* 25 (1993): 1707–1723; and "The Coming Crisis of Public Health in the Suburbs," *Milbank Quarterly* 71, no. 4 (1993): 543–564. See also Rodrick Wallace and others,"Will AIDS Be Contained Within U.S. Minority Urban Populations?" *Social Science & Medicine* 39, no. 8 (1994): 1051–1062.

119. Rodrick Wallace and John Pittman, "Recurrence of Contagious Urban Desertification and the Social Thanatology of New York City," *Environment and Planning Abstracts* 24 (June 1992): 1–6.

120. Wallace and Pitmann, "Recurrence of Contagious Urban Desertification," p. 1.

121. Richard Rothenberg, "Chronicle of an Epidemic Foretold: A Response to the Wallaces," *Milbank Quarterly* 71, no. 4 (1993): 565–574.

122. Mitchell Duneier, *Slim's Table: Race, Respectability, and Masculinity* (Chicago: University of Chicago Press, 1992), p. 75.

123. Rachel Nowak, "WHO Calls for Action Against TB," *Science* 267 (24 March 1995): 1763. See also Stuart B. Levy, "The Challenge of Antibiotic Resistance," *Scientific American* 278, no. 3 (March 1998): 46–53.

124. Charles J. Hanley, "Malaria Stages Comeback," *Associated Press Online* (12 May 1996).

125. Daniel Leviton, "Horrendous Death: Improving the Quality of Global Health," in *The Path Ahead,* ed. DeSpelder and Strickland, pp. 165–168; see also, edited by Leviton, *Horrendous Death, Health, and Well-Being* (New York: Hemisphere, 1991).

CHAPTER 14

1. Quoted in Jeffery L. Sheler, "Heaven in the Age of Reason," *U. S. News & World Report* 122, no. 12 (1997): 65–66.

2. Bertrand Russell, *Unpopular Essays* (New York: Simon & Schuster, 1950), p. 141.

3. See "The Problem of Immortality," in Jacques Choron, *Death and Modern Man* (New York: Collier Books, 1964).

4. Mary Kawena Pukui, E. W. Haertig, and Catherine A. Lee, *Nana I Ke Kumu (Look to the Source)*, vols. 1 and 2 (Honolulu: Hui Hanai; Queen Lili'uokalani Children's Center, 1972). See also E. S. Craighill Handy and Mary Kawena Pukui, *The Polynesian Family System in Ka-'u, Hawai'i* (Rutland, Vt.: Charles E. Tuttle, 1972).

5. Job 7:9, *The Jerusalem Bible*. See also Job 14:7–12.

6. Daniel 12:2, *The Jerusalem Bible*.

7. Stephen J. Vicchio, "Against Raising Hope of Raising the Dead: Contra Moody and Kübler-Ross," *Essence: Issues in the Study of Ageing, Dying and Death* 3, no. 2 (1979): 63.

8. See Lou H. Silberman in "Death in the Hebrew Bible and Apocalyptic Literature," in *Perspectives on Death*, ed. L. O. Mills (Nashville: Abingdon Press, 1969), pp. 13–32. The "Samuel" story is told in the first book of Samuel (28:3–25).

9. H. Wheeler Robinson, "Hebrew Psychology," in *The People and the Book*, ed. Arthur S. Peake (London: Oxford University Press, 1925), pp. 353–382.

10. Earl A. Grollman, "The Ritualistic and Theological Approach of the Jew," in *Explaining Death to Children*, ed. Grollman (Boston: Beacon Press, 1967), pp. 223–245; and Jonathan Boyarin, "Death and the *Minyan*," *Cultural Anthropology* 9, no. 1 (1994): 3–22.

11. See C. Fred Alford, "Greek Tragedy and the Place of Death in Life: A Psychoanalytic Perspective," *Psychoanalysis and Contemporary Thought* 15, no. 2 (1992): 129–159.

12. *The Meditations of Marcus Aurelius*, trans. George Long, *The Harvard Classics*, vol. 2, ed. Charles W. Elliot, pp. 193–301; see especially section II, 5 and 11, pp. 201–202.

13. Carol Zaleski, "In Defense of Immortality," *First Things* (August–September 2000): 36–42.

14. William Barclay, *Introducing the Bible* (Nashville: Abingdon Press, 1972), p. 123.

15. Milton McC. Gatch, *Death: Meaning and Mortality in Christian Thought and Contemporary Culture* (New York: Seabury Press, 1969), p. 78.

16. See Jacques Le Goff, *The Birth of Purgatory* (Chicago: University of Chicago Press, 1984); see also Alan E. Bernstein, *The Formation of Hell: Death and Retribution in the Ancient and Early Christian Worlds* (Ithaca, N.Y.: Cornell University Press, 1993).

17. Richard P. McBrien, *The HarperCollins Encyclopedia of Catholicism* (San Francisco: HarperCollins, 1995), p. 1070.

18. Zaleski, "In Defense of Immortality."

19. Vicchio, "Against Raising Hope," p. 62. See also Gordon E. Geddes, *Welcome Joy: Death in Puritan New England* (Ann Arbor, Mich.: UMI Research Press, 1981); and David E. Stannard, *The Puritan Way of Death: A Study of Religion, Culture, and Social Change* (New York: Oxford University Press, 1977).

20. Salim Mansur, "Delivering Care to Muslims: What We Need to Know to Be Able to Care for Muslims" (invited presentation, King's College 15th International Conference on Death and Bereavement, London, Ontario, 12 May 1997).

21. John L. Esposito, *Islam: The Straight Path* (New York: Oxford University Press, 1988), p. 22.

22. Frithjof Schuon, *Understanding Islam* (Baltimore: Penguin, 1972), p. 16.

23. Alfred T. Welch, "Death and Dying in the Qur'an," in *Religious Encounters with Death: Insights from the History and Anthropology of Religions,* ed. Frank E. Reynolds and Earle H. Waugh (University Park: Pennsylvania State University Press, 1977), p. 184.

24. Huston Smith, *The Religions of Man* (New York: New American Library, 1958), p. 215.

25. Esposito, *Islam: The Straight Path,* p. 35.

26. Welch, "Death and Dying in the Qur'an," p. 193.

27. D. S. Roberts, *Islam: A Concise Introduction* (San Francisco: Harper and Row, 1981), p. 128.

28. Ibid.

29. Abdul Latif Al Hoa, *Islam* (New York: Bookwright Press, 1987), p. 20.

30. Chuang Tzu, *Basic Writings,* trans. Burton Watson (New York: Columbia University Press, 1964), p. 76.

31. T. N. Madan, "Dying with Dignity," *Social Science & Medicine* 35, no. 4 (1992): 425–432.

32. *Bhagavad-Gita* II.27, trans. Swami Nikhilananda (New York: Ramakrishna-Vivekananda Center, 1952), p. 79.

33. Smith, *Religions of Man,* p. 34.

34. E. M. Jackson, "Moksha," in *Key Ideas in Human Thought,* ed. Kenneth McLeish (New York: Facts on File, 1993), pp. 482–483.

35. B*hagavad-Gita* II.22, trans. Nikhilananda, p. 77.

36. J. Bruce Long, "Death As a Necessity and a Gift in Hindu Mythology," in *Religious Encounters with Death,* ed. Reynolds and Waugh, p. 92; see also pp. 73–96.

37. See David R. Kinsley in "The 'Death That Conquers Death': Dying to the World in Medieval Hinduism," in *Religious Encounters with Death,* ed. Reynolds and Waugh, pp. 97–108.

38. "The Meaning of Practice-Enlightenment (Sushō-gi)," in *Zen Master Dōgen: An Introduction with Selected Writings,* trans. Yūhō Yokoi (New York/Tokyo: Weatherhill, 1976), p. 58.

39. Philip Kapleau, *Zen: Dawn in the West* (Garden City, N.Y.: Anchor Press/Doubleday, 1979), p. 296. See also, edited by Kapleau, *The Wheel of Death: A Collection of Writings from Zen Buddhist and Other Sources on Death-Rebirth-Dying* (New York: Harper and Row, 1971) and *The Wheel of Life and Death: A Practical and Spiritual Guide* (New York: Doubleday, 1989).

40. "Awakening to the Bodhi-Mind (Hotsu Bodai-shin)," from the Shōbō-Genzō, in *Zen Master Dōgen,* trans. Yokoi, p. 109.

41. Kapleau, *Zen: Dawn in the West,* pp. 67–68.

42. "The Meaning of Practice-Enlightenment (Shusho-gi)," in *Zen Master Dogen,* trans. Yokoi, p. 58.

43. *The Zen Master Hakuin: Selected Writings,* trans. Philip B. Yampolsky (New York: Columbia University Press, 1971).

44. Kapleau, *Zen: Dawn in the West,* p. 69.

45. W. Y. Evans-Wentz, *The Tibetan Book of the Dead: or, the After-Death Experiences on the Bardo Plane, According to Lama Kazi Dawa-Samup's English Rendering* (New York: Oxford University Press, 1960).

46. Quoted in Kapleau, *Zen: Dawn in the West,* p. 68.

47. Francesca Fremantle and Chögyam Trungpa, eds., *The Tibetan Book of the Dead: The Great Liberation Through Hearing in the Bardo, by Guru Rinpoche According to Karma Lingpa* (Boulder, Colo.: Shambhala, 1975).

48. Christopher Carr, "Death and Near-Death: A Comparison of Tibetan and Euro-American Experiences," *Journal of Transpersonal Psychology* 25, no. 1 (1993): 59–110.

49. Davina A. Allen, "Secularization," in *Key Ideas in Human Thought,* ed. McLeish, p. 668. See also James Turner, *Without God, Without Creed: The Origins of Unbelief in America* (Baltimore: Johns Hopkins University Press, 1985).

50. E. M. Jackson and Kenneth McLeish, "Humanism," in *Key Ideas in Human Thought,* ed. McLeish, pp. 355–356.

51. Kenneth McLeish, "Existentialism," in *Key Ideas in Human Thought,* ed. McLeish, pp. 265–266. See also William Barrett, *Irrational Man: A Study in Existential Philosophy* (New York: Doubleday, 1958); and *Death of the Soul: From Descartes to the Computer* (New York: Anchor/Doubleday, 1986).

52. See Robert J. Lifton, *The Future of Immortality and Other Essays for a Nuclear Age* (New York: Basic Books, 1987).

53. Sheler, "Heaven in the Age of Reason"; see also Jeffery L. Sheler, "Hell's Sober Comeback," *U.S. News & World Report* (25 March 1991), pp. 56–57; and Daniel J. Klenow and Robert C. Bolin, "Belief in an Afterlife: A National Survey," *Omega: Journal of Death and Dying* 20, no. 1 (1989–1990): 63–74.

54. Andrew M. Greeley and Michael Hout, "Americans' Increasing Belief in Life After Death: Religious Competition and Acculturation," *American Sociological Review* 64, no. 6 (1999): 813–835.

55. Quoted in David Cockburn, "Simone Weil on Death," *Mortality* 2, no. 1 (1997): 63–72.

56. Carol Zaleski, *Otherworld Journeys: Accounts of Near-Death Experience in Medieval and Modern Times* (New York: Oxford University Press, 1987).

57. Paul Badham, "Religious and Near-Death Experience in Relation to Belief in a Future Life," *Mortality* 2, no. 1 (1997): 7–21.

58. Bruce Greyson, "Near-Death Experiences," in *Varieties of Anomalous Experience: Examining the Scientific Evidence,* eds. Etzel Cardeña, Steven Jay Lynn, and Stanley Krippner (Washington, D.C.: American Psychological Association, 2000), pp. 315–352; definition pp. 315–316.

59. Kenneth Ring, *Life at Death: A Scientific Investigation of the Near-Death Experience* (New York: Coward, McCann, and Geoghegan, 1980) and *Heading Toward Omega: In Search of the Meaning of the Near-Death Experience* (New York: William Morrow, 1984). See also Bruce Greyson, "Varieties of Near-Death Experience," *Psychiatry* 56 (1993): 390–399; and Raymond A. Moody, Jr., *Life After Life,* and its sequel, *Reflections on Life After Life* (various editions).

60. Bruce Greyson, "Reduced Death Threat in Near-Death Experiencers," in *Death Anxiety Handbook: Research, Instrumentation, and Application,* ed. Robert A. Neimeyer (Washington, D.C.: Taylor & Francis, 1994), pp. 169–179.

61. H. J. Irwin, *An Introduction to Parapsychology* (Jefferson, N.C.: McFarland, 1989), pp. 188–190.

62. William J. Serdahely, "The Near-Death Experience: Is the Presence Always the Higher Self?" *Omega: Journal of Death and Dying* 18, no. 2 (1987–1988): 129–134.

63. William J. Serdahely, "A Pediatric Near-Death Experience: Tunnel Variants," *Omega: Journal of Death and Dying* 20, no. 1 (1989–1990): 55–62. See also William J.

Serdahely and Barbara A. Walker, "A Near-Death Experience at Birth," *Death Studies* 14, no. 2 (1990): 177–183.

64. See Bruce Greyson and Nancy Evans Bush, "Distressing Near-Death Experiences," *Psychiatry* 55 (February 1992): 95–110; and P. M. H. Atwater, "Is There a Hell? Surprising Observations About the Near-Death Experience," *Journal of Near-Death Studies* 10, no. 3 (Spring 1992): 149–160.

65. Ian Stevenson, Emily W. Cook, Nicholas McClean-Rice, "Are Persons Reporting 'Near-Death Experiences' Really Near Death? A Study of Medical Records," *Omega: Journal of Death and Dying* 20, no. 1 (1989–1990): 45–54.

66. For an introduction to the main points of view, see Stephen J. Vicchio, "Near-Death Experiences: A Critical Review of the Literature and Some Questions for Further Study," *Essence: Issues in the Study of Ageing, Dying and Death* 5, no. 1 (1981): 77–89. See also James E. Alcock, "Psychology and Near Death Experiences," *The Skeptical Inquirer* 3, no. 3 (Spring 1979): 25–41; Michael B. Sabom, *Recollections of Death: A Medical Investigation* (New York: Harper and Row, 1981); and Stephen J. Vicchio, "Near-Death Experiences: Some Logical Problems and Questions for Further Study," *Anabiosis: The Journal of the International Association for Near-Death Studies* (1981): 66–87. The history of research into NDEs is traced in Stanislav Grof and Joan Halifax, *The Human Encounter with Death* (New York: E. P. Dutton, 1978), Chapter 7, "Consciousness and the Threshold of Death," pp. 131–157.

67. See Handy and Pukui, *The Polynesian Family System in Ka-'u, Hawai'i*; Donald D. Kilolani Mitchell, *Resource Units in Hawaiian Culture* (Honolulu: Kamehameha Schools Press, 1982); and Pukui, Haertig, and Lee, *Nana I Ke Kumu (Look to the Source)*, vols. 1 and 2.

68. Pukui, Haertig, and Lee, *Nana I Ke Kumu (Look to the Source)*, vol. 1, p. 40.

69. See Roy Kletti and Russell Noyes, Jr., "Mental States in Mortal Danger," which includes a translation of Oskar Pfister's 1930 paper commenting on Heim's observations, in *Essence: Issues in the Study of Ageing, Dying and Death* 5, no. 1 (1981): 5–20.

70. See Russell Noyes, Jr., "Dying and Mystical Consciousness," *Journal of Thanatology* I (1971): 25–41; Russell Noyes, Jr., and Roy Kletti, "Depersonalization in the Face of Life-Threatening Danger: An Interpretation," *Omega: Journal of Death and Dying* 7, no. 2 (1976): 103–114, and "Panoramic Memory: A Response to the Threat of Death," *Omega: Journal of Death and Dying* 8, no. 3 (1977): 181–194; Russell Noyes, Jr., "Near-Death Experiences: Their Interpretation and Significance," in *Between Life and Death*, ed. Robert Kastenbaum (New York: Springer, 1979), pp. 73–78; and Russell Noyes, Jr., "The Encounter with Life-Threatening Danger: Its Nature and Impact," *Essence: Issues in the Study of Ageing, Dying and Death* 5, no. 1 (1981): 21–32.

71. Karlis Osis and Erlendur Haraldsson, "Deathbed Observations of Physicians and Nurses: A Cross-Cultural Survey," in *The Signet Handbook of Parapsychology*, ed. Martin Ebon (New York: Signet/NAL, 1978); and, by Osis and Haraldsson, *At the Hour of Death* (New York: Avon Books, 1977). See also, by Haraldsson, "Survey of Claimed Encounters with the Dead," *Omega: Journal of Death and Dying* 19, no. 2 (1988–1989): 103–113.

72. George Gallup, Jr., *Adventures in Immortality* (New York: McGraw-Hill, 1982). See also Sheler, "Heaven in the Age of Reason"; Greeley and Hout, "Americans' Increasing Belief in Life After Death"; and Klenow and Bolin, "Belief in an Afterlife: A National Survey."

73. Greyson, "Near-Death Experiences," pp. 338, 345.

74. Louis Appleby, *British Medical Journal* 298 (15 April 1989): 976–977.

75. Zaleski, *Otherworld Journeys*, p. 182.

76. Raymond A. Moody, Jr., "An Omega Interview [by Robert Kastenbaum]," *Omega: Journal of Death and Dying* 31, no. 2 (1995): 87–97.

77. From a conversation between Herman Feifel and John Morgan, "Humanity Has to Be the Model," *Death Studies* 10, no. 1 (1986): 1–9.

78. Robert Kastenbaum, "Happily Ever After," in *Between Life and Death*, ed. Kastenbaum, pp. 17, 19.

79. Charles A. Garfield, "The Dying Patient's Concern with 'Life After Death,'" in *Between Life and Death*, ed. Kastenbaum, pp. 52–57.

80. Marie-Louise von Franz, *On Death and Dreams: A Jungian Interpretation* (Boston: Shambhala, 1986), pp. viii–ix.

81. Ibid., p. 156.

82. Ibid., pp. 66–67.

83. Some evidence suggests that LSD may interfere with the transfer of oxygen on the enzymatic level. Anoxia, or diminished levels of oxygen in the bodily tissues, is also found in dying patients as well as in conjunction with certain yogic techniques involving breath control. Thus, anoxia may activate transpersonal matrices in the unconscious, giving rise to experiences associated with near-death experiences, certain yogic states, and LSD sessions. See Grof and Halifax, *The Human Encounter with Death*, pp. 183ff; and Thomas J. Riedlinger and June R. Riedlinger, "Psychedelic and Entactogenic Drugs in the Treatment of Depression," *Journal of Psychoactive Drugs* 26, no. 1 (1994): 41–55.

84. Stanislav Grof, *Realms of the Human Unconscious: Observations from LSD Research* (New York: E. P. Dutton, 1976). See also Robert B. Millman and Ann Bordwine Beeder, "The New Psychedelic Culture: LSD, Ecstasy, 'Rave' Parties, and the Grateful Dead," *Psychiatric Annals* 24, no. 3 (1994): 148–150.

85. See Stanislav Grof, *LSD Psychotherapy* (Pomona, Calif.: Hunter House, 1980), pp. 252ff; Grof and Halifax, *The Human Encounter with Death*, pp. 16ff; and Peter Stafford, *Psychedelics Encyclopedia* (Berkeley, Calif.: And/Or Press, 1977), pp. 23–39.

86. Grof and Halifax, *The Human Encounter with Death*, pp. 120–121.

87. Stanislav Grof and Christina Grof, *Beyond Death: The Gates of Consciousness* (New York: Thames and Hudson, 1980), p. 24.

88. Stanislav Grof and Joan Halifax, "Psychedelics and the Experience of Dying," in *Life After Death*, ed. Arnold Toynbee and others (New York: McGraw-Hill, 1976), pp. 192–193.

89. Grof, *LSD Psychotherapy*, p. 294. On models of human consciousness, see also Seymour Boorstein, ed., *Transpersonal Psychology* (Palo Alto, Calif.: Science and Behavior Books, 1980); Abraham H. Maslow, *The Farther Reaches of Human Nature* (New York: Viking Penguin, 1971); Robert E. Ornstein, ed., *The Nature of Human Consciousness: A Book of Readings* (San Francisco: W. H. Freeman, 1973); Kenneth R. Pelletier and Charles A. Garfield, *Consciousness: East and West* (New York: Harper and Row, 1976); Charles T. Tart, ed., *Transpersonal Psychologies* (New York: Harper and Row, 1975); and Roger N. Walsh and Frances Vaughan, eds., *Beyond Ego: Transpersonal Dimensions in Psychology* (Los Angeles: J. P. Tarcher, 1980).

90. Herman Feifel, *The Meaning of Death* (New York: McGraw-Hill, 1959), p. xiv.

91. International Work Group on Death, Dying and Bereavement, "Assumptions and Principles of Spiritual Care," *Death Studies* 14, no. 1 (1990): 75–81.

92. See Thomas Attig, "Respecting the Spirituality of the Dying and the Bereaved," in *A Challenge for Living: Dying, Death, and Bereavement*, ed. Inge B. Corless, Barbara B. Germino, and Mary A. Pittman (Boston: Jones and Bartlett, 1995), pp. 177–130.

93. Clyde M. Nabe, "'Seeing As': Death As Door or Wall," in *Priorities in Death Education and Counseling,* ed. Richard A. Pacholski and Charles A. Corr (Arlington, Va.: Forum for Death Education and Counseling, 1982), pp. 161–169.

CHAPTER 15

1. Allan B. Chinen, "The Mortal King," in *The Path Ahead: Readings in Death and Dying,* ed. Lynne Ann DeSpelder and Albert Lee Strickland (Mountain View, Calif.: Mayfield, 1995), pp. 335–336.

2. Thomas Attig, "Coping with Mortality: An Essay on Self-Mourning," in *The Path Ahead,* ed. DeSpelder and Strickland, pp. 337–341.

3. J. Eugene Knott and Richard W. Prull, "Death Education: Accountable to Whom? For What?" *Omega: Journal of Death and Dying* 7, no. 2 (1976): 178; see also Joseph A. Durlak, "Changing Death Attitudes Through Death Education," in *Death Anxiety Handbook: Research, Instrumentation, and Application,* ed. Robert A. Neimeyer (Washington, D.C.: Taylor & Francis, 1993), pp. 243–259.

4. Robert Fulton, "Unanticipated Grief" (paper presented at the annual meeting of the Forum for Death Education and Counseling, Philadelphia, 12 April 1985).

5. Darrell Crase, "Black People Do Die, Don't They?" *Death Studies* 11, no. 3 (1987): 221–228.

6. Robert A. Neimeyer and Marlin K. Moore. "Assessing Personal Meanings of Death: Empirical Refinements in the Threat Index," *Death Studies* 13, no. 3 (1989): 227–245.

7. See Robert A. Neimeyer and David Van Brunt, "Death Anxiety," in *Dying: Facing the Facts,* 3d ed., ed. Hannelore Wass and Robert A. Neimeyer (Washington, D.C.: Taylor & Francis, 1995), pp. 49–88.

8. Robert A. Neimeyer, "Death Anxiety Research: The State of the Art" (paper presented at the annual meeting of the Association for Death Education and Counseling, Duluth, Minnesota, April 1991). See also *Death Anxiety Handbook,* ed. Neimeyer; and Adrian Tomer, "Death Anxiety in Adult Life: Theoretical Perspectives," *Death Studies* 16, no. 6 (1992): 475–506.

9. Herman Feifel, "Psychology and Death: Meaningful Rediscovery," in *The Path Ahead,* ed. DeSpelder and Strickland, pp. 19–28.

10. Robert Kastenbaum, "Theory, Research, and Application: Some Critical Issues for Thanatology," *Omega: Journal of Death and Dying* 18, no. 4 (1987–1988): 397–410.

11. Example cited by Kastenbaum, "Theory, Research, and Application," p. 401.

12. Kastenbaum, "Theory, Research, and Application," p. 408.

13. Myra Bluebond-Langner, "Wither Thou Goest?" *Omega: Journal of Death and Dying* 18, no. 4 (1987–1988): 257–263. See also James A. Thorson, "Qualitative Thanatology," *Mortality* 1, no. 2 (1996).

14. Feifel, "Psychology and Death," p. 27.

15. Feifel, "Psychology and Death," p. 28.

16. Robert Fulton and Greg Owen, "Death and Society in Twentieth Century America," *Omega: Journal of Death and Dying* 18, no. 4 (1987–1988): 390.

17. Daniel Leviton and William Wendt, "Death Education: Toward Individual and Global Well-Being," *Death Education* 7, no. 4 (1983): 369–384; and, edited by Leviton, *Horrendous Death, Health, and Well-Being* (New York: Hemisphere, 1991) and *Horrendous Death and Health: Toward Action* (New York: Hemisphere, 1991). See also Richard A. Pacholski, "Teaching Nuclear Holocaust, the Basic Thanatological Topic," *Death Studies* 13, no. 2 (1989): 175–183.

18. International Work Group on Death, Dying, and Bereavement, "A Statement of Assumptions and Principles Concerning Education About Death, Dying, and Bereavement," in *Statements on Death, Dying, and Bereavement* (London, Ont.: IWG, 1994). The three documents on death education prepared by this group were originally published in the following journals: *Death Studies* 16, no. 1 (1991): 59–65 (on education in general); *Omega: Journal of Death and Dying* 23, no. 3 (1991): 235–239 (on education for professionals in health care and human services); and *American Journal of Hospice and Palliative Care* 7 (1991): 26–27 (on education for volunteers and nonprofessionals).

19. "Projections of Resident Population by Age, Sex, and Race: 2000 to 2025," *Statistical Abstract of the United States: 1999,* 119th ed. (Washington, D.C.: Government Printing Office, 1999), p. 25.

20. Ron Crocombe, *The South Pacific: An Introduction* (Auckland, New Zealand: Longman Paul Ltd., 1983).

21. Ibid., p. 73.

22. See Carla J. Sofka, "Social Support 'Internetworks,' Caskets for Sale, and More: Thanatology and the Information Superhighway," *Death Studies* 21, no. 6 (1997): 553–574.

23. Damon Knight, "Masks," in *A Pocketful of Stars,* ed. Damon Knight (New York: Doubleday, 1971).

24. Clifford Simak, "Death Scene," in *The Worlds of Clifford Simak* (New York: Simon & Schuster, 1960); Robert A. Heinlein, "Life-Line," in *The Man Who Sold the Moon: Harriman and the Escape from the Earth to the Moon!,* ed. Heinlein (New York: Shasta Publications, 1950).

25. Kit Reed, "Golden Acres," in *Social Problems Through Science Fiction,* ed. John W. Miestead and others (New York: St. Martin's Press, 1975).

26. Gary Snyder, *The Practice of the Wild: Essays* (San Francisco: North Point Press, 1990), p. 176.

27. Alfred G. Killilea, "The Politics of Being Mortal," in *The Path Ahead,* ed. DeSpelder and Strickland, pp. 342–347.

28. Vernon Reynolds and Ralph Tanner, *The Social Ecology of Religion* (New York: Oxford University Press, 1995), p. 204.

29. Avery Weisman, *On Dying and Denying: A Psychiatric Study of Terminality* (New York: Behavioral Publications, 1972), pp. 39–40; see also, by Weisman, *The Coping Capacity: On the Nature of Being Mortal* (New York: Human Sciences, 1984).

30. This account of Lindbergh's death draws from various sources, including a description by Dr. Milton H. Howell, one of Lindbergh's physicians, reported by Ernest H. Rosenbaum, "The Doctor and the Cancer Patient," in *A Hospice Handbook,* ed. Michael P. Hamilton and Helen F. Reid (Grand Rapids, Mich.: Wm. B. Eerdmans, 1980), pp. 19–43.

31. Sandra L. Bertman, "Bearing the Unbearable: From Loss, the Gain," in *The Path Ahead,* ed. DeSpelder and Strickland, pp. 348–354.

32. Doris M. Schoenhoff, *The Barefoot Expert: The Interface of Computerized Knowledge Systems and Indigenous Knowledge Systems* (Westport, Conn.: Greenwood Press, 1993), p. 100.

Credits and Sources

Prologue and Epilogue: Copyright © 1982 by David Gordon. Used by permission.

Page 6: From "Death in Cades Cove" by A. Crosby, in *Appalachia: When Yesterday Is Today,* ed. students at the University of Tennessee, Knoxville, 1965, pp. 1–3; quoted in *Death and Dying in Central Appalachia: Changing Attitudes and Practices* by James K. Crissman; University of Illinois Press, 1994, p. 27.

Page 11: From the *Los Angeles Times* (21 December 1990).

Page 13: "Grandmother, When Your Child Died," first published by the California State Poetry Society. Used by permission of Joan Neet George.

Page 16: Reprinted by permission of G. P. Putnam's Sons from *Cruel Shoes* by Steve Martin. Copyright © 1977, 1979 by Steve Martin.

Page 27: "One Tree Hill," words and music by U2. Copyright © 1986 by PolyGram International Music Publishing B.V. All rights reserved.

Page 28: "Buffalo Bill's" by e. e. cummings, reprinted from *Complete Poems: 1904–1962* by e. e. cummings, edited by George J. Firmage. Copyright © 1923, 1951, 1991 by the Trustees for the e. e. cummings Trust. Copyright © 1976 by George James Firmage. Reprinted by permission of Liveright Publishing Corporation and Grafton Books.

Pages 38, 210, and 276: Courtesy of Edward C. and Gail R. Johnson.

Page 42: Illustration copyright © 1982 by Eric Mathes. Courtesy of Eric Mathes.

Page 43: From *Death Customs* by E. Bendann; Knopf, 1930.

Page 44: "When Hare Heard of Death" excerpted from pp. 23–24 of *The Road of Life and Death: A Ritual Drama of the American Indians* by Paul Radin, Bollingen Series V. Copyright © 1945, renewed 1973, by Princeton University Press. Reprinted by permission of Princeton University Press and Doris Woodward Radin.

Page 45: Aesop's "Eros and Death" reworked by Steve Sanfield, from *Death: An Anthology of Ancient Texts, Songs, Prayers, and Stories,* ed. David Meltzer; North Point Press, 1984.

Page 48: From *Strange Facts About Death* by Webb Garrison. Copyright © 1978 by Webb Garrison. Used by permission of the publisher, Abingdon Press.

Page 58: Papago song by Juana Manwell. By permission of Smithsonian Institution Press from *Papago Music* by Frances Densmore. Bureau of American Ethnology Bulletin 90. Smithsonian Institution, Washington, D.C., 1929.

Page 58: Dakota song from *The Primal Mind: Vision and Reality in Indian America* by Jamake Highwater; Harper and Row, 1981.

Page 61: Warrior song (Omaha; Hethúska Society) from *The Omaha Tribe* by Alice Fletcher and Francis LaFlesche. Bureau of American Ethnology, 27th Report, Smithsonian Institution, 1911.

Page 62: Burial oration (Wintu) from "Wintu Ethnography" by Cora Du Bois, in *University of California Publications in American Archaeology and Ethnology* 36 (1935). Reprinted by permission of the University of California Press.

Page 65: From *Religions of Africa: A Pilgrimage into Traditional Religions* by Noel Q. King; Harper and Row, 1970.

Page 69: From *Chuang Tzu: Basic Writings,* trans. Burton Watson; Columbia University Press, 1964, p. 113.

Page 71: From *Japanese Death Poems,* comp. Yoel Hoffman; Charles E. Tuttle, Co., Inc., of Boston, Massachusetts, and Tokyo, Japan, 1986. Reprinted by permission.

Page 73: From *The Four Seasons: Japanese Haiku Second Series,* trans. Peter Beilenson. Copyright © 1958 by The Peter Pauper Press.

Page 89: From *Journeys Through Bookland,* Vol. 1, ed. Charles H. Sylvester; Bellows-Reeve Company, Publishers, Chicago, 1922.

Page 92: From *Trinity* by Leon Uris; Doubleday & Company, 1976.

Page 97 (bottom): Drawing by Dominic Horath, created in Mrs. Bronwyn Luffman's classroom at Salesian Sisters School and provided by Linda DaValle. Reprinted by permission of Mary and Frank Horath.

Page 104: From Ruth Walter and Brenda Gameau, "Australia: Its Land, Its People, Its Health Care System, and Unique Health Issues," *Social Work in Health Care* 18, nos. 3–4 (1993): 56–57.

Page 107: "The Shroud" from *Grimms' Tales for Young and Old,* trans. Ralph Manheim. Reprinted by permission of Doubleday & Company, Inc.

Page 124: From the *Honolulu Star-Bulletin* (20 October 1985).

Pages 125 and 197: Used by permission of Elizabeth Bradbury.

Page 128: From *Dying and Death: A Clinical Guide for Caregivers,* ed. David Barton. Copyright © 1977 by the Williams & Wilkins Company. Used with permission of the Williams & Wilkins Company and by courtesy of David Barton, M.D.

Page 134: Reprinted with permission of Simon & Schuster from *To Live Until We Say Good-Bye,* text by Elisabeth Kübler-Ross and photographs by Mal Warshaw. Copyright © 1978 by Ross Medical Associates, S.C., and Mal Warshaw. Photograph copyright © 1978 by Mal Warshaw.

Page 138: From "Medicine and the Question of Suffering" by Richard B. Gunderman, in *Second Opinion: Health, Faith, and Ethics* 14 (July 1990).

Pages 143 and 398: From *You Don't Miss Your Water* by Cornelius Eady, 1995 by Cornelius Eady; Henry Holt, 1995; first published in *Pequod,* no. 35 (1993), p. 114. Reprinted by permission of the author and Henry Holt and Co.

Pages 146 and 238: From *Passing On: The Social Organization of Dying* by David Sudnow; Prentice-Hall, 1967.

Page 147: From *A Gradual Awakening* by Stephen Levine. Copyright © 1979 by Stephen Levine. Reprinted by permission of Doubleday & Company, Inc.

Page 150: From *Experiment Perilous* by Renee Fox; University of Pennsylvania Press, 1974.

Page 152: From "Scream of Consciousness" by Ruth Kramer Ziony; *Neworld* (1977).

Page 153: From "Of Dragons and Garden Peas: A Cancer Patient Talks to Doctors" by Alice Stewart Trillin; *New England Journal of Medicine* (19 March 1981).

Pages 154 and 260: Used by permission of The Centre for Living with Dying.

Page 159: Used by permission of Joan J. Conn.

Page 163: From *Playboy* interview by David Nimmons (September 1993), pp. 61–76.

Page 164: "But You Look So Good" from *No Pain, No Gain.* Reprinted by permission of Judith L. Ellsworth.

Pages 168–169: Adapted from *Living with Cancer* by Ernest H. Rosenbaum; The Mosby Medical Library series, The C. V. Mosby Company, St. Louis, 1982. Used with permission of the C. V. Mosby Company.

Page 174: From *There Is a Rainbow Behind Every Dark Cloud,* compiled by the Center for Attitudinal Healing; Celestial Arts, 1978. Used with permission of the Center for Attitudinal Healing.

Page 177: From "Pain Management on Trial" by Maureen Cushing; *American Journal of Nursing* 7 (February 1992): 21–22.

Pages 184 and 550–551: From *Big Winds, Glass Mornings, Shadows Cast by Stars: Poems 1972–80* by Morton Marcus; Jazz Press, Los Angeles, 1981. Copyright © by Morton Marcus. Used by permission of Morton Marcus.

Page 193: From "Tapping Human Potential" by Norman Cousins; *Second Opinion: Health, Faith, and Ethics* 14 (July 1990).

Page 200: From *Care of the Dying* by Richard Lamerton; Technomic Publishing, 1976.

Page 219: From *Mystics, Magicians, and Medicine People: Tales of a Wanderer* by Doug Boyd. Copyright © 1989 by Doug Boyd. Reprinted by permission of Paragon House.

Page 226: From "Notes on Grief in Literature" by Morris Freedman, in *Loss and Grief: Psychological Management in Medical Practice,* ed. Bernard Schoenberg et al.; Columbia University Press, 1970.

Page 232: From *Nana I Ke Kumu (Look to the Source)* by Mary Kawena Pukui et al.; Hui Hanai, Honolulu, 1972. Courtesy of Queen Lili'uokalani Children's Center, Lili'uokalani Trust.

Page 235: "Twelve Songs IX" from *Collected Shorter Poems* by W. H. Auden. Reprinted by permission of Faber and Faber Ltd. and Random House.

Page 236: From *Living Your Dying* by Stanley Keleman; Random House, 1974.

Page 245: From *Class: A View from Middle England* by Jilly Cooper; Methuen, 1979.

Page 251: From *A Harvest Yet to Reap: A History of Prairie Women* by Linda Rasmussen et al.; Women's Press, Toronto, Ontario, 1976.

Page 252: From *Who Dies?* by Stephen Levine. Reprinted by permission of Doubleday & Company, Inc.

Page 254: From *A Death in the Sanchez Family* by Oscar Lewis; Random House, 1969.

Page 262: "Anguish of Loss," "Sharing the Grief," and "Collapsing" from *The Anguish of Loss,* 2d ed. Copyright © 1992 by Julie Fritsch and Sherokee Ilse. Photographs by Paul Schraub. Reprinted by permission of Wintergreen Press and Julie Fritsch.

Page 271: From "Take Only As Directed" by Wayne Delk; *U.S. Gospel News* (September 1999). Reprinted by permission of the author.

Page 273: Used by permission of Edgar N. Jackson.

Page 277: From *The Loved One* by Evelyn Waugh; Little, Brown & Co., 1948.

Pages 281 and 393: From *The Undertaking: Life Studies from the Dismal Trade* by Thomas Lynch; W. W. Norton, 1997.

Page 284: Athenaeum of Philadelphia Collection.

Page 289: From *The History of American Funeral Directing* by Robert W. Habenstein and William M. Lamers; Bulfin Printers, Milwaukee, 1962.

Pages 294–295: From *Working: People Talk About What They Do All Day and How They Feel About What They Do* by Studs Terkel. Copyright © 1972, 1974 by Studs Terkel. Reprinted by permission of Pantheon Books, a Division of Random House, Inc., and Wildwood House Ltd., London.

Page 298: From *The Papers of Benjamin Franklin,* Volume 1, ed. Leonard W. Labaree; Yale University Press, 1959.

Pages 300–301, 350, and 369: Used with permission of Joe Allen, Brooks Allen, and Janice Laurent.

Page 302: Courtesy of Fritz and Inge Roth, Pütz-Roth, Bergisch Gladbach, Germany.

Page 306: From *To A God Unknown* by John Steinbeck; R. O. Ballou, 1933.

Pages 312–315: Advance directives reprinted by permission of Partnership for Caring, 1035 30th Street, NW, Washington, DC 20007; (800)989-9455.

Page 328: From *The Warming of Winter* by Maxine Dowd Jensen; Abingdon Press.

Pages 330–331: Will of Tomas Antonio Yorba, trans. H. Noya [HM26653]. Reproduced by permission of The Huntington Library, San Marino, California.

Page 335: The Far Side © FarWorks, Inc. Reprinted with permission of Creators Syndicate. All rights reserved.

Page 336: From *You and Your Will* by Paul P. Ashley; New American Library, 1977.

Page 336: From *News from Native California* 4 (August-October 1990).

Page 338: From the *Honolulu Star-Bulletin & Advertiser* (26 August 1990).

Page 342: Caption to cartoon by E. H. Shepard, © Punch/Rothco. Reprinted by permission of Rothco Cartoons, Inc.

Page 343: From "Death Education for Children and Youth" by Dan Leviton and Eileen C. Forman in *Journal of Clinical Child Psychology* (Summer 1974).

Page 345: "Peanuts" reprinted by permission of United Features Syndicate, Inc.

Page 351: From *The Interpretation of Dreams* by Sigmund Freud, trans. and ed. James Strachey; Basic Books, 1953.

Page 354: From *Winesburg, Ohio* by Sherwood Anderson; Viking Press, 1958.

Page 364: From *A Tropical Childhood and Other Poems* by Edward Lucie-Smith. Copyright © Oxford University Press, 1961. Reprinted by permission of Oxford University Press.

Page 365: Used with permission of Christine and Donovan Longaker.

Page 373: From *The Accident* by Carol and Donald Carrick; Seabury, 1976.

Page 375: From *My Grandson Lew* by Charlotte Zolotow; Harper and Row, 1974.

Pages 389 and 445: Used by permission of Maude Meehan.

Page 395: From "Psychological Aspects of Sudden Unexpected Death in Infants and Children" by Abraham B. Bergman; *Pediatric Clinics of North America* 21, no. 1 (February 1974).

Page 397: Transcribed by the authors from an inscription at the National Civil Rights Museum in Memphis, Tennessee.

Page 400: From *Alone: Surviving as a Widow* by Elizabeth C. Mooney; G. P. Putnam's Sons, 1981.

Pages 404–405: Courtesy of Christine Longaker. All rights reserved.

Page 406: From *Love and Profit: The Art of Caring Leadership* by James A. Autry; William Morrow, 1991. Reprinted by permission of HarperCollins Publishers, Inc.

Page 407: From *Chipping Bone: Collected Poems* by Maude Meehan; Embers Press, 1985. Courtesy of Maude Meehan.

Page 416: Edwin Arlington Robinson, "Richard Cory," in *The Children of the Night*; Charles Scribner's Sons, 1897. Copyright under the Berne Convention. Reprinted with the permission of Charles Scribner's Sons.

Pages 420–421: Courtesy of Margaret Macro.

Page 423: From *The Goodbye Book* by Robert Ramsey and Randall Toye. Copyright © 1979 by Robert Ramsey. Reprinted by permission of Van Nostrand Reinhold Co.

Pages 424, 425, 428, 431, 435, and 440: Suicide notes courtesy of Edwin S. Shneidman.

Page 426: Adapted from *Death, Society, and Human Experience*, 2d ed., by Robert J. Kastenbaum; The C. V. Mosby Company, St. Louis, 1981. Used with permission of The C. V. Mosby Company and Robert J. Kastenbaum.

Page 429: Adapted from *Deaths of Man* by Edwin S. Shneidman; Quadrangle Books, 1973. Courtesy of Edwin S. Shneidman.

Page 434: From *The Savage God: A Study of Suicide* by A. Alvarez; Random House, 1972.

Page 443: "Resume" by Dorothy Parker, from *The Portable Dorothy Parker*, revised and enlarged edition, ed. Brendan Gill. Copyright 1926 by Dorothy Parker. Reprinted by permission of Viking Penguin, Inc., and from *The Collected Dorothy Parker* by permission of Gerald Duckworth, Ltd.

Page 449: From *A Hole in the World: An American Boyhood* by Richard Rhodes; Simon & Schuster, 1990.

Page 457: From "Groundfall" by William G. Higgins; *Sierra* (November–December 1979).

Page 460: Reprinted with the permission of Pacific Gas & Electric Company.

Page 464: Courtesy of the Unocal Corporation.

Page 471: From *Murder in Space City: A Cultural Analysis of Houston Homicide Patterns* by Henry P. Lundsgaarde. Copyright © 1977 by Oxford University Press, Inc. Reprinted by permission.

Page 473: From *Custer Died for Your Sins: An Indian Manifesto* by Vine Deloria, Jr.; Macmillan, 1969.

Page 474: From *American Blood* by John Nichols; Henry Holt, 1987.

Page 481: From *A Rumor of War* by Philip Caputo. Copyright © 1977 by Philip Caputo. Reprinted by permission of Holt, Rinehart and Winston, Publishers. Used by permission of Macmillan Press, Ltd., London and Basingstoke.

Page 482: From "The Flesh Made Word," in *Writing in an Era of Conflict: The National Book Week Lectures*; Library of Congress, 1990, p. 6.

Page 484: Copyright © 1981 New York Times Company. Reprinted by permission. Courtesy of Harvey J. Schwartz, M.D.

Page 489: From *Publishers Weekly* (25 October 1985). Copyright © Bowker Magazine Group, Reed Publishing USA. Used by permission.

Page 494: From "Back to a Future: One Man's AIDS Tale Shows How Quickly Epidemic Has Turned" by David Sanford; *Wall Street Journal* (8 November 1996).

Page 503: Courtesy of Barbara J. Paul, Ph.D. All rights reserved.

Page 509: From "Go Down Death—a Funeral Sermon," in *God's Trombones* by James Weldon Johnson. Copyright 1927 by Viking Press, Inc. Copyright renewed 1955 by Grace Nail Johnson. Reprinted by Permission of Viking Penguin Inc.

Page 510: From *Religious Encounters with Death: Insights from the History and Anthropology of Religions*, ed. Frank E. Reynolds and Earle H. Waugh; Pennsylvania State University Press, 1977.

Page 517: From *Zen Mind, Beginner's Mind* by Shunryu Suzuki; 1970. Reprinted by permission of John Weatherhill, Inc.

Page 519: From *Selected Works of Miguel de Unamuno*, Bollingen Series LXXXV, Vol. 4: *The Tragic Sense of Life in Men and Nations*, trans. Anthony Kerrigan. Copyright © 1972 by Princeton University Press.

Page 523: Calvin and Hobbes © Watterson. Reprinted with permission of Universal Press Syndicate. All rights reserved.

Page 530: From *The Gospel at Colonus*. Music by Bob Telson, lyrics by Lee Breuer.

Page 534: From *Harlem Book of the Dead* by James Van Der Zee; Morgan and Morgan, 1978.

Pages 535: Quoted in Gay Becker, "Metaphors in Disrupted Lives: Infertility and Cultural Constructions of Continuity," *Medical Anthropology Quarterly* 8, no. 4 (1994): 383–410.

Page 540: From *The Wheel of Death: A Collection of Writings from Zen Buddhist and Other Sources on Death, Rebirth, Dying* by Philip Kapleau; Harper and Row, 1971.

Page 541: From *The Ancient Child* by N. Scott Momaday; Doubleday, 1989.

Page 545: From "A Last Interview with the Legendary Actor" by Caroline Mangez; *Paris Match*. Published in *Hello!* No. 440 (11 January 1997), pp. 80–82.

Page 549: Reprinted by permission. Advertising agency: Robaire and Hogshead, Venice, Calif. Photography: Michael Ruppert Studios, Los Angeles, Calif.

Page 552: From *At the Edge of the Body* by Erica Jong. Copyright © 1979 by Erica Mann Jong. Reprinted by permission of the poet.

Name Index

Subject Index

648

Mass media *(continued)*
  subcultural influence on, 105
  suicide reports in, 432–433, 439
  war reporting in, 480, 486–487
Mass suicide, 422–423, 438
Mater dolorosa, 225
Mature concept of death, 78, 80, 111,
    113–114, 353–355
Mausoleum, 292, 293
Meaning of death, 41, 533–534. *See also*
    Afterlife concepts
  in childhood, 384–385, 388, 396
  in dance of death, 55–57
  grief and, 242–243
  life-threatening illness and, 151–152,
    161
  literary explorations of, 26–28
  in Mexican culture, 66–69
  social construction of reality and, 103
  suicide and, 433, 438
"Mean-world" syndrome, 22
Medical ethics. *See also* Euthanasia;
    Informed consent
  neonatal death and, 392–393
  organ donation and, 205–209
  principles of, 188–190, 220–221
Medical examiners, 322–323, 325, 415.
    See also Autopsies
Medical paternalism, 122, 539
Medical technology, 11–13, 37, 50, 211,
    544, 546
  costs, 120, 121
  definition of death and, 306–309
  dying trajectory and, 8, 52, 212, 213
  Hippocratic oath and, 188, 195
Medicalization of death, 50
Medicare, 120, 137, 409
Mele kanikau (laments), 26
Memento mori, 52
Memorial societies, 288–289
Memorialization, 10, 31, 32, 53–55. *See
    also* Naming practices
  AIDS Quilt, 31, 32
  costs, 280–281, 295–296
  cross-cultural examples of, 59, 69–74,
    106, 509
Metastasis (defined), 169
Mexican culture, 29, 66–69, 106, 171
"Middle knowledge," 156
Middlescence, 439
Military euphemisms, 14
Miscarriage, 386, 390
Mizuko, 391
Modes of death, 249–253, 320. *See also*
    Accidental death; Homicide; Life-
    threatening illness; Suicide
Morbidity of grief, 233–235
Mortality rates, 8–10, 100. *See also* Causes
    of death
Morticians. *See* Funeral directors
Mortuary, 275, 299, 302
Mourning. *See also* Bereavement;
    Funerals; Grief; Memorialization;
    Notification of death
  artistic expressions of, 23–31
  cross-cultural examples of, 57–74, 106,
    225
  defined, 224
  music and, 23–26
  nineteenth century customs, 49–50, 55
Mourning memorials. *See*
    Memorialization

Mourning restraints (LoDagaa), 65
Movies, 22–23, 71
Multiple losses, 254
Murder. *See* Homicide
Music, 23–26, 55, 63. *See also* Death
    songs
Muslims. *See* Islam
Mutual pretense, 155
Mutual will, 327
Myths and facts about suicide, 450–451

Naming practices, 46–47, 60, 71, 73
Nandi, 62
Narrative models, 161, 242–243
National Organ Transplant Act, 207
Native American culture
  attitudes toward death, 58–62
  definition of death in, 219
  multiple losses in, 254
  origin of death myths, 43–44
  scaffold burial, 40
Native American Graves Protection and
    Repatriation Act, 60
Native Americans
  in Canadian hospitals, 102
  elders, attitude towards, 411
  suicide among, 432, 446–447
  violence against, 470
Natural Death Act (Calif.), 311
Natural death directives. *See* Advance
    directives
Natural disasters, 456, 461–463, 464–465
Navajo, 61, 171
Nazi holocaust. *See* Holocaust
Near-death experiences, 516, 520–528
Necromancy, 46, 503
Neonatal death, 386, 392–393
Neonatal intensive care, 203–205
Netherlands, 199
Neurobiologic markers (suicide), 435
Newborns, seriously ill, 203–205
News reporting. *See* Mass media
Next of kin. *See* Families
Nez Percé, 60
Niche (cemetery), 282, 295
Nirvana, 514, 515
Noncorporeal continuity, 78. *See also*
    Afterlife concepts
Nonmaleficence (ethics), 189
Nonverbal communication, 125–126
Norms (social), 80, 106–107, 113, 225
  wills and inheritance, 328
Notification of death, 6, 12, 38, 267–270.
    See also Death notices
Nuclear threat, 479, 487–489
Nuclearism, 489
Nuncupative will, 327
Nursery rhymes, 89
Nursing homes, 118, 408
Nutrition and hydration, 182, 201–203

Obituaries, 19–20, 268–269, 270
  cross-cultural examples, 66, 67
O-bon (Japanese festival), 70, 73–74, 110
Occupational hazards, 440, 456–457
'Ohana (family), 108, 257–258
Ohlone, 60
Oklahoma City bombing, 15, 20, 128,
    469
Older adults, 10, 407–411, 544
Omaha, 61

Oncologist (defined), 169
Order of lethality (suicide), 443
Ordinary care (ethics), 201–202, 204
Oregon Death with Dignity Act, 318
Organ donation, 205–209, 290
Organ transplantation, 205–209
  in Japan, 217–220
Origin of death myths, 43–44, 45
Orphic mystery religions, 505
Ossuaries, 53, 54
Otherworld journeys, 46, 60, 61, 520,
    529–530. *See also* Near-death
    experiences
Outpatient care. *See* Home care

Pain management, 176–179. *See also*
    Palliative care; Whole-person care
  "double effect" (ethics), 318
  LSD therapy in, 529
Pallbearers, 288
Palliative care, 38, 52, 118, 131–140, 167,
    170, 543. *See also* Home care;
    Hospice care; Pain management;
    Whole-person care
  physician-assisted suicide and, 319
  right to die and, 199–201
Panoramic life review, 523, 525
Papago, 58
Paradise, 504, 508, 510
Paramedics. *See* Emergency personnel
Parent death, 9–10, 79, 80, 225, 241,
    340, 363–366, 398–399
Parental bereavement. *See* Child death
Parental messages about death, 81,
    84–85. *See also* Socialization
Passive euthanasia, 198
Paternalism, 122, 539
Pathological grief. *See* Complicated
    mourning
Patient Self-Determination Act (PSDA),
    316
Patient-caregiver relationship. *See*
    Caregiver-patient relationship
Peekaboo game, 342
Peer support. *See* Social support
Penan Geng (Borneo), 47
Perceived similarity, 248
Perinatal death, 203–205, 386–394
Persian Gulf War, 94, 95, 477, 478, 484
Persistent vegetative state, 196, 211, 309.
    See also Comatose state
Personal death consultants, 38
Pet death, 84–85, 361–363, 594n38
Physician-assisted suicide, 23, 198, 199,
    304, 317–320. *See also* Advance
    directives; Euthanasia; Rational
    suicide
Piagetian model of development,
    347–353
Pidgin (language), 110
Placebos, 192–193
Plague
  Athenian (430 B.C.), 495–496
  emerging diseases as, 489–497
  in medieval Europe, 29, 55, 151, 455–
    456
Play activities (children), 86, 342–343,
    345
Pluralism. *See* Cultural diversity
Political system
  AIDS, 490–491
  medical ethics, 221

Suicide *(continued)*
　prevention and intervention, 439, 443,
　　444–453
　risk factors in, 431–441
　statistical issues, 415–418, 436
　theoretical explanations of, 418–425
　types of, 426–430
Suicide as escape, 426–427
Suicide (definitions), 415
Suicide notes, 443–444
　examples, 420, 424, 425, 428, 431, 435,
　　440, 445
Suicide pacts, 434, 439, 440–441
Support groups. *See* Social support
Surgery, 167. *See also* Organ
　transplantation
Surrogate (advance directives), 311
Survival guilt, 253
Suttee, 421–422
Symbolic healing, 174
Symbolic immortality, 504–505, 519
Symbolic interactionism, 101–103
Symbolic loss (parental bereavement),
　388
Sympathy cards, 14–15

Taboo (death), 151, 415
Tactical socialization, 81
Tahitian culture, 503
"Tamed death," 47–48, 50
Taoism, 70, 108–109, 511
Task-based models
　of coping with grief, 236–240
　of coping with life-threatening illness,
　　160–161
Teachable moments, 35, 91–93
Technological alienation (warfare),
　479–480
Telephone hotlines, 445
Television, 20–22. *See also* Mass media
Terminal care. *See* Palliative care
Terminal illness. *See* Life-threatening
　illness
Terminal sedation, 318
Terrorism, 469, 497
Testator (wills), 326, 328–329
Thanatology, 33–36, 541, 543. *See also*
　Death education
Therapeutic abortion, 386–387, 391–392

Tibetan Buddhism, 515–516
Total care. *See* Whole-person care
Traditional cultures, 42–48, 500–502,
　564n2. *See also* African culture;
　Hawaiian culture
　suicide in, 413
Trajectories of dying. *See* Dying trajectory
Transcendence (near-death experience),
　525
Transmigration of souls. *See* Rebirth
Transplantation. *See* Organ
　transplantation
Trauma care, 143–145. *See also*
　Emergency medical care
Traumatic grief, 233
Treatment issues, 165–179. *See also*
　Informed consent
Triage, 144
Trigger events, 231, 252
Truth telling, 122, 124–125, 190–192. *See
　also* Informed consent
Tsimshian, 59
Tuberculosis, 496–497
Tumor (defined), 169
Tutsi (Rwanda), 478

Undertakers. *See* Funeral directors
Unfinished business, 256–257
Uniform Anatomical Gift Act, 207–208,
　307, 323
Uniform Determination of Death Act,
　307, 308
Unintentioned death, 429
Unorthodox treatment, 175
Urban desertification, 496

Values, 80, 221, 248–249, 499
Veterans, 253, 274, 299, 337, 338,
　483–485
Viatical settlement (insurance), 337–338
Victim-precipitated homicide, 416, 476
Video eulogies, 296
Video game violence, 23
Vietnam War, 477, 481–482, 483,
　484–485
　identification of bodies in, 324
Vigil. *See* Deathwatch
Vigilante stories, 27–28
Violence, 466–476. *See also* Warfare

children and, 93–96, 97, 98–99, 360
　in mass media, 19, 22, 23, 455
　suicide and, 432
Virtual cemeteries, 299
Visual arts, 28–31, 35, 55, 67–68
Visualization, 173, 174
Vital signs, 211–212, 213, 214, 216, 306,
　308–309
Voluntary active euthanasia, 199

Wakes, 5–6, 268, 287, 301
War
　and euphemisms for death, 14
Warfare, 476–489. *See also* Horrendous
　death
　grief from, 241, 483–485, 532
　identification of bodies in, 324
　total war, advent of, 50
Water burial, 290, 291
Weapons. *See* Firearms
Werther effect (suicide), 432
Western European culture, 28–31,
　47–56. *See also* Judeo-Christian
　culture
"Whole-brain" definition of death, 216,
　217, 309
Whole-person care, 127, 131, 148
　afterlife beliefs and, 531
　dying trajectory and, 183–184
　near-death experiences (NDEs) and,
　　527
Widowhood, 49–50, 81, 225, 244, 271,
　421–422. *See also* Spousal
　bereavement
Wills and inheritance, 326–332,
　336–339
Winnebago, 43–44
Wintu, 62
World Wide Web, 120, 299

Xenotransplantation, 205

Yahrzeit (anniversary of death), 503, 504
Yin-yang, 69
Yombe, 64
Yoruba, 15, 66

Zen Buddhism. *See* Buddhism
Zorastrianism, 290